Fifth Edition

The Computer Continuum

Kurt F. Lauckner

Zenia C. Bahorski

Custom Publishing

New York   Boston   San Francisco
London   Toronto   Sydney   Tokyo   Singapore   Madrid
Mexico City   Munich   Paris   Cape Town   Hong Kong   Montreal

Pearson
Custom Publishing
is a division of

www.pearsonhighered.com

ISBN 10: 0-558-34516-6
ISBN 13: 978-0-558-34516-7

Dedication

To our spouses,
Anita and Tom

Contents at a Glance

Table of Contents

Preface

PHILOSOPHY: THE CONCEPTS APPROACH

Higher education has traditionally categorized knowledge into areas such as history, chemistry, physics, and literature. In most colleges and universities, almost all the common major categories have an introduction to their field that is designed for the beginner. The sciences, such as chemistry, physics, and biology, for example, have courses for the nonmajor. These courses are designed to teach the concepts of the individual fields and do not dwell on the tools used to study the field. In chemistry, for instance, courses in glassblowing and apparatus building are not the main introductory core. Instead, the focus is on understanding the concepts, which usually include chemical reactions or the structure of molecules. It is also duly noted by the authors of *The Computer Continuum, Fifth Edition,* that the fields of information systems and computer science are unique. But, the concepts approach is still a valid, if not preferred, means of teaching in these two areas.

During the past decade, the fields of information systems and computer science have focused on the tools. In fact, many colleges and universities continue to offer complete courses in learning the technical aspects of word processing, spreadsheets, and databases. This seems like a misplaced effort, considering what the future holds for the graduate. Continuous speech-to-text input systems will probably make word processors obsolete in a few years, for example. Among those who use spreadsheets to solve real problems, it is well-known that an understanding of modeling and simulation is more valuable than knowing how to make a spreadsheet look pretty. The philosophy of this textbook is to concentrate on the concepts of information systems and computer science, such as data representation, operating systems, programming languages, and algorithms. Software application sections are integrated into every chapter of the book. There also are several laboratory manuals that can be packaged with *The Computer Continuum, Fifth Edition,* to give the student working knowledge of those tools. But ultimately, it is necessary to build a lasting foundation of fundamental concepts to prepare the graduate for the future.

AUDIENCE

The Computer Continuum, Fifth Edition, is primarily for use in college and university undergraduate introduction to computer concepts courses. It is equally appropriate for departments of either information systems or computer science. It is equally appealing to the liberal arts major and the computer science major. This text material has been tested on more than 10,000 college students in both large and small classes.

We think that most of the concepts as presented, will be current even 10 years from now. This lasting power is due to the concentration on fundamental concepts. In fact, simulation and the associated computer concepts introduced in chapter 12, "Simulation: Modeling the Physical World," are the foundation for a new approach to computer science, in addition to the theoretical and experimental approaches.

Unique coverage can be found in chapter 2, "Metamorphosis of Information"; chapter 5, "Hardware and Software: Putting It Together"; chapter 10, "Multimedia"; chapter 12, "Simulation: Modeling the Physical World"; and chapter 13, "Artificial Intelligence and Modeling the Human State."

LEARNING TOOLS

The features of *The Computer Continuum, Fifth Edition,* were designed to create an interactive learning experience and respond to the needs of teachers and students.

Special Features

Many aspects of *The Computer Continuum* will help the student. This book provides a balanced approach to pedagogy, with special features in each chapter.

*The chapter-opening **Puzzlers** pose a question related to the core concepts of the chapter. Hints designed to help the student solve this puzzle are embedded in the chapter, and an end-of-chapter exercise helps tie the concepts together.*

Your computer is on a network consisting of several computers and a printer. Imagine that you've completed a term paper using a word processor and need to print it. But each time you try printing, nothing happens. How can this problem be solved? Create at least two plans of action to solve the problem. The plans should not include calling the network administrator, or taking your disk to a friend's house.

PUZZLER

Amazing Grace

Admiral Grace Murray Hopper was one of the pioneers of computing. At a time when most computer experts believed computers were too complicated for the general public to understand, Hopper's motto was, "If computers were easier to operate, more people could use them." She dedicated her long navy career to computer standardization and demystification.

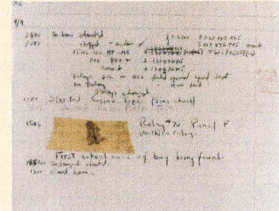

Hopper's formidable skills in mathematics propelled her into the new world of computing machines early in the 1940s, when there were many opportunities to innovate. She worked on the early UNIVACs and became involved in creating computer languages. Recognizing that user-friendly computer languages would entice more people into computer work, she pioneered research to knock down the "Tower of Babel" computer languages had become.

In 1955, Hopper led the committee that invented COBOL (Common Business Oriented Language), a programming language promoting easier access for business application. COBOL allowed English words to be translated into numerals—1s and 0s—that any computer could understand. This revolutionized the computer industry, making it possible for anyone to use a computer to help with his or her daily business needs.

One of Hopper's most famous discoveries was the computer *bug,* in 1945. The term was coined when the navy assigned Hopper to the Bureau of Ordinance Computation Project at Harvard University. Hopper worked on the development of the Mark II computer, used for creating ballistic tables for aiming navy guns, schedules for supplying ships, and top-secret calculations used for the atomic bomb. When evaluating why the new computer wasn't performing, Hopper traced the malfunction down to a short-circuit caused by a moth. The bug was flattened between contacts, preventing the relay from making its connections. Her team taped the dead moth into the log book with this notation, "First actual case of a bug being found." When challenged for not making enough progress, the feisty mother of computing would reply she was busy debugging the computer. The original "bug" is still preserved at the museum of the Naval Surface Weapon Center at Dahlgren, Virginia.

Admiral Grace Murray Hopper died in December 1991, leaving behind an amazing 85-year legacy of accomplishments.

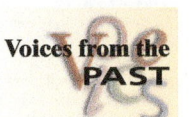

Voices from the Past
boxes feature historical figures, such as John von Neumann, Grace Hopper, and Herbert Simon.

Bots and Intelligent Agents

As our world gets more and more complex, it is difficult for the average citizen to always know the right thing to do. It can be dangerous, for example, to sell your own house. If you forget even a single important word in the contract, then the buyer may back out or force you to pay for something not precisely indicated. That's why there are real estate agents, insurance agents, and other types of experts in a certain area.

The Internet has already produced the precursor of the intelligent agent. Called bots, as in roBOTS, they do menial tasks such as roaming the World Wide Web looking for things. As the following names indicate, they come in many different forms: Web robots, spiders, wanderers, worms, cancelbots, modbots, softbots, userbots, taskbots, chatterbots, knowbots, mailbots, bolo bots, warbots, clonebots, crashbots, floodbots, annoybots, hackbots, Vladbots, Turing bots, gossipbots, gamebots, conceptbots, roverbots, skeletonbots, spybots, spambots, and many others. The bots don't have the intelligence that is expected of the intelligent agent. However, bots that provide services and act as intermediaries between computers and humans could be considered a bottommost class of intelligent agents.

The artificial intelligence community is now developing computerized agents using the model of the human intelligent agents. Alan Kay in his Knowledge Navigator proposed an early classic example of such an agent. His agent was to be a personal assistant that had access to electronic communications. In a simulation of how this agent might behave, the agent took phone calls, made appointments, and would do tasks such as locating individuals by phone or finding research materials. The agent appeared as a talking human form on the monitor screen of the computer. The human would give verbal instructions to the agent in continuous speech, and the agent responded as if it were human. Other researchers have proposed agents that scan the Internet for things of interest to the owner of the agent. This agent would then report back its findings.

Tech Talk *boxes present interesting and more technical computer issues such as graphics formats, use of Java in multimedia, and intelligent agents.*

The Cutting Edge boxes
report on future technology
such as quantum computers,
Internet2, and microbots.

Robots by the Dozen

No, they're not insects! And they're not mechanical vehicles from a child's Lego or Hot Wheels toy set. Instead they are the hottest and newest community of microbots developed at the Artificial Intelligence Lab at MIT. Only one cubic inch in size, these tiny computers have been designed and equipped to lead the next scientific fact-gathering invasion of Mars.

Interplanetary exploration has long relied on robot rovers to collect geological and meteorological samples from planets whose atmospheres may be unfriendly to human scientists. These robots are usually large, clumsy machines, weighing many pounds, and occupying a large percentage of storage space in the exploration vehicle they serve.

They look like vehicles from a child's toy play set, but they are the hottest new development in intelligent microrobots.

Scientists at MIT have been working to develop a microrobot weighing only 10 grams or less to perform the same task. Not only would such computer machines be easier to move and maintain, but because they are used in colonies, they can cooperate to perform more tasks more efficiently than their larger cousins.

Like other computers, the microbots are equipped with specialized hardware for performing their tasks: a Motorola M68HC11E9 microchip as a central processing unit (CPU); a Xicor X68C75 8k EEPROM chip to function as memory, and a variety of sensors (infrared sensors, light sensors, bump sensors, food sensors, tilt sensors, and mandible position sensors) to help with direction of movement and collection of samples. Power is supplied by either solar energy or battery. Locomotion is accomplished by wheels, hopping devices, or tracks—or combinations of all three. Cost? About $300 in parts, and many hundreds of thousands of dollars in research and labor.

Despite the astronomical research and development costs for these tiny robots, the hardware itself can do nothing without software designed especially for them. Developed by Dr. Rodney Brooks at MIT, the software for the robot colonies uses a programming style called subsumption architecture. The program is actually a cluster of many little programs called

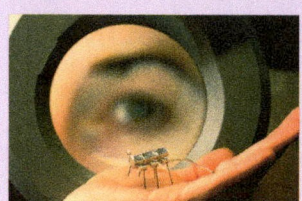

behaviors. Each behavior monitors a few of the robot's sensors and emits an electronic motor command based on the sensor readings. These commands are sent to the motors based on a priority hierarchy: The most important commands override, or subsume, those lower in priority. The result is intelligent behavior highly responsive to environmental elements and capable of cooperative actions when the microbots are used in groups of a dozen or more.

End-of-Chapter Material

The comprehensive end-of-chapter testing material is designed to accommodate different learning and teaching styles. It encourages individual review and reflection, as well as group discussions and problem solving. The end-of-chapter material includes:

1. Matching, true/false, and multiple-choice questions that test basic knowledge.

2. **PUZZLER** Several exercises that provide in-depth problem-solving opportunities. Exercises that support the Puzzler are identified with a puzzler icon.

3. Discussion questions that ask students to think critically about content presented in the chapter.

4. Group exercises that promote working on projects in groups, an important aspect of today's workplace.

5. Web exercises that encourage students to surf the Web for research topics related to the material discussed in the chapter.

Other Helpful Learning Tools

1. Learning objectives previewing each chapter
2. Timelines tracing the evolution of computing as it relates to each chapter
3. Margin term definitions highlighting key concepts
4. Chapter summary
5. Chapter bibliography

ORGANIZATION

The organization of *The Computer Continuum* follows a very natural approach to learning about information systems and computer science. After an introductory chapter, the next five chapters lay down a foundation of theory; the remaining chapters cover some general areas of computer usage. The theory chapters form a solid framework on which the general areas of computer usage and the tools can be supported. The term *general areas* is meant to show that these concepts are used in almost every field of endeavor. A summary of this approach is as follows:

Preliminaries: Where We're Going, consists of chapter 1, "Computers: A First Look."

Part I, The Building Blocks: How Computers Work, consists of chapters 2 through 7 and covers the following:

    Representation of the five kinds of information and its storage
    Hardware components of a computer system
    Programming, algorithms, and computer languages
    Putting together hardware and software in the computer
    Controlling computers through the operating system
    Network communication between computers and people

Part II, Foundations: Applying Concepts, consists of chapters 8 through 12 and covers the following:

    Understanding the Internet and the World Wide Web
    Personal Security and Privacy
    Multimedia from hypertext to streaming audio and video
    Databases: gathering, retrieving, and analyzing information
    Using computers in simulation and modeling

Part III, Empowerment: Extending Our Limits, consists of chapter 13 that covers the following:

    The pursuit of the intelligent computer to extend human abilities
    Using the computer to increase personal knowledge

The rationale for this organization is to first provide an understanding of the basic concepts involved with computers, then to use this understanding to investigate the application of computers in many general areas. To understand the process of image manipulation, for example, it is necessary to understand the concepts of representing images in a computer. The approach is designed to enable the student to first conceptualize, then innovate. Without understanding the underlying concepts, creative work is almost impossible. We truly want our students to innovate!

NEW TO THIS EDITION

The revisions to *The Computer Continuum, Fifth Edition,* are reflections of the recent changes to our society and to computer technology.

Content Changes

Chapter 1, "Computers: A First Look," features now include updated content in use of smart phones and wireless networks, and a new Tech Talk relating past use of abbreviations to the new pop culture usage of abbreviations for text messaging. Chapter 2, "Metamorphosis of Information," includes a new discussion of Unicode and hardware updates. Chapter 3, "Computer Hardware Components: CPU, Memory, and I/O" could not overlook the affordability of larger storage devices for personal computers, the move from floppies to USB storage devices, and the recent updates in CPUs. Chapters 4 and 5, "Computer Languages, Algorithms, and Program Development," and "Hardware and Software: Putting it Together", have minor formatting and editing modifications. Chapter 6, "Operating Systems: The Genie in the Computer," has had updates related to updates in operating system. The new edition discusses Windows XP, Vista, and the Macintosh 10.5 operating systems.

Chapter 7, "Network Concepts and Communications," has included changes that have occurred in the networking concepts. A new "Voices from the Past" discusses Hollywood screen star Hedy Lamarr's patented contribution to wireless communication networks. Chapter 8, "The Internet and the Web: Worldwide Transformation," includes new discussions of social networking and cloud computing, with updated discussion of e-commerce. Chapter 9, now "Personal Security and Privacy," has been moved up from chapter 14 to a more natural placement following Networking, which includes the Internet, and the World Wide Web chapters. Chapter 9 has been updated with information about new threats on security and privacy and includes current methods of guarding our safety and the safety of our computers. Chapter 10, now "Multimedia," includes an expanded discussion of streaming media as well as a new section on the copyright ownership of images found on the Web and of ownership of images taken by the photographer. Education fair use of images is also discussed. Also included in chapter 10 is an updated discussion of digital television, a comparison of HD DVD and Blu-ray technology, and the current state of speech recognition with comparisons of the speech recognition capabilities of Microsoft Word, the inclusion of speech recognition as a part of the Vista operating system, and the speech to text translation of digital audio recorders using Dragon Naturally Speaking.

Chapter 11, now "Databases: Controlling the Information Deluge," has had minor updates to include more current examples. Chapter 12, now "Simulation: Modeling the Physical World," has been updated and now includes a new section on protein folding. The section explains how simulation is used to explore the structure of DNA and how computers are used world wide to assist in new discoveries via a distributed network. A game-like simulator is discussed, which models the folding of proteins.

THE TEACHING PACKAGE

The Computer Continuum, Fourth Edition, has a comprehensive supplements package that is coordinated with the main text and is designed for your teaching convenience. The following supplements are available with the text.

Instructor's Resource Manual

The Instructor's Resource Manual provides learning objectives and lesson outlines for each chapter. The manual also gives the answers to all end-of-chapter material in the main text. For the novice teacher, as well as seasoned instructors looking for new ways

to teach this course, the Instructor's Resource Manual includes Teaching Tips, along with a Sample Syllabus. Lab projects for each of the chapters are included. These consist of a description of the project with sufficient detail to enable the student to work on his or her own. The Instructor's Resource Manual is available for download from the instructor's section of the companion Web site, and is also available on the Instructor's Resource CD-ROM.

Electronic Test Bank

A test databank of more than 1,500 questions is available on the Instructor's Resource CD-ROM or separately. It is also easy to create your own tests using several question types, including true/false, multiple choice, fill-in, and short answer. These questions can be individually selected or chosen at random.

PowerPoint Slides

PowerPoint slides are available as a lecture aid for instructors. There are more than 400 slides available for download from the instructor's section of the companion Web site and on the Instructor's Resource CD-ROM.

Instructor's Resource CD ROM

All of the supplements are conveniently included on one disk. This includes the Instructor's Manual, PowerPoint slides, and Test Manager.

ABOUT THE COVER

Many years ago, one of the authors was privileged to hear British astronomer Sir Fred Hoyle give a talk at a physics colloquium. It was a beautiful talk about an incredible 4,000-year-old scientific project: Stonehenge, considered by many scientists to be the first computer. In fact, Hoyle hypothesized that it must have taken at least 100 years of experiments and data gathering to build Stonehenge. This talk was never forgotten and became the foundation for our examination of the computer continuum from Stonehenge to the millennium.

ACKNOWLEDGMENTS

Projects of this magnitude take the efforts of many people in addition to the authors. We have been working with Pam Moore over a period of several years. This relationship has become a very fruitful forum for ideas and their implementation here at Eastern Michigan University. Teaching these computer concepts several hundred students each year in several different formats has given a special character to our approach. She has also contributed significantly to the supplemental materials for the book.

Finally, this project could not have been completed without the support of our spouses, Anita Lauckner and Thomas Bahorski. The project was hastened along with their patience and encouragement, although these were sometimes given with a little edge by Anita: "Please, get it done so we can return to normal living!"

ABOUT THE AUTHORS

Kurt F. Lauckner received his Ph.D. in physics from the University of Michigan in 1968. His experience with computers began with extensive computer computations for his thesis work in theoretical physics. While a member of the Department of Mathematics, he took the major role in creating the computer science program at Eastern Michigan University.

During the past 30 years, he has developed a concepts approach to teaching computer fluency. The course CoSc 101, Computer Science Concepts and Practical Applications, has

grown into the university's primary computer fluency course and currently enrolls approximately 1,000 students per year. It was used as the model for the university-wide computer literacy requirement in the EMU basic studies program.

Many materials were developed for this freshman-level computer fluency course. They include *Computers: Inside & Out* (in fifth edition), *Student Manual for Computers: Inside & Out,* eight manuals for the tools of computing, and various support materials, such as an instructor's manual and software. Emphasis on concepts was the theme throughout the development of the literacy course and the nine editions of the textbook.

Zenia C. Bahorski received her Ph.D. in Technology from Eastern Michigan University in 2009. She received her master's degree in Educational Psychology with a Concentration in Education Technology in 1990 from Eastern Michigan University. She received her B.S. degree in 1988 in Secondary Teaching of Computer Science and Mathematics and obtained her secondary teaching certificate in 1988. Dr. Bahorski has been teaching as a tenured Instructor in the Department of Computer Science since 1990. Her main teaching interests have been in computer fluency, computer science teacher education, and human-computer interaction. Zenia Bahorski has worked closely with Kurt Lauckner over the past twenty years, contributing to the development of the textbooks and supplemental materials.

The Computer Continuum

chapter **1**

Computers: A First Look

TimeLine

2800–1800 B.C.	Stonehenge is built in several stages to predict the movement of heavenly bodies.
500 B.C.	The abacus is first used to do basic arithmetic.
1920s	The slide rule (a mechanical calculator) is introduced.
1940s	Only a few (fewer than 10) electronic or electromechanical computers exist.
1977	The TRS-80—the first color computer for the home—is introduced.
1977	The first Apple computer is developed.
1977	The Commodore Pet—a text-only computer—is introduced.
1980	The CD player is introduced.
1981	The first IBM Personal Computer is developed.
1998	Chevrolet introduces the Delphi—a vehicle with built-in access to the Internet and e-mail.
2000	Cellular telephones with direct Internet access are generally available.
2047	By this date, all electronically encodable information will be in cyberspace (Gordan Bell's prediction).

Chapter Objectives

- Appreciate how computers pervade our everyday lives.
- Identify which devices are considered computers and which are not.
- Understand why computers use the binary system.
- Understand the differences between electronic and mechanical computers.
- Discern the differences between special-purpose and general-purpose computers.
- Understand the differences between digital and analog computers.
- Be familiar with the major types of software and application programs available.

Lawrence Migdale/Photo Researchers, Inc.

Puzzler: A Trick Question: What IS a Computer?

Accurately defining the term **computer** is tricky because of the great variety of technology we use daily. Is it that box with a video screen we see on every desk? Is it a jumble of tiny electronic circuits? Is it a wonderful invention of the mid-twentieth century? Is it a mysterious power that controls the World Wide Web?

PUZZLER

Before you begin working from this book, take a few moments to write out a list of all the computers in your life. Can you write a definition, in 40 words or less, that fits every item on the list? Be careful, this is a trick question. . . .

1.1 Beyond the Computer Invasion

A DAY IN THE 21ST CENTURY

6:30 A.M. The early beginning of a typical workday. You catapult out of bed when your computerized satellite radio alarm clock sounds automatically. A bleary glance at the clock shows you the LED numerals "6:30."

6:45 A.M. You reach for that first cup of coffee. It's ready, hot, and freshly brewed, because the computerized timer turned on the coffee maker at 6:15.

6:50 A.M. Your computer started automatically, too, and awaits your command. You log into your online broker's Web site to check today's stock prices. Taking advantage of this updated information, you improve your portfolio with two quick transactions, paying the reasonable self-brokering fee with a credit card. The broker's **secure server** protects your credit card transaction as well as your financial privacy.

7:30 A.M. You ease your car away from the curb. The car's computerized diagnostic system indicates that the brakes and air bag are functioning properly and that the oil and fuel levels are okay. An LED light warns that you have not properly closed the driver-side door. A computerized voice reminds you to fasten your seat belt.

8:00 A.M. You turn on your desk computer and log onto your company's network. Your online scheduling calendar acknowledges your presence and sends a list of today's meetings and appointments to your printer. Several e-mail messages are waiting for you, including an order from a customer several hundred miles away. You check the inventory, and through the global community of the Internet, you notify the client that the order has been filled and is on its way.

8:15 A.M. A flashing light on your computer calendar reminds you of your sister's birthday. You send her a quick electronic birthday card and flowers before dashing off to your first meeting.

9:05 A.M. You have just returned to your desk. Your cell phone screen indicates that you received two text messages while you were gone. You retrieve the messages and return one to your associate who is away from the office.

10:00 A.M. The fax machine at the end of the hall beeps to indicate the arrival of an important document. Because an immediate written reply is indicated, you dash one off on your computer's word processor and fax it.

12:00 P.M. You decide to take a few minutes of your lunch hour to buy a wedding gift for a friend. Turning to your computer, you log onto the online bridal registry for an e-retailer and select the item you want to give. You click on its picture to indicate your purchase. The computer informs you that the item you want is available in several colors. You indicate your color choice from the given menu and select to have your package gift wrapped and sent directly to your friend. You enter your friend's address and your name and credit card information and then go to lunch, assured that your gift will arrive on time.

1:15 P.M. Back at your desk, you decide to make airline, car rental, and hotel reservations for a conference you will be attending next month. After surfing the Web for a few moments, you book your reservations with an online travel service and pay by credit card.

3:00 P.M. A message on your computer screen tells you that your paycheck has been deposited electronically into your bank account. An online electronic check stub tells you that the computer has calculated your gross

For an online business, a **secure server** is a dedicated computer that stores, maintains, and protects customer information. The purpose is to keep personal information, such as telephone and credit card numbers, from reaching unscrupulous online predators.

pay as well as net pay after several deductions. Both current and year-to-date amounts are shown. A Web link to the bank allows you to check the arrival of your salary deposit as well as your account balance.

5:15 P.M.   You make a quick stop at the grocery store for a few things you need for dinner. Moving quickly to the self-checkout station, you press the start button on the touch-sensitive screen. A computer voice tells you to pass each selection by the scanner and place the item on the bagging shelf. The bar code scanner reads aloud a description of each product you scan, its weight (if appropriate), and current price. It also calculates your total and gives you payment options. Because the amount is low, you decide to pay with cash and insert a $20 bill into a bill tray. Correct change is dispensed in bills and coins, and a receipt is printed out. You pick up change, receipt, and groceries and head for the parking lot. As you leave, the self-checkout computer politely thanks you for shopping in that store.

6:30 P.M.   Home at last! You activate the voice security, enter the house, and switch on your television to pick up your personal and voice-mail messages from the Web. As you settle into a comfortable chair, you smell the aroma of roast beef. The computerized timer on your oven has started dinner for you. After dinner, you request the day's news summary from your favorite newspaper and update your social networking site.

11:30 P.M.   As the evening news ends, you fall into your bed and turn off the light. The computerized timer on the television will turn off the set in just a few moments. You snuggle down between the thermostatically controlled electric blankets, confident that your computerized alarm will not fail to arouse you tomorrow morning.

Throughout a typical workday, millions of people worldwide interact with computers, often without knowing it. Students, factory workers, homemakers, health care personnel, and even waiters and waitresses in restaurants constantly depend on the machines called computers. Doctors, hospitals, and medical researchers use computers for diagnosis and treatment. Warehouses and department stores use them for sales and inventory control. The U.S. Census Bureau uses computers to store and analyze data on more than 280 million people. Musicians rely on computers to perform, record, and play back their music. Even everyday transportation relies heavily on computers. In the twenty-first century, we have come to depend on computers in every aspect of our lives.

Current Dictionaries Reveal the Pervasiveness of Computers

In 2003 the 4th Edition of the American Heritage Dictionary of the English Language was published. It had about 9,000 new words added, and about 9% of them were related to computers, the Internet and related technology. Among the 800 or so new words are several such as *zine, applet* and *dot-com*. Their definitions from the dictionary are:

zine — **NOUN:** An inexpensively produced, self-published, underground publication.
ETYMOLOGY: Short for magazine.

applet — **NOUN:** *Computer Science* An application that has limited features, requires limited memory resources, and is usually portable between operating systems.
ETYMOLOGY: appl(ication) + -et.

dot-com — **ADJECTIVE: 1.** Of or relating to business conducted on the Internet: *dot-com advertising.*
2. Of or relating to a company whose products or services deal with or are sold on the Internet: *a dot-com brokerage firm.*
NOUN: A dot-com company.
ETYMOLOGY: Pronunciation of .com.

(continued)

Current Dictionaries Reveal the Pervasiveness of Computers *(continued)*

Choosing a word for the dictionary is a rather lengthy procedure. The process involves editors reading magazines, newspapers and other types of common publications. They then put the word, along with how it was used, into a huge database. If a word appears often enough, then it is added to the dictionary, and it will emphasize how important computers and the Internet have become in our society.

Some other facts are rather enlightening:

- It usually takes 10 to 20 years of usage to be sufficient for a word to merit addition to a dictionary. Yet, *dot-commer* made the dictionary in only five years.
- Slang is being adopted increasingly into English language. Words like blog and blogger are recent examples.
- There are many words that are adopted into one dictionary but not another. The word *zine* is in the 4th Edition of the American Heritage Dictionary of the English Language, for example, yet not in the 11th edition of the Merriam-Webster Collegiate Dictionary.

If you think you're tuned into computers and the Internet technology, take a look at the following partial selection of the new words:

applet	feedhorn	personal digital assistant
bit stream	file transfer protocol	point-and-click
caller ID	fire wall	raster
cell phone	flash memory	search engine
cybersurf	home page	shareware
defrag	intranet	subnotebook
dial-up	markup language	taskbar
digerati	multitask	trackball
dot-com	netiquette	Usenet
ethernet	netizen	World Wide Web
expansion board	open source	zine

What percentage of these words do you know, and how many others have you heard but don't know their definitions?

How has this happened? How have we allowed an inanimate machine to become so influential? Why do computers seem to control so much human activity? The reason computers are pervasive is that we can use them in so many different ways. Computers help us perform tasks that are repetitive, that involve calculation or manipulation of numbers, and that involve storage and retrieval of large quantities of information. We use them in business, education, scientific research, and personal record keeping. In fact, we rely on computers because they help us perform more easily and with greater accuracy many tasks that occupy our time day in and day out.

The goal of this book is to prepare you to deal effectively with the rapidly changing world our technology has evolved. To be more specific, one purpose of this book is to understand what a computer is and how it works. Another, is to understand the social ramifications of this technology.

1.2 What Is (and Isn't) a Computer?

The easiest way to discover the qualities and functions that make up a **computer** is to begin with a formal definition:

> A **computer** is a device that takes data in one form, processes it, and transforms it into information that is more useful than the original data.

PUZZLER HINT

PUZZLER HINT

Compare your definition of a computer to the one given here. Are these everyday devices considered computers by your definition: telephone, VCR, microphone, coffeepot, waffle iron, curling iron, fax machine? How can you upgrade your definition to make it cover a broader range of devices?

EXAMPLES FROM HISTORY

The oldest and most commonly known calculating device is the **abacus** (Figure 1.2.1). Many people refer to it as an early computer. The abacus was first used by the Babylonians in 2400 B.C. and later by the Greeks in 600 B.C. primarily as an accounting tool—to calculate the cost of goods being traded or payments owed for services. However, according to the definition given previously, the abacus is not a computer. By our definition, a computer must not only store information, but also it must *change the information* into some other form. The abacus only holds information for the person using it. It doesn't change the form of the information in any way.

On the other hand, Stonehenge, that mysterious monumental structure in England, *is* a computer by our definition. Stonehenge (Figure 1.2.2) takes the movement of the planets, sun, and other heavenly bodies and provides information concerning eclipses and other significant astronomical events. Stonehenge dates back before 1200 B.C. and represented an incredible scientific feat at that time.

SCALES AND CALCULATORS

Even the lowly bathroom scale in Figure 1.2.3 is by our definition a computer. The datum it takes in is the gravitational pull between a human body and the earth. The resulting information of this special-purpose computer is a number, usually expressed in pounds or kilo-

Karen Su/Stock Boston

Figure 1.2.1

The abacus, an early calculating device. Is it a computer?

Figure 1.2.2

Stonehenge, on the Salisbury Plain in Wiltshire, England.

British Tourist Authority

grams. Similarly, scales used in other settings, such as grocery stores and roadside truck weigh stations, perform the same data manipulation, converting the force of gravity on some object or substance into a numeric value, expressed as units of weight.

Another pervasive computer is the mundane calculator. The old electromechanical calculators that had gears and weighed 30 or 40 pounds were replaced in the 1960s by electronic handheld versions (Figure 1.2.4). Originally priced at several hundred dollars, calculators of today cost as little as $2. These lower-priced models add, subtract, multiply, and divide. Some of them also calculate square roots and percentages and have memories. You

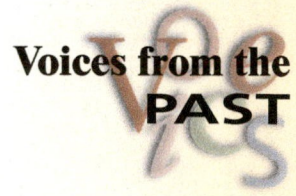

Voices from the PAST

Stonehenge—The First Computer?

Was the 3,500-year-old Stonehenge an astronomical observatory? Computer analysis of the positions of the huge monolithic stones and dozens of other markers reveal that Stonehenge was indeed a complex astronomical computer. Modern computers were used to retrace the positions of various objects in the sky to their positions 3,500 years ago, and it was noted that the positions of the many stones relate to various events. These events include midsummer sunrise and moonrise, midwinter sunrise and moonrise, eclipses, and other occurrences. In fact, while studying how Stonehenge made its predictions, astronomers discovered a 56-year eclipse cycle.

Astronomers hypothesize that it took at least 100 years of observations while recording them using small models to build Stonehenge. The monolithic Stonehenge we know today was then constructed in stages over a period of 300 years. It started in 1900 B.C. with what archaeologists call Stonehenge I. Then came Stonehenge II and Stonehenge IIIA, IIIB, and IIIC. The bursts of building activity ended in 1600 B.C. More than 80 of the large blue stones, weighing up to 5 tons each, were moved 240 miles over water and land from the quarry to the present location. Other stones weighing over 50 tons were quarried only miles away. Stonehenge, one of the first computers, is truly a remarkable example of human ingenuity.

Overview of Stonehenge's Aubrey holes used to predict eclipse seasons.

probably have a prime example of this type of calculator at home, in your pocket, or at work. It is used by thousands of elementary schools to teach concepts of arithmetic. These less expensive calculators are in the category of special-purpose computers; they can do only arithmetic.

More expensive but easily available today are programmable scientific calculators, which can display graphic output in the form of simple charts and graphs in addition to numerical output and text (Figure 1.2.5).

WIRELESS COMMUNICATION AND NETWORK ACCESS

Many exciting computers have been developed over the past few years to serve the communication and networking needs of the worldwide business community. Two pervasive examples are digital pagers and cell phones (Figure 1.2.6). These **wireless communication** devices provide instant **network access** for most business and personal communication needs, including voice mail, e-mail, and fax sending and receiving. Some cell phones even provide built-in Internet access that can be acquired from anywhere, including your automobile.

Other computer devices convert electrical signals into radio frequency signals that allow remote communication between a computer and Internet services such as email and the World Wide Web. One common format is called Wi-fi (Wireless Fidelity) that allows computers with the wireless capability to communicate over the Internet. In addition to communicating over the Internet, Wi-fi can be used to send information to printers or other computers on the network. Special radio frequency hardware must be at both the computer and the network ends.

COMPUTERS LARGE AND SMALL

As you've probably noticed by now, the term *computer* describes many more devices than just the desktop machine we usually visualize. Computers, in fact, come in a variety of sizes and shapes with an equally broad range of differing capabilities. And although today's largest computers, usually called **supercomputers** (Figure 1.2.7), have the highest potential capacity and accuracy, physical size is not always a measure of computing power. Some devices, small enough to fit in a shirt pocket or to hold in your hand, can perform tasks of incredible complexity.

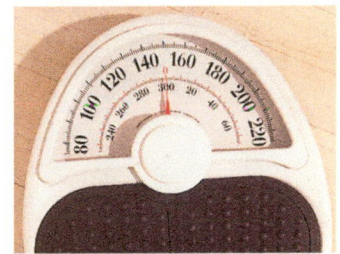

©1996 Michael A. Keller Studios, Ltd./ The Stock Market

Figure 1.2.3
An ordinary bathroom scale.

Casio, Inc.

Figure 1.2.5
More expensive handheld calculators display graphic as well as text and numerical data.

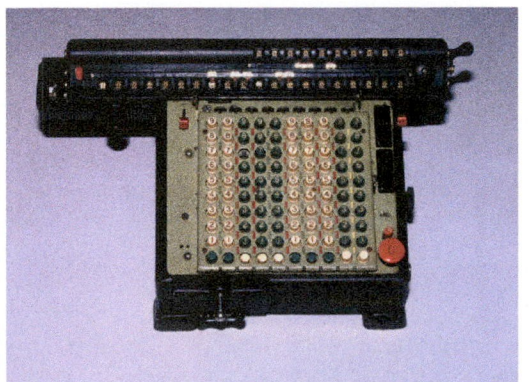

(a) The Computer Museum of America

(b) Courtesy of Texas Instruments Incorporated

Figure 1.2.4
Early desktop calculators, such as (a), were replaced with handheld models (b) in the 1960s.

Courtesy of Nokia

Figure 1.2.6

Paging, voice mail, e-mail, and Internet access are common features of today's wireless cell phones.

Courtesy of Thinking Machines Corporation

Figure 1.2.7

Supercomputers, often occupying an entire room, have today's greatest computing potential and data capacity.

Today's state-of-the-art **handheld computers**, such as PDAs and "smart" phones (Figure 1.2.8), can perform any task done by the desktop machines of a few years ago, and more. Designed primarily for on-the-go business use, they generally incorporate appointment and meeting planners, contact address and phone lists, and report generators and can run a wide variety of off-the-shelf PC software, such as presentation programs, word processors, and electronic spreadsheets. This sort of device is a general-purpose computer and marks the latest generation of palmtop computers. They can be connected to printers, wireless networks, and other electronic devices, and they have extensive memories.

Many cell phones today carry the functionality of a powerful computer. Have you recently tried to find a cell phone that *just* made phone calls? Most cell phones have integrated MP3 players and digital cameras. Although not as powerful as stand-alone digital

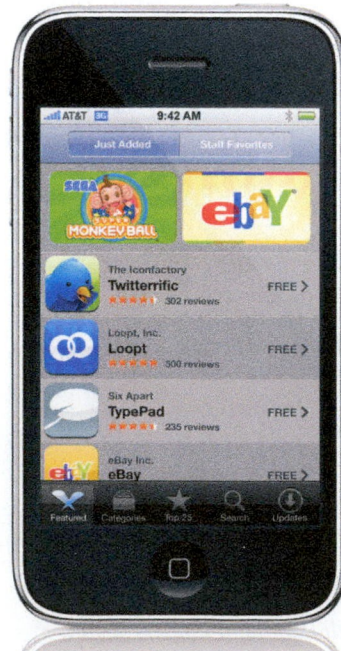

Courtesy of Apple Computers

Figure 1.2.8

Today's smart phones can do tasks performed by desktop machines.

cameras, the digital photographs taken by these cell phones can be used as background images on the phone itself, or sent to another cell phone or email address. Cell phone service contracts may include the sending and receiving of text messages, email services, access to the Web, and acquiring GPS information to determine the current location or for finding turn-by-turn directions to and from another location. With the miniaturization of cell phone components, the expansion and technological advancements to the cell phone networks, and the rise in expectations of services of those who use cell phones, these small handheld devices have become very powerful.

Abbreviations: A New Way to Communicate?

Abbreviations are nothing new. Abbreviations for words and phrases were commonly used by ham radio operators and by telegraph operators when the thrift of words was necessary. Abbreviations are again used as a means of reducing the number of characters necessary to convey text messages. The pop culture of sending and receiving text messages, smileys (text versions of human emotions), and emoticons (graphical representations of human facial emotions) sent by cell phones, in chat rooms, in online forums, in online gaming sites, on blogs, and in emails, has infiltrated the way we communicate in our every day lives.

The list of abbreviations is growing daily. What was once a few hundred abbreviations a few years ago has turned into upward of two thousand abbreviations today. These abbreviations are now commonplace in television advertisements, in printed media, online, in books, and in film. The sheer numbers of text messages has made the learning of this new cryptic language of abbreviations a must.

Telegram abbreviation sampling:

Arv.	Arrive	Thk.	Thanks
Awa.	Away	Tgh.	Telegraph
Bz.	Business	Tgm.	Telegram
Cg.	Seeing	Tnd.	Thousand
G.M.	Good Morning	Tw.	Tomorrow
G.N.	Good Night	U.	You
Hb.	Has been	Uc.	You see
Ixu.	It is understood	Wu.	Western Union
Potus	President of the United States	Ya.	Yesterday

Ham Radio abbreviation sampling:

CQ	Requesting contact of other amateur radio operator
DX	Distance station
XYL	Wife
73	Best regards
88	Love and kisses
161	Best regard to you and your wife

Text message abbreviation sampling:

?4U	I have a question for you	BFFL	Best friends for life
20	Location	BFN	Bye for now
411	Information	BG	Big grin
4COL	For crying out loud	BHL8	Be home late
AAK	Asleep at the keyboard	BRB	Be right back
ATEOTD	At the end of the day	BYOC	Bring your own computer
BF	Boy friend	DTS	Don't think so
BFF	Best friends forever	GL	Good luck

Smiley—Facial emotion text symbol sampling

:-)	Happy face
:-(	Sad face
X)	Laughing really hard
:-O	Surprised face
:-b	Sticking tongue out

More complete lists of text message abbreviations can be found on the Web using the search words "text message abbreviations."

1.3 The Many Kinds of Computers

Although the computer examples described and pictured in the previous section have much in common, they have basic differences as well. First, all except the bathroom scale and the pre-1960 calculator can be described as electronic. That means they need some source of electricity in order to work. The scale pictured in Figure 1.2.3 and the earliest calculators are mechanical and have no need for electricity. Second, some of the examples can be referred to as digital. That means they function using a **binary** (two-state) system rather than the analog system of the scale in Figure 1.2.3. You'll learn more about that in the next chapter. Finally, some computers were described as *general purpose* whereas the others (including the 1960s calculator) were *special purpose.*

Computers can be classified by the three sets of characteristics described previously. To better understand the type of computer we will discuss throughout this book, let's examine the sets of characteristics and see how they are applied to the computers around us. The major comparisons of computers are:

1. Electronic computers versus mechanical computers

2. General-purpose computers versus special-purpose computers

3. Digital computers versus analog computers

When the term **electronic** is used in today's technology, it refers to a device that is constructed from transistors and needs electricity to function. The necessary electrical power might be supplied by connection to a wall socket or generator, or it might come from stored electrical power in the form of batteries. In contrast, the common bathroom scale mentioned earlier is usually **mechanical.** Using a combination of levers and springs, the depression of the top surface of the scale, when someone is standing on it, causes a numbered dial or pointer to rotate and come to rest at some number inscribed on the dial. No electrical power is involved in the transformation of the pull of gravity into numbers of pounds. More expensive bathroom scales sometimes use a combination of mechanical parts to transform the energy and electronic circuits to display final results. This type of scale has electronic digital readouts—that is, instead of a dial with numbers, the individual digits of the number are displayed electronically.

Some common computers might be either mechanical or electronic. A good example is the automotive speedometer. On an older automobile the speedometer has a continuously moving marker, a long needle or pointer that indicates your speed by its position on a numbered dial. The needle is usually controlled by a rotating speedometer cable, which is physically turned by a connection with the rear axle of the automobile. But in most vehicles, speedometers are electronic; speed is calculated directly through the transmission and displayed in digits on a numeric readout on the dashboard.

GENERAL-PURPOSE VERSUS SPECIAL-PURPOSE COMPUTERS

The terms *general purpose* and *special purpose* indicate exactly what these categories of computers represent. For example, the bathroom scale and speedometer are definitely special-purpose computers. The scale can be used only to measure the weight of an object and could not be used to do things such as word processing or controlling the launch of a space shuttle. The speedometer, whether mechanical or electronic, could not be used to weigh something, to make coffee, or to send e-mail.

A **binary** device is one that can be set to one of only two possible conditions. For example, an ordinary light switch can be either ON or OFF—no other options are possible.

An **electronic computer** is a computer built from transistors and electrical circuits. Transistors and circuits must be connected to a source of electricity in order to work.

A **mechanical computer** is a computer built from a variety of different mechanical devices, such as springs and levers.

Most **special-purpose computers** are used to control things. They exist as tiny chips, embedded in some device, which help the device to operate smoothly. Frequently, they control timing (alarms and sparkplug firings), temperature (thermostats, clothes dryers, and dish-washers), digital readouts (speedometers, scales, and watches), various sensors (car door closed and seat belt fastened), and diagnostic devices (echocardiogram machines and fuel-level indicators). Each special-purpose computer performs only the task it was built to do in that specific device.

A **general-purpose computer,** on the other hand, can do many things. For instance, the same general-purpose computer that performs word processing can be used to control an assembly line or to perform statistical analysis of numerical information. The desktop or **laptop computer** we use today is a general-purpose computer of amazing flexibility, capable of performing numerous different tasks, often simultaneously. Its computational power might be compared favorably to that of larger commercially available machines, lacking only the multiple processors that give supercomputers their legendary speed and power. Today, personal computers and **workstations** can do anything supercomputers do, only more slowly.

This book concentrates mainly on the general-purpose computer and how it functions. However, we do mention special-purpose computers because most computing occurs on them. Remember that special-purpose computers are used in modern automobiles, cameras, microwave ovens, dishwashers, CD players, and many other appliances. A special-purpose computer can be categorized as either digital or analog. In the next section, we discuss digital and analog computers and learn why digital is more common than analog.

DIGITAL VERSUS ANALOG COMPUTERS

Analog computers have a rich history. Stonehenge is an analog computer, as are the old-fashioned slide rule, mercury thermometer we use to detect fever, and the already mentioned mechanical bathroom scale. What do all these devices have in common? For all of them, the input consists of quantities that can vary continuously, and the outputs also vary smoothly from one value to another or one position to another. For example, when someone steps on a bathroom scale, the force on the top of the scale starts at zero and increases until the person weighing himself or herself is standing completely on the scale. The number representing that individual's weight is on a numbered scale, which continuously moves until it comes to rest at a certain position. The number opposite a line or mark gives the weight. One interesting feature of the analog scale is its degree of precision, which is usually limited. For example, when you weigh yourself, it isn't possible or even meaningful to read the weight to the nearest one-thousandth of a pound. Better scales such as those found in medical offices have more precision. However, the cost of analog devices increases astronomically with higher accuracy.

The **digital computer** distinguishes itself from the analog computer in that it deals with discretely varying values. That is, the values jump from one value to the next without crossing through any in-between values. For example, digital watches have numerals that jump from value to value. Some digital watches will jump from 12:01 to 12:02 without showing all the 60 seconds between the two values. An analog watch with a second hand will smoothly sweep from minute to minute as the minute and hour hands also smoothly move around the watch dial.

In the past couple of decades, the popularity of digital computers has increased phenomenally. Some of this popularity is caused by fashion—people like to own and use the newest devices available. But the rapid ascension of digital devices over their analog counterparts has an additional, very practical cause: Digital devices are cheaper to build and more reliable to run. Whereas the springs and levers of analog devices require careful balance and tension adjustments, making production time-consuming and complicated, digital devices are made mainly from **binary electronic circuits,** which can be mass-produced inexpensively on assembly lines. Categories of various common devices are shown in Table 1.3.1.

A **special-purpose computer** is a computer designed to be used in a limited way (for example, a bathroom scale or a CD player).

A **general-purpose computer** is a computer that can be used in many situations and for many different and unrelated tasks (such as word processing, playing games, and playing music).

A **workstation** is a personal computer given additional capacity and power through increased memory and faster circuits. It is often connected to other computers and storage devices through the use of a network. It is intended for use by one person.

An **analog computer** functions in continuously varying quantities and produces continuously varying results. Imagine pulling a wagon up a ramp. As the wagon moves continuously forward, its height above ground level varies continuously as well. The ramp is a computer that converts force and forward motion into increased height.

A **digital computer** functions in discretely varying quantities and produces discretely varying results. Imagine carrying a heavy package up a flight of stairs. Each step moves the package (and you) a specific (discrete) distance forward and a specific distance upward.

Although special-purpose digital computers such as digital watches, cellular telephones, fax machines, and CD players have become common elements of our daily lives, it is the general-purpose digital computer on which we have come to depend. Imagine running airline reservation systems or large auto parts warehouses without large powerful **mainframe** computers. Think of the millions of desktop computers used in small businesses to manage payroll programs, accounting systems, and customer information. Consider the millions of computers used in homes and schools and carried in briefcases in cars and airliners. These computers are all digital, general-purpose computers that can be used to perform many different tasks from word processing to game playing, from information management to bidding on auctions.

A **mainframe** is a large, powerful computer used by large businesses, schools, and government agencies. Many users can be connected to a single mainframe computer simultaneously.

Because general-purpose digital computers are so important to us, let's take a brief moment to look more closely at what components comprise them and what makes them work.

Table 1.3.1   *Categories of various common devices.*

Name of device	Is it a computer? Yes/No	Why or why not?	Electronic or mechanical?	Digital or analog?	General or special purpose?
Bathroom scale	Yes	Transforms pull of gravity into pounds	Mechanical	Analog	Special purpose
Speedometer on older vehicle	Yes	Transforms rotation of wheels into miles per hour	Mechanical	Analog	Special purpose
Speedometer on newer vehicle	Yes	Transforms rotation of wheels into miles per hour	Electronic	Digital	Special purpose
Abacus	No	No transformation takes place	Mechanical	Digital	Special purpose
Ramp	Yes	Transforms force and forward motion to height	Mechanical	Analog	Special purpose
Handheld calculator	Yes	Calculates arithmetic results	Electronic	Digital	Special purpose
Echocardiogram	Yes	Converts heart action into visual image and sound	Electronic	Digital	Special purpose
Sundial	Yes	Converts motion of sun into time reading	Mechanical	Analog	Special purpose
Laptop computer	Yes	Converts many types of data, calculates results	Electronic	Digital	General purpose

1.4 The General-Purpose Electronic Digital Computer

A **general-purpose electronic digital computer** is a device that accepts information of many kinds, changes it in a way that is controllable by humans, and presents the result in a way usable by humans. This device is constructed of binary electronic circuits.

After all of this discussion, we can finally define the computer that is discussed throughout the rest of this book: the **general-purpose electronic digital computer.** The words *general purpose* indicate that these computers can be used in many different fields of work, including medicine, atomic research, ecology, payroll, record keeping, sports, retail sales, farming, commercial art, meal planning, and musical entertainment. The word *electronic* indicates that these machines require a source of electricity in order to function. The word *digital* refers to the binary circuitry that comprises the computer's makeup. Finally, the word *computer* reminds us that the purpose of this machine is to accept data in one form and transform these data into some other form that is useful to humans.

Digital computers are conceptually simple and are made up of four major components:

- input units
- memory
- central processing unit (CPU)
- output units

The **input units,** such as the mouse and keyboard, receive information. **Memory** ensures the computer can keep application programs and information ready and available for

Biological Computers Using DNA

William Ditto, Professor

It's been over a decade since Leonard Adleman experimented with his TT-100 computer (Test Tube with 100 microliters of fluid, about 1/50th of a teaspoon). His solution to a type of problem called a directed Hamiltonian path problem was hailed as a breakthrough. An example of such a puzzle is the traveling salesman problem. The salesman wants the shortest path to follow while visiting several cities, yet visiting each city only once. Adleman's biological computer solved the problem in seconds, where it would have taken conventional computers years to solve. However, once the problem was solved it took many hours to extract the answer.

Another researcher, Ehud Shapiro, and his team at the Weizmann Institute in Israel have been entered into the Guinness Book of World Records for creating the smallest biological computing device. The scientists said that two spoonfuls of fluid could hold up to 30 million billion molecular computers and would have 20 times more power than today's fastest supercomputer.

What are these amazing computers that Adleman and Shapiro created? To start with, the present day biological computers are composed of DNA molecules and enzymes. They use DNA molecules as input, output and to provide the programs or software. The "hardware," which corresponds to what we usually think of as hardware, are enzymes that regulate the process. In particular, Shapiro used two enzymes: one enzyme is used to recognize certain sequences of DNA and the other to stick these bits and pieces together in a meaningful way.

What about the memory for this computer? Some type of memory is usually associated with any general purpose computing device. It is interesting to note that a cubic centimeter of DNA can hold the equivalent of a trillion CDs.

Biological computers have the potential to become the smallest and fastest and most powerful computers in the next few decades. The study along the way to this objective will lead to a better understanding of the cell and its mechanisms. It could lead to a point where "cell computers" may be used as a means to watch for trouble in our bodies and possibly synthesize drugs to combat the problem.

The Cutting Edge

use. The **central processing unit,** the brain of the computer, controls all computer operations, processes information, and computes results. **Output units,** such as the monitor and printer, display the results of the computer's computations. We'll take a detailed look at these four computer components in chapter 3. For now, it is sufficient to understand that these four parts are known as computer **hardware.**

The programs that guide the computer through its tasks are collectively known as **software,** which is more complex than hardware. Whether it is a word-processing program or a game, each piece of computer software provides detailed instructions the computer needs to complete a specific task. Without software, the computer cannot function. We'll cover the concept of a computer program and how it manages computer hardware in chapters 4 through 6.

Everything done in a digital electronic computer follows a system of numeration called the binary system. What this means is discussed in the next chapter. Let it suffice to say that numbers in the binary system consist of only ones and zeros. All information put into the computer's memory must be in binary form for the computer to use it.

This overview of the general-purpose computer wouldn't be complete without questioning the magic of why computers work in binary. Digital electronic computers work in the binary system because it is both *cheap* and *reliable*. There is no magic! It's not because the zeros and ones of the binary system can be seen as switches or lights that are either on or off. Building any other type of system is simply too expensive and unreliable.

Our definition of a general-purpose electronic digital computer is pretty general so far. You will need the next five chapters to understand what it means and the remaining part of the book to see how useful the general-purpose electronic digital computer really is.

Computer hardware is the electronics and the associated mechanical parts of the computer. It is distinguished by the fact that it has a physical presence. That is, you can see, feel, and touch hardware.

Computer software consists of instructions that control the hardware and cause the desired outcome. For example, the thousands of instructions that make up a word-processing program allow the user to type words, change the order of the words, and print or save copies of letters.

PUZZLER HINT
PUZZLER HINT

Now that you've completed your definition of computers, you should enhance it by including a clear statement of what kinds of information a computer can manipulate. Use the next section of this chapter to discover five types of computable information and give an example of each.

Because computers deal with information, you will need a clear understanding of exactly what information is before we go much further. In the next chapter, we discuss the five different types of information that the computer uses. By the single word *computer,* we already mean, of course, the general-purpose electronic digital computer. These five kinds of information—numbers, symbols, pictures, sound, and instructions—are then manipulated in some way by something called a program. The program is a set of instructions given to the computer that exerts human control over the process.

Chapter Summary

1.1 Beyond the Computer Invasionm

Millions of people interact with computers daily in numerous and varied ways. At home, at school, and at work, we rely on computers to increase speed and accuracy in performing everyday tasks. Although we seldom think about the computers we use, we can increase our effectiveness by learning more about computers and how they function.

1.2 What Is (and Isn't) a Computer?

A computer is any device that receives data in one form, processes them, and transforms them into a different, more useful form. People have used computers since 1200 B.C., when astronomers built Stonehenge in England. Despite their versatility, computers do not include devices, such as the abacus, which store information but do not process it. Common computers used today include handheld calculators, MP3 players, cellular phones, and bathroom scales. One cannot estimate the power of a specific computer merely by size. Today's smallest handheld computers are more powerful than room-sized computers of only a few decades ago.

1.3 The Many Kinds of Computers

Computers can be classified by describing them in terms of three pairs of characteristics. First, if a computer needs electricity in order to run, it is electronic rather than mechanical. Second, a computer is digital if its quantities vary in discrete units or steps. If the quantities vary continuously like a ramp, the computer is analog. Finally, a computer designed to perform a specific task is special purpose. Those that can be programmed to perform different tasks are general purpose. The computer we have come to depend on is the general-purpose electronic digital computer.

1.4 The General-Purpose Electronic Digital Computer

The computer discussed throughout the rest of this book is the general-purpose electronic digital computer. This device consists of four major components: (a) input units, which receive information; (b) output units, which display results; (c) memory, which stores information and programs; and (d) the central processing unit, which is the "brain" of the computer. These four comprise the computer's hardware. The programs that guide the computer are called software. Digital electronic computers work in the binary system because it is both economical and reliable.

Key Terms

Key terms introduced in this chapter:

1. Abacus, *7*
2. Analog computers, *13*
3. Binary, *12*
4. Binary electronic circuit, *13*
5. Central processing unit, *15*
6. Computer, *7*
7. Digital computers, *13*
8. Electronic computers, *12*
9. General-purpose computers, *13*
10. General-purpose electronic digital computer, *14*
11. Handheld computers, *10*
12. Hardware, *15*
13. Input units, *14*
14. Laptop computer, *13*
15. Mainframe, *14*
16. Mechanical computers, *12*
17. Memory, *14*
18. Network access, *9*
19. Output units, *15*
20. Secure server, *4*
21. Software, *15*
22. Special-purpose computers, *13*
23. Supercomputers, *9*
24. Wireless communication, *9*
25. Workstation, *13*

Matching

Match the number of the key terms introduced in the chapter to the following statements. Each term may be used once, more than once, or not at all.

1. __1__ Although many people think of this as an early computer, it is actually a device that only stores information for later use.

2. __6__ This device takes data in one form, uses the data, and produces a different form of information that is related to (but not the same as) the original.

3. __24__ Cell phones help serve this kind of need in the business community.

4. __23__ This is the name given to today's largest and most powerful computers.

5. ____ These parts of the computer receive the information or programs to be used.

6. __17__ This part of the computer keeps the programs and information ready and available.

7. __19__ These parts of the computer display the results of computation to the human using the computer.

8. __5__ This part of the computer performs calculations, controls all computer activities, and is often referred to as the brain of the computer.

9. __3__ This is the numeration system used by the computer.

10. __16__ This type of computer may use belts, pulleys, or gears to control its function.

11. __9__ This type of computer can be used for several unrelated tasks.

12. __8__ This type of computer is constructed from transistors that use electricity to function.

13. __2__ This type of computer functions in continuously varying quantities and produces or gives results that are continuously varying.

14. __7__ This type of computer functions in discretely varying quantities and produces or gives results that are also discretely varying.

15. __22__ This type of computer is designed to be used in a limited way.

16. __14__ This personal computer is given additional capability by being portable and powered by batteries.

17. __10__ This type of computer can be used for many kinds of work; it is controlled by humans, and it presents results in a way that is usable by humans.

18. __4__ This type of electronic circuit can exist in either one of two states, normally represented by 0 or 1.

19. __6__ This is needed to send and receive e-mail.

20. __12__ This term refers to the parts of the computer that have physical presence—that is, you can see, touch, and feel them.

True or False

Place either T or F on the line provided with each of the following statements. If a statement is false, you should be able to explain what changes would make it true.

1. _F_ The abacus is considered a computer, according to our definition.

2. _T_ Stonehenge is considered a computer, according to our definition.

3. _T_ A bathroom scale is considered a computer, according to our definition.

4. _T_ A CD-ROM drive is considered both an input and output unit.

5. _F_ Magnetic disk storage is considered software.

6. _T_ The programs stored on a floppy disk are considered software.

7. _T_ The binary numeration system consists only of ones and zeros.

8. _F_ Digital computers can use the decimal system familiar to most people.

9. _T_ Digital electronic computers work in the binary system because it is both cheap and reliable.

10. _F_ Building a computer out of electronic circuits that use any base system other than base 2, such as base 10 or 16, has no effect on the reliability of the resulting computer.

11. _F_ An example of an electronic computer is an expensive bathroom scale that has a digital readout.

12. _F_ An example of a general-purpose computer is a newer automobile because it has microchips in it that control air bags, braking systems, and radios.

13. _T_ Stonehenge is an example of an analog computer.

14. _T_ A CD player is an example of a digital computer.

15. _T_ Today's laptop computer has made the use of visual presentations using computer projection systems very common.

16. _T_ Thirty-five years ago, if you wanted a computer to do a specific task, you had to write the software yourself.

17. _T_ Microcomputers are general-purpose electronic digital computers.

Multiple Choice

Answer the multiple-choice questions by selecting the best answer from the choices given.

1. Stonehenge, the old rotating speedometer cable showing car speed, and a watch's smoothly sweeping second hand are all examples of which type of computer?
   a. Analog and special purpose
   b. Digital
   c. General purpose
   d. Electronic
   e. Special purpose and electronic

2. The binary numeration system is used in computers because
   a. computers can't count in decimal
   b. binary is cheap and reliable
   c. humans needed a binary translator when the computer was first created
   d. the zeros and ones of the binary system can be seen as switches that are either on or off
   e. the zeros and ones of the binary system can be seen as lights that are either on or off

3. These are defined as the electronics and the associated mechanical parts of the computer.
   a. Computer software
   b. Programs
   c. Central processing units
   d. Computer hardware

4. These are defined as consisting of instructions that control the hardware and cause the desired process to happen.
   a. Operating system
   b. Numeration systems
   c. Central processing units
   d. Computer hardware
   e. Binary electronic circuits

5. These computers are designed to be used in a limited way.
   a. Electronic computers
   b. Mechanical computers
   c. General-purpose computers
   d. Special-purpose computers
   e. Analog computers
   f. Digital computers

6. These computers function in continuously varying quantities and produce results that are continuously varying.
   a. Electronic computers
   b. Mechanical computers
   c. General-purpose computers
   d. Special-purpose computers

e. Binary electronic circuits

e. Analog computers
f. Digital computers

7. These computers are constructed from transistors that use electricity to function.
   a. Electronic computers
   b. Mechanical computers
   c. General-purpose computers
   d. Special-purpose computers
   e. Analog computers
   f. Digital computers

8. These computers function in discretely varying quantities and produce results that are discretely varying.
   a. Electronic computers
   b. Mechanical computers
   c. General-purpose computers
   d. Special-purpose computers
   e. Analog computers
   f. Digital computers

9. These computers can be used in many situations and for many unrelated tasks.
   a. Electronic computers
   b. Mechanical computers
   c. General-purpose computers
   d. Special-purpose computers

e. Analog computers
f. Digital computers

10. These computers often use a combination of levers, springs, pulleys, or dials. They do not rely on electronic components in order to function.
    a. Electronic computers
    b. Mechanical computers
    c. General-purpose computers
    d. Special-purpose computers
    e. Analog computers
    f. Digital computers

11. Which of the following is not a computer according to the definition given in this chapter?
    a. Bathroom scale
    b. Abacus
    c. Calculator
    d. Automobile speedometer
    e. Cell phone

12. Which of the following terms refers to the largest and most powerful of computers today?
    a. Mainframe
    b. Stonehenge
    c. Palmtop
    d. Workstation
    e. Supercomputer

Exercises

1. Consider your own activities yesterday. How many times did you use a computer? How often did you do something that was affected by a computer?

2. Select any six-hour period of time during which you have been awake. List all interactions you had with computers during that period.

3. Name the four major parts of a computer and explain their relationship to each other.

4. Select any profession or occupation that requires post–high school training or education. Interview someone who does that kind of work and write a report telling how he or she uses computers in the workplace.

5. Name five ways that using computers could help you with your schoolwork.

6. Make a list of brand names of at least one product for each of the following categories and indicate how each is used:
   a. General-purpose computers costing less than $2,000
   b. General-purpose computers costing more than $1 million (commonly called mainframe or super-computers)
   c. Special-purpose digital computers used around the home
   d. Special-purpose analog computers used around the home

7. Make a list of special-purpose computers that are in your home.

8. Name the computer-controlled devices that are in the car you drive.

9. Give three examples of special-purpose computers.

10. Give three examples of general-purpose computers.

11. From the following types of application programs, select three you have used. For each of those you have selected, write the name of the specific program, and describe at least five processes included in that program that you have used.

    Example: If you selected database managers, you might name Filemaker Pro and describe processes for data entry, report formatting, calculations, querying the database, and sorting the information.

    Types of application programs:
    a. Word processors
    b. Database managers
    c. Spreadsheets
    d. Web browsers
    e. Web page builders
    f. Presentation graphics
    g. Operating systems
    h. Utility tools

12. **PUZZLER** For each device named in the following chart, fill in the spaces to answer these questions: (a) Is it a computer? (b) If so, is it digital or analog? (c) Is it electronic or mechanical? (d) Is it special purpose or general purpose?

Device	Is it a computer?	General or special purpose?	Electronic or mechanical?	Digital or analog?
Coffeemaker	_____	_____	_____	_____
Bar code reader	_____	_____	_____	_____
Fax machine	_____	_____	_____	_____
Windup clock	_____	_____	_____	_____
Calculator	_____	_____	_____	_____
Wrist alarm watch	_____	_____	_____	_____
Wrist data bank watch	_____	_____	_____	_____
Home security system	_____	_____	_____	_____
Home computer	_____	_____	_____	_____
Rotary dial phone	_____	_____	_____	_____
Touch-Tone phone	_____	_____	_____	_____
VCR	_____	_____	_____	_____
CD player	_____	_____	_____	_____
Music box	_____	_____	_____	_____
Cell phone	_____	_____	_____	_____
Palmtop	_____	_____	_____	_____
Word processor	_____	_____	_____	_____

Discussion Questions

1. The sundial is obviously related to Stonehenge in a rather trivial way. Is the sundial a computer? Explain your answer.

2. How can software exist only in a person's brain?

3. Why do analog computers cost more than digital computers?

4. Discuss the significance of the fact that binary circuits are cheap and reliable, and why this would lead to their exclusive use over any other type of electronics. Is being cheap and reliable all that important?

5. Are there any reasons why we should fear computers? Think of at least six different reasons for being

concerned or anxious about computers. Do any of these concerns warrant being fearful of them? Explain.

6. Explain how computers have contributed to hospitals and the health care industry in general.

7. How do humans exert control over computers? In other words, how do humans make computers do things, either directly or indirectly?

8. How do computers control our lives? How have we had to change the way we do things because of computers?

9. Which is more important in the field of computer science—software or hardware? Explain you choice.

Group Project

This group project for five people traces the process of computing from its earliest form up through three different generations of computational devices. Each member of the group uses one of the five techniques for calculation.

Perform all three of the following arithmetic problems in each of the five parts of this assignment. Write down any techniques used, such as borrowing in subtraction or how numbers are subtracted on a calculator. *Do the best you can using the capabilities of each device!*

1. Add the following numbers: 24.3, 45, 4, 107.
2. Subtract 65 from 102.
3. Multiply 7 times 13.

Person 1: Long before people invented devices to perform arithmetic, we had to invent the calculation processes and understand them well enough to perform them by hand. As you do the three assigned problems in this part, be aware of the *process* your mind goes through to perform each task, such as borrowing in subtraction. Perform each calculation slowly and write down each step. Do not skip steps that are obvious to you from many years of experience doing similar problems. As you do the three problems, show all the details. You should make little notes about things such as carrying in addition and borrowing in subtraction.

Person 2: The earliest computing device used in this project is an abacus. You may use a real one if you have it, or you may use a virtual abacus located on the World Wide Web.

Select a virtual abacus that includes directions on how to perform simple arithmetic calculations. As you do each of the three problems, write down a summary of the process used in doing the computations.

Person 3: Now we'll jump several centuries to the middle of the twentieth century before the age of electronic calculators. Your next computing machine, called a comptometer, was completely mechanical, performing calculations through the use of springs and levers. Once again, you should find a virtual comptometer on the World Wide Web.

As you do each computation using the World Wide Web virtual comptometer, either sketch the basic layout of the comptometer that is on the computer display or make a screen shot of the computer's display screen. Ask your instructor how to do this. You can then write directly on the printed copy of the screen shot.

Person 4: The development of low-cost electronic calculators represented another quantum leap in the history of calculating machines. For this part of Project 1, you may use either a real calculator or the virtual one included as a desk accessory on most personal computers. When you complete the three problems, write the details on which type of calculator you used and other capabilities that it may have.

Person 5: For this last part of Project 1, you need to use an electronic spreadsheet program. You probably have one installed on the computer you are currently using. Again, use a screen shot of the computer display or sketch in detail how you did each calculation.

 ## Web Exercises

1. Create a photographic time line of the history of computers.
   a. Using your Web browser, search the Web for photos of important computers and people from computer history.
   b. As you find each picture, copy it into your word processor, along with a note naming, dating, and describing the computer. Resize each photo as necessary. Be sure to include a reference to the Web page where you found each photo.
   c. Format your time line document attractively. Print out the document, in color if a color printer is available.

2. Use the World Wide Web to find the information to fill in the following table. For each manufacturer, give the name, memory size, speed, and hard disk size of one computer in each category. If a manufacturer does not make a computer in a particular category, enter "none."

Manufacturer	Web Address	Desktop?	Price	Laptop?	Price	Palmtop?	Price
Hewlett-Packard	_____	_____	_____	_____	_____	_____	_____
Apple	_____	_____	_____	_____	_____	_____	_____
Dell	_____	_____	_____	_____	_____	_____	_____
Compaq	_____	_____	_____	_____	_____	_____	_____
Packard Bell	_____	_____	_____	_____	_____	_____	_____
IBM	_____	_____	_____	_____	_____	_____	_____
Gateway	_____	_____	_____	_____	_____	_____	_____

Bibliography

Bell, David and Barbara M. Kennedy, eds. *The Cybercultures Reader.* New York: Routledge, 2000.

> This book brings together articles covering the whole spectrum of cyberspace and related new technologies to explore the ways in which these technologies are reshaping cultural forms and practices.

Berkowitz, Bruce D. and Allan E. Goodman. *Best Truth: Intelligence in the Information Age.* New Haven, CT: Yale University Press, 2000.

> A reevaluation of concepts of intelligence during the growth and development of the technological era.

Burke, James. *The Knowledge Web: From Electronic Agents to Stonehenge and Back—And Other Journeys Through Knowledge.* New York: Simon & Schuster, 2000.

> This book takes us on a fascinating tour through the interlocking threads of knowledge running through Western history.

Burl, Aubrey. *Great Stone Circles: Fables, Fictions, Facts.* New Haven, CT: Yale University Press, 1999.

> This book examines the facts and mystique surrounding Stonehenge and eleven somewhat similar sites on the British Isles.

Cortada, James W. *Before the Computer: IBM, NCR, Burroughs, and Remington Rand and the Industry They Created, 1865–1956* (Princeton Studies in Business and Technology). Princeton, NJ: Princeton University Press, 2000.

> This volume gives an interesting retrospective of some of the giants of the business information industry before and during the early development of computers.

Denning, Peter J. and Robert M. Metcalf, eds. *Beyond Calculation—The Next Fifty Years of Computing.* San Francisco: Copernicus Books, 1997.

> This book features essays by leaders in the computing community who predict the directions computing will take in the next 50 years.

Hawkins, Gerald S. with John B. White. *Stonehenge Decoded.* New York: Dell, 1965.

> This book explains the development and uses of Stonehenge, with maps and discussions of its scientific significance.

Hobart, Michael E. and Zachary S. Schiffman. *Information Ages: Literacy, Numeracy, and the Computer Revolution.* Baltimore, MD: Johns Hopkins University Press, 2000.

> A sweeping history of information technology from ancient times to the present.

Jones, John Christopher. *The Internet and Everyone.* London: Ellipsis London Press, 2000.

> This work explores the potential of the Internet to act as an instigator of a new kind of life.

Tapscott, Don. *Growing Up Digital: The Rise of the Net Generation.* New York: McGraw-Hill, 1999.

> This book describes how the Net Generation is learning to communicate, work, shop, and play in profoundly new ways—and what implications this has for the world and business.

chapter **2**

Metamorphosis of Information

TimeLine

1000 B.C. The Phoenicians encode language into symbols.

1940 The Bombe computer is created to crack the German Enigma code.

1948 Claude Shannon formulates concepts of information content and communication.

1953 Watson and Crick discover DNA structure.

1974 First digital message sent into space intended for nonhumans.

1988 Hewlett-Packard markets first inkjet printer for $1,000.

2001 Microcomputer chip cycle speeds exceed a gigahertz or 1 billion cycles per second.

2003 The mapping of the human genome is completed.

2013 Extra-solar planet similar to Earth is discovered.

Chapter Objectives

- ⮕ Realize how almost all information fits into one of the following categories: numeric, character, visual, audio, or instructional.

- ⮕ Understand the issues involved in transforming and representing information in a computer.

- ⮕ Know why computers use binary numbers to store information.

- ⮕ Realize why storing any kind of information in a computer requires transformation to binary form.

- ⮕ Identify the differences between the external and internal forms of information.

- ⮕ Understand how pictures can be stored in a computer using pixels.

- ⮕ Recognize several different ways sound can be stored in a computer.

- ⮕ Discern the difference between facts and information.

- ⮕ Know the difference between an opcode and an address.

Arecibo Observatory   David Parker/Science Photo/Photo Researchers, Inc.

PUZZLER

The Arecibo Observatory in Puerto Rico is part of the National Astronomy and Ionosphere Center, a national research center operated by Cornell University. In 1974, scientists at the observatory used the Arecibo Radio Telescope to send a graphical representation of a message into space as shown on page 39. The top lines are counting in binary. What are the numbers and what is the scheme used in their representation? For a description of the Arecibo Radio Telescope, see "TechTalk: An Intergalactic Message" later in this chapter.

2.1 What Is Information?

All the items in the following list represent information of one type or another. The list items are grouped according to five categories. Can you describe the common type of information for each of the following groups?

A chessboard diagram
Satellite photos of the surface of Mars
The fingerprint files of a police department
The blueprint of a Concorde SST wing

The value of pi (π) to 100,000 decimal places
The fuel capacity of a Boeing 747
The total length of cotton thread used in a size 16/33 shirt
The distance between any 2 of the 100 largest U.S. cities
The volume of an electron in cubic light years
The number of Hanes men's briefs sold in January 2005
The annual earnings of a university professor

The text of *Gone with the Wind*
An enciphered diplomatic message
Your seat reservation for an airline flight
The chemical formula for ammonia
A concordance of a Middle English gospel
Your name and address

A Bach fugue in four parts
The sound of pronouncing the word afghanistanbananastand
The echoes sensed by sonar apparatus
A Tarzan yell

A computer program
A recipe for quiche lorraine
Complete directions for building an A-bomb
The menu for a road rally
Directions for assembling a custom wireless computer network

After analyzing this list, you should find that the five categories consist of visual, numeric, character, audio, and instructional information. In this context, the definition of information will be left to your intuition, which will be helped along by the examples. Also, the words *information* and *data* will be used interchangeably until later in chapter 11 where they will take on slightly different meanings. These five kinds of information are the only types of information the computer commonly manipulates. They are summarized in Figure 2.1.1.

Before the computer can use any type of information, it must be stored in the computer's memory, which can be thought of as a place to keep information for later use. Representing different types of information inside a computer presents a seemingly monu-

Figure 2.1.1

Computers manipulate only five categories of information: visual, numeric, character, audio, and instructional.

Visual	Numeric	Character or Symbol	Audio	Instructional or Command

mental task. To accomplish that goal, we must *transform* the information we want to store, converting it into an acceptable *representation* that a computer will accept. To approach the problems of **transformation** and **representation of information** gradually, let's first consider transformation. How can information be transformed from one mode of expression to another? We need to know, first of all, precisely what information we are trying to manipulate. Take, for example, the item "a chessboard diagram" from the preceding list. Such a description obscures a lot of the information, such as

- The pictorial information—that is, the information needed to reconstruct just the visual image of the chessboard diagram.
- The chess information—that is, the chess pieces that are on the board and the squares that they occupy.

To take another example, look at the information implied by the description "the annual earnings of a university professor." This description could include:

- Salary paid to the professor.
- Bonuses awarded for outstanding performance.
- Fringe benefits associated with the job.
- Possibly, additional income earned through sources not connected with the professor's employer. (We have to ask: Is this *any* professor or a *particular* one?)

We need a common form into which all information may be transformed. The form that we choose—numbers—should not be a surprise to you. Before we hastily conclude that all our problems are now solved, let's consider another example: the description "the fuel capacity of a Boeing 747." This clearly refers to a number. However, a **number** is an abstraction or idea and must be represented in order to be described, manipulated, processed, or stored. Unfortunately, numbers may be represented in many different ways. Also, a number may have extra information associated with it, which increases the choice of ways to represent it. The example of the Boeing 747 fuel capacity involves a numeric measure of quantity, and this in turn requires some choice of units. Thus, we might conclude that the airplane's capacity is, say, 46,311 gallons, or 175,306 liters, or 316,307 pounds, or 38,562 imperial gallons. Each representation describes the same amount of fuel capacity, but because different units are used, different numbers become involved.

> A **number** is an abstraction or idea expressing a specific value. It must be represented in some way in order to be described, manipulated, processed, or stored.

Similarly, a number, which has no associated units, may be written or represented in a variety of ways. Think about the number 12, for example. We may represent the number 12 in any of these ways:

~~LHT~~ ~~LHT~~ 11	12/1
XII	twelve
12	12.00

The choices depend on the context. The two representations 12 and 12.00 remind us that there are also different types of numbers: whole numbers, fractions, and decimals.

In this chapter, we'll tackle the problems of transforming information into numbers and choosing the appropriate way to represent the numbers so that a computer can use them. All modern computers work with a system of numbers called **binary numbers.**

Why do computers work using binary numbers? The choice of which form to use for numbers inside a computer system is dictated by considerations of cost and reliability. The electronic devices used in a computer are cheapest and function most reliably if they have to assume only two states or conditions. Such devices are usually referred to as binary electronic circuits.

> **Binary numbers** are similar to decimal numbers. However, binary numbers usually use the two symbols 1 and 0. The digit positions also have different values.

Probably the most familiar example of a binary electronic device is the ordinary light bulb. The light bulb, when controlled by the switch of a lamp or socket, can be in one of two states or conditions: on or off. The light bulb stays on or off until someone turns the switch. Computers contain electronic circuit elements that function in an analogous way: They are in

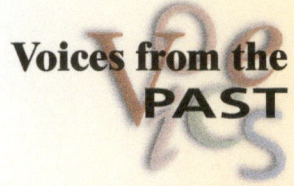

Claude E. Shannon: A Theory of Communication

Claude E. Shannon was born in 1916 in Petoskey, Michigan. He grew up in the small town of Gaylord, Michigan, as a bright and adventuresome youth. One of his early scientific endeavors was to create a communication system between his home and a neighboring farm where one of his friends lived. He cleverly used the barbed wire of the fence line that spanned the farms instead of stringing wires for his Morse code communications system.

Shannon is considered by many to be one of the greatest and most colorful scientists of the twentieth century. His research interests included data communications, cryptography, computers, circuits, games, genetics, and juggling. Dr. Shannon frequently constructed engaging and entertaining devices such as THROBAC (Thrifty ROman numerical BAckward looking Computer). THROBAC performs arithmetic operations in the Roman numerical system. His crowning achievement is the 1948 paper "The Mathematical Theory of Communication." His analysis of information is the first to address the problem of measuring information content and the theoretical limits of its flow over communications channels.

one of two states at any given time. The electronic circuit elements "remember" which state they are in, and this state can be switched from one state to the other. This switching is done by a specific action analogous to flipping the switch for a light bulb. The key to these circuits is that they are cheap to make and reliable in operation when compared to any of the alternatives.

The use of binary circuitry leads to a corresponding use of binary numbers. Such numerals use only 0s and 1s: These two choices may be thought of as corresponding to the off and on states of a light bulb.

Notice that what we have done so far is more than present just another example of information and how it is transformed into numbers. We have described the idea that binary numbers (in this case, 0 and 1) may themselves be associated with electronic devices. This is the connection at the most fundamental level between information and computers.

The use of 0 and 1 will not be confined to this light bulb example but will pervade our entire discussion of computers. The foundation on which the development of all electronic digital computers rests is this: All numbers may be expressed using only 0s and 1s. The system used to represent numbers by 0s and 1s is called the binary system.

2.2 Representation of Numbers

The binary system that makes information readable by computers is really something we all know. You see examples of the binary system of representing information every day. Here are just a few: the *occupied* slide sign in an airplane restroom, the *no* of a *no vacancy* sign, the *bright lights on* indicator of an automobile, the *up down* indicator of an elevator, the *fasten seat belt* sign on an airplane, the *occupied* light of a taxicab, the *flash ready* light on an electronic camera flash unit, the *open* sign at a grocery checkout lane, and the ferry boat *ready to leave* whistle. All these binary information examples have a two-state characteristic. In other words, the information conveyed consists of exactly one of two possibilities: on or off, occupied or unoccupied, yes or no, ready or not ready. Obviously, this is extremely limiting; a single binary device can indicate only one of two possibilities.

To indicate (or represent) more than two possibilities, we will need to use more than one binary device. To see how this works, imagine a bank of three light bulbs, each of which has its own on/off switch. Let's see how many binary combinations we can produce by flipping the switches: Each one of the three lights can be on while the other two are off. That gives us three possible combinations. Alternatively, one light can be off while the other two are on.

Figure 2.2.1

Eight combinations of lights on and off.

That adds three more combinations for a total of six, so far. Finally, the three lights can be either all on or all off. That gives us two more possibilities for a grand total of eight. Figure 2.2.1 illustrates these eight combinations of on/off light bulbs. Can you find any other possibilities?

An example of a three-light system that uses these eight possibilities to record information is a radio tower weather reporting facility. Suppose a local radio station decided to give visual weather coverage to all persons, boats, and aircraft within sight of its radio tower. This could be done by installing three bright lights in the tower. To give weather forecasts, the reporters could turn on or off the individual lights as illustrated in Figure 2.2.2. If the top

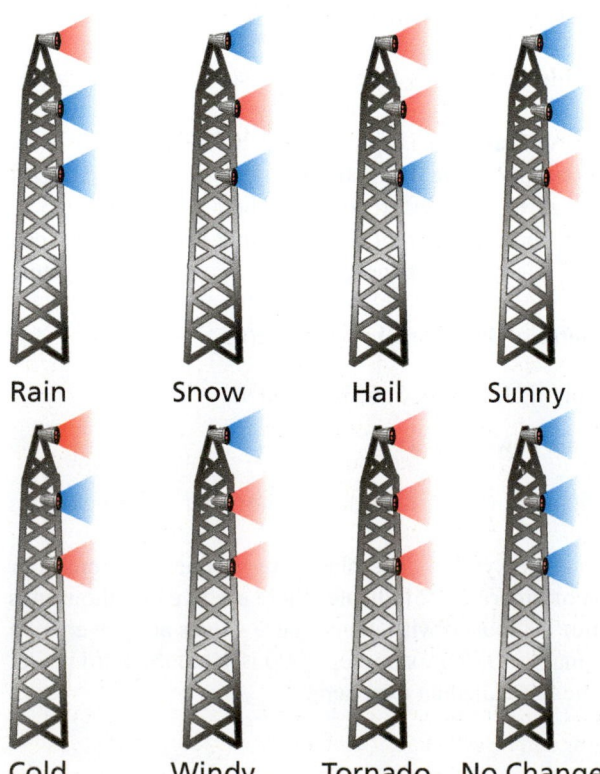

Rain   Snow   Hail   Sunny

Cold   Windy   Tornado   No Change

Figure 2.2.2

Radio tower weather information.

0	000
1	001
2	010
3	011
4	100
5	101
6	110
7	111

light were on and the others off, rain is forecast. The remaining combinations of lights on or off would be recognized as codes for the conditions indicated in the figure.

This example, although possibly interesting, doesn't involve the use of essential information. After all, we can just listen to the weather report over the radio and get more detailed and precise weather information, such as when and how much snow is expected. In addition, the weather tower is restricted to reporting only one condition at a time. (For example, it can't give sunny and windy conditions at the same time.) However, with just a little thought, this example could put us on the track of more vital uses of binary information. Such applications show us that one of the simpler yet important forms of information we have is numbers.

The three-light system could easily be used to indicate the decimal numbers 0, 1, 2, 3, 4, 5, 6, and 7 because there are exactly eight possible combinations of on and off for three lights. We've illustrated just one of many possible methods for numbering the combinations of lights in Figure 2.2.1.

Notice that all possible combinations of on and off have been used. Switching all lights off to represent zero and switching all lights on to mean the largest number, seven, seems logical. If we let the number 1 mean a light is on and 0 mean it is off, then putting these 0s and 1s in the same position as the lights gives us the number representations shown in Table 2.2.1.

These even look like numbers, and in fact, they are called binary **numerals.** Why do we say *numerals* instead of *numbers*? To begin to see why, consider any of the symbols, say, 110. If you had seen this out of context, you would no doubt have identified it as *one hundred ten,* a decimal numeral. In the familiar system of decimal numerals, each digit stands for a multiple of a power of 10 (more about this next). In the system of binary numerals, each digit stands for a multiple of a power of 2 instead. We also note that in the decimal system, each digit may be a number between 0 and 9, whereas in binary, each digit is actually called a **bit** (**bi**nary dig**it**) and may only be either 0 or 1. Thus, the numeral 110 stands for a different number in the decimal system of numerals than it does in the binary system. Look at these examples:

> **Bit** is an acronym for **bi**nary dig**it** and represents a single digit in binary numeration. It can be only either 0 or 1.

$$110_{decimal} = (1 \times 100) + (1 \times 10) + (0 \times 1)$$

$$110_{binary} = (1 \times 4) + (1 \times 2) + (0 \times 1)$$

To understand decimal and binary a little better, let's take an excursion into the realm of numeration systems.

The **decimal** (or *base 10*) **numeration system** is quite useful in our everyday lives. Society considers it so valuable that concepts of the decimal numeration system are taught starting in the first grade, and parents go to great effort to teach their young children to count. How many times have you heard a beaming parent say, "All right now, precious, can you show me how you can count to 10?" Many of the concepts found in our decimal system apply to the binary system.

> The **decimal numeration system** (base 10) assigns values to its digits based on powers of 10. In any given decimal integer, the right-most digit represents values of 10 to the 0 power (ones), the next digit to the left represents values of 10 to the first power (tens), the next represents values of 10 to the second power (hundreds), and so forth. Thus, the numeral 362 in base 10 means 2 ones, 6 tens, and 3 hundreds.

As a reminder, two important features of the decimal system are that

1. Base 10 or decimal uses 10 symbols: 0, 1, 2, 3, 4, 5, 6, 7, 8, and 9.

2. The place values of each position are powers of 10.

Figure 2.2.2 illustrates additional features of the decimal system that are sometimes forgotten.

To represent the various numbers, the symbols are placed in certain positions. For example, the 5 in the leftmost position of Figure 2.2.2 indicates there are five one-thousands in the number. Each position has a value associated with it, and these values are powers of a number called the base, which in decimal is 10. For example, 1,000 is 10 to the third power or 10^3, and 10^3 means $10 \times 10 \times 10$; the 3 is called an exponent.

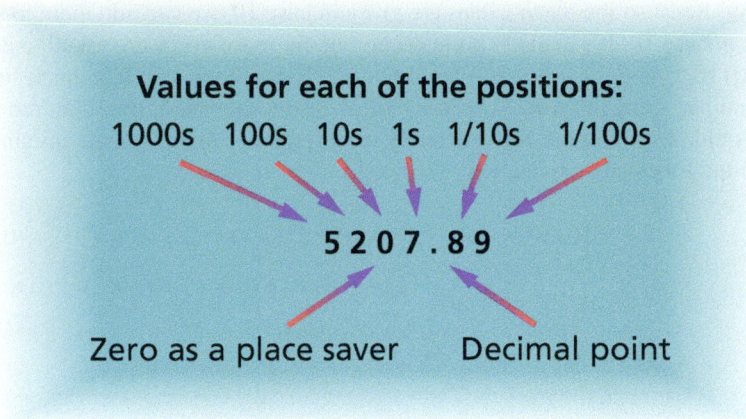

Figure 2.2.2

Place values of a base 10 number.

An **exponent** can be thought of as shorthand notation. It means that you multiply the number it is attached to by the exponent number of times. For example, 10^2 is 100, 2^3 is 8, and 8^2 is 64. An additional requirement for consistency is that anything to the 0 power is 1. For example, 10^0 is 1 and 2^0 is 1.

Using this exponent notation, the base 10 number from Figure 2.2.2 can be written in an expanded form as follows:

$$5207.89 = (5 \times 1,000) + (2 \times 100) + (0 \times 10) + (7 \times 1) + (8 \times 1/10) + (9 \times 1/100)$$

or

$$5207.89 = (5 \times 10^3) + (2 \times 10^2) + (0 \times 10^1) + (7 \times 10^0) + (8 \times 10^{-1}) + (9 \times 10^{-2})$$

After this short review of the base 10 numeration system, understanding another base is less difficult. Rather than give a complete formal mathematical definition, we will let our intuition guide us.

In the binary (or *base 2*) system, these two points seem to follow reasonably from our familiar decimal system of numeration:

1. Base 2 uses only two symbols, 0 and 1.
2. The place values of each position are powers of 2.

For example, the base 2 number 10110 can be written in terms of the familiar decimal numbers as shown in Figure 2.2.3.

Figure 2.2.3

Place values of a base 2 number.

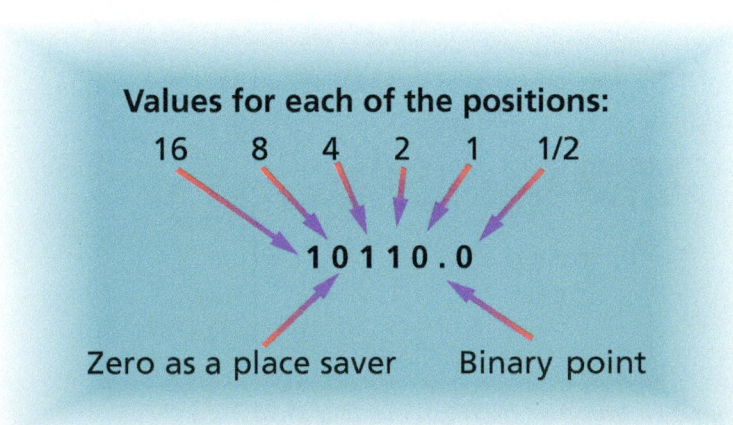

Because the place values are given in base 10, we can add them to see what this number is in base 10. It's actually quite deceiving. Suppose you were asked to go to the store and get 10110_{two} pounds of sugar. Would you need a truck to carry that much sugar? Certainly, if the number were interpreted as base 10, then ten thousand, one hundred ten pounds of sugar would be quite a lot. But it actually represents a relatively small amount in base 2, as shown in the following calculation:

$$10110_{two} = (1 \times 2^4) + (0 \times 2^3) + (1 \times 2^2) + (1 \times 2^1) + (0 \times 2^0)$$
$$= (1 \times 16) + (0 \times 8) + (1 \times 4) + (1 \times 2) + (0 \times 1)$$
$$= 16 + 0 + 4 + 2 + 0$$
$$= 22$$

In fact, the number 10110_{two} represents only 22 pounds of sugar! You could carry this home from the grocery store on your bicycle as shown in Figure 2.2.4.

To get more experience with exponents, let's count in base 2 (binary). First, note that in base 10 when we reach 9, we have run out of symbols, so we put a 0 in the ones place and make the tens place one bigger. In another example, what comes after 99 in base 10? We have all memorized that answer and immediately say 100! If we didn't know, then a way to get the number that is one bigger than 99 is to make the ones place one bigger. It is already at its largest value, so make it a zero and then make the tens place one bigger. The tens place already has a 9, so make it a 0 and then make the hundreds place one bigger. The result is 100!

In binary, the counting is done in the same way. When you run out of symbols in the ones place, change it to zero and make the place to the left one bigger. Table 2.2.2 illustrates counting in both decimal and binary.

Although we've avoided a thorough examination of numeration, this introduction is sufficient to help you understand a key point in how computers store information: No matter what numeration system is used, each number has a single unique representation. This means any base could be used and all results would be equivalent. In today's computers, binary is the numeration system of choice because it is very reliable and economical. No other numeration system, even decimal, would be as reliable and economical. This may change in the future as totally new technologies develop, in particular quantum computers, which we won't attempt to define.

Table 2.2.2 *Counting in decimal (base 10) and binary (base 2).*

Base 10	Base 2
0	0
1	1
2	10
3	11
4	100
5	101
6	110
7	111
8	1000
9	1001
10	1010
11	1011
12	1100
13	1101
14	1110
15	1111
16	10000
17	10001
18	10010
19	10011
20	10100
21	10101
22	10110
23	10111
24	11000
25	11001
26	11010
27	11011
28	11100
29	11101
30	11110
31	11111

10110 lbs
Sugar

10110_{two}
lbs Sugar

Figure 2.2.4

How do we transport 10110_{two} pounds of sugar?

A Serious Conversion Problem

This discussion would not be complete without examining what seems to be an imperfection in the binary representations of decimal numbers. It is obvious that numbers containing 0.1 decimal are important (i.e., one-tenth; the zero before the decimal point is for readability). For example, when representing money, 10 cents is commonly written \$0.10, or one-tenth of a dollar. The problem occurs in the end result of the conversion from 0.1 decimal to its binary form. Without seeing how to do the conversion from decimal fractions to binary fractions, examine the following result:

$$0.1 = .0001100110011001100110011001100110011 \ldots_{two}$$

The simple 0.1 decimal becomes an infinite repeating binary fraction. How is this possible? It's a fact! Just so you don't think this is unusual, remember that the common decimal fractions such as one-third and two-thirds become $0.33333\ldots$ and $0.66666\ldots$, which are also infinite repeating fractions.

A firm, not familiar with this problem, may hire a programmer to write an accounting program that would execute millions of arithmetic operations using 0.1 every day. If not detected, every time a 0.1 is added or subtracted in binary, a tiny part of the binary form of 0.1 would be thrown away. For example, using the first 13 bits of the binary form of 0.1 gives 0.0001100110011_{two}. This is not equivalent to the original number because the remaining part, $0.0000000000000001100110011\ldots_{two}$ is dropped off. Without knowing it, the firm could feasibly lose a lot of money over time on this programming error. This has also been a means of embezzlement by unscrupulous programmers who have intentionally performed this "error" in order to steal from the company.

This problem with 0.1 is not really insurmountable; it simply has to be taken into account. One of the many ways of handling the problem is the BCD (binary coded decimal) representation of numbers. The details of this code aren't of interest here. Let it be sufficient to say that BCD allows exact arithmetic when using 0.1.

2.3 Representation of Symbols and Text

By now, you should have firmly established in your mind the idea that to store any kind of information in a computer's memory, it must first be transformed into binary numeric form. We next consider the problem of storing symbols (characters, numbers, punctuation) or text, as all word processors must do.

Why is storing information important? Consider the information—text—that appears in this book. The authors stored the text using a word processor and the publisher then used it to electronically produce the bound book you are now reading.

One approach to storing text is to assign a different number to every word or grouping of characters that could possibly appear in the text. For example, let *and* be 1, *the* be 2, *this* be 3, and so on. This would be a very compact representation, but unfortunately, it is unacceptable for several reasons. In the first place, you would need a dictionary that provides the numerical equivalent for each possible word or symbol. No matter how big this dictionary was, there would always be new words or symbols popping up and requiring assigned numbers. Also, various punctuation marks and even blank spaces would have to be represented, and there would always be the possibility of new symbols appearing with no assigned numbers. Clearly, the number of revised editions of this dictionary could get annoyingly large. In the second place, the problem of retrieving the original information, once it was represented in numeric form, would present additional difficulties. You would need a *reverse* dictionary that contained the equivalent word or symbol for each possible number. Finally, a subtle difficulty would involve the fact that the numbers used to represent the textual information would, in this scheme, have unequal sizes—needing anywhere from one up to many places. As you might guess, the amount of space or memory needed to store the number 1 is considerably smaller than that required to store, say, 31,519,654. If we reserve enough space in the computer's memory to store numbers the size of 31,519,654, then we waste considerable computer memory for each number we store that is smaller. This difficulty will always be present, but in the interests of economy, it is desirable to minimize its effects.

An alternative way to approach the problem of representing text is to assume the existence of a generalized alphabet or character set for the computer. This set would contain all the single symbols (also known as marks or characters) from which printed text can be constructed. It would include not only the normal alphabetic characters in both upper and lower case, but also marks such as digits (0,1,2, . . . ,9), punctuation (.,!?";:), and special characters (#%&$=*/). A different number would then be assigned to each character. Because there are a relatively small number of possible characters in general use, the numbers assigned would fall into a small range (in contrast to the one to several million of our first attempt), such as 0 to 127 or 0 to 255. A word in a sample of text would be represented as a series of numbers, namely, the numbers assigned to each of the letters comprising the word. For example, if A were assigned the number 1, B the number 2, and so on, then the word *BASIC* would be assigned the sequence of numbers 2,1,19,9,3 (See Figure 2.3.1).

A more mind-boggling example is the task of representing a number itself. If we assign the number 27 to the character 0, the number 28 to the character 1, and so on. Then the symbol for the number 102 would be represented by the sequence 28,27,29 (See Figure 2.3.2). The numbers used here are decimal because we can more easily understand the process. They can always be converted to binary.

In this example, we encounter for the first time one of the fundamental distinctions that lead to confusion when discussing storage of information in a computer. There is a difference between the external form of information—the way we see it in the real world—and the internal form of information—the way the computer sees it. Because we have chosen a binary numeric form for the internal form of information, we must pay special attention to this distinction when talking about the representation of numbers.

Numbers can be put into the computer in two different ways:

ASCII is another numeric code for representing symbolic (text) information in computers. It is used in virtually all personal computers.

1. As pure numbers represented in binary form. For example, 21 decimal is 10101_{two}.
2. As symbols standing for the decimal digits. For example, 21 decimal is 29,28 in the code shown earlier, or using the ASCII code of Table 2.3.1, it is the two seven-digit binary numbers 0110010 and 0110001.

These two binary forms of representing 21 decimal are both valid. When doing arithmetic, we need to use form 1, and when storing numbers as symbols with other letters of the alphabet, we need to use form 2.

EBCDIC is a numeric code for representing symbolic (text) information in computers. It is used primarily in IBM mainframe computers.

An assignment of numbers to the possible characters in a computer's character set is referred to as a *code* (or sometimes as the internal code). As computers have developed, people have realized the need to have a uniform code from one computer to the next. Many computer codes have been created, but only two of these codes have become standardized: EBCDIC and ASCII. The IBM Corporation developed the Extended Binary Coded Decimal Interchange Code (**EBCDIC** for short, pronounced *ebb-suh-dick*). This EBCDIC code is

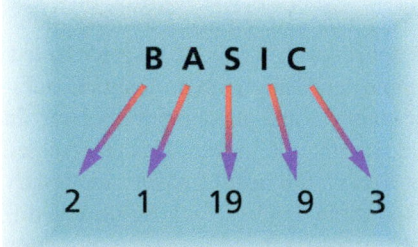

Figure 2.3.1

The word BASIC coded with numbers.

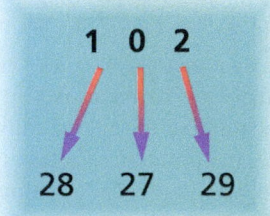

Figure 2.3.2

The number 102 coded with numbers.

used primarily by IBM in its large computers. The other code, which is the more common code, was standardized by the American National Standards Institute (ANSI, or *ann-see*) and called the American Standard Code for Information Interchange (ASCII, pronounced *ask-ee*). The ASCII code, or simply **ASCII,** is used by virtually all non-IBM computers in the United States and Europe. All personal computers use the ASCII code.

The ASCII code is shown in Table 2.3.1. Notice that 128 different characters are represented, and these have been assigned the binary numbers from 0000000_{two} to 1111111_{two}, which are 0 to 127 in decimal. The characters that are represented by the numbers from 0 to 31 decimal (i.e., 0000000_{two} to 0011111_{two}) are probably unfamiliar to you; they certainly do not correspond to any well-known printing or displayable characters. The characters, which these values represent, are referred to as **control characters.** They have a variety of uses including facilitating communication between different computers or between a computer and a device (such as a printer) and control instructions to the computer itself. However, very few control characters are involved in the representation or storage of text.

Control characters are special nonprintable characters used to control execution of commands between a computer and some device connected to it, such as a printer. Most often, they are invisible to computer users.

Table 2.3.1   *ASCII character set in binary.*

ASCII	Binary	ASCII	Binary	ASCII	Binary	ASCII	Binary
Ctrl+@(NULL)	0000000	Space	0100000	@	1000000	'	1100000
Ctrl+A(SOH)	0000001	!	0100001	A	1000001	a	1100001
Ctrl+B(STX)	0000010	"	0100010	B	1000010	b	1100010
Ctrl+C(ETX)	0000011	#	0100011	C	1000011	c	1100011
Ctrl+D(EOT)	0000100	$	0100100	D	1000100	d	1100100
Ctrl+E(ENQ)	0000101	%	0100101	E	1000101	e	1100101
Ctrl+F(ACK)	0000110	&	0100110	F	1000110	f	1100110
Ctrl+G(Bell)	0000111	'	0100111	G	1000111	g	1100111
Ctrl+H(BS)	0001000	(	0101000	H	1001000	h	1101000
Ctrl+I(HTAB)	0001001	)	0101001	I	1001001	i	1101001
Ctrl+J(LFEED)	0001010	*	0101010	J	1001010	j	1101010
Ctrl+K(VTAB)	0001011	+	0101011	K	1001011	k	1101011
Ctrl+L(FormF)	0001100	,	0101100	L	1001100	l	1101100
Carriage return	0001101	-	0101101	M	1001101	m	1101101
Ctrl+N(SO)	0001110	.	0101110	N	1001110	n	1101110
Ctrl+O(SI)	0001111	/	0101111	O	1001111	o	1101111
Ctrl+P(DLE)	0010000	0	0110000	P	1010000	p	1110000
Ctrl+Q(DC1)	0010001	1	0110001	Q	1010001	q	1110001
Ctrl+R(DC2)	0010010	2	0110010	R	1010010	r	1110010
Ctrl+S(DC3)	0010011	3	0110011	S	1010011	s	1110011
Ctrl+T(DC4)	0010100	4	0110100	T	1010100	t	1110100
Ctrl+U(NAK)	0010101	5	0110101	U	1010101	u	1110101
Ctrl+V(SYN)	0010110	6	0110110	V	1010110	v	1110110
Ctrl+W(ETB)	0010111	7	0110111	W	1010111	w	1110111
Ctrl+X(CAN)	0011000	8	0111000	X	1011000	x	1111000
Ctrl+Y(EM)	0011001	9	0111001	Y	1011001	y	1111001
Ctrl+Z(SUB)	0011010	:	0111010	Z	1011010	z	1111010
Ctrl+[(Escape)	0011011	;	0111011	[	1011011	{	1111011
Ctrl+\(FS)	0011100	<	0111100	\	1011100	I	1111100
Ctrl+](GS)	0011101	=	0111101	]	1011101	}	1111101
Ctrl+^(RS)	0011110	>	0111110	^	1011110	~	1111110
Ctrl+_(US)	0011111	?	0111111	_	1011111	Delete	1111111

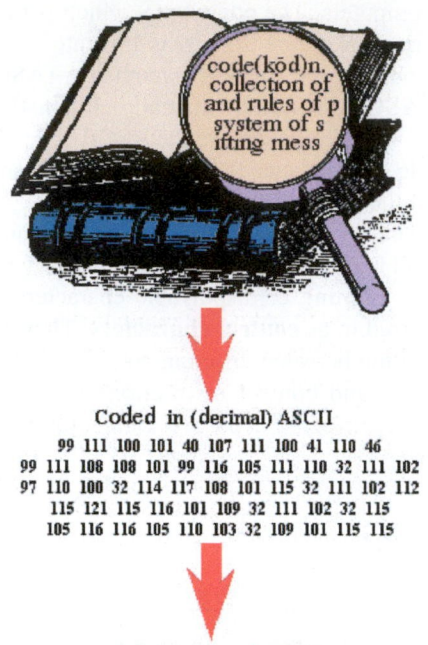

Coded in (decimal) ASCII

```
       99  111  100  101  40  107  111  100  41  110  46
    99  111  108  108  101  99  116  105  111  110  32  111  102
    97  110  100  32  114  117  108  101  115  32  111  102  112
       115  121  115  116  101  109  32  111  102  32  115
       105  116  116  105  110  103  32  109  101  115  115
```

Figure 2.3.3

Representing the text of a book in ASCII code.

Coded in (binary) ASCII

```
                1100011 1101111 1100100 1100101 0101000 1101011 1101111 1100100 0101001 1101110 0101110
          1100011 1101111 1101100 1101100 1100101 1100011 1110100 1101001 1101111 1101110 0100000 1101111 1100110
       1100001 1101110 1100100 0100000 1110010 1110101 1101100 1100101 1110011 0100000 1101111 1100110 0100000 1110000
                1110011 1111001 1110011 1110100 1100101 1101101 0100000 1101111 1100110 0100000 1110011
                1101001 1110100 1110100 1101001 1101110 1100111 0100000 1101101 1100101 1110011 1110011
```

The process of representing printed textual information consists of transforming the sequence of printing characters that constitute the text into a sequence of numbers (the codes that correspond to the printing characters) and, subsequently, storing these numbers in a binary form in a computer's memory. The concept of this process is illustrated in Figure 2.3.3. Some text of this book is enlarged in the magnifying glass. All of the letters beginning with the word *code* are given line by line in both decimal ASCII and binary ASCII. Decimal ASCII is just the binary ASCII number converted to decimal. For example, the lower case letter c has the binary ASCII code 1100011, which converted to decimal is the number 99.

Before the "worldwide" appeal of the World Wide Web opened up the issue of how to represent the graphical characters from languages around the world on our Web pages, a group of researchers in the late 1980's were already looking into this problem. These researchers were determined to come up with a standardized means of representing all of the graphical characters from all of the languages in current use throughout the world. In 1991, the Unicode Consortium finally agreed upon such a list.

The Unicode character set contains over 60,000 graphical characters. An extensive list of languages and symbols are included in the set. Examples of some of the symbols included are those from English, Arabic, Cyrillic, Swahili, Chinese, Braille, currency symbols, music symbols, technical symbols, and mathematical symbols.

Unicode is now an accepted universal standard for displaying graphical characters on Web pages. The expansion of the symbolic character set allows us to view Web pages the way the creator of the page has intended, in his or her own language, or with the symbols relating to their field of work or study.

Cryptography is the science of secret writing. A message is transformed from a readable form into a coded form that is very difficult to read unless you have the knowledge of how to decode it. ASCII code is not secret and is a code for computer communication.

The three codes, EBCDIC, ASCII, and Unicode mentioned in this section were created for computer communication. There are many codes that are used for communication that is very secret, but the basic idea is the same. In fact, the field of **cryptography** is the study of various codes and how to code and decode them. Julius Caesar created a very simple code to communicate with his soldiers; it is called the Caesar Cipher. Another more famous code was Enigma, used by the Germans in World War II. The Allied forces cracked the code near the end of the war and saved many thousands of lives.

2.4 Representation of Images

A simple black-and-white photograph presents an interesting example of how pictorial information can be transformed into numeric form. The basic idea is to subdivide the picture into a grid of squares as shown in Figure 2.4.1. The black squares are easy to see because they are outlined by the white space between them. You will have to extend those lines into the white area to see the white squares. Each of these squares is referred to as a **pixel** (short for picture element). Each square, or pixel, is a very small portion of the original picture. If the squares are small enough, we will see a reasonably good image.

To represent this primitive picture in a computer, the computer needs to record which squares are white and which are black. You probably already realize that this is a simple matter: Simply let the black squares be represented by 1 and the white squares by 0. The piece of a picture shown in Figure 2.4.1 has 39 rows of 48 squares each and, therefore, can be represented by using 0s and 1s, where 1 means a black pixel and 0 means a white pixel. Figure 2.4.2 was made by replacing the black pixels by 1s and the white pixels by 0s.

Making the pixels smaller and showing more of the picture, we see that it is the picture of a baby. The picture is still rather rough and the individual pixels can still be seen. Upon

Pixel is an acronym from the words **picture element**. Pixels are the building blocks of a computer picture. For simple pictures, each pixel is either black or white.

Courtesy of Kurt Lauckner

Figure 2.4.1

Part of a picture showing the pixel structure.

Figure 2.4.3

Picture of baby's face.

Courtesy of Kurt Lauckner

Figure 2.4.2

Black and white pixels represented by 1 and 0.

Courtesy of Kurt Lauckner

Figure 2.4.4

The baby's picture with smaller pixels shows more detail.

Courtesy of Kurt Lauckner

close examination, we can see that Figure 2.4.1 is the baby's right eye. Look closely and see if you can identify it. Now see the baby's entire face in Figure 2.4.3.

Making the pixels even smaller makes the picture in Figure 2.4.4 look better, although it is still not a high-quality image. In fact, the pixels are still visible. The roughness is associated with the size of these pixels. To see this, lean your book up against the wall and stand back about 10 feet. The picture looks quite small, but the image quality appears much better.

PUZZLER HINT

The Puzzler given at the beginning of this chapter involved the Arecibo Radio Telescope message. The Puzzler stated that the top lines in the message are counting in binary. The question is: What are the numbers and what is the scheme used in their representation? To answer this question you should use the basic concept of binary representation along with the idea of a primitive image with pixels that are either black or white. The black and white pixels in this graphical message can be interpreted as 1 for black and 0 for white.

An Intergalactic Message

In 1974 Frank Drake and other staff members of the National Astronomy and Ionosphere Center of Cornell University created a picture that contained a large amount of fundamental scientific data. The information is actually a mixture of numeric and pictorial facts. It is designed as an image 23 squares wide and 73 squares high and, thus, can be represented by a string of 1,679 0s and 1s as shown. This representation was transmitted into outer space using a powerful radio telescope in Arecibo, Puerto Rico. The Earth scientists hoped that their message would be received by intelligent life elsewhere in our galaxy or even in other, more distant galaxies. The message was transmitted repeatedly whenever the telescope sat idle. Its purpose was to give any potential extraterrestrial listener a hint that it originated from intelligent beings on Earth.

If some other life form receives the Arecibo transmission, then it will prove its intelligence by discovering the content of the message. The first step is to discover the message length, 1,679. Eventually, the fact that $1,679 = 23 \times 73$ would be determined. This is the only pair of numbers that could be used to display the 1,679 0s and 1s in a perfectly rectangular space with none left over. Mathematicians easily recognize that 1,679 can be obtained using multiplication with only the prime numbers 23 and 73. Once that step is achieved, the pictures and information contained in the message will become evident. If the receivers of the message have developed computers similar to ours, the decoding of the intergalactic message should be very rapid indeed. Here are two representations of the message, one using 0s and 1s and the second in a more legible form with a black square representing 1 and nothing in the square representing 0. See if you can figure out how the top lines in the message represent counting from 1 to 10. (Hint: It's counting in binary.)

```
0000000000101010100000
0010000000101000001010
0100110100100010010001
0010010010101010101010101
00000000000000000000000000
0000000001100000000000
0000000001011000000000
0000000001011000000000
0000000001010000000000
0000000001111100000000
00000000000000000000000000
0001100001100011100011
0000100110000000000001
0101100001100011000011
11111011111011111011111
00000000000000000000000000
010000000000000001000
00000000000000000000000000
1000000000000000010000
11111000000000000011111
00000000000000000000000000
0001100011100001100011
0000100000000100000001
0101100111000110001011
11111011111011111011111
00000000000000000000000000
01000000001100000010000
0000000001100000000000
1000000001100000010000
11111000001100000011111
0000000001100000000000
0010000001001000000100
00010000001100000010000
00001000001100001100000
000001100001100011000000
00000001100110000000000
0000011000010001100000000
00001000001100011000000
00010000001100001100000
0001000000010000000100000
00100000011000000000100
00100000011000000000100
001000000001100000000010
00101000001000000000010
00001000000100000000100
00000110000000000001000
00000001100000000110000
0000000011010111000100
00000000000100000000100
00000000011111000000100
11011010100101110100000010
1111110010001110011000000
1110110000011100001110011101
110111000010100000000000
111111000001010000000000
000011000010100000000100
0000000001101100000100
00000000000000000000000000
00000000001000001100
1010101010100010101011100
0010101010100000000011100
0000001010000000000000000
00000000011111100000100
0000000111111111000000
00000011100000001110000
00001100000000001100
0000110100000000101100
00011001100000011001100
00010001010000010100010
0001001001000100100010
0000001000101000100000
000000010000100000100000
0000000100000000100000
0000000001010010000000
000111100101111100011110
```

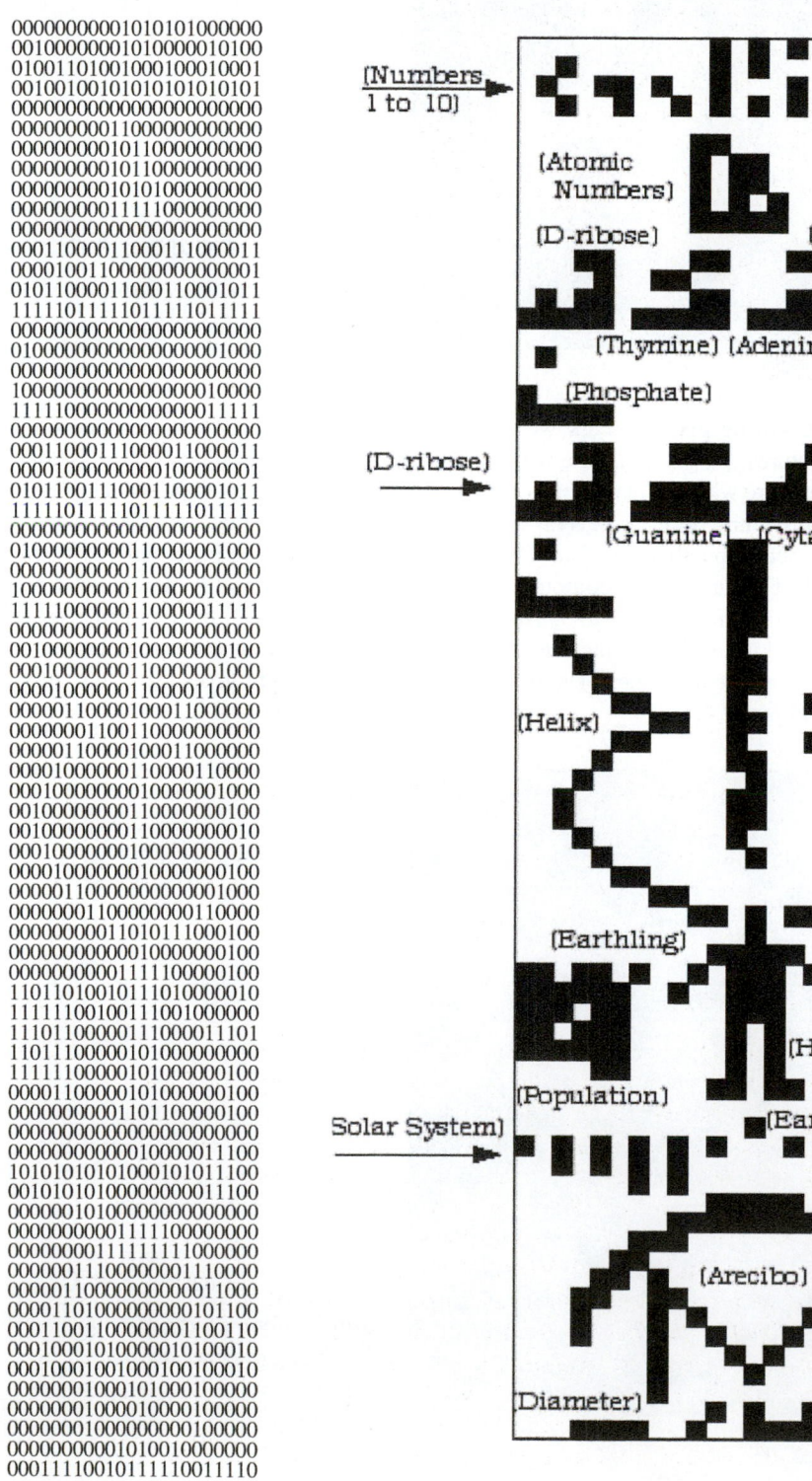

(Numbers 1 to 10)

(Atomic Numbers)

(D-ribose)   (D-ribose)

(Thymine) (Adenine)

(Phosphate)

(D-ribose)

(Guanine) (Cytasine)

(Helix)   (Helix)

(Earthling)

(Height)

(Population)   (Earth)

Solar System)

(Arecibo)

(Diameter)

Figure 2.4.5

Baby's picture with four levels of gray.

Courtesy of Kurt Lauckner

A **gray-scale** is used to represent variations in value of shading between black and white. An eight-level gray-scale includes black, white, and six values (shades) of gray in between.

The simple black/white pixel process we've described, unfortunately, can produce only crude-quality pictures. To get an image with photographic quality, each pixel must assume more shades than pure white or black. In fact, the pixels can have a **gray-scale,** which means that instead of pure white or black, several shades between white and black are used. A four-level gray-scale means that there are four different shades of gray going from white to black. To put this kind of picture into a computer, each level of gray is usually numbered from 00_{two} to 11_{two} or in decimal from 0 to 3. Then each square or pixel will be assigned a value on a gray-scale. Taking the same picture in Figure 2.4.4 and making each pixel be either black, white, or one of two shades of gray between black and white gives the crude gray-scale picture of Figure 2.4.5.

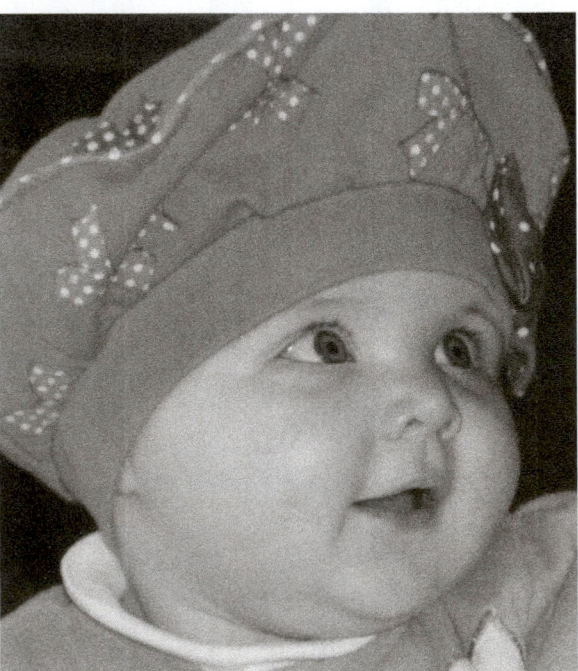

Figure 2.4.6

Baby's picture with 256 levels of gray and smaller pixels.

Courtesy of Kurt Lauckner

Note that we have done two things that make the baby's picture more realistic. First, we reduced pixel size and then we made the pixels two shades of gray plus black and white. Extending both of these techniques results in the picture of the baby shown in Figure 2.4.6. In this image, the pixels use 256 levels of gray and are about one-fourth as large. Eight bits are needed to represent each pixel to get the 256 levels of gray.

The next obvious step is to introduce color. There are three approaches commonly used to display color. Without getting into too much technical detail, we can relate them to some familiar ideas.

Do you remember mixing water colors? By mixing two different colors you could get a third color. For example, mixing yellow and blue in a certain proportion would give green. In theory, by taking three colors that are not too closely related you can create any color from white through the rainbow colors to black.

In the printing industry the three colors used are cyan, magenta, and yellow. But, as is the case with many theories, the practical application requires some modifications. For printed color, in theory black should be possible; however, only a muddy-looking black can be obtained using cyan, magenta, and yellow. To compensate for this, the color black is also included. So using cyan, magenta, yellow, and black will allow any picture to be printed in full color. This is typically referred to as **CMYK,** where each letter stands for one of the colors, with K referring to black. This color theory is often called reflective color because the picture is viewed by reflected light.

> **CMYK** is an acronym that stands for **c**yan, **m**agenta, **y**ellow, and blac**k.** These are the four standard colors of ink used in printing.

The color picture in Figure 2.4.7 is printed using CMYK-colored inks. If you look at the picture with a magnifying glass, you will see the CMYK color dots that comprise each color pixel. This means that four numbers are needed for each pixel, where each number represents the amount of that color. Although there are 7-ink ink-jet printers, which need special calculations to further subdivide the 4 CMYK colors into 7 different colors. This gives better color quality.

Now if you happen to be reading this book on a computer screen, then the CMYK color theory is not what you are experiencing. Only three colors are needed to represent any color on a computer screen. These colors are red, green, and blue, commonly referred to as **RGB.** In fact, if you look at a color monitor with a magnifying glass when it is off, you may be able to see the thousands of small red, green, and blue spots that are illuminated in just the right proportion to make your eye see a particular color. This color theory is called additive color because the three colors are added together to produce a particular color. All that is needed

> **RGB** is an acronym that stands for **r**ed, **b**lue, and **g**reen. They are the three colors used to make the dots on the screen of a color monitor or television.

Courtesy of Kurt Lauckner

Figure 2.4.7

Picture of the baby in full color.

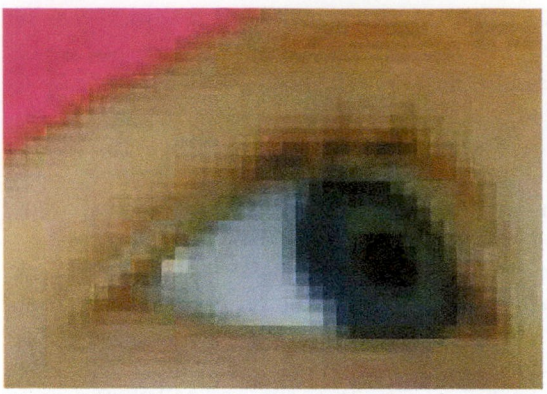

Figure 2.4.8

Picture of the baby's eye with 16 colors.

Courtesy of Kurt Lauckner

to get a picture is to give three numbers for each pixel. These numbers represent the amount of red, blue, and green needed.

Now this is where the story gets a little more complicated. Because illuminating these dots individually would be a messy problem for the computer to handle, a modification of the RGB color system is used.

There are still three RGB color spots, but a single number is used to represent all three of them. From that single number the amount of red, green, and blue is calculated to be displayed on the computer screen. Figure 2.4.8 shows the eye of the baby. In this case each of the square pixels making up the picture is one of 16 colors. This is not an enlargement of Figure 2.4.7 but was intentionally made course with only 16 colors so the technique can be seen. On the screen each of the square pixels has dozens of red, green, and blue trios of color in just the right proportion to give one of the 16 colors.

You may wonder how to obtain the digitized pictures like those of the baby. A digital camera may be used to give these pixels, or a piece of hardware called a **digitizer** or **scanner** can be used to convert the picture to numeric form. There are many types of digitizers. They range in quality from inexpensive home digitizers or scanners to super high-quality commercial digitizers.

A **digitizer** or **scanner** is a device used to convert an image to numbers representing a pixel form of the image.

2.5 Representation of Sounds, Music, and Speech

We have already seen several forms of information including text and pictures reduced to numbers, but there are still more! Sound is also information. For example, a watchdog's bark or the warning shout of a tree trimmer conveys information. Our purpose in this section is quite simple: to show how sound can be reduced to numbers. Let's start with simple musical sounds.

REPRESENTATION OF SIMPLE MUSICAL SOUNDS

A simple example of sound information represented by numbers is illustrated in Figure 2.5.1. This example of numerical coding of musical notes allows children to readily

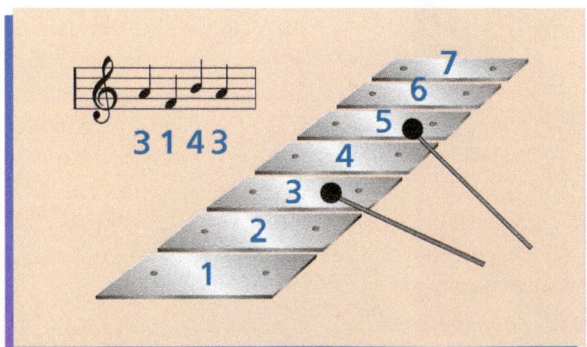

Figure 2.5.1

Relating numbers to musical notes.

play songs on a musical instrument. The numerals on the notes correspond to numerals on the instrument. If you strike the proper numeral in the order given on the sheet of music, the music is reproduced. This simple example, however, leaves out many details: How much time should be taken between notes, and what tempo should be used? Of course, this additional information can also be given in the form of numbers. The tempo, for example, could be the number of beats per minute at which the metronome, a musical timing device, is set. The lengths of the notes themselves already have numerical equivalents: half note (½), whole note (1), quarter note (¼), and so on. So, music that can be written down on paper in the traditional form can also be written out in a numerical form. Then once we have a numerical form, the numbers themselves can be converted to the binary form that is compatible with computers.

This numerical form of music is not in general use by Western musicians because they are trained to read the traditional notation of the five-line staff, which is often referred to as sheet music. But the simple form of Figure 2.5.1 is sometimes used by musical toy manufacturers to make it easy to learn to play their toy pianos and xylophones. Another way to put musical sound into a computer is to use the number associated with the frequency of the sound itself. For example, the tuning fork is often used by musicians to assist in tuning their instruments. Each tuning fork will vibrate at a particular frequency when it is struck. The tuning fork in Figure 2.5.2 is one that sounds middle C, or more appropriately, 256 **hertz.** The number 256, given in the units hertz, is the numerical representation that tells exactly what frequency of sound is produced.

Getting slightly more complex, there is a representation of music that includes note lengths and other attributes. This form of musical representation is called **Digital Alternative Representation of Musical Scores (DARMS)** that is used by some professional musicologists. It is based on the position of symbols on a staff, shown in Figure 2.5.3. The lines of the staff, including ledger lines (lines above and below the staff proper), are represented by numerals 01,02,03, . . ., 49; they are written so that staff line numbers are 21-23-25-27-29 and the spaces on the staff area are 20-22-24-26-28-30. The other details are shown in Figure 2.5.3. The clef, key, and meter are prefaced by an exclamation point. In Figure 2.5.3, !G means treble clef, !Kl- indicates a key of one flat, and !MC indicates the meter C or 4/4 time. The slashes (/) mark the measure boundaries, the Q represents a quarter note, and H a half note. This form of the music can be easily converted to binary using the ASCII code and then manipulated by the computer, but it would certainly take more effort for a musician to learn to play from it! Its main use is by musicologists whose job it is to examine and study musical scores.

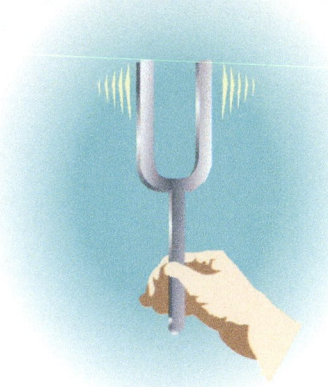

Figure 2.5.2

Frequency as a numerical representation of a pitch.

Hertz is a unit of measurement that indicates the number of cycles per second of a particular sound's vibration.

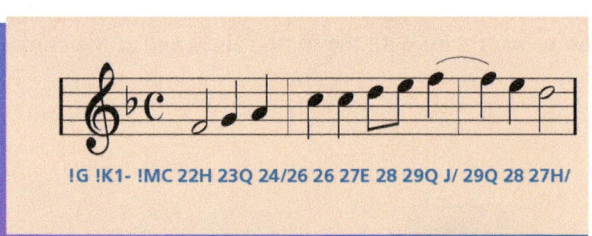

!G !K1- !MC 22H 23Q 24/26 26 27E 28 29Q J/ 29Q 28 27H/

Figure 2.5.3

DARMS: A special case of musical representation.

REPRESENTING MUSIC USING MIDI

A more revolutionary and current coding of music is called **Musical Instrument Digital Interface (MIDI).** In the early 1980s, musicians began to recognize that communication between musical instruments could change the way music was made. MIDI is a set of rules for connecting musical instruments and computers. Although MIDI is much more complex than the previous examples, the concept of representing music in binary form is similar.

The musical information is contained in MIDI messages that are sent over special electronic paths called channels to the various instruments or computer. These MIDI messages can tell instruments, such as synthesizers, what note to play and how long to play it. For example, the message consisting of the three numbers "144,60,64" tells the MIDI device to play middle C on MIDI channel 1 at a medium velocity. The velocity is how fast the sound is to go from no sound to a certain loudness and is referred to as the attack. The type of tone

that is played depends on other messages that set up the MIDI device. To turn off the middle C, the MIDI message is "128,60,00."

These messages are actually sent in binary, but we show them in decimal because it's easier to talk about the message. A complete piece of music can be sent in binary to a MIDI player that will convert the messages into the proper musical sounds. You may wonder who would have time to create all of these numbers. Luckily, it's not necessary to create all these binary numbers one by one. Instead, a musician can simply play the MIDI keyboard and have them automatically generated.

One of the advantages of a MIDI recording is that it occupies thousands of times less space than the standard CD. This also means it can be sent over the Internet in fractions of a second rather than fractions of an hour. We will be coming back to a more detailed look at MIDI in chapter 9.

REPRESENTATION OF ANY SOUND BY DIGITAL RECORDING

Discussion of a very important feature of sound has been ignored. Is there a difference between a violin and a trombone playing the music of Figure 2.5.3? No? Obviously, then, we're leaving something out. The fact is that more than the pure frequency of the notes is produced when different instruments play. It seems natural to want to capture any type of sound. We can do this in a way that is similar to digitizing a picture. However, instead of dividing the image of a picture into tiny cells (pixels), we will divide the time during which a sound is being produced into tiny segments and record some type of information during each of them. What should be recorded? An example is probably the easiest way to understand how this is done.

An ordinary stereo system as shown in Figure 2.5.4 will suit our purpose for this example. What is the information being carried on a wire leading to a stereo speaker? This sound information is in the form of a **voltage.** Because of the variation of this voltage, sound is produced by the speaker.

If it were possible to measure the magnitude of this voltage several thousand times per second, then the sequence of numbers obtained would contain meaningful information as shown in the graph of Figure 2.5.5. Suppose this were done. A typical sequence of numbers, or voltages measured on the wire might be

$$1.2312, -1.2300, -1.2100, 0.9510, \ldots$$

To transform these numbers into sound, a computer need only reproduce them electronically fast enough so that they appear on the speaker wire with the same values and at the correct rate of speed.

Figure 2.5.4

Typical stereo system.

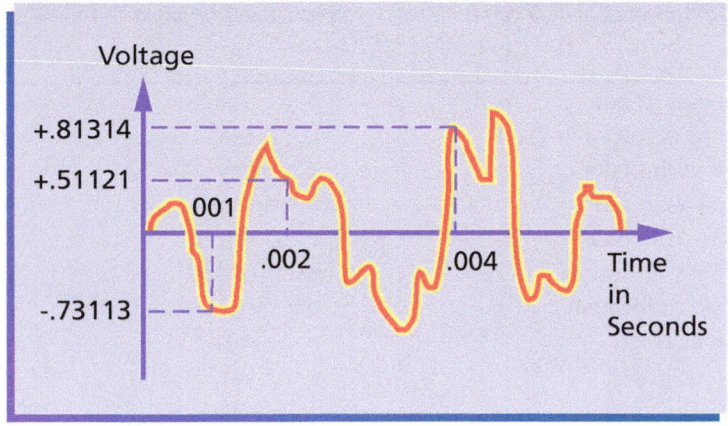

Figure 2.5.5

Graph of voltage appearing in the speaker wire.

As we learned earlier, the more pixels a picture has, the clearer it will be. Similarly, the more measurements we can take per second, the closer the reproduction will be to the actual sound. In fact, to reproduce accurately to 20,000 hertz (frequency in cycles per second), we have to take 40,000 measurements per second. That's just a little fast for a human with a voltmeter. However, electronic circuits can easily do this. Digital stereo systems using these circuits can do exactly what we've been talking about.

A major example of consumer products that represents sound through digital recording is the **compact disc (CD)** recorder/player. Devices of this type have electronics that use the numbers—stored in binary form—to produce the proper voltages up to 40,000 times per second. It's interesting to note that the CD player uses a laser beam that shines on the surface of a disc. If light is reflected back from a tiny spot, that means 0, whereas if the spot doesn't reflect, it's 1. This means that as long as the numbers aren't altered, the recording won't show signs of wear like ordinary cassette tapes. A number is a number!

REPRESENTING SPEECH

Sound-digitizing technique can be used on human speech. In fact, in many large cities the telephone system is completely digital, and our voices are sent over telephone lines as binary numbers. By digitizing the human voice at one end of the telephone line and reconstructing it at the other end, it is estimated that our telephone lines can carry thousands of times more telephone calls. Does this mean our telephone bills will be reduced to one-thousandth their current value? Guess again!

A recorded voice takes a great deal of memory storage space. In addition, there's the very important process of creating speech. An example of created speech is the use of verbal warnings given to passengers of a subway that is about to close its doors. Creating normal-sounding speech using recordings has many problems. For example, the unwritten rules of normal speech would require many different versions of the same words. One such rule is for questions, where the pitch at the end of the sentence rises. The pitch of a normal sentence lowers at the end. Many other special characteristics of speech make creating speech from recorded words difficult.

The problem of creating human speech, or **speech synthesis,** has been studied for many years. This research has been easily applied to the problem of synthesizing speech with the digital computer. Spoken language is broken down into a small number of fundamental sounds called **phonemes.**

Table 2.5.1 gives a simplified list of American English language phonemes found in standard prose. Notice that English sometimes uses two letters to spell one sound, and sometimes one written letter might stand for two or more different sounds in different written words. It should also be noted that the number of phonemes varies considerably from language to language. Hawaiian has only 12 phonemes, whereas dialects of some Pacific Northwest Indian languages have well over 100 phonemes.

Speech synthesis is the process of producing human speech, not by playing back a recording of it, but by creating the right frequencies of sound in the correct timing so as to mimic human speech.

Phonemes are the fundamental sounds of any given human language. There may be two or more words using the same phonemes. The phonemes needed to pronounce the word *there,* for example, may also be used to say *their.*

Table 2.5.1   *The phonemes of American English.*

Vowels		Consonants		
ee as in bee	p	pea	b	bee
i as in mitten	t	tea	d	Dee
e as in make	k	key	g	gone
eh as in led	f	fee	v	vee
ae as in had	s	see	z	zip
ah as in father	sh	sheep	zh	vision
aw as in small	tsh	chest	dzh	jaw
o as in go	r	rate	m	me
u as in put	y	yet	ëm	chasm
oo as in tool	w	Wales	n	not
uh as in the	hw	whales	ën	Eden
er as in anger	h	he	ng	sing
ai as in while			l	lee
ou as in how			ël	cradle
oi as in toy				
iu as in fuse				

Once the phonemes for a particular language are defined, we can assign a binary number to each of them. Then to construct natural-sounding words and phrases it would seem to be a relatively easy task of stringing together the proper phonemes. Unfortunately, that is not true. Three additional factors have a great affect on how a word or phrase sounds. The first, **inflection,** involves the rising or falling pattern of pitch on an individual phoneme. The second factor affecting the way a particular word sounds is the **duration** of one or more phonemes. Finally, the two or more phonemes that make up a word or phrase must be spliced so that when one of them ends and the next begins, the connection will sound natural. This is called **elision.**

A major challenge in digitizers of human speech is that we unconsciously introduce stresses and pauses into our speech. The linguistic rules that determine these stresses and pauses are specific to whatever native language we speak and are learned from childhood. One such habitual rule in American English, for example, involves lowering both pitch and volume for the period at the end of a sentence, but raising the pitch slightly at a comma, to indicate that the sentence continues. Rules of this type are very difficult to program into the computer, making natural speech difficult to synthesize. However, computer-synthesized speech is becoming better and is almost always quite understandable. Before long we will have computers that can talk as well as HAL the computer in the movie *2001: A Space Odyssey.* HAL used a recorded human voice.

2.6 Representing the Instructions of Programs

The types of information treated so far in this chapter have been factual in nature. Instructions are imperative; they command action whereas information is a declaration of fact. Examples of instructions include the *fasten seat belt* command in automobiles and airplanes; the *pull over* command of a highway patrol officer; and the *mix ingredients thoroughly* instruction of a cooking recipe.

What, then, is the difference between facts and instructions? The difference is a matter of use or purpose. The purpose of most types of information is declarative—to impart knowledge. The purpose of an instruction is manipulative—to control information or activity. Instructions are always directed at someone or something that is capable of carrying them out. To be effective, each instruction must be clearly understood by its intended receiver, and the information needed to process that instruction must be readily accessible.

So far, our discussion has concerned how the computer handles various types of information including text, pictures, sound, and speech. The computer's main function, however, is not merely to *store* information. Its main purpose is to *manipulate* information—to use it for calculations, queries, and reports. To perform these manipulations, the computer must follow a series of commands or instructions.

As with all of the other types of information, the computer's instructions must be stored within the computer before they can be used. They must be stored, like all other information, in binary form. A set of binary instructions, which the computer can follow, or **execute,** is called a **program.** That is why today's computer is commonly called a stored program computer.

THE WORD HUNT INSTRUCTION SET

To understand how a series of instructions can be stored in the computer as a group of binary numbers, we've devised a set of instructions that will allow us to read a message hidden in chapter 1, "Computers: A First Look." Our instruction set is called the **Word Hunt.** Table 2.6.1 lists the Word Hunt instructions and an explanation of what each one means.

The six instructions comprise an **instruction set**—in this case, a word hunt. Notice that each instruction (except the STOP) has the same format, or **syntax:** ACTION—OBJECT. The ACTION is a verb that tells you to do something and the OBJECT modifies the verb, telling you where, or how much, or what the verb requires. The first four instructions merely move a pointer (your finger) to a specific word. The fifth tells you to record or display the word you find, one word at a time. The last tells you when the message is completed.

Figure 2.6.1 shows a typical Word Hunt puzzle. See if you can carry out the instructions and find a simple message.

Having followed a series of instructions from the Word Hunt instruction set, we are now ready to see how these instructions can be converted into a form the computer can store in its memory. Suppose we assign a number to each of the different commands in our instruction set. Figure 2.6.2 shows what that would look like.

Now, if we want to write a Word Hunt program, we can do it with numbers. For example, *1 37* would mean *GOTO 37,* or *go to the top of page 37.* And *4 5* would mean the same

To execute a program means to perform the commands that make up the program.

A **program** is a collection or list of commands designed for a computer to follow, which gives some desired result.

GOTO	11
SELECT	7
FORWARD	1
WRITE	*word*
SELECT	1
FORWARD	16
WRITE	*word*
GOTO	12
SELECT	33
FORWARD	8
WRITE	*word*
BACKUP	7
WRITE	*word*
STOP	

Figure 2.6.1

A Word Hunt puzzle program (above). Follow the instructions and find the message.

Table 2.6.1   *The six instructions used in Word Hunt.*

GOTO #	Turn pages either backward or forward until you get to the page number indicated in the instruction.
SELECT #	Counting down from the top of the page, move the pointer (your finger) to the beginning of the line indicated by the instruction's number. The top line of main body text is line 1. Blank lines don't count.
FORWARD #	Beginning with the word immediately to the right of your current position, count forward the number of words indicated in the instruction. On each new line, begin with the pointer before word 1, the first word on the line. If you move forward three, the pointer will then be on the third word in that line.
BACKUP #	Beginning with the word immediately to the left of your current position, count backward the number of words indicated in the instruction.
WRITE *word*	Write a copy of the current word (that's the one the pointer is on) on a piece of paper.
STOP	The message is now completed. You can stop searching for words.

1	11
2	7
3	1
5	
2	1
3	16
5	
1	12
2	33
3	8
5	
4	7
5	
0	

Figure 2.6.3

Decimal code form of the program shown in Figure 2.6.1.

1 stands for	GOTO #
2 stands for	SELECT #
3 stands for	FORWARD #
4 stands for	BACKUP #
5 stands for	WRITE *word*
0 stands for	STOP

Figure 2.6.2

Assigning a number code to each Word Hunt instruction.

001	001011
010	000111
011	000001
101	
010	000001
011	010000
101	
001	001100
010	100001
011	001000
101	
100	000111
101	
000	

Figure 2.6.4

Program in Figure 2.6.3 translated into binary code.

An **operation code** or **opcode** is the part of an instruction that tells the computer what to execute. If any additional information is needed to perform the instruction, this is contained in a second part of the instruction called the operand.

as *BACKUP 5,* or *move the pointer 5 words back along the line.* Let's look at the previous Word Hunt program written in the new numeric code we've devised. See Figure 2.6.3.

Can you still follow the instructions? Do you get the same message using the numeric code as you did with the word commands? It should be identical. We can now perform the final task of transforming the instructions into a form that the computer can use.

As you found out earlier in the chapter, all information, whether factual or instructional, must be converted into binary form before it can be stored in the computer's memory. Now that we have created a numeric version of our instruction set, conversion into binary form is easy. All the numbers in the program in Figure 2.6.3 can be translated into binary code using the chart given in Table 2.2.2 earlier in the chapter. The resulting program, shown in Figure 2.6.4, is ready to be stored in the computer.

ABOUT COMPUTER INSTRUCTIONS

There are four main differences between our Word Hunt program and a computer program:

1. The computer's program would have originally been written in a programming language (there are lots of them) rather than in English.
2. Each instruction in the instruction set would have to be a task that the computer was capable of performing.
3. The computer would check the program's instructions for errors and then translate the program (written in a programming language) into binary code.
4. The computer can then take the binary version of the translated program, and, upon instruction to do so, execute the program to produce the desired results.

Every one of the instructions in a computer program is acted upon or executed in the given order to accomplish the desired result, just as our Word Hunt program instructions had to be followed in their proper order to get the correct hidden message.

Each of the many types of computers has a unique collection of instructions that it can understand. Even though instruction sets for different computers vary widely, they all contain the classes of instructions shown in Table 2.6.2.

With the various types of instructions arranged in a certain order, computers can perform such tasks as printing payroll checks, controlling a robot's mechanical arm for a factory assembly-line job, or even controlling the landing of a rocket on Mars. What these collections of instructions or programs do and how they do it are topics for chapter 4, "Computer Languages, Algorithms, and Program Development." At present, we're more concerned with how the instructions are represented in the computer.

All instructions must have an identifying code called the **operation code** or **opcode.** This opcode tells the computer which operation is to be performed. The number of bits needed to give this information depends on how many different instructions the computer is capable of executing. If the computer has only eight instructions, then only three binary bits are needed to represent each of them. Why? It's because eight different binary numbers can be expressed with three digits. Suppose the computer has over 100 different instructions. If there are fewer than 128 of them, then seven bits will do the job because with seven binary digits, we can count in binary from 0000000_{two} to 1111111_{two}. This is equivalent to counting in decimal from 0 to 127. A particular meaning or instruction could be assigned to each different number.

Table 2.6.2   *Basic types of instructions.*

Instruction Type	Description
Arithmetic Instructions	Addition, subtraction, multiplication, division, and other number-type operations.
Data Movement Instructions	Move numbers from place to place in the computer. For example, they may copy a number from a memory location to a place in the computer where it can be added.
Logical or Comparison Instructions	The decision-making instructions that cause various results to happen depending on certain conditions. For example, suppose a program is to count from 1 to 10. The computer will have a number in its memory that changes from 1 to 2 . . . until it reaches 10. An instruction that will stop it at 10 would be used to compare the current value of that number with 10, and when it reaches 10, the program stops counting.
Control Instructions	Control the order in which instructions are performed or stop the program.
Input/Output Instructions	Allow the computer to communicate with the outside world. They provide a means for getting information into and out of the computer.

In addition to the opcode, the computer must know the location of the object of the operation. For example, if an instruction is to add a number, the computer must know the memory location of that number. The object of the operation is commonly called the operand. Its location is most often given by means of an **address.** This address is analogous to our home address that the U.S. Postal Service uses to deliver mail. In the computer, the address indicates the location in the computer's memory where either a number is to be stored or retrieved or some other operation is to be performed.

The classes of operations that are not arithmetic need additional information, usually in the form of an address. Before getting too complicated, however, let's examine an actual instruction.

Let us assume, for this simple example, that we have a small computer capable of executing only eight instructions and containing 32 different locations to store things such as numbers. The instructions could be represented in a total of eight bits, three for the opcode and five for the address. A typical instruction for this computer is shown in Figure 2.6.5.

This particular instruction tells the computer to add the number in location 11010_{two} to the accumulator. The other seven instructions for this simple computer would also have the same opcode and address form.

Before we leave the subject of the representation of instructions for now, a last and very important point must be made. How does the computer know that the eight bits 01011010 for the ADD instruction shown represent an instruction? In fact, if we interpret them as an integer, it corresponds to the decimal number 90:

$$01011010_{two} = 2^6 + 2^4 + 2^3 + 2^1 = 64 + 16 + 8 + 2 = 90$$

We could even interpret the rightmost seven bits as an ASCII letter Z (see the table of ASCII codes in Table 2.3.1), or maybe it could correspond to a particular sound or part of a picture.

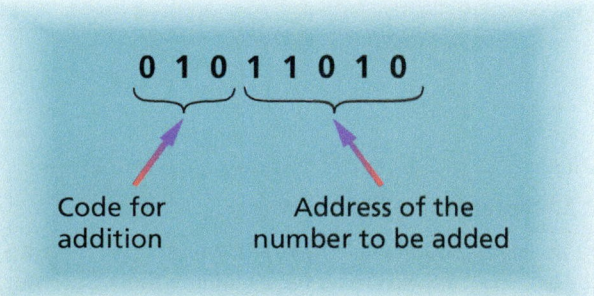

Code for addition

Address of the number to be added

Figure 2.6.5

A typical instruction for a simple computer.

All of these interpretations are possible. After examining all of the possibilities, it is certain that we need a solution to this dilemma. The solution is simple. We must tell the computer, within the program, exactly how the number is to be interpreted, whether it is an instruction, number, ASCII symbol, or whatever else. In other words, the program itself is written with the interpretation already determined.

Representation of the Human Genome

As we have learned in this chapter, there are five kinds of information that are commonly represented in a digital computer using the binary system of numeration. However, there are many other types of information in this world, which are represented in many different ways. The human genome is probably the most complex collection of information we currently know about. It is the string of DNA that represents an individual's complete plan for development and contains all the inheritable traits of that individual. The human genome is represented in a sequence of over

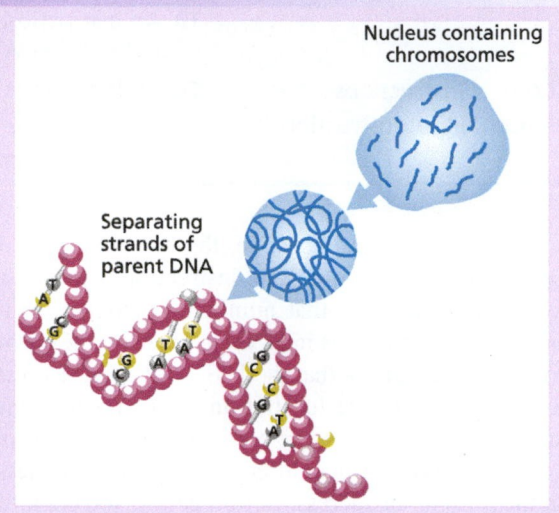

3.5 billion base pairs consisting of the four bases adenine, thymine, cytosine, and guanine (abbreviated A, T, C, and G). This huge string of base pairs is often referred to as the double helix. It is the order of these 3.5 billion base pairs that contains the information for making a copy of you! It's also amazing that each of the trillion cells that make up your body have a complete copy of this string of DNA. The DNA string is organized into 23 pairs of chromosomes that are further subdivided into over 100,000 genes. This is a huge amount of information that is copied over and over again to make up the more than 1 trillion cells of your body. A major project to map this representation of information was started in 1995 by the U.S. federal government. Called the Human Genome Project, it was completed in 2003. From the human perspective, our DNA is certainly the ultimate representation of information.

PUZZLER HINT

PUZZLER HINT

The Arecibo Radio Telescope message Puzzler given at the beginning of this chapter involves counting from either 1 to 10 or from 10 down to 1. Important things to remember are that binary numbers involve the place values of 1, 2, 4, 8 . . . and all numbers have some recognizable starting point. In decimal numbers it is the right edge of the number, which is sometimes marked by a decimal point.

Chapter Summary

2.1 What Is Information?

Computers work with five kinds of information: numbers, symbols or text, images, audio, and instructions. Because computers work in binary, it is necessary to represent the five kinds of information in binary form.

2.2 Representation of Numbers

Representing numbers in binary can be simple, if we just use the decimal rules to create binary numeration. Each position in a decimal number has a value, such as 1, 10, 100, and so forth. This value in decimal is based on the number 10, and note that there are 10 symbols in decimal: 0, 1, 2, 3, 4, 5, 6, 7, 8, and 9. Similarly, the base 2 position values are based on multiples of 2, and the two symbols used are 0 and 1. The important thing to note is that each decimal number has exactly one binary equivalent and vice versa.

2.3 Representation of Symbols and Text

Representing symbols and text is a matter of assigning a binary code to each symbol that is needed. A binary code is a combination of 0s and 1s that stands for the symbol. The most common code used in personal computers is the ASCII code. It consists of seven bits or binary digits, and represents 128 different letters, punctuation, numerals, and special codes.

2.4 Representation of Images

Representing images in a binary form is done by dividing the picture into tiny squares called picture elements or pixels. In black-and-white images a number is assigned to the pixel, which indicates the darkness or lightness of that pixel. Color can be either CMYK or RGB. CMYK is used in printing and RGB in color monitor displays. It takes four numbers to give a description of a CMYK pixel and only three for an RGB pixel. The numbers can be represented in binary and, therefore, are compatible with the computer.

2.5 Representation of Sounds, Music, and Speech

Representing sounds, music, and speech is done in different ways, but each method results in a series of numbers that can be translated to binary numbers and is, therefore, compatible with the computer. Digitizing sound is similar to digitizing images. The sound is digitized by taking the value of the voltage in the electronic recorder at each fraction of a second. This gives a series of numbers that can then be translated to binary. MIDI is another way of representing sound. It consists of a series of commands to play predetermined notes, whose volume and other attributes are controllable. Speech synthesis is done using the fundamental sounds of a language, which are called phonemes. Each language has its own set of phonemes that can vary in number from about 12 to over 100.

2.6 Representing the Instructions of Programs

Programs consisting of a series of commands or instructions can be coded in a binary form that can be executed by a computer. Each of the binary instructions contains the command to be performed, which is called the operation code or opcode, and additional information that may be needed called the operand. A program consisting of combinations of the instructions is written to accomplish some desired result when executed by the computer.

Key Terms

Key terms introduced in this chapter:

1. Address, *49*
2. ASCII (American Standard Code for Information Interchange), *34*
3. Binary numbers, *27*
4. Bit (Binary digIT), *30*
5. CD (compact disc), *45*
6. CMYK (cyan, magenta, yellow, and black), *41*
7. Control characters, *35*
8. Cryptography, *36*
9. DARMS (Digital Alternative Representation of Musical Scores), *43*
10. Decimal numeration system, *30*
11. Digitizer, *42*
12. Duration, *46*
13. EBCDIC, *34*
14. Elision, *46*
15. Execute, *47*
16. Exponent, *31*
17. Gray-scale, *40*
18. Hertz, *43*
19. Inflection, *46*
20. Instruction set, *47*
21. MIDI (Musical Instrument Digital Interface), *43*
22. Number, *27*
23. Numeral, *30*
24. Opcode (operation code), *48*
25. Phoneme, *45*
26. Pixel (picture element), *37*
27. Program, *47*
28. Representation of information, *27*
29. RGB (red, green, blue), *41*
30. Speech synthesis, *45*
31. Scanner, *42*
32. Syntax, *47*
33. Transformation of information, *27*
34. Unicode *36*
35. Voltage, *44*
36. Word Hunt, *47*

Matching

Match the number of the key terms introduced in the chapter to the following statements.
Each term may be used once, more than once, or not at all.

1. ____ This must first be done to information before it can be stored or used by a computer.

2. ____ This is the number system that modern computers use to represent information.

3. ____ Electronic devices used in computers that assume only two states contain these numbers.

4. ____ This is another name for base 10.

5. ____ This is another name for base 2 numbers.

6. ____ This is the name given to each digit in binary.

7. ____ All personal computers use this code.

8. ____ IBM mainframes use this code.

9. ____ These special characters are generally not printable.

10. ____ This is known as the building block of a picture.

11. ____ This is also known as a picture element.

12. ____ This device converts a picture into numeric form.

13. ____ When each pixel assumes more shades than pure white or black, it is said to have this.

14. ____ This is a form of musical representation.

15. ____ This electrical value produces sound on the speakers of a stereo system.

16. ____ This is the name given to a set of binary instructions, which the computer can follow.

17. ____ This unit of measurement indicates the number of cycles per second a particular sound vibrates.

18. ____ This is a field of study that deals with secret codes.

19. ____ This is the color system used when printing in color.

20. ____ This is the process of creating human speech.

True or False

Place either T or F on the line provided with each of the following statements. If a statement
is false, you should be able to explain what changes would make it true.

1. ____ Information must first be transformed into a binary representation of that information before it can be stored in the computer's memory.

2. ____ Number means the same as numeral.

3. ____ ANSI standardized the character set that is now being used by all personal computers.

4. ____ Standard codes such as EBCDIC assign a different number to every word or groupings of characters. These words are recorded in a large dictionary that is accessed each time words are entered in a word-processing document.

5. ____ The standard EBCDIC codes and the standard ASCII codes are identical.

6. ____ The ASCII set of codes includes all of the characters that can be typed at the keyboard plus others that represent characters you can't even see.

7. ____ In a picture, only those pixels that have values of 1 need to be stored. Pixels that have the value of 0 need not be stored because ink will not be necessary at that spot.

8. ____ More memory is needed for gray-scale pictures than for pictures that have black and white pixels.

9. ____ Because the pixels of gray-scale images can be one of many shades of gray, gray-scale pictures need more memory than color pictures.

10. ____ RGB or red/green/blue are the colors of ink used when printing color photos.

11. ____ *MIDI* is a term used to describe digitizing a picture.

12. ____ All current music stored within the computer uses the form of musical representation called DARMS.

13. ____ CD recorder/players use binary information to produce sounds through the speakers.

14. ____ All human languages have the same number of phonemes.

15. ____ Because CD players read the information from the disc using a laser beam, eventually the recordings will show signs of wear.

16. ____ Another name for operation code is opcode.

17. ____ The two parts of an instruction are the operation code and the address.

Multiple Choice

Answer the multiple-choice questions by selecting the best answer from the choices given.

1. Which of the following is not one of the five types of information that can be stored in a computer?
   a. Numbers
   b. Visual
   c. Audio
   d. Tactile
   e. Characters

2. How many different symbols are used in the binary system?
   a. None
   b. 1
   c. 2
   d. 4
   e. Infinite number

3. How many different symbols are used in the decimal system?
   a. None
   b. 9
   c. 10
   d. 100
   e. Infinite number

4. How would the number 40 be represented in the computer? (You need to translate it into a binary number.)
   a. 11_{two}
   b. 101_{two}
   c. 10100_{two}
   d. 101000_{two}
   e. 100111_{two}

5. Translate the following base 2 number to base 10: 110011_{two}.
   a. 24
   b. 25
   c. 50
   d. 51
   e. 99

6. For what does the acronym EBCDIC stand?
   a. Extended Binary Coded Decimal Interchange Code
   b. Extensive Binary Character Decoding Interface Code
   c. Easy Binary Characteristic Decision Installation Code
   d. Einstein's Binary Conditional Decoding Intellectual Code
   e. Everyday Binary Commercial Dedicated Interface Code

7. For what does the acronym ASCII stand?
   a. Associated Society Coded Instruction Interface
   b. Annotated Script Coded Instruction Icons
   c. American Standard Code for Information Interchange
   d. American Sentry Character Internal Information
   e. Assignment of System Codes for Internal Information

8. Which of the following Word Hunt commands instructs you to find a particular page?
   a. GOTO #
   b. FORWARD #
   c. SELECT #
   d. BACKUP #
   e. PAGE #

9. The two parts of each instruction are
   a. Inside and outside
   b. High end and low end
   c. Command and operative
   d. Opcode and operand
   e. Control and comparison

Exercises

1. Classify the following items into one of the five categories of information:

   A clap of thunder
   Automobile mileage
   Tarzan's yell
   A satellite weather map
   A recording of a flute solo
   A special fudge recipe
   The shape of traffic signs
   The text of *Crime and Punishment*
   Honking of a car horn
   The score of a football game
   Computer-animated cartoon
   Pattern in a stained-glass window

2. Consider the following:
   1001110 1001111
   a. What is it when interpreted as ASCII symbols?
   b. What is it when interpreted as a binary number or numbers?
   c. Would the answers to (a) and (b) change if it were written as 10011101001111?

3. Decode the following ASCII message:

1010100	1001000	1001001	1010011	0100000
1001001	1010011	0100000	1000001	0100000
1010011	1010100	1010101	1010000	1001001
1000100	0100000	1010000	1010010	1001111
1000010	1001100	1000101	1001101	0100001

4. Decode the following ASCII message:

1010100	1101111	0100000	1100010	1100101
0100000	1101111	1110010	0100000	1101110
1101111	1110100	0100000	1110100	1101111
0100000	1100010	1100101	0101100	0100000
1110100	1101000	1100001	1110100	0100000
1101001	1110011	0100000	1110100	1101000
1100101	0100000	1110001	1110101	1100101
1110011	1110100	1101001	1101111	1101110
0100001				

5. Find and use a table of EBCDIC codes to decode the following message: (Why can't you use the ASCII table?)

C7 C1 D9 C2 C1 C7 C5 40 C9 D5 6B 40

C7 C1 D9 C2 C1 C7 C5 40 D6 E4 E3 4B

6. Name three ways pictorial information can be stored in a computer.

7. Name three ways audio information can be stored in a computer.

8. Represent each of the following words as a sequence of binary numbers using the ASCII code from Table 2.3.1:
   a. JUMP
   b. TAKE
   c. HELLO
   d. ZIP

9. When typing the number 173 at a computer keyboard, the actual binary information sent to the computer is (assuming an ASCII character set)

0110001 0110111 0110011

If we could peer into the storage and see how the computer actually saved the information (assuming the computer was expecting to take a number), we would see

10101101

Why do you suppose these two are different?

10. If it takes 1 bit to store a pixel that can be only black or white, how many bits would be necessary to store a pixel that can be
   a. A shade of gray between 0 and 63?
   b. A shade of gray between 0 and 255?
   c. A shade of gray between 0 and 1,023?

11. Explain why the pixels in a gray-scale image commonly have shades from 0 to 63, 0 to 255, or 0 to 1,023, where, in the second example, 0 is the number representing white, 255 is black, and 127 would be a gray halfway between black and white. Why not 0 to 320?

12. Why is the process of printing color pictures called four-color printing? Explain why four colors are necessary. In theory, isn't it true that to get color it only takes three colors?

13. Look at a TV screen with a magnifying glass. Describe what you see when the set is on and when it is off. Can you identify the pixels? What are the colors used in the pixels, and can you actually see them?

14. Design your own three-initial monogram using a 9 ˘ 12 size block for each letter.

15. Give some examples of phonemes in a particular language that give difficulty to those who are learning it as a second language.

16. Use the library to research and identify the 10 to 12 phonemes of the Hawaiian language.

17. Identify the African tribe that uses clicking sounds in its speech. Research linguistics books to try to identify its function.

18. Identify the phonemes in the words *shall, can't, mesmerize,* and *pumpkin.*

19. Create a Word Hunt program that will give the message:

   MIDI is a common application of the computer.

   Use this textbook for the source of the words that the Word Hunt program finds.

20. **PUZZLER** In the figure that describes the message from the Arecibo Radio Telescope in section 2.4 there are 10 black-shaded areas directly to the right of the arrow labeled "solar system." Duplicate the 10 shaded areas on a piece of paper and label what each of them represents. Note that "Earth" is already labeled for you. Why are some of the shaded areas bigger than others?

Discussion Questions

1. Aside from DNA, can you think of any information that does not fit into one of the five categories mentioned in this chapter?

2. Explain what is meant when the sales pitch for a certain computer monitor says that it has millions of colors.

3. Why do some games such as SimCity request that you change your monitor from millions of colors to 256 colors?

4. Why are print colors different from video colors?

5. How can you decide whether sound you hear from a cash register or other machine is synthesized speech using phonemes or a prerecorded digitized message?

6. In the Word Hunt program, do you see any problem with using the BACKUP instruction immediately after using the FORWARD instruction? What are all the possibilities of what might happen? What would be the best of those possibilities and why is it the best one?

7. Are thoughts and emotions information? Do they fit any of the five categories? Is a thing or entity (such as a chair) information?

Group Project

Each person in a group of four is to research and prepare materials for the group about a single cryptographic system. Some suggestions include Caesar cipher, Morse code, Playfair square, and semaphore signals. Each individual should encode a single message using all four cryptographic schemes. The other members of the group will decode the message as a team under the guidance of the author of the coded message.

Web Exercises

1. One of the codes for symbol or text information mentioned was EBCDIC. It is still in use, but because personal computers use ASCII, EBCDIC isn't as well known. EBCDIC codes are usually given in base 16 or hexadecimal, which you should learn about from the Web site for the Computer Continuum. Use a search engine on the World Wide Web (WWW) to find this site.
   a. What does the acronym EBCDIC stand for?
   b. What company or individual created the EBCDIC code?
   c. Where is the EBCDIC code used?
   d. Use the WWW to find a table of the EBCDIC code, and then find the coding for the letters of the word *symbol*. Write out the letters in binary, base 10, and base 16.
   e. Write the word *symbol* as ASCII.

2. Music over the WWW has become very popular. In particular, MP3 is the standard most often used. Use the WWW to answer the questions:
   a. What does the acronym MP3 stand for?
   b. Why is MP3 useful and how did it relate to Napster?
   c. Download software that will allow you to play MP3 files on your computer. List the URL where you found it, its name, and whether it is shareware or freeware.
   d. MP3 music files can be played on a computer, but small players are available that can easily be carried in your pocket. Find and list the cost, name, and size of at least three different MP3 players.

Bibliography

Bauer, Frederich Ludwig. *Decrypted Secrets: Methods and Maxims of Cryptology*. London: Springer-Verlag, 2000.

   This book deals with secret codes and their uses in cryptography.

Bosme, Josephine Nettime. *ReadMe! ASCII Culture and the Revenge of Knowledge*. Brooklyn, NJ: Autonomedia, 1999.

   This is a thought-provoking look at words, thoughts, and the effects of ASCII code on the Internet.

Shannon, Claude Elwood et al. *Claude Elwood Shannon: Collected Papers*. Los Alamitos, CA: IEEE Press, 1993.

This collection includes the many scholarly writings of Shannon and some of his contemporaries.

Singh, Jagjit. *Great Ideas in Information Theory, Language and Cybernetics*. Toronto: Dover, 1966.

   This book explores the links connecting three foundational fields of computer theory.

Singh, Simon. *The Code Book*. New York: Doubleday, 1999.

   A very understandable book about cryptography, from Mary, Queen of Scots, to quantum cryptography.

chapter **3**

Computer Hardware Components: CPU, Memory, and I/O

TimeLine

1936 Konrad Zuse develops the concept of a computer memory to hold binary information.

1944 The first electronic digital computer, ENIAC, performs its first computations.

1962 Integrated circuit is nicknamed the "chip."

1964 The first successful supercomputer, the CDC 6600, is produced.

1965 Douglas Englebart creates the mouse at Stanford Research Institute.

1970 A chip 1/10" square contains 1,000 transistors.

1980 The Osborne 1, a "portable" computer weighing 24 pounds, is introduced.

1983 The capacity of floppy disks is expanded to 360 KB.

1985 Supercomputer speeds reach 1 billion operations per second.

1986 The 3½" disk, introduced for Macintosh, becomes popular with other computers as well.

1995 DVD format jointly invented by nine big companies including Sony, Panosonic, Toshiba.

2000 First gigahertz personal computer becomes available.

2011 Quad core computers are the standard.

Chapter Objectives

- ➡ Understand the concept of the von Neumann computer.
- ➡ Know what is meant by input/output (I/O) and its significance.
- ➡ Discern the difference between primary and secondary memory.
- ➡ Recognize the four fundamental characteristics of secondary memory devices.
- ➡ Identify the four basic components of a typical computer.
- ➡ Understand the difference between a von Neumann computer and a supercomputer.
- ➡ Identify the three basic components of a CPU.
- ➡ Understand how the fetch and execute cycle works.
- ➡ Know the relationship between bits, bytes, and words.
- ➡ Identify the many types of digital electronic computers.

SuperStock, Inc.

Computers need both hardware and software to function. If the hardware isn't properly connected or fails, you need to be able to determine what the problem is and plan a course of action to solve it. Make a plan of action to solve each of the following hypothetical problems.

PUZZLER

- My scanner doesn't seem to be there when the scanner program looks for it, even though it has power and is connected to the computer.
- I keep getting out-of-memory messages.
- The computer seems to be working because I can hear the usual sounds. But nothing shows up on the video monitor.
- When I turn on the power on my computer, it starts running okay, but after 10 minutes it freezes, no matter what program I'm running.
- My connection to the Internet via the cable modem from my broadband connection doesn't work after a power failure.
- I try to run programs but they crash at random times.
- My printer doesn't print, but the ready light is on.

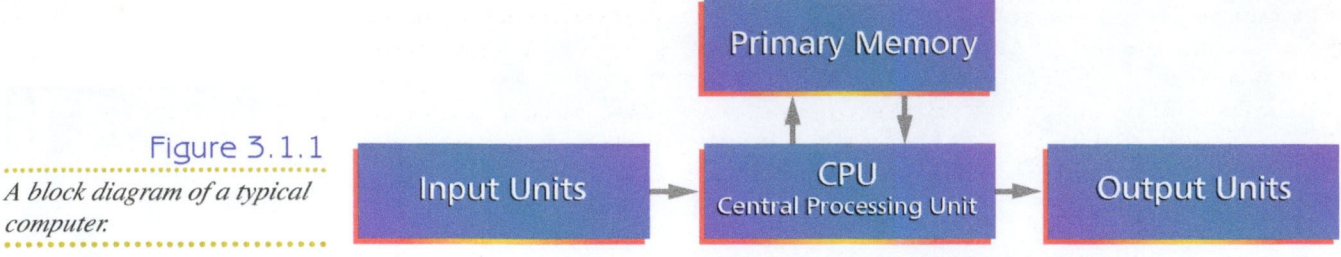

Figure 3.1.1

A block diagram of a typical computer.

3.1 Basic Concepts of Computer Hardware

The majority of digital computers are conceptually quite simple and are based on the structure shown in Figure 3.1.1: primary memory, input units, output units, and the central processing unit. For each box of the diagram there are additional classifications. For example, under the classification of input units are the mouse, keyboard, and floppy drive.

This model of the computer is often called the **von Neumann-type computer,** or architecture, after the brilliant mathematician John von Neumann. The block diagram in Figure 3.1.1 illustrates two key points about the von Neumann computer: First, programs and data that are currently in use are stored in the same location, called the **primary memory.** This point led to the computer being called a **stored-program computer.** The primary memory gets its name from the fact that it is the main memory of the computer and will be defined more formally in a later section. Second, the computer can perform only one instruction at a time. In other words, the von Neumann computer is a stored-program computer with a single program counter. The program counter keeps track of which instruction is supposed to be executed next. The single program counter is commonly referred to as the **von Neumann bottleneck,** because it limits the speed of the computer.

Those parts of the computer receiving information or programs to be used are called the **input units.** The computation is performed in the central processing unit. Other parts of the computer provide the results of computation to the person using the computer; these are called the **output units.** The **input/output** of a computer is often referred to as **I/O.** The computer must also have memory and storage units so that it can keep the programs and information ready and available.

The programs, called computer software, are quite a bit more complex than the conceptual computer itself. Whether it is a word-processing program or a game, the computer hardware must be controlled by software to perform the desired task. We'll cover the concept of a computer program and how it functions in conjunction with the hardware in chapter 4, "Computer Languages, Algorithms, and Program Development," and chapter 5, "Hardware and Software: Putting It Together."

Software is more ephemeral than **hardware.** It consists of programs that make the computer function. Programs can exist in a human's brain, written on paper, or stored magnetically on disk. Hardware, on the other hand, is something you can touch and feel. This chapter will examine the various hardware components necessary to allow the software to do its job.

A **stored-program computer** is a computing device with a place to keep information needed for computing—the **primary memory** of the computer. This memory stores both programs and data that are currently in use.

Input/output or **I/O** refers to the process of getting information and data into and out of the computer.

3.2 Sources of Data for the Computer

Almost any type of information that you can absorb can also be a source of information or data for the computer. For example, computers can deal directly with printed text, visual information, unrecorded sound, and other common information and data. These can include things such as engine temperature sensors or the atmospheric pressure. Note that we are using the words *data* and *information* interchangeably, which is okay for now, but later when we talk about computers and database systems the terms will differ in meaning.

There are many forms of data that only computers can readily work with. These consist of the various binary forms coded especially for the computer. Some familiar examples include data stored on floppy disks, DVDs, and music CDs. We cannot make direct use of them except with the help of a computer.

The first category of hardware we'll discuss includes input devices. Input devices are used to enter both original and previously stored data in the computer. Without input, the computer can't do anything that would remotely meet our needs.

3.3 Input Devices

One of the most commonly used input devices is the **keyboard.** You probably use a keyboard to enter data into a computer. As each key is struck, a special code called a scan code is sent in binary form to a program in the computer that processes it. Depending on the program that is expecting the keystroke, the scan code might be converted to an ASCII code for a letter in a word processor. Or, in the case of striking an arrow key, the scan code may cause the cursor on the screen of your computer to move. Keyboards generally use the QWERTY keyboard, which are named after the first 6 keys above the homerow of the keyboard. There are some differences possible in extra keys, the presence of a numeric keypad, the ergonomic shape shown in Figure 3.3.1, or even the wireless keyboard of Figure 3.3.2.

The **mouse** is another common input device for original data. Invented by Douglas Englebart at Stanford Research Institute in 1965, the mouse is used interactively to move the cursor on the screen and to signal the operating system to do certain things by clicking the buttons on the mouse. Note that the operating system of a computer is the master control

A **keyboard** is the most common piece of hardware used to input data into a computer. It has letters of the alphabet, numerals, punctuation, and many special function keys. The typical keyboard has a QWERTY form and sometimes has special numeric keypads to the right side to make it easier to enter numbers.

The **mouse** is one of the most common ways for the user to communicate commands to the computer. It usually has two buttons that are used to signal the computer to perform a task.

The **Bluetooth** standard was created to replace desktop cabling. It uses radio frequencies with a typical range of about 30 feet and is commonly used to allow connections between computers, keyboards, printers, celphones and many other devices.

Figure 3.3.1

An ergonomic keyboard.

Shahn Karmani/Liaison Agency, Inc.

Figure 3.3.2

A Universal Bluetooth folding keyboard for use with smartphones, PDAs, and other computers.

Courtesy of Freedom Input USA

Table 3.3.1   *Some hardware used to create data or information.*

keyboard	Used to input ASCII characters and control commands
touch pad	Used to move the cursor on the screen by moving fingertip on an active pad
touch screen	Touching the screen does the same as a mouse click
light pen	Pointing to the screen with a pen and clicking by pushing pen
digitizing mouse	Allows position information from drawings to be entered
voice recognition software, microphone and sound card	Allows voice control of computer and word input to word processors
scanner	Digitizes slides and photographs or any other type of visual image
CD-ROM drive	The device that accepts a CD-ROM disc, then uses a laser to read binary information
pen scanner	Passing a pen scanner over a line of text will digitize the image, which is then converted to words with software
MIDI synthesizer	The MIDI device (e.g., keyboard) sends MIDI messages to the computer for musical control of other devices
video digitizer	Live or VHS video signal is fed to hardware that digitizes the video sound/picture, and stores it for playback/editing
digital camera	Photographic images are created in the camera in digital form and can then be transferred to your computer

SuperStock, Inc.

Figure 3.3.3

Two-button mouse.

Voice recognition hardware is an electronic device connected to the computer that receives analog voice data. Using software, the computer can then separate the words and display them in written form on the screen or use them directly as commands.

Digitizing is the process of taking a visual image, including video, or audio recording, and converting it to a binary form for the computer. This binary form is then used as data for programs to display, play, or manipulate the digitized data.

A **digital camera** is similar to ordinary cameras. However, instead of using film, it immediately digitizes the scene being viewed and records it in binary form.

program for the computer, and it carries out activities that the user commands. Operating systems will be discussed in chapter 6, "Operating Systems: The Genie in the Computer." There are three versions of the mouse—with one, two, or three buttons. The most common mouse used with Microsoft Windows has two buttons, as shown in Figure 3.3.3.

Table 3.3.1 contains a list of many pieces of hardware that are sources of data or information. Let's examine some of them.

One of the most novel input devices that creates data is **voice recognition hardware** (see Table 3.3.1). The hardware consists of a device that digitizes analog audio information. Then special software is used to divide the continuous stream of sound into words, which are then converted to ASCII code and can be used by a word processor. The hardware could also be used for simple digital voice recording involving no recognition of the words. Can you see the major difference? The latter case with the voice digitally recorded can only be used for playing back the sound. A voice recognition system can be used to control the computer or input text to a word processor because the actual words are picked out of the stream of sound. There is a huge difference in what this means. In fact, it may mean that keyboards will eventually disappear and we won't have to develop typing skills!

Another very useful input device in Table 3.3.1 for students and others doing research with written text is a pen scanner. This battery-powered device scans the lines of text in eight languages and converts the images to ASCII characters. The QuickLink Pen shown in Figure 3.3.4 allows up to 1,000 pages of ASCII text to be stored, which can then be downloaded into your personal computer. It can also read the text aloud.

More general forms of a scanner allow **digitizing** photographs, pages of text, slides, and other visual flat objects. Note that the generic term *digitizing* means to take pictures, video, or audio data and put them into a binary form for the computer to process or display. Scanners for photographs and other flat objects are relatively inexpensive and have become very popular. Using them can be simple, but the process can become quite complicated because there are many options as to quality and even manipulation through special software. An inexpensive home scanner is pictured in Figure 3.3.5.

A final example from Table 3.3.1 is a popular piece of input hardware that is replacing the classic film camera. It is the **digital camera.** Taking digital pictures has the advantage of flexibility. You can take a picture and immediately see it, then send it to anyone in the world

Figure 3.3.4

Pen scanner inputting a line of text that is stored and then downloaded to the computer.

WIZCOM Technologies Ltd.

Figure 3.3.5

An inexpensive home scanner.

Porter Novelli Convergence Group

over the Internet. A typical midrange camera costs several hundred dollars and produces pictures that look reasonable when enlarged to 8" x 10". The Olympus D-545 Zoom shown in Figure 3.3.6 is a popular midrange camera. Many digital cameras have the added features of video clips and audio notes that can be recorded along with the digital images.

CONNECTING HARDWARE TO THE COMPUTER

Each device attached to a computer requires two important elements: access to the computer through some general input/output connections, and software on the computer that can service the device. Let's take a brief look at these two components.

Computer scientists have created many computer connection standards to allow users to use external devices such as printers and monitors. The actual connecting point on the computer is called a **port.** The word *port* itself is similar to how *seaport* is used to describe a sea entrance to a country. Examples of computer ports include DB-25, USB, DB-15, RJ-11, RJ-45, firewire, video, stereo, and RCA, or a special interface card that can be used for a custom input/output port. Figure 3.3.7 shows a few of these common standard plugs used to connect printers, keyboards, disk drives, scanners, digital cameras, and many other devices. The ports follow standards that define how each of the wires is used. Names for some of these standards are SCSI, RS-232, USB, and IDE. All of them except the **SCSI (Small Computer**

A **port** is a pathway for data to go into and out of the computer from external devices such as keyboards. There are many standard ports as well as custom electronic ports designed for special purposes.

Figure 3.3.6

Olympus D-545 Zoom 4 megapixel camera.

Connector

DB-25, 25-pin female

DB-25, 25-pin male

DIN, 6-pin female

DB-15, 15-pin female

RJ-11

RJ-45

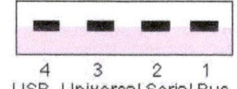

4   3   2   1
USB Universal Serial Bus

Figure 3.3.7

Standard I/O ports.

A **peripheral device** is a piece of hardware such as a printer, disk drive, or CD player that is outside the main computer. It is peripheral to the computer.

A **device driver** is a software addition to the operating system that will allow the computer to communicate with a particular device, such as a printer, hard disk, scanner, or many other input/output devices.

System Interface, pronounced "scuzzy") and **USB** (**Universal Serial Bus**) are for connecting individual **peripheral devices** or hardware such as printers and disk drives.

Both the SCSI and USB can be used to hook up more than one peripheral device in **daisy chain** fashion. This means that the first device is connected to the computer, the next device connects to the previous device, and so on until all peripheral devices are connected. These special connections require the appropriate connecting cables that have the right shape and correct number of wires.

The other important element for connecting a computer to a device is the software needed to recognize and service the device. This software is called a **device driver.** The purpose of the device driver is to allow communication between the device and the operating system that controls the computer. Drivers can access all functions of the device and allow control of the device by the operating system. If you were to install a CD player on your computer, you would also need a driver. Along with the CD player will be a disk with software that you must add to your computer's operating system. This is called installing the driver for the CD player. Most companies provide an installation program that will do all the work of installing the driver by just the click of a mouse button.

PUZZLER HINT

When a peripheral device doesn't function properly, it could be due to the connection, driver, or the failure of the device itself. You need to determine which of these is causing the problem.

COMMON TECHNOLOGIES FOR STORING BINARY INFORMATION

Before we investigate the next major category of input devices, it will be less confusing to look at the basic technologies used in input devices for information that was previously stored by the computer. The three most common technologies are

- electronic
- magnetic
- optical

You probably encounter each of these storage technologies daily. *Electronic input* is the source for Microsoft's X-Box and Sony PlayStation II games. Those little game cartridges you plug into the game are made up of electronic circuits. The hard drives in your computer on which you save your papers and other schoolwork use *magnetic impulses* to store the information. Even more common are the CDs on which your favorite music resides. Those data are stored using *optical* (laser) *technology.* Let's look at how these three forms of technology work.

Electronic circuits are the most expensive of the three forms for storing binary information. They were in use in the first electronic digital computers. Figure 3.3.8 shows **flip-flop circuits** using vacuum tubes from the Electronic Numerical Integrator and Computer (ENIAC). The term *flip-flop* is a description of what happens in the electronic circuit when a 0 or 1 is stored in it. The circuit has either one electronic status or the other, and it is said to flip-flop from one to the other. Believe it or not, the early flip-flops shown in Figure 3.3.8 could only store a handfull of bits. The ENIAC had 20,000 vacuum tubes, many of which were used to store bits.

We've come a long way from the vacuum tube flip-flop. The tiny microchip shown in Figure 3.3.9 contains over 8 million flip-flop circuits. These electronic circuits' means of storage come in two forms: permanent and nonpermanent. In the permanent form, the information is permanently contained in the circuits and it can't be changed. This is the form that the game cartridges use. The other form is nonpermanent and can be used to store information that can be replaced with different information at a later time. The latter is commonly referred to as RAM memory (non-permanent) and the former as ROM memory (permanent).

Magnetic technology is used in many ways to store binary information. Unlike the electronic circuits, there are two parts to most of the magnetic forms of information storage. For

The Computer Museum of America

Figure 3.3.8

Flip-flop circuits from ENIAC circa 1948.

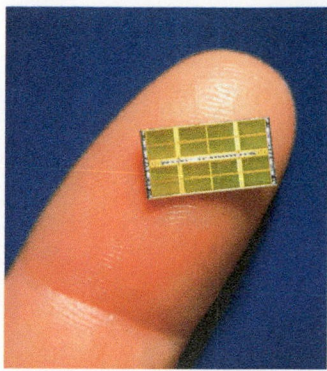

Corbis/Sygma

Figure 3.3.9

Microchip electronic circuit storage.

convenience, the medium that actually stores the magnetic information is separate from the device that is able to read the magnetic information. The hard drive shown in Figure 3.3.10 has its cover removed so the disk can be seen. The round mirror polished metal surface revolves very fast. Note the slender arm shown over the disk. It has a sensor on it that floats over the surface of the disk on a cushion of air. As the disk spins, the arm can move from the center to outside edge of the disk. This allows the sensor to reach any spot on the disk, and then read or store data there.

The keyword to note here is *magnetic* because tiny spots on the disk are magnetized to represent 0s and 1s. It is easiest to visualize these individual 0s and 1s as very tiny compasses that point only north and south. One direction (either north or south) corresponds to 1 and the other would be 0. We will discuss other magnetic storage devices in the next section.

The magnetic storage technology has a very unique feature. It performs nondestructive reading of the information contained. Let's consider an example to see what this means. Suppose you've written a term paper and stored it on the hard disk. Now you would like to rewrite your paper, so the computer takes a copy of the paper and puts it into the memory leaving the original copy on the hard disk. It will, however, destroy the old copy when you save your changes, and the paper stored on the hard disk will be the term paper with the changes you made.

The third technology commonly used is optical. It uses lasers to read the binary information from the medium, usually a disc, such as the one shown in Figure 3.3.11. Millions of tiny holes are "burned" into the surface of the disc. Then when the disc is inserted into the disk drive the holes are interpreted as 1s while absence of a hole is 0. This technique is used on both CDs and DVDs. Note the unusual convention of using the words *disk* for magnetic

Seagate Technology, Inc.

Figure 3.3.10

Hard drive with its cover removed.

Figure 3.3.11

A music CD containing binary information.

Fotopic International/West Stock

media and *disc* for optical media. There are several types of optical disc systems that we will look at later in this chapter.

SECONDARY MEMORY INPUT DEVICES

Next, we discuss the type of input devices used by a computer to store information and then to retrieve that information as needed. These input devices are often referred to as **secondary memory.** The term *secondary memory* suggests that it is not the main or primary memory of the computer, and it is used to store information that must later be transferred to the main memory of the computer when needed. Secondary memory is often called secondary storage.

Secondary memory is important. Without it, you couldn't use the computer to do most of the computing done today. It's the place where almost all of the programs are kept when they are not in use. The three basic technologies we discussed earlier are most commonly used for secondary memory. Of course, this means that secondary memory uses the binary form. The usual unit of measurement is called the **byte,** which contains eight binary digits.

Each secondary memory device has unique features and satisfies certain computer storage needs. Their four most important characteristics are

A computer's **secondary memory, or storage,** is where the original data and programs needed for the computer are stored. Secondary storage is on media external to the computer and commonly consists of hard disk drives, CD-ROMs, or flash memory.

■ speed and access time

■ cost/removable versus nonremovable

■ capacity

■ type of access

A **byte** consists of eight binary digits or bits. The byte is the standard unit of data used by the computer.

Speed and Access Time   First, let's examine the characteristic of speed. What does the speed of a storage device indicate? It tells how fast the information can be taken from (read from) or stored onto (written to) the storage device. The speed of a device is sometimes referred to as its **access time,** although these characteristics are technically different.

The vast differences in access time for the various storage devices can be easily appreciated by looking at two extremes. The fastest devices for holding binary information are certain types of electronic circuits. The fastest have access times of about 10 billionths of a second. At the other extreme are the old floppy disks, which take up to ½ second to reach full speed. At full speed, a floppy disk needs several thousandths of a second to access

The **access time** of a storage device is either (1) the time it takes to get information from the device (read time) or (2) the time it takes to put information into the device (write time).

information. The vast difference in speed between these two devices probably doesn't seem significant, but maybe an analogy would help to make it meaningful. Suppose a speed-reader capable of reading a 200-page book in one hour is similar to the fastest electronic storage device. The slower floppy disk would then be equivalent to a person reading only four words per year! Now that's quite a difference! It should be obvious that fast storage devices are needed to utilize the computer fully; otherwise, it would be sitting idle most of the time, waiting for data.

It is important to remember that there are two parts to the floppy disk system: (1) the media or floppy disk where the information is stored, and (2) the device called the floppy disk drive where the disk is inserted. As previously discussed, the high-density floppy disk uses magnetic technology.

Cost/Removable versus Nonremovable

Cost is another way to characterize secondary storage devices. In many secondary storage devices the actual medium or place where the binary information is stored is removable. With removable storage media there are actually two parts to the cost. The first part is the cost of the actual medium used to store the bits. The second cost is the price of the drive unit that accesses data on the medium. In the case of the CD and DVD systems, the disc itself costs only a few cents. The drive can be $49 to $129; however, only one of them is needed to access any number of storage disks.

There are other types of removable memory devices. One in particular has become very common, it's the USB flash drive, sometimes referred to as a "thumbdrive." It comes in a variety of sizes that range from 64 MB up to 128 GB. They are relatively small and are priced from a few dollars into the hundreds of dollars. The "USB" in the name refers to the fact that it plugs into the USB (Universal Serial Bus) port on the computer. Being quite small, they are often provided with a ring for attaching to your keychain. Figure 3.3.12 shows the SanDisk Cruzer extended (ready to plug into the computer's USB port) and also in the retracted ready to travel format.

The need for even larger volume secondary storage is satisfied by what is commonly referred to as the hard drive. The reason for the term *hard drive* is that the disk itself is hard and inflexible. This allows much greater densities of bits to be stored because it allows greater precision with much faster access time than a floppy drive. Without exception, all new personal computers sold today have hard drives. A typical hard disk drive is shown in Figure 3.3.13 with its cover removed. They are usually sealed in a box to keep dust and dirt out.

Finally, the most economical form of information storage in a removable form is the CD-ROM and DVD. The music CD shown in Figure 3.3.11 is the same as the CD-ROM

> The term **megabyte** means a million bytes. **Gigabyte** refers to a billion bytes.

Figure 3.3.12

Flash

Courtesy of SanDisk Corporation

Figure 3.3.13

Hard drive with its cover removed.

used for computer secondary storage. It costs just a few cents to duplicate CD-ROMs and they hold over 600 megabytes of information. As mentioned earlier, to make an original CD-ROM, a laser burns tiny craters in the surface of the disc. A crater means 1 and no crater means 0. When retrieving information from a CD-ROM, a low-power laser, which can't burn craters, is used to "see" the craters. The low-power laser's beam is reflected (no crater) or not reflected (with the crater). A schematic of the CD-ROM's construction is shown in Figure 3.3.14. Note that ROM is an acronym that stands for read only memory. Once the holes are burned into the disc, no new information can be put there and, therefore, the designation of read only is appropriate. The DVD is described later in this chapter (see Fig. 3.6.5).

For a few hundred dollars, drives are available that can write onto either blank CD-ROMs or DVDs. They use a more powerful laser, one that can burn holes in the disc. Then when reading the CD-ROM, the laser power is reduced so that it only reads the data that have been previously burned in.

It should be pointed out that CDs and DVDs are not considered to be archival. According to some sources, degradation could start as soon as 10 years. However, more important is the fact that as technology changes the formats and reading devices may change.

Figure 3.3.14

A CD-ROM's layout.

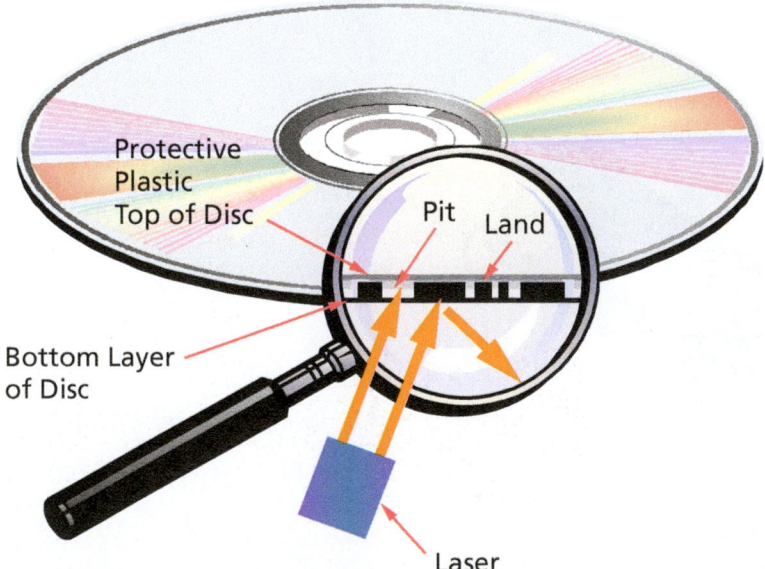

Table 3.3.2   *Common terms used to describe capacity.*

Terms	Value
1 byte	8 bits
1 kilobyte	1,024 bytes
1 megabyte	1,048,576 bytes
1 gigabyte	1,073,741,824 bytes
1 terabyte	1,099,511,627,776 bytes

Capacity   The capacity of a secondary storage device ranges from the very old slow, cheap, and removable 1.4 megabyte floppy disks to the more expensive, fast, and nonremovable hard drives. The hard drive capacities range from hundreds of megabytes to several hundred gigabytes, and DVDs can contain up to 17 gigabytes.

An interesting note should be made here. When referring to the capacities in bytes or other numbers in binary, a megabyte isn't 1 million bytes, but it is 1,048,576. This seems rather strange until you recognize that multiplying 2 times itself 20 times yields 1,048,576, and remember that in binary each additional bit doubles the size of the number that can be represented. Table 3.3.2 shows the terms used to describe capacity.

Type of Access   There are two types of access that a computer's storage or memory uses: **random access** and **sequential access.** With random access storage, we can go directly into any part of the storage to either retrieve (read) information or write it. Hard disks are considered random access, although a short wait may be necessary to allow the disk to rotate to where the information is located. Most secondary memory used today is random access.

Random access to storage allows information to be obtained directly rather than by sifting through other information to reach it.

In contrast, with the sequential access storage, we must start at the beginning and go through the storage until we reach the information of interest. The very old magnetic tapes are examples of sequential access storage. As an example of what this means, imagine that we have stored the *Encyclopedia Britannica* on the magnetic tapes needed to get every word recorded. Now suppose we need information regarding Vladimir Kosma Zworykin, the U.S. electronics engineer acknowledged as the inventor of television. We would have to wind through the tape that contains the z entries from the beginning to reach the desired information. That would be analogous to flipping through all the pages one by one until page 1027 of Volume 23 of the 1970 edition appears. How tedious! Random access, on the other hand, corresponds more closely to the way we usually use the encyclopedia. We can go right to where the information is stored because we know that Zworykin would be at the end. Figure 3.3.15 shows some half-inch-wide, 2,400-foot-long magnetic tapes. Note that a CD-ROM can store about 55 times more bits per disc than the entire reel of tape pictured at a fraction of the cost.

Sequential access to storage allows the desired information to be obtained by starting at the beginning of a list of information and then proceeding item by item until it is reached.

Figure 3.3.15

Several magnetic one-half inch tapes up to 2,400 feet long.

Courtesy of BASF

TABLE 3.3.3   *Relationships among various types of storage.*

	Magnetic	Optical	Other
Nonreusable	Magnetic ink	CD-ROM	Bar code
	Optical character recognition media	Laser disk (analog)	Punched paper
		DVD	Hollerith cards
Reusable	USB Flash Drive	Holographic	
	Hard disk	CD-RW	
	Removable disk cartridge	DVD-RW	
	Digital magnetic tape		

It should be noted that the IRS has switched from the 40-year-old magnetic tape–based master file system to the CADE (Customer Account Data Engine) database system.

Table 3.3.3 summarizes the relationships among various types of storage. It is divided into storage that can be used over and over again (reusable) like a chalkboard with an eraser and storage that can be used only once (nonreusable) like writing on a chalkboard with non-removeable paint. The two main categories of storage are magnetic and optical.

3.4 Primary Memory

The previous section examined input devices for the computer, particularly secondary memory. The term *secondary memory* itself indicates that there is another kind of memory that is more important. Indeed, the **primary memory** of the computer is where we store information currently in use, whereas the secondary memory stores information that will be used at some future time.

> A computer's **primary storage**, or **memory**, is where the data and program that are currently in operation or being accessed are stored during use. Primary storage is most commonly made from electronic circuits.

The primary memory of the computer consists of electronic circuits that are extremely fast and expensive. The analogy used in the previous section of the speed-reader reading a book in one hour compared with reading 4 words per year seems extreme. Primary memory is very fast with access times about a billionth of a second. This is necessary so as not to slow down processing done by the electronics that make up the main part of the computer where all the actual computing takes place. In Figure 3.3.9, we saw a silicon microchip that contains 64 million bits of fast electronic circuit memory. Other memory chips are shown in Figure 3.4.1. Each bit is represented by an electronic switch that is on or off, corresponding to the 0 or 1 in binary. This circuitry-type memory costs about .00000002 cent per byte, whereas other storage media are much less expensive. The music

Photo courtesy of Intel Corporation

Figure 3.4.1

Two memory chips "pose" with a Pentium microprocessor.

CD pictured in Figure 3.3.11 costs .00000005 cent per byte. An even less expensive secondary storage is the DVD shown in Figure 3.6.5 at only .00000000006 cent per byte.

Another important distinction in the types of electronic storage must be made between permanent and nonpermanent primary storage. The two common types of memory are **RAM** (random access memory) and **ROM** (read only memory). If the power plug to a computer is accidentally pulled, all of the data in the RAM (nonpermanent memory) disappear. The ROM (permanent memory) maintains its data even though the computer is turned off.

The RAM memory is where programs such as word processors reside when they are being "used." In fact, any program that is to be "used" in the computer has to be in primary memory, either RAM or ROM. The programs that process the keyboard input and sense when the mouse is moved are kept in ROM (permanent) memory. These programs are needed to start up the computer, and are seldom updated, because they are so fundamental.

It should be pointed out that game cartridges are ROM memory of the electronic variety because of the need for access speed.

There is a very rich history of the development of primary memory for computers. For digital electronic computers it began with hardwired memory, where the programs were put into memory by wiring boards that were much like what the old-fashioned telephone switchboard operator used. There was also the mercury delay line and the cathode tube memory. They were very slow by today's standards and also had very small capacity, usually measured in dozens of bits. However, the concepts involved are the same today as they were then.

3.5 The Central Processing Unit

The **central processing unit** (**CPU**) is often referred to as the brain of the computer. It is responsible for controlling all activities of the computer system, performing all calculations, and executing all instructions. In the simplistic view of Figure 3.5.1 are shown the three major components of the CPU:

- arithmetic unit
- control unit
- instruction decoding unit

RAM (random access memory) is a part of the primary storage, or memory, of the computer. Its contents are not permanent and can be changed. This characteristic is necessary so that different programs and data can be stored there. Also, if the power shuts off, RAM loses everything that was stored in it.

ROM (read only memory) is a part of the primary storage, or memory, of the computer. It is permanent memory. It keeps its contents forever and can never be changed, unless you unplug and replace it.

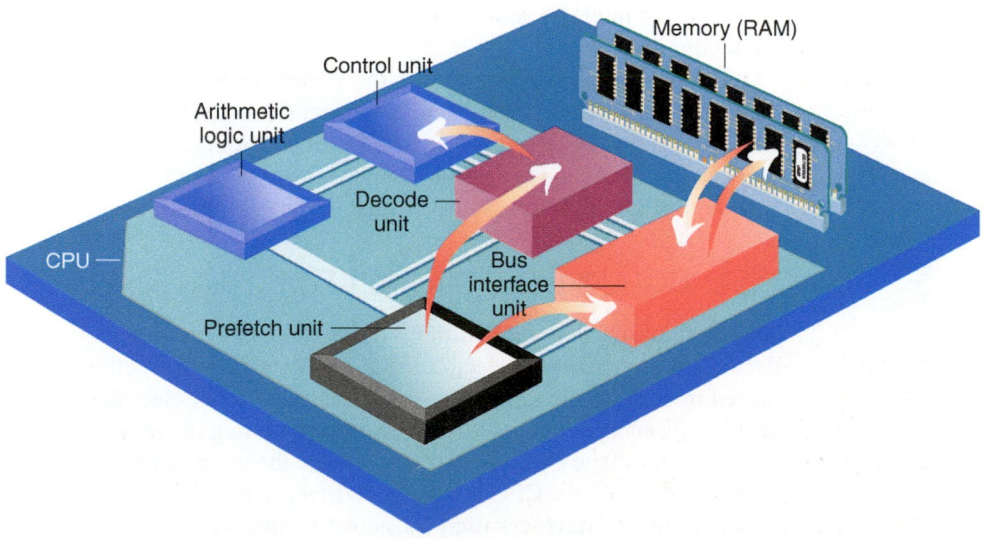

Figure 3.5.1

The three major parts of the central processing unit.

The **arithmetic unit** is the part of electronic circuitry in the CPU where arithmetic operations such as addition and subtraction are performed.

The **control unit** controls what is done in the CPU. It coordinates actions such as putting instructions to be done in the instruction register (IR) and using the program counter (PC) to keep track of where to go when ready to get the next instruction.

Registers are places right in the CPU where special numbers are temporarily kept. Examples include the **instruction register, program counter,** and the accumulators.

The **instruction decoding unit** takes the instruction in the instruction register and causes it to be executed.

Courtesy of Intel Corporation

Figure 3.5.2

An Intel ® Core ™ i7 processor with and without cover.

Figure 3.5.1 shows the arrangement of these components that facilitate the work of the CPU: prefetch unit, bus interface unit, and memory. The names are quite suggestive. The arithmetic unit is where addition and subtraction are done, the control unit controls the action of the CPU, and the instruction decoding unit decodes the instructions of a program as they are brought into the CPU through the bus interface.

In personal computers, the CPU is on a **chip.** The word *chip* originated because the circuits are etched—as is a paint chip or wood chip—on a small piece of thin silicon. The chip is mounted on a piece of plastic with "legs" or edge contacts that are connected to the chip by tiny wires. Figure 3.5.2 shows a Intel ® Core ™ *i7* used in many desktop computers.

ARITHMETIC UNIT OF THE CPU

The **arithmetic unit** is the part of the CPU where arithmetic is done. It has a place where calculated results are accumulated, called the **accumulator.** The accumulator results are then stored in RAM memory. This is a simplistic view of the CPU, as it may have several accumulators, but the concepts are the same.

CONTROL UNIT OF THE CPU

The **control unit** has two locations where important numbers are kept: the instruction register (IR) and the program counter (PC). There may be many other registers related to instructions and the instruction register, depending on the computer's design. The **instruction register** is where a command to do something is placed for analysis by the instruction decoding unit. An example of an instruction might be adding a number in memory location 2,337,298 to the accumulator.

The **program counter** contains the address or location in the RAM memory where the next instruction to be executed resides. The control unit will carry out or execute the desired operation residing in the instruction **register.** It will then go to the address in memory contained in the program counter to fetch or get the instruction that is to be performed next.

Courtesy of Intel Corporation

Figure 3.5.3

The interior surface structure of an Intel® Core ™ i7 processor.

INSTRUCTION DECODING UNIT OF THE CPU

The **instruction decoding unit** is the part of the computer that will decode the instruction. It electronically analyzes each instruction as it is placed in the instruction register and causes the proper electronics to be activated to make the instruction happen. This is referred to as executing the instruction.

In computing we often refer to the CPU as everything inside the main cabinet. Actually, this cabinet usually contains not only the CPU but the hard drive, CD-ROM drive, modems, and other electrical circuits called **interfaces** used for network connections and other purposes. Even though this seems rather complex, it is nothing compared to the microprocessor

Fetch/Execute and the Clock

The **fetch/execute cycle** refers to how programs run in a computer. The CPU must first retrieve the next instruction from the memory (the fetch), and then the CPU can do what the instruction commands (execute). This cycle is controlled by the clock of the computer. Analogous to the metronome of a practicing musician or the drums in a marching band, the clock keeps time for the computer. It usually takes several clock ticks to complete some of the more complicated instructions. In everyday terms, the clock speed of the computer is measured in megahertz (MHz). A 600 MHz computer is 50 percent faster than a 400 MHz computer. The megahertz unit represents millions of clock ticks per second. A one gigahertz (GHz) computer has a clock that ticks 1 billion times per second. Of course, you can't hear an electronic tick; this term is from the days when the escapement of a mechanical clock or watch actually made ticking sounds. The fastest microcomputers are almost 4 gigahertz. Larger computers go much faster.

Because the number of clock cycles needed to execute an instruction varies, a more descriptive measurement of speed is the number of instructions executed per second. A computer that can execute 5 million instructions per second would have its speed indicated as a 5 Mips computer. The most time-consuming type of instruction is one that can deal with fractional numbers, called **floating-point numbers.** This has led to the measurement of speed by the number of floating-point instructions per second. A computer that can do 1 trillion floating-point instructions per second is a one Tflop computer. A supercomputer that can do a thousand trillion instructions per second has its speed denoted as 1 petaflop or Pflop.

chip itself. Figure 3.5.3 shows a microphotograph of the inside surface of the Intel® Core™ *i7* processor. This processor has millions of transistors that carry out all the duties of the CPU and contains the instruction registers, program counter, various accumulators, instruction decoding unit, and clock.

The CPU, interface electronics, primary memory and other support electronics are all placed on a single piece of plastic called the **motherboard.** This single sheet of plastic has tiny wires etched on the surface that carry the electrical signals between the components.

The **motherboard** of a computer is the place where most of the electronics including the CPU are mounted. It is a piece of nonconducting plastic that has wires etched on the surface.

3.6 Output Devices

The input/output units allow the computer to communicate with hardware outside the CPU and primary memory. The input unit allows the computer to receive information (both data and instructions) from the outside world, whereas the output unit stores and displays information (calculated results and other messages) for us to see and use.

USB FLASH DRIVES AND HARD DRIVES

The USB flash drives and hard disks discussed in section 3.3 also function as output devices. The CPU stores the results of computations onto a flash drive and/or hard drive. This includes Internet-related information that may be requested by the computer user. The most often used storage for computer output is the hard drive. Almost all computers have a hard drive, which is the workhorse of computer storage. In the 1990s hard drives weren't standard and their capacities were small, usually around 20 megabytes. In the beginning of the twenty-first century capacities are thousands of times larger, with 40 to 320 gigabytes being the norm. A high-capacity, 1.5 TB(terabyte) hard disk drive from Seagate costing just under $130 is shown in Figure 3.6.1. It should be pointed out that most hard drives are mounted inside the main computer box and can't be seen.

Figure 3.6.1

Seagate 1.5 terabyte (TB) Barracuda 7200.11 hard disk drive.

DISPLAY MONITORS

The **cathode ray tube (CRT)** and **liquid crystal display (LCD)** are the two most common ways for the computer to visually display results. The CRT is a large vacuum tube in which streams of electrons make phosphors glow on the tube face. The LCD is a flat panel display that uses crystals to let varying amounts of different colored light pass through it.

The most visible of all of the output devices is the video monitor. Without a way for us to view and understand information, decisions can't be made and computers would be useless. Because the major input to the human brain is visual, it is not surprising that computer companies have designed a vast array of monitors. Standard analog television sets don't have the quality to display text—it's just too fuzzy. In the computer field we say that the resolution isn't high enough. However, with the development of digital television, the resolution issue will disappear.

The high-resolution monitors used with computers come in two major types. The least expensive uses a large picture tube called a **cathode ray tube (CRT),** just like standard television. These display monitors are quite bulky and occupy a good portion of your desktop. An example of the tube-type high-resolution display is shown in Figure 3.6.2. The other type of display monitor is the **liquid crystal display (LCD),** which was created primarily for portable computers. Every laptop computer uses an LCD display as shown in Figure 3.6.3. Laptop displays differ somewhat in technology but operate conceptually in the

Figure 3.6.2

Tube-type, high-resolution display monitor.

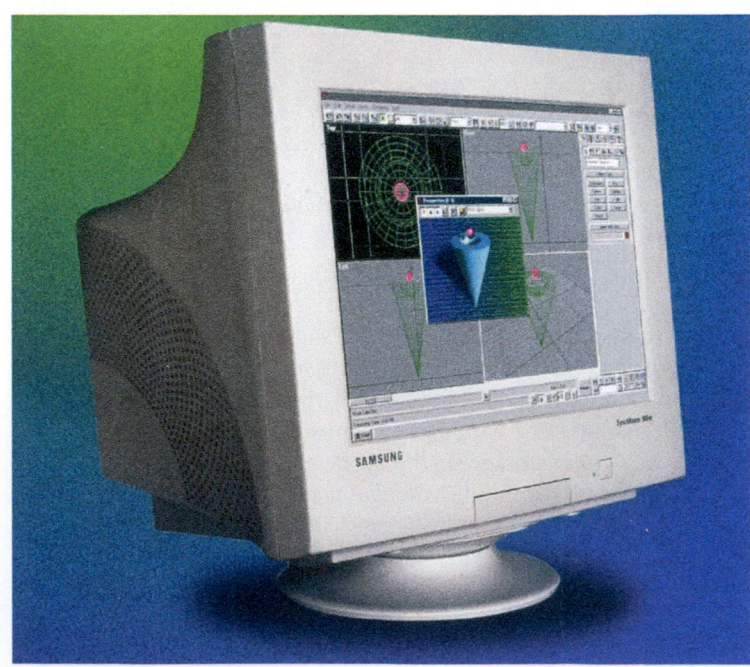

Samsung Electronics America, Inc.

same manner. In spite of their cost, under $300 for a 17" display, these liquid crystal displays are making their way onto the desktop. This is because they don't take up the space that tube-type monitors require, as can be seen in Figure 3.6.4.

AUDIO OUTPUT DEVICES

Vision is undoubtedly the most important of our senses; however, hearing is also important. Computers have become mainstream when it comes to sound. More people have been exposed to music on CD than have been exposed to the general-purpose computer, and after all, the CD player is a computer! Most personal computers have a CD drive that can access both music CDs and CD-ROMs containing all types of information. Computers such as the Macintosh have audio playback built into them. Windows machines need a special audio card for audio output.

Aside from music CDs, audio output from computers has been relegated to specialized tasks, such as fighter pilot information updating and building elevators' floor announcements. But voice synthesis is becoming more human sounding, and with speech recognition programs becoming popular, speech output is also likely to follow closely behind. Multimedia is also an area in which sound is being used. In chapter 10, "Multimedia," we will examine audio output in more detail.

OPTICAL DISKS: CD-ROM AND DVD

All of the secondary storage input units discussed in section 3.4 are also output devices, with the exception of the CD-ROM and DVD drives that will only read information from the CD-ROM and DVD. However, there are special CD-ROM and DVD drives that will not only read CD-ROMs and DVDs but will also *burn* information into blank CD-ROMs and DVDs. The term *burn* is used because the laser used to make the craters in the surface to represent a binary 1 literally burns a tiny hole in the surface. When this type of device is used for reading, the laser is used with reduced power so as to not burn more craters in the surface. Key specifications of CDs are:

- Storage: They can store a maximum of 650 megabytes.
- Time: It takes much more time to burn a CD-R than to record on a hard drive.
- Software: They need special software to record, whereas with a hard drive you can "drag and drop."

But, what was originally called digital video disc and is now known as **digital versatile disc (DVD),** allows up to 17 gigabytes of storage. This is made possible by packing information closer together. There are four versions of the DVD, which include a single-sided, single-layer (4.7 GB), single-sided, double-layer (8.5 GB), double-sided, single-layer (9.4 GB), and double-sided, double-layer (17 GB). Figure 3.6.5 illustrates the four types of DVD.

DVD-Video has been quite successful due to the excellent quality of video and audio recording possible on DVD and the fact that full-length movies can be put onto a single disc complete with sound. Another very important feature of the DVD drive is that it is compatible with the older CD technology. This means older CDs can be used with today's DVD drives.

STORAGE CAPACITY

The physical size or capacity of storage devices with their inherent cost is certainly a significant factor and depends on how the storage is to be used. For example, storing the total contents of the Library of Congress on electronic circuit–type storage would be costly. On the other hand, optical mass-storage memories can hold trillions of bits and could easily fit into a small room. These optical storage systems can easily contain the total contents of the 35-acre, 20,000,000-volume Library of Congress. See Table 3.6.1.

The term *mass storage* is intuitively understandable but deserves further discussion. Mass storage involves storing huge amounts of information. Until the late 1980s, magnetic

FPG International LLC

Figure 3.6.3

Laptop computer with liquid crystal display.

Samsung Electronics America, Inc.

Figure 3.6.4

Desktop liquid crystal display.

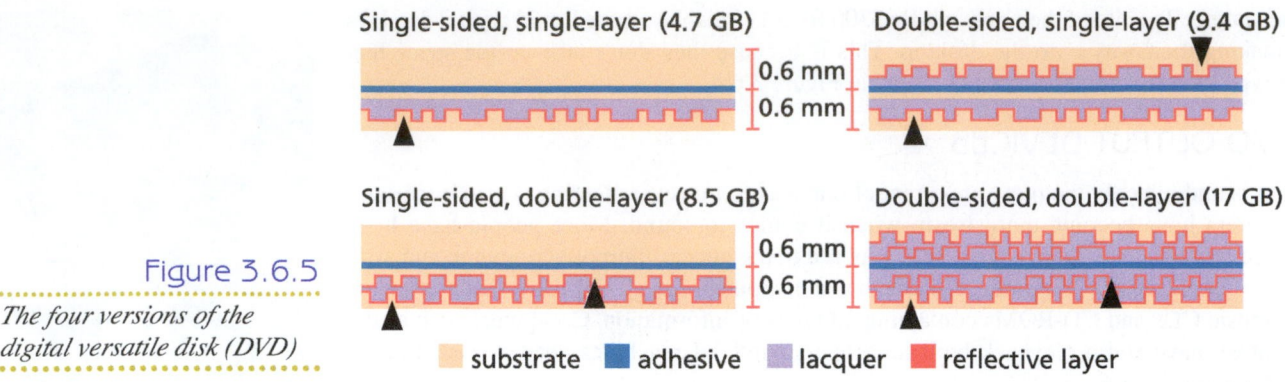

Figure 3.6.5

The four versions of the digital versatile disk (DVD)

tape was the most common form for storing large amounts of data cheaply and in a relatively small space. When all the factors such as cost, capacity, and speed were taken into account, this seemed to be the most reasonable mass-storage medium. DVD-ROMs have replaced magnetic tapes for mass storage because of their smaller size, lower cost, higher capacity, and greater reliability. A single DVD-ROM can hold the equivalent of over 1,300 of the 1980s vintage 2,400-foot magnetic tapes.

Table 3.6.1   *Comparative storage requirements and capacities.*

How much computer memory does it take to store . . .	
One keystroke from the keyboard	1 byte
One line of word-processed text*	4 kilobytes (2,740 bytes)
One page single-spaced, unformatted text	40 kilobytes
Nineteen pages of formatted text with heads and subheads	75 kilobytes
Word processor, program alone	883 kilobytes
Spelling dictionary	258 kilobytes
Word-processing help file	468 kilobytes
Complete word-processing package	8.4 megabytes (the latest versions take more)
Full-page, black-and-white drawing	18–67 kilobytes, depending on complexity
Full-page color photo	4–6 megabytes
The word *good-bye*	3.2 kilobytes
One second of high-fidelity sound	95–110 kilobytes
This book, text only, no pictures	4.6 megabytes
How much data can be stored on . . .	
One inch of ½-inch wide magnetic tape	4 kilobytes
One 5¼" floppy disk, double-sided, double-density (MS-DOS)	360 kilobytes
One 3½" floppy disk, double-sided, double-density (Macintosh)	800 kilobytes
One 3½" floppy disk, high-density	1.44 megabytes
One compact disc (CD-ROM)	650 megabytes
One 12" laser video disk (analog)	55,000 still color images, each taking 4–6 megabytes if digitized
One DVD	Up to 17 gigabytes

*This varies according to hard drive size and the minimum allocation used.

Figure 3.6.6

Holographic data, stored and displayed by Star Wars *droid R2-D2.*

Lucasfilm Ltd.

STORAGE DEVICES OF THE FUTURE

An advanced research project on storage devices at IBM sounds like science fiction. Remember the crystal storage devices from *Star Trek,* the holographic storage cubes in Isaac Asimov's *Foundation* series, or the holograms of *Star Wars*? (See Figure 3.6.6.) IBM research, GE and several other companies are currently working on holographic technology. You may be familiar with the two-dimensional holographic stickers used on credit cards for security. The new device will be in disc format and use laser light to read and write it. Researchers believe they can store 500 gigabytes of data on a disc. It would also be faster than today's fastest mass-storage devices.

3.7 Moving Information within the Computer

In chapter 2, we saw how the five forms of information can be represented by binary numerals and where these binary numerals can be stored or kept for use by the computer. Another important part of how computers work involves how these binary numerals are moved into, out of, and within the computer.

First, let us take a look inside the computer. Because of the great speed of the electronic circuitry inside the computer, moving binary information bit by bit from one place to another is very inefficient. Instead, the information is moved about in bytes or multiple bytes, which in large computers are called **words.** These words are the fundamental units of information, passed around inside the computer. The number of bits per word varies greatly. A word length is 32 bits for the older large IBM mainframe systems.

The number of bits necessary to store a single alphanumeric character is six, seven, or eight bits, depending on the system of representation. (Chapter 2, "Metamorphosis of Information," showed only the seven-bit ASCII code.) Because of this, many words are subdivided into units called **bytes,** which are usually eight bits long. The division of a common 32-bit word into bytes is shown in Figure 3.7.1.

To further complicate matters, computers can be designed with many different word sizes. When the word size becomes as small as eight bits, then such words are referred to as bytes. For example, most early microcomputers had only eight bits as the fundamental unit of information that was passed around inside them. The eight-bit microcomputer words are referred to as bytes, mainly because the eight-bit byte is too small to contain the information usually contained in the words of larger computers.

The bits that compose a word are passed in **parallel** (that is, together as a group) from place to place inside the computer. If we were to open the main box containing the computer's electronics, then we could see some of these parallel data paths over which the words

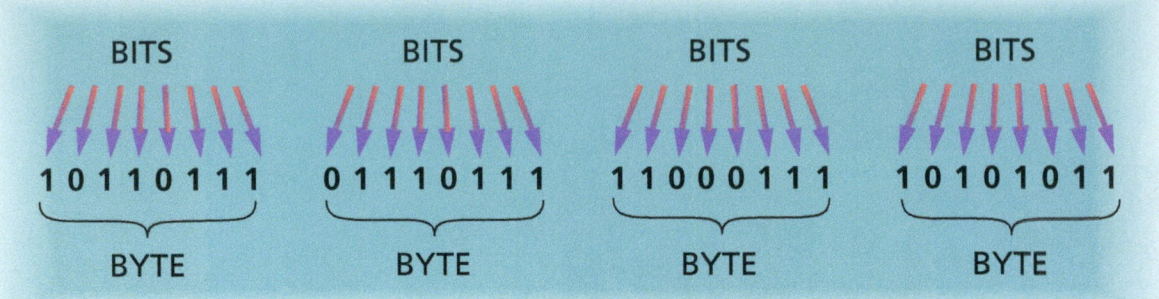

Figure 3.7.1

The relationship between bits, bytes, and a word. These four bytes make up a word.

are passed. One of the more visually obvious paths is in the form of **ribbon cables.** These ribbon cables consist of several wires molded together, side by side, one for each bit of the word or byte, plus some additional wires to coordinate the activity of moving the information. Figure 3.7.2 shows a ribbon cable in a microcomputer for connection between the motherboard and disk drive. It consists of several wires, each carrying one bit of information in the form of a voltage pulse. Included are the wires carrying the eight-bit byte. These pulses are voltages that are applied to the wires for a very short time, millionths of a second. Typically, the voltages are 5 to 12 volts.

As an example of how this ribbon cable would function, suppose the computer moved the ASCII letters *WOW* over the ribbon cable. Voltage pulses corresponding to the ASCII coding would flow through the cable, as shown in Figure 3.7.3. The ASCII code is only seven bits, so the extra bit on wire 8 isn't used, except in special cases.

Another major point is that the information flowing inside a computer can be checked for errors. In the more sophisticated computer systems, the errors are not only detected but also the appropriate corrections can be made on the information moving around inside the computer.

How bytes flow into and out of the computer is also related to the information flow within a computer. This type of communication is done via input/output (I/O) devices. A

Figure 3.7.2

Ribbon cable used for electronic connection.

Christopher Lauckner

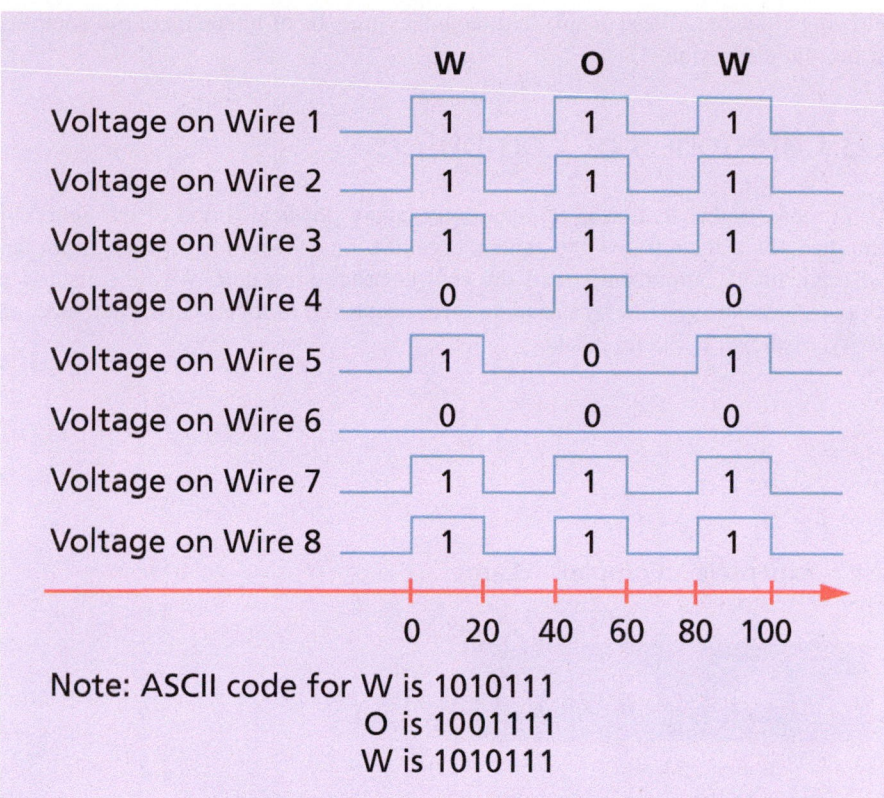

Note: ASCII code for W is 1010111
O is 1001111
W is 1010111

Figure 3.7.3

ASCII characters WOW on ribbon cable with the voltage on wire 8 fixed at 1.

familiar input device for a computer is a keyboard. Typing on the keyboard sends ASCII characters to the CPU (central processing unit) of the computer.

As a simple example, suppose you would like to type the number –23 (-10111_{two}) into a letter. Typing the –, 2, and 3 on the keyboard causes these symbols to appear on the screen of your computer. The reason the symbols appear is that the seven-bit ASCII codes for the –, 2, and 3 are sent by the keyboard to the word-processing program, which in turn saves them in memory and makes the symbols appear on the screen. Table 3.7.1 (a) illustrates this case. Incidentally, the ASCII information is not usually sent in parallel to and from I/O devices in most microcomputers. Sending it bit by bit in **serial** is fast enough. This saves wires and reduces problems with bad connections.

The –23 entered into the microcomputer would end up as a string of voltage pulses as shown in Table 3.7.1 (b). It should be pointed out that this picture is somewhat simplified. The computer must be ready to receive a character at any time; otherwise, it could miss the

Table 3.7.1   *ASCII characters and codes for –23.*

(a) Character information to be sent representing –23.

Order Sent	Symbol	ASCII Code
1st	–	0101101
2nd	2	0110010
3rd	3	0110011

(b) Voltage pulses coded as 0s and 1s for –23.

Voltage code	0 1 0 1 1 0 1	0 1 1 0 0 1 0	0 1 1 0 0 1 1

Voltage pulses actually sent, where 0 means no voltage and 1 means high voltage or 0 means off and 1 means on.

following character. These details, although they may be of interest, are too complicated for our present discussion.

3.8 Categories of Computers

Our purpose in this section is to discuss the many physical forms of the general-purpose computer. All of them follow the general organization shown in Figure 3.1.1: primary memory, input units, output units, and the central processing unit. We will discuss general-purpose computer systems by grouping them according to their speed, cost, size, and complexity, as shown in Figure 3.8.1.

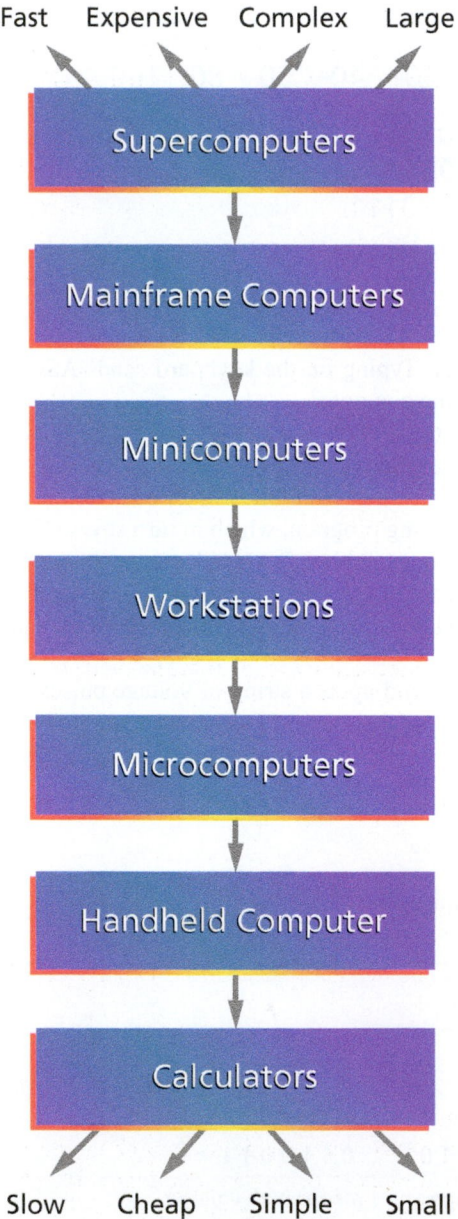

Fast   Expensive   Complex   Large

Supercomputers

Mainframe Computers

Minicomputers

Workstations

Microcomputers

Handheld Computer

Calculators

Slow   Cheap   Simple   Small

Figure 3.8.1

Computer systems' speed, cost, complexity, and size.

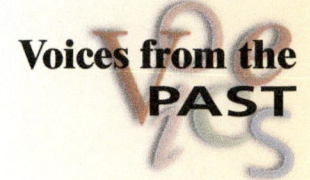

The Father of the Electronic Digital Computer

Think of it: Suppose you owned the patent rights to 99.9 percent of all electronic digital computers ever made! Indeed, you would be one of the richest people in history. A disagreement on the patent rights to the electronic digital computer started with the designers of the ENIAC, J. Presper Eckert and John W. Mauchly. They also wanted exclusive patent rights to the EDVAC, which they claimed was based on ENIAC. The patent dispute carried on into 1947 when the meeting of the principal players in the issue agreed that the von Neumann report put the concepts of the stored-program computer in the public domain. But it also left the door open to additional individual patent claims and the discovery of the true father of computing. Eckert and Mauchly went on to sell their patent rights to Sperry Rand corporation.

The real father of electronic computing was discovered to be Dr. John Vincent Atanasoff. His identity surfaced during the patent fight between Honeywell and Sperry Rand. When Sperry Rand tried to collect hundreds of millions of dollars in license fees for the use of the von Neumann computer concepts, it was revealed that Atanasoff and his associate Cliff Berry had constructed a computer at Iowa State College between 1939 and 1941. This computer, called the ABC (Atanasoff Berry Computer), was seen by Mauchly in a visit to Atanasoff's laboratory in 1941. This visit by Mauchly lasted five days, and through court testimony, it is clear that many of the major ideas were incorporated in the Atanasoff Berry Computer.

So goes the story of the electronic digital computer. The invention was claimed by Eckert and Mauchly, actually invented by Atanasoff, and named after John von Neumann. As a footnote, it should be mentioned that, independently, Konrad Zuse in Germany finished creating his first of several electromechanical computers in 1938, which was designed to crack enemy codes during World War II. It contains some of the same ideas as the von Neumann computer.

CALCULATOR

The lowest on the list are the familiar handheld calculators, which are the cheapest, slowest, simplest, and smallest general computers discussed here. However, as limiting as these calculators are, they are still more powerful than the ENIAC, which is shown in this chapter's Voices from the Past. The larger calculators, such as the one shown in Figure 3.8.2, are programmable. Calculators and programmable calculators are convenient but aren't designed for high performance, and they have limited memory storage.

HANDHELD COMPUTER

The **handheld computer** is almost as small as a calculator but is really a full-blown computer. Figure 3.8.3 shows a handheld computer with display and running Microsoft Windows. It has the power of the larger personal computers, but the keyboard is very small and the input/output units are limited.

MICROCOMPUTER

A **microcomputer** or the personal computer contains a **microprocessor** or "micro-CPU," which is a small central processing unit. The microprocessor is made using a photographic process that exposes and layers semiconductor materials in order to make incredibly tiny transistors. These transistors are so small that millions of them can be placed on an area

Hewlett-Packard Company

Figure 3.8.2

A programmable calculator with display.

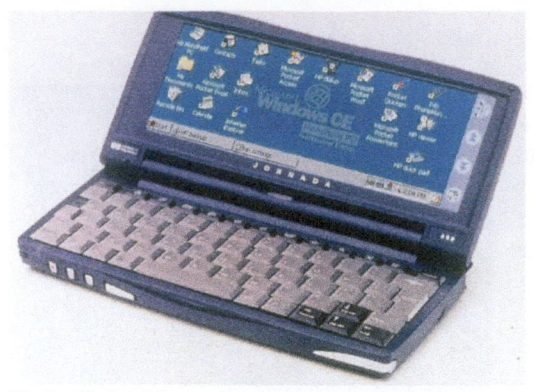

Figure 3.8.3

A handheld computer running Windows.

Hewlett-Packard Company

smaller than a bumblebee's shadow at noon! Examples of the microprocessors that are in the personal computers of today are worth a little time investigating.

The microprocessor shown in Figure 3.8.4 is the Motorola Power PC chip. Believe it or not, this small half-inch square area contains the equivalent of about 200,000 transistors. Designed originally by IBM, this design is the basis for not only the Macintosh Power PC computers from Apple Computer but also personal computers by IBM and other manufacturers.

Another popular microprocessor chip used in many microcomputers is the Pentium 4 by Intel. It is almost a complete computer on a chip and is much more sophisticated than its early predecessors, some of which now cost only a few cents. Figure 3.5.2 shows the Pentium 4.

These two popular microprocessors—the Motorola Power PC and the Pentium 4—are the latest in a long line of microprocessors that started in the 1960s. The technology that makes them possible is also responsible for the personal computer revolution, which is now so evident. For just a few hundred dollars, you can purchase a computer system that only a

Figure 3.8.4

The Motorola Power PC microprocessor.

Motorola, Inc.

Quantum Computers

What is a quantum computer? This is a common question that must be prefaced with another question: What is quantum mechanics? In the theory of how the universe works, which, of course, includes everything on Earth, one of the most powerful of all theories is quantum mechanics. This theory gave rise to atomic energy and the frightening nuclear arms race. It was the brilliant physicist Richard Feynman who first suggested the idea of quantum computers in 1982.

IBM's Almaden Research Center

One of the reasons that quantum computers have such great power can be seen in the way information would be stored. In the von Neumann computers of today, the bit is the fundamental unit of information. A bit can be either 0 or 1 and several bits strung together are needed to represent numbers or pictures. In quantum computers the fundamental unit is the qubit or QUantum BIT; it can hold many numbers and, therefore, is no longer a binary system. A second reason is that unlike the von Neumann computer that can work on only one number at a time, the quantum computer can work on thousands of numbers at one time. This may not seem like a big deal. However, put in another way, the qubit and how it is manipulated would allow quantum computers to work thousands to millions of times faster.

In what areas can quantum computers perform functions that can't be done by ordinary binary-based computers? The three most often mentioned are code cracking, database searching, and simulation of quantum systems in physics. It isn't hard to see why the U.S. government has an interest in code cracking. This capability is necessary to track criminals and foreign governments' activities, both of which often use secret messages for communication. Major improvements in database searching would benefit business, government, and the individual. These improvements would translate into cost savings and increased capability. When there are a billion Web pages to search, how can the Web search engines of today even begin to cope?

Now for a reality check. There are no working quantum computers! However, researchers have been able to simulate them, which is how the fantastic predictions were made. There are many universities and research laboratories working on the problem of building quantum computers—in particular, Oxford University in the United Kingdom, Quantum Information and Computing Institute at MIT, Caltech, and the University of Southern California. No predictions are forthcoming about when the first quantum computer will be available, but at the speed at which the computer field advances, it wouldn't be surprising to see a working quantum computer within a decade.

few years ago cost $50,000 or even $1,000,000. Many microcomputer manufacturers, numbering in the dozens, entered the competitive home-computer market. A few of the early computers were the Apple II, Commodore PET, Commodore VIC, TRS-80 Model III, IBM PC, and TRS-80 Color Computer. Later, the Macintosh Power PC and Pentium-based computers came with hundreds of times the power of the earlier personal computers. With millions of these computers in homes, schools, and businesses, it is no wonder that learning about them is crucial to job opportunities and advancement. The end is not in sight. Even newer methods and materials are on the horizon.

Most people are unaware of how the microprocessor has invaded our consumer society. For example, these devices are used quite commonly in dishwashers, washing machines, dryers, microwave ovens, and automobiles. The older mechanical methods of performing the necessary actions for these products are much more expensive and not as reliable as the microprocessor. In the case of automobiles, the microprocessor is fast enough to tell each

Micron Electronics, Inc.

Figure 3.8.5

*Micron Electronics Millennia
MME Pentium-based
personal computer with
several input-output units.*

spark plug when it is supposed to spark. While it is doing this, measurements such as engine temperature are taken to make adjustments in the timing of the spark. This means, in effect, that a cold car seems to run as if it were already warmed up. Now let's return to the discussion of the microcomputers, most often called personal computers (PCs), that make use of these microprocessors.

The microcomputer can be outlined by using essentially the same block diagram as shown in Figure 3.1.1. In fact, similar block diagrams can generally describe 99.9 percent of all computers. An example of one such microcomputer is the Micron Electronics Millennia MME Pentium-based computer shown in Figure 3.8.5. It is called a Pentium-based PC because the microprocessor chip that is the heart of this computer is a Pentium microprocessor.

WORKSTATION AND MINICOMPUTER

A step up in speed, cost, complexity, and size is called the **workstation.** It has more power than a microcomputer, but it is still used by only one person at a time. It is usually connected to other computers and a large storage device. An example of a popular workstation manufactured by Sun Microsystems is shown in Figure 3.8.6. The speed and storage capacity of the workstation allow it to manipulate more data than a microcomputer.

At the next level up in speed, cost, complexity, and size is the **minicomputer.** The main characteristic that distinguishes workstations from minicomputers is that workstations are single-user systems, whereas a minicomputer is most often used by several people who access the minicomputer over a network using their desktop microcomputers. Minicomputers don't look much different from workstations; however, they usually have even more storage and complex multiuser software.

MAINFRAME COMPUTER

Closer to the top of the diagram in Figure 3.8.1 are **mainframe** computers. They have increased size, speed, complexity, and cost. A mainframe costs hundreds of thousands of dollars as compared to hundreds of dollars for the microcomputer. It also follows the same basic computer system configuration illustrated in Figure 3.1.1. An example of a mainframe is shown in Figure 3.8.7. It's in the IBM 9600 family of mainframes.

Courtesy of Sun Microsystems

Figure 3.8.6

Sun Microsystems Ultra 60 workstation.

Courtesy of International Business Machines Corporation.
Unauthorized use not permitted.

Figure 3.8.7

IBM 9672 mainframe computer.

The primary RAM memory of the larger mainframe computers may vary from under 100 million bytes to over a billion bytes. Their speed is considerably faster, too, on the order of billions of instructions per second.

SUPERCOMPUTER

However, the ultimate speed in computing is found in the **supercomputer,** which executes several instructions in parallel, giving effective speeds measured in trillions of instructions per second. Applications such as weather simulation, large data storage systems, and airplane reservation systems need computers with extremely high capability. Before looking at an actual supercomputer, an understanding of the basic structure that most supercomputers follow would be helpful. The supercomputer has many CPUs working together as a team to calculate or perform some program. Current supercomputers have up to 130,000

Figure 3.8.8

The Blue Gene/L supercomputer.

CPUs working together. A typical configuration for IBM's Blue Gene/L supercomputer is shown in Figure 3.8.8.

Even though these monolithic boxes seem mysterious, in principle, it has a block diagram closely related to Figure 3.1.1. The major difference is that the Blue Gene/L shown in Figure 3.8.8 has up to 130,000 processors working in parallel as a team. Each of these processors is like a von Neumann computer, except it shares some common memory and peripheral devices, such as disk drives, with the other processors. The Blue Gene/L supercomputer is also referred to as a massively parallel computer because it has a large number of microcomputers all hooked together to work in parallel. A block diagram with only four processors instead of 512 is shown in Figure 3.8.9 and the resemblance to Figure 3.1.1 is quite clear.

The incredible speed (trillions of instructions per second) allows the larger computer to deal with much larger programs and at the same time control all of the input/output devices, such as the line printer, terminals, magnetic tapes, and disks. To fully describe this computer worth millions of dollars is beyond the scope of this book; in fact, programmers working with large systems such as the one shown in Figure 3.8.8 need access to hundreds of reference manuals that, if printed out, would reach heights measured not in inches but in feet!

The extreme complexity of this supercomputer is managed by the operating system. The concept of the controlling program or operating system is discussed in the next chapter.

Figure 3.8.9

Block diagram of a four-processor supercomputer.

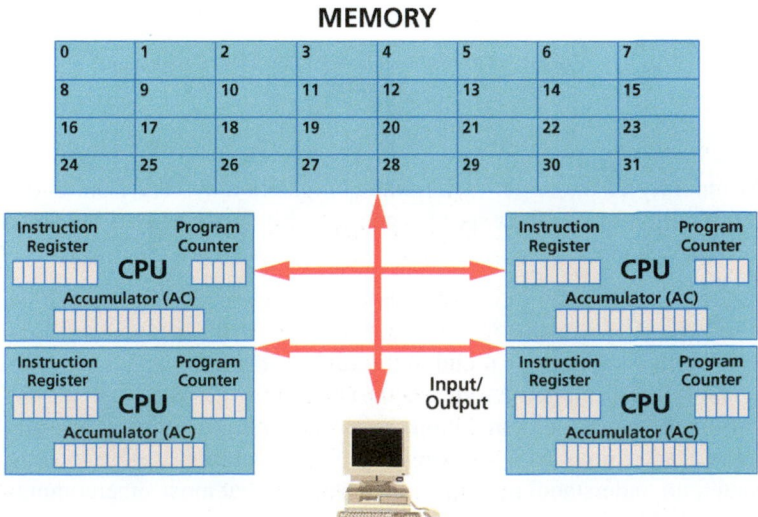

Chapter Summary

3.1 Basic Concepts of Computer Hardware

The von Neumann computer is the classic model for the vast majority of computers. It consists of the primary memory where both data and programs are stored. Called a stored-program computer, it has a place for input and output commonly referred to as I/O, and a main section of electronics called the central processing unit, where all the computing takes place.

3.2 Sources of Data for the Computer

The data or information used by computers comes from many sources. The original data comes from sources not associated with the computer, whereas previously stored data comes from a place where the computer previously stored the data.

3.3 Input Devices

Data or information can come from many sources including the keyboard, mouse, scanner, audio digitizer, digital camera, and many other devices. The three most common technologies used for storing binary information are electronic circuits, magnetic systems, and optical systems. Secondary memory devices have four important attributes: speed and access time, cost/removable versus nonremovable, capacity, and type of access. The most common secondary memory input devices make use of special hardware called drives, which read floppy disks, hard disks, CD-ROMs, and DVDs.

3.4 Primary Memory

The primary memory of the computer consists of random access memory (RAM) and read only memory (ROM). The RAM is nonpermanent memory and anything stored in it will disappear when the power is turned off. On the other hand, ROM is permanent memory and is always there. The primary memory is what is used by the CPU when it is executing programs.

3.5 The Central Processing Unit

The central processing unit is the most important part of the computer. This is where all the work is done. It consists of three major parts: arithmetic unit where arithmetic is done, the control unit that controls the operation of the CPU, and the instruction decoding unit that analyzes the instruction so it can be performed.

3.6 Output Devices

Many of the input devices are also used as output devices. The floppy disk and hard disk drives are used to store data after processing is done by the CPU. Other output devices include display monitors, audio systems, and optical discs such as CD-ROMs and DVDs. Each device and its media satisfy some use based on cost, capacity, and speed. In the future holographic storage may be possible.

3.7 Moving Information within the Computer

Moving binary data about in the computer is usually done in parallel rather than bit by bit. It's just like having multilane expressways rather than two-lane roads. The parallel paths allow much faster execution of instructions and transfer of data.

3.8 Categories of Computers

Computers come in many forms and sizes. They can easily be categorized by the attributes of speed, cost, complexity, and size. The following list of computer systems is arranged from the slow, cheap, simple, and small to the fast, expensive, and complex: calculator, handheld, microcomputer, workstation, minicomputer, mainframe, and supercomputer.

Key Terms

Key terms introduced in this chapter:

1. Access time, *64*
2. Accumulator, *70*
3. Arithmetic unit, *70*
4. Byte, *64*
5. Bytes, *75*
6. Cathode ray tube (CRT), *72*
7. Central processing unit (CPU), *69*
8. Chip, *70*
9. Control unit, *70*
10. Daisy chain, *62*
11. Device driver, *62*
12. Digital camera, *60*
13. Digital versatile disc (DVD), *73*
14. Digitizing, *60*
15. Fetch/execute cycle, *71*
16. Flip-flop circuit, *62*
17. Floating-point numbers, *71*
18. Floppy disk drive, *63*
19. Gigabyte, *65*
20. Handheld computer *79*
21. Hardware, *58*
22. I/O (input/output), *58*
23. Input units, *58*
24. Instruction decoding unit, *70*
25. Instruction register (IR), *70*
26. Interface, *70*
27. Keyboard, *59*
28. Liquid crystal display (LCD), *72*
29. Mainframe, *82*
30. Megabyte, *65*
31. Microcomputer, *79*
32. Microprocessor, *79*

33. Minicomputer, *82*
34. Motherboard, *71*
35. Mouse, *59*
36. Output units, *58*
37. Parallel, *75*
38. Peripheral devices, *62*
39. Port, *61*
40. Primary storage or memory, *68*
41. Program counter (PC), *70*

42. RAM (random access memory), *69*
43. Random access, *67*
44. Register, *70*
45. Ribbon cable, *76*
46. ROM (read only memory), *69*
47. SCSI (Small Computer System Interface), *61*
48. Secondary memory or storage, *64*
49. Sequential access, *67*

50. Serial, *77*
51. Stored-program computer, *58*
52. Supercomputer, *83*
53. USB (Universal Serial Bus), *62*
54. Voice recognition hardware, *60*
55. Von Neumann bottleneck, *58*
56. Von Neumann-type computer, *58*
57. Words, *75*
58. Workstation, *82*

Matching

Match the number of the key terms introduced in the chapter to the following statements. Each term may be used once, more than once, or not at all.

1. ___ The name of the concept that governs the cycle by which programs are executed.

2. ___ A characteristic of the way data stored on a hard drive are accessed.

3. ___ The results of computations are accumulated in this part of the CPU.

4. ___ This computing device has a place to keep information needed for computing.

5. ___ This part of the computer is often referred to as the "brain" of the computer.

6. ___ These allow the computer to communicate with things outside itself.

7. ___ This type of computer is named after "microprocessor."

8. ___ An example of this type of computer is manufactured by Sun Microsystems. It is usually connected to other computers and a large storage device.

9. ___ The general term for this type of memory that is used to store data when not in use by the computer.

10. ___ This type of computer is moderately priced.

11. ___ This type of computer can be held in your hand.

12. ___ This type of computer is used by a single user and is a standalone computer.

13. ___ Several people can use this physically larger type of computer at one time.

14. ___ This type of memory is used directly by the computer.

15. ___ This computer has many CPUs.

16. ___ This type of computer was named after its large metal cabinet.

17. ___ This is the most powerful of all computers.

18. ___ This type of access allows information to be obtained directly.

19. ___ This type of access allows information to be obtained by starting at the beginning of a list of information and then proceeding item by item until it is reached.

True or False

Place either T or F on the line provided with each of the following statements. If a statement is false, you should be able to explain what changes would make it true.

1. ___ When an instruction is to be executed by the CPU, the CPU removes the instruction from memory (clearing that instruction from memory) and places it into the instruction register.

2. ___ The control unit keeps a copy of the instruction that is to be performed now and knows which instruction is to be performed next.

3. ___ Computers are compared in their speed, cost, complexity, and size.

4. ___ The microprocessor was partially a result of the development of miniaturized technology for the space program.

5. ___ The Intel Pentium microprocessor chip is the only chip being used by computer manufacturers in the microcomputers of today.

6. ___ ROM memory is nonpermanent memory.

7. ___ A DVD holds more data than a CD-ROM.

8. ___ CRT displays are used on laptop computers.

9. ___ Whereas microcomputers, minicomputers, and mainframe computers typically have only one CPU (one program counter), a supercomputer can have thousands!

10. ___ The four most important characteristics of memory devices are speed, cost, capacity, and manufacturer.

11. ___ The memory storage that has the fastest access time is also the least expensive.

12. ___ Storing the contents of the Library of Congress on electronic circuit–type storage would take up less room than storing the same amount of information on optical mass-storage media.

13. ___ RAM memory is nonpermanent memory.

14. ___ ROM memory is accessed in a random access fashion.

15. ___ Random access type of storage is synonymous with RAM.

16. ___ An example of a device that uses random access is the popular magnetic disk.

17. ___ An example of a device that uses sequential access is magnetic tape.

18. ___ LCD displays are very heavy and would never be used on a laptop computer.

19. ___ DVD drives use magnetic technology.

Multiple Choice

Answer the multiple-choice questions by selecting the best answer from the choices given.

1. The least expensive means to store information is
   a. CD ROM
   b. Electronic circuitry
   c. Magnetic tape
   d. Hard disk
   e. Floppy disk

2. Stored-program computers are also commonly called this type of a computer.
   a. Pascal computers after Blaise Pascal
   b. Ada computers after Ada Lovelace
   c. von Neumann computers after John von Neumann
   d. Hollerith computers after Herman Hollerith
   e. Babbage computers after Charles Babbage

3. This part of the CPU has a place where all results of computations are accumulated.
   a. Control unit
   b. Accumulator
   c. Instruction register
   d. Program counter
   e. Instruction decoding unit

4. This part of the control unit is where an instruction is placed for analysis by the instruction decoding unit.
   a. Arithmetic unit
   b. Accumulator
   c. Instruction register
   d. Program counter
   e. Memory

5. This part of the control unit contains the address of where the next instruction to be executed resides.
   a. Arithmetic unit
   b. Accumulator
   c. Instruction register
   d. Program counter
   e. Instruction fetching unit

6. When executing a program, the CPU of the computer identifies which instruction is to be performed, gets the next instruction to be performed, decodes the instruction, performs calculations if necessary, and executes the instruction. The process is then repeated until the program is finished. This name of this process is the
   a. Fetch and execute cycle
   b. Nondestructive reading cycle
   c. Analyzing cycle
   d. CPU cycle
   e. There is really no name for this process. It is just done by the CPU.

7. Which of the following lists of the types of computers is in order of cheapest and slowest to most expensive and fastest?
   a. Minicomputer, microcomputer, mainframe computer, supercomputer
   b. Microcomputer, minicomputer, mainframe computer, supercomputer
   c. Supercomputer, mainframe computer, microcomputer, minicomputer

d. Minicomputer, microcomputer, mainframe computer, supercomputer

e. Microcomputer, mainframe computer, minicomputer, supercomputer

8. Which of the following is not true of a CD-ROM?
   a. It can contain a maximum of about 650 megabytes.
   b. It can contain over an hour of music.
   c. It can contain a full-length movie.
   d. It is used to store games.
   e. It is used to distribute software such as word processor programs.

9. Sending information bit by bit to and from I/O devices is referred to as sending in
   a. Voltages
   b. ASCII

c. Parallel
d. Serial
e. Bytes

10. When a von Neumann computer runs a program it takes instructions from the memory and then does them. What is this process called?
    a. Clock cycle
    b. Fetch and execute cycle
    c. Memory cycle
    d. Process control
    e. Random access process

Exercises

1. Estimate the number of letters in your favorite dictionary. (a) How many bytes of information is this, assuming one character or letter per byte? (b) How many floppy disks would be needed to store them?

2. Estimate the number of ASCII characters it would take to represent all the books in your school library. Ignore pictures and things that don't have ASCII codes. (a) How many bytes of information is this, assuming one character or letter per byte? (b) How many floppy disks would be needed to store them?

3. In Table 3.3.3, one kilobyte is 1,024 bytes, and one megabyte is 1,048,576. Why aren't they exactly 1,000 and exactly 1,000,000? Hint: It has to do with binary numbers, in particular, powers of 2. Show how these results are obtained.

4. What is the major concept related to RAM and ROM memory that

   (a) they have in common in how information is accessed,
   (b) they have regarding information's everlasting nature.

5. Name several hardware storage devices that are used for both input and output.

6. What is the significant difference in usage of primary and secondary memory.

7. Suppose you would like to buy a computer. Make a list of pros and cons regarding purchasing a laptop portable computer or a desktop computer. Be sure to include cost, convenience, security, and special devices such as scanners and DVD drives.

8. Make up a table of typical storage capacities for various devices, and calculate the number of units of each needed to store information described in Exercises 1 and 2.

9. **PUZZLER** Begin a trouble log for your computer. The log can refer to either your own computer or any computer you use regularly in a lab or other location. Using your word processor, create a table with five columns. Label the columns Date/Time, Description of Problem, Software Being Used, Diagnosis, Fixed Date/Time. Your table should look something like the following

Date/Time	Description of Problem	Software Being Used	Diagnosis	Fixed Date/Time
January 4, 2001	Printer does not respond to print command	Microsoft Word	Print driver missing	New print driver installed January 5, 2001

Continue with your table until you have at least five problems reported, along with their fixes.

Discussion Questions

1. When the technology for computer memory improved, the price to the consumer dropped accordingly. Do you think improvements in communication technology will cause a drop in communication rates (such as telephone, fax, pagers, and so on)? Why or why not?

2. Why is ROM primary memory necessary? What would a computer be like without it?

3. Will the DVD ever replace the CD-ROM? What are the issues?

4. Discuss the significance of the von Neumann bottleneck. Why does the supercomputer solve that particular problem? Can you see any problems that a programmer must face when writing the programs for it?

Group Project

Each person in a group of four should choose one of the following types of computers: personal computer, workstation, mainframe computer, and supercomputer. Research in the literature or through the Web the fastest speed computer in each category. Using a spreadsheet, make up a table with the four categories along both the top and side. Then fill in the matrix with speed ratios of column heading over row heading.

Each person researching a type of computer should get the time it takes for that type of computer to do a particular problem. For example, how long does it take to make a five-day weather forecast using a supercomputer? Make up another spreadsheet with the types of computers along the top and the specific problems along the left. Suppose a problem takes one minute on a supercomputer. Fill in the matrix with the length of time it would take each of the other types to do the same problem.

Web Exercises

1. Browse the Web to find information about three different types of memory devices. For each one, list the product name and manufacturer, the type of device (hard disk, CD-ROM drive, etc.), access speed, capacity, cost, and type of access. Place this information into a document created with a word processor, along with a picture of each device downloaded from the Web.

2. **PUZZLER** Create a poster for your classroom or lab with at least 10 tips for trouble-shooting computer hardware problems. Search the Web to find the tips. Be picky—include only those items you think are helpful. Use a word processor or layout program to create the poster.

3. Here is an opportunity to design your "dream machine" computer. Search the Web to find the best set of computer hardware components you can find for your own personal computer. Find the microprocessor you'd like, the monitor, disk drive, hard disk, CD-ROM drive, modem, mouse, printer, scanner, digital camera, and anything else you'd like to add to your dream setup. Don't be satisfied with package deals offered by specific retailers or manufacturers. Make your own decisions! When you are done, list all of the components you've chosen. For each one list the features that made you choose it, the manufacturer and model number, and the cost. When you are all done, add up the cost to see what you've "spent."

Bibliography

Bigelow, Stephen J. *Troubleshooting, Maintaining and Repairing PCs, Millennium Edition.* New York: McGraw-Hill, 1999.

This book combines authoritative reference material on IBM-standard personal computers with condition-specific troubleshooting advice.

Dugrenier, Ronald J. *CST-Computer Service Technician: The Definitive Guide to Software and Hardware Troubleshooting.* San Bruno, CA: CF Publications, 1998.

This is a comprehensive PC troubleshooting book that is often referred to as the ultimate reference tool.

Computer Languages, Algorithms, and Program Development

TimeLine

1943	First "bug," a moth that caused a relay failure, is found by Grace Murray Hopper.
1954	First FORTRAN compiler is devised by John Backus and others at IBM.
1958	The program language Lisp is developed for artificial intelligence work.
1959	The computer language COBOL is created by the CODASYL committee.
1969	BASIC is developed for a mainframe time-sharing system at Dartmouth College by Kemeny and Kurtz.
1969	The programming language Pascal, a precursor to Modula-2, is developed by Niklaus Wirth.
1972	The programming languages Prolog, Smalltalk, and C (so named because it came after B) are developed.
1975	BASIC is adapted for the Altair 8080 microcomputer by 19-year-old Bill Gates and Paul Allen.
1980	The programming language Ada emerges, designed by the U.S. Defense Department.
1983	An object-oriented version of C called C++ is introduced by Bjarne Stroustrup.
1995	Java, an object-oriented language developed for Internet work, is released.
2000	Software-defined radio, which allows single devices to access many different frequency ranges, is introduced.
2010	Large programs, no longer written by human programmers, are grown in a computer through evolutionary programming.

Chapter Objectives

- Discern the reasons why programming languages are necessary to communicate with computers.
- Know the definition of semantics and how it relates to computer programs.
- Know the definition of syntax and how it relates to computer programs.
- Identify the five generations of the program language continuum.
- Know the differences between an assembler, an interpreter, and a compiler.
- Understand how scripting relates to programming in general.
- Know the steps necessary to build a computer program.
- Know four criteria for analyzing a program's quality.
- Identify the steps taken to test a program after its initial creation.
- Appreciate the amount of time and effort it takes to complete a large, intricate computer program.
- Understand how easy-to-use software such as HTML can create other, more complicated results.

Jackson Smith/Pictor

Shedding Some Light on Computer Communication

Communicating a series of instructions to a computer is a precise, careful activity, and success depends entirely on the person providing the instructions. To ensure success in solving a computer problem, the program instructions must be correct and complete, they must be expressed in the proper form, they must be general enough to solve all similar problems, and they must produce the desired result.

PUZZLER

To experience some sense of the enormity of the programming task, let's try a little experiment. Suppose you were instructing a friend on how to change a household lightbulb. We can assume your friend is of average intelligence and speaks the same language as you do but is unfamiliar with the lightbulb-changing process and needs exact instructions. Write out for your friend a detailed description of how you would go about changing a bulb at home. Be complete—don't leave out any steps. Try to include every thought process and decision you would have to make. Be efficient—get the light changed as quickly as possible with as little effort. Account for every possible variation.

Speaker encodes information

Listener decodes information

Listener returns
feedback to speaker

Figure 4.1.1

The communication cycle usually represents a face-to-face conversation between two people.

Communication cycle refers to one complete unit of communication. It includes the following parts: an idea to be sent, an encoder, a sender, a medium such as air through which the idea travels, a receiver, a decoder, and a response. The full process recurs as a cycle because the response itself is an idea, which must be encoded in turn, sent out over a medium, received, decoded, and so forth.

4.1 Communicating with a Computer

The process of communicating with a computer appears similar to that of conversing with people, as illustrated in Figure 4.1.1. Both require the same activities: We must plan out what we want to say, figure out how to phrase it clearly, and then actually say it. Then we wait for a response from the other party. Of course, if the other party is a computer, the response may be in the form of a printout or some symbols appearing on the monitor screen. See Figure 4.1.2. Whatever form the response takes—lights, symbols, or spoken words—we must understand the response before we begin a new round of communication.

Whether we are dealing with a computer or another person, good communication requires that every step in the process be completed successfully. Unfortunately, the communication process is prone to failure. A breakdown can occur any place along the cycle, causing communication to halt. Here are three examples of communication failure between people:

- If the person you are speaking with cannot hear you, no message can get through.
- If a phone connection is broken, there is no medium to carry your words.
- If the message is phrased in French and the listener understands only Japanese, neither person will understand the other.

Communication success is even more tenuous when the participants are one person and one computer. Computer hardware is susceptible to failure. Communication would be interrupted, for example, if any of the following occurred:

Figure 4.1.2

If we substitute a computer for one of the people in the communication cycle, the process remains basically the same, although some of the elements are greatly transformed.

User encodes information

Computer decodes information

Computer returns
results to user

Figure 4.1.3

Programming languages bridge the gap between human thought processes and computer binary circuitry.

- The power supply was suddenly interrupted.
- An internal wire or transistor burned out or was disconnected.
- A keyboard, mouse, or printer malfunctioned.

When we are trying to communicate instructions to computers, however, the areas of greatest difficulty are not the hardware and technology but the encoding and decoding processes. Thus, our problem of communicating with computers boils down to this: How can we translate our human thoughts, usually expressed as words, into computer "thoughts," which must be expressed as binary numbers? (See Figure 4.1.3.)

Translating instructions into binary code one by one is a time-consuming task because people don't work in numbers like computers do. The need to facilitate this task has led to the development of an amazing number of **programming languages.**

4.2 The Role of Languages in Communication

Designed by computer scientists to solve the problem of communicating data manipulation instructions (such as read, add, store, print) to computers, programming languages play the same role in the communication process as do **human languages**. However, many subtle differences can be seen in how programming languages are developed and used. To illustrate both similarities and differences, we'll examine three fundamental elements of language that contribute to the success or failure of the communication cycle: **semantics,** syntax, and participants.

SEMANTICS (MEANING)

Languages have no meanings of their own. They get their meanings from the human beings using them. We give a language its meaning by associating each language unit—word—with a particular object or experience. When the association between a particular word—tree, for example—and a specific object—like the one with branches and leaves—is recognized by a group of people, that word can be used to communicate the associated idea. Thus, words and expressions in every language gain meaning by repeated, consistent use. Let's look at how human languages and programming languages differ in terms of semantics.

A **programming language** is a series of specifically defined commands designed by human programmers to give directions to digital computers. The commands are written as sets of instructions called programs. Each program enables a computer to solve a particular problem or perform a specific task. All programming language instructions must be expressed in binary code before the computer can perform them.

Semantics refers to meaning. It is the content of a language unit. In user-to-computer communication, **semantics** refers to the specific commands (e.g. input, output, print) that you wish the computer to perform.

Translation is the porting of ideas, instructions, and concepts from one language form to another with no change of meaning.

Semantics in Human Languages	Semantics in Programming Languages
Human languages are not created—they develop and gain meaning haphazardly as needed for humans to communicate their ideas and feelings with each other.	Programming languages are designed (very carefully) by computer scientists for the purpose of giving instructions to computers.
Words and expressions get their meanings from the humans using the language.	Words and expressions get their meaning from the human scientists creating the language.
Words and phrases often are given multiple meanings. That is, the same word may be used to relate to two or more different ideas. 'Tree' can refer, for example, to the growing thing with green leaves on the top and roots on the bottom, or to an object meant to hold coats and hats in a hallway.	Each 'word' or command is given one and only one meaning. The scientists who devise a particular programming language, assign only one very specific meaning to each group of characters. Once that has occurred, no other meaning can be given to the same word or command.
Words and expressions in human languages sometimes have idiomatic meanings, peculiar to a particular region or culture. This leads to confusion in meaning, which can be resolved by context or discussion.	Words and commands in programming languages have no idiomatic or regional meaning. Each has a specific meaning to perform a specific task. No confusion is tolerated.
People can evaluate context to determine which of several meanings a particular word has.	Computers know nothing about context. Each command must have a specific meaning regardless of context, and that meaning must always remain the same.
All human concepts, ideas and feelings of a particular culture can be represented by word units of human language of that culture.	Not all human concepts can be represented by computer languages. Communication units of programming languages are primarily associated with commands for data manipulation and retrieval.

Syntax is the grammatical structure or form of a language. In both human and computer languages, sentence structure, spelling, and punctuation are all part of a language's syntax.

SYNTAX (FORM)

To form an understandable message, people join several words into sentences. To form an instruction to input, process, or print data, a programmer joins a computer language command with a piece of data or the memory location where it can be found. In any case composing a complete sentence (or instruction) follows particular rules. In human written language, for example, we know that a complete sentence begins with a capital letter and ends with a period. Similarly, each computer language has specific rules regarding the format of an instruction in that language. In both types of language, human and computer, the rules of structure used to form complete units are called syntax. In human languages we refer to syntax as grammar. Let's take a look at how human language syntax and programming language syntax differ.

The greatest syntactic difference between human languages and their computer counterparts is a matter of **tolerance**. Humans have a great deal of freedom in how they use language. We can say the same thing in many different ways, choosing from large selections of words with similar meaning. Often we use inflection or body gestures to completely change the meaning of an utterance. (Can you say no so that it means maybe?) We can even be creative, using new words or putting words together in unique ways. These possibilities make human language flexible and rich in expression. (See Figure 4.2.1.)

In contrast, computer languages are spare and economical. There is no room for ambiguity and redundancy. Each computer command can have only one meaning. No two commands can have the same meaning. Syntax is ironclad! Misplacing a comma or period or misspelling a word can drastically affect the output from a program, or cause it not to run at all.

Syntax in Human Languages	Syntax in Programming Languages
To form an understandable message, people join several words into sentences.	To form a programming instruction, a programmer joins a computer language command with a piece of data or the memory location where it can be found.
A complete sentence begins with a capital letter and ends with a period.	Each computer language has specific rules for formatting an instruction in that language.
Human languages have rules governing pluralization, tense, agreement of subject and verb, pronunciation, and even gender.	Programming language syntax governs things like repetition, subdivision of tasks, identification of variables, and definition of memory spaces.
Human languages have thousands of rules and many exceptions to each rule.	Each programming language has at most a few hundred rules and tolerates no exceptions. Syntax is ironclad.
Humans can say the same thing in many different ways, choosing from large selections of words with similar meaning.	Computer languages are spare and economical. There is no room for ambiguity and redundancy. No two commands can have the same meaning.
Often we use inflection or body gestures to completely change the meaning of an utterance.	Computers can neither produce nor understand inflection or body gestures. (Does it help to yell or shake a fist at your computer?)

J. Sapinski/The Stock Market

Figure 4.2.1

People can use facial expressions and gestures to enhance or even change the meaning of a phrase or sentence. Computers can make no such modifications.

PARTICIPANTS

The most significant difference between human language and computer language is the most obvious one: Human languages are used by people to communicate with each other; while programming languages are used by people to communicate only with machines.

Let's look at the ramifications of this difference. First, when we input a message written in a programming language to the computer, that message must be translated into the only form the computer can 'understand'—**binary code**. Only after this translation process is complete can the computer respond.

Participants in Human Languages	Participants in Programming Languages
Human languages are used by people to communicate with each other.	Programming languages are used by people to communicate only with machines.
Only people use programming languages.	The computer never uses anything but binary code—1s and 0s.
Sometimes, a message written in one human language (such as English or French) must be translated into another human language (Spanish? Japanese?) for a particular person to understand the message.	All instructions written for the computer in programming languages must be translated into the only form the computer can 'understand'—binary code—before they can be followed.
Humans have many choices of how to respond to a message, and can select one that best suits their needs.	Computers can make only two possible responses to any instruction. It must either obey your command or indicate to you that it does not understand your message.
In human communication both speaker and listener share responsibility for making each message clear and correct.	In computer communication, the human must assume responsibility for any errors that are made, as well as for resubmitting corrected messages.

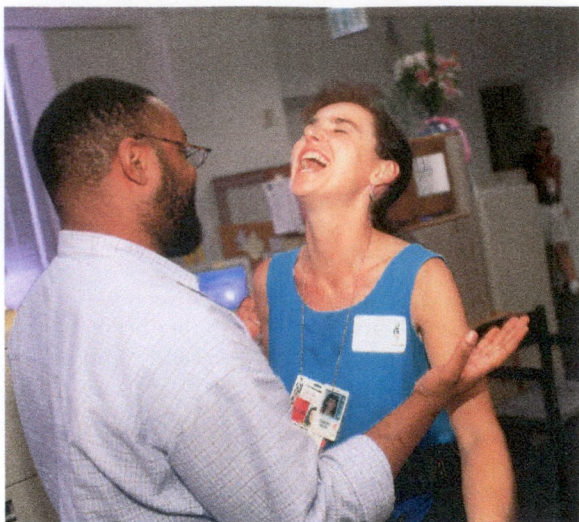

Figure 4.2.2

In face-to-face communication people can tailor their responses based on feedback from their listeners. Computers have no such choice.

How the computer responds to a communication is another important issue. When you speak a message to a friend in face-to-face conversation, your friend (the listener) has many choices of how to respond and will select one that best suits his or her mood, your message, and the general situation. The computer has no such choice. It must either obey your command or indicate to you that it does not understand your message. (See Figure 4.2.2.)

Notice that the burden of successful communication with the computer lies only with you. Often a listener can understand your meaning even if you use an incorrect word, pronounce something strangely, or make a grammatical error. The computer can do none of these. If the message you entered is translated into a string of 1s and 0s that is not recognized by the computer, all it can do is tell you that you have made an error. Thus, if the computer gets an unrecognizable user name in an e-mail address, it promptly informs you that you have made an error. The result? The e-mail letter bounces back to you! If you wish to send the letter you wrote, you (not the computer) must correct the error and send it again.

A **program** is a series of instructions for the computer. Once translated into binary code, the instructions can be performed by the computer to accomplish a specific task, such as organizing a file or calculating a mathematical result.

4.3 The Program Language Continuum

IN THE BEGINNING . . .

In the twentieth century, when digital computers were being developed, software **programs** such as Microsoft Word, Excel, and PowerPoint did not exist. Computers consisted of special-purpose computing hardware. Each different computer was designed to perform a particular arithmetic task or set of tasks. To get a particular computer to function, a skilled engineer

Hardwiring instructions into a computer was a very painstaking process of using a soldering iron to create electronic circuit boards with the connections needed to perform a specific task. The work required skill and precision and was performed only by electrical engineers and physicists.

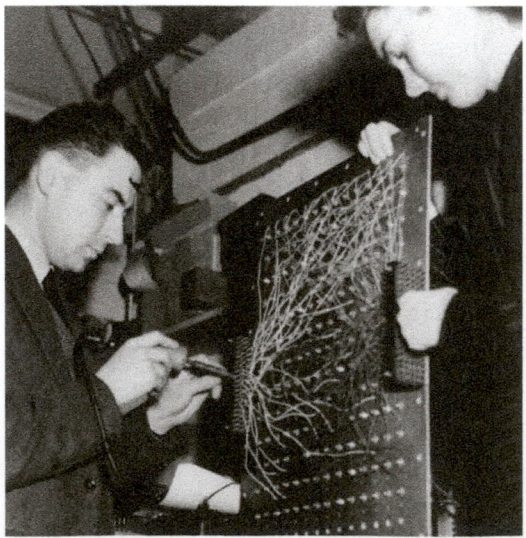

Figure 4.3.1

Early logic boards were composed of digital relays, which could be programmed using manual switches or soldered connections.

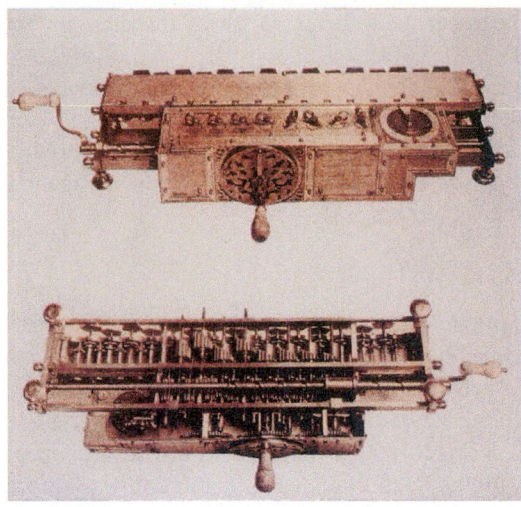

Corbis/Sygma

Figure 4.3.2

Early computing machines, like this Stepped Reckoner, had no software. They were operated by direct physical manipulation of the machine's hardware.

had to manipulate some parts of the computer's hardware directly. Sometimes this was done by "fat-fingering"—using human fingers to position electrical switches in either off or on position, representing the binary digits 1 and 0. Other computers, such as the one pictured in Figure 4.3.1, required programs to be hardwired into the computer, using a soldering iron and other tools to create the needed circuits to perform desired tasks. Still others used holes punched or burned in paper or plastic tape to represent the 1s and 0s needed to program the computer.

The manipulations needed by early computing machines were often ingenious. For example, Gottfried Wilhelm von Leibniz of Leipzig, Germany, in 1674, designed a machine called the Stepped Reckoner to perform multiplication. This machine, pictured in Figure 4.3.2, used a movable carriage that could multiply numbers up to 5 and 12 digits long and calculate a result of up to 16 digits. To perform a multiplication, the user manipulated a large hand-driven dial to enter the multiplicand into the Reckoner's carriage, then turned a crank once for each unit of each digit in the multiplier. A fluted drum translated the turns into additions. The carry mechanism required additional user intervention.

Two and a half centuries after von Leitniz performed multiplications by cranking his Stepped Reckoner, scientists at the University of Pennsylvania, in Philadelphia, developed a more flexible computer called **ENIAC.** ENIAC was able to perform a number of different mathematical tasks through the use of a program, a set of instructions. The program was entered into ENIAC by plugging connector cables into particular sockets on a plug-board. The setup was complicated and took hours to accomplish. The resulting tangle of cable, seen in Figure 4.3.3, was intricate and error-prone. Once the program setup was complete, it

The Computer Museum of America

Figure 4.3.3

ENIAC, a digital computer built in 1944, was programmed by using wires to connect relay switches.

would generally be used for weeks at a time before a different set of instructions was needed.

Today, most computer users never have to write a computer program. Thousands of programs exist and can be entered into computers electronically with virtually no effort from the user. What was once an arduous task attempted only by scientists and electrical engineers can now be accomplished in minutes by virtually anyone. Let's take a few moments to discover how such a change was accomplished.

MACHINE CODE—THE FIRST GENERATION

The first computer language, **machine language,** was only a small step beyond the hardwired programs of the earliest machines. Machine language programs were made up of binary code, the 1s and 0s of the computer's "native language." Each instruction consisted of two parts: an operation code, which specified the action to be carried out, and an operand, or memory address relevant to that instruction. A few computer instructions had several operations. Both parts were represented in binary digits. In addition, each instruction was accompanied by the binary representation of the memory address where the instruction itself would be stored. A typical program looked like two or three columns of 1s and 0s, unintelligible to all but a few computer experts. The machine language program was easily executed by the computer but was difficult for people to decipher and extremely error-prone. In addition, if the programmer wanted a different computer to perform the same task, the program had to be completely rewritten using the machine code peculiar to the new computer. Computer languages that could be performed by only one type of computer with a particular CPU are often referred to as **low-level languages** and said to be **hardware dependent.**

Table 4.3.1 shows part of a machine language program that calculates the sum of two integers and places the result in the computer's memory. Notice that each instruction occupies three columns: the instruction location in the left-hand column, an operation code in the center, and an operand (machine memory address) on the left. A fourth column, not part of the machine language, has been added to explain the function of each step.

Machine language is the first language used to write programs. Instructions are represented as **binary codes** that can be directly executed by the computer.

A **low-level language** is a programming language written to be used with a particular type of computer with a particular CPU. It is referred to as a **hardware-dependent** language.

Mnemonics refers to anything used as a memory-assisting device. In assembly language it refers to easily memorable three- and four-letter abbreviations signifying specific opcodes.

Table 4.3.1   *Part of a machine language program that calculates the sum of two numbers.*

Instruction Address	Opcode	Operand	Explanation
00000001	10000000	00001110	Load contents of memory location num1 into accumulator.
00000010	01100000	00001101	Add the contents of memory location num2 to accumulator.
00000011	10100000	00001111	Store the result in memory location sum.

ASSEMBLY LANGUAGE—THE SECOND GENERATION

Rather than forcing the programmer to write in the binary code native to the computer, an **assembly language** allows the use of convenient alphabetic abbreviations called **mnemonics** to represent operation codes and abstract symbols to represent operands (memory addresses and data items). The resulting program is still in two or three columns but is somewhat more intelligible to programmers and, thus, less error-prone.

Because the program is no longer written in 1s and 0s, the computer cannot directly understand it. Assembly language made programming easier for us but one step harder at the computer's end of the communication cycle. Before the computer can execute an assembly language program, the program must first be translated into binary code.

In the example in Table 4.3.2, notice how alphabetic abbreviations that are easier to decipher and remember are used in the opcode column rather than binary numbers. More significant, alphabetic symbols are used in place of actual memory addresses in the operand column. This greatly simplifies programming because the programmer has no need to know or remember exact storage locations of data and instructions. Like machine code, however, assembly languages are written for specific computers and cannot easily be transported from one type of computer to another.

Table 4.3.2   *Alphabetic mnemonic opcodes and symbolic operands make assembly language easier than machine code for programmers.*

Mnemonic Opcode	Symbolic Operand
load	num1
add	num2
store	sum

Amazing Grace

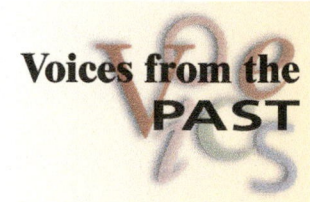

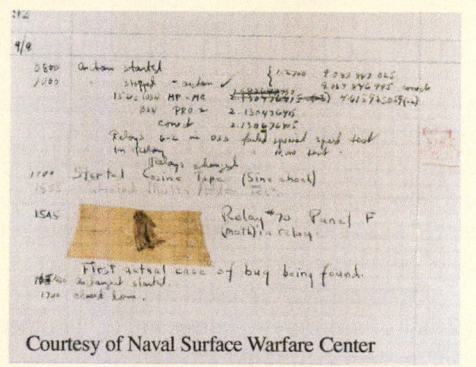

Admiral Grace Murray Hopper was one of the pioneers of computing. At a time when most computer experts believed computers were too complicated for the general public to understand, Hopper's motto was, "If computers were easier to operate, more people could use them." She dedicated her long navy career to computer standardization and demystification.

Hopper's formidable skills in mathematics propelled her into the new world of computing machines early in the 1940s, when there were many opportunities to innovate. She worked on the early UNIVACs and became involved in creating computer languages. Recognizing that user-friendly computer languages would entice more people into computer work, she pioneered research to knock down the "Tower of Babel" computer languages had become.

In 1955, Hopper led the committee that invented COBOL (Common Business Oriented Language), a programming language promoting easier access for business application. COBOL allowed English words to be translated into numerals—1s and 0s—that any computer could understand. This revolutionized the computer industry, making it possible for anyone to use a computer to help with his or her daily business needs.

One of Hopper's most famous discoveries was the computer *bug,* in 1945. The term was coined when the navy assigned Hopper to the Bureau of Ordinance Computation Project at Harvard University. Hopper worked on the development of the Mark II computer, used for creating ballistic tables for aiming navy guns, schedules for supplying ships, and top-secret calculations used for the atomic bomb. When evaluating why the new computer wasn't performing, Hopper traced the malfunction down to an open-circuit caused by a

Courtesy of Naval Surface Warfare Center

moth. The bug was flattened between contacts, preventing the relay from making its connections. Her team taped the dead moth into the log book with this notation, "First actual case of a bug being found." When challenged for not making enough progress, the feisty mother of computing would reply she was busy debugging the computer. The original "bug" is still preserved at the museum of the Naval Surface Weapon Center at Dahlgren, Virginia.

Admiral Grace Murray Hopper died in December 1991, leaving behind an amazing 85-year legacy of accomplishments.

High-level languages are programming languages that are independent of any specific computer hardware. Before programs written in these languages can be executed by a computer, they must be translated using a compiler or interpreter.

```
program sums2 (input, output);
var
num1, num2 sum: integer;
begin
        read (num1, num2) ;
        sum: = num1 + num2 ;
        write 1n (sum)
end .
```

PEOPLE-ORIENTED PROGRAMS—THE THIRD GENERATION

The third generation in program language development produced the first programming languages that are people oriented rather than machine oriented. Instructions in these languages are called statements. Third-generation statements resemble English phrases combined with the mathematical terms needed to express the problem or task being programmed. The syntax (grammatical form) and semantics (meanings) of such statements do not reflect the internal machine code or instruction set of any one particular computer. They are, therefore, said to be **machine independent** and are often referred to as **high-level languages.** Programs written in a high-level language require very little reprogramming when transferred to a different computer.

The programming example in Figure 4.3.4 is written in a high-level language called **Pascal.** It illustrates how close to the English language a high-level program statement can be.

Figure 4.3.4

High-level languages, such as this sample of Pascal, brought computer programming closer to human thought processes.

NONPROCEDURAL LANGUAGES—THE FOURTH GENERATION

As computers became more popular for personal, business, and at-home use, people wanted to be able to control them without the difficulty of learning complex programming languages. This led to the development of many categories of programming language–like systems, each of which aimed at simplifying the programmer's task of imparting instructions to a computer. Many of these systems are associated with specific application packages and enable people unfamiliar with programming to describe tasks to be performed by the computer. Common **fourth-generation languages** include query languages, report writers, and application generators.

- **Query languages**—Usually embedded within database management programs, query languages enable users to specify exactly what information they require from the database.

- **Report writers**—These take the information retrieved from a database and format it into attractive, usable output. Many report writers can perform a limited number of calculations, including totals, subtotals, averages, and counts. Some also enable the users to enter custom calculation formulas.

- **Application generators**—These enable the user to specify a problem and describe the desired results. When the user is done, the application generator creates the program (usually in assembly language or binary code). Many powerful microcomputer programs today include specialized application generators called macrolanguages.

OBJECT-ORIENTED PROGRAMMING

A **procedure** is a precise sequence of steps that, when performed in a particular order, will accomplish a specific programming task. A **procedural language** is one that expresses a computer problem as a series of discrete tasks and the instructions needed to accomplish those tasks.

Although most of the languages examined earlier are concerned with defining **procedures**—sequences of instructions for performing tasks—**object-oriented programming** is concerned with defining **objects**—entities contained within a particular system—and how they relate to one another. Because this methodology closely resembles the way people think, it has brought the task of programming a computer even closer within the reality of human endeavor.

An object is a representation of whatever you need to model or manipulate in the development of a program. For example, an object might be a window on your screen that you want to change in some way or a list of names you wish to organize. Whatever the object is, you can think of it as a black box, like a VCR, with some buttons and lights on its surface. To use an object, you must know what the buttons do, which buttons you must press to get the object to do what you want, and what the lights can tell you about the status of the object. The inside construction of the object is irrelevant when you are using it. Similarly, you do not need to know what the wiring is like inside a VCR to use one.

An **object** is an entity contained within a particular system. An **object-oriented language** is one that expresses a computer problem as a series of objects a system contains, the behaviors of those objects, and how the objects interact with each other.

In object-oriented programming, using a software object is not much different from using a VCR. It has well-defined ways of interfacing with other objects in its environment and with the outside world and can provide information about its current state. The internal workings of the object—representation, algorithms, and data manipulation—are all hidden from programmers and users in the outside world.

Several object-oriented programming languages have been developed and are in use today. Some of the most popular include Smalltalk, Eiffel, C++, and Java. The language of choice for many object-oriented applications is C++. This is because C++ is derived from an earlier language, C, and therefore has a heritage of success performing real tasks on real computer systems. rapidly expanding use of the World Wide Web has greatly increased interest in Java, which may supercede C++ in popularity before long.

IS THERE A FIFTH GENERATION?

Many more computer languages are being developed and will be introduced during the next several years. Some crystal balls foresee that such languages will one day make computer programming effortless. Communicating with a computer via **natural language** would be as easy as ordinary conversation in one's native language. Unfamiliar syntax and special meanings would be eliminated, making error-free programs much easier to achieve.

Table 4.3.3   *Computer language genealogy: Traversingthe generations.*

Generation	Class	Description	Examples	Dates
First	Machine language	■ Binary representation of operation codes in 1s and 0s ■ Machine specific	ROBOT Instruction set	1940s
Second	Assembly language	■ Mnemonic representation of operation codes ■ Machine specific	Pencil and Paper Instruction set	1950s to 1960s
Third	High-level languages	■ Code resembles English language–like structure ■ Transportable from one machine to another	COBOL, FORTRAN, BASIC, Pascal, Ada	1960s to present
Fourth	Nonprocedural languages	■ Query languages ■ Application generators ■ Very-high-level languages such as Turbo Pascal, other 4GLs	PROLOG, QBE, SQL, Hypertalk, Smalltalk, QUEL, C++, Lisp, Java	1980s to present
Fifth	Natural languages	■ Treats problems as humans do ■ Allows inheritance of characteristics from previously defined objects ■ Encourages modular development	Visual Basic, Ada 95, HotJava, CASE tools	21st century

Much research and experimentation toward this goal are being done in the area of natural languages. Programs called intelligent compilers are now being developed to translate natural language (spoken) programs into structured machine-coded instructions that can be executed by computers. Progress is being made, but so far we are a long way from speaking any but the most trivial programs directly into the computer. Producing worthwhile programs is still one of the most complex intellectual tasks we have. Although a natural language compiler might save programmers the task of typing thousands of lines of program instructions on a keyboard, it cannot save us the involved planning and thought processes that produce useful programs. Truly effortless, error-free natural language programs are still some distance into the future, but some attemps have been made. Table 4.3.3 summarizes the five generations of programming languages.

4.4 Assembled, Compiled, or Interpreted Languages

Except for those written in machine code, the computer's native language, all programs must be translated before their instructions can be executed. We can group computer languages according to which translation process is used to convert their instructions into binary code. Table 4.4.1 summarizes the three types of translators discussed here.

■ Assembled languages—The translation program used with an assembly language is called an **assembler.** In the translation process, each assembly language statement, most often yields a single line of binary (machine) code. The entire program is assembled before the program is sent to the computer for execution.

■ Interpreted languages—An **interpreter** translates the high-level program statements one at a time. Each programming language statement (called **source code**) may yield several lines of **object code** (instructions in binary) as a result of the interpretation process. As each statement is translated, it is checked for errors. If there are none, the object (binary) code is sent to the computer's central processing unit for execution. Once executed, the binary coded instruction is discarded before the next statement is translated. As a result, the program must be reinterpreted each and every time it is run. This is a slower process, but it is especially helpful if you are trying to locate errors in the original program.

Table 4.4.1   *Comparative characteristics of computer language translators.*

	Assembler	Interpreter	Compiler
Source code languages	Assembly language program.	Third-generation language program.	Third-generation language program.
Object Code languages	Each line of source program yields one line of binary (machine) code.	Each line of source program yields several lines of binary (machine) code.	Each line of source program yields several lines of binary (machine) code.
Translation pattern	Entire program is translated before program is executed.	Program lines are translated and executed one by one.	Entire program is translated before program is executed.
Hardware Orientation	Machine specific.	Machine independent.	Machine independent.
Advantages	Address hardware functions directly for increased speed.	Error messages line specific, easier to debug.	Quicker and more efficient than interpreters.
Disadvantages	Assembly language harder to learn than third generation.	Interpretation process takes longer than compilation.	Error messages often hard to decipher, not line specific.

■ Compiled languages—A **compiler** reads and translates the entire high-level language program before anything is sent to the CPU for execution. As each line is translated, it is set aside until the entire program translation is complete. The whole program in object (binary) code form is then saved to disk. If the compiler has detected no errors during compilation, the whole program is ready to be executed. Like the interpreter, the compiler may produce several lines of object code for each statement in the original language. A compiled program is more efficient than an interpreted one, but it is not as helpful in the finding and correcting of program errors. After a program has been correctly compiled, its binary coded form (already stored on disk) can be reused as often as desired without recompilation.

4.5 Programming for Everyone

From the first part of this chapter you learned that programming has come a long way from the days of hand-wiring special boards as a means of programming. The previous section discussed some history about how the process of programming has become more people friendly by using high-level and object-oriented programming languages. Yet, the currently popular languages that professionals use to program, such as C++ and Java, still require extensive training.

Most computer users have no desire to undergo years of training to become skilled programmers. They want to acquire the application programs they need in a ready-to-use state, having been written and tested by someone else. Thousands of programs are available exactly like that. But no matter how good an application is or how perfectly suited to a particular user's needs, there is always some tweaking to be done.

In the late 1970s, tweaking an existing program required the assistance of a professional programmer. The typical user couldn't do it and most likely was afraid to try. Today, however, several programming-like alternatives are available even to the casual user. Customization is now possible in many applications without the help of an expert programmer. This section will describe several different ways you can control what your computer does or the way it accomplishes a particular task. The topics to be discussed include the following:

■ Using macros
■ Using HTML to create Web pages
■ Scripting

USING MACROS

A **macro** is a set of operations within a computer application that has been recorded for later execution. Once saved, the macro could be used repeatedly on any document within that application.

The earliest occurrence of user programming within a computer application was called the **macro.** Macros were an advanced feature found initially in **electronic spreadsheet** pro-

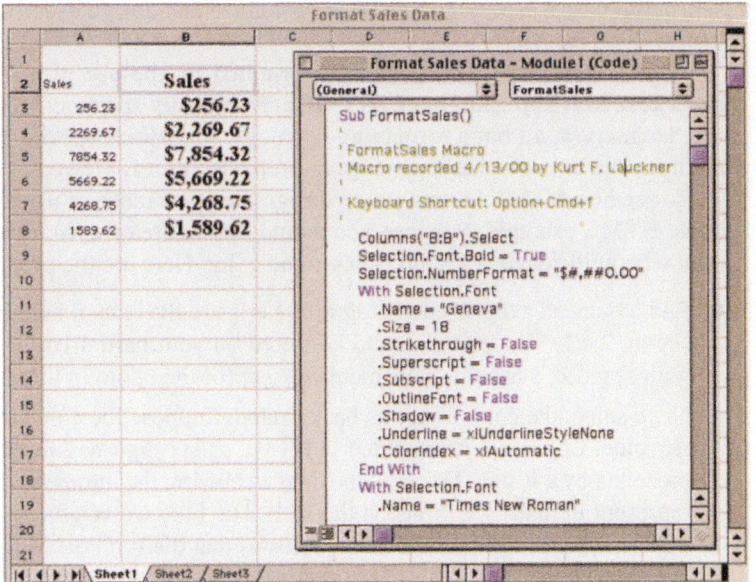

Figure 4.5.1

Here is an example of macro programming included in an electronic spreadsheet application.

grams and word processors and were used primarily to help users achieve ease and speed performing repetitive tasks. Their most common use was for consistent formatting and typing automatic text. Here is an example:

Suppose you worked in a business setting and were responsible for writing many letters. At the bottom of each and every letter, you had to type the following signature:

Sincerely,

James R. Emmelsohn
Director of Public Relations
Martin Electronics, Detroit Division

A word-processing macro would allow you to type all of this out, exactly as you wanted it to appear at the bottom of each letter, spacing and all. You would then save it as a macro and assign it a code name, say, SIG. Then, when you were finished with the message, instead of typing out the entire signature, you would merely enter the macro name, SIG. The signature would appear exactly as you entered it.

Perhaps the best thing about using a macro is that once you have entered it and checked to see that it was exactly the way you wanted it, you can use just a few letters to recall it again and again in any document created by the same application program.

Creating and performing a macro requires no knowledge of a programming language. You merely "define" the macro by performing the desired operations and then saving them as a macro. Once it has been saved, you can use the macro operation by referring to the macro by name. Different applications prescribe different steps for defining, saving, and using a macro. Some applications also allow the use of macros created outside the application program using a language such as Visual Basic. Popular program companies incorporating macros into their software include Corel, Lotus Corporation, and Microsoft. (See Figure 4.5.1.)

USING HTML TO CREATE WEB PAGES

A computer scientist would most likely tell you that creating a Web page is not actually programming. Nevertheless, Web page creation belongs in this section because it allows the user (in this case a Web page author) to customize and design exactly what a viewer will see when visiting the author's page.

What a Web page looks like is determined by the use of a special language called **HyperText Markup Language (HTML).** Technically speaking, HTML is not a programming language at all but a formatting language. It contains special codes that allow you to determine the layout—markup—of your Web page as it is viewed in a Web **browser.**

To see how HTML allows you to design the appearance of a Web page, let's examine a simple HTML example. Suppose you would like to create a Web page to display a photograph with a title against a solid background color. Here are the preparatory steps:

- First you need a digitized photograph. Let's use the baby image from chapter 2 found in Figure 2.4.7. This photo should be stored on your hard drive under a file name ending with .jpg. Let's use the filename *Annie.jpg* for the photo in this example.

- Next, select the color to use as background. Suppose the color we wish to use is a light sky blue. Colors are represented in HTML as six-digit hexadecimal (base 16) numbers preceded by a # sign. You can find charts showing the number codes and the colors they represent in many locations on the Web. The blue we've chosen happens to be the six-digit number #99ffff, where the # indicates that the symbols following represent a number in base 16.

- Finally, you must decide what text you want to use as the caption of the picture and what size and color you wish to use. If you do not specify size and color, default values will be used, and the text will be small and black.

Once these three steps are accomplished, you are ready to write out the HTML to create your Web page. Figure 4.5.2 shows the HTML program, and Figure 4.5.3 shows the resulting Web page as displayed by the Microsoft Explorer browser.

As you examine this Web page and its HTML, notice that every feature of the page as you see it was created by one line of HTML. Almost every line of HTML contains a **tag.** Each tag is marked at its beginning by the symbol < and at its end by the symbol >.

Let's see what each tag does in Figure 4.5.2:

- <html>—This is always the first tag of an HTML layout. It indicates to the Web browser program that the information following is an HTML program.

- <body>—This tag denotes the beginning of the main HTML program, whereas </body> indicates the end of the main body of the program.

HyperText Markup Language (HTML) is a computer language consisting of special codes intended to design the layout (or markup) of a Web page. World Wide Web browsers interpret the HTML codes and display the resulting Web pages.

The **browser** is a program that interprets and displays information from the Internet, especially the World Wide Web. WWW-related information is most commonly in the form of HTML programs.

A **tag** is a formatting instruction in HTML, the language that specifies the design and layout of Web pages. Each tag is delineated by angle brackets before and after to set the tag apart as complete.

```
<html>
<body bgcolor=#99ffff>
Loveable Annie
<img src="Annie.jpg">
</body>
</html>
```

Figure 4.5.2

HTML program to display the Web page of Figure 4.5.3.

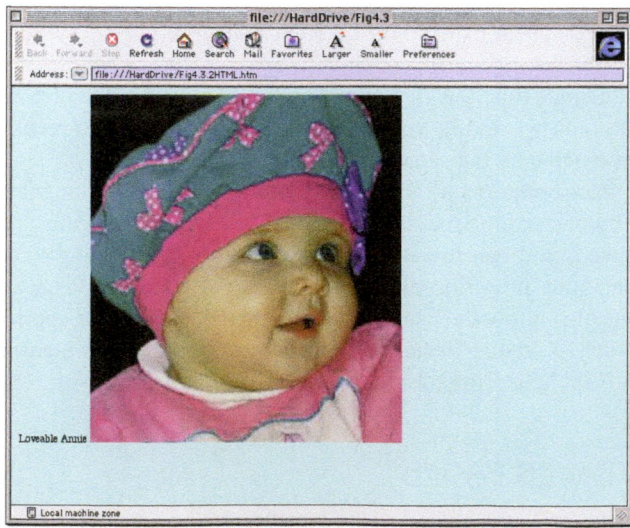

Screen shot reprinted by permission from Microsoft Corporation

Figure 4.5.3

Web page resulting from HTML program in Figure 4.5.2.

- The special modifier bgcolor is used with the <body> tag to indicate background color.
- The letters *Loveable Annie* are then printed in black in a small font because no tags were used to format this text or define its color.
- <img>—This tag produces the image of Annie's photo.
- The special modifier *src= "Annie.jpg"* identifies the name of the file where the photo is stored on the hard disk.

We can improve the design of this Web page by including more tags with the appropriate modifiers. Figure 4.5.4 is a modification of the previous HTML program. Some new tags—<head> and </head>—mark the beginning and end of some heading information that can be useful. The <title> tag titles the Web page, as can be seen in Figure 4.5.5, where it causes *ANNIE* to appear at the very top of the MS Explorer title bar. Also note that the words *Loveable Annie* are larger, colored pink, and centered above the image, which is also centered. It is rather easy to pick out the tags that cause these things to happen.

Our HTML program was not viewed over the Internet. For one example, the browser was used to display it directly from the hard disk of the computer. Additional steps having nothing to do with the HTML that produced the page would be needed before our creation could be viewed over the Internet.

SCRIPTING

We will use the term **scripting** to indicate a means by which programmers add extensions or additional capabilities to an application. Many word processors, database programs, and operating systems have scripting capability.

A list of several scripting languages is shown in Table 4.5.1. These languages range from Perl and C++, which are general-purpose, full-scale programming languages, to VBScript, a subset of Microsoft's powerful Visual Basic, to **JavaScript,** a scripting language designed for enhancing the functionality of Web pages.

Many people think that JavaScript is derived from the programming language **Java.** Not so. JavaScript is related to Java in name only. Java is a full-featured programming language beyond the realm of our discussion. JavaScript is a special scripting language used to enhance an existing Web page. To write a JavaScript routine, you must know the commands

> A **script** is a series of commands written to accomplish some task. It is very similar to the concept of a program, but it is not as large or comprehensive. The purpose of a script is to extend the capabilities of the application where it is used. **Scripting** is the process of writing a script.

> **JavaScript** is a scripting language that allows the Web page designer to add functional features to a formatted Web page created with HTML.

```
<html>
<head>
<title>ANNIE</title>
</head>
<body bgcolor=#99ffff
   text=#FF0099>
<center>
<h1>Loveable Annie</h1>
<img src="Annie.jpg">
</center>
</body>
</html>
```

Figure 4.5.4

HTML program to display the Web page seen in Figure 4.5.5.

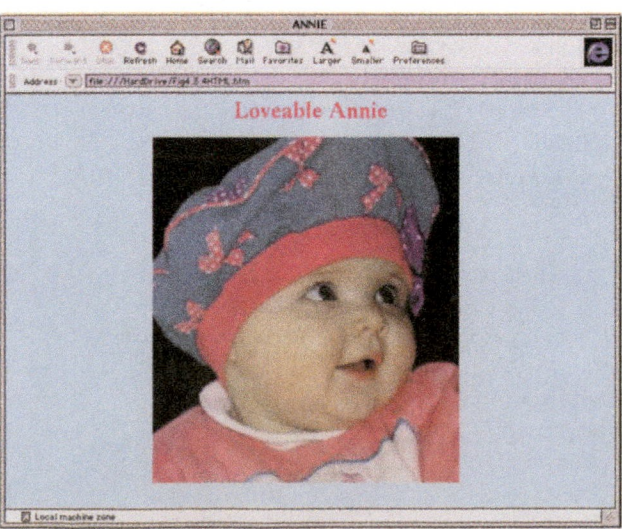

Screen shot reprinted by permission from Microsoft Corporation

Figure 4.5.5

Web page resulting from HTML program in Figure 4.5.4.

Table 4.5.1   *Some scripting languages.*

Scripting Language	Used With	Common Purpose
AppleScript	Macintosh	Extending Opsys
Euphoria	DOS, Windows, Linux	Extending Opsys
JavaScript	Most systems	Web Browsers
Perl	Most systems	Web/Internet
VBScript	Windows and Unix	Extending Opsys

of the language and how they work. To use such routines, however, you have only to find them and copy them into your own Web pages. The WWW has thousands of JavaScript routines that you can use without knowing much about how they work.

As an example, let's take the HTML in Figure 4.5.4 and create a banner below the words *Loveable Annie*. The HTML for this looks much more complicated with the JavaScript added! However, doing even simple tasks in programming often requires many statements. Figure 4.5.6 shows the HTML code that produces an identical page to the one in Figure 4.5.5 with the words *Annie is a wonderful child* scrolling in a banner below the title *Loveable Annie.*

JavaScripts can be much longer than the one we've used and create much more complex design features. Many long and involved JavaScripts creating attractive and exciting effects have already been written by others and are available free over the WWW. Use Google on the WWW to search for "java scripts."

Figure 4.5.6

JavaScript added to HTML of Figure 4.5.5 to give flashing words.

```
<html>
<head>
<title>ANNIE</title>
<SCRIPT LANGUAGE="JavaScript">
ScrollSpeed = 200;
ScrollChars = 1;

function ScrollMarquee() {
window.setTimeout('ScrollMarquee()', ScrollSpeed);
var msg = document.scrollform.box.value;
document.scrollform.box.value = msg.substring(ScrollChars) +
        msg.substring(0, ScrollChars);}
//End—>
</script>
</head>
<body bgcolor=#99ffff text=
        #ff0099 OnLoad="javascript:ScrollMarquee()">
<center>
<h1>Loveable Annie</h1>
</center>
<form method=get name=scrollform>
<input name=box type="text" size="25" value=
    "    Annie is a wonderful child!  "
    onFocus="javascript;this.value=";ScrollSpeed=99999;">
</form>
<img src="Annie.jpg">
</center>
</body>
</html>
```

4.6 Building a Program

As we have seen, computer programmers write instructions that allow us to use computers to solve computational problems and to prepare documents and spreadsheets. Some computer problems fit into the traditional mold of mathematical problems. For example, you may have to solve the following problem at your job: "Calculate the weekly salaries of all the employees in the Corporation." Other problems may not seem at all like math problems in the traditional sense: for example, "Access information, music, or a video clip from a CD-ROM disc." Whatever type of problem needs to be solved, a carefully thought out strategy is needed before a computer solution can be determined.

THE FIRST STEP: UNDERSTANDING THE PROBLEM

Writing a computer program to accomplish even the simplest task involves the skills of analyzing problems and devising plans for their solutions. You must first state the problem clearly and precisely. Suppose we wanted to perform this task:

Print out the names of the students in your class.

That sounds like an easy task. But do we know enough about the problem to be able to solve it? Do we know, for example, how many names are on the list? Do we want the names to appear one after the other in paragraph form or each on a separate line in a list? Where can we find the names? Do we want them to appear on a monitor or on paper? None of this information appears in the simple statement of our problem. We don't even know for sure that we want to use the computer as part of the solution. Until these questions and others like them have been answered, we cannot begin to work on a solution. The problem must first be restated, providing all the information we need to proceed.

So let's try again:

Write a program that will instruct the computer to accept the names of 30 students, one at a time, as we type them in on a keyboard, and print them out in the same order on paper in a numbered list.

There! That's better! The new problem statement contains the answers to all those troublesome questions. Now we can move on to devising a solution. One word of caution before we continue, however: Not all problems are this simply restated. The more complex the problem, the more time and care must be spent producing an accurate statement of the tasks required.

PUZZLER HINT

How is your light-bulb-changing description coming along? Have you accounted for all possible bulbs (fluorescent as well as incandescent) in all possible fixtures (desk lamps and ceiling installations)? Did you remember a ladder for the ceiling? Did you remember to get the bulb out of the closet before starting up the ladder? Is it a good, working bulb?

When you are certain you have considered and described all possibilities, change your written description into a series of one-line instructions. Each line must be an imperative—command—statement expressing one step in the process. For example, one statement might be "Get bulb out of its wrapper" or "Place ladder against wall." Don't worry about how many steps the process takes. Concentrate on being complete.

Building a program requires five major steps:

1. Understanding the problem
2. Developing an algorithm
3. Writing the program
4. Documenting the program
5. Testing and debugging the program

DEVELOPING THE ALGORITHM

An **algorithm** is a detailed description of the exact methods used for solving a particular problem.

After the problem to be solved has been clearly stated, the next step is to devise a plan of attack for writing the program. Computer programmers call a plan such as this an **algorithm.**

To develop an algorithm, the programmer must first analyze which data users need. Two questions should be asked. First, "What data have to be fed into the computer?" These are called the **input data.** For our class-list program, the input data consist of the names of the 30 students in the class.

The second question is, "What information do I want to get out of the computer?" For the class-list problem, that's easy. We want to get out the same data that we put in: the students' names, numbered consecutively from 1 to 30. This printed list of the student names will be the **output data** of our program.

Now that we know our data needs, we must plan the processing that will cause our input data to become our output data. The processing part of the program algorithm is called the **logic** of the program. For the class-list program, our processing will consist of generating the numbers from 1 to 30, one at a time, so that they can be printed with the names. Because our problem is a very easy one, our algorithm contains only one processing step. Most problems require many more processing steps to complete their logical development.

Logic is the processing part of the program algorithm. It contains the instructions that cause the input data to be turned into the desired output data.

Although we have now identified the input data, the output data, and the processing steps needed for the class-list program, we are still not ready to begin writing in a programming language. We must produce a more detailed, step-by-step plan of everything we want the computer to do. The computer must follow these steps, for example, for the class-list program:

- Start a name-counter at 0.
- Get a name from the keyboard.
- Add 1 to the name-counter.
- Print the value of the name-counter and the name.
- Go and get a new name, unless all 30 are done.
- When all 30 are done, stop processing.

We can write out a step-by-step program plan in many ways. Nothing is wrong, for example, with a straightforward sentence outline such as the preceding one. Programmers, however, often use one of three major notations for planning detailed algorithms: flowcharts, Nassi-Schneidermann charts, and pseudocode.

- **Flowcharts** have been part of program development almost as long as there have been programs. A flowchart consists of a series of visual symbols representing the logical flow of a program. Each type of programming instruction (input/output, executable, control, and so on) is represented by a differently shaped symbol. Notice, for example, that a diamond shape represents a decision (conditional) statement. Figure 4.6.1 is a flowchart showing the logic of the class-list program we have been solving.

- Two research programmers working in the field of psychology developed another method of visualizing program algorithms. **Nassi-Schneidermann charts** use specific shapes and symbols to represent different types of program statements. Figure 4.6.2 shows a Nassi-Schneidermann chart for the class-list program.

- **Pseudocode** is also a verbal shorthand method of detailing the steps of a program. It consists of statements that closely resemble those of a programming language but do not have to follow a rigid syntax structure. The programmer can pattern his or her pseudocode after any programming language. Many select the language in which the final program will be written. For our program, the pseudocode in Figure 4.6.3 is modeled after Pascal.

WRITING THE PROGRAM

By this point in the programming process, the difficult tasks of analysis and planning have been completed. If the analysis and planning of the program have been done thoroughly,

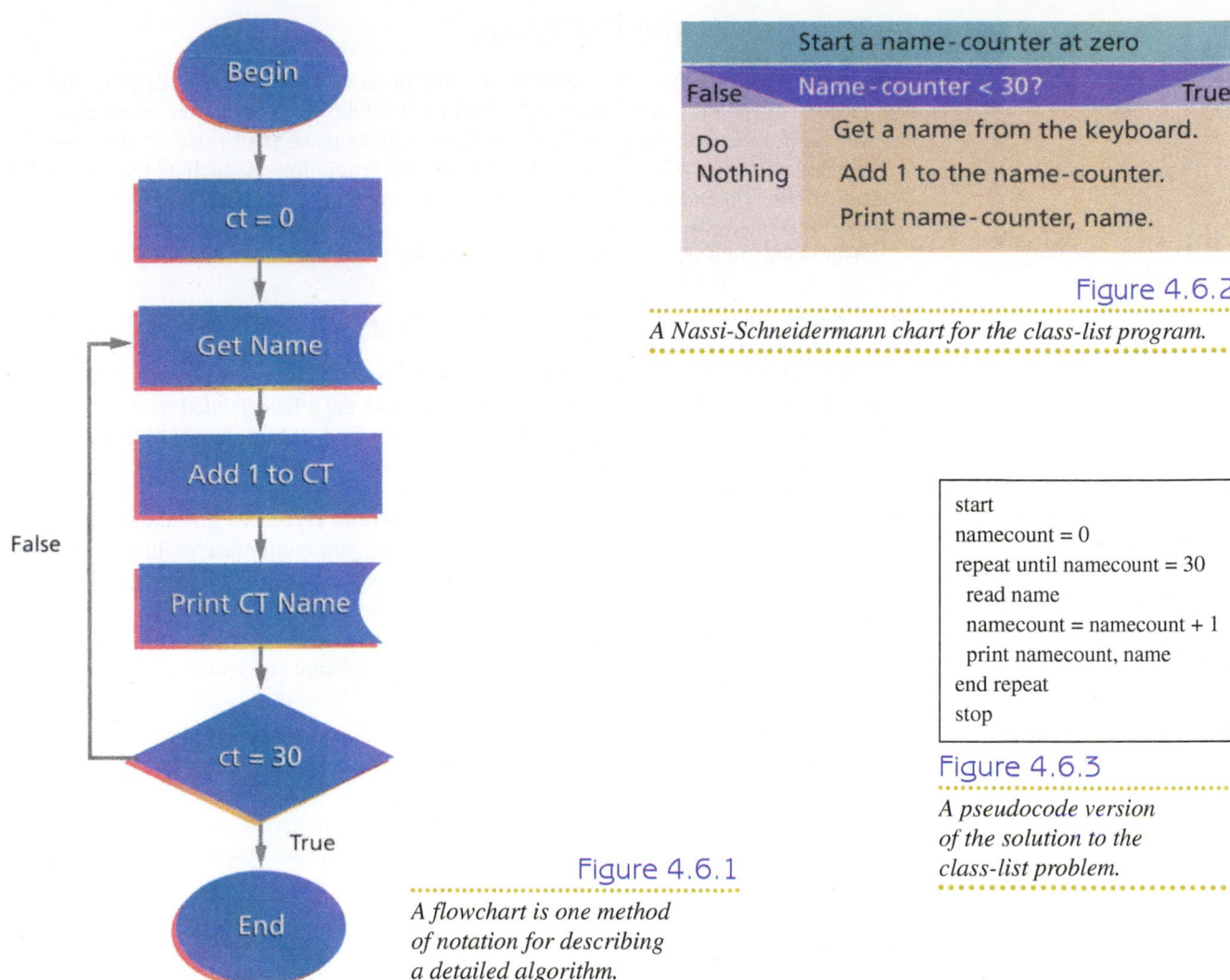

Figure 4.6.2

A Nassi-Schneidermann chart for the class-list program.

```
start
namecount = 0
repeat until namecount = 30
  read name
  namecount = namecount + 1
  print namecount, name
end repeat
stop
```

Figure 4.6.3

A pseudocode version of the solution to the class-list problem.

Figure 4.6.1

A flowchart is one method of notation for describing a detailed algorithm.

translating our detailed, step-by-step plan into a programming language should be a quick and easy task. Table 4.6.1 illustrates the results of this step as they would appear in three different programming languages.

Table 4.6.1   *Three sample programs.*

Pascal	C	FORTRAN
Program Name_List (input, output);	main ( )	Character * 15 Name
var	{	Integer Count
count: integer;	int count;	Do 27 Count = 1,30,1
name: packed array [1..15] of char;	char name{15};	Read, Name
begin		Write, Count, Name
for count:= 1 to 30 do	for(count=1; count<=30; ++ count)	27 Continue
begin	{ gets(name);	Stop
readin (name);	print("%2d %\n",count,name);}	End
writeln (count:3, name:20)	}	
end		
end.		

DOCUMENTING THE PROGRAM

During both the algorithm development and the program writing stages of programming, explanations called documentation are added to the code. Such documentation helps users as well as programmers understand the exact processes to be performed by the computer. Documentation usually includes technical notes for programmers, such as explanations of variable definition and usage. It also often includes notes for the end user, such as instructions for installation and program execution.

But we're not done yet. The final step in building a program is correcting its flaws.

TESTING AND DEBUGGING THE PROGRAM

During this phase, the programmer tries to discover and eliminate any errors—programmers call them **bugs**—in the finished product. The program must be executed many times using different data sets. The purpose of extensive testing and **debugging** is to establish four important elements that determine the program's quality:

- The program must be free of syntax errors. A **syntax error** is a mistake in the form or grammar of the program statements. For example, you might have omitted a comma or semicolon at the end of a statement. Such an error would make that statement unrecognizable to the compiler. Eliminating syntax errors is fairly easy and must be completed early in the testing activities. A program cannot be translated into machine language unless there are no syntax errors, and the computer cannot execute it until translation has been completed.

- The program must be free of logic errors. A **logic error** is a mistake the programmer introduces into the algorithm or processing plan of the program. For example, in the class-list program, if you added 3 each time the loop was performed instead of only 1, only some of the names would be printed and their numbering would be incorrect. The program would still run because there would be no syntax errors, but incorrect output would result. Logic errors are more difficult to detect than syntax errors and are harder to correct.

- The program must be **reliable.** A program is considered reliable if it correctly performs the task(s) defined by the statement of the problem. It must be able to produce correct results with every possible combination of appropriate data. Reliability errors are usually caused by flaws in the logic or plan of the processing.

- The program must be **robust.** that means it should be able to detect execution errors such as improperly typed data or insufficient memory, warn the user, and allow the error to be corrected or terminate the run. Suppose a name were missing in the input data of our list program, leaving a blank line someplace in the middle of the list. A robust program would detect the absence of input, print an appropriate message, then continue with the processing until the list was complete. A less robust program would simply crash in the middle.

Even with tasks as trivial as the class-list problem, program development is both time consuming and exacting. The larger and more complex the problem, the more difficult the job of developing an algorithm to solve it. Our problem was solved in an hour's time and yielded a program only 8 to 10 lines long. Real-life programs may have several hundred thousand lines and take a team of highly skilled programmers up to several years of development time. See Table 4.6.1 for three sample programs that solve the class-list problem.

Many computer catastrophes have shown that as programs grow in size and complexity, we must be careful and prepared for failure. A sophisticated operating system may be well over several million lines of code with very complex logic. In a project of such vast size, no one can possibly predict how safe and reliable the program will be until it has been extensively tested. Even then, testing every single eventuality in a complex system is virtually

Introducing Java: A Software System for Online Multimedia

Tech Talk

Java: A simple, object-oriented, distributed, interpreted, robust, secure, architecture-neutral, portable, high-performance, multithreaded, and dynamic language.

That's how JavaSoft, parent company of the Java programming language, describes its product. But that's not how it began.

In 1991, a special project team of six software developers from Sun Microsystems went into self-imposed seclusion to attack a difficult hardware problem: Computerized/electronic devices such as VCRs, Nintendo Game Boys, stereos, and TV set-top control boxes were all made with different central processing units. Because of their difference in microprocessor chips, the devices could not communicate with one another. The Sun team, code-named Green, went to work on a fresh approach to software programming and developed a new object-oriented programming language called Oak. Based loosely on C++, Oak was a spare, stripped-down language compatible with small, handheld electronic devices and designed to enable programmers to more easily support dynamic, changeable hardware.

After extensive development and several explorations into marketable products based on the Green team's research, Oak might have fizzled into oblivion. In 1991, however, Mosaic was introduced by the National Center for Supercomputing Applications (NCSA). The World Wide Web was born. More Web technology soon followed, and the Internet, used formerly only by scientists and educators, exploded with additional traffic.

Within a year, Oak's development team refocused its resources, developing what they called a "language-based operating system" for online multimedia applications. The language they produced, renamed Java because of a trademark conflict, was given away free on the Internet. With Java in the hands of the Internet community at large. Netscape began to support it as a Web development tool. The result? Millions are developing Java applications (called applets) that reside on centralized servers and can be called on as needed. A new generation of exciting interactive Web sites has been born.

impossible. There are no guarantees that some unexpected condition will not cause the program to fail at some point in the future. To understand these problems, let's look at how commercial software is created. Usually the project is broken down into small segments called subprograms. Each **subprogram** is analyzed, written, and tested individually. Then, when the complete program has been designed and coded (that is, put into some computer language), the final testing begins.

At this point, the program is at the **alpha testing** point. This is normally done within the company that created the program. The process will uncover any major problems, which the programmers identify and correct.

Because it is impossible to check all possible conditions that could occur in a large program, it makes sense to subject it to testing that involves an even wider number of conditions. This is referred to as **beta testing.** The program is sent out to possibly hundreds of sophisticated users outside the company who will test the program under an enormous number of conditions. The motivation to do this beta testing is to get the software into a segment of the marketplace and to start gathering initial user feedback. After both alpha and beta testing problems have been resolved (and this may take several months and produce many versions of the program), software is usually ready for the commercial market.

> A **subprogram** is a small but logically independent module of a large programming project. Breaking a large project into subprograms allows each to be designed, written, and tested individually before the finished product is reassembled and tested as a whole.

PUZZLER HINT

When your list of instructions is finished, try translating them into a flowchart similar to the one illustrated in this chapter. Use one visual symbol for each step. You might try using rectangles for performing tasks, diamonds for making decisions, and ovals for getting an object or

continues

leaving one someplace. Try to make the flowchart as clear and easy to follow as the list of instructions was.

If you have solved this puzzler, you should end up with a fairly complex set of directions and an illustration for what seemed at the start to be a very simple task—changing a light bulb. The exercise demonstrates the level of detail needed to provide complete, accurate directions for solving a seemingly simple general problem. Computer programs demand this same level of detail.

4.7 Software Development: A Broader View

We have spent a lot of time in this chapter explaining programming languages and the process of writing a computer program. Our approach has been, however, admittedly simplistic. Although the use of short, simple examples is a good teaching and learning tool, it does not give an accurate picture of problem solving and computer programming in the real world. Before we go on to explore the many ways computers are being used today, let's consider a broader view of real-world programming.

How long, then, are real programs? How long, for example, is a standard word processor or spreadsheet program? How long is a compiler? Hold onto our hats! The numbers in Table 4.7.1 are out of sight.

Another measure of the effort spent on real-life programs, as compared with those written as student exercises, is time. How long does it take to write a computer program?

Students writing programs usually work alone on their projects and measure the time spent in number of hours. In the real world, commercially written programs are seldom, if ever, the product of one person working alone. More often they are the work of project teams, who measure their time in units called **person-months** and **person-years.** A person-month is equivalent to one person working 40 hours a week for four weeks. Therefore, a team of five people working for eight weeks would be 10 person-months.

Large projects, those in the 1 million-line size range and up, measure time in person-years. Twelve person-months make up one person-year. It is not at all unusual for a large programming project to take two years or more to complete, with a project team of 6 to 10 people.

As you read further in this book, you will discover how computers are being used in art, music, business, education, and everyday life. Keep in mind that the programs, which make the computers usable, are incredibly long and complicated and that they took a lot of time and effort to write. Work it out for yourself. If it took you an hour or so to work out the program for the word-search game in chapter 2, how long would it take to write the 10,000 or so lines of a small compiler?

Table 4.7.1   *Comparative sizes of real-life programs.*

Type of Program	Number of Lines
The ROBOT simulator (see ROBOT, Chap. 5)	Over 1,000 lines of code
The compiler for a language with a limited instruction set	Tens of thousands of lines of code
A full-featured word processor	Hundreds of thousands of lines of code
A microcomputer operating system (Windows XP)	Over 40 million lines of code
A military weapon management program (missile defense, for example)	Estimated 100 million lines of code

Software-Defined Hardware

The title "Software-Defined Hardware" seems a little contradictory. But, in fact, new concepts in both hardware and software have been developed that make it possible to change how hardware is constructed by using software. The idea has been around for several years in a powerful form called programmable gate arrays. We won't try to define them here, but suffice it to say that the hardware is configured or changed by software to do the desired function.

UPI/Bettman/Corbis
The early radio and its use

An additional concept that should be mentioned to put things into perspective is the convergence of technology. This refers to a converging of multimedia telecommunications technology such as voice, data, video, and visual imagery. They will all be readily accessible and managed from a desktop computer. In this scheme, technologies such as VHS players. CD players, radios, and television tuners won't be necessary because all of these forms of information will be digital and accessible by your desktop computer.

In this scheme of things the Federal Communications Commission (FCC) has begun the process of evaluating the concept of software-defined radio. Because the FCC is the governmental agency that is responsible for allocating and licensing any use of radio frequencies, it has to develop policies and rules on how the radio frequency spectrum is used. Its responsibility includes cell phones, radio, TV, ham radio, pagers, CB radio, and any device that broadcasts radio frequencies.

Software-defined radio would allow devices such as cell phones to be programmed to become radio transmitters or to make use of uncrowded frequencies to facilitate any type of communication, including wireless Internet access. You would only need to have a single piece of hardware that could act as a cell phone, pager, or any number of other devices. The changes would be a simple matter of obtaining the software, probably over the Internet, which would in turn make the device act as desired. It is another step in the convergence of all communication systems.

Chapter Summary

4.1 Communicating with a Computer

Despite some surface similarities, communication between a person and a computer is distinctly different from person-to-person communication. The computer's binary circuitry does not closely resemble the symbolic thought processes of the human mind. Special languages, called programming languages, have been devised to bridge the gap between what the user wants to do and the way an electronic digital computer does it.

4.2 The Role of Languages in Communication

The major differences between human languages and computer languages involve three facets of the communication cycle: semantics, syntax, and participants.

Semantics refers to the meaning conveyed by a communication. Computer languages are imperative: They convey only instructions from the human to the computer.

Syntax refers to the form and structure of language. We have great leeway in how to express our thoughts. In contrast, computer instructions are expressed in narrowly defined patterns: Computers are intolerant of variations in syntax.

Computers respond to communication only after translation of instructions is complete. They have no choice of how to respond. If a computer understands the translated instruction, it must obey. Only computer users can correct errors and submit instructions for retranslation.

4.3 The Program Language Continuum

Pre-twentieth-century computers were programmed in machine code by direct hardware manipulation. Succeeding generations of programming languages have increased the ease with which humans program a computer but require program translation before the computer can perform a task. Most recently, language research is investigating ways to speak instructions directly into the computer. Such programs are, however, still a long way in the future.

4.4 Assembled, Compiled, or Interpreted Languages

With the exception of those written in binary code (machine language), all computer programs must be translated before they can be executed by the computer. Three types of translators are used. Assemblers translate programs written in assembly language. Interpreters and compilers translate high-level languages. Interpreters translate and execute one instruction at a time, whereas compilers translate an entire program before execution. Compilers are more efficient than interpreters, but assemblers execute fastest because of direct machine code addresses.

4.5 Programming for Everyone

It is now possible for many of us to do programming in various forms. The simplest programming produces the macros of word processors, data management programs, and spreadsheets. More complex programming can be done in the various forms of scripting used to enhance an operating system, word processor, spreadsheet, database, or Web page.

One of the most popular forms of programming is creating Web pages using HTML. This process is becoming easier with programs that create the HTML through a WYSIWYG visual programming environment.

4.6 Building a Program

Computer programs are written to solve specific problems. Accurate understanding of the problem will result in the development of a good plan, or algorithm, for a solution. A well-developed algorithm can then be expressed in a program language. Careful documentation ensures clearer understanding of the program processes when the development stage is done.

4.7 Software Development: A Broader View

Although simple examples of programs are best suited for instructional purposes, actual programs are both long and complicated, often requiring full-time attention by expert teams of several programmers. Good documentation and communication among team members are needed for programming success.

Key Terms

Key terms introduced in this chapter:

1. Algorithm, *108*
2. Alpha testing, *111*
3. Application generators, *100*
4. Assembler, *101*
5. Assembly language, *98*
6. Beta testing, *111*
7. Binary code, *95*
8. Browser, *104*
9. Bugs, *110*
10. Communication cycle, *92*
11. Compiler, *102*
12. Debugging, *110*
13. Electronic spreadsheets, *102*
14. ENIAC, *97*
15. Flowcharts, *108*
16. Fourth-generation languages, *100*
17. Hardware dependent, *98*
18. Hardwiring, *96*
19. High-level languages, *99*
20. HyperText Markup Language (HTML), *104*
21. Human language, *93*
22. Input data, *108*
23. Interpreter, *101*
24. Java, *105*
25. JavaScript, *105*
26. Logic, *108*
27. Logic error, *110*
28. Low-level language, *98*
29. Machine language, *98*
30. Machine independent, *99*
31. Macros, *102*
32. Mnemonics, *98*
33. Nassi-Schneidermann charts, *108*
34. Natural languages, *100*
35. Object code, *101*
36. Object-oriented language, *100*
37. Objects, *100*
38. Output data, *108*
39. Pascal, *99*
40. Person-months, *112*
41. Person-years, *112*
42. Procedures, *100*
43. Programs, *96*
44. Programming languages, *93*
45. Pseudocode, *108*
46. Query languages, *100*
47. Reliable, *110*
48. Report writers, *100*
49. Robust, *110*
50. Script, *105*
51. Scripting, *105*
52. Semantics, *93*
53. Source code, *101*
54. Subprogram, *111*
55. Syntax, *94*
56. Syntax error, *110*
57. Tag, *104*
58. Tolerance, *94*
59. Translation, *94*

Matching

Match the number of the key terms introduced in the chapter to the following statements.
Each term may be used once, more than once, or not at all.

1. ____ This type of language is spoken by people to communicate with each other.

2. ____ This term refers to meaning.

3. ____ This term refers to the grammatical form or structure of a language.

4. ____ This refers to a language that has been written by people for the express purpose of being able to communicate with digital computers.

5. ____ This is the porting of ideas, instructions, and concepts from one language to another.

6. ____ This is the form that all information must be translated into before the computer can "understand" it.

7. ____ The term given to instructions when they are written in binary code.

8. ____ A language that expresses a problem in terms of objects and their behavior/interactions.

9. ____ This category of languages uses alphabetic abbreviations called mnemonics.

10. ____ This category of languages encompasses a wide range of programming-language-like systems, each of which aims at simplifying the task of imparting instructions to a computer.

11. ____ This category of languages uses structure closely resembling human thought processes.

12. ____ This category of languages has statements that resemble English phrases combined with mathematical terms needed to express the problem or task being programmed.

13. ____ This layout language is used to create Web pages.

14. ____ This language is used to write scripts that enhance an already developed Web page.

15. ____ Research is being done in this area that will enable a person to speak instructions into the computer instead of writing them in some programming language.

16. ____ Except for programs written in machine language, this must be done to all programs before their instructions can be executed.

17. ____ This translation program translates an entire high-level language program into machine code before sending it to the CPU for execution.

18. ____ This is the term given to programming language statements that are still in their high-level language form.

19. ____ This is the term given to programming language statements that have been changed to machine language form.

20. ____ This is a detailed description of the exact methods used for solving a particular problem.

21. ____ This is an error in the planning or algorithm of a program.

22. ____ This is the name given to computer errors by Grace Hopper in 1943.

23. ____ This name is given to a formatting instruction in HTML.

24. ____ This term is used to describe computer languages written only for a specific type of CPU.

25. ____ This is a mistake in the form or grammar of the program statements.

True or False

Place either T or F on the line provided with each of the following statements. If a statement
is false, you should be able to explain what changes would make it true.

1. ____ In contrast to human language that is tolerant of minor grammatical errors in communication, programming languages are intolerant of grammatical errors.

2. ____ Programming computers has become easier because they no longer need instructions to be translated into binary code.

3. ____ Before programming languages were developed, computers could be programmed only by experts manipulating the hardware directly.

4. ____ ENIAC was the first computer to respond to natural language programming.

5. ____ Recently developed computer languages do not need translation into binary code.

6. ____ As shown in the diagram in the chapter, each assembly language instruction may produce several lines of object code.

7. ____ As shown in the diagram in the chapter, each high-level language instruction may produce several lines of object code.

8. ___ Compiled languages are more efficient than interpreted languages.

9. ___ When using an interpreted language, it is easier to find errors than in a compiled language.

10. ___ An assembler is used to translate only assembly language programs into machine code.

11. ___ Only compilers are used to translate high-level languages to machine code.

12. ___ Whereas interpreters translate one line of a program into one line of object code, a compiler may translate one line of a program into several lines of object code.

13. ___ Nassi-Schneidermann charts are often used by programmers for planning detailed algorithms.

14. ___ To use programs such as Dreamweaver, you must first learn HTML.

15. ___ Object-oriented program languages are used primarily to simulate objects existing in real life.

16. ___ Bugs are strictly syntax errors found by the compiler.

17. ___ Sophisticated users outside the company who will test the program under an enormous number of conditions do alpha testing.

18. ___ Communicating with a computer is no more difficult than communicating with other people.

19. ___ Object-oriented programming is useful because it resembles the thought process of the human brain.

20. ___ Consumers do beta testing after the manufacturer has released the software for public use.

21. ___ For a program to be reliable, it must correctly perform the defined tasks with every possible combination of data.

22. ___ For a program to be robust, it must be able to detect improperly entered data and other execution errors such as insufficient memory. It would warn the user of a problem and enable the user to correct or terminate the run.

23. ___ Using JavaScript requires that you understand the commands of the language before you use the script on a Web page.

24. ___ A person-month is equal to four people working for one week at 40 hours or one person working for four weeks at 40 hours.

25. ___ Large projects measure time in person-months.

Multiple Choice

Answer the multiple-choice questions by selecting the best answer from the choice given.

1. This type of language falls under the first generation of programming languages.
   a. Assembly language
   b. High-level language
   c. Machine language
   d. Natural language
   e. Query language

2. This computer was programmed by plugging cables into plug-boards to complete the connections needed for a task.
   a. Interpreter
   b. ENIAC
   c. CPU
   d. Compiler
   e. Assembler

3. Three- or four-letter names given to opcodes in assembly language programs.
   a. Mnemonics
   b. Logic
   c. Input data
   d. Object code
   e. Bugs

4. This language is used to define the style and appearance of a Web page as seen in a browser program.
   a. Assembly language
   b. Natural language
   c. HyperText Markup Language
   d. Fourth-generation languages
   e. Human languages

5. Three ways to represent an algorithm are:
   a. Mnemonics, logic, debugging
   b. Translation, scripting, macros
   c. Beta testing, flowcharting, semantics
   d. Flowcharting, Nassi-Schneidermann charts, pseudocode
   e. Macro language, Nassi-Schneidermann charts, pseudocode

6. This type of language falls under the second generation of programming languages.
   a. Assembly language
   b. High-level language
   c. Machine language
   d. Natural language
   e. Query language

7. This type of language falls under the third generation of programming languages.
   a. Assembly language
   b. High-level language
   c. Machine language
   d. Natural language
   e. Query language

8. This type of language falls under the fourth generation of programming languages.
   a. Assembly language
   b. High-level language
   c. Machine language
   d. Natural language
   e. Query language

9. This type of language falls under the fifth generation of programming languages.
   a. Assembly language
   b. High-level language
   c. Machine language
   d. Natural language
   e. Query language

10. This translation program changes a high-level language into machine code one line at a time, executing each line as it goes.
   a. Assembler
   b. Compiler
   c. Interpreter
   d. Source code
   e. Object code

11. This translation program changes second-generation programming languages into machine code.
   a. Assembler
   b. Compiler
   c. Interpreter
   d. Source code
   e. Object code

12. A high-level program using this translation program will not be allowed to execute until after all of it has been changed to machine code.
   a. Assembler
   b. Compiler
   c. Interpreter
   d. Source code
   e. Object code

13. This is the term given to the translated machine code version of a program.
   a. Assembler
   b. Compiler
   c. Interpreter
   d. Source code
   e. Object code

14. This is the term given to the high-level language version of the program.
   a. Assembler
   b. Compiler
   c. Interpreter
   d. Source code
   e. Object codel

Exercises

1. Name and briefly describe the four major generations of computer programming language.

2. Write a sentence that is semantically correct but syntactically wrong. Explain the difference between semantics and syntax.

3. How do words in human languages get their meaning? How does this process change for computer languages?

4. Name several human concepts (such as age or affection) that cannot be represented by computer languages. Why can't the computer deal with ideas such as these?

5. Give a few examples of syntax rules in a human language.

6. What do we mean when we say that computer languages have very low error tolerance?

7. Make up a chart showing one of the differences between human languages and computer languages.

8. Explain the concept of feedback in human communication. How does this concept change when we are communicating with a machine?

9. What is meant by natural language? Explain some of the possible problems involved in using natural language with computers.

10. Why are machine language and assembly language considered machine dependent?

11. Why can compiled and interpreted computer languages be machine independent?

12. Name the one most important difference between an interpreted and a compiled language.

13. Examining Figures 4.5.4 and 4.8.2, answer the following questions. (a) What are the base 16 codes for the background color and the color of the lettering? (b) Compare the two figures and resulting Web pages. (c) Give the key information that determines the size of the text *Loveable Annie*.

14. What kinds of data can be handled by symbolic computer languages?

15. **PUZZLER** Pick any two of the following problems. List, in correct order, all of the steps needed to accomplish these tasks. On the list of steps, mark any loops and repetitions needed to implement your directions:

Climb a flight of steps.
Dial a telephone.
Order food in a restaurant.
Lace and tie a pair of shoes.
Total up the amount of change in your pocket or purse.

16. What are the three general things we humans want computers to do for us?

17. Why do computer programs need documentation?

18. Explain what is meant by the word *algorithm*.

19. What are the four measures of program quality discussed in this chapter?

20. Describe the three methods of representing an algorithm explained in this chapter.

21. Explain how object-oriented language and program development closely resemble human thought processes.

22. What is the difference between a syntax error and a semantics (or logic) error in a program? Give an example of each.

23. Explain how a program might be hardwired into a computer.

24. Explain what is meant by a computer bug.

25. Explain the concept of machine independence in computer languages.

Discussion Questions

1. How might it be to the economic advantage of a programmer to become an expert in a high-level programming language rather than an assembly language for a particular model of computer?

2. Can you think of any circumstances under which it might be economically advantageous for a programmer to be an expert in the assembly language for a particular model of computer?

3. How might it be to the economic advantage of the people who pay for programs to be written to have them written in high-level languages?

4. Discuss why flowcharts and/or Nassi-Schneidermann charts might be considered helpful in planning programs and in documenting how they work.

5. What is the purpose of programming languages (that is, why do we need them)?

6. Explain how the syntax of a programming language relates to the grammar of a human language.

7. There is a move toward a sixth generation of programming languages. What do you think it might entail? What kinds of questions should it answer?

Group Project

1. A group of four students is assigned the task of designing a software system that helps manage a small retail store. The type of store will be selected by the students as a group. For example, the store could be a music store, comic book store, sports equipment store, ice-cream shop, coffee shop, or even a specialty bookstore. The software design should be modular and include at least the following: financial system (accounts payable, accounts receivable, internal reporting, banking, bud-

geting), inventory with automatic reordering, and personnel/scheduling.

The purpose of the project is to specify completely a system that would enable the store to run smoothly. Details as small as the layout of a computer screen for inventory are necessary. It should be specified so that a programmer could take the design and write the program implementing the system.

Web Exercises

1. Use bookmarks (Netscape Navigator) or favorites (Microsoft Internet Explorer) to create a JavaScript or Java applet resource for your own use. Search the Web for sites that offer free downloads of scripts and applets for use on your computer platform (Windows, Unix, or Macintosh) using your browser program (Netscape

Navigator or Internet Explorer). Maintain a list of 10 or more useful sites in a separate folder in your bookmarks or favorites file.

2. Grace Murray Hopper was one of a few women in the twentieth century who achieved fame and success in the male-dominated worlds of computer science and electrical engineering. Use the Web to find the names and biographies of other women who made significant contributions to computer development, languages, and programming. Use the Web resources you find to create a Web page highlighting these pioneering women and their contributions. Be sure you cite the location of any photos and text you decide to use on your Web page.

3. Using the HTML tags illustrated in this chapter, create a Web page with text and an image similar to the Loveable Annie page created in the Programming for Everyone section of this chapter. Display your page in your Web browser. Then modify your Web page by adding two or more JavaScripts or applets to the HTML to enhance the page's appearance. Look at the page again. Be sure it looks the way you want it to look.

After your page looks good to you, start all over. Create the page again, this time using a Web design edit-

ing program such as Dreamweaver. Try to recreate the same effects and appearance as you did using HTML and JavaScript. When you are done, print out the three pages you have created and compare them. Write a brief description of the differences you see and what has caused them.

4. Find and download a personal Web page that you think is well designed. Print it out. Then view the source code that created that page. For every line of HTML, decide what effects that line had in the Web page. For example, did it display a photo or graphic image? Did it center or enlarge text? Did it draw a horizontal line? Highlight any HTML tags that are new to you and learn how they are used. (There are lots of Web sites to help you learn and understand HTML.) Then incorporate those tags into your next Web page.

Bibliography

Boumphrey, Frank et al. *Beginning XHTML.* Ashburton, UK: Wrox Press, 2000.

A step-by-step book for learning a current version of HTML.

Chabert, Jean-Luc et al., eds. *A History of Algorithms: From the Pebble to the Microchip.* London: Springer-Verlag, 1999.

This book presents a non-language-dependent study of the classic algorithms in the computer field and how they were developed.

Hopper, Grace Murray, Steven L. Mandell, and Clyde Perlee, eds. *Understanding Computers.* Belmont, CA: West/Wadsworth, 1990.

Written by "the mother of programming," this book presents the timeless concepts that have controlled the development of computer software from its beginnings.

Jager, Rama Dev and Rafael G. Ortiz. *In the Company of Giants: Candid Conversations with the Visionaries of the Digital World.* New York: McGraw-Hill, 1997.

This book offers readers an insider's view into the history and people behind today's greatest digital successes.

Kohanski, Daniel. *Moths in the Machine: The Power and Perils of Programming.* New York: Griffin Trade Paperback, 2000.

This book explains what computer programming is all about, why it is so important—and so difficult—and what practical and ethical problems programmers face.

Rothstein, Michael F. *Ace the Technical Job: Programming.* New York: McGraw-Hill, 1999.

This book helps promote professional advancement in a highly competitive field.

Warner, Janine and Paul Vachier. *Dreamweaver 3 for Dummies.* Foster City, CA: IDG Books Worldwide, 2000.

A step-by-step introduction to effective use of this Web design software.

Whitelaw, Nancy. *Grace Hopper: Programming Pioneer.* New York: W. H. Freeman, 1995. Although intended for children, this well-presented and well-illustrated book contains a wealth of information about a remarkable woman.

chapter 5

Hardware and Software: Putting It Together

TimeLine

1945 John von Neumann introduces the concept of a stored program in a draft report on the EDVAC computer.

1952 Univac I predicts the outcome of the presidential election on television, and the public consciousness about computers is raised.

1961 IBM's Stretch supercomputer runs 30 times faster than the 704. This spurs further research in supercomputing.

1964 The first successful supercomputer, the CDC 6600, is produced.

1971 The "computer on a chip," the Intel 4004 microprocessor, is developed.

1972 Slide rules become obsolete as handheld calculators become popular.

1977 The benchmark for personal computers, the Apple II, is announced.

1982 The Cray X-MP supercomputer proves to be three times faster than a Cray-1.

1985 Supercomputer speeds reach 1 billion operations per second.

1994 The concept of DNA as a computing medium is demonstrated by Leonard Adleman.

2000 MiniRobots designed at the Artificial Intelligence Labs are destined for use in data collection on interplanetary explorations.

2015 First commercially available quantum computer.

Roger Ressmeyer/Corbis

Chapter Objectives

- Realize how programs enable computer hardware to perform tasks.
- Understand how the stored-program computer stores both programs and needed information.
- Know how the ROBOT's instruction decoder converts a ROBOT instruction into an operation code and an address.
- Recognize how a computer's instruction set defines the computer's uses and capabilities.
- Know how a program is loaded into a computer's memory.
- Recognize how the four basic components of a computer system are implemented in the ROBOT and Pencil and Paper computer simulations.
- Understand how the three basic units of a CPU function to execute a Pencil and Paper computer program.
- Understand how the fetch and execute cycle works.
- Recognize the difference between loading a program and executing a program.
- Understand the importance of programs and algorithms in empowering the hardware capabilities of computers.
- Understand the purpose and special features of electronic spreadsheet software.

A Double Whammy

In this chapter, you'll meet two highly simplified computers—the **ROBOT** and the **Pencil and Paper computer.** Each one can be programmed to perform a variety of tasks within limited capabilities.

PUZZLER

The instruction set for the ROBOT computer severely restricts the kinds of movements it can make.

Nonetheless, you can create a sequence of instructions causing the ROBOT to move diagonally across its domain. Here is the ROBOT puzzler:

Write a program for the ROBOT that will cause it to begin at the upper right corner of the domain and proceed diagonally across the room until it reaches the lower left corner. The ROBOT should stop there with its arms down, facing a wall. Assume the room is square (x tiles by x tiles) and that there are no doorways.

In its own way, the Pencil and Paper computer is just as restricted as the ROBOT, providing no commands to perform multiplication or division. Both, however, are possible. Here is the Pencil and Paper computer puzzler:

Write a program for the Pencil and Paper computer that will do the following:

- Read two integers from the imaginary keyboard and place them in the memory.
- Multiply the first integer by the second and place the result in the memory.
- Print out both original numbers and the result on the imaginary monitor.

Reminder—Each computer has only 32 memory locations!

5.1 Reviewing Key Concepts

In the previous four chapters, we discussed computers from several different viewpoints.

- We looked at different types and sizes of computers.
- We examined different types of information and how that information could be stored in computers.
- We defined the basic hardware components of computers, what each does, and how it works.
- We explored person/computer languages and how to develop software to perform a particular computer task.

In this chapter, we'll put these viewpoints together and answer a complex question: How do **programs,** written by programmers, work with the computer's hardware components to manipulate the information in the computer's memory, producing a desired outcome or result?

Before we try to answer this question, let's first review a few important concepts from the earlier chapters:

- Computers are not able to do anything with the data they have stored until they are given instructions for processing them.
- All data that computers contain and manipulate must be in binary form. This means that any instructions used by the computer must also be represented in binary code.
- Computer instructions must be performed sequentially, in the order presented. If the instructions in the Word Hunt program developed in chapter 2 were performed out of order, you would find a wrong message. Similarly, computer instructions executed out of order would not produce the desired results.
- Every instruction in a program must have one and only one meaning. Neither the person following the Word Hunt nor the computer following a program would get far if the instructions given were ambiguous or unclearly defined.
- Computer instructions are divided into two segments. In computer terminology, these are usually called the **opcode**, or **operation code**, and the **operand**.
- In every computer language there are some instructions (such as the WRITE and STOP instructions in the Word Hunt) that make no use of the operand part of the instruction.
- It is possible to translate computer programs written in any language into binary form by first assigning a numeric value to each instruction, and then converting each numeric value to its binary equivalent.
- Once a program is expressed in binary form, the computer can use it directly. It is then referred to as a **machine language** program. Machine language can be used immediately by the computer with no further translation or conversion. The machine language for all computers is written in binary form.

> A **program** is a collection of instructions for the computer to perform sequentially, one by one.

> **Machine language** is the form in which all instructions must be written before the computer can follow them. This form consists of binary numbers or binary code.

5.2 Two Conceptual Computers

In the next few sections of this chapter, we will examine two conceptual computing devices—a robot and a simplified model of the most common computer. Each of them will help illustrate parts of the answer to the question posed at the beginning of this chapter:

> How do programs, written by programmers, work with the computer's hardware components to manipulate the data in the computer's memory, producing a desired outcome or result?

You might wonder why we have chosen to use imaginary computers to examine how computers work. Today's real computers are incredibly complex machines with huge memories, large instruction sets, and nearly limitless options and flexibility. Using conceptual computers rather than real ones allows us to strip away the complexity, thus revealing the underlying simplicity of computer operation. Our two conceptual computers are "no-frills" machines. Each is designed with very limited capabilities, just enough memory to illustrate how programs and data are stored and manipulated, and a small, minimally functional instruction set. By eliminating everything else, we can focus our attention on the few concepts fundamental to understanding how computers and programs work together to accomplish tasks.

Both conceptual computers are examples of what are commonly called **von Neumann computers**, which were introduced in chapter 3. Each illustrates some of the principles fundamental to the **stored-program computer,** generally attributed to von Neumann. The conceptual computers presented in the next two sections each contain a minimal configuration: input units, memory, central processing unit, and output units. Each can store a program and the data it needs within its own memory. Each executes instructions in a program sequentially.

The first of these special imaginary computers is a programmable robot. Robots seem to have a universal appeal. People can relate to a robot because of the robot's similarity to themselves, yet still feel superior because the robot merely acts and does not think. Our ROBOT is very limited indeed. It can neither see nor speak nor count and includes no keyboard or printer. The ROBOT can perform only one kind of task, moving around its domain in response to the instructions in a program.

The other conceptual computer in this chapter is actually a simplified abstraction of an ordinary computer. We call it the Pencil and Paper computer. It has all the functional units and capabilities needed to qualify it as a classic digital computer, but it functions only as we execute the steps of its program one by one. The Pencil and Paper computer can accept numeric data, perform the simple arithmetic tasks of addition and subtraction, and display a result on its imaginary monitor screen.

A study of the ROBOT and the Pencil and Paper computers will help you understand how computers obey instructions and how they manipulate data. Although these are two simplified imaginary machines, many similarities exist between them and all other computers.

> A **stored-program computer** is a computing device with a place to keep information needed for computing—the memory of the computer. This memory stores both the programs (instructions for what to do) and the data needed for the program to compute.

5.3 The ROBOT Computer: Programs and Algorithms

Our first example of a computer, the ROBOT, is shown in Figure 5.3.1. Our ROBOT is rather specialized and not very useful. It can move around its domain, raise and lower its arms, and "know" whether it is facing a wall. To call the ROBOT a computer at all is a little pretentious; however, our objective is to introduce you to some of the typical concepts of the computing world.

THE ROBOT'S DOMAIN

Being very limited in its capabilities, our ROBOT can function only in its own special environment. Before we can understand the ROBOT or tell it what to do, we must first have a clear picture of the **ROBOT's domain,** or environment in which it operates. Imagine, first, an

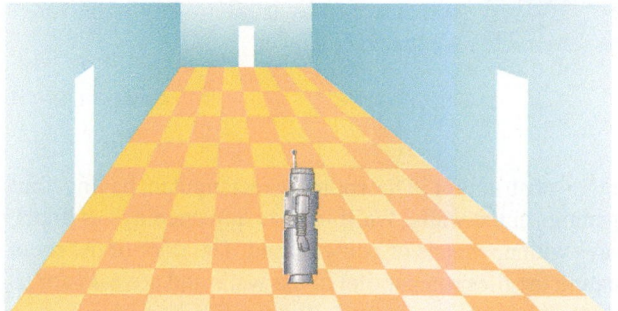

Figure 5.3.1

The ROBOT in its domain.

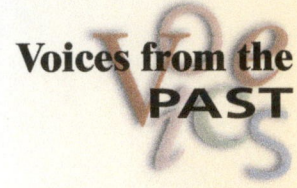

Voices from the PAST

John von Neumann

Courtesy of RAND Corporation

"If people do not believe that mathematics is simple, it is only because they do not realize how complicated life is."
—John von Neumann

Born into a banking family in Budapest, Hungary, John von Neumann (1903–1957) was unmistakably one of the brightest minds of the twentieth century—a true genius. When only six years old, he could divide eight-digit numbers in his head; at 18, he published his first scholarly paper. A mathematician by training, he made major contributions in many fields of science, including computer science. He became a United States citizen in 1933, and was appointed one of the original six professors of mathematics at the Institute for Advanced Studies at Princeton University. He retained that position for the remainder of his life.

Von Neumann's interest in computers differed greatly from that of his peers. He quickly perceived that the importance of computers would be in their application to specific scientific problems rather than in the development of mathematical tables. During World War II, von Neumann had the responsibility to seek ways to make calculations in several areas of science for the war effort. His expertise in hydrodynamics, ballistics, meteorology, game theory, and statistics was put to good use on many projects. Late in the war years, he served as a consultant on several national committees, applying his amazing ability to see through problems to rapid (and effective) solutions. Through this means he brought together the needs of the Los Alamos National Laboratory and the Manhattan Project with the computing capabilities of several computing engineers nationwide, including the developers of ENIAC at the University of Pennsylvania and the IAS computer at the Institute for Advanced Studies.

After World War II, von Neumann concentrated his efforts on further development of the Institute for Advanced Studies and its copies around the world. His work with the Los Alamos group continued, and he continued to develop the synergism between computer capabilities and the use of computational solutions to nuclear problems related to the hydrogen bomb.

Despite his collaboration with the Manhattan Project and the University of Pennsylvania, von Neumann was too late to be involved with ENIAC's design, which had started in 1943. Brilliance and understanding of the problems to be solved made him a major player in the subsequent computer called the EDVAC (Electronic Discrete Variable Automatic Computer). This project resulted in a report authored by von Neumann titled "First Draft of a Report on the EDVAC." The report, written in the spring of 1945, detailed the concepts of the stored-program computer and was a summary of many individuals' ideas. In spite of this, von Neumann was given credit for most of the concepts, and in fact, the general form of almost all other computers today is referred to as the von Neumann computer.

Courtesy of Institute for Advanced Study

empty room, free of furniture or other obstruction. The room is rectangular, having four walls. There may be one or more openings in the walls. We'll refer to any openings as doors, although technically they are doorways with no means of being closed. The floor of the room is paved in square tiles. Lines delineating the tiles run parallel to the walls and are easy for us to see. Any doors present are exactly one tile wide, as shown in Figures 5.3.1 and 5.3.2.

Figure 5.3.2

The ROBOT, standing one square away from a wall with its arm extended. The ROBOT cannot move further forward—there isn't enough room.

Most of the ROBOT's movements and capabilities are closely related to the characteristics of its domain. For example, when the ROBOT takes a step, it moves from one square floor tile to an adjacent tile. When it turns, it pivots its body but remains standing on the same tile. The ROBOT can never straddle two tiles or come to a stop standing on a line. Likewise, the walls limit certain activities of the ROBOT. They determine how far it can go in any one direction. Because the ROBOT's arms are exactly as long as the side of a tile, the ROBOT is unable to raise its arms if it is standing next to the wall it is facing. It cannot take a step if it is facing a wall and right up against it, unless it is in a doorway. A step through a doorway leads to destruction.

Although the ROBOT's room is always rectangular, its size is unknown to us at any given time. It can be any number of square tiles wide by any number of square tiles long. The rectangle may be a different size and shape for every different problem the ROBOT faces. The doors in the walls may be positioned differently, depending on the room's size. We can be certain in advance of only two things: first, that the room's dimensions will not change during the execution of a program and, second, that any doors present will never be located in the exact corners of the room.

HARDWARE—DEFINING ROBOT CAPABILITIES

To "program the ROBOT" means to devise a sequence of instructions designed to accomplish some particular task. To know what tasks are reasonable for the ROBOT, we need to know the ROBOT's characteristics and capabilities. Once we know what individual actions the ROBOT can perform, then we can speculate on what types of tasks it is capable of doing.

The ROBOT's capabilities are defined by its hardware. For example, the ROBOT has no eyes or cameras built in; therefore, it cannot "see" its surroundings. It has no numerical capacity; therefore, it cannot count the number of squares or steps needed to reach a wall. This is a very minimal ROBOT—we cannot use it to perform a task that is beyond its capabilities.

External Hardware Features The ROBOT is equipped with a special locomotion device at its bottom, where it comes in contact with the floor of its domain. This device allows the ROBOT to move from one square to an adjacent square within its domain. We refer to a single such action as a step. All steps are taken in a direction parallel to two walls of the room and in the direction that the ROBOT faces. Diagonal and reverse steps are not possible, nor can the ROBOT step sideways. The ROBOT can also pivot, but only to the right and only 90 degrees at a time—no more and no less.

The ROBOT has two mechanical arms—one at each side of its torso. An arm can be raised in front to shoulder height and lowered back to the ROBOT's side. When raised, the arm is at a right angle to the ROBOT's torso and parallel to the floor of the room. When the ROBOT's arm is extended, it reaches to the far edge of the next square in front of the ROBOT. (That is, the ROBOT technically occupies two squares when its arm is extended.) A consequence of this is that if the ROBOT is in a position such as that shown in Figure 5.3.2, it cannot take a step forward because the arm is touching the wall in front of it. In fact, when the ROBOT occupies a square that is immediately adjacent to a wall, it is impossible for it to raise its arm. There just isn't enough room!

The ROBOT is equipped with special sensors, located at the ends of its arms. These devices are capable of sensing the presence of a wall when the ROBOT is positioned as shown in Figure 5.3.2. The sensors activate if the ROBOT is directed to carry out the command SENSE, which causes it to try to sense the wall.

ROBOT Characteristics   The ROBOT has no intelligence. It cannot think or plan its own activities. The ROBOT is capable only of following a program of instructions that it retrieves from its memory and then executes, one instruction at a time.

That last sentence sounds simple enough but contains several difficult—and important—concepts. Let's analyze the internal hardware of the ROBOT a little more closely in terms of that statement. The ROBOT has a **memory.** In that memory are stored the **instructions** that make up a program. In addition, the ROBOT is equipped with circuits, which enable it to **fetch** instructions from its memory, interpret or **decode** their meaning, and **execute** them. Let's define further all of the terms printed in boldfaced type:

- **Memory**—The ROBOT's built-in memory is quite tiny. It contains 32 memory locations, numbered consecutively from 0 to 31. Each memory location is capable of storing a single ROBOT instruction.

- **Instructions**—The ROBOT does not understand human speech or any written language. It responds only to binary numbers, each eight bits (binary digits) in length. Each possible combination of the eight binary digits is a meaningful instruction to the ROBOT.

- **Fetch**—The ROBOT's electronic circuits cause it to fetch (or retrieve) its instructions from memory, one at a time, and usually in the order in which they are stored. The only exception to this rule involves the GOTO command from the ROBOT's instruction set. For the full story, see the explanations of the individual ROBOT commands, the sample programs, and Table 5.3.1.

- **Decode**—The ROBOT knows what action to carry out for a given binary number because the ROBOT's hardware contains an instruction decoder. Such a unit is present in one form or another in all digital computers. The instruction decoder is a set of circuits that causes the appropriate actions to be taken based on the particular binary number instruction that is received as input.

- In most cases, the decoder circuits may be required to split apart a given binary number into two or more parts in order to interpret the instruction represented by the number. Each ROBOT instruction must be split into two segments as shown in Figure 5.3.3. The operation code or command part of each instruction is represented by the first three binary digits, starting from the left. The remaining five bits are ignored by the ROBOT except when used with the GOTO command.

- **Execute**—The ROBOT executes the instructions by carrying out the action or command that each individual instruction represents. Each instruction has its own particular purpose and characteristics. Some instructions cause the ROBOT to take an observable action. For example, 00000000 causes the ROBOT to take one step forward. Instructions of this type may cause different results depending on where the ROBOT is located; this is what makes programming the ROBOT both interesting and a little tricky. For example,

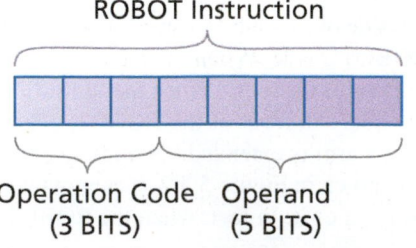

ROBOT Instruction

Operation Code   Operand
(3 BITS)   (5 BITS)

Figure 5.3.3

Each ROBOT instruction is split apart into two segments or fields: the operation code, or action, and the operand, or address.

Robots by the Dozen

No, they're not insects! And they're not mechanical vehicles from a child's Lego or Hot Wheels toy set. Instead they are the hottest and newest community of microrobots developed at the Artificial Intelligence Lab at MIT. Only one cubic inch in size, these tiny computers have been designed and equipped to lead the next scientific fact-gathering invasion of Mars.

Interplanetary exploration has long relied on robot rovers to collect geological and meteorological samples from planets whose atmospheres may be unfriendly to human scientists. These robots are usually large, clumsy machines, weighing many pounds, and occupying a large percentage of storage space in the exploration vehicle they serve.

Donna Coveney/MIT

They look like vehicles from a child's toy play set, but they are the hottest new development in intelligent microrobots.

Scientists at MIT have been working to develop a microrobot weighing only 10 grams or less to perform the same task. Not only would such computer machines be easier to move and maintain, but because they are used in colonies, they can cooperate to perform more tasks more efficiently than their larger cousins.

Like other computers, the microrobots are equipped with specialized hardware for performing their tasks: a Motorola M68HC11E9 microchip as a central processing unit (CPU); a Xicor X68C75 8k EEPROM chip to function as memory, and a variety of sensors (infrared sensors, light sensors, bump sensors, food sensors, tilt sensors, and mandible position sensors) to help with direction of movement and collection of samples. Power is supplied by either solar energy or battery. Locomotion is accomplished by wheels, hopping devices, or tracks—or combinations of all three. Cost? About $300 in parts, and many hundreds of thousands of dollars in research and labor.

Despite the astronomical research and development costs for these tiny robots, the hardware itself can do nothing without software designed especially for them. Developed by Dr. Rodney Brooks at MIT, the software for the robot colonies uses a programming style called subsumption architecture. The program is actually a cluster of many little programs called behaviors. Each behavior monitors a few of the robot's sensors and emits an electronic motor command based on the sensor readings. These commands are sent to the motors based on a priority hierarchy: The most important commands override, or subsume, those lower in priority. The result is intelligent behavior highly responsive to environmental elements and capable of cooperative actions when the microrobots are used in groups of a dozen or more.

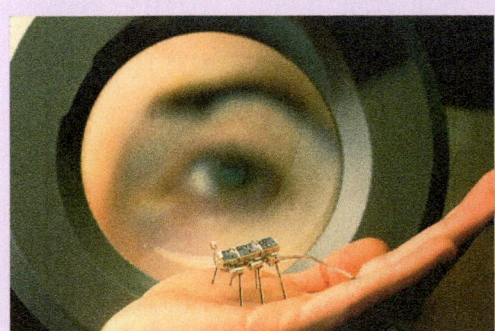

Peter Menzel/Stock Boston

if the ROBOT is directly in front of a wall, the 00000000 instruction causes it to spin its wheels and wear them out, much to the detriment of the ROBOT and the wall!

SOFTWARE—THE ROBOT'S LANGUAGE

The ROBOT's language consists of eight different commands. These commands are referred to as the ROBOT's **instruction set.** Like the ROBOT and the Word Hunt game in chapter 2, every different type of computer has its own instruction set.

An **instruction set** includes all of the different possible commands available to us in a particular programming language.

A **statement** is a single instruction in a particular program.

Each ROBOT instruction consists of an eight-bit binary number. Up to 32 ROBOT instructions may be stored in the ROBOT's memory, one in each memory location. Thus, the maximum number of **statements** in any one ROBOT program is 32.

Each ROBOT instruction consists of two separate portions or fields. This is illustrated in Figure 5.3.3. The first three bits form the command or opcode field. The opcode, or operation code, dictates the action to be taken by the ROBOT as a result of the instruction. The last five bits are almost always ignored, except in one instruction. These last five bits form the so-called argument or operand field, which is the address of a position in the memory. This argument or operand is extra information required in order to carry out the action indicated.

ROBOT Programs

The list of instructions, which the ROBOT has stored in its memory, can be determined and changed by the person who operates the ROBOT. The particular list of instructions that is currently stored is referred to as the ROBOT's program, and it must be placed into the ROBOT's memory before any execution can take place.

A **toggle switch** is a binary switch with only two positions—on and off. The most familiar type of toggle is the common household light switch.

To place programs into the ROBOT, you must have some sort of access to the ROBOT's memory. On our ROBOT, the memory unit is located on the left side of its torso. A door on that side opens to allow access. Each memory location is represented by a row of eight **toggle switches,** in which one eight-bit binary number representing an instruction can be stored. When one of these switches is turned on, the bit in that position has a value of 1; when the switch is off, the bit has a value of 0 (zero). In this case, a bit is on when the switch is up and off when the switch is down. Figure 5.3.4 shows the memory unit with six eight-bit instructions. At the moment, we're not concerned with what actions these represent, just

Figure 5.3.4

The ROBOT's memory switches.

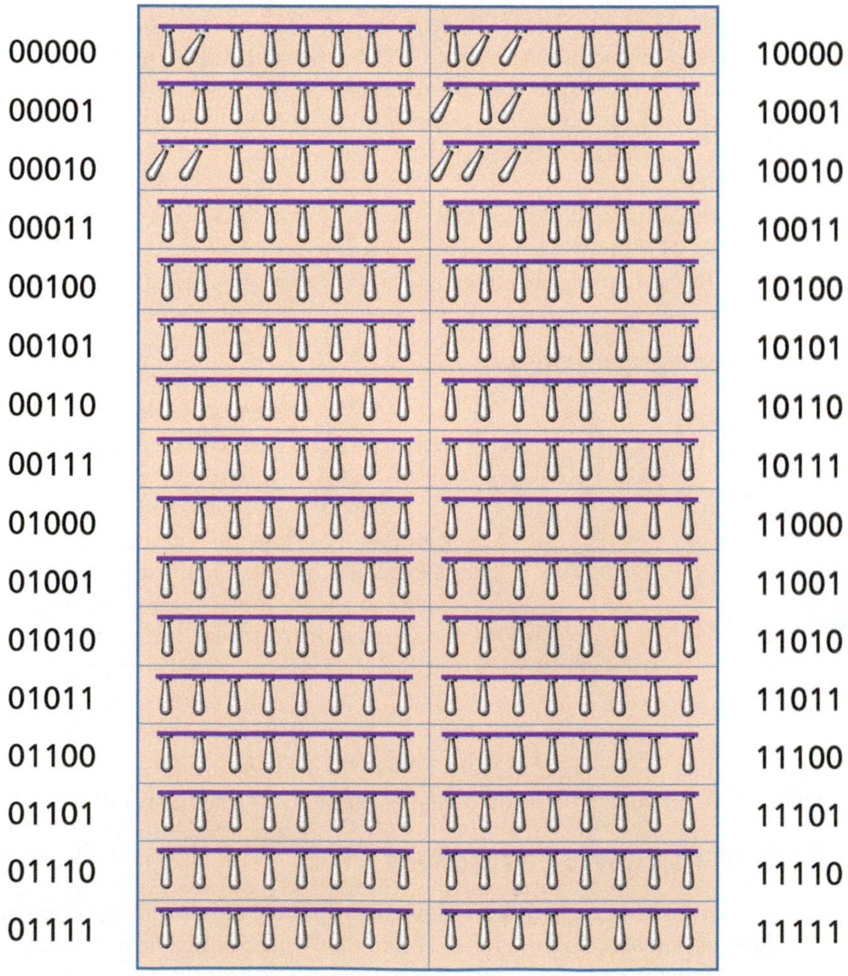

00000	10000
00001	10001
00010	10010
00011	10011
00100	10100
00101	10101
00110	10110
00111	10111
01000	11000
01001	11001
01010	11010
01011	11011
01100	11100
01101	11101
01110	11110
01111	11111

how they are entered. The top-right configuration 01100000 (at memory location 10000), for example, represents the instruction for the ROBOT to lower its arms.

The process of setting the value in each memory location to conform to a particular program is referred to as **loading** the program. All computers must load programs before they can execute commands. When all the instructions of a program are loaded, the programmer closes the door to the memory bay and presses the ROBOT's START button. The ROBOT can then begin to execute the program.

As noted earlier, there are exactly 32 memory positions. They are numbered from 0 to 31, using the binary numerals from 00000 to 11111. The memory position numbers in the ROBOT's memory bank in Figure 5.3.4 start in the upper left and are numbered down the first column and then on to the second column. When a program is executed, the instructions are performed in the order of step number, starting with the instruction stored at location 00000.

One of the ROBOT commands—the GOTO command—is designed to allow the ROBOT to take instructions out of normal order. This command or opcode has the binary code 101. When used within an instruction, its operand (the last five bits of the instruction) indicates the step number (memory location) from which the next instruction is to be taken.

Table 5.3.1 lists each value possible for the three-bit opcode of an instruction along with a single English word that suggests the action taken by that ROBOT command. Opposite each opcode is an explanation of the possible actions that can result from using that command in an instruction. We will refer to this set of commands as the ROBOT's instruction set.

Finally, the ROBOT is equipped with a special red warning light on top of its head. When the ROBOT's power switch is activated, the warning light is off, but certain situations cause it to be turned on. When the warning light is on, the ROBOT ignores all instructions except one, the one containing the LIGHT command. As we shall see, this feature gives the ROBOT a limited decision-making capability.

The ROBOT language is an example of a low-level language, also known as machine language. You should notice two distinctive features of this type of language:

- It is distinctly nonsymbolic. Usually, it consists entirely of binary numbers.

- Each instruction in the language produces a small effect. Getting the machine to perform any given task takes multiple instructions.

Table 5.3.1   *The ROBOT's instruction set.*

Command	(English)	Action
000	(STEP)	The ROBOT takes a step forward if possible. If not, the ROBOT remains where it is. A step is considered to be impossible if the ROBOT faces a wall and is up against it with arms lowered or if the ROBOT faces a wall and is one step away with arms raised.
001	(TURN)	The ROBOT turns 90 degrees to the right if it is able. It is considered unable to turn if there is a wall to its immediate right and its arms are raised.
010	(RAISE)	The ROBOT raises its arms if possible. If it cannot raise its arms, it turns on its warning light. If its arms are already raised, it does nothing.
011	(LOWER)	The ROBOT lowers its arms if they are raised; otherwise, it does nothing.
100	(SENSE)	If the ROBOT's arms are raised and it is a step away from the wall it is facing, then this command will cause it to turn on its warning light. (It senses the wall.) In any other circumstances, the command is ignored.
101	(GOTO)	The ROBOT will take its next command out of normal order. (The last five bits of this command tell it from which memory location to take the command.)
110	(LIGHT)	If the warning light is on, this command causes the ROBOT to turn it off. Important note: When the warning light is on, the ROBOT ignores every instruction except LIGHT. Also, when the ROBOT first has its power switch turned on, the warning light is set to off.
111	(STOP)	The ROBOT shuts off its own power.

As you develop the algorithm for the ROBOT puzzler, remember that the room could be any size, so long as it is square. So it might be 1 square by 1 square, or 7 squares by 7 squares, or 23 squares by 23 squares. Your solution must be general enough to accommodate any square room. Don't forget to check for a wall before every step.

A good way to proceed is to use graph paper and draw your solution to help visualize the actions of the ROBOT. Remember, that for our ROBOT to turn left, it must make three right turns.

USING THE ROBOT

We now know a lot of detail about the ROBOT but hardly anything about how to make it perform. The best way to learn how to use a machine-level language is to solve a series of **problems** of gradually increasing difficulty. That is exactly what we are going to do with the ROBOT now. Because certain concepts that have general application in any computing situation will arise as we proceed, we will highlight those ideas as they occur. These concepts follow:

> A **problem** in the context of this discussion is a well-defined task to be performed by the computer.

- Program
- Problem
- General solution
- Algorithm
- Conditions
- Loops
- Infinite loops
- Escape from loops

Let's first review a few key ideas from previous chapters: A program is a sequence of instructions designed to carry out a task. We'll refer to a potential task for the ROBOT as a problem. The solution to the problem is provided by the program. However, to arrive at the program, we must proceed through fairly detailed logical thinking, and in so doing, devise a general method for approaching the problem. Such a method, expressed in clear and precise logical steps, is called an **algorithm.** This term is one of the words most commonly used by computer scientists and programmers.

> An **algorithm** is a step-by-step process used to solve a problem. Essentially, the algorithm is the solution to the problem and is usually implemented by a program.

To illustrate these ideas, let's examine a series of problems for the ROBOT and then plan their solutions (algorithms). Finally, we will write the program that follows each algorithm.

Problem 1. Cause the ROBOT to walk to the wall it is initially facing and then stop with its arms lowered and facing against the wall. Assume the ROBOT is not initially facing an open doorway.

A few thoughts may occur to you during the process of solving this problem, or as we should say, creating the algorithm to solve the problem. Does *stop* mean turn off power or just come to a halt? Should we assume that the ROBOT's arms are lowered to begin with? How far is the ROBOT from the wall to begin with?

If you thought of any of these, pat yourself on the back! You are properly analytical. Let's establish some of the necessary ground rules by answering these questions:

- By *stop*, we mean literally turn itself off by executing the instruction 11100000.
- We will make only two assumptions about the ROBOT's initial or starting configuration. We can assume its arms are down at the start of any program and it is not facing a doorway.
- We make no assumptions about the distance of the ROBOT from the wall.

Let us begin our problem analysis by addressing the last point: We don't know how far the ROBOT is from the wall. The obvious way to solve this problem is to count the number of squares to the nearest wall and then enter the program with the correct number of steps. A program that causes the ROBOT to stop at the wall if it is three squares away is shown in Table 5.3.2.

Table 5.3.2   *Program to get the ROBOT to the wall if it begins three steps from the wall.*

Memory Location			
Binary	Decimal	Command	Explanation
00000	0	00000000	STEP
00001	1	00000000	STEP
00010	2	00000000	STEP
00011	3	11100000	STOP

In other words, we could just instruct the ROBOT to take the correct number of steps and then stop. There are at least two difficulties with this: First, it won't work if the ROBOT is more than 31 steps from the nearest wall, and second, it is not very general. It will work only with a specified number of steps. We would have to write a separate program for every possible number of steps the ROBOT can be from the wall. A good algorithm or solution to the problem should be *general*.

What we are after is a single program that will work in all circumstances. Let's attack the problem of not knowing how many steps from the wall the ROBOT is to begin with. What if we could put one 00000000 (STEP) instruction in the program and get the ROBOT to repeat STEP until it gets to the wall? That way, we wouldn't need to know exactly how far from the wall the ROBOT was to begin with. We need a way to make the ROBOT repeat an instruction. What we have in mind is called a **loop**.

The ROBOT has an instruction that will cause it to repeat some earlier instructions in a program. The opcode 101 (**GOTO**), followed by a five-bit address, causes the ROBOT to repeat the sequence of instructions starting at that address. Let's try the program shown in Table 5.3.3.

An algorithm for a specific problem should be **general**. That means it should solve the stated problem for all possible sets of circumstances.

In programs, a **loop** is a sequence of instructions that is repeated one or more times when a program is executed.

Table 5.3.3   *Program to get the ROBOT to the wall using a loop.*

Memory Location			
Binary	Decimal	Command	Explanation
00000	0	00000000	STEP
00001	1	10100000	GOTO location 0
00010	2	11100000	STOP

It certainly is short! The instruction at 00000 causes the ROBOT to step (does it always?), and the instruction at 00001 causes the ROBOT to go back and do step 00000 over again. Then the instruction at 00010 causes the ROBOT to stop. Well, it sounds good. What's wrong with this program? Hint: There is more than one thing wrong!

Our second try certainly overcomes the objection to our first try regarding the distance to the wall. The second program does not put any limit on the number of times the 00000000 (STEP) instruction is carried out—and there is its difficulty. The first two instructions in this trial solution will be executed over and over and over and over and. . . . This is an

An **infinite loop** occurs when a program is repeating the same group of instructions again and again and again, with no possible way of stopping the repetition. Intervention by the person overseeing computer operation is necessary.

example of an **infinite loop**. There is no way to escape from the loop. Running this program is going to be hard on the ROBOT's batteries! Besides, when the ROBOT does reach a wall (and it could do that at any time), it will wear out its wheels trying to take steps that are impossible.

We now seem to be caught in a dilemma. We need a loop to account for different distances to the wall, yet our proposed solution loops forever! We need some way to have the ROBOT stop as soon as it reaches the wall. Let's look back at everything we know about the ROBOT and see if there is any way it can "know" when it gets to a wall.

Reviewing the commands or opcodes in the table of instructions given earlier, we see that the opcode 010 (RAISE) causes the ROBOT to turn on its light if it is against the wall—just what we're after! In describing the ROBOT's characteristics, we promised that the ROBOT's warning light would give it a decision-making capability. Great, that's just what we need—a way to identify the wall and a way to decide when to escape from the loop.

Recall the way the warning light works: Once the light is turned on, the ROBOT ignores all instructions except for 11000000 (**LIGHT**). The 110 opcode tells the ROBOT to turn off the warning light. If the warning light is on for any reason, this is the only opcode that has any effect.

Getting the ROBOT Out of a Loop
Now, let's attack the problem again by using the 010 (RAISE) opcode to solve our dilemma. To get the ROBOT out of its deadly loop, one of the instructions inside the loop must sooner or later cause the warning light to be turned on. That instruction contains the 010 (RAISE) command. The ROBOT tries to raise its arms and cannot (because it is up against a wall), so the light goes on. When that occurs, the 101xxxxx (GOTO) instruction, which normally causes the ROBOT to begin repeating the loop (assuming the loop begins at a step number xxxxx), will be ignored because the light is on. The ROBOT will then execute the instruction following the 101xxxxx instruction, thereby escaping from the loop!

The new program with both the binary machine language and the English language explanation about what the instructions do is shown in Table 5.3.4.

Table 5.3.4   *Program to get the ROBOT to the wall using a better algorithm.*

Memory Location			
Binary	Decimal	Command	Explanation
00000	0	01000000	Try to RAISE arms.
00001	1	01100000	If it can, LOWER arms.
00010	2	00000000	Take a STEP.
00011	3	10100000	GOTO location 0.
00100	4	11000000	Turn off the LIGHT.
00101	5	11100000	STOP.

This one really does work. To convince yourself, run the program on a ROBOT simulator if one is available; otherwise, run it in the classroom with a classmate acting the part of the ROBOT.

Problem 2. Have the ROBOT locate any corner of the room and stop there with its arms lowered. Assume the ROBOT is not initially facing an open doorway.

One of the aspects of programming that lets us solve complicated problems more easily is that we can reuse pieces of programs that have already been written. We just wrote a useful program that allows the ROBOT to find the wall. This new example will build on that program, nicely illustrating the idea of reusing parts of programs.

To find a corner, the ROBOT must find two walls. We have it first find the wall it's facing—which we already know how to do—and then turn it 90 degrees and repeat the process to find the second wall. That's a reasonable algorithm stated in words. Hence, using the last problem's solution with some additional details, we get the complete solution shown in Table 5.3.5.

There are two separate loops in this program, one to find each wall. They are indicated by the braces shown in Table 5.3.5.

Note that in the second loop of Problem 2, the ROBOT is moving along the wall with the wall on its left side.

Table 5.3.5 *Program to get the ROBOT to a corner of the room no matter where it is initially positioned.*

Memory Location			
Binary	*Decimal*	*Command*	*Explanation*
00000	0	01000000	Try to RAISE arms.
00001	1	01100000	If arms are raised, LOWER them.
00010	2	00000000	Take a STEP.
00011	3	10100000	GOTO memory location 0.
00100	4	11000000	Turn off the LIGHT.
00101	5	00100000	TURN to face new wall.
00110	6	01000000	Try to RAISE arms.
00111	7	01100000	If arms are raised, LOWER them.
01000	8	00000000	Take a STEP.
01001	9	10100110	GOTO memory location 6.
01010	10	11000000	Turn off the LIGHT.
01011	11	11100000	STOP.

5.4 The Pencil and Paper Computer

The ROBOT computer of the previous section is not a general-purpose computer. Its only purpose is to perform specialized tasks such as stepping around a room or finding a doorway. The conceptual computer discussed in this section, the Pencil and Paper computer, comes a bit closer to being a general-purpose computer, but it isn't completely general. It can perform only a limited set of arithmetic calculations. However, it contains so many features of a general-purpose computer that it allows us to leave computer abstractions behind and discuss genuine, real-world computers.

In chapter 3, we examined the hardware components of a typical computer. Almost all computers can be broken down into the fundamental units shown in Figure 3.1.1. Let's revisit that diagram, and see how the four major parts of a computer manifest themselves in the ROBOT and in the Pencil and Paper computer. We repeat this diagram in Figure 5.4.1.

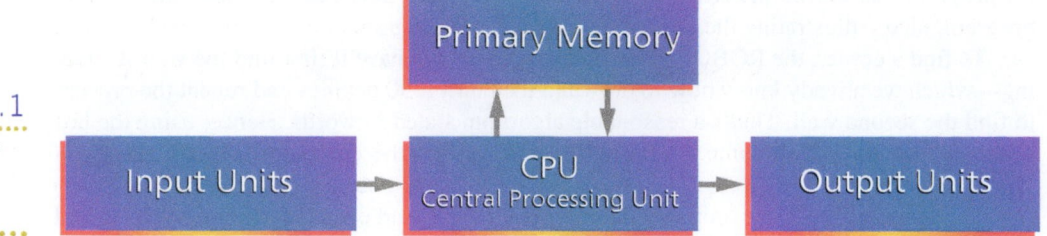

Input and Output Units

1. In the ROBOT computer, the **input and output units** are easily recognizable, as shown in Table 5.4.1. The toggle switches that comprise the ROBOT's memory allow us to enter instructions into the computer. The ROBOT uses only instructions—no other data are needed. The only other information needed from the outside world is the presence of a wall. This information enters the ROBOT in two ways: through sensors at the ends of the ROBOT's arms, and through the inability of the ROBOT to raise its arms when facing against a wall.

2. ROBOT output is provided to the programmer visually through the movement of the arms and legs and through the light turning on or off at the top of the ROBOT's head.

3. The Pencil and Paper computer needs numeric data to manipulate as well as instructions on how the manipulation or calculations should be done. Both the data and the instructions are entered into the computer's memory through an imaginary input device—a keyboard.

4. Pencil and Paper output presents the results of arithmetic calculations performed on the data. It is provided by an equally imaginary output device—a monitor screen.

Memory

- In the ROBOT, the memory is the switch panel shown in Figure 5.3.4. Instructions are entered into the memory using the toggle switches as input devices. Once the program is loaded, the toggle-switch memory stores the instructions awaiting execution time.

- The memory of the Pencil and Paper computer, like that of the ROBOT, has 32 locations. Data and instructions are entered directly into available memory locations through the imaginary keyboard. Each memory location can store either one instruction or one numeric data value for calculation.

Central Processing Unit (CPU)

- You might have some difficulty identifying the CPU of the ROBOT. This is due to our deliberately incomplete discussion of it. Because of the ROBOT's limited use, there was no advantage in including a more detailed explanation of its CPU. We know only that it fetched each instruction from the next memory location and executed it.

- The Pencil and Paper computer, however, performs tasks similar to those performed by real computers, although much simplified. Because its CPU so closely resembles that of a real computer, we will take a much closer look at all aspects of the Pencil and Paper CPU and functioning.

Table 5.4.1   *ROBOT input and output units.*

Input Units	Output Units
Toggle switches located on left side of ROBOT	Movement of legs and arms
Sensor on arms	Light on and off

A schematic drawing of the Pencil and Paper computer is shown in Figure 5.4.2. We've already talked about the input/output devices and the 32-compartment memory. Now let us move on to less familiar territory. The **CPU**, or **central processing unit**, consists of three parts: the arithmetic logic unit, the control unit, and the instruction decoding unit.

The **arithmetic logic unit** is where arithmetic is done. It has a place where all the results are accumulated, called the **accumulator**. Real computers have much more detail and several accumulators, but the idea is the same. Notice that the accumulator is more than eight bits in size. When the accumulator calculates answers, the results produced may be higher values than decimal 255, thus needing more than eight binary digits to accommodate the answer. The Pencil and Paper computer's accumulator is 14 bits long. This means the largest number it can contain is 4095 (in binary this is 11111111111111_{two}). It should also be noted that the Pencil and Paper computer can store and manipulate only positive integers between 0 and 255. The reason for this is that it can store only eight bits in each memory location, and 255_{ten} is the highest value than can be stored in eight binary digits. Although a computer such as this one is not very practical, it will help us understand the overall operation of more versatile computers.

The **control unit** has two locations where numbers are kept: the **instruction register (IR)** and the **program counter (PC).** The eight-bit instruction register is where an instruction is placed for analysis by the **instruction decoding unit.** The program counter contains the five-bit address of the memory location where the next instruction to be executed resides. The control unit will carry out the operation given by the opcode in the instruction register. It will then go to the five-bit address in memory contained in the program counter to find out what instruction must be performed next.

The instruction decoding unit is the part of the computer that decodes the instruction. In a real computer, it electronically analyzes each instruction as it is placed in the instruction register and causes the proper electronics to be called upon to execute the instruction. During program execution, the control unit gets the instruction from the instruction register, sends it to the instruction decoding unit, and then adds one to the value of the program counter to determine the address of the next instruction.

The **arithmetic logic unit** is a part of the CPU where all arithmetic calculations are done. The results of each calculation are stored in a special location of the arithmetic logic unit, called the **accumulator**. The accumulator can store only one result at a time.

The **control unit** is the part of the CPU responsible for carrying out the operations demanded by the program's instructions.

The **instruction register** contains the eight-bit binary code of the current instruction.

The **program counter (PC)** contains the binary value representing the address of the next instruction (the one to be executed after the current one is finished).

The **instruction decoding unit** analyzes the instruction in the **instruction register** and then causes the appropriate electronic connections to be made that cause the instruction to be executed.

MEMORY

0	1	2	3
4	5	6	7
8	9	10	11
12	13	14	15
16	17	18	19
20	21	22	23
24	25	26	27
28	29	30	31

CPU

Instruction Register (IR):

Program Counter (PC):

Accumulator (AC):

Input/Output

Hello

Figure 5.4.2

Schematic representation of the configuration of the Pencil and Paper computer.

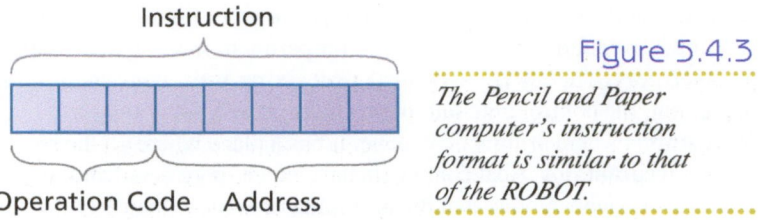

Figure 5.4.3

The Pencil and Paper computer's instruction format is similar to that of the ROBOT.

THE PENCIL AND PAPER COMPUTER INSTRUCTION SET

As with any other computer, the Pencil and Paper computer has its own unique set of commands to be used within instructions. The instructions are the lifeblood of any computer and are the means for causing the computer to do things. Also, as with the ROBOT computer, each instruction must ultimately be represented as a binary number. In the Pencil and Paper computer, these instructions are similar to those of the ROBOT because they consist of only one byte—eight binary digits—as shown in Figure 5.4.3.

The instruction format for the Pencil and Paper computer, like that of the ROBOT, contains a three-bit operation code (opcode) and a five-bit address, or operand. The three-bit opcode allows us a total of eight different commands in the instruction set, whereas the address portion allows access to 32 memory positions, numbered 0 through 31. This is a very limited size for both memory and number of commands. In fact, most personal computers have many megabytes (MB) of memory. This size is rather awesome when compared to the 32 bytes (.032 KB) of the Pencil and Paper computer. As you might suspect, a larger number of bits in the address is required to reference so many memory locations. In fact, 16 to 32 bits are used in a personal computer for the address rather than the five used by the Pencil and Paper computer. Personal computers also have several hundred commands in their instruction sets.

The complete instruction set for the Pencil and Paper computer appears in Table 5.4.2. As you can see, the instruction set doesn't even have multiplication or division. Of course, repeated addition and subtraction can do these operations.

How does the CPU work with instructions using these commands? Let's see what happens when two numbers need to be added: One number must first be placed in the accumulator. The instruction decoder then separates the ADD instruction into its two components, the opcode and the operand. When the ADD opcode is executed, the number stored in the

Table 5.4.2   *The Pencil and Paper computer's instruction set.*

Instruction	Opcode	Description
ADD	001	Add the contents of the referenced memory location to the current value in the accumulator.
SUB	010	Subtract the contents of the referenced memory location from the current value in the accumulator.
LOAD	011	Place a copy of the value currently stored in the referenced memory location into the accumulator. This overwrites or destroys the previous contents of the accumulator.
STORE	100	Place a copy of the contents of the accumulator into the referenced memory location. This overwrites or destroys the previous contents of that memory location.
READ	101	Obtain a value from the keyboard of the terminal and store it into the referenced memory location. This overwrites or destroys the previous contents of that memory location.
PRINT	110	Display the value in the referenced memory location on the computer screen. This does not alter what is in that memory location; a copy of the value is displayed on the screen.
PJUMP	111	Jump to the referenced memory location if the accumulator contains a positive nonzero number.
STOP	000	This causes the computer to stop executing the program.

Plug and Play

When a new hardware device, such as a sound card, is added to a personal computer many things need to be done so that it can function. With Plug and Play the necessary additions and changes are dynamically made using a combination of the system BIOS, operating system, device drivers, system resources, and other hardware devices. The beauty of Plug and Play (PnP) is that all of these changes are done automatically. This means the unsophisticated user can just plug the new hardware device into the computer and immediately begin using it.

Before PnP, adding a hardware device often involved hours spent reading manuals, loading the proper drivers, setting configuration switches and configuring the operating system. This was indeed such a burden that in 1993 a group of software and hardware manufacturers formally introduced the idea of Plug and Play, which has since become a common feature of personal computers. It involves standards for the BIOS, operating system, the computer bus and the serial/parallel ports. These standards allow the various manufacturers to cooperate in creating new products using the PnP approach.

Plug and Play makes adding hardware components to your personal computer very easy. Scanners, printers, sound cards, and many other devices can just be plugged in and you can begin playing with them.

---

memory location described by the operand is added to the one already in the accumulator. The sum is placed back in the accumulator. Suppose the accumulator contains the binary number 00011011 when the instruction ADD 27 is executed. Assuming that location 27 of the memory contains the number 00000001, after the ADD 27 is executed, the number 00011100 (00011011 + 00000001) will be in the accumulator. Location 27 still has the 00000001 because of the **nondestructive reading of memory**. (That is, only copies of numbers are taken from memory; the original is still there.) Nondestructive reading is almost universal in the operation of computers.

PUZZLER HINT

To solve the Pencil and Paper puzzler, remember that multiplication is really a series of additions. The second number tells how many of the first number to add together. Here's an example: 5 times 3 means 5 + 5 + 5. Here's a partial algorithm for performing the multiplication part of this problem:

1. Place numB into the accumulator.
2. Subtract 1 from numA.
3. Add numB to the accumulator.
4. Store result.
5. Pjump to step 2.
6. Print result.

Let's now see how the Pencil and Paper computer works. Addressing the simple problem of adding two integers and printing out the result seems a reasonable first program. The essential elements of solving this problem with the Pencil and Paper computer can be outlined in the following algorithm:

■ Read two numbers from the keyboard and put them in memory locations X and Y. The actual memory locations X and Y are chosen by the computer at execution time.

Table 5.4.3 *Mnemonic assembly language program that sums two integers and prints out the results.*

READ	X
READ	Y
LOAD	X
ADD	Y
STORE	Z
PRINT	Z
STOP	

Table 5.4.4 *Machine language version of the summing program in Table 5.4.3.*

10111101
10111110
01111101
00111110
10011111
11011111
00000000

Memory labels allow the computer, rather than the programmer, to select where data values and results will be stored. This frees the programmer from having to keep track of the exact locations used. With the large memories of today's real computers, this is an important aid to the programmer.

A **loader** is one of the programs within a computer's operating system (see chapter 6) that places into memory a program that is to be executed. The loader also places the address of the first instruction to be performed into the computer's program counter..

- Put one of the numbers into the accumulator.
- Add the other number to the one already in the accumulator.
- Copy the result from the accumulator into the memory at the location identified by Z.
- Print the sum of the two numbers.
- Stop running.

We'll write this program first using the one-word, English-like or **assembly language** form of each instruction we need. Assembly language is a historical term used to identify English-like mnemonic forms that represent each machine language instruction. This makes it easier to program and allows us to label memory positions using names. The result is shown in Table 5.4.3.

Before the Pencil and Paper computer can execute this program, it must be translated to machine language form, which consists only of eight-bit binary numbers for each instruction. A program called an assembler does the work of translating the program. Doing the translation by hand gives more insight into the problems that must be solved: First of all, to what do the X, Y, and Z refer? The letters X, Y, and Z are **memory labels** that refer to locations in the memory of the computer. Using labels such as these allows the computer to select where the values will be stored. In unusual cases, such as the Pencil and Paper computer, the programmer can pick the memory locations to be used. For this program, let's assume memory locations 29, 30, and 31 are used in place of X, Y, and Z. This choice is completely arbitrary. We could have just as easily used 11, 23, and 28, unless, of course, instructions are stored in these memory locations.

Once memory locations have been chosen for X, Y, and Z, we must then begin at the top of the program and number the steps of the program. Usually, the step numbers begin with position 0 (that's zero) of the memory. But that's another arbitrary choice. You can begin at any location, placing each instruction one location number higher until you run out of instructions or memory locations. Remember not to exceed step 31 for a Pencil and Paper program. After the memory locations (step numbers) have been assigned, the actual translation of the English-like instructions into binary (machine) code can begin. Start at the top of the program, and translate one instruction at a time. You can get the binary codes for each instruction using the opcodes of Table 5.4.4. The machine code result of the hand translation of the program in Table 5.4.3 is given in Table 5.4.4.

LOADING AND EXECUTING A PENCIL AND PAPER PROGRAM

The next problem with the Pencil and Paper computer is to place the program into the memory of the computer so that it can be executed. This job is usually the duty of a program called a **loader.** The loader will store the program into memory and place the memory address of the first instruction to be executed into the program counter. It should be noted that this starting address is not always the first location of the memory.

Another function of the loader is to start the **fetch and execute cycle.** The instruction whose address is in the PC (program counter) will be fetched and placed in the IR (instruction register). The instruction in the instruction register will then be executed (in the example we have been using, a number is read from the keyboard and placed in memory location 29). Then, the fetch and execute is started again, reading the next address from the program counter and fetching the next instruction. The cycle is repeated until an instruction with the STOP command is reached. This fetch and execute cycle is represented in Figure 5.4.4.

A more detailed account of the fetch and execute cycle is shown in flowchart form in Figure 5.4.5.

You should take the program as shown loaded into the memory in Figure 5.4.6 and execute it via the fetch and execute process. In other words, play computer and see what results. Note that all memory locations not containing the program have been set to zero. This is quite common in most computers. Also note that locations 29, 30, and 31 are zero. This is because the numbers to be summed are read in while the program is executing and not during the loading phase. It is important to understand completely the difference between load-

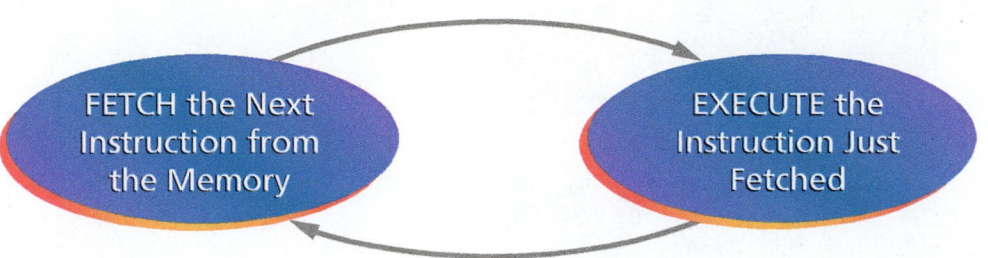

Figure 5.4.4

The fetch and execute cycle.

ing a program into the memory of the computer and executing the program (that is, performing each instruction as the fetch and execute cycle works its way through the program).

In this example, the numbers to be read are supposed to be typed on the keyboard. This is rather difficult to actually do on an imaginary paper computer, so just use your imagination. Consider a computer that beeps to prompt you to enter a number on the keyboard. Let's assume that when the computer beeps, you would type a 12, and when it beeps a second time, you would type a 17. Figure 5.4.7 shows a snapshot of the memory just after the program has executed. Because 12 and 17 were typed on the keyboard, it should be no surprise that the sum 29 appears in memory location 31.

Figure 5.4.5

Detailed flowchart of the fetch and execute cycle.

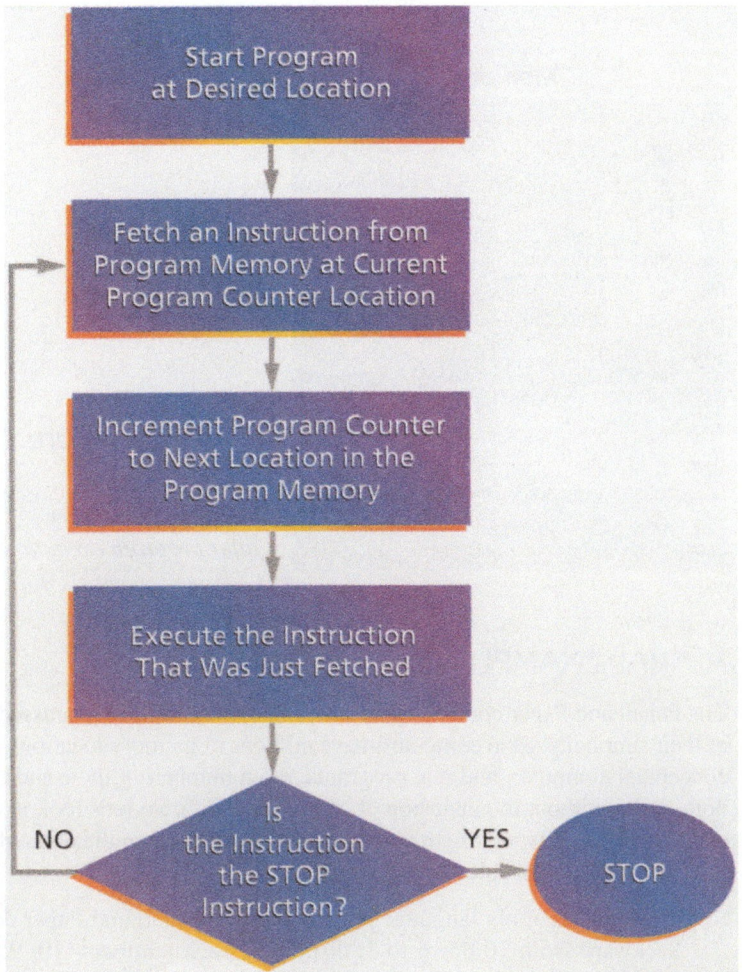

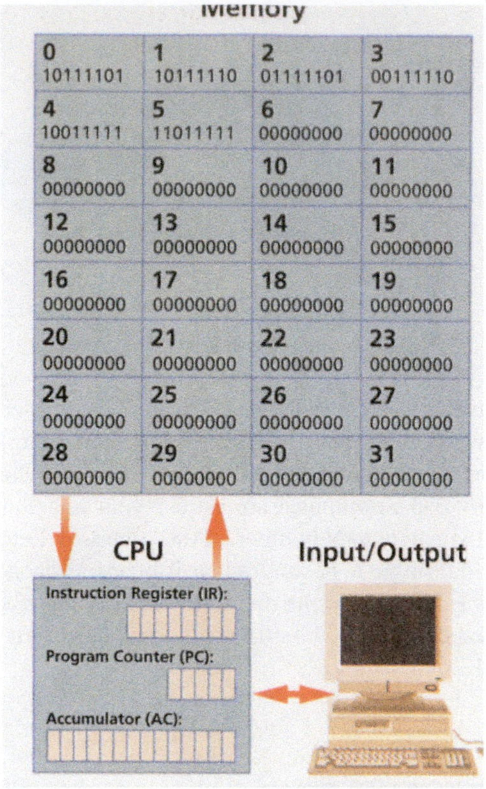

Memory

0 10111101	1 10111110	2 01111101	3 00111110
4 10011111	5 11011111	6 00000000	7 00000000
8 00000000	9 00000000	10 00000000	11 00000000
12 00000000	13 00000000	14 00000000	15 00000000
16 00000000	17 00000000	18 00000000	19 00000000
20 00000000	21 00000000	22 00000000	23 00000000
24 00000000	25 00000000	26 00000000	27 00000000
28 00000000	29 00000000	30 00000000	31 00000000

CPU

Instruction Register (IR):

Program Counter (PC):

Accumulator (AC):

Input/Output

Figure 5.4.6

Pencil and Paper computer before program execution.

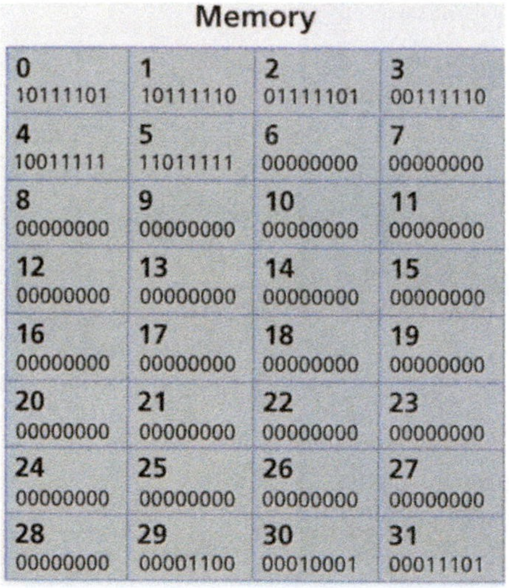

Memory

0 10111101	1 10111110	2 01111101	3 00111110
4 10011111	5 11011111	6 00000000	7 00000000
8 00000000	9 00000000	10 00000000	11 00000000
12 00000000	13 00000000	14 00000000	15 00000000
16 00000000	17 00000000	18 00000000	19 00000000
20 00000000	21 00000000	22 00000000	23 00000000
24 00000000	25 00000000	26 00000000	27 00000000
28 00000000	29 00001100	30 00010001	31 00011101

Figure 5.4.7

Pencil and Paper computer's memory after program execution.

A FINAL EXAMPLE

The Pencil and Paper computer and the sample program just discussed are nontypical because of their simplicity. Real computers have millions of memory locations rather than the 32 of our conceptual computer, and real programs, often numbering thousands of instructions, are seldom useful without the inclusion of at least one loop. So let's look at one more programming example to see how we might accommodate these two complexities of real-life computing.

Consider this problem:

Write an assembly language program for the Pencil and Paper computer that will count backward from 10 down to 1, displaying each number—10, 9, 8, . . . ,3, 2, 1—on the imaginary monitor.

A quick analysis of this problem reveals two important pieces of information that are different from what we learned in the previous example:

1. As in the earlier example (summing two numbers), the computer needs two pieces of information in order to begin. In this case, however, the values needed are the numeric constants 1 and 10, rather than two variables to be entered in from the keyboard.

2. The problem calls for a repetitive task—the display of a value from the memory several times.

Our first task is to set aside memory locations for the necessary information. In the earlier example, the programmer selected memory locations 29, 30, and 31 for the needed information, and labeled them X, Y, and Z, respectively. We were able to do this because there were so few possible locations available, and none of them were already being used by another program. In a real computer, however, tracking the use of millions of individual memory locations is daunting. Therefore, we will leave the selection of memory locations to the assembler—the program that translates assembly language instructions into binary code.

Most assembly languages allow the programmer to label positions in the memory without actually specifying where they are. You can do this by using a memory label followed by a colon to mark a position in memory. After the colon, a value can be entered to initialize the specific memory location. When the program is translated, the assembler will assign specific memory locations to each of our labels and will place the indicated values into those memory locations. See Table 5.4.5 to see how this looks in the program.

We've already noted that this new problem calls for the performance of a repetitive task—printing a number. Problems requiring repetition demand that we answer at least two questions:

- What steps must be repeated over and over again?
- How do we know when we have performed enough repetitions?

As with the ROBOT, the performance of a repetitive task is called a loop. Answering the first question will give us the body of the loop, whereas answering the second question will give us what we need to get out of the loop. Here are the steps we need to perform for each number from 10 down to 1:

1. Print out the number.
2. Place the number in the accumulator.
3. Subtract one from it.
4. Place the new number in the memory at the same place where the old number was stored.
5. Repeat step 1 until the last number has been printed.

Table 5.4.5   *The assembly language solution to the counting backward problem.*

Assembly	Language	Program	Explanation
ONE:	1		Set aside and name a memory location to hold the number 1.
COUNT:	10		Set aside and name a memory location to store the counter.
START:	PRINT	COUNT	Identify the first instruction to be executed.
	LOAD	COUNT	Place the value stored at COUNT into the accumulator.
	SUB	ONE	Subtract the value stored at ONE from the value in the accumulator. Result will be in the accumulator.
	STORE	COUNT	Place the value in the accumulator into memory location COUNT.
	PJUMP	START	If the accumulator holds a positive value, go to START and repeat instructions. If the accumulator is at or below zero, proceed to next step.
	STOP		

The statement of the problem itself provides the answer to our second question. We are told to write a program that prints out the numbers from 10 down to 1. Therefore, our loop must stop repeating after the number 1 has been printed but before the number 0 is printed. The Pencil and Paper statement that will help us accomplish this is the PJUMP command. The **PJUMP** command will allow us to keep repeating a group of instructions as long as the accumulator has a positive—above zero—value. This will remain true until we have printed the number 1. Once that has been printed, we will subtract one from it, leaving the value 0 in the accumulator. Because 0 is not a positive number, the repetition will stop, and our task is finished. Table 5.4.5 shows the complete assembly language program.

Our two conceptual computers have allowed us to study many of the important concepts of computers and computing without having to fight the complexities of large computers in the real world. The remainder of this chapter will give us a chance to compare how real computers handle numeric problems with the help of a real-life application program called an electronic spreadsheet. Then chapter 6 will help us to see how operating systems enable real-life computers to perform the tasks of our conceptual computers—and beyond.

Chapter Summary

5.1 Reviewing Key Concepts

After studying essential fundamentals of computers and computing for four chapters, a brief review focuses attention on a few important concepts before examining the process of how programs work together with computer hardware to accomplish tasks. Especially important is the realization that computers, without software—programs—can accomplish nothing at all.

5.2 Two Conceptual Computers

In order to understand the process of loading and executing computer programs, we have chosen to study two imaginary computers. Both are stored-program computers, closely related to computers commonly in use today. The advantage we gain is that the conceptual computers have been stripped of the complexities characteristic of real computers, leaving only carefully simplified essentials.

5.3 The ROBOT Computer: Programs and Algorithms

The ROBOT computer is a very simple special-purpose computer, capable of performing a narrow range of tasks. Operat-

ing only within its own domain, the ROBOT can move around its room and locate doorways and walls. It has a built-in memory with space for up to 32 eight-bit instructions. Programming the ROBOT helps us learn the following concepts: developing a general solution, writing a loop, escaping an infinite loop, using machine language, and testing a solution.

5.4 The Pencil and Paper Computer

The Pencil and Paper computer is modeled on a simplified general-purpose computer with imaginary components common to most computers. Its memory has 32 locations, each of which can store one data value or one eight-bit instruction. Pencil and Paper programs are similar to assembly language programs. Programming the Pencil and Paper computer allows us to study the parts of the central processing unit, how each functions, and how the fetch and execute cycle works.

Key Terms

Key terms introduced in this chapter:

29. Pencil and Paper computer, *121*
30. PJUMP, *142*
31. Problem, *130*
32. Program, *122*
33. Program counter (PC), *135*
34. ROBOT, *121*
35. ROBOT's domain, *123*
36. Statement, *128*
37. Stored-program computer, *123*
38. Toggle switch, *128*
39. von Neumann computer, *123*

Matching

Match the key terms introduced in the chapter to the following statements. Each term may be used once, more than once, or not at all.

1. ___ This is a collection of instructions for the computer to perform one by one.

2. ___ This term refers to all different commands that a particular computer can perform.

3. ___ This is the form in which all instructions must be before the computer can do them.

4. ___ This imaginary computing device has a place to keep information needed for computing, as well as program instructions.

5. ___ This imaginary computing device stores program instructions but has no need to store data for calculations.

6. ___ These are sequences of instructions that are repeated one or more times when a program is executed.

7. ___ This is a step-by-step process used to solve a problem.

8. ___ This command enables the ROBOT to continue after leaving a loop.

9. ___ This is a situation in which a group of instructions is repeated over and over with no way of stopping it.

10. ___ This should be simple. It should solve the stated problem in all situations.

11. ___ This command allows the Pencil and Paper computer to get out of a loop.

12. ___ This term refers to the way a computer gets a command, executes it, and then gets the next command.

13. ___ This part of the CPU deciphers the meaning of an instruction and then sets up the circuits needed to perform that instruction.

14. ___ This part of the computer contains the control unit and the arithmetic unit.

15. ___ These allow the computer to communicate with things outside itself.

16. ___ This is the term used to describe the environment in which the ROBOT can function.

17. ___ This part of the CPU stores the address of the next instruction to be executed.

18. ___ This historical term is used to identify English-like mnemonic forms of instructions.

19. ___ This program's function is to get a program into the memory of the computer so that it can be executed.

20. ___ The results of computations are placed in this part of the CPU.

True or False

Place either T or F on the line provided with each of the following statements. If a statement is false, you should be able to explain what changes would make it true.

1. ___ Machine language programs need to be translated into binary before the computer can execute them.

2. ___ The ROBOT is limited to 32 instructions in a single program.

3. ___ The ROBOT is limited to understanding only eight different commands.

4. ___ A ROBOT instruction has four fields: operation code, opcode, argument, and operand.

5. ___ The first three bits of a ROBOT instruction correspond to the operation code.

6. ___ The last five bits of a ROBOT instruction correspond to the operand.

7. ___ ROBOT instructions are performed in a top-down fashion, never going out of order unless directed otherwise by a GOTO command.

8. ___ The ROBOT is a simplified example of a general-purpose computer.

9. ___ Computer hardware alone enables the computer to perform a number of different tasks.

10. ___ In a ROBOT set of instructions, every GOTO command signifies a loop.

11. ___ The Pencil and Paper computer is a simplified example of a general-purpose computer.

12. ___ When an instruction is to be executed by the CPU, the CPU removes the instruction from memory (clearing that instruction from memory) and places it into the instruction register.

13. ___ The Pencil and Paper PRINT command prints the value currently in the accumulator on the imaginary monitor.

14. ____ Assembly language programs need to be translated into binary before the computer can execute them.

15. ____ Current general-purpose computers can do nothing at all without software programs to control them.

16. ____ In a Pencil and Paper program, only the computer can define where data are stored.

17. ____ In a Pencil and Paper program, the addition or subtraction of values takes place in memory, where those values are stored.

18. ____ When a value is moved from the Pencil and Paper computer's memory into the accumulator, the memory location is left empty until another value is placed there.

19. ____ The control unit keeps a copy of the instruction that is to be performed next.

20. ____ To speed up very involved scientific calculations, a second processing chip, called a math coprocessor, is sometimes added to a computer running an electronic spreadsheet program.

21. ____ Let's assume that the contents of memory location 15 has the value of 3. Let's also assume that the accumulator has the value of 6. In the instruction ADD 15, the value 15 is added to the contents of the accumuator.

Multiple Choice

Answer the multiple-choice questions by selecting the best answer from the choices given.

1. Another name for opcode is
   a. Optical codifier
   b. Operation code
   c. Operand code
   d. Optional code
   e. Optimal instruction set code

2. Stored-program computers are also commonly called
   a. Pascal computers after Blaise Pascal
   b. Ada computers after Ada Lovelace
   c. Von Neumann–type computers after John von Neumann
   d. Hollerith computers after Herman Hollerith
   e. Babbage computers after Charles Babbage

3. This is a step-by-step process used to solve a problem. It should be a general solution able to solve the problem in all situations.
   a. Program
   b. Problem
   c. Algorithm
   d. Loop
   e. Infinite loop

4. This sequence of instructions repeats a section of a program in a way that was intended by the programmer.
   a. Program
   b. Problem
   c. Algorithm
   d. Loop
   e. Infinite loop

5. This sequence of instructions repeats a section of a program in a way that was probably not intended by the programmer. Intervention is necessary to stop this process of repetition.
   a. Program
   b. Problem
   c. Algorithm
   d. Loop
   e. Infinite loop

6. This part of the CPU has a place where the result of each computation is placed. What is the name of this place?
   a. Control unit
   b. Accumulator
   c. Instruction register
   d. Program counter
   e. Instruction decoding unit

7. This part of the control unit is where an instruction is placed for analysis by the instruction decoding unit.
   a. Arithmetic unit
   b. Accumulator
   c. Instruction register
   d. Program counter
   e. Memory

8. This part of the control unit contains the address of where the next instruction to be executed resides.
   a. Arithmetic unit
   b. Accumulator
   c. Instruction register
   d. Program counter
   e. Instruction fetching unit

9. When executing a program, the CPU of the computer identifies which instruction is to be performed, gets the next instruction to be performed, decodes the instruction, performs calculations if necessary, and executes the instruction. The process is then repeated until the program is finished. This name of this process is the
   a. Fetch and execute cycle
   b. Nondestructive reading cycle
   c. Analyzing cycle
   d. CPU cycle
   e. There is really no name for this process. It is just done by the CPU.

Exercises

ROBOT

All the ROBOT exercises assume that there are no doors in the corners of the room. Note also that the size of the room is unknown. Another important fact is that the ROBOT may or may not be facing an open doorway. The asterisk (*) indicates the ROBOT is not initially facing an open doorway.

1. Design an algorithm and then write a program that will cause the ROBOT to find the wall it is initially facing and stop one step away from it, facing it with arms raised.*

2. Design an algorithm and then write a program that will cause the ROBOT to find the wall it is initially facing and end up facing away from the wall with its arms lowered and its back against the wall.*

3. Design an algorithm and then write a program to make the ROBOT take a step. You will probably conclude that this problem is logically impossible under one circumstance. What is it?*

4. **PUZZLER** Design an algorithm and then write a program that has the ROBOT locate any corner of the room and stop there with its arms lowered. Unlike Problem 2 in the text, have the ROBOT move toward the corner with the wall on its right side. This means when viewed from overhead, the ROBOT is moving counterclockwise.*

5. Have the ROBOT locate a door, not knowing which wall the door is on. Make sure your ROBOT stops without going through the door. Don't use the SENSE command at the beginning.*

6. Repeat Exercise 4, using the 100 opcode (SENSE).*

7. Have the ROBOT find any wall and stop facing the wall against it. However, the ROBOT may or may not initially be facing a open doorway. Assume there are no doors located in any corners of the room. Also assume that each doorway has corners and the ROBOT may go one step through the doorway. (Hint: A search pattern must be developed around each square.)

8. Have the ROBOT find a door in any wall; however, the ROBOT may or may not initially be facing a open doorway. Assume there are no doors located in any corners of the room. Also assume that each doorway has corners and the ROBOT may go one step through the doorway. (Hint: A search pattern must be developed around each square.)

9. What is the difference in effect (if any) between the instructions 00000000 and 00011111?

10. Why are the ROBOT's memory locations numbered starting from 0 instead of from 1?

11. What is a field? How many fields are there in a ROBOT instruction?

12. What are the names of the fields in a ROBOT instruction? How many bits are used in each field?

13. How many memory locations could the ROBOT use if the address field were six bits long?

14. How many instructions could the ROBOT have if its opcode were four bits rather than three bits long?

15. Why do we refer to the ROBOT as a stored-program computer?

16. Why can't we program the ROBOT using the English words that stand for the instructions (STEP, SENSE, RAISE, LOWER, and so on)? Is it nonetheless valid to think in terms of the words when solving ROBOT problems? To what extent and in what way?

Pencil and Paper Computer

Unless otherwise indicated, each of the following problems assumes the program will be loaded starting at memory location 0.

1. Design an algorithm and then write a Pencil and Paper computer program that adds two numbers, which are already located in memory locations 20 and 21, and then prints out their sum.

2. Design an algorithm and then write a Pencil and Paper computer program that prints the numbers from 10 down to 1. Use only one PRINT command. This means you must use a loop.

3. Design an algorithm and then write a Pencil and Paper computer program that prints the numbers from 1 to 10. Use only one PRINT command. This means you must use a loop.

4. Do exercise 3, but make the necessary changes assuming the program is to be loaded starting at location 9.

5. Design an algorithm and then write a Pencil and Paper computer program that prints the numbers from N down to 1, where N is input from the keyboard using the READ command.

6. Design an algorithm and then write a Pencil and Paper computer program that prints the numbers from 1 to N, where N is input from the keyboard using the READ command.

7. **PUZZLER** Design an algorithm and then write a Pencil and Paper computer program that prints the numbers from N to M, where both N and M are input from the keyboard using the READ command. Assume that M is greater than N.

8. **PUZZLER** Design an algorithm and then write a Pencil and Paper computer program that adds all the counting numbers starting with 20 and going down to 1. Hint: Start at 20 and count down to 1.

9. **PUZZLER** Design an algorithm and then write a Pencil and Paper computer program that adds all the counting numbers starting with 1 and going to 20. Print out only the final total. Hint: Start with 1 and count up to 20.

Discussion Questions

1. Why should algorithms be general?

2. What would happen to the computer industry if the world ran out of silicon?

3. Arrange the following in an order that makes sense and discuss why each precedes the next.

a. Write the program.
b. Debug the program (find errors).
c. Analyze the problem.
d. Devise an algorithm.

Group Project

Suppose we could enlarge the configuration for instructions for both the ROBOT and the Pencil and Paper computer, so that instead of each instruction being limited to 8 binary digits, each could occupy 12 binary digits. This would allow a 4-digit opcode and an 8-digit operand.

➡ What is the maximum number of memory locations the operand could address?

➡ What is the maximum number of different commands that could be included in the instruction set?

➡ What commands would you add to the instruction set of either computer, now that you have the capacity for more?

➡ How would the addition of these commands change the capabilities of either of these computers?

➡ Once you have designed the new instruction sets, write a program to perform a task that was impossible when there were only 8 opcodes but is now possible with the increased selection of commands.

Web Exercises

1. Computerized robots, more or less related to the conceptual ROBOT studied in this chapter, have been used in many ways and in many areas of endeavor. Browse the Web and see if you can find articles and descriptions of robots used in some of the following areas: art, automotive manufacture, medical research, safety research, entertainment, assistance for people with physical disabilities, education, literature, simulations, and warfare. For each one you find, paste its Web address into a word-processing document, and write a brief summary describing the site. You can add pictures, if you wish, as long as you are sure to cite the Web address of the source.

2. How many different tools for performing mathematical tasks can you find on the Web? For example, can you find an abacus, a calculator, a slide rule, a decimal-to-metric converter, a miles-to-kilometers converter, a program for calculating mortgage and loan interest, a budget-builder, and so on? For each one you find, paste its Web address into a word-processing document and write a brief summary describing the site. You can add pictures, if you wish, as long as you are sure to cite the Web address of the source.

Bibliography

Goldberg, Ken, ed. *The Robot in the Garden: Telerobotics and Telepistemology in the Age of the Internet.* Cambridge, MA: MIT Press, 2000.

   This book examines how remotely operated machines affect our beliefs and interactions with each other and the environment.

Hillis, W. Daniel. *The Connection Machine.* Cambridge, MA: MIT Press, 1989.

   In this book, the author puzzles over the nature of information and the mechanisms by which information is put to use.

Hillis, W. Daniel. *The Pattern on the Stone: The Simple Ideas That Make Computers Work* (Science Masters Series). New York: Basic Books, 1998.

   This glorious book simply and elegantly reveals the nature of logical machines.

Lunt, Karl. *Build Your Own Robot!* London: A. K. Peters, 2000.

   This book provides rare coverage of all the basics involved in building a robot.

Macrae, Norman. *John von Neumann.* New York: Pantheon Books, 1992.

This book gives a detailed biography of John von Neumann.

Raucci, Richard. *Personal Robotics: Real Robots to Construct, Program, and Explore the World.* London: A. K. Peters, 1999.

Step-by-step instructions to build and program a robot, starting from scratch.

Reader's Digest. *How to Do Just about Anything on a Computer.* Pleasantville, NY: Reader's Digest, 2000.

This book teaches computer novices that they need to know, assuming absolutely no knowledge of computer technology on the part of the reader.

White, Ron. *How Computers Work: Millennium Edition.* New York: Macmillan, 1999.

This book demystifies the PC-CPU, drives, printers, mouse—every component—with down-to-earth, step-by-step descriptions and exceptional illustrations.

Wise, Edwin. *Applied Robotics.* Indianapolis, IN: Howard W. Sams, 1999.

This starts with the basics and moves into more advanced and interesting robot behaviors.

chapter 6

Operating Systems:
The Genie in the Computer

TimeLine

Chapter Objectives

- Appreciate why an operating system is necessary in today's computers.

- Describe how the process of booting a computer affects the operating system.

- Identify the types of duties performed by an operating system.

- Recognize the difference between a warm boot and a cold boot.

- Know the difference between a command-line user interface and a graphical user interface.

- Appreciate the advantages of a hierarchical file system over a flat file system.

- Understand why files from one type of machine won't always work on another type of machine.

- Discern the difference between cache memory and virtual memory.

- Recognize how context switching is used in conjunction with multiprogramming.

- Appreciate how distributed processing makes networks efficiently use computing power and memory.

Ron Chapple/FPG International LLC

Common everyday problems in computing come in many forms. Those problems regarding the operating system and how application programs use the operating system can often be solved when the user has some knowledge of what the operating system is and what it does. See if you can solve the following problems. The answers can be found or derived using the material from this chapter.

PUZZLER

- **Problem 1.** It's 2 A.M., you have a 20-page paper due tomorrow, and your printer isn't working. What do you do? Someone down the hall has a computer system; he's still awake and offers to help. But he uses a different word processor and it doesn't recognize your word-processing file. There are three things that you can quickly try. What are they?

- **Problem 2.** You notice your program is running abnormally slow, or a message on the screen indicates there is not enough memory to run a program. What can you do?

6.1 What Is an Operating System?

In the earlier chapters, we discussed how computers work and the nature of information. We'll now review how a computer is controlled. For a computer to run a particular program, many tasks must be performed, ranging from simple tasks such as loading the program into RAM or printing a document to complex ongoing tasks such as virtual memory management. These topics will be discussed later in the chapter.

The operating system is a collection of programs that manages and controls applications and other software, and coordinates the various hardware components to perform tasks requested by the user.

The program that takes care of these details is called the **operating system.** If you understand how the operating system functions, it will make it easier for you to know how to communicate with the computer. As the definition of the operating system indicates, many parts of it act as a helper to anyone using the computer. On most computers, the operating system resides on the hard drive when the computer is off, and then on starting up the computer, a copy of the operating system is transferred to the RAM.

COMPUTERS WITHOUT OPERATING SYSTEMS

Before getting into the details of an operating system, let's look at how a computer would be used without one. A good example of a computer without an operating system is one of the first microcomputers. Introduced in 1975, the **Altair 8800** was a personal computer without an operating system. Figure 6.1.1 reveals the many switches where information had to be entered to control the use of this computer. These switches were necessary to enter information directly into RAM (nonpermanent memory). The lights let the person using the computer know what was going on inside. The first thing that the computer user had to do was to "fat finger" a program into the RAM. This means that a program had to be entered by flipping the switches, up for a 1 and down for a 0. This was difficult to do even with small fingers because the switches were close together, hence the expression "**fat fingering**" a program.

The very first program loaded into the Altair allowed a larger program to be read into RAM from a paper tape reader. This larger program usually allowed the use of a keyboard. In fact, until the larger program read from paper tape was in the computer's RAM and running, the keyboard was unusable. Once the keyboard was active, it could be used to read in a still larger program, which could be something such as the **BASIC** language system. Then programs written in BASIC could be run. This whole process could take up to 30 minutes, depending on whether the paper tape reader was accurate or had a misread. A misread means that somehow errors were present, so the process had to be started over.

The BIOS (basic input/output system) is a collection of programs that has the capability of communicating with peripheral devices such as keyboards, disk drives, printers, display/monitor, and other I/O devices. However, the most important task it performs is to load the operating system into RAM and turn control of the computer over to it.

BIOS (BASIC INPUT/OUTPUT SYSTEM)

Today's personal computers have a relatively small, unchangeable part of the operating system in the ROM. In the Macintosh and Windows systems, this permanent part of the operating system is often called the **BIOS** (basic input/output system). Because the ROM is permanent

Figure 6.1.1

The Altair 8800 hobbyist computer.

Christopher Lauckner/PERTEC

memory, its contents don't disappear when the power is turned off. The ROM typically contains the BIOS programs that allow use of the keyboard and both floppy and hard disks. The process of starting up a modern personal computer activates the BIOS programs in ROM; they immediately search for the rest of the operating system, usually on the computer's hard drive. If no operating system is found, the personal computer will not function.

As stated in the definition, an operating system consists of a collection of programs that helps you communicate with the computer's hardware. It not only makes a computer easier to use, but it also allows the computer to run efficiently. It acts like a smart proactive assistant that moves information around the computer and performs other odd jobs as needed. Here's a partial list of the numerous activities that the operating system performs:

- Using the keyboard
- Using the mouse
- Printing to a printer
- Choosing different printers on a network
- Starting up programs
- Changing colors on the screen
- Using modems for communications
- Managing the files of the computer
- Finding things for the user
- Allowing more than one program to be open at the same time
- Allowing more than one program to run simultaneously (such as printing while still doing word processing)
- Formatting secondary storage devices
- Burning CDs and DVDs
- Loading programs into RAM so they can perform

This fundamental idea of controlling the computer system using programs rather than a human is an important point to understand. The operating system is the traffic cop of the computer. Depending on the context, it has also had many different names. In earlier years, synonyms used for the operating system were *monitor, supervisor,* and *executive.* Now operating systems are referred to by their commercial names or simply called the *operating system.* Some common operating systems you may have heard about are Windows XP, Windows Vista, Mac OS X, UNIX, Linux, and MS-DOS.

To understand more fully what an operating system does, we will begin with booting up a computer, which is the starting place for all the things a computer does.

6.2 Booting the Computer

Booting up a computer means that a program in the permanent ROM is loading the operating system into RAM from a secondary storage device, such as a hard drive. Booting up a computer is the start-up of a computer or getting the computer ready to do useful work.

Among the reasons why the Altair computer previously discussed was not too useful included the fact that it lacked permanent memory or ROM, and it had no secondary storage devices such as a hard drive. But even more important was the lack of a program to assist in running the computer. It was difficult for the user to manage the computer without help. In fact, the user had to know where every program was in memory so he or she could tell the computer where to go to run it. It was a tedious process.

If the computer is already running, **rebooting** is the term used to indicate starting up a computer that was already turned on. There are two different ways to perform a reboot: cold boot and warm boot.

Booting up a computer is the process of automatically running a program located in ROM, which in turn loads the operating system into RAM and leaves the operating system in control.

COLD BOOT

The **cold boot** of a computer is booting up when the power to the computer is originally off.

If the power is off, starting the computer is called a **cold boot.** This term makes sense when you realize the computer is cool when off. When the computer is on, it is warm from the hot electronics.

In the case of the cold boot, when the power is turned on, a stripped-down miniature operating system in ROM (permanent memory) looks for the rest of the operating system. After finding it, the stripped-down operating system loads the remaining part of the operating system into RAM.

WARM BOOT

The **warm boot** of a computer is booting up when the power to the computer is originally on, and a command is given to put a fresh copy of the operating system into RAM.

On the other hand, a **warm boot** is used when the computer has the power on with the disk drive spinning. For the warm boot, a restart command must be given to the part of the operating system that is in ROM. The warm boot doesn't shut off the power. You can perform a warm boot by holding down a combination of keys simultaneously (such as Alt + Ctrl + Delete). The hard disk keeps spinning, and the power supply is still operating. The warm boot reloads a fresh copy of the operating system into RAM and allows the user to begin again but without turning off the power to the disk or power supply. It is used when something may have accidentally altered the operating system or maybe a defect in the operating system was encountered, each of which would cause problems. Many other factors can also cause the operating system to cease functioning, including memory fragmentation, bad memory chips, and defects in application programs. In fact, sometimes the computer just locks up for no apparent reason, and it is impossible to communicate with the operating system. This is the ideal occasion to use the warm boot.

Why is it important to know about the difference between a cold and warm boot? This may seem like one more nitpicking computer detail. In fact, users who switch their computers off and quickly on again run the risk of doing damage to their computer. How can this be? Power surges can actually damage the power supply electronics, which are expensive to replace. Therefore, be sure to leave the power off for at least a couple of seconds before you power back up.

Diagnostic programs look for problems in the computer and its peripheral hardware. They serve the same function as a physician does when giving a physical examination. In this case, the patient is the computer.

When a computer is booted up, a set of **diagnostic programs** in the ROM is run. Before the operating system is brought into the RAM, these diagnostics check the RAM, video card, the bus, and any other cards that may be in the computer. The user is alerted to any problems that may be present. However, the diagnostic programs don't check everything. Programs that do additional checking can be purchased.

BOOTING WITH MULTIPLE OPERATING SYSTEMS

It is sometimes desirable to have more than one operating system on a computer. This is because certain programs may run only under a particular operating system. The situation could arise in which your company computer runs one operating system, and you need to sometimes work at home. Yet, the operating system on your home personal computer is different from that of the company, and your home software may not be compatible with the company's software. Having both operating systems on the same computer would solve the problem.

Another common situation occurs because older Windows or Macintosh OS programs won't run under the latest Windows operating system. This means it is very important to understand which software upgrades may be necessary when you start using another operating system. To alleviate this problem, there are utility programs that will check your computer system for any hardware or software that is incompatible with an operating system you would like to use.

Any time a change from one operating system to another is made, it is important to have a way to get back to your original operating system. This can be done by making an identical copy of data and programs on the hard drive, which can be used to restore the previous system.

Figure 6.2.1 shows the process of setting up a computer with two different operating systems. This is especially valuable for those who like to try out an operating system over a long period of time without permanently committing to it. The **Windows** operating system,

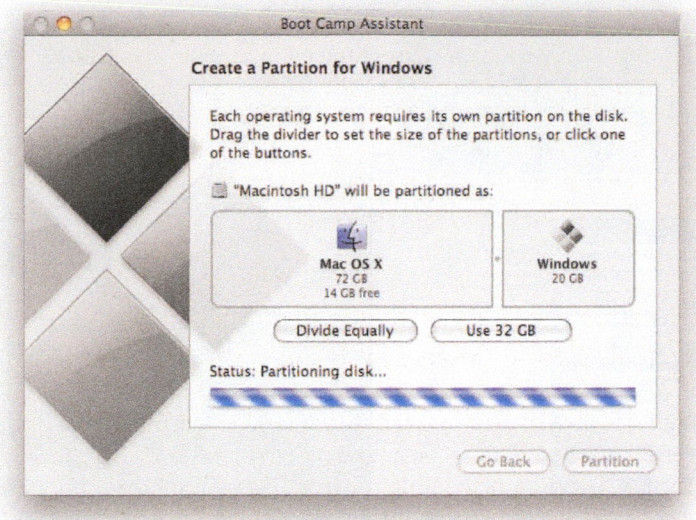

Reprinted by permission of VMware, Inc.

Figure 6.2.1

The partition decision in the process of installing windows on a Macintosh using "Boot camp."

for example, could be tested out on the same computer running Macintosh OS X through a technique called partitioning. **Partitioning** the hard drive can be thought of as dividing a hard drive so that it appears to the computer to be two separate hard drives. At boot-up time the computer can be set to automatically boot up from a certain partition with a particular operating system. More sophisticated systems let you make the selection of the desired operating system at the time of booting up. This partitioning process is done with software and no physical changes are made to the hard drive. The utility software that does this partitioning is commonly available for most operating systems.

There are many details involved in partitioning and putting multiple operating systems on the same computer. One of the more complex issues involves the way information is organized on the hard drive. Different operating systems use differing filing systems. If file organization is not recognized, then the partitioning will not work.

Although partitioning seems to be a rather advanced concept, it is sometimes necessary and not difficult when using the proper software tools or utility programs. It also has the advantage of efficiency, especially in the case of very large hard drives. Password security can also protect certain partitions and still allow the use of the computer by authorized personnel.

The **partitioning** of a hard drive is the process of separating the hard drive into independent partitions, which individually act as though they are separate hard drives.

6.3 User Interfaces

The **user interface** is the part of the operating system that the computer user sees and interacts with. The two basic kinds of operating system interfaces are called command line and **graphical user interface (GUI).**

THE GRAPHICAL USER INTERFACE (GUI)

Figure 6.3.1 illustrates a typical view of the Windows XP GUI. A mouse controls the access to various menus and window activity. The Macintosh GUI, first introduced in 1984, has gone through several revisions. Figure 6.3.2 shows Mac OS X version 10.5 with the same folder opened in three different views. On the left side is the "dock" that allows quick access to applications, such as iTunes and MS-Word. Note the cursor is on iTunes and is magnified for easy selection. The **version number** indicates the version of the operating system software being used. It is important to know the version of the operating system because programs such as word processors, spreadsheets, and others are written for a particular version of the operating system. These programs make use of some of the hundreds of parts of the operating system to function properly. Of course, this means if you upgrade

The **graphical user interface** or **GUI** (pronounced goo-ee) is an operating system interface in which commands are usually given through a mouse. The mouse is used to move a pointer on the screen to point at an icon (a small picture representing things or commands). Commands to the operating system are given by clicking the mouse's button while the pointer on the screen is over the desired icon.

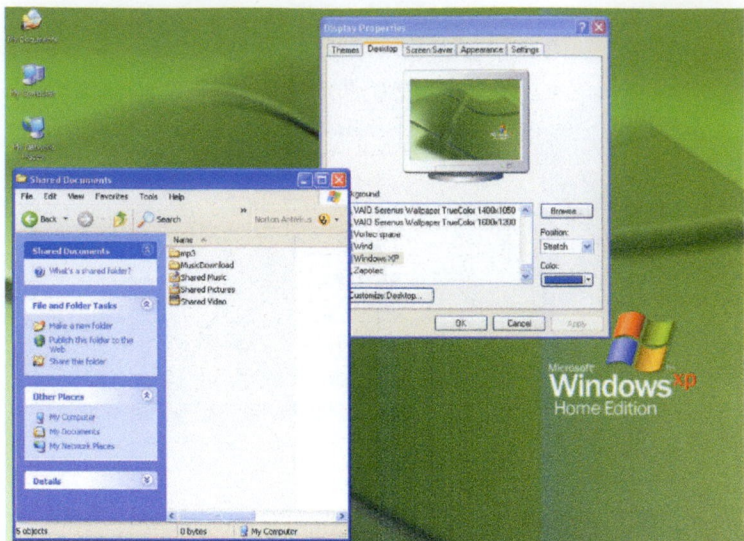

Screen shot reprinted by permission from Microsoft Corporation

Figure 6.3.1

Typical view of a Windows XP graphical user interface.

The **version number** of a program is an identification number given to a program to indicate in a precise way the variant of the program being considered. Programs also have the release and modification numbers that give even more specific information about the program variant.

your operating system to a newer version, your programs might not work. When buying software, such as word processors or even games, it is important to know under which version of the operating system it was designed to run. This is particularly important if you are running an operating system such as Linux because many of the most common applications cannot run under the Linux operating system. Figure 6.3.3 shows the Gnome GUI for Linux.

In a GUI-type interface, you can see graphical images (such as a small icon or picture representing the disk and another icon representing an English paper) on the screen of the computer. To copy the English paper onto the floppy disk, you simply use the mouse to move the pointer over the icon of the English paper and hold the mouse button down while moving the mouse, until the icon of the paper is over the icon of the disk. If you release the mouse button at this point, the GUI operating system automatically makes a copy of the

Figure 6.3.2

View of Macintosh desktop running under Mac OS X.

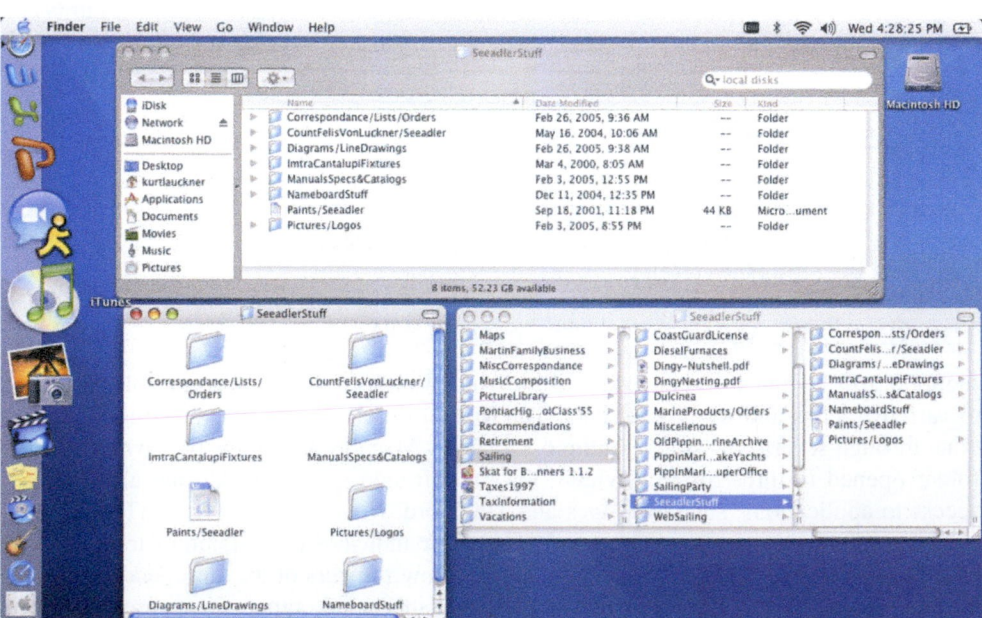

Screen shot from Macintosh OSX version 10.5

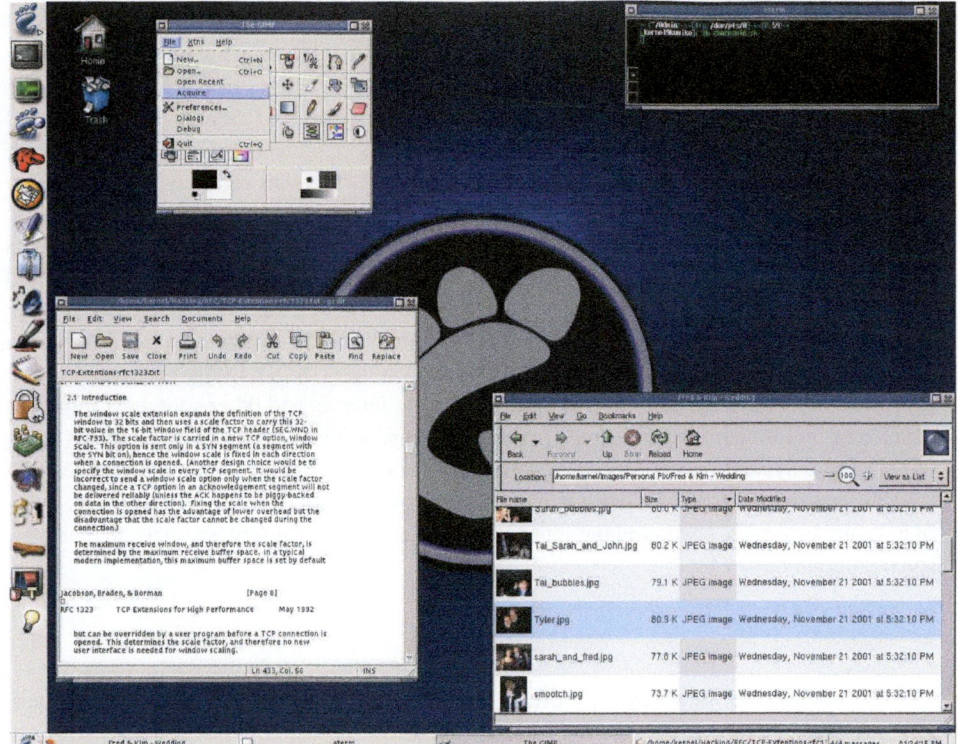

Source http://shots.odir.com/slideshow.php?release=276&slide=15

Figure 6.3.3

A view of a Linux graphical user interface called Gnome.

English paper and places it on the floppy disk. The process is sometimes referred to as **drag and drop.**

COMMAND-LINE INTERFACE

A common **command-line interface** is the older MS-DOS. Command-line interfaces take time to learn because they are not intuitive. For example, suppose you want to copy an English paper you wrote onto a floppy disk so that you can work on it at home. To do this, you must know the name of the disk drive on which it currently resides (such as drive C) and that of the disk drive in which your floppy resides (such as drive A). The command line that you type is

copy C:Paper A:

This command assumes you know whether to type "C:Paper" or "A:" first after the word *copy.* Also, accidental extra spaces could make this command unintelligible to the operating system. Command-line interfaces are not very intuitive.

Intuition is very important to make computers easier to use and to prevent serious errors. The concept is referred to as being **user friendly.** An illustration of the user-friendly concept is found in the completely different field of weather reporting. Do you immediately know what is meant by *tornado watch* and *tornado warning* as used by the U.S. Weather Service? Every time these terms are used on the radio, the announcer has to define them. More user-friendly terms might be *tornado possible* and *tornado sighted.* These terms need no explanation; they are self-defining. Careful crafting can result in intuitive and user-friendly computer operating system interfaces.

UNIX AND LINUX

A large number of professional high-powered computer users in business, science, engineering, and networking choose the **UNIX** operating system for their computers. Its popularity is due to its flexibility in doing computing jobs and the fact that it is extremely well

In a GUI, the process of dragging one icon over the top of another and releasing the mouse button is called **drag and drop.**

The **command-line interface** is one in which communications are given to the computer by typing commands on the keyboard.

UNIX—Operating System of Choice for Professionals

UNIX is one of the most influential operating systems in the history of computer science. It was created along with the language C by Ken Thompson and Dennis Ritchie at Bell Laboratories more than three decades ago. It is a much more powerful and flexible operating system than most personal computer operating systems. UNIX was certainly instrumental in the development of the Internet and is also the operating system of choice for many academic computer scientists. One of the major reasons for this is the vast number of software tools that have been developed for UNIX. Included in this list is X Window, which is a GUI and networking interface to UNIX.

 Some versions of UNIX do run on personal computers. One such example is Linux, a UNIX-compatible operating system (that is, it acts just like UNIX). Linux is free and represents the zenith in free software. It is available on the Internet and other sources. Linux was developed by Finnish student Linus Torvalds. Because it doesn't directly contain any parts of the UNIX system (all of Linux is original, written by Torvalds, and only behaves like UNIX), this means Torvalds had complete control over it and decided to give Linux away free. Linux is quickly becoming the standard operating system for professionals on their personal computers.

written. It doesn't fail or crash very often. Even more compelling, some versions, such as Linux, are free.

 The UNIX operating system can have either a command-line or GUI type of user interface. However, it has its roots in the command-line type of user interface. Popular and historic command-line interfaces to UNIX include these:

- Korn shell
- C shell
- Bourne shell
- Bourne-again shell

The word **shell** is another way of describing the interface between the user and the computer.

 An example of a GUI (graphical user interface) to UNIX is called X Window. X Window was designed with networking in mind. However, most UNIX users use it as a GUI to UNIX. It is much easier to use than the command-line version of UNIX.

 The Linux operating system can be used with both command-line and graphical user interfaces. It should be noted that Linux is free and the original program is available, which means that anyone can make changes to suit his or her computing needs. This is called **open-source software** and has been a great success with Linux. It has resulted in the two popular GUIs called Gnome and KDE. Each of these GUIs is similar to Windows and the Macintosh OS. Figure 6.3.4 shows the home Web page for Linux.

 Operating systems of the future will be more powerful but easier to use than current operating systems. Eventually, special intelligent programs called **agents** will most likely assist the user. It would be like having a human expert sitting with you and telling you what to do. For example, suppose you want to write a letter to your mother. All you might have to do is tell the agent you want to write a letter to Mom. The agent will find the word processor, open it, save as you write, and do all the chores that you normally have to do when communicating with the operating system. Intelligent agents will be discussed in a later chapter.

Open-source software means that the program has copies of the original source code available so that changes can be made. This is in contrast to most software, such as word processors, in which only the translated version of the program is available. Changes to this translated software are almost impossible.

6.4 Files and File Management

A **file** is a collection of data that is treated as a single unit and is referred to by its file name.

The word **file** is the name given to any program or chunk of data that is stored on floppy disk, hard disk, CD-ROM, or other storage medium. There are two distinct and very different areas to the subject of files and file management. The one area most computer users are

Figure 6.3.4

Web page for the Linux operating system.

familiar with is the graphical file system interface found in GUI operating systems. It is designed to make managing your computer files easier.

Underneath any file interface is a very different file system used by the operating system to manage the files internally. For the vast majority of computer users, knowledge of this internal or invisible file system is necessary only if they are going to partition hard disks and install two different operating systems that may not have compatible formats for the internal file structure. Acronyms such as FAT16 (File Allocation Table), FAT 32, or NTFS (NT File System) refer to these hidden file systems that we will not discuss. As a computer user, you need only be concerned with the file system interface because that is what you must deal with directly.

NAMING FILES

Both serious work and just playing games demand an understanding of where things are kept and how to save material. A letter to Mom or Dad, for example, can be saved as a file and is usually given a name by the user that suggests what it is. Examples of file names that might be used are:

- MomDadLetter
- LetterHome10-2-00
- Letter#1Home
- MomDad11-6-00
- MomDad#1
- Home11-6

In the early days, some operating systems of personal computers allowed only eight-letter names. The modern operating systems allow the user to name a file with as many as 256 letters. This means that a complete description of the file can be contained in its name. It is very important to name files with names that tell what they contain.

Historically in the older MS-DOS world, which has a command-line user interface, the file can't have the name *SandyLetter12-1-00*. The file names are restricted to eight characters, so the actual names shown would have to be changed. By changing *SandyLetter12-1-00* to SandyDec and eliminating any back slashes, the user could access the letter by typing

C: /MyDisk/Correspondence/Friends/SandyDec

This seems rather clumsy and difficult compared to the Windows and Macintosh computers, where it is only necessary to visually locate the file by using the mouse and clicking.

The **extension** or **file name extension** is the ending of a file's name, and it is usually three letters appearing after a period. It identifies what type of data makes up a file and, often, what program created it.

Another feature of file names is called the **extension,** or more properly the **file name extension.** The extension is added to the file name but separated from a three-letter extension by a period. The file extension helps the operating system identify the type of file. For example, if the letter to Sandy was in MS-Word, then the usual extension to Word files is DOC. So the file name would become SandyDec.DOC. In more modern operating systems the complete name SandyLetter12-1-96.DOC would be used. Incidentally, DOC is an abbreviation for document. Common file extension names are listed in Table 6.4.1.

Table 6.4.1   *Common file extension names.*

doc	Microsoft Word
rtf	Rich Text Format MS Word
xls	Microsoft Excel
jpg	Joint Photographers Expert Group file
gif	Graphics Interchange Format WWW
pict	Macintosh bit-mapped image
mov	Quick Time movie
aif	Audio file for Mac, Windows, UNIX
wav	Default audio standard for Windows

THE HIERARCHICAL FILE STRUCTURE

In the early years of computing, computers didn't have many files to organize. They were selected by the user from a simple list. This was referred to as a **flat file structure.** It is inadequate for today's computing needs. It was quickly replaced by the **hierarchical file structure.**

A **flat file structure** is a filing system that organizes files in one list, usually in date or alphabetical order. It is not subdivided in any way, and access to the list must be obtained by looking at the complete list.

A simple example will illustrate why the flat file system is no longer in use. Suppose that you have more than a thousand different files on your computer, which consist of various documents such as correspondence home, school papers, a résumé, budgets, and so on. In a flat filing structure, these items would all be stored in a single list of a thousand file names. This means that when one of them is needed, the list of more than a thousand items must be scanned by the user and identified. If 32 lines were visible at one time on the screen of the computer, viewing all 1,000 items would take 32 screens full of names. This was certainly not satisfactory, and it led to a much more efficient way to organize the files on a computer—a hierarchical file structure.

A **hierarchical file structure** is a filing system that organizes files in a treelike structure or hierarchy. Finding a file involves starting at the root or beginning of the structure and following a path through the hierarchy group by group until the file is found.

The hierarchical file structure organizes files into groupings. For example, let's suppose a student has a floppy disk to store school and home information. All correspondence home could be put together under a single named grouping, commonly referred to as **folders** or **file folders,** such as LettersHome. Then any budget items could be grouped and named as BudgetStuff. Groupings can also be made within groupings. For example, suppose papers and homework from several courses are stored in files on the computer. The diagram in Figure 6.4.1 shows how these files could be organized.

In Figure 6.4.1 there are 23 files, all of which are listed below the blue boxes. The boxed items represent the hierarchy of the data. In this particular case, the files are stored on a hard disk drive called HardDisk. Then on this HardDisk are created three major subdivisions to store files, namely: Correspondence, JobSearch, and School. Under Correspondence and School categories, further subdivisions are made, but under JobSearch, the four files are stored with no further subdividing of the hierarchy. Locating the desired file on HardDisk organized in this manner is easy and logical. When many files are saved, organizing files in this hierarchical structure is absolutely necessary. Most hard drives of serious computer users have several thousand files organized in this manner. It is also very important to choose names for both files and the folders that tell exactly what they contain.

A **folder** or **file folder** is a grouping of files or other folders under a single name. It is analogous to the office file folder that contains several files related to the name on the label.

Working with files in a graphical user interface is much simpler and more intuitive than with a command-line interface. In fact, locating the Budgets folder in Windows is done by opening HardDisk and visually selecting Budgets from the list in the window as shown in Figure 6.4.2.

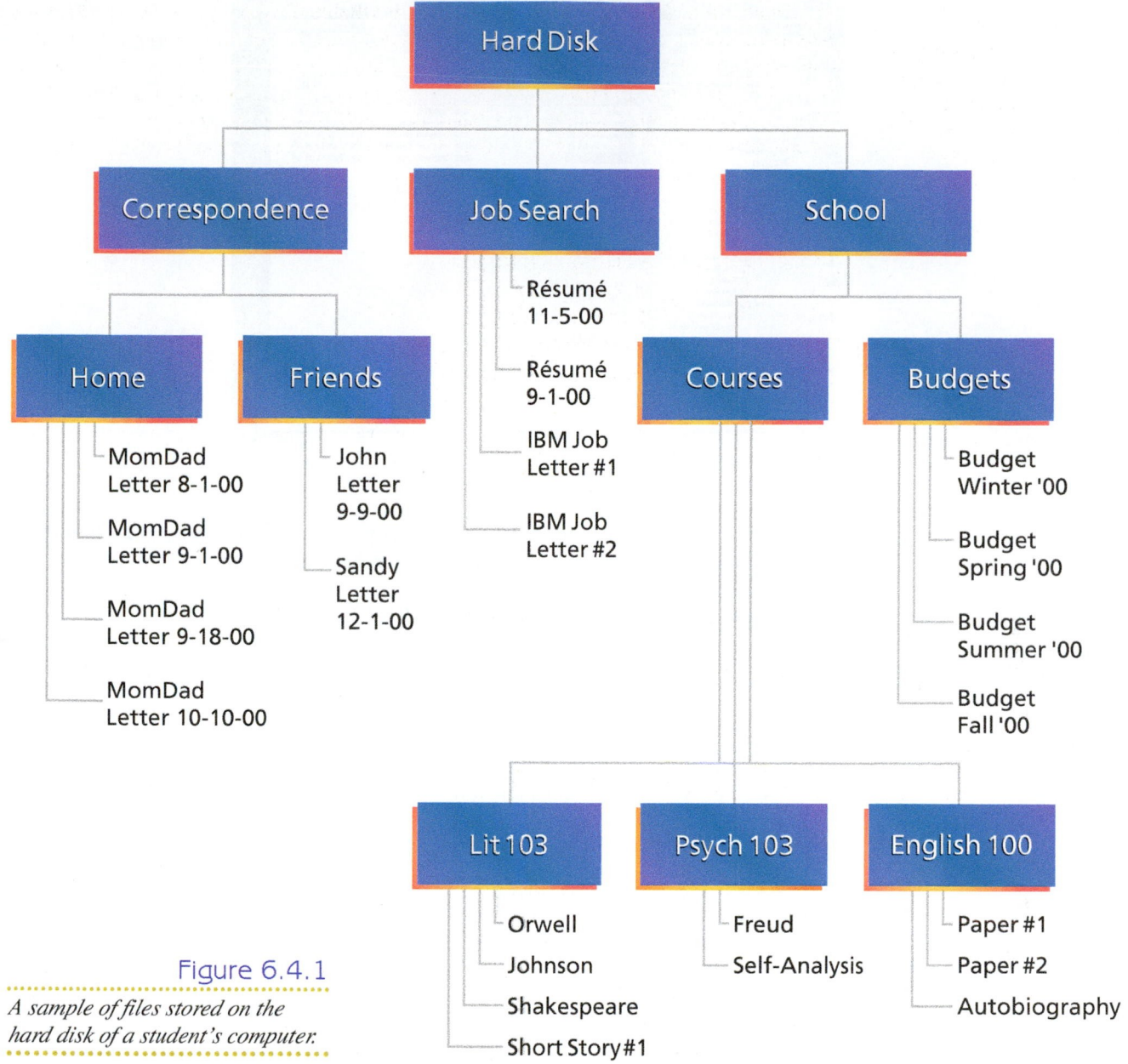

Figure 6.4.1

A sample of files stored on the hard disk of a student's computer.

6.5 Input and Output of Information

Input/output of information, or I/O, as it is commonly called, refers to getting information into the computer and also back out of the computer. In chapter 2, we identified the five basic kinds of information:

- Numbers
- Text or characters
- Visual information
- Audio information
- Instructions

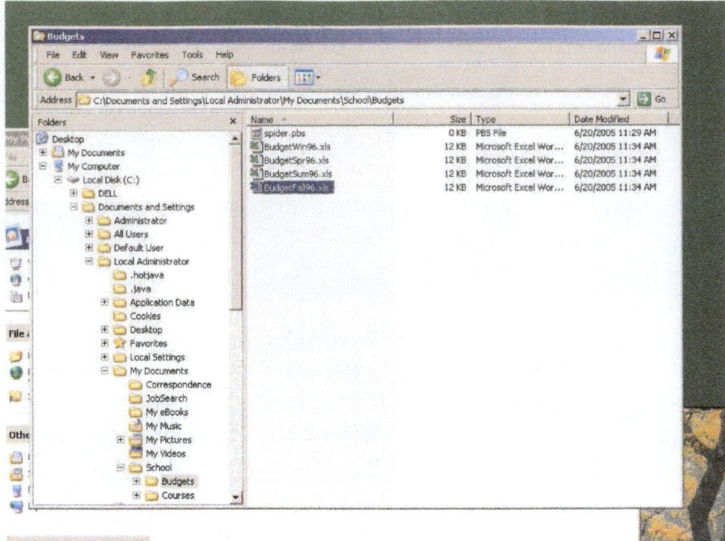

Figure 6.4.2

Finding the Budgets folder in Windows XP.

These five kinds of information are used in I/O. As you'll recall from chapter 2, all of these types of information are in the binary form. What makes them different to the computer?

GENERAL ISSUES IN PROCESSING FILES

The computer has no way of "knowing" which of the five types of information is contained in a particular binary file. The person or the application using the computer must supply the information in the proper form. For example, what happens when you try to use a Microsoft Word file from a Macintosh on a Windows machine with a different or even the same word processor? The file is probably in the wrong form, and the computer won't open it. The file must first be converted to a compatible form.

PUZZLER HINT

Puzzler Hint for Problem 1: The problem of sharing word-processing files is simple when the concept of file formats is understood. The following discussion clarifies this statement.

PUZZLER HINT

Puzzler Hint for Problem 2: Sometimes there are other applications that are in RAM and not in use, or several windows and directories are open on the desktop.

Let's look at a hypothetical example illustrating how file incompatibility might affect you and your work. Suppose you and a friend are working on a project together. Each of you is working at home on your own part of the project. When the time comes to put the two parts together, your friend brings his or her thumb drive to your house. You slide it into your computer and double click on the project file. You wait for the file to open so that you can combine it with yours. Disaster! Your word processor cannot open your friend's file. What do you do now? How are you going to get your work done? Do you have to retype everything?

The first thing to do is take a deep breath and understand what has caused the problem: Most word processors, (and many versions of the same word processor) use different file formats for storing text files in memory. As a result, files created by one word processor often are not recognized by another word processor. Their file formats are incompatible. But once you understand the problem, there is hope. Actually, there are three common solutions to this problem that you can try:

1. Instead of double-clicking on the file itself, try opening your word processor and using the word processor's OPEN command to open the file. This might work, because you identify the word processor rather than having the operating system go out looking for it. An operating system is usually smart enough to search for and find the application that actually created the file, if it is available, but if that exact application isn't there, the operating system doesn't know what to do next, or where else to look.

2. This possible solution involves the flexibility of the word-processing program that created the document. Most current word processors will allow you to save a document in any of several different file formats. Send your project partner back to the computer that created his or her file. Once the file has been successfully opened in the word processor that created it, have your friend call and read off the list of possible SAVE AS formats, comparing that list to what formats are available in your word processor. It may be possible for your friend to save the document in a form that your word processor will recognize.

3. If all else fails, have your friend save the document as a **text-only** file. Most word processors allow this option, saving only the ASCII characters making up the content of the document. The problem with saving a word-processing document as a text-only file is that all information regarding formatting—margins, type fonts, indents, tabs, etc., is stripped away. You will have to reproduce the formatting after you open the document in your own word processor. The formatting characters are frequently the cause of incompatibility among word processed files.

> A **text-only file** is a file consisting of only ASCII-coded symbols. All of the formatting, graphics, and other special coding are eliminated, which leaves only the ASCII symbols.

What concept does this example illustrate? The main point is that the user should know what form of information a particular program expects, so problems that may be encountered can be solved in advance. As programs are getting more user friendly, they are becoming more tolerant of errors or users trying to feed the wrong type of information into a particular program. Today, most current operating systems allow the user to open any file by double-clicking it. The operating system then searches for a program that will translate that particular type of information and start the program, input the file, and even show it on the screen. Figure 6.5.1 illustrates what happens when the Windows XP operating system can't find a program that would open the file selected.

DEVICE DRIVERS

Another important point should be made about input and output. The process of using the external hardware for I/O requires special software that will recognize and follow the appropriate protocol for successful communication. The **driver** is the generic name for this

> A **driver** is a program that will allow communication between the operating system and another part of the computer, usually a peripheral device such as a printer or scanner. It is an addition to the operating system.

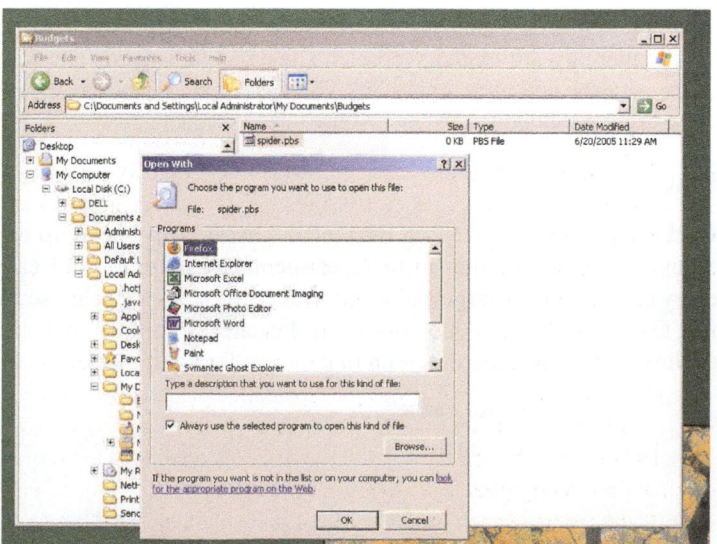

Figure 6.5.1

Dialogue box indicating that the operating system can't find an application to open the file selected.

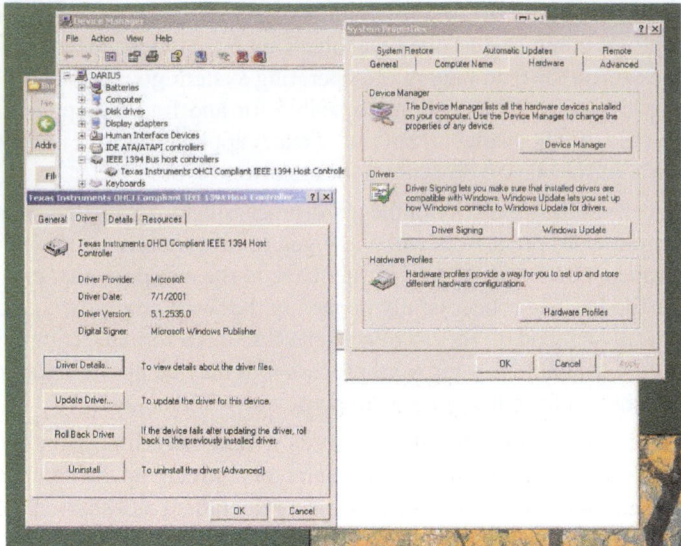

Figure 6.5.2

Installing a driver for a new piece of hardware.

software. In order to use some new piece of hardware, such as an external hard drive, a scanner, or other peripheral device, you must first install it. This means that not only must the physical connection be made to the peripheral, but the proper software drivers must be added to the operating system's collection of programs.

The driver is a program that directs the flow of information to and from a specific piece of hardware such as a thumb drive, CD-ROM player, hard disk, printer, laser printer, color laser printer, ink jet printer, video interface, or modem. Sometimes the driver is included as part of the operating system. Such is the case in communication between a keyboard or mouse and the computer, where a movement of the mouse or a keystroke on the keyboard sends data to the respective drivers. The driver will then pass these data on to the operating system as appropriate. On the other hand, to use special pieces of hardware such as printers or scanners, the software driver must be installed on the computer so the operating system can use it to communicate with them. The installation process is sometimes automated with dialog boxes helping guide the user as shown in Figure 6.5.2.

6.6 Memory Limitations: Cache and Virtual Memory

Insufficient primary memory size and the slow transfer of data between primary and secondary memory are memory problems that can be solved. The solution can be provided by cache memory and virtual memory. These concepts surface in the personal computer through names such as video RAM, cache, pipeline burst cache, and disk cache.

CACHE MEMORY

Cache memory is a faster memory. Its purpose is to speed up processing of the programs.

Cache memory is used when the memory access can't keep up with the CPU's needs. This access can involve either primary or secondary memory and can improve speed. Almost every computer both large and small uses cache memory because RAM speeds have become fast and the secondary memory is inadequate. Computer manufacturers such as Intel are dealing with the problem as seen in their ads for computers, which include phrases such as:

- "Advanced transfer cache"
- "Level 1 primary cache"

- "Level 2 cache on processor"
- "Backside level 2 cache"

The idea of the cache memory is to provide a cache of faster than normal memory that can keep up with the CPU. With the faster memory the operating system will try to keep required data and instructions in the cache memory as much as is possible, thereby speeding up the process of computation.

There are two major categories of cache memory: secondary cache memory and RAM cache memory. The former involves the interaction between secondary memory such as hard disks and ordinary RAM. The latter category involves ordinary RAM and special superfast RAM. Each has the goal of putting data and programs into memory with faster access.

Disk/Secondary Memory Cache

One common type of cache memory in the first category, which deals with secondary memory and RAM, is called **disk cache.** The disk cache speeds up processing by automatically saving the most frequently used parts of the program being run or executed in the normal RAM. The basic idea is that the CPU may need to access the data in that same area of the program again. The information will be there ready to go, saving the CPU from repeatedly retrieving it from the disk, which takes time to reload into RAM. The disk cache wouldn't be necessary if the RAM were large enough to hold all of the information, both data and program, required by the program. A good example of something that is frequently held in the disk cache is the hard disk directory. This is especially useful if you happen to be looking for a file on the hard disk or communicating with the operating system in a way that needs information from the hard disk directory.

Disk cache is a type of memory that allows data normally accessed directly from a disk to move to the normal RAM, where the CPU can obtain it more quickly.

RAM Cache Memory

RAM cache memory involves the same concept as the disk cache we just discussed. But, in the case of RAM cache memory, the interaction is between ordinary RAM and a special type of very fast and expensive RAM. To understand how this works, let's first look at what happens without RAM cache. The process is as follows:

- The program and data are taken from the disk and placed in RAM.
- The CPU takes program instructions from the RAM.
- Data needed by the program are also taken from the RAM.
- The CPU performs the instructions of the program.
- The results of the computation are placed back in the RAM.
- When complete, the final results are placed back on the disk.

RAM cache memory is very fast memory that is used by the operating system to house the data and instructions that are currently being used. The CPU can then run faster than if it needed to access normal RAM, which is much slower.

With present-day CPUs, however, the RAM is relatively so slow that the CPU is waiting most of the time for instructions and data to be transferred from the RAM to the CPU for computation. The solution to this bottleneck is to provide some much faster and expensive RAM called the cache. Then, because today's sophisticated operating systems have ways of predicting what data or instructions will be needed next, it can load them into the RAM cache so that it doesn't take so much time to get the instructions and data into the CPU. The process is similar to the preceding one with two extra steps:

- The program and data are taken from the disk and placed in RAM.
- The cache controller loads instructions and data from the RAM into the cache.
- The CPU quickly takes program instructions from the cache memory.
- Data needed by the program are also taken from the cache memory at a very high rate.
- The CPU performs the instructions of the program.
- The results of the computation are placed back in the cache memory at very high speed.
- Those results are then placed back into ordinary RAM.
- When complete, the final results are placed back on the disk.

There is a similar bottleneck problem involved with video display information. With the high-resolution large monitors, the data needed to create the picture must be moved very quickly from memory to the display circuits. Ordinary RAM isn't fast enough to make quick changes in the display, so over the last few generations of PCs, the video memory has gone from ordinary RAM to **video RAM** (**VRAM).** By putting the image data into this faster video RAM, delays can be minimized. As VRAM has matured, it has also been optimized for video, which means it is organized differently than ordinary RAM. In other words, you can't just interchange the memory chips. However, the concept we call RAM cache is the same concept used with the VRAM.

VRAM or **video RAM** is memory used by the operating system to house video display data that allows quicker and better video display. It is usually located on the video electronics card called the video controller.

VIRTUAL MEMORY

The other end of the spectrum from cache memory problems occurs when a program and its data are too big to fit in the available RAM. Trying to manipulate a large photograph in Adobe's Photoshop program, for example, may need more RAM than you have in your computer. This problem is solved with **virtual memory.** Whereas cache memory addresses the concerns of speed and efficiency, virtual memory addresses the problem of a program being too big to fit into the available RAM.

Virtual memory allows an application program to run even though there isn't enough RAM for it. This is accomplished by using a portion of the hard drive memory or other secondary memory as if it were the additional RAM needed by the program. The operating system controls the management of the virtual memory.

Before we discuss modern-day virtual memory use, it is important to know some historical facts. The Burroughs Corporation produced the first commercially available computer with virtual memory. The B5000 was way ahead of its time in 1961, but because of poor marketing it wasn't successful. Then about a decade later IBM introduced its virtual memory operating system, which was a big success. The virtual memory concept didn't appear in the personal computer field until the early 1990s. It is now quite common in personal computers.

The virtual memory capability of an operating system will "fool" the application into thinking that a portion of the hard disk is RAM. When the RAM is not large enough, the data and instructions will be put onto the hard drive by the operating system. This will, of course, slow down the processing of information because time is needed to go to the disk to get the various pieces of the program.

The virtual memory feature of an operating system can usually be turned on or off by the user. It should be used with care because using the virtual memory mode of an operating system can sometimes result in an extreme slowdown in processing. The amount of virtual memory can also be specified to the operating system, which manages the virtual memory. It is wise to refer to the application's suggestions regarding how it uses virtual memory.

6.7 Context Switching and Multitasking

In the personal computer world, context switching and multitasking are concepts that the average user should understand. Each of these concepts solves the problem when more than one program is needed to accomplish some goal. You may need to transfer data between word-processing, spreadsheet, and graphics programs, for example. Without context switching this could be very frustrating.

CONTEXT SWITCHING

Context switching allows having more than one program in RAM at one time and being able to switch contexts easily from one program to another. Figure 6.7.1 shows several programs in RAM on a Macintosh computer. By clicking the mouse on any one of them, the operating system switches you to that program at the place where you left off. An example will show the need for having two or more programs in RAM at the same time.

Context switching allows several application programs to be in RAM at one time. Each is ready to continue or start computing on command.

Suppose you are writing a letter and need to get something from a spreadsheet to insert in the letter. Without context switching, you would have to follow these steps:

1. Save the current copy of the letter.
2. Quit the word-processing program.

3. Start the spreadsheet.

4. Create the spreadsheet data.

5. Save it in a form that is acceptable to the word processor.

6. Quit the spreadsheet program.

7. Restart the word processor and return to the letter.

8. Insert the spreadsheet data.

With context switching, you could temporarily leave the word processor and go to the operating system. This is done without losing the status and current work on the letter, which means that the word processor and letter are still in RAM. Next, you start the spreadsheet program and do the required calculation. At this point, because of context switching, the word processor, letter, spreadsheet, and spreadsheet calculation are all in RAM at the same time. However, only the spreadsheet is active. It would be possible to switch from the word processor to the spreadsheet and back without exiting or quitting either one or losing any work. In other words, you could switch from the context of the word-processing program to the spreadsheet context and work on either, but only one at a time. In fact, it is quite common for a computer user to keep half a dozen programs in memory ready to be used. These programs might include a word processor, spreadsheet, database, drawing program, communications program, and, of course, the operating system—all in RAM, ready to be activated.

The concept of context switching has one major limitation: The only active program is the one just switched to; all others are inactive. An example will help explain what this means and why it's sometimes important. An illustrator working on a magazine cover using Adobe Photoshop may start a manipulation that takes several minutes to perform. If context switching was used, the manipulation would cease at the instant the illustrator switched to another program. Another, more powerful concept called multitasking solves this problem.

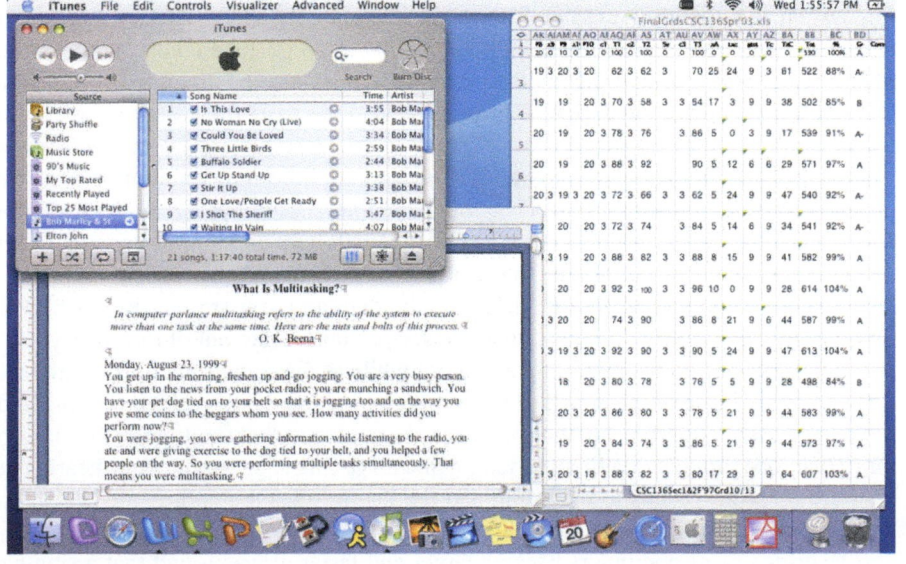

Figure 6.7.1

Menu from Macintosh operating system showing several applications in RAM, ready for context switching.

Multitasking allows several application programs to be in RAM at one time. Each of them will be allowed CPU time as needed, even though only one of them is currently being used by the person at the keyboard. All of this is controlled by the operating system.

MULTITASKING

It was mentioned that the illustrator's problem referred to in the previous paragraph is solved with **multitasking.** Remember, the problem is that the illustrator would like to do something

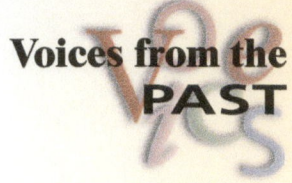

Voices from the PAST

Multics, the Granddaddy of Operating Systems

The director of the MIT computer center received a memo from John McCarthy in 1959 that proposed a form of time-sharing for a computer. The result was the CTSS project (Compatible Time Sharing System) at MIT. This became the spark that gave birth to the modern-day operating system. The first outgrowth of this work was the Multics operating system.

Multics (Multiplexed Information and Computing Service) was a time-shared computer operating system developed by a consortium consisting of Bell Laboratories, General Electric, and MIT in the mid-1960s.

It was clearly one of the most ambitious operating system projects up to that time. Multics contained operating system features such as virtual memory, hierarchical file system, and many more concepts in use today. In fact, Bell Laboratories took many concepts of Multics and created a smaller, more manageable operating system called UNIX. It's interesting to

MIT Museum and Historical Collections

note that UNIX is a pun on the word *Multics,* and it was indeed focused on one goal rather than multiple goals. Also, Digital Equipment Corporation based its VMS (Virtual Memory System) family of operating systems on Multics.

But back to John McCarthy. He went on into another area of computer science and coined the term *artificial intelligence (AI).* McCarthy is best known for the language LISP (LISt Processing), which has had an enormous effect on the field of artificial intelligence. He is a very important figure in the field of AI, but his involvement in early operating systems is also significant.

on the computer rather than waiting for the photo manipulation to finish. With a multitasking system the operating system allows the illustrator to go on with some other program, such as a word processor, while the photo manipulation goes on computing. This is accomplished by the operating system's taking any idle time of the CPU and using it to continue with the Photoshop computation. It literally steals time from the CPU to work on the photo while the illustrator is still using the word processor. *Background execution* is the term professionals use to indicate this process. It means the photo manipulation is not in the foreground where the illustrator is working on a word processor, but it is in the background.

An analogy taken from everyday experience will help explain the concept of multitasking. Suppose you just got home from work or school. You grab an energy bar, put on your tennis shoes/walking gear, put the leash on the dog, and you are out the door. Oops, don't forget your water bottle. Now, the analogy: As you take a bite out of the energy bar, you are holding back the dog from chasing a squirrel while at the same time opening the water bottle and taking a slug of water. All of these things are done while you are walking and talking to the dog. Analyzing the situation, it is easy to conclude that the human brain is able to do more than one thing at one time. In fact, while all of this is going on, your heart is pumping, eyes are relaying visuals to the brain, and the leg muscles are coordinated to walk. This is analogous to multitasking by computers.

Historically, as computers became larger and faster, it was found that a single program couldn't keep the CPU busy. Too much time was needed to get information into and out of the computer. This so-called I/O-bound situation was not economical, so computer designers had the idea that maybe the CPU could run more than one program or task at a time. To have a program do all of the things it's supposed to do generally requires many tasks. This means that several programs would be stored in the main memory so that when one of them had to wait for data from outside the CPU, the CPU could be used to work on another program or task that was already there. This was made feasible by having "smart" input or output devices that didn't need the help of the CPU to accomplish this work, thereby freeing the CPU. As you might suspect, it was necessary for the operating system to make decisions on which programs or tasks to run and keep the CPU working smoothly.

In multitasking, as opposed to context switching, when you switch from the word processor in the middle of doing something, it continues performing the task in the background. This means it will get some time on the CPU whenever the multitasking operating system schedules it. You might occasionally notice a slowdown when the operating system is stealing a few cycles of CPU time from the program you are currently using. All of this is done under operating system control with little control exercised by the computer user.

Printing is a common example of multitasking. Suppose that a long printing process has just been started from a word processor. Instead of waiting, the user can switch to another program and continue working. In the meantime, the multitasking operating system will continue the printing process. Actually, many printers now have the capability of taking the printing job from the CPU into their own memory, where it is processed and printed. Another example of multitasking occurs when your Web browser automatically downloads your e-mail at regular intervals while you are using some other program such as a word processor.

With a true multitasking operating system such as UNIX or Linux, many tasks, or processes, as they are often called, will be used by the operating system itself. Also, other users can run programs or tasks on that computer through a networking system. All in all, a multitasking operating system is capable of running several hundred processes simultaneously. Even though they seem to be running simultaneously, only one process at a time can use the CPU because of the von Neumann bottleneck previously discussed. The bottleneck is due to the fact that the CPU can only process a single instruction from any one task at a time, no matter how many tasks there are.

6.8 Operating Systems for the Networked World

There are many types of operating systems. Remember that the purpose of the operating system is to efficiently manage the computer and make it easy for users to tell the computer what to do. The computer may be a relatively simple von Neumann computer, or it may be a supercomputer. Regardless of the type, the operating system is exceedingly complex, as is illustrated by its millions of lines of programming instructions. This section examines the principles behind a wide variety of operating systems.

PARALLEL PROCESSING

There are two categories of operating systems: the single CPU (such as a von Neumann computer) and the multiprocessor system that has many CPUs (such as a supercomputer). **Multiprocessing** systems are more difficult to program because it is necessary to divide a program into pieces. Each of these pieces of a program gets processed by one of many processors. At the same time, the other parts of the program are being processed by the additional processors.

The complexity of the operating system for the supercomputer Blue Gene/L shown in Figure 3.8.8 of chapter 3 is immensely greater than that of the personal computer. This supercomputer has over 100,000 processors to organize and keep running efficiently. The operating system of a personal computer has only one processor to control. Because of the multiple processors, developing operating system software for parallel processing machines is exceedingly difficult. An even more daunting challenge is sharing many processors over a network. This is called **distributed processing.** Distributed processing also includes grid computing along with the new paradigm "cloud computing" discussed in chapter 8.

Parallel processing or **multiprocessing** is computing that takes place on a computer that has many processors or CPUs. Many different parts of a program are computed by different processors at the same time.

Distributed processing makes use of a network to decentralize and distribute the computing needs over several interconnected computers.

NETWORKS AND DISTRIBUTED PROCESSING

In today's networked world, it's not too hard to realize that the next reasonable extension of operating systems will make use of networks. With networks, individual people can access and use several computers besides their own computer. That is, several computers are connected by the network and share each other's resources. For example, suppose you are working on a group project. With a network and its operating system, it is possible for the entire group in the project to share results and communicate.

As you might suspect, there are operating systems specifically designed for the computers in such a network. One example is Sun Microsystem's Solaris 10 Unix operating system. Not only must the network operating system be able to handle all the normal single-computer chores, but it must also be able to communicate with other computers in the network.

The desire to keep a single copy of a file that can be used by many people has created a further modification of networking. Suppose you're in a group of five people working on a long report, for example. Each of you is writing a section, but the sections aren't completely independent, which means you have to compare your writing progress quite often. Using paper and passing copies back and forth would be very time-consuming. With a network, however, the work can be shared electronically with all the changes color coded and attributed to the various authors, as shown in Figure 6.8.1.

Inexpensive systems have been devised to allow one computer on a network to act as a shared storage unit. Its function is to serve and control the interactions of other computers on the network. This shared computer is commonly referred to as a **server,** and the total system follows a client/server architecture. We'll consider these concepts with more detail in chapter 7, "Network Concepts and Communications."

The networking idea can be modified to provide distributed processing. Each computer contains only a portion of the data or programs used. The other computers on the network can access these programs and data as needed and even tap into unused computing power. The goal is to distribute both information and processing capability around to the computers in the network and then to allow each of them to access the others as needed. This trend toward distributed processing is a direct result of the new smaller and cheaper computers, especially the microcomputer.

> A **server** is a computer that provides data and programs on request from multiple clients. These clients may be other programs or individual users. A server is always on a network and accessible to many computers.

Figure 6.8.1

A document during the editing process. Note the colored text indicating different authors.

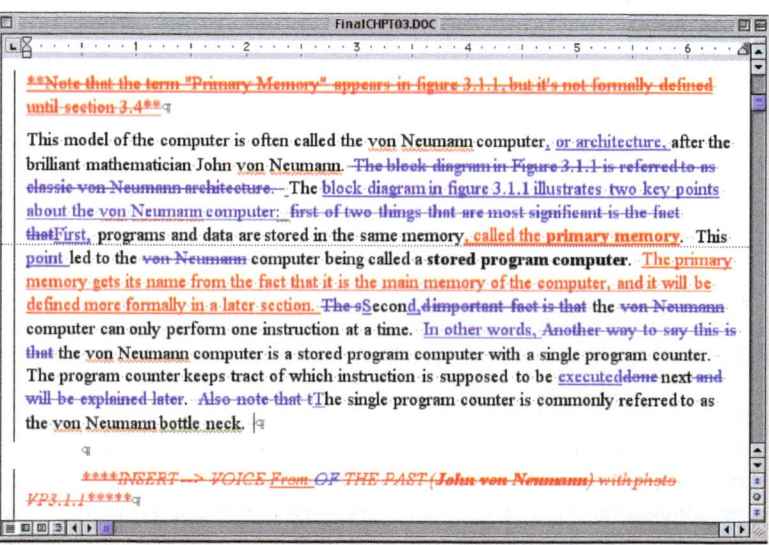

Screen shot reprinted by permission from Microsoft Corporation

Distributed Processing and Operating Systems

In the early years, mainframe computers with huge, monolithic programs "fed" these programs to terminals often referred to as "green screens." All activity was controlled by the mainframe's operating system. Then along came the PC in the early 1980s, and this started a revolution. Within a decade a dramatic paradigm shift began as the client/server architecture developed and allowed individual PCs to take over some of the processing of data. Along with these events, there was a proliferation of UNIX-based servers that gave more cost-effective computing than did the mainframes. So, with the database residing on a UNIX-based server and the processing done on the client PC, the stage was set to separate the dependence of the PC on any server changes. This is because the software was layered, which means changes can be made in a particular layer without knowing the details of the layers above and below. This allows changes in the server software without having to make changes in the PC or client software. The effect is dramatic because major changes in the database software don't require subsequent changes in the hundreds of PC clients' software. This independence given by the decentralized distributed architecture has led to a need for standardization. As with all new technologies, there is a proliferation of standards, and the distributed operating systems are not an exception. Here is a list of standards for distributed computing to illustrate the variety of standards that have evolved in just the past 20 years:

CentOS Community ENTerprise Operating System

Common Object Request Broker Architecture (CORBA)

Application Programming Interface (API) using socket programming

Remote Procedure Call (RPC) using sockets indirectly

Distributed Computing Environment (DCE) from Open Software Foundation (OSF)

Distributed Component Object Model (DCOM) from Microsoft

Jini Connection Technology from Sun Microsystems

Any one of these standards can be followed to create custom distributed operating system environments, whose purpose is to allow individual PC users to feel like they have one giant machine at their disposal. This means that all of the computing power of the computers on the network with the distributed operating systems is available to any single PC.

The last standard on this list is Jini from Sun Microsystems. Among its many characteristics is the concept of a connection technology. What is a connection technology? For one thing, the technology doesn't need complicated software protocols, such as drivers, which must be added to an operating system for proper communication to some device such as a printer. Instead, when a new device is added to a network, "it goes through an add-in protocol, called discovery and join-in." This means the device itself finds the equivalent of its driver and sets up the proper communication link to the network. With many other features, the Jini connection technology has the potential to revolutionize distributed operating systems.

REAL TIME AND PROCESS CONTROL

Real-time processing systems are another innovative form of computing requiring a rather complex operating system. The term *real time* indicates that the computing performed must be done in a way that is compatible with the world outside the computer. In other words, information is fed to a real-time computer system and computations must be performed quickly enough so that the results are still useful. One example from the business world is the automated teller machine (ATM). When you use it, you want your cash back now, not tomorrow. Another example is the airline ticket reservation system, which typically may have several thousand computers and terminals connected to it throughout the United States. The system must accept reservation information and respond quickly enough so that the

Real-time processing in the business world is computing that involves humans interacting with the computer in a situation in which quick or timely return of results is important. Real-time processing in the engineering and manufacturing world is computing that controls processes in a timely fashion.

Figure 6.8.2

Process control of robots on an assembly line.

Process control refers to the control of some process by a computer in real time. It is necessary for the computer to accept information, perform calculations using the information, and then execute the task on the basis of these calculations.

response is useful; waiting an hour or even 10 minutes for a response would be intolerable. Some reservation systems are so complicated that they even check to see if the individual has any other reservation in the same name. Airline reservation systems use millions of dollars' worth of computer equipment. And it costs several more millions of dollars to develop the computer programs for these applications.

Process control systems are needed to perform timely and accurate computations. An interesting example of process control is the microcomputer that controls the engine in an automobile. All major automobile companies have some engines with spark timing, fuel injection, and other engine functions controlled by a microcomputer. In spark timing, the microcomputer is fast enough to sense when each cylinder is ready to ignite while taking into account other things such as engine temperature. Other examples include assembly-line control in factories, control of traffic in a railroad freight yard, control of automobile traffic in a city, flood control on rivers, satellite rocket launches, and lunar landings of space capsules. Closer to home are the thermostats and environmental controls in the home heating/cooling system.

Other examples of process control are from the field of robotics. Maneuvering a robot's arm is just one of the many tasks accomplished through process control. We are assuming that the robot can sense the environment and as a result of the sensing move the arm appropriately in a timely fashion. Figure 6.8.2 shows a robot assembly line controlled by computers running a process control operating system. Some robots used in industry can even see. This introduces some special problems for the robot's computer. However, discussing these problems is more appropriate for chapter 13, "Artificial Intelligence and Modeling the Human State."

Chapter Summary

6.1 What Is an Operating System?

Without an operating system, you would need at least several minutes to get a computer system running even minimally. The operating system is like a personal assistant: It does a lot of detailed work to make it possible for someone to use a computer with a minimum effort. It all starts when the computer's power is turned on. This process starts by running a program in permanent memory, which will look for the complete operating system that is usually found on the hard drive of the computer. The ROM BIOS of the computer contains all of the program components needed to use the keyboard and display activity on the screen.

6.2 Booting the Computer

The process of putting a copy of the operating system in the RAM of the computer is referred to as booting up the computer. There are two basic types of booting a computer. The cold boot is when the power to the computer is turned on after previously being off. The warm boot is when the computer is on, but for some reason a fresh copy of the operating system is needed in the RAM. If a user needs more than one operating system, the hard drive of the computer can be partitioned or divided into sections or partitions, each of which can have a separate operating system. It is not unusual for a computer professional to have two or three different operating systems on his or her computer.

6.3 User Interfaces

You communicate with the operating system through the computer interface. There are two major types of interface: command line and GUI (graphical user interface). Command-line interfaces are much less intuitive than GUIs and require considerably more expertise to use. As operating systems develop, their interfaces also change, which means it's very important when requesting help to know the version number of whatever operating system is being used. Commercially released software starts with version 1.0, and higher version numbers indicate newer programs. In spite of its age, UNIX is still the choice of computer professionals, with both command-line and graphical user interfaces available. A UNIX look-alike called Linux is becoming very popular, which is due in part to its being open-source software. Open-source software is when complete details including the original program of the software are available so anyone can make changes to it. Usually software is only available in binary form, known as compiled code, and this makes it impossible to make changes or understand how the program works.

6.4 Files and File Management

It is important to be able to find and use already created files on your computer. This means that the names you give to the files should be descriptive, so it isn't necessary to open the file just to see what it is. The organization of these files on a hard drive is usually in the form of a hierarchical structure rather than a plain list or flat file structure. The hierarchical file structure allows the nesting of folders within folders.

6.5 Input and Output of Information

Processing computer files consists of not only moving them around from CPU/RAM to various peripherals but also recognizing them so you or the computer can access them quickly. It is important to understand the different ways the operating system can be directed to open files. This will allow the use of files from different computers and application programs. The user must also understand the basic concept of communication between the CPU and peripherals and how they make use of software drivers. This will allow troubleshooting problems of a certain type.

6.6 Memory Limitations: Cache and Virtual Memory

Cache memory is a memory design technique used in computers when the memory access can't keep up with the CPU's needs. Access to cache memory can involve either primary or secondary memory, where the cache memory provides faster than normal memory that can keep up with the CPU. At the other end of the spectrum from the cache memory problem is the one in which a program and its data are too big to fit in the available RAM. This problem is solved with the concept of virtual memory. Whereas cache memory addresses the concerns of speed and efficiency, virtual memory addresses the problem of a program being too big to fit into the available RAM. The virtual memory capability of an operating system will fool the application into thinking that a portion of the hard disk is RAM. It usually results in a significant slowdown in processing speed.

6.7 Context Switching and Multitasking

Context switching occurs when there is more than one program in the RAM at one time and the operating system can easily switch from one application to another. In multitasking, as contrasted with context switching, when you switch from a program in the middle of doing something, it continues performing the task in the background. A multitasking operating system allows the user to start up many tasks that will be worked in the background while the user is doing something else. Each task gets a slice of computing time as scheduled by the operating system.

6.8 Operating Systems for the Networked World

The standalone operating systems used in personal computers may eventually be replaced by special networking distributive operating systems. This means your individual computer may not have all the capability that you need; however, as you would normally be connected to a network, that capability would automatically be given to you over the network.

There are some unique cases that require different types of operating systems. In the case of multiple processors, the management problems are much different from those of a standalone computer with a single CPU. In fact, the Connection Machine supercomputers could have up to 64,000 processors. This introduces all types of problems that need special operating systems.

Finally, there are real-time and process control computers that have yet different requirements. Operating systems are often designed to solve their unique problem needs.

Key Terms

1. Agents, *156*
2. Altair 8800, *150*
3. BASIC, *150*
4. BIOS, *150*
5. Booting up a computer, *151*
6. Cache memory, *162*
7. Cold boot, *152*
8. Command-line interface, *155*
9. Context switching, *164*
10. Diagnostic programs, *152*
11. Disk cache, *163*
12. Distributed processing, *167*
13. Drag and drop, *155*
14. Driver, *161*
15. Fat fingering, *150*
16. File, *156*
17. Flat file structure, *158*
18. File folder, *158*
19. File name extension, *158*
20. GUI (graphical user interface), *153*
21. Hierarchical file structure, *158*
22. Multiprocessing, *167*
23. Multitasking, *165*
24. Open-source software, *156*
25. Operating system, *150*
26. Parallel processing, *167*
27. Partitioning, *153*
28. Process control, *170*
29. RAM cache, *163*
30. Real-time processing, *169*
31. Rebooting, *151*
32. Server, *168*
33. Shell, *156*
34. Text-only file, *161*
35. UNIX, *155*
36. User friendly, *155*
37. User interface, *153*
38. Video RAM (VRAM), *164*
39. Version number, *153*
40. Virtual memory, *164*
41. Warm boot, *152*
42. Windows, *152*

Matching

Match the number of the key terms introduced in this chapter to the following statements.
Each term may be used once, more than once, or not at all.

1. ___ A collection of programs that makes the computer easier to use and allows the most efficient use of the computer.

2. ___ This term had been given to the clumsy way a computer had to be activated by first flipping many tiny switches to directly enter start-up information into RAM.

3. ___ This term is used to indicate the process of starting up the computer when its power is initially turned off.

4. ___ This term is used when a fresh copy of the operating system is needed in the RAM.

5. ___ This acronym is used to identify a part of the operating system that is in the ROM.

6. ___ The name given to the user interface that uses only text for commands.

7. ___ The name given to the user interface that is graphical.

8. ___ This is the part of the operating system with which the computer user interacts.

9. ___ The name of an operating system that is modeled after UNIX.

10. ___ The name of a file system that, when sketched out in a diagram, looks like an upside-down tree.

11. ___ The name of the software that is needed when the CPU communicates with a peripheral device.

12. ___ The name given to a file that represents a group of files.

13. ___ This is the process of clicking the mouse over an object, moving it over to another object such as a disk, and releasing the mouse button.

14. ___ This term refers to the ease of use of a computer, one that is intuitive to use, needing little explanation.

15. ___ This type of file system lists everything stored in an area in a single, all-inclusive list.

16. ___ This type of file system organizes files into groupings.

17. ___ This type of file is saved in its ASCII form. It is generally saved this way when transporting it from one type of computer system to another or from one word-processing product to another.

18. ___ This type of cache memory is used to store video display data.

19. ___ This type of cache memory speeds up processing by automatically saving the most frequently used parts of the program being run in the part of RAM that is used for cache.

20. ___ This type of multiprogramming entails two programs running at the same time, each taking up time on the CPU. You may be running one program and have the computer run another in the background.

True or False

Place either T or F on the line provided with each of the following statements. If a statement is false, you should be able to explain what changes would make it true.

1. ___ In modern computers, a part of the operating system can be found in ROM, ready for use before the computer is turned on.

2. ___ In modern computers, a part of the operating system can be found in RAM, ready for use before the computer is turned on.

3. ___ In modern computers, a part of the operating system can be found in secondary memory, ready for use, whether it's on a floppy or the hard disk drive, before the computer is turned on.

4. ___ Without the operating system, the computer is almost useless.

5. ___ The operating system has also been known as the monitor, supervisor, and executive.

6. ___ Only one operating system can be stored on the hard disk, ready to be booted.

7. ___ A flat file system allows files to be arranged hierarchically.

8. ___ Cold booting and warm booting the computer are similar in that they both reload the operating system.

9. ___ Cold booting and warm booting the computer have the same effect on the hardware of the computer.

10. ___ Learning to make the computer do what you want using a command-line interface takes less time than learning to use GUI commands.

11. ___ UNIX strictly uses a command-line interface.

12. ___ Text files allow the transportation of documents from one computer platform to another or from one word processor to another.

13. ___ All peripheral devices need a device driver.

14. ___ When buying a piece of hardware that is a newer technology than your computer, such as a digital camera or scanner, the device must come with a driver program. The driver program is necessary for the operating system to communicate with the new hardware.

15. ___ Disk cache is synonymous with RAM cache.

16. ___ More than one program can be in the RAM at the same time.

17. ___ Multiprocessing refers to having more than one program in memory at a time.

18. ___ One benefit of networking is that it provides access to shared resources.

19. ___ A server's function is to allow access to individual computers on a network by an administrator who needs to check employee productivity.

20. ___ An airline reservation system is an example of real-time processing, whereas controlling engine temperature is an example of process control.

Multiple Choice

Answer the multiple-choice questions by selecting the best answer from the choices given.

1. Which of the following is not a function of the operating system?
   a. Using the keyboard
   b. Sending a file to a printer
   c. Turning on the computer
   d. Saving a file to a disk drive
   e. Managing the files of a computer

2. This is an acronym used to identify the software in ROM that is needed for input/output in the computer.
   a. I/O
   b. BIOS
   c. RAM
   d. HFS
   e. UNIX

3. Restarting the computer by powering off and then powering the computer back on is known as:
   a. Loading the computer
   b. Driving the computer
   c. A warm boot
   d. A cold boot
   e. Surging the computer

4. Restarting the computer by pressing a combination of keys simultaneously while the computer is still running so that an interruption of power does not occur is known as:
   a. Loading the computer
   b. Driving the computer
   c. A warm boot
   d. A cold boot
   e. Surging the computer

5. This type of interface recognizes typed commands almost exclusively.
   a. GUI
   b. Interactive graphics interfaces
   c. Text-based interface
   d. Command-line interface
   e. Interactive iconoclastic interface

6. This type of interface recognizes commands given by a mouse or other pointing device. Activities are selected by using a mouse to point and click on icons.
   a. GUI
   b. Interactive graphics interface
   c. Text-based interface
   d. Command-line interface
   e. Interactive iconoclastic interface

7. This is an indicator of the age of a program. The higher the number, the newer the software.
   a. Report number
   b. Version number
   c. Procedure issue number
   d. Primer number
   e. Model number

8. This addresses the problem of a program's being too big to fit in RAM. The program is divided up into pieces, which are brought into memory as needed.
   a. Cache memory
   b. Disk cache
   c. RAM cache
   d. Virtual memory
   e. Virtual reality

9. This refers to several processors or CPUs in the same computer simultaneously working on a program.
   a. Multiprocessing
   b. Multitasking
   c. Context switching
   d. Multiprogramming
   e. Distributed processing

Exercises

1. List at least six things that an operating system does for you.

2. Put a formatted disk without an operating system into both a Macintosh computer and a Windows-based computer. Turn on the computer and observe what happens. Describe the results and explain the actions of the computer.

3. List the steps involved in cold booting a computer.

4. What is the difference between a warm boot and a cold boot?

5. In general terms, describe the process used in any GUI to
   a. Copy a floppy disk's contents to a hard drive
   b. Save a file to a floppy disk that is currently on the hard drive
   c. Create a hierarchical file structure with file folders

6. In general terms, describe the process used in any command-line interface to
   a. Copy a floppy disk's contents to a hard drive
   b. Save a file to a floppy disk that is currently on the hard drive
   c. Create a hierarchical file structure with file folders

7. Suppose you are writing a letter home to Mom and Dad. The file name under which this letter will be saved can have many forms. Which of the following names are most desirable for naming a file? You should assume several letters will be written to them. Explain your answer.

MomDadLetter	Letter A
LetterHome10/2/96	Letter#1Home
Letter	Budget#1
XYZ	MomDadLetter12/1/96
MomDad11/6/96	Stuff#1

8. Suppose you may only use eight characters to name the file containing the correspondence home. Give six examples of good file names.

9. What has to be done to use a word-processing document created with a Macintosh computer on a Windows computer? What are all the options? Include the option in which you know that the document is to be used on a Windows computer before you save the document on the Macintosh computer.

10. Considering the general duties of an operating system, make up several appropriate names for operating systems (such as master control program).

11. Describe the two methods given in section 6.5 for converting a file from one type of machine so it can be used on another type of machine.

12. Why does the computer upon start-up always search for the rest of the operating system on the floppy disk drive first, before looking on the hard drive?

13. Determine the amount of RAM cache and video RAM in the computer that you use.

14. Draw diagrams showing the basic concepts of how a computer uses RAM cache memory. Use arrows to indicate the flow of data.

15. Why doesn't the operating system manufacturer put all drivers ever needed into the operating system, so driver installation wouldn't be necessary?

16. Give two examples of distributed processing.

17. Make a list of at least three applications that use real-time processing in the business sense.

18. Make a list of at least six things that use real-time process control computers (such as a dishwasher).

19. Study the following string of binary numerals:

1011010001111100

By looking at the string of binary numerals, can you guess to what it belongs? Is it part of a picture? Is it a number? Can it be a couple of letters from an ASCII text file? Could it possibly represent a couple of sounds? With these questions in mind, explain how a computer's operating system would identify what is saved in a file and why this is important.

20. Design a problem-solving scenario that would pinpoint why a particular program is running abnormally slowly on your computer. It should consist of a list of things to do, which might even include e-mailing the manufacturer.

21. Make a list of requirements needed to run Linux on your computer. This should include things such as minimum RAM, hard disk space, CPU speed, and so on. Hint: Find a manual or an ad for Linux, or interview some computer professionals.

22. Find someone who has a software hard disk analyzer such as Norton Utilities on his or her computer. Describe the steps needed to check how fragmented the hard drive is, and report the hard drive's fragmented status.

23. **PUZZLER** For your favorite word processors, make a list of all of the possible formats under which a word-processing document can be saved.

Discussion Questions

1. Why isn't the entire operating system stored in ROM? Wouldn't it be easier for the user and the machine?

2. Describe a situation in which a command-line interface would be preferable to a GUI.

3. Why does the operating system need to use a disk cache in RAM instead of just using the disk?

4. Is multiprocessing necessary for multiprogramming? Why or why not?

5. For the computer you use, make a list of things you would like the operating system to do. Don't use examples from the book. Think of the operating system as your assistant. This means you can think of the question as requesting a list of things you would like your assistant to do in helping you use the computer.

Group Project

A group of four students with relatively little experience with computers should each keep a log of all the difficulties in using the computer for their assignments. This log should be kept over a period of approximately four weeks or at least three assignments. The log should keep track of any confusing details, such as the following:

➡ I couldn't get the computer to save my essay to the disk.

➡ I needed help in starting the word processor.

➡ When I tried to copy a picture from the Internet, it wasn't clear what I should do.

As each difficulty is solved, the solution should also be noted in the log along with possible things that could have been done to avoid the problem. For example, "I tried to save my essay on a disk, but the disk wasn't formatted, and no one told me I had to format it."

At the end of this four-week period, the students should share their experiences and fit them into a small number of categories such as the following:

➡ Difficulty in getting a program started

➡ Saving results

➡ Finding things

Keep the log until the end of the semester. Then, during the last week of the term, reevaluate and write a report with suggestions that would have made your life easier.

Web Exercises

1. Search the World Wide Web for reviews or tutorials for five operating systems, such as Windows XP, Linux, Plan 9, Jini, and Macintosh X. Make a list of these sites and describe what each Web site contains.

2. Search the Web for sites dealing with GUI interfaces for UNIX and/or Linux. Make a list and describe each Web site.

3. Search the Web for frequently asked questions (FAQs) about any three of the operating systems mentioned. Hint: Look at the manufacturers' Web sites and/or user groups.

Bibliography

Brooks, Frederick P., Jr. *The Mythical Man-Month: Essays on Software Engineering.* New York: Addison-Wesley, 1995.

The Twentieth anniversary edition of this classic collection of essays on software engineering and managing complex projects.

Cooper, Alan. *About Face: The Essentials of User Interface Design.* Foster City, CA: IDG Books Worldwide, 1995.

This book is a must-read for anyone serious about user interface design, especially for Windows.

Cooper, Alan. *The Inmates Are Running the Asylum: Why High Tech Products Drive Us Crazy and How to Restore the Sanity.* Indianapolis, IN: Sams, 1999.

This book is about the many user-hostile concepts deeply embedded within the software development process.

Farley, Jim and Mike Loukides, eds. *Java Distributed Computing.* Cambridge, MA: O'Reilly, 1998.

This thorough guide explains how to harness the power of Java to create distributed systems.

Laurel, Brenda, ed. *The Art of Human–Computer Interface Design.* Reading, MA: Addison-Wesley, 1990.

This book is a collection of essays from industry luminaries such as Alan Kay, Nicholas Negroponte, and Ted Nelson.

Lewis, Rita, Simon Hayes and Bill Fishman, eds. *Mac OS in a Nutshell* (Nutshell Handbook). Cambridge, MA: O'Reilly, 2000.

Mac OS in a Nutshell is a comprehensive, compact reference that systematically reveals what serious users of Mac OS will find interesting and useful.

Meghabghab, George. *Introduction to UNIX.* Indianapolis, IN: Que Education and Training, 1999.

A detailed yet easy-to-read introduction to Unix for the serious user.

O'Hara, Shelle. *Easy Microsoft Windows 2000 Professional.* Indianapolis, IN: Que, 2000.

This is a task-based tutorial that gives you full-color, step-by-step solutions to your Windows 2000 questions.

Organick, Elliott Irving. *The Multics System: An Examination of Its Structure.* Cambridge, MA: MIT Press, 1972.

Although this book is out of print, it is a classic. Studying the grandfather of all operating systems gives great insight into their purpose and functionality.

Pogue, David. *Mac OS 9: The Missing Manual.* Cambridge, MA: O'Reilly, 2000.

This book touts itself as the guide that should have come with your copy of Apple's operating system. It offers a wealth of information from the basics to some of OS 9's more esoteric functions.

Rosenfeld, Gary, Robin Walshaw, and Eriq Oliver Neale. *Deploying Windows 2000 with Support Tools.* New York: Syngress Media/Harcourt, 2000.

This book provides a clear, expert guide to using Microsoft's new operating system to its full potential.

chapter 7

Network Concepts and Communications

TimeLine

1957 USSR launches Sputnik. The United States responds by forming the Advanced Research Projects Agency (ARPA).

1962 Paul Baran and a group at Rand Corporation begin research into a new communication network using packets.

1965 ARPA sponsors research into a cooperative network of time-sharing computers.

1969 Organization of the first four hosts of the ARPAnet takes place: UCLA, UC Santa Barbara, University of Utah, and Stanford Research Institute.

1973 File Transfer Protocol (FTP) is developed.

1979 Usenet news implemented decentralized model—grandfather of peer-to-peer.

1981 Minitel (Teletel), a national messaging network over phone lines, is deployed across France by French Telecom.

1982 TCP/IP is established as an Internet standard.

1984 Domain name system (DNS) is introduced.

1990 The World provides the first commercially available dial-up Internet access.

1999 Napster peer-to-peer MP3 file sharing was extremely popular.

2013 The majority of network traffic will be in the form of grid and cloud computing.

Chapter Objectives

- Understand how the human need to communicate has motivated the development of networking technology.

- Identify the various types of physical connections possible in a network.

- Know the five basic properties of a network link and how each contributes to the link.

- Know different ways of connecting computers in a network (bus, ring, star, tree, and fully connected).

- Identify the uses and benefits of DANs, LANs, MANs, and WANs.

- Understand how protocols control the flow of information between networks.

- Understand how information is packaged and repackaged for each intervening network when it is sent on the Internet.

Richard Falco/Black Star

PUZZLER

Your computer is on a network consisting of several computers and a printer. Imagine that you've completed a term paper using a word processor and need to print it. But each time you try printing, nothing happens. How can you solve this problem? Create at least two plans of action. The plans should not include calling the network administrator, or taking your disk to a friend's house.

7.1 Introduction: "Everything Is Connected to Everything" (John F. Akers, Former President of IBM)

During the early 1990s, a new phenomenon seized the United States and the world. By 1995 it had developed into a full-blown frenzy. Every day, computer users in hundreds of thousands of homes and offices turned on their desktop machines and went *online*, which is a term used to indicate connecting to a collection of interconnected computers called a **network**. A few keystrokes or mouse clicks quickly brought an astonishing variety of information and services to their computer monitors. People can do their banking, pay bills with a credit card, plan and book vacation travel, send messages across the office or around the world, participate in free-wheeling discussions, play "live-action" games, or purchase anything from flowers to houses. In fact, it is not uncommon for college students to obtain a course syllabus and get assignments via computer as a result of these networks. Of course, the biggest use of networks is in business. Corporate networks keep vital sales, manufacturing, and market information within reach of CEOs and other managers who need to make decisions in a fast-paced and competitive environment.

> A **network** is of a collection of computers, display terminals, printers, and other devices linked either by physical or wireless means.

The seeds of networking were planted in the fertile ground of scientific research. Germination was slow, however, until 1966, when ARPA (Advanced Research Projects Agency) focused major development effort on computer networking. ARPA is the United States Defense Department's research organization for advanced future technology that may be used to defend the United States. Its goal is to promote research on these technologies by funding university and industry research proposals.

Thousands of databases became available to the public because of the work of ARPA. Computer users can now access weather predictions, stock market quotations, lyrics to popular songs, telephone books, maps and itineraries, and contents of entire magazines and newspapers including both text and pictures. The magic that provides this wealth of information and services is called computer networking. Computer networking reaches its peak in a phenomenon called the Internet. Today most of us access the Internet through the World Wide Web, which is the most popular service provided over the Internet.

An informal naming standard that has become popular concerns the use of the words Internet and internet. This naming standard stems from an old naming convention standard. When television and radio were first introduced, "Television" and "Radio" were always capitalized. This was because it was presumed that television and radio made up new communication environments. This too has happened to the terms Internet and internet. The lowercase I in the spelling of internet referred to any collection of linked networks that is owned and controlled by a single group. Whereas the capital I in Internet conventionally refers to the collection of thousands of networks linked together under special rules. As the Internet has become more popular, more and more people are beginning to refer to it as the internet, without using the uppercase I.

> The **Internet,** commonly spelled with the uppercase *I,* is a worldwide network connecting millions of computer networks for the purpose of exchanging data and communications using special rules of communication.
>
> An **internet,** commonly spelled with a lowercase *i,* is any network connecting two or more computer networks.

There's no telling how far the Internet and the World Wide Web will take us or how quickly, but they continue to grow and are at the center of a communication revolution. As more and more links are added, and more and more services are accessible, we move inexorably closer to the time predicted by John F. Akers, when he was president of IBM, a time when "everything is connected to everything." We will examine the Internet and World Wide Web in detail in this and the next chapters.

The human need to communicate—to connect with others—has motivated humanity's creativity from the earliest prehistoric times throughout history. As shown in Figure 7.1.1, cave dwellers drew pictures on the walls of their caves, primitive peoples used smoke signals and drum rhythms, American pioneers developed the Pony Express and Wells Fargo, and Alexander Graham Bell invented the telephone.

All were answering a basic driving force of humanity—the need to share information, be recognized, and give warnings—that is, establish connections to others in the known world.

Drumbeats and puffs of smoke have given way to visual images and electronic pulses. Yet, the drive for one human being to connect and to pass information to another continues unabated. As the need for human connectivity grows, human ingenuity has developed the

(a) Jean Clottes/Corbis/Sygma

(b) Deborah Davis/PhotoEdit

(c) Equity Management Inc. (EMI)

(d) Mark Marten,
Photo Researchers, Inc.

Figure 7.1.1

(a) Cave drawings, (b) signal drums, (c) mail by stage coach, (d) Alexander Graham Bell, inventor of the telephone.

technology to enhance that connectivity. There is no doubt that we can today share more information more quickly than ever before by using computer networks.

7.2 Communication Basics of Networks

To understand computer communications we must become familiar with several concepts that permit the connection of computers into networks. Once you understand these concepts, it will be much easier to learn about the Internet and the World Wide Web, which we cover in the next chapter.

TYPES OF CONNECTIONS—PHYSICAL CONNECTION VERSUS WIRELESS

The technology that supports computer communication is neither magical nor mysterious. In fact, the conceptual idea is reasonably simple: just physically connect a bunch of computers together! This means using wires or optical cables to connect the various computers and call it a network. These connections will be referred to as **network links.**

Network links are connections between computers and other electronic devices. These network links are created with various types of physical media such as **twisted pairs** of wires (used to connect telephones), **coaxial cables** (used to connect most cable TV), **fiber-optic cables** (used in modern telephone and cable TV systems), and space (radio frequency, microwave, and laser beams traveling through space).

Physical Network Links

The three most common physical links used to create networks are:

- Twisted pair
- Coaxial cable
- Fiber-optic cable

Of the three, the easiest to visualize is the **twisted pair.** It consists of two wires twisted together to make them less susceptible to acting like an antenna and picking up radio frequency information, such as radio station signals, appliance electrical noise, or even household 60-cycle power signals from the power lines in the home or building. The telephone system uses twisted-pair copper wires to link telephones. Figure 7.2.1(a) illustrates four standard twisted pairs plus a green ground wire.

Coaxial cable also uses two wires, but the design is quite different from the twisted pair. To make the pair of wires in coaxial cable more impervious to outside electrical noise, the better cables have a mesh made of fine strands of wire, forming a tube that is electrically grounded. The other is a solid copper wire that runs down the center of this tube, and the space between is filled with a special nonconducting material. Figure 7.2.1(b) shows a single coaxial cable.

Wire or cable has definite limitations on how much information it can transmit. Light is also electromagnetic, however, and because of its higher frequencies, can transmit a lot more information through a single strand. Experiments on using optical cable have been carried out for many years. The result is the **fiber-optic cable** that both cable TV and telephone companies are now using. Figure 7.2.1(c) shows a bundle of fiber-optic cable. It is more economical to bundle several individual optical fiber strands together in many applications. Each individual cable can carry the equivalent of several thousand phone conversations or computer communications.

The three cables types just discussed are all physical forms of electronic links. You can touch and hold twisted pair, coaxial cable, or fiber-optic cable in your hand.

Wireless Network Links

Another form of equally useful links is wireless. That means the link or connection is made using electromagnetic energy that goes through space

Figure 7.2.1

Three physical types of links used in networks: (a) twisted pair, (b) coaxial cable, (c) fiber-optic cable bundle.

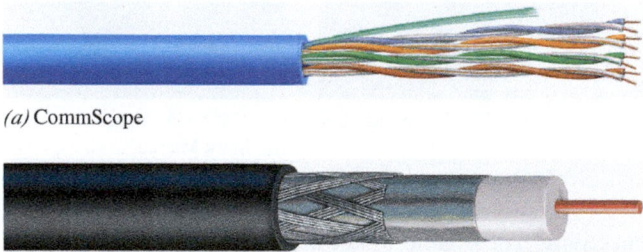

(a) CommScope

(b) CommScope

(c) © 1997 George B. Diebold/The Stock Market

instead of traveling along wires or cables. The following three types of wireless communications are commonly used in networking:

- Infrared
- Radio frequency
- Microwave

Infrared communication is commonly used in TV and VCR remote controls. One of the characteristics of infrared communication is that both devices must be in line of sight. If someone is between you and the TV, for example, your controller won't work unless it has a strong enough signal to bounce off a wall to reach your TV. Infrared frequencies of electromagnetic radiation behave almost the same as visible light. In the computing world, keyboards and mice can use infrared for the link so that you aren't restricted by wires. Figure 7.2.2 shows a Bluetooth folding keyboard ready for action.

Radio frequency links can function even though the line of sight is interrupted. The benefits of this are obvious. Suppose, for example, that you park your car in a huge parking lot and can't remember where. Some automobile electronic keys that use radio frequencies can be used to flash the car lights when you press the correct button on the electronic key, thereby making the car's location obvious. Cell phones also use radio frequencies but at different wavelengths so that they don't interfere with automobile usage. This form of communication between computers is becoming very popular. The two most recent standards being used are **bluetooth** and **Wi-Fi.** The bluetooth standard developed in 1994 was designed to eliminate the cabling used for connections that are such a nuisance. It has a range of about 30 feet and is often used to hook keyboards and mice wirelessly to the computer. It has, however, made a big impact in the cell phone communication area, with remote head sets and the synchronization of cell phone address books with computers leading the way.

The second standard is referred to as Wi-Fi, or technically as the IEEE 802.11 family (Institute of Electrical and Electronics Engineers). These standards were designed for computer access to local area networks and the Internet. One of Wi-Fi's more visible applications is in many of the coffee shops, where they offer free Internet access. There are others offering this service in airports and hotels, sometimes for a fee. Wi-Fi has a range of about 300 feet and is faster than bluetooth communication. Wi-Fi first surfaced in products in 1997.

As it is often necessary to establish communication with distant locations, **microwave** frequencies and satellite links are quite useful for large-volume communication. The obvious advantage is that physical wires or cables don't have to be strung from one location to the other. In today's communication world, microwave towers and dish antennas dot the landscape. One of the main disadvantages of microwaves is that they can only be used in the line of sight. No obstructions may exist between the transmitting and receiving antennas. In

Infrared communication is wireless and uses infrared frequencies of electromagnetic radiation that are just beyond human visibility at the red end of the light spectrum. It works only in the line of sight, much the same as TV channel changers.

Radio frequency communication is wireless and uses radio frequencies of electromagnetic radiation. Connected devices do not have to be in the line of sight. It's much like AM/FM radio that can be heard on radio receivers inside many buildings.

The **bluetooth** standard was created to replace desktop cabling. It has a range of about 30 feet and is commonly used to allow connections between computers, keyboards, printers, cell phones and many other devices.

Wi-Fi is a standard created to allow wireless networking and access to the Internet. It has a range of about 300 feet.

Figure 7.2.2

A Bluetooth folding keyboard for use with smartphones, PDAs, and other computers.

Courtesy of Freedom Input USA

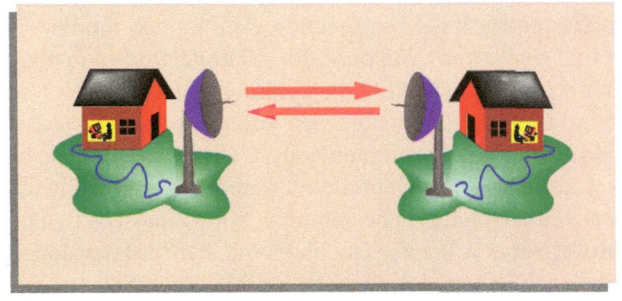

(b)

Figure 7.2.3

(a) Microwave towers, (b) two microwave towers in line of sight.

fact, heavy rainfall sometimes can have deleterious effects on microwave communication. The photograph in Figure 7.2.3(a) shows a cluster of typical towers with microwave antennae. We can't easily see the other towers they communicate with because they are so far apart, but their relationship is shown in the accompanying diagram in Figure 7.2.3(b).

Communications satellites also use microwaves, but a satellite has its own receiving and transmitting antennas and links together two or more Earth stations. Figure 7.2.4(a) shows a typical communications satellite. The satellite acts as a relay station between one Earth-based microwave station and one or many others, as shown in the diagram of Figure 7.2.4(b).

PROPERTIES OF TRANSMISSION

Both types of communication links mentioned in the previous part of this section—physical and wireless—have some common attributes that should be discussed. These attributes are important whether dealing with cable TV or telephone and computer communications.

There are five basic properties of both the physical and wireless links:

1. Type of signal communicated (analog or digital)
2. The speed at which the signal is transmitted (how fast the data travel)
3. The type of data movement allowed on the channel (one-way, two-way taking turns, two-way simultaneously)
4. The method used to transport the data (asynchronous or synchronous transmission)
5. Single-channel (baseband) and multichannel (broadband) transmission

Digital signals are those signals that vary in steps or jumps from value to value. They are usually in the form of pulses of electrical energy.

Analog signals are those signals that vary with smooth, continuous changes.

Type of Signal   The signal can be in one of two forms: digital or analog. **Digital signals** consist of pulses of electrical energy that represent 0s or 1s (that is, binary numbers). On the other hand, the **analog signal** is a continuously changing signal similar to that found

(a) PhotoDisc, Inc.

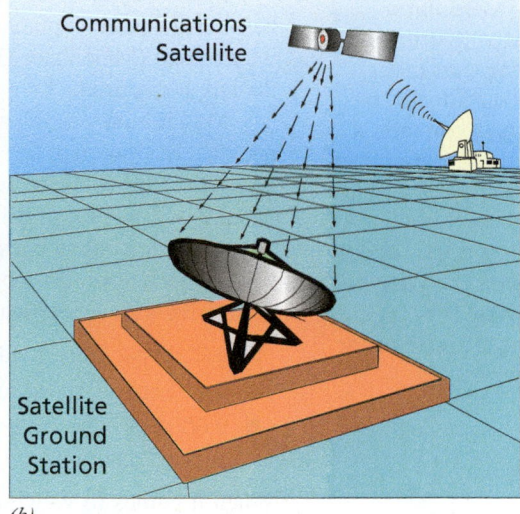

Communications Satellite

Satellite Ground Station

(b)

Figure 7.2.4

(a) Communications satellite, (b) base station linking to satellite.

on the speaker wires of a high-fidelity audio system. Figure 7.2.5 shows these two basic types of communications signals.

Analog signals are typically of lower quality than digital signals. This is evident in audio cassette tapes and vinyl record formats, which suffer from wear and limitations of fidelity. The phone system was mostly analog, but is now being converted to digital. This move to digital systems is also evident in the stereo recording field where compact discs (CDs) are digital. And, in the television industry, the production of televisions and the transmission of television signals has moved to digital. Why is it inevitable that these changes from analog to digital formats are taking place? It is easier to maintain quality and control over noise and errors with a digital system.

Speed of Signal   The speed at which the data can be transmitted is important. Currently, it is impossible, for example, to transmit a complete TV broadcast signal through a telephone line. The speed at which signals are fed to the channel and the enormous amount of data in the TV signal would limit the picture to TV snapshots taken several seconds apart.

The speed of transmission in digital systems is measured in **bits per second (bps).** Bits per second is a measure of how fast binary digits can be sent through a channel, that is, the number of 0s and 1s that travel down the channel per second. Whereas Bps is the number of 8-bit bytes traveling down the channel per second, another term frequently used to describe transmission speed on a digital channel is called the **baud rate.** The baud rate, often confused with bps, is a number indicating how many times the signal on a channel changes per second.

Bits per second (bps) is a measure of how fast binary digits can be sent through a channel (that is, the number of 0s and 1s that travel down the channel per second). The **baud rate,** often confused with bps, is a number indicating how many times the signal on a channel changes per second.

Figure 7.2.5

Analog and digital signals.

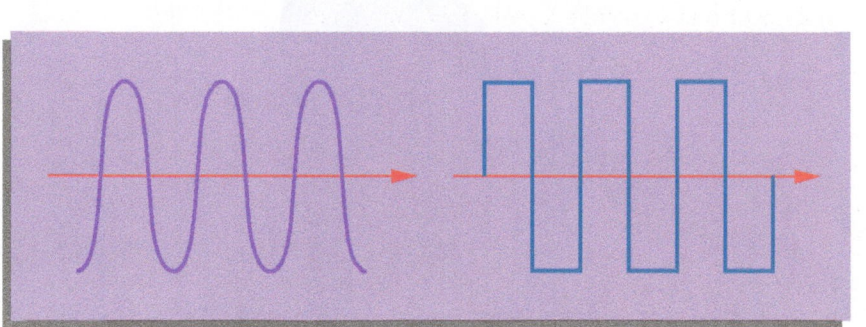

A **modem** (MOdulator DEModulator) is an electronic device that takes the binary data from the computer and converts them to analog data (modulates) so that they can be sent over telephone lines. The receiving-end modem then converts the data back (demodulates) from analog to digital so the computer can use them.

In the personal computer field, communicating data over the analog telephone system between a microcomputer and some destination is achieved through an electronic device called the **modem** (MOdulator DEModulator). The modem allows the computer to be connected to the link being used.

Modems are usually rated in bits per second. The speed of modems commonly used with personal computers is 56 Kbps. Kilobits per second (Kbps) means a thousand bits per second. For efficient World Wide Web communication, 56 Kbps is the minimum speed to use. Telephone lines are of different qualities. It is not unusual for 56 Kbps modems to be used with better telephone lines. To put communication speed into perspective, assume someone is watching a news release being sent to a computer screen. Different bps rates would cause the news release to appear with the following effects:

- 1,200 bps: Good readers can keep up with words printed.
- 2,400 bps: A speed reader would get the gist of the words.
- 9,600 bps: The words fly past the screen in a fraction of a second and would be impossible to read unless a pause occurs.

When it comes to viewing on the World Wide Web, each of the following bps rates would have delays for a reasonably sized graphic image, as indicated:

- 14.4 Kbps: Quite common in communications; a 10- to 20-second delay waiting for graphics.
- 28.8 Kbps: A 5- to 10-second wait for graphics.
- 56 Kbps: Minimum for World Wide browsing with full graphics.
- 2 Mbps: Rate at which slower cable modems operate, depending on the number of users connected.
- 5 Mbps: Higher rate at which cable modems operate. Great connection speed with little delay.

Modems for microcomputer communication come in many forms. But, for personal computer users there are basically three types. The older dialup phone systems require one type used on either digital or analog phones, whereas much faster access to the Internet via broadband is either the cable modem for cable TV systems or the DSL modem for the telephone companies' Digital Subscriber Line. Both of these broadband types of access make use of excess channel capacity of cable TV line or the DSL line respectively.

Modems for microcomputers are made in both external and internal forms. The external form is in a box separate from the computer and the internal form plugs into the motherboard of the computer.

Simplex transmission is one-way communication of data.

Type of Data Movement on the Link

Three basic types of data movement can occur on the link. The most basic movement is called **simplex transmission.** This is a one-way transmission of data. It is usually used for displaying information. An example is the display of flight arrivals and departures on TV monitors found at most airports. Information appears on them, but the observer cannot make changes or send information back to the source (sender).

Half-duplex transmission is two-way communication of data but only in one direction at a time.

A more general form of data flow is found in **half-duplex transmission.** In this form, the data can flow one way or the opposite way on the channel but not in both directions at the

Figure 7.2.6

External cable modem for use with broadband connection.

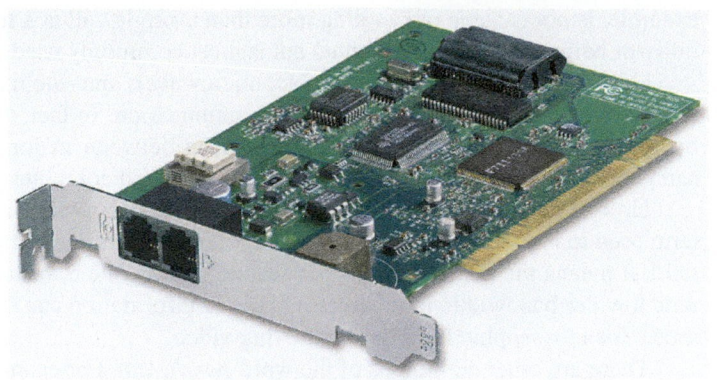

U.S. Robotics Corporation

Figure 7.2.7

Internal modem, which is inserted into the computer.

same time. Push-to-talk cell phone services with a "walkie-talkie" type transmission currently use this type of data movement. **Full-duplex transmission** allows transmission in both directions at the same time. The telephone and the computer are the most familiar examples of full-duplex transmission. Figure 7.2.8 depicts these three types of data movement.

Full-duplex transmission is communication of data in both directions at the same time.

Method of Transmission

There are two basic methods of data transmission, each requiring a different type of modem. One is called asynchronous transmission; the other is called synchronous transmission. In **asynchronous transmission,** information is sent in individual bytes, one byte at a time. As each byte is sent, it is preceded by a start bit, which alerts the receiving computer that the byte is being sent. Transmission of a message consisting of several bytes may take some time because the bytes are not connected together. After all bytes have been received, the message must be reassembled before it can be read. Asynchronous transmission is cheaper than synchronous and is commonly used in data entry via keyboard to CPU or main memory.

Asynchronous transmission is when data are sent byte by byte without regard to how much time elapses between bytes.

In **synchronous transmission** data are sent in large blocks rather than in small pieces. Each block is preceded by special information concerning error detection and block size. Synchronization bits are used to organize the block, which is made up of bytes that flow along just like a train. Synchronous modems are quite expensive, but they are very fast. This method of transmission is used for transporting large amounts of information, and it is more efficient than asynchronous transmission.

Synchronous transmission is when data are sent in a stream with the bytes precisely timed so that they can be received without the need for starting and stopping signals for each byte.

Single-Channel versus Multichannel Transmission

Each of the physical or wireless means of linking can carry at least one channel of communication. A channel is a path for the signal, just like a TV channel. In the case of both twisted-pair and coaxial cable, a single signal is most common. The normal telephone line coming into your home, for

Figure 7.2.8

Simplex, half-duplex, and full-duplex transmission.

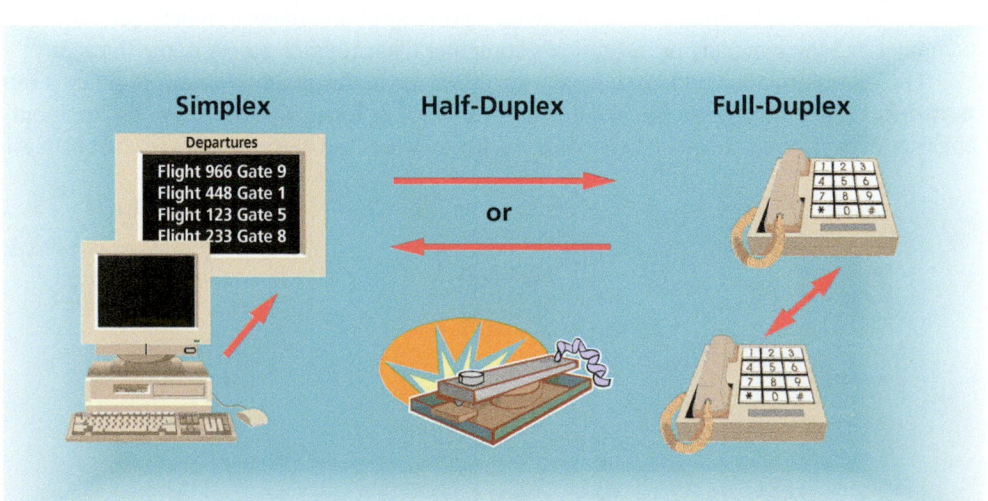

Simplex   **Half-Duplex**   **Full-Duplex**

Departures

Flight 966 Gate 9
Flight 448 Gate 1
Flight 123 Gate 5
Flight 233 Gate 8

or

The **bandwidth** of a communications link is the number of bits per second (bps) that can be sent over that link.

Table 7.2.1 *Typical cable bandwidths used in local area networks.*

Cable	Typical Bandwidth
Twisted pair	10 to 100 Mbps
Coaxial cable	10 to 100 Mbps
Fiber-optic cable	100 to 2,400 Mbps

Table 7.2.2 *The bandwidth of different services offered by phone, broadband cable, and satellite companies.*

Service	Bandwidth (Mbps)
ISDN	0.064 /channel
DSL(dn)	1.5
DSL(up)	0.64
Cable	10–30
Satellite(dn)	0.6–1.4
Satellite(up)	0.064
T1	1.5
STS-1	51

Node is the generic name given to all devices hooked up to a network. Each one must have a unique address assigned to it by the network.

Direct-connect networks are those whose nodes have direct connections through either physical or wireless links. They can also be referred to as **connection-oriented networks**.

example, is not capable of handling more than a single call at a time. Infrared has the capability of being used for multichannel but is most commonly used as a single-channel device.

On the other hand, fiber-optic cable, microwaves, and satellite transmissions most commonly carry more than one channel of communication. In fact, the microwave signals used by telephone companies to carry phone traffic between major cities can simultaneously carry thousands of individual phone conversations and computer communications.

How is it possible to measure the capacity of communication links? **Bandwidth** is a term used to measure the capacity of a link to send information. In the computer-networking field, it means the number of bits per second that can be transmitted on the link. Note that with a wider bandwidth, more diverse kinds of information can be sent—the simplest being voice, the most sophisticated being moving video.

There are other definitions of the word *bandwidth*. For example, in the analog world, it means the difference between the highest and lowest frequencies that can be sent over an analog link. The measurement is given in hertz (Hz). However, for both definitions, a wider bandwidth means more information can flow over the channel.

The bandwidths of several common cable links used in networks and also telephone services are shown in Tables 7.2.1 and 7.2.2. Note that Kbps means kilobits per second (thousands of bits per second); Mbps means megabits per second (millions of bits per second); and Gbps means gigabits per second (billions of bits per second). Also note that the acronym STS (synchronous transport signal) indicates the link is optical fiber.

7.3 The Physical Organization of Networks

Now that we are familiar with the basic concepts of networks, let's see how computers get connected together to form networks. There are two parts to this: hardware, which physically hooks the computers together, and software, which controls the hardware.

LINKING COMPUTERS TOGETHER—DIRECT-CONNECT NETWORKS

When two or more devices are linked, the total collection is called a network, as defined in section 7.2. Each individual device, whether it is a computer, terminal, or printer, is called a **node** of the network. The nodes are linked to each other by physical or wireless means. It is important to differentiate between **direct-connect networks** and those networks that are not directly linked, such as the Internet. The telephone system is an example of a directly connected network. When you are talking to someone, a connection is maintained between you and the person to whom you are talking.

The simplest of all networks is obtained by connecting two computing systems, one at each end of the communications link as shown in Figure 7.3.1. This is a common type of network but somewhat limiting. It is referred to as a **point-to-point network.** This is how some of us connect to the Internet from home, with a point-to-point connection between our home computer and the company or institution's computer that provides access to the Internet.

The most common and inexpensive way to link the nodes of any network is called a **bus network.** Figure 7.3.2 shows an example of this simplest form. The bus network commonly consists of an optical fiber or twisted-pair wire to which all the devices are attached. All

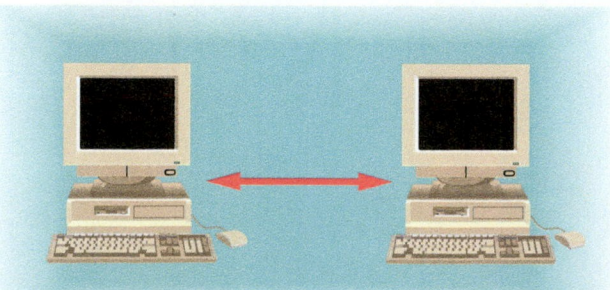

Figure 7.3.1

Computing systems connected by a point-to-point link.

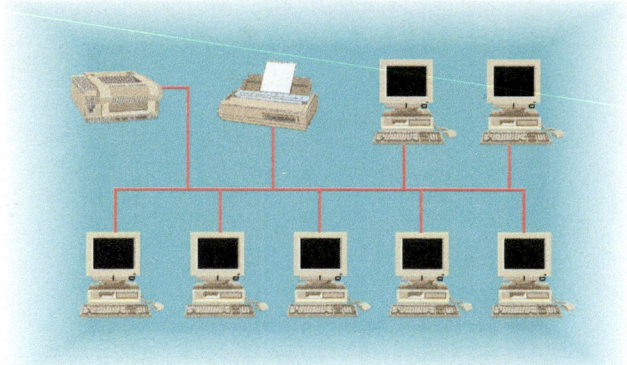

Figure 7.3.2

The bus network.

nodes (devices) on the bus can detect all messages sent along the bus at the same time. As a message is sent from one node (for example, a computer) to another (for example, a printer), a special part of the message (address) is used to select the destination (printer) and let the data through (to be printed). All the other devices will ignore the data not meant for them.

The **ring network** consists of nodes linked together to form a circle as shown in Figure 7.3.3. A message is sent from one node, usually a computer, to the next until it reaches its destination. As each node receives the message, it either carries out the action specified by the message or retransmits it to the next node on the ring.

The **star network** shown in Figure 7.3.4 has each node linked to a central node. All messages must be routed through the central node. The central node acts as a controlling device and will route the messages properly between the other nodes.

Figure 7.3.5 shows what looks like an upside-down tree and is, in fact, called a **tree network.** It is also sometimes referred to as a hierarchical network. The end nodes are linked to interior nodes that allow linking through to another end node. End nodes are the last nodes on each line; in other words, they are the leaves of the tree. This network arrangement is used in

Bus, ring, star, tree and **fully connected networks** are all different ways of electronically connecting computers together.

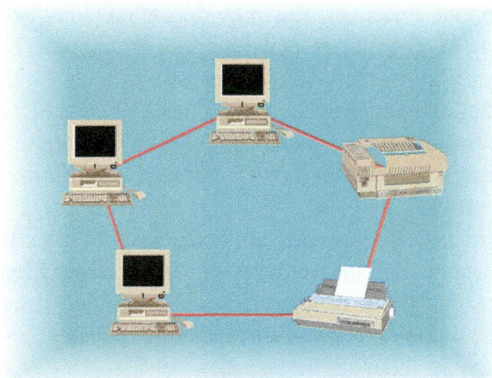

Figure 7.3.3

The ring network.

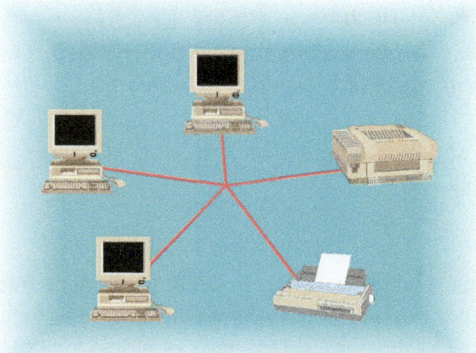

Figure 7.3.4

The star network.

Figure 7.3.5

The tree network.

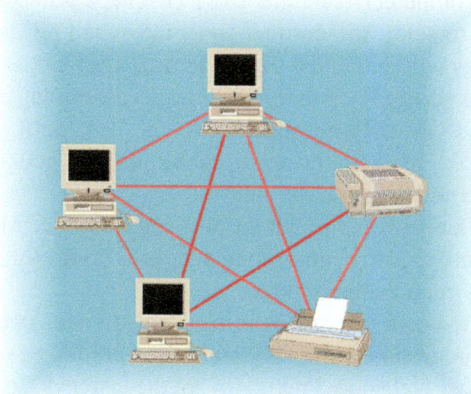

Figure 7.3.6

The fully connected network.

the telephone system. The end nodes in the telephone system are the individual telephones, and the interior nodes are the nodes that allow linking to other end-node telephones or computers.

The **fully connected network** is shown in Figure 7.3.6. It is the most complete of all networks. All nodes are linked to all other nodes. This means each node has a direct link to all other nodes. This would indeed be a very expensive type of network to build, and it is seldom used except when extreme speed and reliability are needed. No companies or corporations could afford or need fully connected networks.

In addition to direct-connect networks, there are also those networks that are not directly linked. This important and revolutionary concept is called internetworking. **Internetworking** consists of providing links between any number of any type of the direct-connected networks. The result of internetworking is as small as just linking any two of the direct-connected networks previously discussed, or it can be the largest of them all, the Internet.

Internetworking is the term used when direct-connect networks are connected together.

NETWORKS ON DIFFERENT SCALES

A common way to categorize networks is according to their size. Each size category has its own set of limitations and requirements. There are four common categories of networks:

- DAN (desk area network)
- LAN (local area network)
- MAN (metropolitan area network)
- WAN (wide area network)

A **desk area network (DAN)** consists of the parts of a single desktop computer that are linked by their normal connections. The most useful are the CPU, display, and hard drive. These components can be made available to any other computer on the network.

Desk Area Networks   The most recent networking category is **DAN (desk area network).** The basic idea behind DAN is to make all components of your desktop computer available to all other computers on the network. The most important parts of a desktop computer that are useful to other people on the network are as follows:

- *CPU.* Unused computing power could be used by other computers.
- *Hard disk.* Items stored on your hard drive might be needed by others, or someone may want to put some information on your hard drive.
- *Video display.* Alert messages from a central source, such as the arrival of an e-mail message, might be important to you sitting at your computer.
- *Other items.* Printers, cameras, or other I/O devices connected to your computer might be needed by others.

Local Area Networks   Communication between computer-related devices became necessary as working groups of individuals needed to share information and computer peripherals, such as printers, fax machines, and hard disk drives. Because most of the equipment was located within a relatively small geographic area—a campus, a building, or even a room—a type of interconnection called a **local area network (LAN)** was created.

The simplest of these LANs is the bus network arrangement as shown in Figure 7.3.2. This system is popular because it is inexpensive and easy to connect. Rings and other linking arrangements are also used. In all cases, however, each node will need a special interface card to connect to the LAN. A LAN is usually contained within a building and is used to connect users and their computers to file servers, the Internet, printers, and other peripherals. LANs never extend beyond a few kilometers. In fact, one type of network design, called an ethernet, can cover only up to one-half mile. The ethernet was originally designed at the Xerox Palo Alto Research Center and has become very popular.

A **local area network (LAN)** is a collection of nodes within a small area. The nodes are linked in a bus, ring, star, or tree arrangement.

PUZZLER HINT

Your printing problem is on a network called a LAN. There may be other services, such as e-mail, that are provided by the network. Check to see if these other services are working. At least this will tell you if your computer has a working connection to the network.

Computer Networks: The Beginning

Networking computers was only a dream for many computer scientists until Bob Taylor, director of computer research at ARPA (Advanced Research Projects Agency), focused sponsored research on what was to become the Internet. Building on the ideas of many others, Taylor organized ARPA research funding, including the hiring of Larry Roberts as program manager, to create a major computer networking effort in 1966. Key to the development of computer networks were the ideas of Paul Baran and Donald Davies, who independently came up with the idea

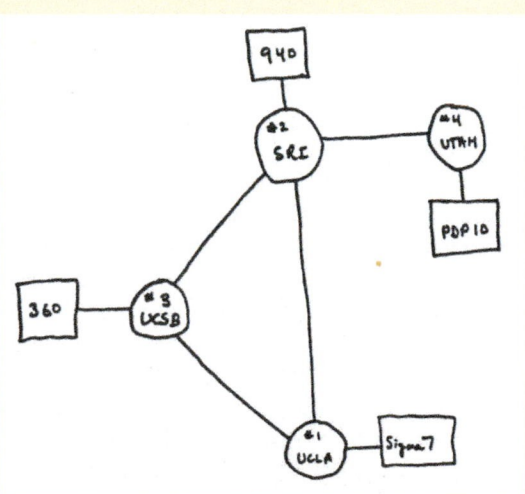

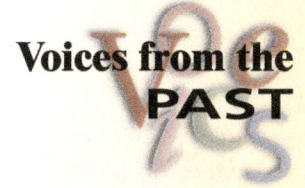
Voices from the PAST

of packet switching in the early 1960s. Unlike the direct-connect telephone system, this revolutionary idea was to divide messages into smaller pieces or packets. The next step is to send the packets to their destination, not hooked together like a train, but independently like bees going back to the hive. The principle purpose of ARPAnet was to share expensive computing resources. Computer researchers needed more and more computers to perform the ARPA-sponsored research, and sharing resources seemed to offer some budget relief to ARPA. In 1969 ARPAnet became operational with the first four nodes at UCLA, UC Santa Barbara, SRI (Stanford Research Institute), and the University of Utah. By the mid-1970s, ARPAnet linked together several military sites and about 20 universities.

LANs can be used not only to share resources but also to enable communication between individuals through the use of networking applications. One widely used application is e-mail, or electronic mail, where, for example, a supervisor can electronically send a memo to all employees at one time. Another networking application is groupware, which allows individuals to send e-mail messages and files, and leave voice mail for each other while collaborating on a project. Following are the main benefits of local area networks.

- Hardware resource sharing (laser writer, hard drive)
- Software and data sharing (applications software)
- Consolidated wiring/cabling
- Simultaneous distribution of information
- More efficient person-to-person communications

A **metropolitan area network (MAN)** consists of many local area networks linked together. They normally span distances of just a few miles.

Metropolitan Area Networks

When developing networks that span distances of several miles or about the size of a large metropolitan area, it is necessary to use higher-speed links than LANs. These **metropolitan area networks (MANs)** must be designed so that information flow is not affected by failure of links or other minor disruptions, such as a major information traffic route being disabled by an accidental cable cutting. One design solution is called DQDB (Distributed Queue Dual Bus). Its name describes the essence of the solution. DQDB means that two electronic links have information flow distributed evenly between them. It's like having two lanes for traffic rather than just one.

Wide area networks (WANs) consist of a number of computer networks, including LANs, that are connected by many different types of links.

Wide Area Networks

As is suggested by the name, **wide area networks (WANs)** are spread out over a wider area. In fact, the Internet-wide area network spans the Earth. WANs usually consist of a number of computer networks connected together over various communication channels such as telephone lines, microwave links, and satellite transmissions.

Examples of wide area networks abound, but the Internet is the most influential new WAN. The most familiar example is the old but reliable telephone network. Both of these WANs cover every country on Earth. As networks have proliferated, various corporations, government agencies, and other enterprises have created their own internal networks. These are referred to as intranets or enterprise networks. An **intranet** or **enterprise network** is a network used and controlled by a single corporation or government agency for internal communication. Intranets have their own special set of problems to be solved. Security of the network, for example, is usually considered a top priority. This is easy to understand when considering the importance of research and financial records. Corporate spies have been known to try cracking into a competitor's networks. Some have even succeeded. One of the most talked about solutions to this security problem is something called a **firewall.** In simple terms, a firewall is a set of programs that monitors all communication passing into and out of a corporation's intranet. This helps prevent but doesn't eliminate unauthorized access or use of corporate data. The term *firewall* can be used to indicate a protective shield between any two networks, but it still allows authorized communication.

An **intranet** or **enterprise network** is a network used and controlled by a single corporation or government agency for internal communication.

Firewall is a term used to describe software that shields or guards a network from outside unauthorized communication.

7.4 Software Architecture of the Network

In the beginning of this book we introduced the concepts of hardware and software. It is quite clear that without software, nothing can happen. This section examines the software side of networking and the standards necessary for computers on a network to be compatible.

Hedy Lamarr: Inventor of Spread Spectrum

Who would have ever believed that a Hollywood film star sex symbol co-created one of the most important inventions of this century? Spread spectrum or frequency hopping is the major feature that allows Bluetooth, Wi-Fi, cordless phones, GPS and other wireless systems to communicate efficiently without error. The main concept is that instead of a communications signal remaining on a singe frequency throughout its transmission, the stream of binary information "rides on" frequencies that "jump around" in a prescribed manner such that the receiving device is listening on the right frequency at the right time. This avoids the very nasty problems of radio interference, which can be caused by things such as electric hand tools, microwave ovens, heavy electric machinery, automobile ignition noise and many other origins. Without frequency hopping there would be major problems with cell phones, Bluetooth, Wi-Fi and other wireless communication.

Hedy Lamarr was born in 1913 as Hedwig Eva Maria Kiesler in Vienna, Austria-Hungary. She was recognized for both her beauty and talent at an early age. Not as well known were her mathematical and scientific abilities. Rather than leaving her at home to pursue acting, a jealous industrialist husband took her to many military technology meetings where she learned a great deal of science. It is not exactly clear how she got out from under Hiltler's influence. One version is that she disguised herself as one of the maids and escaped to Paris in 1937. Hollywood mogel Louis B. Mayer recognized her ability and beauty and persuaded her to come to Hollywood under the name Hedy Lamarr.

At this point in World War II, the Axis forces were radio jamming the Allied radio controlled torpedoes. Recognizing the inherent problem, she and and another actor came up with a scheme that prevented the jamming. The idea of frequency hopping was hers, and her partner provided implementation strategy. She and her partner received a US patent in 1942 for the concept, but it was never used in WWII. Not long after her patent expired the US used the concept during the Cuban missile crisis. The spread spectrum concept was kept secret by the US government until the 1980s. The idea is hailed today as a fundamental breakthrough.

THE RULES OF OPERATION: PROTOCOLS OF A NETWORK

The concept of connecting a bunch of computers with wires is simple enough to imagine. What happens after that is not quite as intuitively simple. This is the problem:

> Connect several computers that may be different and running different operating systems such as Windows, Linux, Macintosh, UNIX, or any number of other operating systems. Now find a way to get things such as e-mail, data, and files exchanged between them. Then allow for connections to other networks running an unknown combination of operating systems.

A **protocol** is a set of rules that allows an orderly exchange of information between nodes on a network. It is implemented in the form of a collection of programs called a **protocol suite.** These programs must be on all computers or nodes in the network. The necessary programs from the suite are executed when needed to prepare information to be sent over the network.

A **network's architecture** is the overall organization of the rules of the network and is implemented in a set of programs called the protocol suite. The protocol suite is organized into parts that make it easier to implement a particular network architecture.

TCP/IP (Transmission Control Protocol/Internet Protocol) is a collection of over 100 programs that must be on any computer that is part of the Internet. Among the many tasks these programs do are to prepare data for sending over the Internet and to receive data from the Internet.

The problem is solved by creating a set of rules or **protocols** that, when followed, will allow an orderly exchange of information. Each computer or node in the network must have copies of the network protocols. These protocols are in the form of a collection of programs sometimes called a **protocol suite.**

When information is sent over the network by one computer to another computer, the protocol program on the originating computer will execute. It will "package up" the information so that it can be sent on its way. As the "packaged up" information makes its way along the network, it may be "repackaged" by other nodes, such as gateways and routers (described later in the chapter). When the packaged information reaches the destination, it then has to be unpackaged by the protocol suite programs to a form that is compatible with the receiving computer or other device.

The protocol suite and the general scheme that guides its rules are called the **network architecture.** It is analogous to the design of a building being called its architecture. The difficulty in creating a network architecture for particular networks was made easier by breaking down the network into smaller pieces that could be more easily programmed. Several years ago some experts created a very complete protocol called OSI (Open System Interconnect) that was broken down into seven layers or parts. The computer industry generally adopted this model, but it is not the most popular. In 1980 the University of California at Berkeley made available a four-layer architecture implemented in a protocol suite called **TCP/IP,** which is named after the two protocols TCP (Transmission Control Protocol) and IP (Internet Protocol). It was especially easy to obtain and written for the very popular operating system called UNIX, which ran on thousands of computers throughout the country. This huge base of computers with TCP/IP gave the beginning of the Internet a jump start.

Many protocol suites are commercially available and in use on LANs and WANs. AppleTalk and Novell NetWare IPX, for example, are both LAN related. For WANs there are the SNA and ATM architectures. Each of these products solves the most important problems of network management in its own way.

PUZZLER HINT

Your printing problem is still not solved. Check to see if others on the network are having printing problems. At least you can determine if it's your computer or one that affects everyone.

Of the many network management problems that must be faced, one of the easiest to understand involves the collision of information. The collision of information is caused by two computers simultaneously attempting to send information to the network. There are many ways to take care of this problem; let's examine three such solutions:

1. **AppleTalk** protocol (created by Apple Computer)—Collisions are handled by using a concept called handshaking, which the following example illustrates. Device-A sends out a request for communication to device-B, and if device-B receives this request it will acknowledge the request. This will essentially reserve the link for their communication. If some other device simultaneously sent out a request to different device for communication, neither request gets through. With no response, device-A waits a random amount of time and tries again. Eventually the exchange is made.

2. **Token Ring** Protocol (originated by IBM, many variations available)—A token, a special piece of information, is passed around the nodes of a ring network. Collisions are avoided completely because an individual node can send only when it possesses the token.

3. **Ethernet** Protocol (originated by Xerox, many variations available)—Collisions are not avoided; they are taken care of when they occur. Suppose two nodes simultaneously attempt to send a message over the network that originally looked available. As they

both start to send out information, each detects the other's presence. At that point, they both stop and wait for a randomly assigned time period and then again attempt to send information.

THE ARCHITECTURE OF THE INTERNET

The Internet has become a pervasive part of our lives. Regardless of your background or career, you will have some contact with its terminology. Almost everyone who has "surfed the Net" is familiar with the acronyms HTTP, TCP/IP, and FTP. These are designations for Internet protocols. What they do and where they are in the architecture of the Internet will help you understand how the Internet works.

As mentioned earlier, the Internet architecture can be interpreted as being based on a four-layer protocol suite. These rules, or protocols, are in the form of programs that must be on all computers that are part of the Internet. Figure 7.4.1 illustrates the four-layer architecture, and the definitions of acronyms used are in Table 7.4.1.

It should be noted that these protocols are not owned by a particular company or individual and are, therefore, in the public domain. Protocols are well defined and can be used by anyone to write programs or use applications following the rules that they represent.

It is necessary to understand another major concept before examining how the Internet works. This is the concept of packaging information before it goes out to the Internet. All network protocols require information to be packaged in a form that can be moved around on the network. For efficiency, a single standard size unit of information must be used. This size is fixed, so if something to be moved over the network is larger than the standard size for that particular network, it must be divided up into units called **packets,** frames, or segments.

Unlike the direct-connect telephone system, this revolutionary idea involves sending the packets making up each message to their destination, not hooked together like a train, but independently, like bees going back to the hive. The concept of packets and **packet switching** provided the foundation for what would one day grow to become the Internet. For that reason, the Internet is referred to as a packet-switched network. Each packet contains important information regarding its content, where it came from, and where it is supposed to go. Unfortunately,

> A **packet** is a collection of bytes containing various types of information that usually includes where it came from and the address of where it's going. **Packet switching** is the process of moving packets in a network from node to node until the destination is reached.

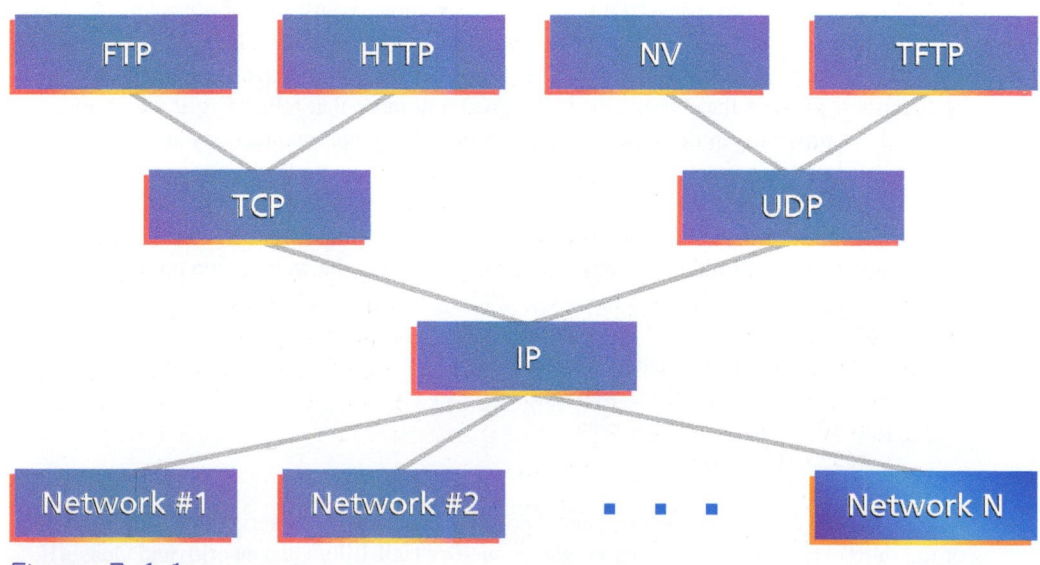

Figure 7.4.1

The Internet's four-layer architecture.

Table 7.4.1   *Four-layer architecture definitions.*

FTP (File Transfer Protocol)	Allows the transfer of files between two computers over the Internet.
HTTP (HyperText Transport Protocol)	Allows the use of browsers such as Netscape Navigator and Microsoft's Internet Explorer. These browser programs and others are usually written with the HTTP built in to them. This allows information to be sent out to and received from the Internet.
NV (Network Video)	Allows the use of live videoconferencing that runs over MBone. (MBone or Multicast backBone allows multicast routers to send live video across the Internet).
TFTP (Trivial File Transport Protocol)	Allows the use of Telnet for remote logon, SMTP (Simple Mail Transfer Protocol), and e-mail communication.
TCP (Transmission Control Protocol)	Provides a very reliable channel over which a stream of bytes is passed up to the application running on the computer.
UDP (User Datagram Protocol)	Provides a less reliable channel than TCP to programs running on the computer where it resides. Used mainly for audio- and video-related information that can tolerate small errors. A datagram can be thought of as a message.
IP (Internet Protocol)	Translates a particular network's interactions into the standard Internet formats to be used by TCP and UDP.
Network #N	A particular network's protocol (for example, Ethernet).

to make things even more complicated, each network that a packet goes through also has its standard packet or frame sizes. As an Internet packet makes its way to a destination, it is constantly being packaged and repackaged to fit the network that it is passing through.

A **connectionless** network is one that uses packet switching to perform communication. It is in contrast to the direct-connect or connection-oriented networks.

It is important to note that this **connectionless** network could have some direct-connect components. But this does not mean it is a directly connected or **connection-oriented** network. Signing onto the Internet, for example, often involves using the telephone system to reach a computer that is on the Internet.

TCP/IP and Application Ports

The TCP/IP protocol consists of programs that are used for many different applications. Downloading MP3 files using FTP protocol, for example, is just one of a possible 65,535 possible programs in the TCP/IP program suite. There aren't nearly this many programs in the TCP/IP program suite, so there is plenty of room for future expansion allowing other applications. Each of these programs is assigned a number that tells TCP/IP which of the hundreds of programs in the suite is needed to handle the communications at hand. When you are surfing the Internet using the World Wide Web, for example, the program numbered 80 is used, or more often we say that port 80 is used. There are three categories of port numbers: (1) well known ports, (2) registered ports and (3) dynamic/private ports. The well-known ports are numbered between 0 and 1023. Included in the well-known ports are:

    port 23   Telnet
    port 69   Trivial file transfer protocol
    port 80   The World Wide Web (http)
    port 107   Remote Telnet service
    port 523   IBM-DB2

Port 1433 is an example of a registered port that Microsoft SQL server uses. An example of the third category are Quake-based games such as Half-Life, Quakeworld, and QuakeIII, which use numerous ports in the 26000-28000 range.

In summary, the term port with an associated number refers to a program that is part of the TCP/IP program suite. Its purpose is to handle the network communications for a specific use, such as email.

Figure 7.4.2 illustrates how a packet travels on a network. A woman named Lucinda is running a World Wide Web browser program on her computer, which is linked to Network A. She is requesting a home page located on the hard drive of Lena's computer. A home page is information collected at a single address on the World Wide Web. Lena had to have some additional software added to the HTTP program so that her computer can deliver the requested home page. Lena's computer is linked to Network B. All the boxes inside the rectangles labeled as Lucinda's and Lena's computers represent programs on those respective computers. There are, of course, many other programs, such as the operating system, but the purpose of this example is to focus on the Internet part of the process.

These programs—FTP, HTTP, NV, TFTP, TCP, UDP, and IP—are part of the Internet protocol suite, which has over 100 programs. The figure also shows that the two computers are indirectly linked through many nodes and networks represented by the cloud-shaped object, the Internet.

Another amazing fact is that not all the packets will travel along the same path through the Internet. They have all been numbered so that reassembly of the original request for Lena's home page can be accomplished.

This is a good time to reinforce a key concept describing how the Internet works. To do this, let's first look at the telephone system. When you make a telephone call, a direct connection to the person with whom you are talking is established. You dial a number, the connection is made, you talk, and finally you hang up and the connection is broken. This is called a connection-oriented network. On the other hand, the U.S. Postal Service is a connectionless system. Individual letters or packets are addressed to a particular location and arrive there eventually after passing through various parts of the postal system.

Networks, including the Internet, use the connectionless form of operation. On the Internet, packets are addressed to some location and will make their way there by various routes. Upon arrival at the destination, they have to be reassembled to give the form of the information originally sent. How these packets make their way is more complicated because each network they go through may have a different packet size and the packets may have to be repackaged. But it is a dynamic and a changing routing system, which satisfies the original intent of the Internet started by ARPA (Advanced Research Projects Agency of the Pentagon) in 1962. The intent of ARPA was to create a communications system that was robust and could not be destroyed by eliminating computers or links in the system. The Internet can't be eliminated; it may slow down, but it is here forever!

CLIENT/SERVER MODEL

It is now time to look at some special-purpose nodes that inhabit networks. Some of these nodes have a special significance for the individual. If someone wants his or her own World Wide Web site, for example, he or she must find a home for it. This means finding a computer that has an Internet address and can, therefore, act as a destination for Internet packets. Then space on that computer's hard drive must be allocated for the Web site. The result is the concept of a **server,** which was born many years ago when networks needed to store information and produce copies as needed. The information could be data, programs, or even home pages for the World Wide Web.

This leads to another major concept in networking referred to as the **client/server model.** In the example shown in Figure 7.4.2, Lucinda's computer is acting as a client; she is requesting Lena's home page be "served" to her. Client computers can run any type of operating system, so long as they have the ability to use the Internet protocols.

A very common analogy is used to understand the client/server model. Suppose Lucinda is in a restaurant and orders a cup of tea. The waiter's purpose in the restaurant is to "serve" the tea Lucinda has ordered.

A server on a network, linked to the Internet, is a perfect place for World Wide Web pages to reside. Universities will often allow students free space on a server for their Web pages. Outside the university, many commercial services not only provide access to the Internet but also often allow Web pages to be stored on their server. Of course, this costs extra. In some cities, community networks not only give free access to the Internet but in addition allow free space on their server for a Web page.

A **server** is usually a dedicated computer that is part of a network. A server's hard drive contains files that are "served" to whatever requests them. The server normally also runs the networking software that implements the network's protocols, which means it helps manage the network.

In the **client/server model** one computer, the client, requests information from another computer, the server. There are usually many more clients on a network than there are servers. The servers are usually running a shared network operating system and help manage the network.

Lucinda's Computer

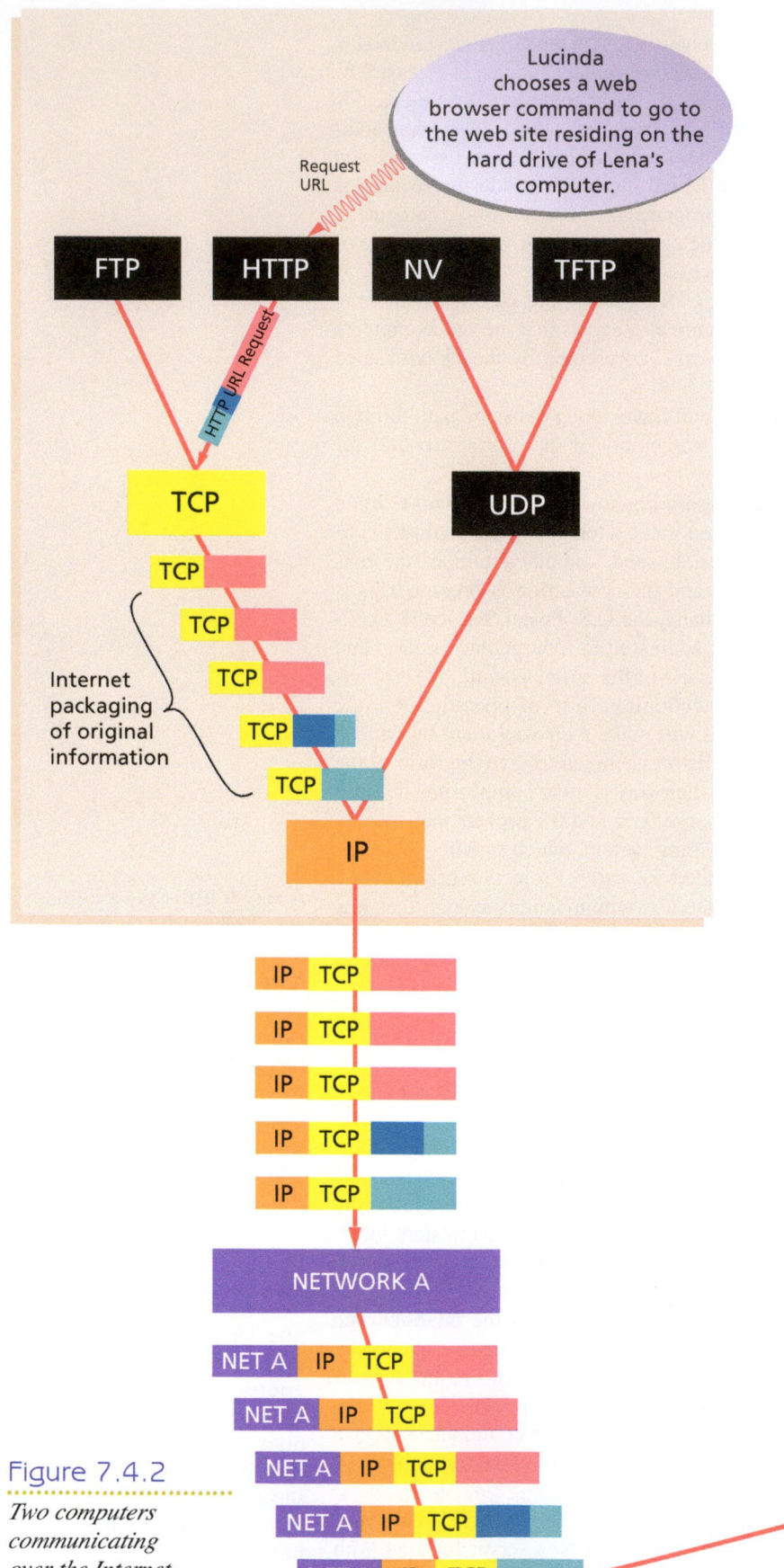

Lucinda chooses a web browser command to go to the web site residing on the hard drive of Lena's computer.

Request URL

FTP HTTP NV TFTP

HTTP URL Request

TCP UDP

TCP

TCP

TCP

Internet packaging of original information

TCP

TCP

IP

IP TCP

IP TCP

IP TCP

IP TCP

IP TCP

NETWORK A

NET A IP TCP

NET A IP TCP

NET A IP TCP

NET A IP TCP

NET A IP TCP

Figure 7.4.2

Two computers communicating over the Internet.

- Lucinda chooses to access a World Wide Web page that resides on Lena's computer. Lucinda's computer is referred to as the client and Lena's the server.

- Lucinda's browser already contains the necessary HTTP program that implements the HTTP protocols or rules. The HTTP program passes this request for Lena's Web page on to the TCP program.

- The TCP program receives information from HTTP and packages it into Internet packets. It then feeds these packets to the IP program.

- The IP program's main job is to send the Internet packets over Network A. Network A's protocol is well known to the IP program. Network A then passes the packets on to Router A.

- Router A reads the addresses of each packet, not knowing they are even related, and sends them in the direction of Network B.

- Finally, out on the Net, the packet or packets requesting the home page make their way toward Lena's computer. Dozens of routers will undoubtedly read the packet addresses and reroute each of them as they go from Lucinda's computer to Lena's computer. One of many amazing facts is that not all of the packets will travel along the same path through the Internet. Fortunately, they have all been numbered so that reassembly of the information can be accomplished at the other end.

The Internet

Router A

- The packets arrive at Network B and are fed to the IP program on Lena's computer. However, the network operating system residing on the Network B system will strip off Network B's information before passing on the packets.

- The IP program in turn strips away all information, leaving the original Internet packets from Lena's computer. The IP program then passes these Internet packets to the TCP program.

- The TCP program then unpackages the Internet packets and reassembles them to their original form and passes this information to the HTTP program.

- Because Lena's computer is acting as a server, her HTTP program has some additions to it. These additions to the HTTP program allow it to act as a server. In fact, it acts much like a butler serving tea. The appropriate Web page is passed back to the HTTP program.

- Now the process goes in reverse until the Web site home page reaches Lucinda's computer where the browser displays the home page from Lena's computer.

- Seems a little tedious doesn't it? It seems almost ridiculous when you realize that a simple home page may take several hundred Internet packets! If there are a large number of photographs, it could be thousands of packets. It may also happen that the original Internet packets have to be broken into pieces to go over other networks in the path.

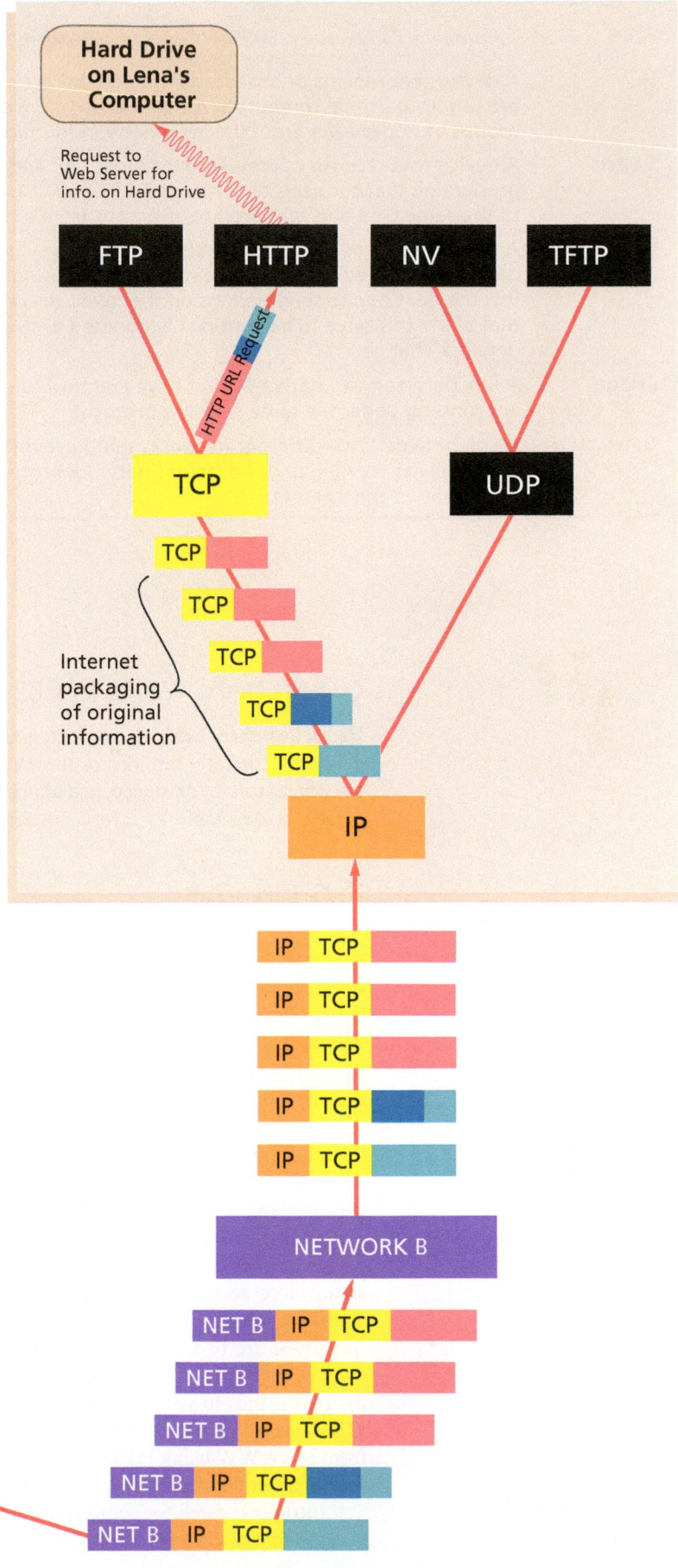

Lena's Computer

Table 7.4.2   *Hardware components commonly used in networking.*

Hub	A device that repeats or broadcasts the network stream of information to individual nodes that are usually personal computers. A hub is an economical way to get the network information to groups of nodes away from the main networking facilities.
Switch	A device that receives packets from its input link and then sorts them and transmits them over the proper link that connects to the node addressed. It is primarily used to connect nodes or networks of the same type and is, therefore, different from a router.
Router	A node that sends network packets in one of many possible directions to get them to their destination. A key feature of the router is its routing table or dynamic address book, which lists the next hop to send packets on their way. Routers exchange messages with each other that allow this table to be continually updated as the network topology and traffic on the network change.
Bridge	A link between two networks that have identical rules of communication. That is, the networks are running under the same network protocol.
Gateway	A link between two different networks that have different rules of communication. That is, the networks are running under different network protocols. For example, America Online provides a gateway to the Internet.

OTHER HARDWARE NECESSARY FOR NETWORKS

Hubs, switches, bridges, routers, and **gateways** are additional types of nodes that inhabit networks. Literally millions of these nodes are scattered throughout the Internet. Each has its own reason for existence, and almost all will run the TCP/IP protocol suite or appropriate parts of it. See Table 7.4.2 for a description of each type of node.

7.5 Firewalls

All of us face some inherent dangers in a networked world. Because of the nature of the Internet, there is a very real threat from intruders that can attack our personal computing systems. The resulting damage can be anything from access to private information, destroying valuable information, to using your computer as a platform to mount a "denial of service" attack on some high profile company's Website. The latter has happened to the Websites of eBay, Yahoo, and Microsoft.

It is possible to minimize these dangers by instituting what is called a firewall on our computers. It isn't guaranteed, but doing nothing is inviting trouble. In fact, some have made the analogy that a computer connected to the Internet without a firewall, is like leaving your car unlocked with the keys in it in a crime ridden neighborhood. And those computers that are connected to the Internet 24 hours a day via cable companies or other network services face even greater danger. Before we discuss the concept of a firewall it is necessary to understand more about how communication over networks occurs. You should first read the TechTalk sidebar on TCP/IP ports in this chapter.

There are two basic ways to penetrate your computer from the Internet. Examine the layer in Figure 7.4.1 that has both TCP and UDP directly connect to the IP layer. These are the two entries to your computer. Each one consists of a large number of programs in the TCP/IP program suite that are labeled by their port numbers. For example, any access to and from the WWW using HTTP is done via port 80 of TCP. A firewall can be made to inspect every packet that enters or leaves your computer through these ports.

Intruders search for computers by scanning the Internet for systems that will respond to packets sent to different ports. The scanners are often called port scanners and represent the means by which the intruder probes your PC. A program that gets into your computer by attaching itself to another legitimate program or data is referred to as a Trojan horse. Some of these Trojan horse programs are called Trojan servers and will take residence in your computer waiting for an intruder using a scanner to probe a predetermined port. There are lists of known Trojan programs that can be searched out on your computer and eliminated. One group of hacker called Back Orifice has many Trojan horse programs associated with ports 80, 8787, 31337, 54341, and many others. Table 7.5.1 is a short list from hundreds of known Trojan horse ports. If a port is closed, then the intruder cannot enter through that port. The next question to be examined is: how are ports opened and closed?

TCP/IP ports are only opened if the first packet going to that port requesting to establish a connection is responded to by your computer. If your computer doesn't respond to the

An Internet address or **IP address** is a unique string of numbers that identifies each specific computer attached to the Internet. Every node on the Internet has an IP address, although the string of numbers is often replaced with a character string identifying a specific server.

Table 7.5.1   *List of port numbers and the related Trojan Horse programs.*

20 Senna Spy FTP server
21 Back Construction, Blade Runner, Juggernaut 42, Larva, Motlv FTP
22 Shaft
30 Agent 40421
80 AckCmd, Back End, Back Orifice 2000 Plug-Ins, Cafeini, CGI Backdoor
81 RemoConChubo
99 Hidden Port, NCX
110 ProMail trojan
113 Invisible Identd Deamon, Kazimas
119 Happy99
1269 Matrix
1313 NETrojan
1338 Millenium Worm
1703 Exploiter
1777 Scarab
1807 SpySender
1999 Back Door, SubSeven, TransScout
2001 Der Späher / Der Spaeher, Trojan Cow
2023 Ripper Pro
2115 Bugs
2130 (UDP) - Mini Backlash
2140 The Invasor
2255 Nirvana
2300 Xplorer
2339 (UDP) - Voice Spy
2345 Doly Trojan
2565 Striker trojan
2583 WinCrash
2600 Digital RootBeer

2716 The Prayer
3024 WinCrash
3031 Microspy
3150 The Invasor
3456 Terror trojan
3459 Eclipse 2000, Sanctuary
3700 Portal of Doom
3777 PsychWard
4000 SkyDance
4092 WinCrash
4242 Virtual Hacking Machine - VHM
4444 Prosiak, Swift Remote
26274 (UDP) - Delta Source
26681 Voice Spy
27444 (UDP) - Trinoo
27573 SubSeven
29104 NetTrojan
29891 The Unexplained
30000 Infector
30029 AOL trojan
30100 NetSphere
54283 SubSeven, SubSeven 2.1 Gold
54321 Back Orifice 2000, School Bus
55166 WM Trojan Generator
57341 NetRaider
60001 Trinity
60068 Xzip 6000068
64101 Taskman
65390 Eclypse
65421 Jade
65535 RC1 troj

VisualRoute is a trademark of FORTEL, Inc. Product information is available at www.visualroute.com. Reprinted by permission.

request to open a connection, then that port will be invisible or closed. A firewall essentially controls the opening and closing of ports. This is done using several different criteria that are determined by the user. For example, only certain IP addresses may be allowed to establish a connection via some port, or maybe packets from certain IP addresses aren't responded to.

Good firewalls must be properly configured or they are worthless. A set of criteria for your own system will depend on the degree of exposure of your PC. The degree of exposure from least exposed to most exposed is in the list:

- Continuous connection
- Sending files via FTP
- Accessing your files remotely
- Using your computer as a Web server
- When using remote access programs such as: PC Anywhere, Laplink, or Wingate

The firewall that you decide to use should fit your needs. (By examining your usage and picking the product which is best for your system.)

The Maturing of the Client/Server Model

The client/server model is one of the foundation concepts of networks: A client requests some data from a server, which responds to the request. This model allows several computer users to share files on demand over networks. Over the years, the model has evolved from the mainframe and minicomputer environments, where data were centralized in large computers that served them to dumb terminals that had no computing power of their own.

The client/server model's second stage was made possible by the personal computer. Almost all the computing was done on the client PC using data and application files served over LANs. A major disadvantage of this approach is that the network has to send a very large amount of data from which the client PC distills the required information. A request from the server for a part number for a product, for example, could cause the complete catalog of products to be transferred to the PC, where the PC's program would search for the product number. This leads to a network overloaded with data traffic, most of which isn't used.

When distributed network environments came on the scene, a third variation of the client/server model was born. The third variation has a more sophisticated division of labor that will reduce the data traffic over the network, yet retains the centralization of the data as in the early mainframe model. In this case the server will respond to the client's request for data, but will do some processing to eliminate irrelevant data that the client doesn't need. Suppose there is a request for employee salaries, for example. Instead of sending all employee records with other information such as phone numbers, addresses, and other items, the server will extract just the salary data and send them alone. This would be just a fraction of the data otherwise sent to the client. The client PC's computing power would then be used to display data and maybe do some analysis, such as calculating average salaries.

Chapter Summary

7.1 Introduction: "Everything Is Connected to Everything"

The human need for communication is one of our most important necessities. This need is today being answered by computer networks. In particular, the Internet and the World Wide Web service that it provides are changing the world. These networking concepts came into focus when ARPA (Advanced Research Projects Agency) started putting money into network research in the mid-1960s. By the mid-1990s the effect of the World Wide Web began to reveal the new revolution in human communication.

7.2 Communication Basics of Networks

The nodes of a network can be linked with either physical connections or wireless connections. The physical connections consist mainly of twisted-pair wires, coaxial cable, and fiber-optic cable. The wireless links between the network nodes are made with infrared, radio frequency, and microwaves. In both the wire and wireless links there are five basic properties of transmission in common: type of signal (analog or digital), speed (bps, baud), type of movement (simplex, half duplex, full duplex), method of transport (asynchronous or synchronous), and channel size (single, multichannel). These basic concepts about the links between nodes provide the basis for hooking together networks into various configurations.

7.3 The Physical Organization of Networks

The nodes of a network can be connected in many different ways. There are several unique geometries that the networks can use. They have suggestive names such as bus, ring, star, and tree. There are two major concepts in how communication takes place on networks. One concept is the direct link in which a definite connection is made from one computer to another, or from point to point. These networks are catego-rized by function, from the smaller, such as DANs and LANs, to larger conglomerations often connected to each other through gateways. The larger collections of networks are called MANs and WANs.

7.4 Software Architecture of the Network

A network must have software that controls the flow of information. All of the computers and other hardware connected to a particular network must follow the same rules or operation called protocols. The rules of operation are divided up into layers so that a programmer need only be concerned with the layer with which the program is communicating. The Internet is a four-level architecture that is best known by the protocols TCP/IP, which all computers connected to the Internet must have. Otherwise they wouldn't be part of the Internet. Another very important concept is the packet, which is the unit being passed around the Internet. Packet switching is the process of packets moving from node to node in the direction of the destination.

A concept that has become synonymous with networks is the client/server model. It suggests by its name that the rules of the network can be viewed as clients requesting services/information and servers providing them. Any computer can be considered to be server or client depending on whether it is providing information or requesting it. The nodes of a network include not only the client/server computers but also hubs, switches, bridges, routers, and gateways. Each of these is a special-purpose computer performing necessary functions to make the Internet work.

7.5 Firewalls

Firewalls are a means of protecting a computer from unauthorized access through networks. When installed they must be configured to match the users needs, otherwise they are almost worthless.

Key Terms

Key terms introduced in this chapter:

1. Analog signal, *184*
2. AppleTalk, *194*
3. Asynchronous transmission, *187*
4. Bandwidth, *188*
5. Baud rate, *185*
6. Bits per second (bps), *185*
7. Bluetooth, *183*
8. Bridge, *200*
9. Bus network, *188*
10. Client/server model, *197*
11. Coaxial cable, *182*
12. Connectionless, *196*
13. Connection-oriented, *196*
14. Desk area network (DAN), *190*
15. Digital signal, *184*
16. Direct-connect network, *188*
17. Ethernet, *194*
18. Fiber-optic cables, *182*
19. Firewall, *192*
20. FTP, *195*
21. Full-duplex transmission, *187*
22. Fully connected network, *190*
23. Gateway, *200*
24. Half-duplex transmission, *186*
25. HypertText Transport Protocol (HTTP), *195*
26. Hub, *200*
27. Infrared, *183*
28. Internet, *180*
29. internet, *180*
30. Internetworking, *190*
31. Intranet (enterprise network), *192*
32. IP, *194*
33. IP address, *201*
34. Local area network (LAN), *191*

35. Metropolitan area network (MAN), *192*
36. Microwave, *183*
37. Modem, *186*
38. Network, *180*
39. Network architecture, *194*
40. Network links, *181*
41. Node, *188*
42. NV, *195*
43. Packet, *195*
44. Packet switching, *195*

45. Point-to-point network, *188*
46. Protocol, *194*
47. Protocol suite, *194*
48. Radio frequency, *183*
49. Ring network, *189*
50. Router, *200*
51. Server, *197*
52. Simplex transmission, *186*
53. Star network, *189*
54. Switch, *200*

55. Synchronous transmission, *187*
56. Transmission Control Protocol/Internet Protocol (TCP/IP), *194*
57. TFTP, *195*
58. Token Ring, *194*
59. Tree network, *189*
60. Twisted pair, *182*
61. UDP, *195*
62. Wide area network (WAN) *192*
63. Wi-Fi, *183*

Matching

Match the number of the key terms introduced in the chapter to the following statements. Each term may be used once, more than once, or not at all.

1. ___ Wireless communication used to connect keyboards and mice.

2. ___ Wireless communication used by satellites.

3. ___ Connections between computers and other electronic devices.

4. ___ Electronic signal that is continuously changing.

5. ___ Indicates the number of times a signal on a channel changes per second.

6. ___ Electronic signal that consists of pulses representing 0s or 1s.

7. ___ Method of transmission that sends information more quickly and is more expensive.

8. ___ Device that changes digital information to analog so that it can be sent over the telephone.

9. ___ A network category that spans the distance of just a few miles.

10. ___ A generic term used when referring to a device that is connected to a network.

11. ___ Data movement that can go in only one direction at a time, such as that used by a fax machine.

12. ___ Data movement that can go in only one direction, such as that used by television or radio.

13. ___ A set of rules that allows an orderly exchange of information on a network.

14. ___ The network with a central node that acts as a controlling device.

15. ___ A transmission protocol that allows the use of browsers on a network, including the Internet.

16. ___ A link between two networks that may be using different network protocols.

17. ___ A computer that contains files that are "served" on request.

18. ___ A link between two networks that are using the same network protocols.

19. ___ A collection of programs that must be on a computer to allow access to the Internet.

True or False

Place either T or F on the line provided with each of the following statements. If a statement is false, you should be able to explain what changes would make it true.

1. ___ Other than face-to-face vocal communication, the earliest form of long-distance communication was the telegraph.

2. ___ Network links that use twisted-pair wires can suffer from interference caused by appliances or other electric devices in the home or office.

3. ___ Network links use only one type of physical media to connect computers and other electronic devices.

4. ___ Coaxial cables are as susceptible to interference from outside noise as twisted pairs of wires.

5. ___ Fiber-optic cables can carry more signals than either twisted-pair or coaxial cable.

6. ___ Of the three types of wireless communications used in networking, only the infrared type needs to have the sending and receiving units in the line of sight of each other.

7. ___ Radio frequencies are not commonly used as wireless communication between computers because of the fear of other devices causing interference.

8. Although microwave wireless communication needs to be in the line of sight, nothing else really causes any interference.

9. ___ The properties of communication signals do not vary among the differing communication links.

10. ___ Although commonly confused, bits per second is not the same as baud rate.

11. ___ A modem is necessary to send information from one computer to another computer over current telephone lines.

12. ___ A broadband communication path carries much more information than a baseband communication path.

13. ___ A network only accounts for those computers that are directly connected by physical means.

14. ___ Networks range in size from one that makes the use of the functionality of components on an individual computer to one that spans the earth.

15. ___ The terms *Internet* and *internet* have the same meaning.

16. ___ One of the functions of a protocol suite is the management of collisions of information that might occur on a network.

17. ___ The beauty of a packet that travels along the Internet to a destination is that it is not changed anywhere along the way.

18. ___ A bridge requires that both networks being linked run under the same network protocol.

19. ___ All packets on the Internet have a lifetime of over a week during which they can travel over the Internet.

Multiple Choice

Answer the multiple-choice questions by selecting the best answer from the choices given.

1. Ring, star, and bus are categorized as being
   a. Types of wireless transmission
   b. Transmission protocols
   c. Types of data movement
   d. Types of networks
   e. Devices connected to a network

2. Digital versus analog, simplex, half-duplex, or full-duplex, asynchronous versus synchronous are all
   a. Types of wireless transmission
   b. Properties of transmission
   c. Types of data movement
   d. Types of networks
   e. Devices connected to a network

3. Nodes are
   a. Types of wireless transmission
   b. Transmission protocols
   c. Types of data movement
   d. Types of networks
   e. Devices connected to a network

4. Microwave and infrared are examples of
   a. Types of wireless transmission
   b. Transmission protocols
   c. Types of data movement
   d. Types of networks
   e. Devices connected to a network

5. The rules governing how information travels along a network are included under
   a. Types of wireless transmission
   b. Transmission protocols
   c. Types of data movement
   d. Types of networks
   e. Devices connected to a network

6. This is where files are stored so that connections to the Internet are possible.
   a. HTTP
   b. Internet
   c. WWW
   d. Packets
   e. Server

7. This began as a government-funded project.
   a. HTTP
   b. Internet
   c. WWW
   d. Packets
   e. Server

8. This is how information is grouped together when it is sent from one computer to another along the Internet.
   a. HTTP
   b. Internet
   c. WWW
   d. Packets
   e. Server

9. This is the name given to a growing part of the Internet.
   a. HTTP
   b. Internet
   c. WWW
   d. Packets
   e. Server

10. This protocol allows information to be displayed on a screen after it has been received from the Internet.
   a. HTTP
   b. Internet
   c. WWW
   d. Server

Exercises

1. If you were given the job to design a multiuser electronic game for the school classroom, which of the several types of wire or wireless connections would be your choice? State the reasons for your choice and at least one negative reason for not choosing each of the other forms.

2. What is a potential problem for using infrared keyboards in an office without walls? How could the problem or problems be eliminated?

3. A telephone line, which is most commonly a twisted pair, handles only one conversation at a time. How does call waiting work? Call waiting is when a call is in progress and you're interrupted by a second call, which produces a click. Explain how this is possible.

4. What is the concept behind conference calls? This is when more than two people at different telephone locations can be talking at once, just as if everyone is on the same telephone line.

5. Determine whether each of the scenarios described here is classified as simplex, half-duplex, or full-duplex transmission. Explain your answer.
   a. An engaged couple has listed the items they wish to receive as wedding presents in a department store's computer. This department store has conveniently positioned information kiosks with access to the couple's list at several places around the store. Using the touch pad, you can choose to see the items that have been purchased and the items remaining on the list.
   b. A fax machine receives and sends faxes one at a time but not at the same time.
   c. Traffic-flow display devices are attached to overpasses on an expressway, showing the drivers which lanes are open.
   d. A person can speak over a citizen's band radio (CB) only when the button on the microphone is depressed. During the time when the button is depressed, however, the speaker cannot hear the other voices over the radio.
   e. A television receives a signal over the airwaves.
   f. A television attached by cable is connected to the Internet by the use of a special device that enables the person viewing it to also send requests for new sites to view.

6. Assuming the following physical bus network connection:

```
      B       D
      |       |
 |    |       |        |                    |
 A    C       E        F
```

   a. Can device B send information to device A at the same time that device D is sending information to device E? Justify your answer.
   b. If device C were not there, could device B send information to device A at the same time that device D is sending information to device E? Justify your answer.
   c. Can device A send information to device E even if device C is turned off?

7. Would you expect a bridge or a gateway to be more complex? Why?

8. Portable telephones use radio frequencies to transmit information. Some portable (cordless) telephones are listed as 900 MHz machines. Is this a frequency or is this a measure of the strength of the signal produced? Of what advantage is the 900 MHz phone over the earlier models?

9. List the four types of physical media used for network links that were described in this chapter. For each of them, include an example of its use.

10. When will modems become unnecessary?

11. What is another name for a tree network configuration? How does the meaning of the name relate to the actual network configuration?

12. 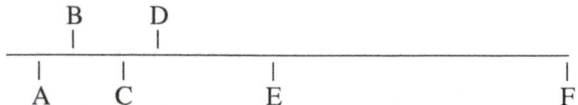 When printing a document over a network, there are usually several clues leading to successful printing that can be observed. These clues might include the printer's light blinks, the printer icon on your desktop flashes, or the printer makes a little noise like it is starting up. Make a list of clues that happen when you are printing from the computer you regularly use.

13. Use the following chart to help determine the answers to the following questions:

How long would it take to send a 1 MB file using a modem that is

    2,400 bps
    9,600 bps

    14.4 Kbps
    33.6 Kbps
    56.8 Kbps

Why might these optimal times not be attainable in the real world?

SPEED OF MODEM		TIME IT TAKES TO SEND A FILE		
bps (bits per second)	How many bytes per second	1 KB (1,000 bytes)	10 KB 2 pages (dbl)	36 KB 1 simple picture
2,400 bps	300	3.3 sec	33.3 sec	120.0 sec
9,600 bps	1,200	8.3 sec	30.0 sec	833.3 sec
14.4 Kbps	1,800	0.6 sec	5.6 sec	20.0 sec
28.8 Kbps	3,600	0.3 sec	2.8 sec	10.0 sec
33.6 Kbps	4,200	0.2 sec	2.4 sec	8.6 sec
56.8 Kbps	7,000	0.1 sec	1.4 sec	5.1 sec

Discussion Questions

1. If TV and VCR remote controls have some problems with infrared signals, can you think of some reasons why manufacturers of these devices don't use radio frequency links instead?

2. Which of the network configurations described in section 7.2 would be the best choice if security of the transmitted message was an important consideration? Why?

3. Which of the network configurations described in section 7.2 would be the best choice if reliability and getting the message delivered was the most important consideration? Why?

4. Describe a situation in which a DAN would be useful.

5. Could MBone be used for an alternative to TV sent to your computer? Why or why not?

6. A very long telephone message may have to be left on a telephone answering machine in "pieces" because of a limited amount of time permitted by the machine for each message. Discuss the analogous situation for a network.

Group Project

This project is designed for a group of four people. Each of you should select a role to play in a small business that is about to invest in a network for its office. Choose one role from among these four network users: president and CEO—needs current information on employees, sales, orders, and also needs to communicate with employees and people outside the company; vice president of marketing—needs to design marketing materials and communicate with staff and World Wide Web sites; office manager—manages office staff and ensures things are running smoothly; vice president of sales—needs to keep track of salespeople and their sales and provide feedback to marketing. The company has six other employees who are divided into office staff and salespeople. Each needs his or her own computer. The four of you should decide what basic type of network you would like. Should it be a bus, ring, star, tree, or fully connected? Also, would you need twisted pair, coaxial cable, fiber-optic cable, or wireless links? How many computers, printers, servers, and connections to the Internet would you need? Try to stay general in your overall design. Good luck, and remember small businesses have a limited amount of money to spend.

Web Exercises

1. Locate a copy of a traceroute program on the Web and then download it and install it on your computer. If it isn't your computer, you should ask permission to do this. Read the tutorial and report some interesting results that you find.

2. Use a traceroute program to trace packets between your computer and computers in Europe, Russia, South America, and Africa.

3. Search the Web for history of the Internet and try to find estimates of the number of computers that are on the Internet.

Bibliography

Black, Uyless D. *Internet Architecture: An Introduction to IP Protocols.* Upper Saddle River, NJ: Prentice Hall, 2000.

This book focuses on the Internet architecture and the principal protocols that make up this architecture.

Blank, Andrew G. *TCP/IP Jumpstart: Internet Protocol Basics.* Alameda, CA: Sybex, 2000.

This book provides everything you need to know about TCP/IP to get started in Internetworking. It clarifies complex topics with simple explanations and realistic, easy-to-understand examples.

Busby, Michael. *Demystifying TCP/IP.* Plano, TX: Wordware, 1999.

A book/CD-ROM package introducing topics fundamental to the TCP/IP networking standard, including user services, Telnet, FTP, SMTP, ICMP, World Wide Web, and Internet.

Groth, David and Jim McBee. *Cabling: The Complete Guide to Network Wiring.* Alameda, CA: Sybex, 2000.

This book provides all the information you need to know to work safely and effectively with networking cables.

Horak, Ray, Mark A. Miller (Editor), Harry Newton. *Communications Systems and Networks.* Foster City, CA: IDG Books Worldwide, 2000.

A comprehensive explanation of current and developing communications systems and networks. Explores the current range of communications systems, including wired and wireless voice, data, and video; and features recently developed and emerging technologies.

Leiden, Candace and Marshall Wilensky. *TCP/IP for Dummies.* Foster City, CA: IDG Books Worldwide, 1999.

This book is for anyone who wants to explore what really makes the Web tick. In a lighthearted style, the authors explain the basics of TCP/IP and other technologies.

Wilson, Ed and James Naramore. *Network Monitoring and Analysis: A Protocol Approach to Troubleshooting.* Upper Saddle River, NJ: Prentice Hall, 2000.

This book discusses Windows NT network troubleshooting from the ground up using real-world scenarios, understandable examples, and plenty of illustrations.

chapter

8

The Internet and the Web: Worldwide Transformation

TimeLine

358	The foundations of HyperText are demonstrated in the Talmud.
1972	*Electronic mail* is coined and used to send messages across the ARPAnet.
1982	*Internet* is coined to designate a connected set of networks.
1990	First commercially available Internet access—the World.
1991	Gopher, an Internet menu-style file finder, is released by University of Minnesota.
1992	CERN, the European Laboratory for Particle Physics, releases the World Wide Web.
1992	An act of the U.S. Congress allows commerce on the Internet. This milestone is credited with explosive growth of the Internet in the 1990s.
1993	First graphics-based Web browser Mosaic becomes available.
1996	Internet connects a consortium of 100+ research universities.
1997	The Internet connects 150 countries.
2002	E-commerce business-to-business transactions reach $286 billion, up from $5.6 billion in 1997.
2005	The number of Internet users worldwide reaches 817 million, up from 300 million in May 2000.
2016	Fifty percent of all commerce in the world will be conducted over the Internet.

Chapter Objectives

- Know the historical beginnings of the Internet.
- Identify some of the tasks the Internet can perform.
- Realize how the human need to communicate helped motivate the development of the World Wide Web.
- Understand the concepts of hypertext and hypermedia and their uses in a multimedia environment such as the Internet.
- Recognize the separate parts of URLs and what each represents.
- Understand how search engines enable convenient access to the information available on the Internet.
- Identify the issues involved with downloading software from the Internet or putting together your own Internet page.
- Recognize the issues, concepts, and uses of e-commerce and of accessing the Internet as a business tool.
- Understand what is meant by the deep web.

Gary Hush/Stone

Spinning an E-Commerce Web

PUZZLER

Every day, hundreds of new online businesses are springing up on the Web. Many are "dot com" companies with no physical home. They exist only on the Web, and in the minds and home computers of their creators. Your task for this puzzler is to design such a company and specify its online activities.

You can start by answering the questions on this list. The list is by no means complete—each question is a stepping-off point.

a. What will you call your company, and what will its domain name and Web address be?

b. Will you have a company logo? Motto? Protocol? Philosophy?

c. What products or services will your company provide? What price structure will you use? Who will your customers be, and how will they find you?

8.1 A Powerful Voice

In the transition of the last decade of the twentieth century and the first decade of the twenty-first century, the Internet and the Web continue to emerge as powerful tools of influence and persuasion. Let's consider three examples:

1. Just after the 1989 Tiananmen Square massacre, Chinese students in the United States were worried they would have to interrupt their education and return to China when their visas expired. They organized an e-mail campaign over the Internet to lobby Congress for protective legislation. Their campaign worked—they were allowed to stay.

2. In the fall of 1993, when Russian President Boris Yeltsin suspended parliament, many civilians were caught in the political chaos. In particular, three prominent Russian labor leaders were arrested while trying to prevent further bloodshed. They were kicked and beaten by Moscow police until word of their fate reached Vassily Balog, the deputy head of Russia's major labor confederation. As an active e-mail user, he sent Internet e-mail to friends in the United States and United Kingdom with appeals for support and the phone number of the police station. Australian journalist Renfrey Clarke reporting from Moscow estimated the first phone call to the police station came about 30 minutes after the e-mail was sent. The first phone call came from Japan, and then others followed from all over the world. The international pressure brought about by the phone calls caused the release of the three men.

3. During the U.S. presidential primaries from 1999 to 2000, John S. McCain, a candidate for the Republican nomination, sought new sources of campaign support. He posted a letter requesting financial contributions on his campaign's World Wide Web home site. Money poured in. Before the end of 1999, online contributions exceeded $750,000. Online support peaked in February 2000, when McCain won the New Hampshire primary. Despite raising millions via the Internet, McCain's candidacy failed. His Web-based fund-raising efforts, however, produced a history-making change in political campaign methodology.

You need only skim media sources to find convincing evidence of Internet and Web influence in the worlds of business, education, politics, agriculture—any field we can name.

In chapter 7, "Network Concepts and Communications," we discussed the technology and protocols that made the Internet possible. For this chapter, let's start with the **ARPAnet** as it appeared in the early 1970s, and trace its development into the Internet as we know it today.

8.2 The Internet: Struggling to Maturity

The seeds of what we know as the Internet were planted in the early 1960s. At that time, most computer scientists considered the idea of networking computers only a dream. As noted in the previous chapter, ARPA researchers Paul Baran and Donald Davies took the first key steps toward realization of that dream. Working independently, these two researchers each devised the idea of packet switching in the early 1960s. The concepts of packets and packet switching, described in chapter 7, were the foundation for what would one day grow to become the **Internet.**

By the early 1970s, ARPAnet had grown from its first four research nodes into a nationwide network linking several military sites and about 20 universities, as shown in Figure 8.2.1.

At this point it became clear that guidance and support of a different type were needed. ARPA started an effort to sell off the ARPAnet to an academic or corporate consortium. Before any sale could take place, federal rules required the Defense Department to determine whether ARPAnet was needed for national defense. The Defense Department recognized the potential importance of computer networking, so the ARPAnet was never sold but was instead transferred to the Defense Communications Agency in 1975.

When ARPAnet became part of a defense agency, its resources were not open to all researchers and were heavily restricted. Only about 15 university research centers were given access. To correct this, the National Science Foundation (NSF) started **CSnet** in 1980. Its purpose was to provide a resource-sharing network opportunity to computer science research at

CSnet was a resource-sharing network available to the computer science departments of all universities. It was started in 1980 by the National Science Foundation.

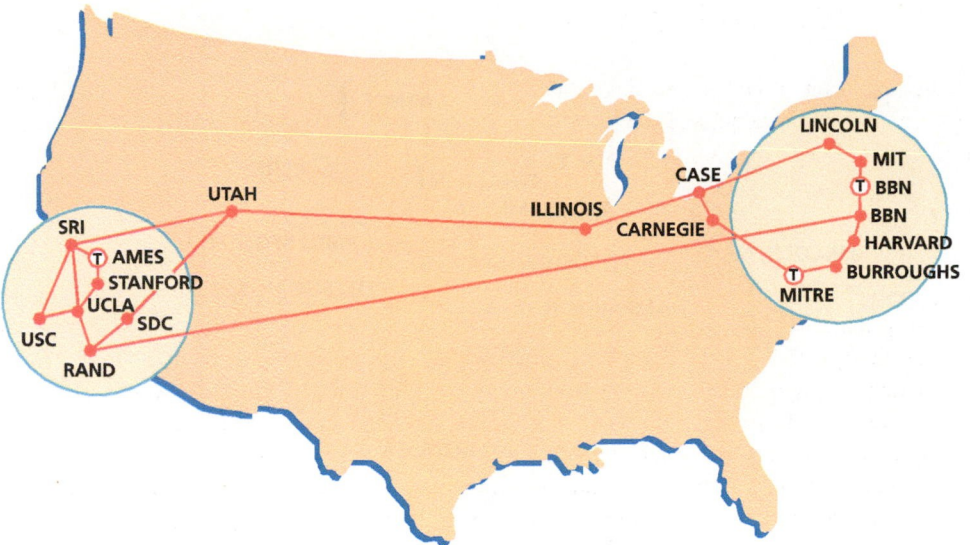

Figure 8.2.1

This map is a geographical depiction of ARPAnet, as it was configured in September 1971.

all universities. By 1986, almost all of the country's computer science departments were connected to CSnet; a large number of private companies were also connected. CSnet used the **TCP/IP** protocol, unlike ARPAnet, which used the Network Control Protocol.

The success of CSnet fueled interest in creating a more comprehensive network to link all scientific communities, not just the computer sciences. But, like ARPAnet, this would take millions of dollars per year, which was more than NSF could support. The solution came with the advent of the five supercomputing centers spread out over the United States. NSF would build a very fast connection, called a **backbone,** linking the five supercomputer centers, and then each region surrounding them would develop its own community network. NSF would allow the regional community networks exclusive access to the backbone.

Meanwhile, ARPAnet had grown so big that the Defense Communications Agency decided security was an issue. Figure 8.2.2 shows the rapid expansion ARPAnet achieved by 1980.

Every network, considered by itself, has a backbone, which is the main traffic route of the network and usually the fastest.

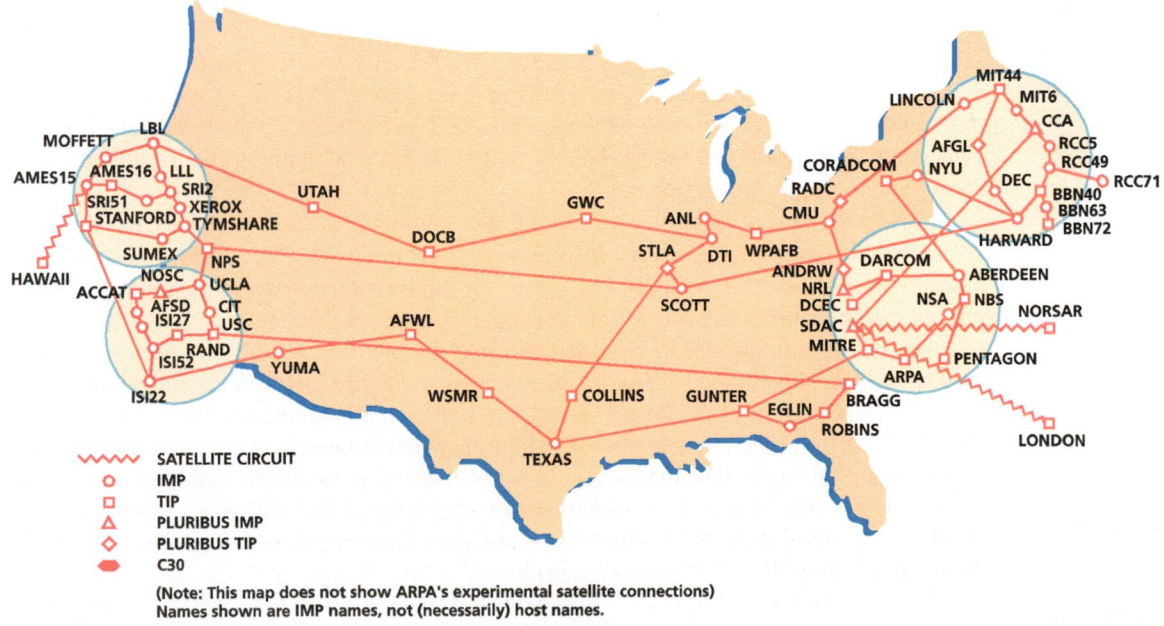

Figure 8.2.2

By October 1980, ARPAnet had grown vastly and included links to London.

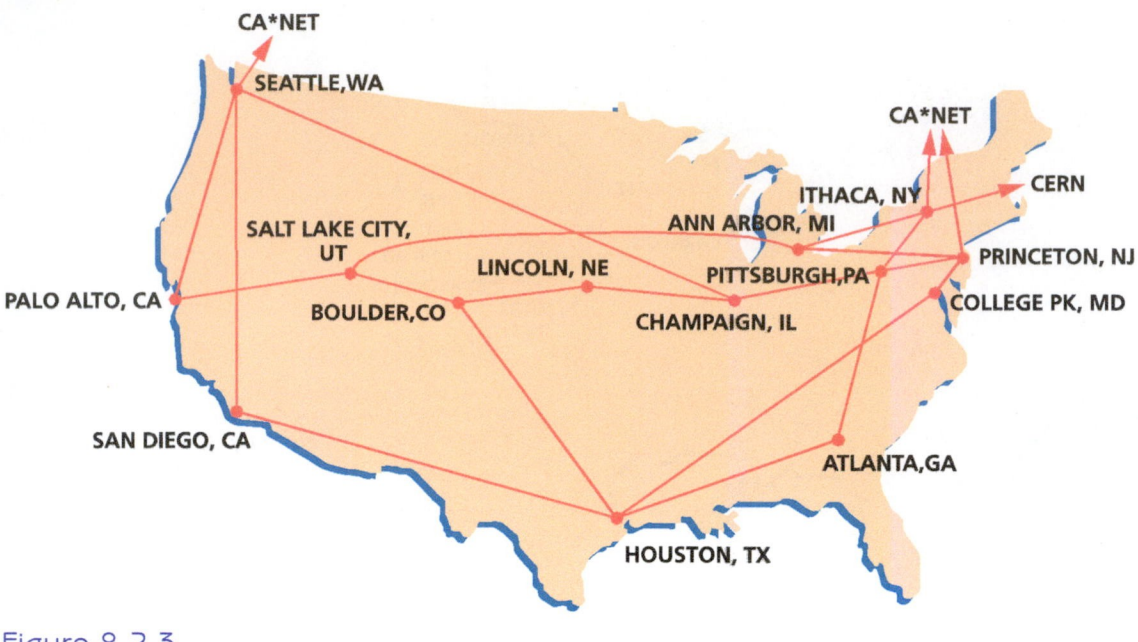

Figure 8.2.3

In 1991, NSFnet's high-speed T1 backbone spanned the nation.

The **Milnet** (Military Network) was a large portion split off from **ARPAnet** in 1983 to be used for nonclassified military information.

NSFnet was a very fast network providing the backbone connecting the five regional supercomputing centers. Regional research centers and community networks were allowed exclusive access to the backbone.

So the Defense Communications Agency split off a portion of ARPAnet in 1983 and called it **Milnet** (Military Network). The smaller part retained the name ARPAnet and consisted primarily of university researchers. Milnet was used for nonclassified military information. With special gateways between the two parts, however, researchers with proper access could use the system as if it hadn't changed. At the same time as the split, ARPAnet converted from the Network Control Protocol to the TCP/IP protocol.

By the late 1980s, the number of networks running TCP/IP protocol and connected to the **NSFnet** made it far larger than ARPAnet had ever been. And it was still growing. NSFnet was also faster and easier to connect to than ARPAnet, so NSFnet became the system of choice for researchers everywhere. By then, ARPAnet was costing $14 million per year to keep up and running, even though it had outlived its usefulness. The financial plug was pulled, and by 1989 the majority of ARPAnet sites were connected to the NSF backbone through the regional community networks, as shown in Figure 8.2.3. This vast internetwork consisting of thousands of LANs, WANs, and computers all running the TCP/IP protocol soon became known as the Internet.

In its early stages, what was to become the Internet was used primarily for scientific research and exchange of scientific information. Information exchange was exclusively text based without images or sounds. The users were universities, research institutes, science-related corporations, and a few enterprising information-gathering companies that had foreseen the mountains of data available through the Internet. As the Internet became recognized as an unparalleled information resource, it began to reach its full potential. In 1992, with the advent of the World Wide Web, both visual and audio information could be shared via the Internet. In early 1995, the Internet became known as the information superhighway, and as such, began to draw users from every population sector with computer access. By 1999, Internet access was approaching universal status, as shown in Figure 8.2.4, and the great information resource had become universally recognized. The ARPA-planted seeds had grown to maturity.

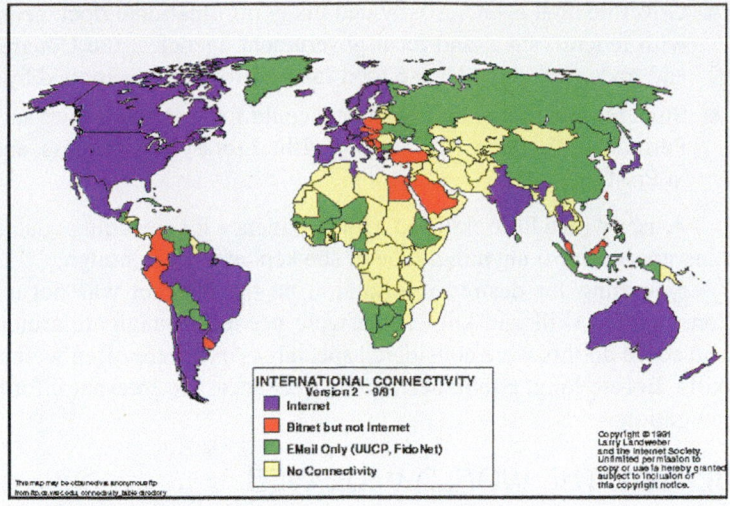

(a) Copyright © 1991 Larry Landweber and the Internet Society www.cs.wisc.edu/lhl/maps

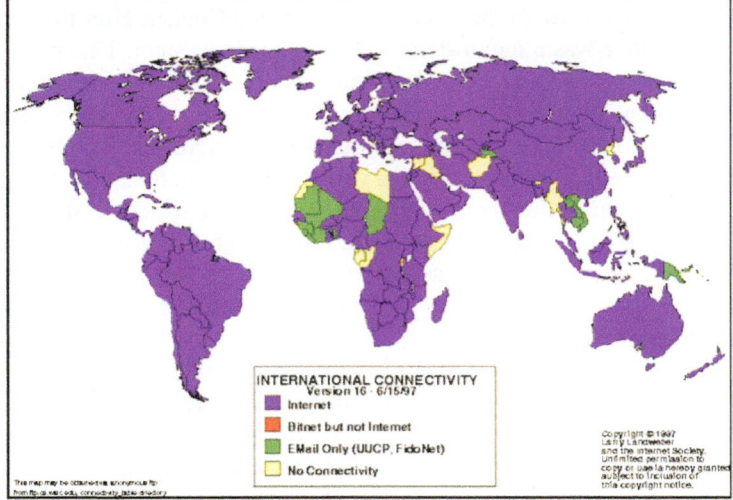

(b) Copyright © 1991 Larry Landweber and the Internet Society www.cs.wisc.edu/lhl/maps

Figure 8.2.4

These two maps highlight the dramatic growth of Internet connectivity by country. Figure 8.2.4(a) shows countries with Internet access in September 1991. Figure 8.2.4(b) shows countries with Internet access in June 1997.

8.3 The Internet: Early User Interfaces

After beginning as a scientific research tool for sharing computer resources, the Internet rapidly reached the stature of a multipurpose tool. By the end of the 1980s, many users from educational and governmental communities had found ways to put the Internet to work for them. The variety of tasks that tapped the Internet's computing power is truly astonishing. The following four examples of popular Internet functions illustrate the diversity of Internet use in the early 1990s:

- University sites provided class and faculty information, books, periodicals and lists of government documents in their libraries' collections (titles, descriptions, and summaries were usually available).

- Employment offices provided vacancy notices and job descriptions for jobs on and off campus—full- and part-time jobs, student through professional level, local or international.

- Governmental agencies provided many informational documents including job listings with federal, state, and local government agencies; the Congressional Record; patent and trademark records; and food safety information supplied by the FDA.

- Students and academic researchers could find bibliographies such as Readers' Guide to Periodical Literature, the catalog of the Library of Congress, and most recently, Books in Print.

A user with a little skill and a lot of patience for searching could, in fact, find out something about almost anything, if he or she kept at it long enough.

Searching for desired information on the Internet was not a simple, intuitive task. Considerable skill and knowledge were needed to navigate around the Internet. People who could do this were considered specialists and were often well paid for the use of their skills. Before long, public desire for direct access to Internet information led to improved navigation.

BEFORE THE WORLD WIDE WEB

With its popularity growing, the Internet needed improvements in user friendliness. The University of Minnesota, home of the Golden Gophers, introduced the first major improvement in navigation of the Internet. It was called Gopher, after their mascot.

Gopher was a **menu-driven** Internet access system. This means that when you access Gopher, your monitor displays a main menu containing all the choices available to you from that screen. To move through the menu, you use the up and down directional arrows on your keyboard. To select from a menu, you move the highlight bar to the item you want and press the Return key. This in turn gives you another menu that goes to yet another menu, and so on, until you get to the desired information. Figure 8.3.1 shows how the University of Minnesota's main menu page looked. Although it consisted only of text in menu form, Gopher became very popular. With menus, almost anybody could navigate on the Internet. Gopher's popularity mushroomed, and at one time there were over 5,000 Gopher servers established throughout the world.

Veronica (Very Easy Rodent-Oriented Netwide Index to Computerized Archives) was a searching system that indexed all of the entries in all known Gopher menus. With the development of the Veronica index, users no longer were forced to visit all 5,000 Gopher servers, each with its own set of menus. Instead, they queried Veronica to find only those sites related specifically to the topic of interest. About twice a week, the Veronica system scanned all

Gopher was an older Internet service, often hosted by a university, that allows communication and data access over the Internet.

A **menu-driven** access system allows you to view a selection—menu—of choices available from a particular screen. Using the keyboard arrow keys, you can select the menu item you want and press the Return key.

In a **command-line** driven system, you must type in a command at the keyboard to access specific information or instruct the computer to perform some task. Of course, you must know what command to type, and you must enter it without errors.

Veronica (**V**ery **E**asy **R**odent-**O**riented **N**etwide **I**ndex to **C**omputerized **A**rchives) was a Gopher search program that allows you to enter one or more keywords from the keyboard. Veronica then searches Gopher space to find Gopher menus that contain those keywords.

Figure 8.3.1

A typical opening menu of a Gopher site.

```
         Internet Gopher Information Client v2.1.3

         Home Gopher server: gopher.tc.umn.edu

  —>  1. Information About Gopher/
       2. Computer Information/
       3. Discussion Groups/
       4. Fun & Games/
       5. Internet file server (ftp) sites/
       6. Libraries/
       7. News/
       8. Other Gopher and Information Servers/
       9. Phone Books/
      10. Search Gopher Titles at the University of Minnesota <?>
      11. Search lots of places at the University of Minnesota <?>
      12. University of Minnesota Campus Information/

  Press ? for Help, q to Quit, u to go up a menu>
```

Reprinted by permission of University of Minnesota

Gopher servers in the world and added any new entries to the several million already in the index.

The great grand-daddy of the search engines in use today was called Archie. At the time of Archie's birth in the early 1990s, users' main interest was finding downloadable data files located in some computer on the Internet. Originally, Archie was designed to search FTP archive sites, which are computers on the Internet containing repositories of data and programs. Archie is no longer in use. Finding information that can't be obtained from popular WWW search engines is done by deep search engines, which we will discuss later in this chapter. Most WWW search engines, such as Google or Yahoo search only Web pages. Thousands of files on the Internet, however, are not Web pages. Archie identified this harder-to-find information, so that an FTP program could download it.

> **Archie**—short for archived data files—was the name of an automated search service on the Internet. It was originally designed to search repositories of downloadable files anywhere on the Internet.

8.4 USING TODAY'S INTERNET

Today, the Internet is the largest and most widely used network in the world. And yet, Internet activity is constantly changing. According to a Nielsen report dated March 2009, the top five uses of the Internet as of December 2008 are: 1) Searching reaching 85.9% of Internet users, 2) General Interest Portals and Communities reaching 85.2% of Internet users, 3) Software Manufacturers reaching 73.4% of Internet users, 4) Member communities (Social networking) reaching 66.8% of Internet users, and 5) E-mail reaching 65.1% of Internet users. Surprisingly, social networking has surpassed E-mail in Internet activity! And, according to the Nielsen report, the largest growing sector of the population who are audiences of social networking sites is "shifting from the young to the old" with the largest percentage of new activity among the 65 and over group (increasing by seven percent). The youngest population, the group that comprises the two to 17-year-old audience, has decreased by seven percent.

E-MAIL

Email generates much of the Internet traffic produced today — more than 2.5 trillion messages per year in the United States alone.

The email concept is quite simple—it consists of correspondence between two or more individuals connected on a network. In theory, using email is very similar to using its predecessors, land-mail and airmail. In all three mail-modes, a message is sent from one person to another. When it is delivered, it is placed in a holding area, called a mailbox. Finally the addressee picks it up from the mailbox, thus receiving the message.

Similarities stop there. Most people use email to take advantage of three mail service differences:

- **Efficiency**—Communicating via email allows you to send messages from virtually any computer to any other computer, wasting very little of your time or effort

- **Speed**—Whether you are communicating from across the street, around the world or within the same building, e-mail communication is easier and faster than telephone, notes, or in-person delivery

- **Cost**—With email, users can send any number of messages, anywhere, any length and any time with no additional charges beyond the cost of Internet service

Despite the many advantages of using email, electronic communication has a dark side also. When we drop an ordinary letter into a mailbox, we have every reason to believe that it will be delivered to the person addressed, and that only that person will read it. Email does not provide the same degree of privacy we expect from regular mail. This is partially because the computer makes it easy to copy and snoop into unprotected computer files, such as email messages. For example, many corporate executives and managers—over 28% of them—regularly monitor personal e-mail communications of their employees. Company security, customer service quality control and cost effectiveness are some of the reasons managers give for prying into employee email. We'll address issues of privacy and security later on, in chapter 9.

FTP AND PEER-TO-PEER FILE SHARING

Peer-to-Peer file sharing is a decentralized model for directly sharing files between computers without control of a third party, like a server. Usenet was the first of this type of program, but Napster brought it to the masses.

Some Internet historians will undoubtedly say that in the year 2000, the Internet reverted to its original mission of file sharing, and in particular **peer-to-peer file sharing** (P2P). Because of the WWW, the client/server model of the Internet was overshadowing file sharing, but when Napster came along things changed. The illegal copying and sharing of copyrighted songs was so pervasive that one large Midwestern university indicated sometimes up to 80% of their massive network's traffic was Napster downloads. Many other file sharing applications soon followed: Gnutella, Freenet, Fundamentally, Kazaa, Kazaa Light, eDonkey, Overnet, Morpheus and BitTorrent.

The last of these P2P applications, BitTorrent was created by Bram Cohen, and is a true phenomenon. It is estimated in 2002 that one-third of the data sent over the Internet is done using BitTorrent. By that time over 20 million copies had been downloaded, and by 2006 the expected number of downloads of BitTorrent will be about 40 million. Many types of data, legal and illegal, are posted as "torrents." Maybe you missed your favorite popular TV show, but no problem, as someone has probably posted it as a "torrent."

Peer-to-peer file sharing is characterized in many ways. Dave Winer, a Web services evangelist and co-author of SOAP (Simple Object Access Protocol), has identified seven basic attributes of general peer-to-peer file sharing. From his blog of September 2000:

1. A network app that doesn't run in a web browser
2. The user's machine is a client and a server
3. It includes some kind of tool for creating your own content
4. Networks with other users, creating a community
5. Does something *new* with networks
6. Supports cross-network protocols such as XML-RPC, SOAP
7. Deeply integrated for ease of use, lots of connections between the components

One of the problems for the usual implementation of P2P, such as Kazaa, is that they have upload speed problems. Downloading is not a problem because most broadband cable companies have very fast downloading rates. However, your computer uploads files (sends out files) relatively slowly. This means that an MP3 song is capable of downloading to your computer at about 1.5 megabytes per second or just a few seconds; however, it is sent at a far slower rate because only one computer is sending the file. This creates a bottleneck, thereby slowing file transfer down to the speed of the sending computer.

This is where the BitTorrent concept really pays off, because instead of sharing the file from a single computer, chunks of the file come from many different computers. This allows the receiving computer to download at full speed. Bram Cohen's approach can be explained as outlined by Clive Thompson in a *Wired* magazine article:

1. A single source file within a group of BitTorrent users, called a swarm, spreads around pieces of a film or videogame or TV show so that everyone has a chunk to share.
2. After the initial downloading, those pieces are then uploaded to other needy users in the swarm. The rules require every downloader to also do some uploading. Thus the more people trying to download, the faster everything is uploaded.
3. Before long, the swarm has shared all the pieces, and everyone has their own complete source.

LISTSERVS, NEWSGROUPS, AND USENET

One of the most useful two-way communication vehicles on the Internet are the many mailing list systems. Before email lists started, dial-up access was the only way to reach the thousands of bulletin board systems (BBSs). These were named after the classic bulletin

Internet2 and the Evolving National Lambda Rail

When the World Wide Web was initiated in 1990, few suspected how successful it would become. By spring 2000, over 300 million people browsed the Web, surfing millions of Web sites and over 1 billion Web pages. The traffic jams of the early Internet days grew to staggering proportions. The technology was unable to keep pace with the skyrocketing demand.

In October 1996, 100 research universities joined together with corporations and government agencies to form UCAID (University Corporation for Advanced Internet Development). Their purpose was to create a nationwide virtual research facility for developing and testing emerging technologies. The project is called Internet2. It's working to invent new network applications that can't be run using existing technology, and then develop the infrastructure to support those applications.

Internet2 is not a single network but a consortium of hundreds of high-speed networks linked by fiber-optic backbones that span the United States. It transmits data at speeds up to 2.4 gigabits per second—45,000 times faster than a 56 Kbps modem. This high speed will enable scientists to test their laboratory discoveries in the real world.

Internet2 is not intended to replace the Internet but to enhance it. With increased bandwidth, Internet2 will have the speed essential for simultaneous transmission of voice, video, and data. In fact, it has been stated that the difference between the existing Internet and Internet2 will be the difference between a country road and a multilane interstate highway.

One of the problems with Internet2 is that it doesn't own the infrastructure. This means that researchers can't always experiment for future innovations. The National Lambda Rail (NLR) is an all optical fiber infrastructure that will be owned by the NLR consortium. Its main purpose is to link research universities with thousands of miles of fiber optic cable. Some have even argued that this is the most important network project since the 1969 creation of the ARPAnet, grandaddy of the Internet. It will be capable of carrying high-definition video. In fact, it will be able to download a complete DVD movie in 4 seconds.

boards still found in many public spaces. Individuals would post useful information for specific topics, such as professional photography tips, to an electronic bulletin board.

As the needs of those who network changed and matured, the conferencing system was created. Special software would allow multiple topics, and individuals would read those of interest and possibly respond.

A **computer conference,** or **electronic conference,** is a clearinghouse for information. It is similar to a typical meeting where people sit at a table and discuss issues, review reports, plan strategy, and schedule events. For a face-to-face conference involving people, however, everyone must be in attendance. Corporations still spend large sums of money to fly geographically dispersed people together for a conference. A computerized conference, on the other hand, can take place with the participants located anywhere in the world. They don't even have to be participating at the same instant in time. A computerized conference is a place where individuals can post questions, get answers, communicate private or public messages, and perform traditional e-mail communications at their own convenience. It allows almost all the traditional events that occur at face-to-face meetings.

One system that has some unique and interesting conferences is called the WELL (Whole Earth 'Lectronic Link). The WELL has thousands of registered users, accessing more than 100 public conferences (topics). There are also many private conferences, including one exclusively for women, a men-only conference, and several private corporation conferences. The conferences range anywhere from the Grateful Dead Conference to a conference to design T-shirts for the WELL. The variety of conferees is what gives the WELL its character. They include artists, writers, hackers, Deadheads, knowledge workers, educators, programmers, lawyers, and musicians. It is no longer necessary to dial by phone directly into this conference because it is now on the Internet and also has its own World Wide Web site.

A **computer conference,** or **electronic conference,** is an electronic meeting that can take place at the convenience of the participants. Conference participants (members) can type questions or comments so that other members can see them and respond. A member can visit a conference at any convenient time to read both comments and responses.

Usenet is a major older vehicle for sharing news about particular topics over the Internet, and provides a means of downloading movies, music, video and other file types. Topics that individuals may subscribe to are often referred to as **newsgroups**.

Listserv or **newsgroup** is a cross between straight e-mail and conferencing. It allows two way communication through mailing lists that are kept on the listserv server. **Posting** to the list means sending an e-mail from one member to all the others.

Chat rooms or chat forums are real-time text "conversations" over the Internet. The Internet Relay Chat (IRC) was the first to gain widespread use. Software on the participant's computer allows communication to IRC server computers that send the messages to all participants on a certain chat group or channel.

Another prime example of a conference is **Usenet** (Users' Network), which has hundreds of individual conferences. The individual conferences are organized by topics such as the following:

- World events
- New technology
- National elections
- Privacy issues
- Entertainment
- Computer viruses

Usenet is a richly featured, distributed conferencing system that generates over 100 MB of new text each day. This is equivalent to more than 10 copies of *Webster's New Collegiate Dictionary* every day. Usenet doesn't reside in any one computer. Copies of the Usenet news conferences are distributed on networks throughout the world.

Usenet was started in 1979 by two graduate students at Duke University interested in sharing information about the UNIX operating system. A reader was then developed by a graduate student at the University of North Carolina. This combination started Usenet. It should be remembered that the Usenet service is accessed over the Internet, and was before the WWW and browsers. It wasn't long before this conference type newsgroup became extremely popular. They require a Usenet reader or newsreader that are sometimes given free by the Usenet server service. It doesn't use the WWW HTTP protocol, but now most often uses the Network News Transfer Protocol (NNTP), which is software designed to handle the Usenet data. Huge volumes of data, estimated at 2 terabytes daily, require the use of many Usenet server sites that have copies of both current and archival data.

A cross between e-mail communication and conferencing is referred to as a **newsgroup** or **listserv.** Actually, LISTSERV is a trademark owned by L-Soft, the company who markets a series of products including LISTSERV, LISTSERV Lite and a free limited version LISTSERV Free Edition. In spite of this, the concept of a mailing list with interest groups is generically often referred to as a listserv. The mailing list is kept on the listserv server, and individuals who would like to join can have their name automatically entered. Typically what occurs is someone will make a **posting** to the list, which means they send an e-mail that is automatically sent to all others on the list. Upon reading the post, an individual user may want to respond. They do this by posting their response that pertains to that original posting.

Many of the almost 300,000 LISTSERV using institutions and companies are public. They range from the Federal government's Social Security Administration (over 340,000 subscribers) to music fans of the Beatles (over 50,000 subscribers), Pink Floyd (over 17,000 subscribers), and SnoopDogg (over 50,000 subscribers).

Other applications such as Majordomo, Google Groups, and Yahoo Groups use the same concept and are popular. However, these applications including listservs usually reside on a single systems control.

As technology marches on, new innovative ideas have come to the Internet. These new concepts caused AOL to discontinue its integrated Usenet service in early 2005. Among these new innovations are blogs (Weblogs), chat forums, and online conferencing. Let's first examine chat forums.

INSTANT MESSAGING AND CHAT ROOMS

The Internet allows two major types of real-time (synchronous) communication: **chat rooms** and **instant messaging**. Both types of service exist on many public and commercial servers. An early forerunner of both chat rooms and instant messaging was called The Internet Relay Chat (IRC). Developed in 1988 by Jarkko Oikarinen in Finland, IRC is the Internet's version of a real time chat facility. The term real time means that the communicating parties must be connected to the system at the same time. Communication is accomplished via typed text over a network connection.

Here is the way IRC works: Individuals anywhere in the world can join an IRC. Chats are usually organized by topic or purpose. To communicate with others in the chat room, a member (let's call her Pam) logs on to the IRC by entering her username and password. Because the discussion is ongoing, Pam can read what others have entered and then type in a comment of her own. The text Pam has typed appears on the screens of any IRC members who happen to be signed in at that time. As soon as Pam's comment appears, other members can read it and respond, if they so choose. Everyone in that "room" sees all the comments as soon as they are typed, and a single comment may elicit many simultaneous responses, which appear consecutively on screen as they are received.

Today's chat rooms have changed somewhat from the IRCs of the late 1980s and early 1990s. Communication is still accomplished via typed text and 'smilies'—little typed images (like this: ;) that are used to convey emotions in typed messages. Because of the extreme popularity of chat rooms, most chat services limit the number of members who can be in a room at a given time, so that all have the opportunity to participate in the discussion. The newest technologies for chat rooms gaining in popularity are voice messaging and video imaging to accompany members' discussions.

Instant Messaging is an interesting variation on chat room technology, and the current craze in real time communication. In addition to allowing two people to communicate via the Internet, at a speed faster than the pace of email, Instant Messaging software also allows you to track when another person logs on and logs off the Internet. Some software even provides the convenience of sending files back and forth to one another.

Here's how it works: When you log onto the instant messaging server, the system verifies your identity and registers you as being online. Then when other users register and connect, they will know that you are logged on because the server maintains a list of everyone who is online. Therefore you can send anyone who is on the 'online list' an Instant Message rather than phoning or emailing them. This saves time, and increases productivity.

AOL's instant messenger was the first to be widely used. Many others have followed, but not all the software use compatible protocols. Apple Computer's iChat allows both voice and video in real-time.

These examples represent a very small portion of the types of activity on the Internet. Some of the activity is on a rather small scale, but the use scale of the Internet is about to rise dramatically, and this is primarily due to the Web. We are about to experience . . . the Web!

Instant Messaging (IM) is a form of chat room where the chat participants can have their presence automatically announced to a prearranged group of buddies. Their "chat conversation" is shared among the buddies signed on the Internet, or one-to-one. This is done in real-time, which is analogous to "talking" in a group face-to-face. Some chat software allows voice and video in real time, and is like talking on a video phone.

BLOGS

"**Web Logs**" or **blogs** are a Web phenomenon that started in the late 1990s and have had a huge impact on communication. Blogging has grown at a rapid rate. By 2005, there were over 2 million active blogs. By 2009, this number has swelled to over 100 million. In many cases they are like public diaries, and are related to Web pages. In other examples they are a filtering of mainstream news events giving a certain point of view. But, they differ from the classic Web pages in four major aspects, namely:

- up to date content (assuming an active blog)
- presentation is a chronological ordering of content
- simple automatic distribution (interested parties can subscribe via RSS)
- feedback through reader's comments that are easily added

Web pages tend to go out of date, mainly because of the effort needed to change them. Added to this is another more practical difference: blogs are usually very informal. Content and timeliness are considered more important than polish.

The importance of blogs is reflected in the fact that the Merriam-Webster dictionary selected "blog" as the word of the year in 2004. This is in part due to the millions of blogs, on all conceivable topics such as do-it-yourself-type blogs on jewelry making, glass blowing, metallurgy, woodworking, blogs that include political commentaries, personal blogs, and blogs intended to release information or up-to-the-minute news about some current event. In April of 2007, soon after a Virginia Tech student opened fire on school grounds for example, bloggers were actively updating posts dealing with the shooting. Some students at Virginia Tech used blogs as a means of communicating with their families to let them know that they were safe. Soon bloggers posted comments regarding information that was released to the public to try to understand why it all happened. After the tragedy, other students from around the country tried to send some sort of comforting messages to those who were affected by the shootings.

Blogs are a worldwide phenomenon. The terrible Asian tsunami of 2004 was almost instantly reported on by many bloggers. They included many photos and even some video. It should be clear that the quality of these blogs varies. They reported with pictures, comentary and video on the tsunami and its aftereffects. Yahoo! News listed 37 different blogs, many of which dealt with missing persons pictures and their last known location. One in particular, The South-East Asia Earthquake and Tsunami Blog at http://tsunamihelp.blogspot.com, has organized reader/responder comments by these categories: tsunami help general, enquiry, missing persons, news updates, help needed and help offered.

It should also be note that the unscrupulous leeches of the porno industry have taken advantage of the comments area of blogs to insert links to pornographic sites, and spammers insert key phrases like "buy viagra" which are links to sales sites. This is one of the detractions due to the fact that most blogs allow comments by any participant. In spite of these weaknesses, Professor Dan Hunter of the Wharton School of the University of Pennsylvania commented in the newsletter Knowledge@Wahaton: "This is not a fad. It's the rise of amateur content, which is replacing the centralized, controlled content done by professionals." He also put the concept of the blog on a par with the invention of the printing press.

The corporate world has taken advantage of blogs, which are often password protected. This allows group input and decision making to be more time efficient. Suppose, for example, a potential employee is being interviewed by a group. Then the blog with its potential interaction of the participants can be a lot more efficient than having a meeting. Another more important issue is archiving a company's internal communication. Blogs easily do this, whereas, companies that use instant messaging lose the communications content when the chat window is closed.

To start a blog and to use them efficiently, it is very helpful to understand how they work. The first task is to create the blog site. Similar to creating Web pages, there are software tools that allow their creation. These tools are often in the form of templates and formatting choices. Several software platforms are available including Movable Type (free personal version), Blogger (free Google company), Radio Userland (small fee), Greymatter (free, open source), Xanga (free) and several others.

The second step is to find a place for the blog to reside, which can be on your own computer or usually through one of the blog service providers or hosts. Using your own computer raises similar issues to those involved with hosting your own Web page. Needless to say, it is much easier to use a service provider. The software sources mentioned above are sometimes coupled to hosting services, which may be free if you can tolerate ads or upgrade to a premium service without ads. Hosting services include Blog*Spot, LiveJournal, Radio UserLand, TypePad, Webblogger, and Xanga. Even cell phone access is available. Most include both software and a hosting service.

RSS (**R**eal **S**imple **S**yndication) protocol is one of a family of web syndication protocols, based on XML. RSS allows subscription to news feeds and blogs among others. In some cases, this information is provided to the user with summaries and links to complete versions.

Another attribute that makes blogging different from Web pages is syndication. This means anyone who subscribes to your blog will automatically receive all new additions to your blog as you publish them. This feature is referred to as RSS (real simple syndication, a dialect of XML) and is software that has two purposes. First, a blog site with RSS capability is programmed to send subscribers any updates to the blog. These updates are sent either to a blog reader on your computer or to a Web hosting site, called an aggregator. The aggregator service will receive updates from all of the blogs that you subscribe to and send them to the blog reader on your computer. Blog readers are included as part of some browsers. Finally, RSS is often used by newspapers and other information services to provide up to date news and other information.

Blogging is maturing and sometimes includes video and audio presentations. It has grown immensely since 1999, when there were fewer than 100 bloggers. In 2005 an estimated 4 million blogs exist. About 2 million are active.

SOCIAL NETWORKING

Social networks are environments where people can share thoughts, experiences, and expertise on a wide range of topics. Social networks come in an array of flavors. Some are general environments where people communicate with like-minded individuals who are interested in social causes, meeting old friends, or meeting new friends. Others have members who are interested in a narrower focus of topics, such as photography, religion, educational issues, or political issues, among others.

Some organizations have had great success in integrating Web 2.0 social networking technologies into marketing campaigns, with applications directly linked to feature films, soft drinks, and other pay-per-use web services. The rise in popularity in social networking sites have made them vehicles for political campaigns, volunteer management, and non-profit donations.

There are many social networking sites. A few well-known social network environments are CouchSurfing, Facebook, Flickr, LinkedIn, Live Journal, MySpace, Ning, Second Life, and Twitter. Most of these sites have opened their doors to the general public, which limits the extent to which the sites may guarantee identity and security.

The Facebook environment is based on a user's "social networks," which are built upon real-life, school, work, and personal relationships. Originally restricted to .edu-based accounts and higher education, Facebook has since opened its doors to the general public.

A personal Facebook network can be built in one of several ways. One way to build a network of friends is to allow Facebook to gain access to the user's Yahoo, AOL, Hotmail, or Google email accounts using the sites' "Friend Finder" tools. The site can also determine which of their friends on various instant-messaging tools are Facebook users. Additionally, a new user can find networks through prior employers, class schedules, and personal interests.

While much of the allure to Facebook stems from building and maintaining networks, third-party applications are what keep users coming back to the site. These may range from applications that compare movie taste, tell others what books you are reading, various quiz results (What "Sex and the City" Character Are You? Which "Lost" Cast Member Are You?), or which friends (or friends of friends) you would be willing to date.

Anyone wishing to create a Facebook "presence" must divulge personal information or Facebook will not allow them to create that presence. Some of the information that is requested is the person's name, address, telephone number, email address, and school attended. Other information divulged to Facebook will also be included with their personal information, such as personal preferences information. Facebook recommends that parents of children over the age of thirteen who wish to have a Facebook presence should speak to their children about the dangers of having an online presence and also recommends that the parents might consider adding software that will monitor what they do online

Second Life is another social networking site. In this "virtual world", people can, with the help of their browser, go into the world for entertainment, or to meet for business, political, or educational purposes. Second Life has millions of registered users. In order to explore this virtual world, one would first need to create a virtual person, called an Avatar, The Avatar has a physical presence that is selected by the user.

The Second Life environment has many features of the real world. Money is exchanged for goods and services. Land is purchased and sold. Clothing shops with virtual clothing created by software can be bought, all using the world's Linden Dollar currency. Although Linden Dollars are exchanged in this virtual environment, these Linden Dollars are purchased with real monetary currencies on the Lindex, which is Second Life's currency exchange. For currencies that are not U.S. dollars, the Lindex includes a "value added tax".

Twitter is another rapidly growing social network. This site allows users, or tweeters, to post streams of short real-time text messages. Others who are interested in catching up on whatever is happening to that person in their life will follow and read the streams of postings using instant messaging, their web browsers, or cell phones. Tweeters include people from politics, business, education, media industries of radio, television, movie industry, and printed media, to students, mothers, fathers, children, and friends. Some famous Tweeters include Barack Obama, Britney Spears, Eddie Izzard, Ellen Degeneres, John Cleese, John McCain, and Oprah Winfrey.

Twitter, along with Facebook, performed an amazing communications feat in the summer of 2009. After a strongly contested election, thousands of Iranians organized communication via both Twitter and Facebook. People from around the world rallied in support to try to help cover the Iranian communications by changing their "home" addresses to Iran. The government did all they could to try to stop them. But, to no avail. Information still circulated in Iran and to the outside world.

Still other social network sites have a more limited purpose. For example, CouchSurfing is a networking site for people who are looking for a place to stay while visiting cities almost anywhere in the world. Flickr includes people interested in photography but is used mainly for the sharing of digital photographs. Live Journal is a social networking site that is mainly used as a blogging platform. Ning is a site that lets you create your own social networking web sites. LinkedIn is a networking site mainly for professional who are interested in sharing information and keeping informed of their professions. There will always be a place for communication of ideas in our fast-paced, wired society.

8.5 The World Wide Web: Internet's Most Common Access

HTTP—HyperText Transfer Protocol is a set of rules that allows the transfer of visual and audio information as well as text over the Internet.

The year 1989 ushered in a new era of Internet communication. At that time, Gopher was the best tool we had for Internet navigation, but it displayed only textual materials. Other types of information, such as pictures and sound, were still out of reach in 1989. The need to access visual and audio information became the next obvious step in communications on the Internet.

Tim Berners-Lee, a physicist at the European high-energy physics laboratory (CERN) in Switzerland, recognized this need in 1989. He created the **HTTP—HyperText Transfer Protocol,** which we discussed in chapter 7. HTTP's ability to communicate images and sound in addition to text led to the creation of major developments in Internet usage—the **World Wide Web** (WWW, or simply the Web).

The **World Wide Web (WWW)** is a communications protocol that allows multimedia information to be accessed and transmitted via the Internet.

Unlike earlier protocols, HTTP could convert not only text but also visual and audio information into packets to traverse the Internet. The result forever transformed the Internet from being simply a useful tool for scholars and professionals to being the vehicle for global multimedia communication.

Let's take a moment to see why this happened. Why did the addition of visual and sound capabilities cause an Internet revolution? The answer is buried deep within the human need to communicate.

From the beginning of time, the need to communicate has been an essential aspect of human endeavor. Humans continuously reach out to others, sharing feelings, ideas, and information. This need for communication is instinctual and, indeed, motivated such ingenious creations as the printing press, the telegraph, and the Internet itself.

We communicate best when we can use several means of communication at once. The word *help* written on a piece of paper does not attract the same attention as the word *HELP* shouted in a loud voice. And the shout becomes even more effective when accompanied by wide eyes and wildly waving arms. What makes the World Wide Web effective as a communication conduit is its ability to convey simultaneously the word, the shout, the gesture, and more. Effective human communication simultaneously employs several senses; similarly, effective computer communication demands **multimedia.**

Multimedia involves the communication of several different types of information, such as text, sound, graphics, and video animation, simultaneously over several different communication media.

WHO OWNS THE WEB?

No single entity, government, or corporation can own the World Wide Web because it is a collection of millions of computers and networks with diverse ownership that are all part of the Internet. The Web is a means of accessing the many physical connections of the Internet. Each of the computers connected to the Internet follows a set of protocols and standards accepted worldwide. Included in this set of protocols is HTTP, which allows WWW multimedia communication.

Next question: If no one can own the Web or the Internet, how can it be managed or controlled? Well, no one controls the Internet, either, or at least, not all of it at once. The Internet is made up of hundreds of thousands of computers that are all connected together. Although an individual or organization may own and control a small piece of the Internet (its own network and the computers connected to it), many others also own their piece of the Internet and exercise control over that. There are as many managers and controllers of the Internet as there are networks connected to it.

The more pertinent issue here is not ownership at all but access. Through the mutual acceptance of TCP/IP and HTTP protocols, computer and network owners around the world agree to let others access certain files and documents. The access is limited to **read-only access.** When you access a Web page, you can view the page, read it, or even print it out. What you cannot do is *change* it. Only the specific owner of that page can make any changes or delete the page.

> **Read-only access** allows viewers to see, read, or print a Web page or Internet file but not to change it. Only the owner can modify or delete Internet information.

8.6 Navigating the Web

The ability to convey multimedia information was not the only contribution the World Wide Web protocol brought to the Internet. It brought also its own unique techniques for navigating the Internet's complexities.

Vannevar Bush (1890–1974)—An Enigma

As in every major event in human history, there are those whose work stands out as being an essential foundation. A former MIT Professor of Electrical Engineering, Vannevar Bush is one such individual. His influence is associated directly with the formation of the Manhattan Project, which created the atom bomb. He also conceived ARPA (Advance Research Projects Agency) and NSF (National Science Foundation) through the OSRD (Office of Scientific Research and Development). In OSRD Vannevar Bush set up an ultrasecret research group, which was the precursor of the CIA.

His most public influence is found in the 1945 *Atlantic Monthly* article "As We May Think." In this article he proposes a device called the "memex," whose major aspects are yet to be realized. However, the Hypertext links and organization of the WWW are directly related to his memex device. It was a personal information system with links between items of information. It addressed one of the most pressing problems in today's World Wide Web—a vast amount of junk must be sifted through to get something of value. Memex handled this type of problem and addressed others not yet part of the World Wide Web in three significant ways:

First, the memex would allow a great reduction in the information overload that is currently found when surfing the Web.

Second, the memex would keep track of "associative trails," which are connections between items of information and reasons for making them. These connections are needed to make sense of what has been explored and how thoughts mature as the thinking process moves forward.

Third, the memex would be a mind amplifier. It would become a thinking aid and assist in forming a human-machine consciousness that would literally amplify an individual's thinking efforts.

As the World Wide Web matures, several companies are trying to tame the chaos. Their efforts seem to be involved with the same points that memex addresses: recording relationships of an individual's associations. As quoted in *Wired* magazine, Brewster Kayle states: "Bush's great insight was realizing that there's more value in the connections between data than in the data itself." Exploration and use of this insight is going to make the World Wide Web even more revolutionary and influential in our daily lives.

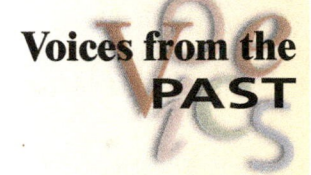

Voices from the PAST

Consider, for a moment, how Gopher worked. Even when accessed through the Web, Gopher was awkward to use. To find information on Gopher, you navigate textual menus and select options by typing a letter or two until you find whatever you are seeking. When you wish to consult another reference, you back up through the menus, sometimes to the beginning, and select different options. Navigation from one item of information to another is clumsy and inconvenient.

Navigation on the Web is another matter. Because of its point-and-click technique, the Web is much more user friendly. Unlike Gopher, the World Wide Web allows you to type a known Web address, or URL, into a command-line box on the Web browser screen. If you do not know a specific address for the information you wish, you can search for it using one of several available search programs. When you find the Web site you are seeking, you point to it, click the mouse button, and presto, you are *there*. This magic is accomplished by the use of two concepts: hypertext and hypertext links.

HYPERTEXT, HYPERMEDIA, AND HOT LINKS

Hypertext is any word or phrase in an electronic document, which can be used as a pointer, or **link,** to a related text passage. **Hypertext links** are any text or image that has been designated as a means of accessing related material.

The term **hypertext** refers to any word or phrase in an electronic document, which can be used as a pointer, or link, to a related text passage. This is done by making that word or phrase into an active spot, or **hypertext link,** within its document. To use hypertext, the reader moves the mouse cursor to the linking word and clicks the mouse button. Whether the related passage is in the same document or another, it immediately appears.

Hyperlinks are embedded into Web documents as they are written. Here are the steps.

- Identify the specific words that will be useful as links.

- Search for and locate the related text or additional information the hypertext will access.

- Set pointers containing information on how to find the document containing the related material.

- Have the selected words printed in a special color and underlined, so the reader can recognize them as hypertext.

Let's see how hypertext works by following Figure 8.6.1. If you were reading a World Wide Web page about Christopher Columbus, you might encounter Queen Isabella's name.

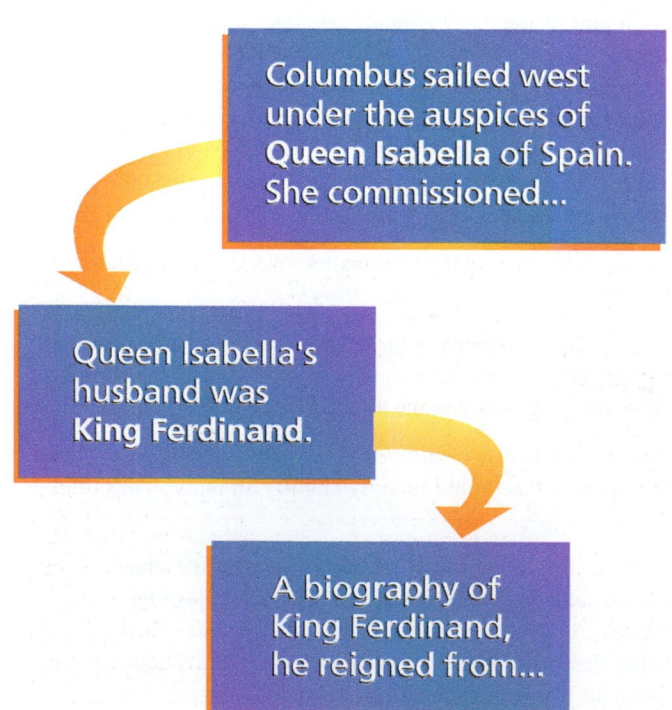

Columbus sailed west under the auspices of **Queen Isabella** of Spain. She commissioned...

Queen Isabella's husband was **King Ferdinand.**

A biography of King Ferdinand, he reigned from...

Figure 8.6.1

In hypertext, you follow the links to additional related information.

The author could easily have used her name as a link to the history of her reign as the Queen of Spain. That description tells you that she was the wife of King Ferdinand. Clicking on his name might give his biography. By following the author's preset links, you could easily explore as much or as little as you wanted.

The history of the hypertext concept has roots that go back to humankind's early critical writings. *The Talmud,* for example, contains interpretations and annotations referring to the first five books of the Bible and the laws of Judaism. Figure 8.6.2 shows a typical page of this ancient document. An important passage from Jewish law is printed in the center of the large page. Commentaries referring to that passage are arranged in a border around it. The reader can read and study not only the original passage but also the possibly conflicting interpretations that have been collected through the centuries. The convenience of these comments being visually connected so closely to the text makes them easy to read and compare. The Talmud's visual layout contains the essence of our modern-day electronic computerized hypertext.

Figure 8.6.2.

The Talmud, a work that records interpretations of Jewish law, shows early use of the hypertext concept.

Hypermedia refers to using the concept of hypertext linking with other media, such as pictures and sound. **Hypermedia links** are often referred to as **hyperlinks**.

With the advent of the World Wide Web, the linking of text to other text was not sufficient. Internet navigation needed to go one step more: It stretched to encompass multimedia linking.

The concept of using hypertext linking with other communication media is called **hypermedia.** Whereas in hypertext only phrases or words could be used as linking points to related text, hypermedia is more complex. It allows visual objects and text to be linked to other visual objects, animations, text, or even sound. The result is a kind of free-form navigation of the Web, limited only by the vast reaches of the Internet and the endless variety of the human imagination.

Today, World Wide Web access to the Internet provides the most extensive form of hypermedia experience. As with hypertext, the major responsibility for the success of using multimedia linking rests with an author, or whoever set up the links. In this case there is no single author. Individuals, businesses, and organizations put their own audio, animations, video, and images online for anyone to access. Navigating via the Web takes advantage of the hypermedia linking of many entities and thereby becomes a hypermedia resource.

PUZZLER HINT

Visit the Web sites of several successful e-commerce businesses to see how they have handled business needs similar to yours: eBay, Amazon, Barnes & Noble, 1800Flowers, and many others have created ways to handle navigation, fees, catalogs, multiple purchases, customer information, security, credit card sales, and so on.

Here are two more helpful questions:

a. What kind of Web page space do you need? How many pages will your Web site entail? How will customers navigate from page to page? Be sure to provide "go back" capabilities.
b. Will you use images? Video? Sound? Photos? How much Web space do you need? Who will provide it?

8.7 Understanding Web Addresses (URLs)

Surfing is the slang term used to describe the free-form navigation from place to place on the Internet by following hyperlinks.

A **Web page** is a document especially created for Web viewing. It usually contains at least some of the following items: text, photographic images, graphics, animation, sound, and hyperlinks.

Uniform Resource Locator (URL) is the name given to the worldwide standard for expressing the unique address of a specific Web page.

Well, now we know that the Internet consists of hundreds of thousands of physical connections linking computers and networks around the world. Because of these connections, you can send mail, view files, and gather information by using computers located everywhere. The way to do this is by **surfing** the Web.

Links appear in documents called **Web pages,** especially created for World Wide Web viewing. If you mouse-click a link on one Web page, you will soon be viewing a different Web page. That's because the link you clicked on the first Web page contained two things:

1. an instruction to locate and display the second page
2. the location, or address, where to find it

Because millions of Web pages exist on the Internet, we must have some way to be sure that each one has a unique address. Originally, CERN set up a registration system called InterNIC to issue and monitor Web addresses. Subsequently, this has been taken over by ICANN (Internet Corporation for Assigned Names and Numbers). The technical name for a Web address is **Uniform Resource Locator (URL).** A URL consists of three parts:

Table 8.7.1   *Examples of networking protocols.*

Name	Definition	Description
http	HyperText Transport Protocol	Language used to construct Web pages
ftp	File Transfer Protocol	Used for transferring files between computers
mailto	E-mail protocol	Used to send or create an e-mail link
file	Local file access	Used to view an HTML file on your computer
gopher	Name of Internet access system	Transfer type used by the Gopher menu system
wais	Wide area information service	A tool for searching information databases
telnet	Telephone Networking	A service for logging into remote computers

1. The type of connection—specific protocol to be used.

The protocol to be used is determined by how you use the Web resources. A colon (:) appears after the name of the protocol. Because the World Wide Web is only one of the many Internet protocols available, you might find it helpful to know a few additional protocol names. Table 8.7.1 shows some of the other protocols you might use and the kinds of services they provide.

2. The Internet address of the computer you are trying to reach.

This one's a bit trickier. A computer's Internet address is called a **domain name** and is preceded by two slashes (//), as seen in Figure 8.7.1. The domain is divided into two or more **subdomains,** separated by periods. The domain segment(s) on the left identify the Web **server,** a computer permanently connected to the Web. The rightmost subdomain, called the **top-level domain,** identifies the type of organization owning the computer. Table 8.7.2 shows top-level domains and what kinds of organizations they signify.

Here is an example of a possible domain: www.eds.com. To read this out loud, you would say "W W W dot E D S dot com." Notice that the periods separating the segments of the domain are pronounced "dot." The domain name for Eastern Michigan University is www.emich.edu.

In countries outside the United States, the top-level domain specifies a two-letter code for the country. For example, the URL for the Royal Canadian Mounted Police is www.rcmp-grc.gc.ca/ where the ca stands for Canada.

3. The path and name of the file.

Whereas the Internet address, or domain, locates the specific computer you wish to reach, the path and name identify the specific **file** you want to see. A slash (/) separates the path from the domain. Typically, the **path** names any directories and subdirectories you'll need to go through to find the desired file. The **file name** identifies the specific document creating the Web page you need. If the person who owns a Web page titled it index.html, a path and file name need not be included in the URL.

Now that we've examined the parts of a Uniform Resource Locator (URL), let's take another look at the complete Web address in Figure 8.7.1: Pronounced aloud, this URL reads as follows: "H T T P colon slash slash W W W dot E D S dot com slash home slash E D S underscore home dot H T M L." That's quite a mouthful, but it does uniquely identify a specific Web page.

A **domain name** is the specific Internet address for a particular computer.

Subdomains are the segments of a domain. They are separated by periods. The leftmost segment(s) identify the Web **server** for that computer. The rightmost segment is the **top-level domain.**

A Web **server** is a computer permanently connected to the Web, providing Web access to other computers networked to that server.

A **top-level domain** is the part of a URL that identifies the type of organization owning a specific Web site.

A computer **file** is a document saved on a computer's hard disk. For the purposes of this discussion, a file is a document creating a specific Web page.

The **path** names any directories and subdirectories you have to go through to find a particular file.

Table 8.7.2   *Some of the most commonly encountered top-level domains.*

Domain	Usage
com	commercial (profit-making) organization
edu	educational institution
gov	government agency
mil	military
net	networking organization
org	nonprofit organization
biz	business
museum	museums
coop	cooperatives

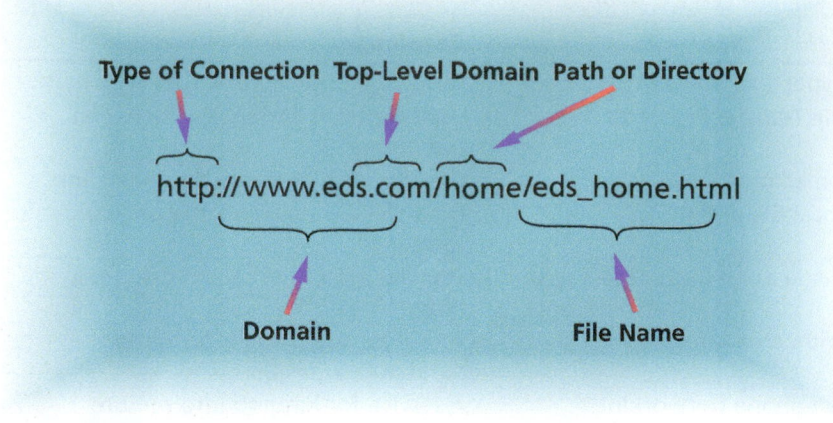

Figure 8.7.1

Annotated diagram of a Uniform Resource Locator.

A **file name** identifies the specific document creating the Web page you need.

Internet Service Provider (ISP) is a company or institution that provides access to the Internet.

A **Web browser** is a program that follows the rules of HTTP protocol, enabling the user to find and view files created for the Web. Netscape Communicator and Internet Explorer are two popular browsers used to access information on the World Wide Web.

8.8 The Web and You

Establishing your relationship with the World Wide Web is a strangely personal experience, requiring you to select your own set of preferences and choices. The result is an Internet identity as uniquely yours as an electronic signature. You should take great care making the choices that comprise your online persona.

ACCESSING THE WEB (INTERNET SERVICE PROVIDERS)

Before you can connect to the Internet and use the World Wide Web, you must first arrange to be connected to an Internet Service Provider. **Internet Service Providers (ISPs)** are companies that have networks and WWW servers linked to the Internet, and that allow you to connect to their servers, usually for a fee. There are thousands of local ISPs to choose from. In effect, when you hook up to an ISP, your computer becomes part of the ISP's network and the Web. The service provider assigns you a username and password, so that only authorized personnel can use its network connections. You are responsible for any actions taken or charges incurred under your username.

Suppose you own computer A, which occupies your desk at Hometown College, USA. You most likely pay a technology fee to your college. One of the things this fee provides is access to the Internet. Your college is an Internet Service Provider for its staff and students. We'll call the college ISP B. If you want to view a particular Web page on the Internet, let's say a file on computer C, which is hooked up to ISP D, how does this happen? Figure 8.8.1 gives a schematic representation of a typical Web transaction.

SURFING THE WEB

After you have acquired the physical networking components described in the previous section, you must turn your attention to software. As you've already discovered, computers need software to make things work. The software needed for surfing the Web is called a **Web browser.** The common browsers are Safari from Apple and Internet Explorer, a Microsoft product.

Because Web browsers support HTTP protocols, they enable you to use hypermedia links to see and hear information from distant Internet documents. A typical document prepared in accordance with HTTP protocol may have text, sounds, music, and still and moving images, all on the same Web page. When you see a Web page on your computer screen, you

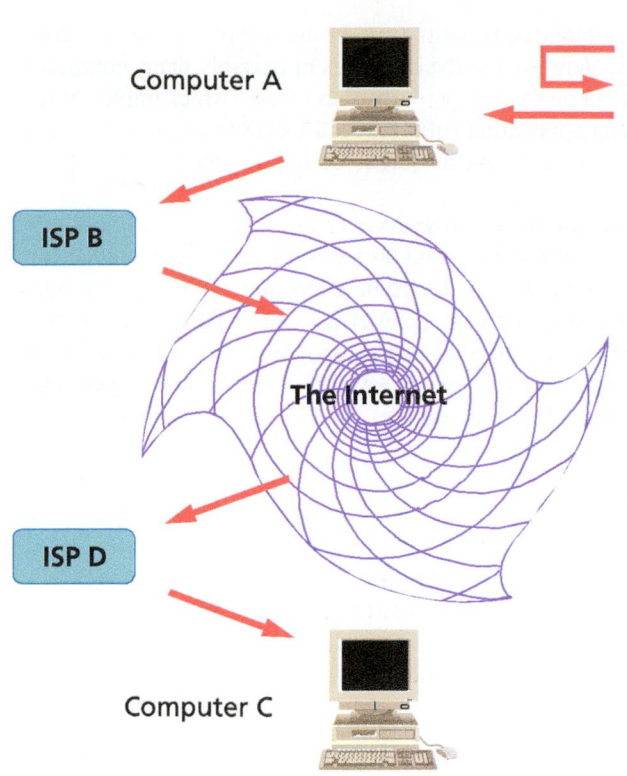

Computer A

ISP B

The Internet

ISP D

Computer C

1. You determine what Web page you want to view.
2. You request to view the desired page by clicking on a link or by typing the page's URL on the keyboard of computer A.
3. Using a modem and a phone line or a wireless connection, computer A sends your request to your Internet service provider, ISP B.
4. ISP B passes your request and URL along its network to the Internet.
5. Following many Internet links and telephone lines, your message reaches ISP D and its network.
6. ISP D activates its hookup to computer C, enabling a search for the path and file named in your URL.
7. When the file is found, the Web page is sent back through the Internet and appears on the screen of computer A.

Figure 8.8.1

Following the link to a Web page.

may notice highlighted or underlined words or images. These are hypermedia links. When you click on one, your browser software activates the link and issues a request to find and show you the file named in the link's URL. This allows you to surf effortlessly from one Web page to another, viewing related information.

In addition to providing software for Web surfing and viewing, browsers serve several other useful functions. For example, they do the following:

- Read the contents of Web documents and format them to be viewed on your screen.
- Enable you to make a paper copy (printout) of documents as they appear on your monitor.
- Enable you to copy text from a Web page and paste it into a word-processing document.
- Enable you to save still and moving images from Web pages as files on your computer's hard disk.
- Provide arrows and buttons (hyperlinks) to assist in moving back and forth through Web pages you have already visited.
- Support e-mail, File Transfer Protocol, Internet Relay Chat, and other Internet services.
- Keep an address book of your favorite Web pages, so you can find them easily without typing in their URLs.

CLOUD COMPUTING

In the Internet environment, information flies around from computer to computer, and from server to server. Oftentimes, this is called **cloud computing**. In cloud computing, we know that these computers and servers exist, but we don't know where they are located. In other words, in cloud computing, we really don't care where the computers are as long as they *work* and they give us the information or services we need.

Cloud Computing is an off-site, server-based, computing environment. It can provide data storage, computing power, and application software services.

One of the major ways cloud computing benefits us is in the use of the massive computing power of other organizations. Here, we use the resources of possibly many computers instead of having the programs or data on the computer in front of us. Two examples of this cloud computing concept are 1) using application software on a server in a remote location, and 2) using the computational power and data resources of one or many computers in remote locations.

As an example of using application software on a server in a remote location, Google^{TM} allows access to web-based document, spreadsheet, and presentation applications, which are available online for anyone to use with an Internet connection and a browser. Looking specifically at the online word processing application, with Google^{TM} Docs you can open existing documents, create new documents, store them in a Google^{TM} account, save a copy to your computer, email the documents as attachments, export them as Web pages, PDF files, Microsoft Word files, OpenOffice files, or as zip files. In addition, the author of a document can invite others to view or update the document from within Google^{TM} Docs. This flexible environment means that you do not need to purchase their specific application software or load it onto your own computer. This server-based application software makes use of the Internet and the computing power of the computers at Google^{TM}.

Another example of cloud computing is the use of the Wolfram Alpha^{TM} computational knowledge engine. Wolfram Alpha^{TM} is not merely a search engine. The server, residing in Champaign Illinois, takes free-form requests in the form of queries. Entering a query is very much like asking Wolfram Alpha to use its computational power to analyze data for you, like "Compare Microsoft and Apple". Then, by making use of the power of its thousands of processors and knowledge engine, produces its results. In a simplistic way of looking at it, the use of the knowledge engine is much like using the calculating power of a spreadsheet program. However, with the Wolfram Alpha^{TM} engine, the calculations use massive amounts of current and historical data for its massive number of computations.

Expanding on the previous example, namely comparing Microsoft and Apple, by entering the names of the two publicly traded companies, the Wolfram Alpha^{TM} engine returns graphical and charted comparisons of the companies' stock market worth, the number of employees in each company, their net income, their annual dividends, projections of growth based on previous history, and other information about the two companies. The Wolfram Alpha^{TM} computational knowledge engine is useful in the fields of mathematics, chemistry, geography, economics, statistics, socioeconomics, geology, physics, health, lotteries and card games, comparing stocks, conversions of unit measurements, and much, much more. This site, in its infancy, has already shown the computer's awesome power and effectiveness of mathematical computation.

DOWNLOADING SOFTWARE

It's true that different people use the World Wide Web in different ways, but most users find it a useful source of software. Many software companies advertise on the Web and make their products available electronically. Figure 8.8.2 shows a page from Microsoft's Download Center, which provides access to software supporting their Windows products. If you wish to acquire a software product available over the Internet, you just copy it to your own computer. This process is known as **downloading** the software.

Downloading is the process of receiving a program, document, or file via a network from another computer. A download always comes from an outside source to your computer electronically. Moving a program or document in the other direction, from your computer along a network to a remote node, is known as **uploading**.

Free Downloads   Many different kinds of software are available free over the Internet. The most popular include technical support assistance, utility programs such as drivers, virus checkers and hard disk optimizers, electronic games, and visual enhancements for your own documents, such as icons and other images, fancy fonts, and animated cartoons. Sometimes sample and trial versions of popular software are also offered.

Free downloads (freeware) are exactly that—free! You, however, must do all of the work and take the responsibility for getting your copy (not that there is very much work involved). Here are the steps:

Tech **Talk**

The Deep Web

Usually when we talk about search engines and the number of Web pages they index, it should be remembered that these are static Web pages. A static Web page is one that is constructed with HTML and saved on a server. These Web pages constitute the surface Web. Google, Yahoo!, AOL and other search engines mainly *see* this surface Web. Contrast this with an eBay query, for example, when you request all item titles that match your particular interest. The list of items that pops up is a Web page created just for you. It didn't exist until eBay software searched its data base for item titles matching your specifications and then created the custom Web page for you.

It is estimated, when including only the publicly accessible databases, that this invisible Web or deep Web is about 500 times larger than the surface Web of static pages. Special search engines are needed to probe these public records. One company that has created such a search platform is BrightPlanet.

BrightPlanet's software was originally available as a PC program. However, the market for data from the deep Web is not something the common Web user appreciated. BrightPlanet's product line is aimed at larger entities, which include governmental agencies, Fortune 2000 companies, national associations, and the intelligence community. In reference to their Deep Query Manager (DQM), BrightPlanet's Website quotes an ACT Intelligence Staff Officer of NATO:

> NATO has been using DQM for several years and has found it to be the single most effective means of systematically exploiting the vast amount of information available through the Deep Web.
>
> DQM has repeatedly proven its unparalleled power to analysts at NATO's strategic command in Norfolk, VA and in the theatre of operations when other sources have failed.

However, it's not as simple as search engines dealing only with the surface Web and those whose purpose is to probe the deep Web. For example, the search engine Alta Vista includes access to phone databases through Yellow Pages and People Finder links. It also has news, jobs, items for purchase, and auctions that are accessible by ordinary search engines. Google includes pdf files and images in its access to more than just surface Web stuff. Typing "World Trade Center" into Google's search box and then selecting the image tab will yield a large number of photos of the 2001 WTC attack.

Deep Web content is often given through subject directories on many search engine sites. There are also static Web pages that give access to the deep Web through subject categories, such as:

Complete Planet   http://aip.completeplanet.com
Invisible Web Directory   http://www.invisible-web.net/

1. Be sure you are connected to your ISP.

2. Search the World Wide Web to find the free download you want, or go to Web sites specializing in freeware, such as www.download.com.

3. When you've found a program you want, click on its name or icon to begin the download process. Because many products are available for several different computer configurations, be sure you select the one set up for your computer and operating system.

4. Downloading may require the use of **FTP (File Transfer Protocol).** This is included with most Web browsers, and many download providers use it without your awareness.

5. After the download begins, it may take several seconds, several minutes, or even hours. The time needed is determined by the size of the item you are downloading, the density of network traffic at that particular time, and the speed of the transaction.

Free downloads (freeware) are computer programs available over the Internet at no cost to the user. They may be downloaded and copied to your hard disk and used or distributed freely.

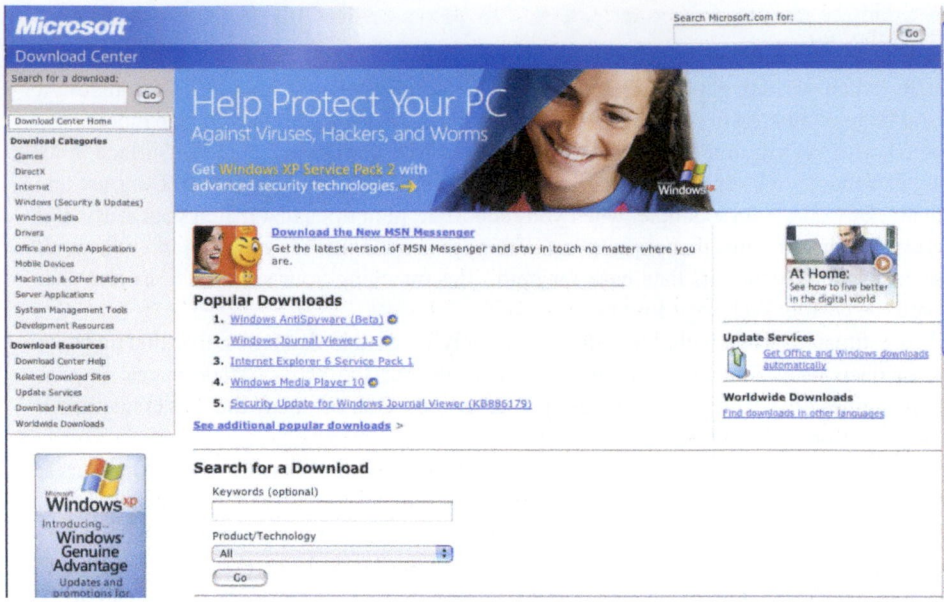

Figure 8.8.2

Microsoft offers an extensive list of free downloads and updates from its technical support home page.

A file in **compressed format** has been made smaller by condensing space-wasting features of the original file. Before you can use or read a compressed file, you must **decompress** it back to its original format.

6. For speed and efficiency, many downloads are transferred in **compressed format.** Downloading a compressed file takes less time, but the result is a file or document you cannot use without decompressing it. Sometimes the downloaded file is self-decompressing and will be ready for installation on your computer. Other downloads will require you to perform the **decompression,** using a program such as WinZip, for the Windows computer, or StuffIt Expander for the Macintosh. Both of these products, by the way, are available in their latest versions as free downloads.

7. Downloaded software usually is accompanied by a readme file. This will likely contain licensing and use agreements, instructions for installation, if needed, any known problems or incompatibilities, and help on getting started. Take the time to read these files. They can save hours of frustration.

8. Be especially aware of any time and usage limitations of free downloads. Alpha and beta versions (that means they are still being tested) of commercial software frequently limit your use of the programs to 60 or 90 days. Introductory and sample packages, designed to let you try a program before you buy it, often "cripple" their free downloads by leaving off key segments. You can explore these samples but cannot do any serious work using them. Distribution of such samples to other potential users is also frequently forbidden. Read the limitations of your license and comply with them!

Shareware is software that is legal to distribute and copy but is not free. The receiver is allowed to try it, usually for a limited period of time. If you decide to keep the shareware, you must pay a royalty to the author.

Shareware   Unfortunately, not everything you download will be free. An important service found at many Web sites is the collection and distribution of **shareware.** Shareware writers request payment for their products. They allow users to download their materials for free, use them for a limited period of time, and then pay a nominal fee for their continued use. Sometimes shareware producers offer technical support in the form of user manuals or phone-in service after the requested fees have been paid.

Two final words about downloading shareware from the Web:

First—software downloads come with no guarantee of quality. For every 10 downloads you do, you may find only one or two really good ones, and even fewer that meet your specific needs.

Second—The sad truth is that viruses can inadvertently or purposefully be distributed along with free downloads and shareware. To protect yourself, install and use a good virus checker on your system and download software only from reputable sources. A good place to start for shareware is the following World Wide Web location: http://www.shareware.com.

CREATING A WEB PRESENCE

Creating and maintaining your own Web home page is perhaps the ultimate way to communicate with the world. After your page is up (that is, once it is displayed on the World Wide Web and visible to anyone), you can expect Web surfers to visit your site, follow the hyperlinks you set up, and perhaps send you e-mail about interests you have in common.

Web pages can be created in a multitude of ways. For instance, Web pages can be created using software specifically intended for such a purpose. The cost for commercial prepackaged software can cost near $400.00. Other options include shareware or server-based Web creation tools. The benefit of the server-based software is that you can use the software on the organization's server to create your pages. Most word processors have the capability of translating a document into a Web page. To do this, you would create a document and add text, links, images, and color features that you would like to see in your browser's window. Then, you would save the document as a Web page. One disadvantage to this method is that it may be difficult to update your pages. The last two options to create Web pages includes text editors specifically written for the creation of Web pages, and the option of creating a Web page using a simple text editor.

> **HyperText Markup Language (HTML)** uses a series of codes or tags to format materials on Web pages.

One of the best ways to appreciate the work that goes into creating Web pages and to understand more fully how to edit pages later is to use a simple ASCII text editor to create a Web page. As you may remember from chapter 2, the ASCII chart discussion showed how the computer stores symbols and special characters. Therefore, an ASCII text editor simply stores these symbols and special characters. Examples of ASCII text editors include NotePad in the Windows environment and TextEdit on the Macintosh computer. We'll be using this type of text editor to create our Web pages in this section.

One of the coding schemes for creating Web pages uses a special formatting language called HTML, or HyperText Markup Language. This formatting language uses special codes, called tags, to control the objects that are to be a part of the window. Some of the items that are controlled can be as simple as the color of the window's background, the color of the text, the size of the type of each letter in the window, the fonts that are used, where images are to be displayed in the window, and where links are to be directed. Other more animated objects need special written program commands. Some of these commands, for example, could control the placement of a clock on the screen or a counter for the number of visitors a site has had.

Figure 8.8.3 shows an example of a document as it was typed into an ASCII text editor. Notice that the HTML elements are traditionally typed in all lower case letters and enclosed in angle brackets. Here is an example: <head>. A single HTML element, with its brackets, is called a **tag**.

An HTML document is created in two sections, the head and the body. The head, beginning with <head> and ending with </head>, contains global styling information which affects the entire document. The body, beginning with <body> and ending with </body>, contains the actual formatting instructions for the text, images, and links that are to be included on the page, within the browser's window.

Some of the commands used to control the formatting on a page include:

> **Tags** are special HTML codes that specify formatting or layout for a Web page. Each tag is enclosed in angle brackets, such as these: < >.

  This tag centers the text that follows it. Its termination tag is .

<h1>   This is a header tag. The size of the lettering of this header will be the largest possible. This tag is delineated with </h1>.

<h6>   This is also a header tag. The size of the lettering for this header will the smallest possible. This tag is delineated with </h6>

```
<html>
  <head>
    <title>My First Web Page</title>
  </head>

  <body text="silver" bgcolor="2d763a" link="yellow" vlink="yellow">
    <center>
      <h1>Welcome</h1>
      <h2>to my</h2>
      <h3>Web Page</h3>

      <img src="stressrelief.jpg" height="250" alt="stressrelief">
      <br>
      <hr size="5" color="003300">
      <br>
    </center>

    <h3>My Favorite Links:</h3>
    <ul>
      <li><a href="http://www.google.com">Google Search Site</a></li>
      <li><a href="http://www.microsoft.com">Microsoft Home Page</a></li>
      <li><a href="http://www.apple.com">Apple Home Page</a></li>
    </ul>

    Thanks for visiting! Come back soon!
  </body>
</html>
```

Figure 8.8.3

HTML code and what it produces. (a) The HTML code for the page; (b) the Web page result.

Courtesy of Zenia Bahorski

<img>   This tag is used to include an image on the page. The name of the image, as well as alternate text (if images are not viewable by the browser) are included as part of this tag.

         This "break" command forces what follows onto the next line.

<hr>   This tag stands for "horizontal rule". The result of this tag is a horizontal thin line. This tag does not need a termination tag. Adding the size element will let you increase the size of the line as shown in figure 8.8.3b.

<li>   This tag makes up a bulleted list. The list items, or bulleted items in this case, are enclosed within the <li> and </li> tags.

<a>   This is an "anchor" tag. This tag is used when some action is required, like the inclusion of a hyperlink. In this case, the hyperlink would look like: <a href="http://www.google.com">Google</a> Where the text within the quote marks is the action that is to be taken when the visitor clicks on the word Google.

The market has become flooded with Web page builders for people who do not know HTML. They provide a template, a series of questions for you to answer, and some choices for you to make. When you have finished with the decisions requested, the wizard creates the page, all ready to place on the Web. Others offer a broad range of tools for more creative Web design. Adobe's GoLive is an example of a full-featured Web page design program.

Whichever way you create your home page, your HTML document and any photos or other images you have used should be saved together on a hard disk or other secondary memory device. As long as they remain on your drive, they are viewable only by you, using a browser such as Safari or Internet Explorer. No one can use the Internet to view your page while it resides only on your drive. To be seen by others, your page must first be uploaded to an Internet-accessible account. Your Internet Service Provider will be able to tell you how to access your own account and upload files. Putting a personal home page on the World Wide Web is exciting and satisfying, but there are a few risks involved: Remember that a Web page is on the Internet for the world to see. Anything you put there is as public as it can get. To protect your privacy, include only pictures and information you are willing to reveal to *everyone*. The Web is no place for secrets.

8.9 The Web in Business: The Growth of E-Commerce

Soon after President George H. W. Bush signed the High-Performance Computing act of 1991 into law, the Internet was opened up to the commercial marketplace. The business world quickly recognized the potential benefits of having a **Web presence.** Many individual companies rushed to create commercial Web sites. Their main purpose was to give the company an electronic presence—an accessible, online place to do business. Companies such as IBM, Sony, L.L. Bean, Proctor & Gamble, and many others created Web sites touting their company's products and image. Figure 8.9.1 shows screen shots of some of these Web sites.

Because of the high cost of creating and maintaining a Web site, outsourcing (that is, hiring outside consultants) these services became cost-effective. Web page designers, online advertising salespeople, Web masters, and others banded together to provide Web production services. The race to reach the Web-surfing consumer was on, causing a frenzy of electronically conducted business transactions.

This business medium that swept the country and the world is called **electronic commerce** or **e-commerce.** E-commerce has spawned an avenue of performing business operations, combining good traditional business practices with the speed and convenience of Internet communication. The result is an automated way to conduct marketing, retail sales, advertising, inventory management, customer relationship management, and in-house information transfer through company intranets.

The three main drivers behind the power of e-commerce are:

A business is said to have a **Web presence** if it has its own Web site, usually including its trademark or logo, products or services available, philosophy, and policies. Having a Web presence is like having a branch store or office online, allowing customers to discover the company, view its products, and purchase and pay for merchandise, all on the Internet.

Electronic commerce (e-commerce) is the online advertising, buying, and selling of goods and services.

Figure 8.9.1

Web sites of several large corporations: (a) L.L. Bean; (b) IBM.

1. Lower transaction costs for both business and client.

2. Larger purchases per transaction, and more transactions per client.

3. Integration of Internet activities into the business cycle. A business cycle is a complete transaction, from the time a product is ordered to the time it reaches the consumer's hands.

Let's look at a few of the many factors that help achieve these goals for companies doing business over the Internet:

■ E-commerce eliminates many barriers between merchants and customers. This results in a shortened business cycle, so that services and goods change hands fewer times before reaching customers.

■ Web sites cost less for companies to establish and maintain than do physical stores or catalog sales.

- Web sites entice customers to purchase larger numbers of items by providing links to related goods and complementary items.
- Online merchants can provide extensive customer services using consumer time rather than salaried employee time. These services include allowing customers to place complicated custom orders, to search through very large catalogs of selections, and even to return unwanted items to existing local outlets rather than incur costs of return mail.

PUZZLER HINT

You might find it helpful to chart out a map of your company Web site, showing how pages are linked to each other. List information or images that are needed on each page. How will your customer navigate from one place to another to learn about your products or services? How will you calculate charges? How will you collect what is owed to you?

Here's a last question to answer: How much will it cost you to set up and operate your business? List the various costs (exact amounts are not important) you expect to have.

Another major facet of e-commerce is encouraging potential customers to visit your site and to return to buy additional items. Business Web sites must be easy to find and convenient to use, or customers will not return. One way businesses attack this problem is to have links to their company's site on some of the more popular sites on the Web. Many Web service companies, such as Yahoo! and Google, sell ad space on their home pages. Each ad takes the form of an icon, banner, or picture. By clicking on a specific ad, a viewer can immediately be linked to the company's Web site. Competition for ad space makes the home pages for Google and others similar to the advertising space in newspapers and magazines.

PAYING FOR E-COMMERCE PURCHASES

New methods of buying and selling products using e-commerce demand a reexamination of the methods of payment possible for online transactions. Let's look at some of the payment methods commonly used in electronic business today, as well as a few innovative proposals for the future.

Using a credit card over the World Wide Web causes consumers to experience moments of uncertainty and doubt. They fear being the victims of electronic theft. However, most credit card companies cover losses after the first fifty dollars. A more serious problem of using credit cards online concerns the credit rating of the cardholder. Several thousand dollars erroneously charged to a person's account could conceivably affect his or her credit rating. Even though such a problem is immediately corrected, any delay of payment could show up in credit reporting systems as a bad debt. The result could be a refusal for financing a new car or house. Secure channels over the Web that handle credit card transactions are one way of preventing such an occurrence.

Many payment methods developed for e-commerce are more convenient than the traditional credit card or surface-mailed check. The most popular is PayPal. But, both buyer and seller must be registered. The buyers' purchases are paid directly from their registered checking accounts. Once set up, it becomes a very conveninent procedure.

In the near future, electronic wallets may be used to pay for small charges at Internet sites. Included in Web browser or PDA software, an **electronic wallet** is a program that acts like a rechargeable debit card or phone card. The purchaser will preload his or her electronic wallet, paying into it by check or credit card. Fees for small purchases or services can then be deducted from the amount in the wallet until the preloaded amount is exhausted. Periodically, the purchaser must reload the electronic wallet with another check or credit card payment.

There are a growing number of alternate methods of collecting for e-commerce goods and services on the merchant's end. The top five alternative online payment-processing companies in 2009 were 2Checkout, AlertPay, Digital River, E-Junkie, and TrialPay. These payment-processing companies use a special encryption scheme to collect the amount owed for the companies selling goods and services online. As a result, buyers and sellers are more secure in their transactions. The privacy of the purchaser is protected. In addition, because these payment-processing companies check for fraudulent credit information, the investments of the sellers are protected as well.

PRIVACY AND CONSUMER PROFILING

Consumer profiling is the business practice of collecting consumer information from online-based activities and using that information to create targeted marketing efforts.

A huge problem connected to small transaction-type commerce on the Internet is consumer privacy. E-commerce businesses can collect very extensive information about their customers in an attempt to closely define consumer needs and desires. This activity is called **consumer profiling.** Some consumers and commerce regulators consider profiling unethical because of the ease of online data collection.

Many believe that consumer profiling for e-commerce should be regulated by the government. Although legislators in Congress have repeatedly considered this issue, no laws have yet been passed. In a poll conducted in February 2000, 93 percent of online customers surveyed considered consumer profiling at least a potential threat to their personal privacy. In contrast, by September 2008, in a Consumer Reports National Research Center poll, this number had been reduced to 72%. In the same 2008 poll, 93% of Americans would like to be able to specify how online information about them is to be used. Because of such survey results, many companies are moving quickly to increase consumer control of their own data.

8.10 Software Applications: Search Engines

Searching the World Wide Web for specific information is a daunting task. Trillions of Web pages exist, posted to the Internet in no specific order. In fact, by July 2008, Google had found 1 trillion unique Web-pages, and there are certainly many more that haven't been included. Most pages contain masses of information irrelevant to your needs. Only a few pages contain valuable nuggets of relevant information. The frustrating problem is harvesting the relevant nuggets without sifting through mountains of junk. Fortunately, many free search services have sprouted up on the Web providing a series of Web-searching utilities called search engines. Like library catalogs and indexes, **search engines** sift through the Internet's digital data and guide us to the useful information we seek.

A **search engine** is a program available through World Wide Web browsers that enables the user to search the Internet for information on specific topics.

WHAT ARE SEARCH ENGINES AND HOW DO THEY WORK?

Search engines on the Web, such as Google, Yahoo!, MSN, and AskJeeves, work by calling on special programs and indices to scan the Web for specific types of information. Although several types of search programs have been written, most use the same underlying technology—the spider.

A **spider** is a piece of Web software that constantly searches for new Web pages and follows any links found on them. It enters Web addresses, page titles, and significant words and topics into a huge database that is accessed by search engines.

Like its namesake pictured in Figure 8.10.1, **spider** software automatically searches from site to site on the Web, perpetually seeking new pages. When the spider finds a new site or one that has recently changed, it sends information about that site and its contents back to the search software's database. What information is sent and how much depend on the search engine being served by the spider. Some spiders are selective, submitting only the titles of pages found, whereas others send back every word in every document. This impacts the kind of results you will get from any search query.

When you type a word or phrase into the search string text box, the search engine canvasses its data bank of Web pages, seeking the words you entered. When it finds matching entries, it compiles them into a list of links to the matching sites. This list is displayed on the screen.

Different search engines utilize different methods of producing their indexes. Here is a list of indexing techniques:

- **Subject or Topic Search:** This type of search begins with a list of classifications, which are further divided into a hierarchical system of several levels of subclasses. Web pages

Figure 8.10.1

Like its arachnid namesake, the software spider searches the Web for new conquests.

Wernher Krutein/Photovault

are categorized by subject. You can have the engine search for your topic in a single category or throughout the entire classification.

- **Keyword Search:** This kind of search engine is a close relative to a Biblical concordance. Like a concordance, it uses a technique called an inverted index to index every word in every document it finds on the Web. To initiate this search, you type in some keywords relevant to your topic. The search engine then produces a list of documents containing those words. The number and quality of results depend on how well you select your keywords.

- **Concept-Based Search:** This system maintains a matrix of which words commonly occur together or near each other in a document. For example, when it finds the words *film* and *director* in close proximity to each other, it assumes the document has something to do with the movies. It uses related words such as these to select documents that fit your search query.

- **Text Analysis Engine:** This system analyzes the content of a document's text and comes up with a specific classification from its classification hierarchy. It then adds that item to its directory of that category. Searches are then made by matching desired concepts to those of specific classifications.

- **Image Content Search:** This incredible search technology analyzes specific features, such as color, texture, patterns, and content of images within a digital photograph. For example, if you were searching a database of wallpaper samples and wanted to see samples that had a green background tint and a floral pattern, you could request a color search and a content search to find matching images.

USING A SEARCH ENGINE EFFECTIVELY

To perform a search for some specific information you need, you simply type a **query** into the search engine's text box. A query is made up of one or more **keywords** that can be used to identify the information you want.

Selecting keywords and queries that correctly specify the information desired in the search is the single most important insurance of a successful search. The goal is to get the information you want without having to sort through irrelevant material. Several pitfalls could cause your search to be less than successful. Suppose you were interested in purchasing a particular breed of dog—say, an Australian shepherd. Table 8.10.1 shows a progression of keywords you might select for your search queries and what results you would get.

Multiple attempts at framing a satisfactory query are common, especially when you first begin to use search engines. Remember that the ultimate goal is to find exactly the

A **query** is a request specifying what information is to be sought in a search operation. Most often, queries are made up of one or more keywords. The **keywords** are criteria selected to identify and narrow the specific information desired in a search.

information you want without having to waste time shuffling through unnecessary junk. The few moments spent in refining a query until you achieve the desired results will save time and effort on the overall task.

Here are a few tips for refining a Web search query:

- Use more than one word to make your query more specific and weed out undesired Web sites in advance. Example: *leather handbag* rather than *handbag*. A search on *handbag* alone will include vinyl handbags as well as leather ones.

- Use quotation marks to indicate that the search engine needs to match an exact phrase rather than two individual words. Example: *"leather handbag"* rather than *leather handbag*. Using quotation marks as indicated will eliminate items such as handbags with leather trim, and leather-look handbags.

- Use a plus sign to indicate that one or more specific words must be in all items found. Example: *+leather handbag*. All items found will contain the word *leather*, but they may or may not contain the word *handbag*. Notice that there is no space after the + sign in the query.

- Use a minus sign to indicate a word that must not be in any items found. Example: *+handbag+leather-vinyl*. All items found will include the word *handbag* and the word *leather*, not necessarily in that order, but no items will contain the word *vinyl*.

Table 8.10.1   *An example of how to refine a Web search query to produce useful and manageable results.*

Enter This Query	Expect This Result	Analysis of Results
dog	About 368 million Web sites containing the word *dog* in text or title	Keyword accurate, but too broad—you'd need a lifetime to scan the results
Australian Shepherd	About 1.4 million sites, some of which contain *Australian,* some of which contain *shepherd,* and some of which contain both keywords	Still too many results. You want the search engine to consider only pages with both keywords
+Australian+Shepherd	About 1.4 million or so Web sites are found, some of which relate to the dog you want, and some of which relate to shepherds who raise sheep in the Australian outback	Much better—but you did not specify the order in which the keywords had to occur
"Australian Shepherd"	About 1.4 million sites, only a few of which deal with humans who are also Australian Shepherds	Actually this is pretty close—you just have to eliminate sites dealing with nondog examples
+dog+"Australian Shepherd"	About 1.1 million sites, all related to your topic, although some related only marginally	Still a lot of sites to read—can we be more specific?
+dog+breeder+"Australian Shepherd"	About 68,000 Web sites, all very specific to your interests	Finally, the desired results!

It's a good idea to try your search queries on several different types of search engines to see which give the best (and most relevant) results. Because they organize their indexes differently, different search engines produce different lists of Web pages for the same query.

Chapter Summary

8.1 A Powerful Voice

In the short time since its inception, the Internet has grown beyond the wildest dreams of its originators. In the transition period that encompasses the last decade of the twentieth century and the first decade of the twenty-first, the Internet and the Web continue to emerge as powerful tools of communication, influence, and persuasion.

8.2 The Internet: Struggling to Maturity

What we now call the Internet began in the 1960s, when four university research facilities joined together to form ARPAnet. Their purpose was to share expensive computing resources. After suffering growing pains through the 1970s, ARPAnet evolved into NSFnet in the late 1980s. By the early 1990s, most research and education interests had switched to CSnet, using the TCP/IP protocol. This was the foundation for what became known as the Internet.

8.3 Internet Services

Before the inception of the World Wide Web, all Internet services were text based. Gopher, developed at the University of Minnesota, provided a menu-driven index for finding information on the Internet. Archie and Veronica, two early Internet search tools, greatly eased the pain of finding specific information on the free-form Internet.

8.4 Using Today's Internet

Whether Internet activity is done in the context of a small office network or a worldwide internetwork, similar communications resources exist. Major uses made of the Internet include e-mail, bulletin boards and conferencing, and Internet relay chat rooms. Although all of these existed on a smaller scale in the all-text world of the Internet, they grew instantly more popular with the advent of the World Wide Web.

Web Logs or blogs are a Web phenomenon starting in the late 1990s with over an estimated 2 million active blogs in early 2005, which grew to over 100 million by 2009. They are related to Web pages in certain respects, but have some major differences. For example, they are noted for being current and usually informal. Also, the protocol called RSS or Real Simple Syndication has allowed convenient and automatic subscriptions to the blogs by anyone. Sometimes readers are encouraged to comment on the content.

8.5 The World Wide Web: Internet's Most Common Access

The human need to use several communication media simultaneously helped motivate the development of the World Wide Web. HTTP (HyperText Transfer Protocol) used by the Web could convert not only text but also visual and audio information into packets to traverse the Internet, making multimedia communication possible. Although anyone can access the Web, no single entity owns or controls it. Visitors to Web sites can read or print them out but cannot modify or delete their contents.

8.6 Navigating the Web

Navigation on the Web is accomplished through the use of hyperlinks—images or pieces of text that can be used as pointers to related Web pages. To use a hyperlink, the reader moves the mouse cursor to the linking word and clicks the mouse button. Whether the related passage is in the same document or another, it immediately appears.

8.7 Understanding Web Addresses (URLs)

Each of the millions of Web pages that exist on the Internet has a unique address called a Uniform Resource Locator, or URL. Used all together, the parts of a URL uniquely identify a specific Web page by specifying the protocol used, server, computer, domain, path, and file for that page.

8.8 The Web and You

In order to use the Web, you must first sign up with an Internet Service Provider. The hardware you need includes a computer with adequate speed and hard disk capacity, a modem, and a telephone connection. Necessary software is a Web browser program. A special layout language called HTML is needed to develop documents readable by Web browsers. Web page development software can help you design pages without learning HTML. To be seen by others, a Web document must be made accessible to the Internet.

8.9 The Web in Business: The Growth of E-Commerce

E-commerce, a rapidly growing area of World Wide Web use, includes all phases of doing business over the Internet. Although online business has many of the same concerns as traditional commerce, several additional problems exist. Companies doing business over the Web must address the issues of customer privacy, credit card security, attracting and retaining customers, and payment methodology.

8.10 Software Applications: Search Engines

The goal of Web searches is finding relevant information without having to sift through mountains of junk. To accomplish this, you type a query into the text box of a search engine, which then searches its indexes to find items that match your query. Most search engines use a program called a spider to keep their indexes updated. Specific, carefully defined queries produce the best search results.

Key Terms

Key terms introduced in this chapter:

1. Archie, *217*
2. ARPAnet, *212*
3. Backbone, *213*
4. Blog, *221*
5. Chat room, *220*
6. Cloud computing, *231*
7. Compressed format, *234*
8. Command-line system, *216*
9. Computer conference, *219*
10. Concept-based search, *242*
11. Consumer profiling, *240*
12. CSnet, *212*
13. Decompression, *234*
14. Deep Web, *231*
15. Domain name, *229*
16. Downloading, *232*
17. Electronic commerce (e-commerce), *237*
18. Electronic conference, *219*
19. Electronic mail (e-mail), *217*
20. File name, *229*
21. Free downloads, *232*
22. FTP (File Transfer Protocol), *233*
23. Gopher, *216*
24. HTML—HyperText Markup Language, *234*
25. HTTP—HyperText Transfer Protocol, *224*
26. Hypermedia, *228*
27. Hypertext, *226*
28. Image content search, *241*
29. Instant Messaging, *220*
30. Internet, *212*
31. Internet2, *219*
32. Internet address (IP), *216*
33. Internet Relay Chat (IRC), *220*
34. Internet Service Provider (ISP), *230*
35. Invisible Web, *231*
36. Keywords, *241*
37. Keyword search, *241*
38. Link, *225*
39. Listserv, *220*
40. Menu-driven, *216*
41. Milnet, *214*
42. Multimedia, *224*
43. National Lambda Rail, *217*
44. Newsgroup, *220*
45. NSFnet, *214*
46. Path, *229*
47. Peer-to-Peer (P2P) file sharing, *218*
48. Posting, *220*
49. Query, *241*
50. Read-only access, *225*
51. Real Simple Syndication (RSS), *222*
52. Search engine, *240*
53. Server, *229*
54. Server, *229*
55. Social networking, *223*
56. Spider, *240*
57. Subdomains, *229*
58. Subject search, *240*
59. Surfing, *228*
60. Tag, *235*
61. TCP/IP, *213*
62. Text analysis engine, *241*
63. Topic search, *240*
64. Top-level domain, *229*
65. Uploading, *233*
66. URL (Uniform Resource Locator), *228*
67. Usenet, *220*
68. Veronica, *216*
69. Web browser, *230*
70. Web page, *228*
71. Web presence, *237*
72. World Wide Web (WWW), *224*
73. Yahoo Groups, *214*

Matching

Match the number of the key term introduced in the chapter to the following statements.
Each term may be used once, more than once, or not at all.

1. ____ This type of Internet communication accessed only textual materials.

2. ____ This communication protocol allows text, visual, and audio information to be accessed and transmitted via the Internet.

3. ____ A slang term used to describe the free-form navigation from place to place on the Internet by following hypermedia links.

4. ____ Any word or phrase in an electronic document that can be used as a pointer or link to a related text passage.

5. ____ The electronic connection between text or image and another text passage or image.

6. ____ These links use visual objects and text to be linked to other visual objects, animations, text, or even sound.

7. ____ Links appear in these documents that have been created for the World Wide Web.

8. ____ This is the name given to the worldwide standard for expressing the unique address of a specific Web page.

9. ____ This protocol is used for transferring files between computers.

10. ____ This type of access refers to the ability to view a page without being able to make any changes to it.

11. ____ The general name given to software that allows access to the World Wide Web.

12. ____ This important network was transferred to the Defense Department in 1975.

13. ____ The National Science Foundation started a network using this protocol in 1980.

14. ____ This network was created by the National Science Foundation to provide a resource-sharing network opportunity to computer science researchers at all universities.

15. ____ This menu-driven system consists of programs that display text-based lists of accessible information.

16. ___ This search system on Gopher specialized in finding data files.

17. ___ This search system on Gopher specialized in indexing the entries in all the Gopher menus.

18. ___ The military formed this network after it split off a portion of ARPAnet in 1983.

19. ___ This is an example of an Internet chat facility.

20. ___ This is currently the most visible activity on the Internet.

True or False

Place either T or F on the line provided with each of the following statements. If a statement is false, you should be able to explain what changes would make it true.

1. ___ Like the Gopher system, Veronica and Archie were two other systems that allowed the navigation of the Internet via text menus.

2. ___ Gopher systems are no longer accessible on the Internet.

3. ___ Gopher was, and still is, primarily a text-based system that allows access to some information on the Internet.

4. ___ An Internet address that identifies where a person can be found must be supplied with the message in order to send a message to someone on the Internet.

5. ___ The Internet has the potential of infecting millions of computers with viruses.

6. ___ IRCs require that people "chatting" on the IRC be connected to the network at the same time.

7. ___ Every computer on the Internet must have a unique individual IP address.

8. ___ The only links that are displayed on Web pages appear as highlighted text passages.

9. ___ The World Wide Web is a protocol that not only allows textual information to be accessed on the Internet but also visual and audio information.

10. ___ The World Wide Web uses multimedia communication.

11. ___ The prefix or leftmost part of a URL identifies the type of Internet protocol requested.

12. ___ The Internet and the World Wide Web are one and the same.

13. ___ A URL contains the address of the computer you are trying to reach.

14. ___ A URL address for any computer within the United States must contain the two-letter code: us.

15. ___ Because no one owns the World Wide Web, no one includes service charges for accessing the Web.

16. ___ A spider is synonymous with a search engine.

17. ___ Free downloads are exactly that—free!

18. ___ Once a download has begun, it can never be interrupted.

19. ___ Many downloads are sent in a compressed format and need to be decompressed before installation is possible.

20. ___ Unless a document includes specific formatting codes, it cannot be viewed on the World Wide Web as a Web page.

Multiple Choice

Answer the multiple-choice questions by selecting the best answer from the choices given.

1. This network was started for computer science researchers.
   a. ARPAnet
   b. CSnet
   c. NSFnet
   d. Internet
   e. CSResearchNet

2. In 1975, ARPAnet was transferred to
   a. NASA
   b. NSF (National Science Foundation)
   c. A Defense Department agency
   d. An IBM holding company
   e. The Internet board

3. The NSFnet with its internetwork running the TCP/IP protocol became known as
   a. ARPAnet
   b. Milnet
   c. Internet
   d. UNIX
   e. Phishnet

4. The term *Gopher* came from:
   a. Going Over Piles of Hideous Erroneous References
   b. Georgia's Office of Physical Health OpERations
   c. Gopher (UNIX programmers typically work in basements)
   d. Gopher (mascot of University of Minnesota)

5. The operating system of choice for specialists who originally used the Internet was
   a. MS-DOS
   b. OS/2
   c. VMS
   d. UNIX
   e. MacOS

6. This real-time communication system enables people to "talk" to one another over the Internet by using the keyboard in places called chat rooms.
   a. IRC
   b. E-mail
   c. Bulletin Boards
   d. Gopher
   e. Phonehome

7. This term is used to describe information being communicated through several different media simultaneously.
   a. Medium
   b. Media
   c. Multimedia
   d. HyperText

8. This term is used to describe any word or phrase in an electronic document that can be used as a pointer to a related passage (restricted to text only).
   a. Medium
   b. Media
   c. Hypertext
   d. Multimedia
   e. Hypermedia

9. Which of the following is not included in a URL?
   a. The type of connection to be made
   b. The Internet address
   c. The name of the Web server
   d. The HTML tags
   e. The domain

10. When searching the WWW, this looks for specific requested information.
    a. Web browser
    b. Search engine
    c. Spider
    d. HTML
    e. Tag

11. This will search for sites that have changed or have been recently added to the World Wide Web.
    a. Web browser
    b. Search engine
    c. Spider
    d. HTML
    e. Tag

12. This program allows access to the WWW.
    a. Web browser
    b. Search engine
    c. Spider
    d. HTML
    e. Tag

13. Applying these to a document will allow us to share the document with others on the World Wide Web.
    a. Web browsers
    b. Search engines
    c. Spiders
    d. HTTP protocols
    e. HTML tags

14. The top-level domain name that would be included in the address of any corporate Web page would be
    a. edu
    b. com
    c. gov
    d. mil
    e. org

15. Some examples of this type of communication include CD-ROM, WWW, television, theater, and movies.
    a. HyperText
    b. Hyperlinks
    c. Multimedia
    d. Medium
    e. Internet

Exercises

1. What is the difference between a text-based accessing method and a multimedia-based accessing method?

2. Name three text-based information-accessing methods mentioned in this chapter.

3. People join IRCs (Internet Relay Chat) to exchange information with others on a topic of interest. When you send a response to another's message, your contact information may or may not be included. What would you do if someone posted a message with which you totally disagree, but you would rather not have that person know who you are?

4. Which is bigger, the Internet or the World Wide Web? Why?

5. What is the difference between a path and a domain?

6. Mark each of the following as either hardware, software, or other:
   a. Web browser
   b. ISP
   c. hypertext
   d. protocol
   e. modem
   f. HTTP
   g. FTP
   h. shareware
   i. search engine

7. Check the following box indicating the top-level domain identifier for each organization listed.

	org	com	edu	gov
Sony				
The FBI				
Greenpeace				
Harvard				
IBM				
The CIA				
The Salvation Army				
E.F. Hutton				

Discussion Questions

1. Explain why censorship on the Internet would be hard to police.

2. Discuss possible advantages and disadvantages of people meeting in a virtual space/location using newsgroups, bulletin boards, and IRCs versus actually meeting in person.

3. Discuss the exact ways in which IRC is similar to and different from a telephone conference call.

4. If information is stored on computers (rather than printed books, magazines, handwritten notes, and so on), it can be easily changed. This can make it easy to correct, update, or delete information. Discuss the potential social, political, or psychological conse-

quences of "falsifying the past" in this fashion. Such tampering with history was predicted in the novel *1984,* and even done without computers in the Soviet Union and in China, by inserting and removing individuals as they fell into or out of favor or power.

5. What kept the early Internet from achieving the popular success enjoyed by the Web?

6. How would you go about setting up a "private" chat room for yourself and your friends?

7. WWW site names are registered with domain organizations and then owned by the persons who have registered them. Some people have registered as site names the names of other famous people, corpora-

tions, and products. They hope to sell them to those people or corporations for a lot of money or possibly place misleading or embarrassing content on those sites. Discuss the ethics of such activity and, if you see this as wrong, what do you think should be changed to prevent this?

8. Discuss possible ways to pay individuals who make the results of their creative efforts (music, books, etc.) available on the WWW.

9. What business issues can you see with unlimited access to the Web?

10. What legal issues can you see with unlimited access to the Web?

Group Projects

1. A group of four students is to share responsibility for a presentation about services carried over the Internet. Each person of the group will take two of the services from the list:

- ➡ HTTP (HyperText Transfer Protocol)
- ➡ FTP (File Transfer Protocol—include anonymous FTP and Archie)
- ➡ E-mail (include MIME and SMTP)
- ➡ Gopher (include Veronica)
- ➡ WAIS (Wide Area Information Service)
- ➡ Telnet (Telephone Networking—include PPP and SLIP)
- ➡ Usenet (How does it compare in form and function to IRCs?)

The presentation should use Microsoft PowerPoint, or other presentation software, and include an example in which the presenter used the service and shows the result. It should outline what the service is used for and

how to use it. Research for these topics can be found on the World Wide Web. Each slide should be short and not include a lot of text.

2. **PUZZLER** A group of four students should pick an area of common interest and create a Web site on the school server. If possible, make use of a Web HTML publishing tool. Each person in the group should pick one of the following jobs and be responsible for recording and organizing information related to that task. The four areas are:

Layout and design

Research for content materials

HTML program for the Web page

Logistics for getting Web page up on school system

Ideas for each of these areas should be discussed within the group. Each student should record the group's wishes for his or her areas. A general layout and map of the Web site should be designed by the group.

Web Exercises

1. These Web exercises take the form of a virtual treasure hunt. Each item on the list can be found by using one of the Web's search services and carefully created queries. Some items are more difficult to find than others. For each item you find, print out the item or answer the question. Annotate each item by giving the URL where you got the item or information needed, the name of the search service you used, the query you created to find the item, and the number of results your query produced.

Hint: The best answers are those found by detailed, specific queries producing only a few very relevant results, and no inappropriate junk!

Find these items:

a. A place in the United States where you can purchase voodoo dolls.

b. Japanese language lessons (online) for American children.

c. The most important event that happened on your birthdate during any year from 1900 to the present year.

d. A current job listing relevant to your major or minor field of study.

e. The home page for a dog or cat rescue society.

f. The best place to go for an Australian bicycle trip.

g. A definition of *mirepoix,* with directions for finding and using it.

h. A complete worldwide listing of the two-character country codes used in international Internet addresses.

i. The best place to go shopping for vintage classic equipment used in your favorite sport or hobby.

j. The history of bagels.

k. Detailed instructions for creating a working electric motor out of easy-to-get "found" objects.

l. A "Teaching Tip for the Day" aimed at parents who home-school their children.

m. A place where you can get free information on how to create a healthy pond ecoenvironment.

n. Creation myths of cultures other than your own.

o. Makeup and fashion tips (both male and female) from famous entertainment, business, or sports celebrities.

2. Using a Web browser of your choice, go first to the following location: http://gopher.tc.umn.edu. This site lists the resources available on the University of Minnesota's Gopher server. It is not quite up to date. Second, find when the weather for your area was last updated. Third, find a recipe that you might like. Write down the URL of the recipe you have found.

3. **PUZZLER** Design a Web page that would be appropriate for the welcoming page of the Web site of a small retail business. Be sure to provide links to important business departments, products, services, personnel, and payment options. Your Web page should include at least the following items: a company logo or slogan, a photograph or other relevant graphic image, an animation, several sizes and/or colors of text, links to other pages, a counter, date last revised, name and e-mail address of Web master (you), and contact person with title and e-mail address.

4. **PUZZLER** Find the Web sites of three companies in your geographic area that seem similar in size and interests. Examine their Web sites and describe the effectiveness of their Web presence. If you were designing their sites, what would you change that would improve their customer appeal?

5. Use whatever search service is set as a default on your Web browser and see how many other search services you can locate. Identify at least five different services and describe the differences among them. Why should there be so many search services?

Bibliography

Berners-Lee, Tim. *Weaving the Web: The Original Design and Ultimate Destiny of the World Wide Web by Its Inventor.* New York: Harper San Francisco, 1999.

This book, written by Tim Berners-Lee, provides a no-nonsense account of how he invented the World Wide Web.

Comer, Douglas E. *The Internet,* 2nd ed. Upper Saddle River, NJ: Prentice Hall, 1997.

A good, readable overview of how the Internet works.

Deitel, Harvey M., Tem Nieto, and Paul J. Deitel. *Complete Internet and World Wide Web Programming Training Course* (with CD-ROM). Upper Saddle River, NJ: Prentice Hall, 2000.

This book provides comprehensive coverage of Web-development techniques designed for beginners, programmers moving into Web development, and pros that want better skills.

Gurian, Phil. *E-Mail Business Strategies and Dozens of Other Great Ways to Take Advantage of the Internet.* New York: Grand National Press, 2000.

This book goes beyond e-mail to provide great tips on using a host of Internet services.

Hafner, Katie and Matthew Lyon. *Where Wizards Stay Up Late: The Origins of the Internet.* New York: Touchstone, 1996.

This is a readable, amusing, but accurate history of the Internet.

May, Paul Richard. *The Business of E-Commerce: From Corporate Strategy to Technologies.* New York: Cambridge University Press, 2000.

This book gives a fairly detailed explanation of how to develop a business plan and set up an online business.

Saunders, Rebecca. *Business the Amazon.com Way: Secrets of the World's Most Astonishing Web Business.* London: Capstone, 1999.

This book reveals the secrets, deals, schemes, and dreams of one of the world's Web superstars.

Smith, Rob et al. *Complete Idiot's Guide to e-Commerce.* Indianapolis, IN: Que, 2000.

A beginners-level book for developing an online business.

Trinkle, Dennis A. and Scott A. Merriman, eds. *The History Highway 2000: A Guide to Internet Resources.* Armonk, NY: M. E. Sharpe, 2000.

This volume cites by topic of interest some 2,500 sites for historians, history teachers, students, discussion groups, and researchers.

Sherman, Chris and Gary Price. *The Invisible Web.* Meford, NJ: Cyberage Books, 2001.

This is a look at the Deep Web.

Hewitt, Hugh. *Blog—Understanding the Informative Reformation that's Changing Your World.* Nashville, TN: Thomas Nelson, 2005.

This is a complete discussion of blogs.

chapter 9

Personal Security and Privacy

TimeLine

1981 First successful undocumented computer virus occurs on Apple II at Texas A&M.

1982 First documented computer virus by Fred Cohen as a student project.

1988 Robert Morris Jr., a graduate student, releases a worm program into the Internet, revealing the need for greater network security.

1991 Phil Zimmermann creates Pretty Good Privacy, a cryptography program to protect the privacy of an individual's email.

1999 Melissa virus infected computers when a Word document was opened.

2000 Distributed denial of service (DDoS) stops activity at Yahoo!, eBay, and several other popular sites.

2004 Mydoom is a mass-mailing worm that arrives as an attachment, causes denial of service attacks.

2013 By 2013 somewhere in the world a major catastrophe will be the result of some cyberterrorist attack.

Chapter Objectives

By the end of this chapter, you will:

➡ Understand what computer viruses are and how to protect against them.

➡ Describe the differences between computer viruses, worms, and Trojan horses.

➡ Appreciate the vulnerabilities of personal computers.

➡ Understand what spyware is so as to protect yourself from it.

➡ Know how wireless devices work so you can invoke the proper protection schemes.

➡ Discern the difference between legitimate and illegitimate access to your computer.

➡ Identify the tools needed to protect your personal computer from invasions of privacy and make it secure from unwanted tampering.

- **Problem 1.** Over a period of several weeks you notice that your computer is slowing down. Also, any time you're surfing the Web a lot of ads keep appearing on the screen. It gets so bad that getting anything done is almost impossible. What is the problem? How can you get your computer back to normal?

PUZZLER

- **Problem 2.** Many of the problems caused by worms, viruses, Trojan horses, phishing emails, and other malicious programs can be solved by how you use computers. What personal habits in the use of any computer should you develop? Make a list.

9.1 Introduction to Issues of Personal Security and Privacy

Before we can discuss the issues regarding personal security and privacy, it is first necessary to understand the source of these invasions and the techniques that they employ. We can categorize the security and privacy attacks as coming from three major sources: individuals commonly referred to as hackers, the business community, and the government. These individuals and groups use many techniques and special software. The attacks can be serious or just annoying problems. Figure 9.1.1 is a partial list of the common difficulties.

It is important that those who use the Internet, wireless devices and computer networks understand their vulnerabilities and the issues they create. We examine these technologies in the following sections and we will investigate how they can be used to invade our personal security and privacy.

There are also several techniques and programs that can be used to protect against attacks on our personal security and privacy. Understanding them will allow intelligent choices in organizing personal protection. They include:

- Agent and bot eradication programs
- Cryptography
- Filtering
- Firewalls
- Virus protection programs

This chapter will discuss these techniques and programs along with their limitations so that users can be better prepared for the future.

SERIOUS & PERSONAL	PERSONAL PRIVACY	ANNOYING TO US
Trojan Horses	Chat Rooms	Spam
Viruses	Spyware	Popups
Worms	Data mining	Parasitic computing
Phishing	Email sniffing	Denial of service attacks
Agents & Bots	Instant Messenger	
Bluebugging	Lifelog	
Bluesnarf	RFID	
	Search engines	

Figure 9.1.1

Three areas of concern that are serious, affect our privacy, or are annoying.

A computer **virus** is programming code intentionally designed to reproduce itself. It is attached to a host program or file and when program is executed or the file opened, the virus will find other hosts to attach itself to. Its effect ranges from harmless to very destructive. Human action is part of the process, whether it is inserting a disk, opening a file, or opening an infected email.

9.2 Fundamental Concepts in Personal Security

The majority of the issues relate to the Internet. However, other networks and certain wireless type systems also are of concern. The three problem areas listed in Figure 9.1.1 have some overlap. In fact, the personal privacy issues listed can become serious and lead to both financial and physically harmful problems. Let's now examine several of these intruders.

VIRUSES, WORMS AND TROJAN HORSES

The three "malware" or malicious software elements—viruses, worms and Trojan horses—are related and sometimes overlap in how they work. In fact, worms can be thought of as a subclass of viruses. They got their names in rather straightforward ways. In the case of viruses there are many parallels between real world viruses, such as the common cold, and computer viruses. Hence the name itself: computer virus.

The first successful computer virus is attributed to "Joe," a member of an undocumented group at Texas A&M. They were speculating on how to use evolution and natural selection to reproduce good Apple II computer games, while disposing of poor ones. As reported by Robert Slade

> It was spread on Apple II floppy disks (which contained the operating system) and reputed to have spread from Texas A&M. …we know the virus was named Elk Cloner and displayed a little rhyme on the screen:

Elk Cloner: The program with a personality

> It will get on all your disks
> > It will infiltrate your chips
> > > Yes it's Cloner!

> It will stick to you like glue
> > It will modify ram too
> > > Send in the Cloner!

Phil Zimmermann: Email Privacy for Everyone

In 1991, security via encryption was available only to governments and large corporations. Anyone else who wanted to protect the privacy of his or her email was out of luck. Programs the ordinary person could use to encode email simply did not exist.

Then along came Philip R. Zimmermann.

Philip R. Zimmermann was an experienced software engineer specializing in cryptography and data security, data communications and real-time embedded systems. He received his bachelor's degree in computer science from Florida Atlantic University in 1978. He then embarked on a lifetime of professional and personal service protecting the individual security and privacy essential to American life. Today, he is a member of the International Association of Cryptologic Research, the Association for Computing Machinery, the League for Programming Freedom, and the Union of Concerned Scientists. He serves on the board of directors of Computer Professionals for Social Responsibility, and the Advisory Panel of Americans for Computer Privacy.

In 1991, Philip R. Zimmermann was the target of a three-year criminal investigation. His crime? He invented a cryptographic software system called *Pretty Good Privacy* (PGP). PGP allowed the average person to encode his or her email. At the time, cryptographic software was considered essential to US national security, and could not be exported to foreign nations. The government held that these restrictions were violated when PGP spread all around the world following its 1991 publication as freeware. Despite the lack of funding, the lack of any paid staff, the lack of a company to stand behind it, and despite government persecution, PGP nonetheless became the most widely used email encryption software in the world. After the government dropped its case in early 1996, Zimmermann founded PGP Inc, which was acquired by Network Associates in December 1997. Zimmermann is now a Senior Fellow at Network Associates, as well as an independent consultant in matters cryptographic.

Zimmerman has received numerous technical and humanitarian awards for his pioneering work in cryptography. In 1999, he received the Louis Brandeis Award from Privacy International. In 1998, he received a Lifetime Achievement Award from Secure Computing Magazine, and in 1996 the Norbert Wiener Award from Computer Professionals for Social Responsibility for promoting the responsible use of technology. He also received the 1995 Chrysler Award for Innovation in Design, the 1995 Pioneer Award from the Electronic Frontier Foundation, the 1996 PC Week IT Excellence Award, and the 1996 Network Computing Well-Connected Award for "Best Security Product." PGP was selected by *Information Week* as one of the Top 10 Most Important Products of 1994. *Time* Magazine also named Zimmermann one of the "Net 50", the 50 most influential people on the Internet in 1995.

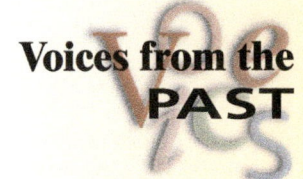

Voices from the PAST

The first documented computer virus was in 1983. The virus was a seminar project done by Fred Cohen on the Unix operating system to prove the virus concept could spread. His seminal paper, *Computer Viruses – Theory and Experiments* written in 1984 defines and describes how computer viruses are viable. History has proven his work a valid prediction.

From Cohen's original paper, the following pseudocode shows a general scheme that a simple virus program labeled "V" can follow. This is a somewhat difficult example, but with some patience and concentration the understanding of how one virus works is a worthy reward.

```
program virus:=
    {1234567;

subroutine infect-executable:=
    {loop:file = get-random-executable-file;
    if first-line-of-file = 1234567 then goto loop;
    prepend virus to file;}

subroutine do-damage:=
    {whatever damage is to be done}

subroutine trigger-pulled:=
    {return true if some condition holds}

main-program:=
    {infect-executable;
    if trigger-pulled then do-damage;
    goto next;}

next:}
```

His paper goes on to describe in words what this program does:

This example virus (V) searches for an uninfected executable file (E) by looking for executable files without the "1234567" in the beginning, and prepends V to E, turning it into an infected file (I). V then checks to see if some triggering condition is true, and does damage. Finally, V executes the rest of the program it was prepended to. When the user attempts to execute E, I is executed in its place; it infects another file and then executes as if it were E. With the exception of a slight delay for infection, I appears to be E until the triggering condition causes damage.

A triggering condition might be a certain date, such as the 4th of July, 2009. The damage done when the condition is true might be something only annoying like displaying a waving flag on the screen, or it could be the malicious destruction of the contents of the computer's hard drive.

This simple scheme is often enhanced and made more complicated with additional features. The **worm** is one of the special modifications. It should be noted that the simple virus discussed above needed a human to originally introduce it to the computer. Automating this feature to make this virus self replicating transforms it into what is commonly called a worm.

In 1988 Robert Morris, Jr., a 23-year-old computer science doctoral student at Cornell University, created one of the first and most pervasive worms to be unleashed on the Internet. It infected as many as 6,000 computers all running the UNIX or SunOS operating systems. It wasn't intended to do damage, however, the "cleanup" cost was estimated at between 10 and 100 million dollars. As an interesting sidelight to the story, his father was head of the National Computer Security Center that was part of an NSA (National Security Agency) computer security project to educate the public. It is also said that Morris's exploits introduced the word "hacker" to the vernacular. He was convicted under the computer Fraud

A computer **worm** is a form of computer virus that can replicate itself without human action or a host program. Once it is introduced to a computer or computer network, it spreads, consuming memory and communications bandwidth. The effect due to worms ranges from annoyingly slowing down computers to very destructive behavior.

and Abuse Act (Title 18) and sentenced to 3 years probation, a $10,050 fine, and 400 hours of community service. One final note before examining how the *Internet Worm* worked: Morris is now an Associate Professor of Electrical Engineering & Computer Science at MIT.

The *Internet Worm* used a three part attack with a program of about 3,000 lines of C programming language code. To execute the *Internet Worm* attack, the program had to be reconstructed from the binary code. This process is called disassembling. The three parts of the worm that made use of holes in the operating systems components are commonly known as *sendmail, fingerd,* and *rsh/rexec*. Each part had a unique approach:

The Sendmail Attack:

The worm on the infected computer opens a TCP connection to another computer's sendmail or SMPT port that it has obtained from itself. This process causes a transfer of data that allows the attacking computer to gain access to the uninfected computer. The uninfected computer then requests that data from the attacking computer be transferred. This data is the seed that when processed by the uninfected computer, causes it to do the same thing to other computers given to it by the attacking computer. This process repeats over and over again mushrooming into a gigantic traffic jam on local networks and the Internet.

The Fingerd Attack:

In UNIX type operating systems the *fingerd* program is used to obtain information of users on the network. There was a bug in this program that allowed the greatest success of the three attacks. The information being read was stored in memory near the *fingerd* command. The bug in the UNIX operating system permitted the information to be put in locations beyond the normal storage area. This allowed the attacker to replace the finger command by one that would transfer the infecting program from the attacker to the newly infected computer. Then the process started all over again, but this time the newly infected computer became the attacker.

The Trusted Host Attack:

The main objective of this attack was to get into people's accounts and to find the *trusted hosts* list where the worm could migrate to. The *trusted hosts* list is a list of other computers that are accessible from the computer under attack, which in turn have *trusted hosts* lists. Since the attacking computer doesn't have special privileges, it also needs a password. To circumvent this problem a password attack is launched. The Internet Worm's *trusted hosts* attack would guess passwords, first by trying user names, nicknames, the name in the GCOS field, and a list of over 400 popular passwords found in Figure 9.2.1. If this search for the correct password failed, the program opened the UNIX user dictionary and started trying the words in it. Using these methods the password search was often successful, mainly because of the poor choices made by computer users. Once the program found the password then it ported over the necessary files needed to start the Internet Worm attack on the new computer.

This look into one of the first worms that caused widespread damage shows what it takes to exploit holes in an operating system. The damage in human labor and loss of service was estimated at between 10 and 100 million dollars. Current operating systems are still vulnerable to worms and viruses, and the attacks are becoming more sophisticated and sometimes more sinister.

The **Trojan horse** is the last of the three general types of invasion discussed in this section. The concept has a long history going back to the Greek's Trojan horse, which the Greeks put in front of the gates to Troy as a gift. The Trojans took it inside the walls of the city and that night a small number of hidden solders emerged and opened the gates so that the Greek solders could enter and sack the city.

The client/server model discussed in Chapter 7 is the basis for the Trojan horse attack. The unsuspecting victim downloads a song (e.g., MP3 file), a jpeg image, opens an email attachment, or possibly follows a spam link. This, in turn causes the running of a program attached to the file. One scenario would allow this hidden program to turn their computer

A **Trojan horse**, named after the Trojan horse in Greek mythology, is a program that pretends to be some legitimate program, game, email, image, or other file. They do not replicate themselves, but must have human assistance in getting downloaded to other computers. They are often destructive, but may not affect the perceived operation of the computer, while doing other unscrupulous things.

aaa	carmen	engineer	herbert	minimum	rainbow	super
academia	carolina	enterprise	hiawatha	minsky	raindrop	superstage
aerobics	caroline	enzyme	hibernia	moguls	raleigh	support
airplane	cascades	ersatz	honey	moose	random	supported
albany	castle	establish	horse	morley	rascal	surfer
albatross	cat	estate	horus	mozart	really	suzanne
albert	cayuga	euclid	hutchins	nancy	rebecca	swearer
alex	celtics	evelyn	imbroglio	napoleon	remote	symmetry
alexander	cerulean	extension	imperial	nepenthe	rick	tangerine
algebra	change	fairway	include	ness	ripple	tape
aliases	charles	felicia	ingres	network	robotics	target
alphabet	charming	fender	inna	newton	rochester	tarragon
ama	charon	fermat	innocuous	next	rolex	taylor
amorphous	chester	fidelity	irishman	noxious	romano	telephone
analog	cigar	finite	isis	nutrition	ronald	temptation
anchor	classic	fishers	japan	nyquist	rosebud	thailand
andromache	clusters	flakes	jessica	oceanography	rosemary	tiger
animals	coffee	float	jester	ocelot	roses	toggle
answer	coke	flower	jixian	olivetti	ruben	tomato
anthropogenic	collins	flowers	johnny	olivia	rules	topography
anvils	commrades	foolproof	joseph	oracle	ruth	tortoise
anything	computer	football	joshua	orca	sal	toyota
aria	condo	foresight	judith	orwell	saxon	trails
ariadne	cookie	format	juggle	osiris	scamper	trivial
arrow	cooper	forsythe	julia	outlaw	scheme	trombone
arthur	cornelius	fourier	kathleen	oxford	scott	tubas
athena	couscous	fred	kermit	pacific	scotty	tuttle
atmosphere	creation	friend	kernel	painless	secret	umesh
aztecs	creosote	frighten	kirkland	pakistan	sensor	unhappy
azure	cretin	fun	knight	pam	serenity	unicorn
bacchus	daemon	fungible	ladle	papers	sharks	unknown
bailey	dancer	gabriel	lambda	password	sharon	urchin
banana	daniel	gardner	lamination	patricia	sheffield	utility
bananas	danny	garfield	larkin	penguin	sheldon	vasant
bandit	dave	gauss	larry	peoria	shiva	vertigo
banks	december	george	lazarus	percolate	shivers	vicky
barber	defoe	gertrude	lebesgue	persimmon	shuttle	village
baritone	deluge	ginger	lee	persona	signature	virginia
bass	desperate	glacier	leland	pete	simon	warren
bassoon	develop	gnu	leroy	peter	simple	water
batman	dieter	golfer	lewis	philip	singer	weenie
beater	digital	gorgeous	light	phoenix	single	whatnot
beauty	discovery	gorges	lisa	pierre	smile	whiting
beethoven	disney	gosling	louis	pizza	smiles	whitney
beloved	dog	gouge	lynne	plover	smooch	will
benz	drought	graham	macintosh	plymouth	smother	william
beowulf	duncan	gryphon	mack	polynomial	snatch	williamsburg
berkeley	eager	guest	maggot	pondering	snoopy	willie
berliner	easier	guitar	magic	pork	soap	winston
beryl	edges	gumption	malcolm	poster	socrates	wisconsin
beverly	edinburgh	guntis	mark	praise	sossina	wizard
bicameral	edwin	hacker	markus	precious	sparrows	wombat
bob	edwina	hamlet	marty	prelude	spit	woodwind
brenda	egghead	handily	marvin	prince	spring	wormwood
brian	eiderdown	happening	master	princeton	springer	yaco
bridget	eileen	harmony	maurice	protect	squires	yang
broadway	einstein	harold	mellon	protozoa	strangle	yellowstone
bumbling	elephant	harvey	merlin	pumpkin	stratford	yosemite
burgess	elizabeth	hebrides	mets	puneet	stuttgart	zap
campanile	ellen	heinlein	michael	puppet	subway	zimmerman
cantor	emerald	hello	michelle	rabbit	success	
cardinal	engine	help	mike	rachmaninoff	summer	

Figure 9.2.1

A list of common passwords used by the Internet Worm.

into a server that would allow the "bad guy/girl" client to start using the Trojan horse program. It would connect the client to the server using the TCP/IP or UDP protocol (see Figure 7.4.1). The hidden program could then listen to certain TCP or UDP ports waiting for the attacker to communicate, or possibly use some other type of automatic startup.

In 2004 one such attack, called Backdoor-CGT, started in the form of an email received on the unsuspecting user of Microsoft's Outlook email program. Clicking on an embedded link in the email the user was led to a series of Web sites. Each site carried out a stage of the attack using the Outlook flaw that hid these redirections to other sites, while invisibly downloading and installing the Backdoor-CGT program. The name **back door** comes from the fact the program randomly chose one of the 65,535 ports, opened it and then communicated with a server on the Internet controlled by the attackers. In just a two hour period the security company MessageLabs received over 3,600 email messages that linked to the Backdoor-CGT Trojan horse.

The program installed in a Trojan horse attack can be capable of almost anything from turning a computer into a spam "zombie" sending thousands of spam emails to remotely controlling the computer and looking through a connected Web camera.

In June of 2004 the network equipment company Sandvine Inc. said that these "spam zombies" are responsible for up 80% of the spam. The senior director of Symantec Security Response at Symantec Corporation said that people controlling the "zombies" rent them out to spammers for 3 to 8 cents per PC per week. The zombie PCs can used for whatever the renter wants to do, whether it is creating more zombies, spamming, delivering porn, or sharing copyrighted music.

Another example of a Trojan horse actually taking over a computer is found in the "JPEG of Death" Trojan horse. In this case when a poisoned jpeg image is opened, it uses a jpeg file that is formatted to trigger an overflow in a Windows program routine called GDI+ JPEG decoder. This overflow causes the computer that is about to be infected to contact the sending computer, which in turn connects to an ftp site where a copy of the Radmin program is downloaded to the unsuspecting computer. Radmin is a legitimate commercial program whose company states on their homepage (www.radmin.com): "With Radmin you can work on a remote computer exactly as if you were right there at its keyboard." With this program the attacker can take full control of the infected computer.

One rather intrusive example of a Trojan horse taking over a computer was in Spain, where a 37-year-old man was arrested. The Spanish police said they caught him red-handed "with documents stolen from computers, as well as photos and recordings, many of them compromising for their owners." This particular individual used peer-to-peer file sharing networks to distribute images and music that contained Trojan horses. Among other things, the Trojan horse would remotely take over the infected computer and activate the victim's **Webcam** to view whatever it was pointed at.

Viruses, worms, and Trojan horses are all considered to be on the dark side. They almost always have either mischievous or destructive behavior. Other less destructive, but none the less undesirable programs can steal valuable computing resources from you. This form of theft is called **parasitic computing**.

SPYWARE

Spyware can be thought of as a Trojan horse that is specifically designed to gather information and report it to the person spying. These programs can be categorized by their goals into three basic types:

- Gathering data for marketing by companies
- Spying by hackers, companies, and government
- Monitoring of children by parents

The ethical nature for any of these reasons ranges from somewhat benign to extremely intrusive. A company may, for example, gather information about all programs on your com-

A **back door**, **trap door** or **wormhole** is a hole deliberately left or created in a program by the programmer or hacker for future access. The intentions can be as benign as allowing maintenance programming on operating systems, or for the more sinister reasons. They are used by viruses, worms and Trojan horses.

Parasitic computing gets its name from the fact that someone is making unauthorized use of the computing power of another computer. The most common form takes advantage of a process in the TCP program subroutine called checksum, which tricks an attacked server computer into doing some desired computations.

Spyware is a program that surreptitiously gathers data about your computer use or personal information. This information is sent back to a data base controlled by an individual, company or the government.

puter and Web sites that you have visited. This information is used to build a marketing profile that is very valuable for advertising.

The more unethical and even criminal spying that hackers may do is to record your every keystroke and thereby get passwords, credit card numbers and other sensitive information. Correspondence, spreadsheet files, and other sensitive information can be sent to the "spy." Even chat room logs can be gathered. Some major software vendors have been accused of having spyware installed in their software. The main purpose of this intrusion is to insure the software is not a pirated copy. Still in the realm of hacking is the government's long-time process of corporate espionage. The FBI has spyware as a form of "digital wiretap" to gather evidence against individuals or corporations. Corporations themselves sometimes spy on each other using spyware.

The monitoring of children by parents is a third type of spyware use that also has its ethical issues. A child's Internet action, chat room conversations and email can all be monitored by parents using spyware.

Adware is one of more frustrating forms of spyware. It is done by certain businesses to send popup ads to your Internet browser, with hope that you will influenced by them. A classic example of adware is *Gator*. This program is offered as some free service, such as storing passwords, which makes it easier to keep track of different passwords. Upon installation, a dialog box appears on the screen asking permission to install the free application. If the user says yes, then the application and adware are installed. The result is that unsolicited ads start appearing on the screen, which may be tolerable in small numbers. But, when hundreds of these adware programs have invaded the computer, it almost impossible to get any work done because they appear in large numbers and can lock up the computer. There are many cases where some individual computers have had thousands of adware programs causing thousands of popup ads to appear. The Symantec corporation, a well known creator of computer security software, has a very succinct technical description of Gator that can shed some light on how adware gets established:

When Adware.Gator is installed, it does the following:

1. Inserts a file in the %System% folder. The file name appears to differ depending on which program installs Adware.Gator. Some known file names are:

   - Fsg.exe
   - Fsg_3202.exe
   - Trickler.exe.

Note: %System% is a variable. The adware component locates the System folder and copies itself to that location. By default, this is C:\Windows\System (Windows 95/98/Me), C:\Winnt\System32 (Windows NT/2000), or C:\Windows\System32 (Windows XP).

2. Creates the registry key:
   HKEY_LOCAL_MACHINE\Software\Gator.com

Note: There will be several subkeys under this key.

3. Creates the value: "Trickler" in the registry:
   HKEY_LOCAL_MACHINE\Software\Microsoft\Windows\CurrentVersion \Run so that the Adware runs when you start Windows.

4. Displays advertisements in pop-up windows.

5. Connects to the following server [Random name].gator.com on port 80 and submits Web browsing habits the server, and then download advertisements from it:

Note: Other programs download Adware.Gator to allow them to download and display advertisements in pop-up windows.

The technical description above about how Gator works may seem difficult to understand. But with just a little examination, an appreciation of how one adware program functions is worth the effort.

Step#1 says that Gator inserts a file into the system folder.
Step#2 when the operating system starts up it will run the file in step#1. This causes the a special insertion into the "registry key database."
Step#3 sets the auto-start so that Gator will be run on startup of the computer.
Step#4 Gator will display ads in popup windows that have already been downloaded.
Step#5 The Gator program connects to some preset sever through port 80, and uploads web browsing habits of the infected computer, then downloads popup ads that are displayed in pop-up windows.

Although not trivial, understanding this process will help individual users begin to understand the problems, and will be better able to select a defense from this type of malware.

But, popup ads are not nearly as serious as the spyware that steals online banking passwords. At the beginning of 2005 the anti-virus company Sophos detected a Trojan horse called BankAsh-A. What makes this program noteworthy is the fact that it is the first incidence of software designed to disable Microsoft's new AntiSpyware. It does this by first attempting to suppress warning messages of impending spyware invasions and then it tries to delete AntiSpyware files. The spyware BankAsh-A then targeted users of United Kingdom banks, including Barclays, Cahoot, Halifax, HSBC, Lloyds TSB, Nationwide, NatWest, and Smile. The bank passwords and account information were then sent back to the malware instigator. This is a very sophisticated approach. Another simpler way that criminals gain bank account and credit card information is by phishing.

PHISHING

The concept of **phishing** is not new. This concept of pretending to be something you're not is a ploy that has been used for thousands of years. As applied in this situation, the Internet is used to solicit communication that tries to trick the receiver into revealing sensitive information, such as bank account numbers and on line passwords. The typical situation is where thousands of emails are sent randomly to individuals with the hope that they have accounts at a certain bank or other institution. The usual message is that your account may have been accessed without permission and you should immediately click a link in the email that looks official. In reality, the link is to a harvesting site that will ask you to type in your account number and password. These unscrupulous characters will then take money electronically out of your account. By the time you find out, it's too late.

The author has received hundreds of these email attacks. One particular series of phishing emails was from the "TCF Bank" at which the author had an account several years ago. Of course the TCF Bank had no connection with this email, only the name and logo match. Another example of a common phishing technique is to request that email recipients change their email account passwords. These requests look as though the institution's Technology Administrators are requesting the changes. Many have been fooled by these requests. See Figure 9.2.2 for a sample of one of these requests.

The URLS of these phishing emails are usually short lived, but can do a lot of damage. In one case a Brazillian group of 53 men were arrested for stealing more than $30 million dollars from online banking customers. In another case German police arrested five men for a phishing scam that netted about 30,000 euros from Postbank customers. And then there were the Australian high school students who were arrested for stealing bank account numbers and passwords for a global Internet gang operating out of Australia and Russia. But, the U.S. is still the world's leading host for phishing scams with an estimated 32% of the phishing sites. Even sites in China (12%) and Korea (11%) were hosts as reported by the APWG (Anti-Phishing Working Group).

A list of institutions that were used in phishing schemes is shown in Figure 9.2.3 (from the APWG Web site).

Phishing or **spoofing** is an old scam implemented on the Internet. It is usually in the form of an email that falsely represents a particular person or organization to get information such as bank account numbers and passwords.

From: "Upgrade Team" <the_hana@singnet.com.sg>
Sent: Monday, June 1, 2009 7:53:36 PM GMT -05:00 US/Canada Eastern
To: info@upgrade.com
Subject: Upgrade Your Email Account

This message is from the Database Information Technology service messaging center, to all our e-mail account holders. All Mailhub systems will undergo regularly scheduled maintenance. Access to your mailbox via ourmailportal will be unavailable for some period of time during this maintenanceperiod.

We shall be carrying out service maintenance on our database and e-mail accountcenter for better online services. We are deleting all unusede-mailaccounts tocreate more space for new accounts.In order to ensure you do not experience service interruptions/possibledeactivation Please you must reply to this email immediately confirming your email account details below for confirmation/identification.

_____

1. First Name & Last Name:
2. Full Login Email Address:
3. Username & Password:
4. Confirm your Current Password:

_____

Failure to do this may automatically render your e-mail account deactivated from our email-database/mailserver. to enable us upgrade your email account,

please do reply to this mail.

Thanks.
Upgrade Team

Courtesy of Zenia Bahorski

Figure 9.2.2

Courtesy of Zenia Bahorski

2checkout.com	Lloyds TSB	TCF Bank
Amazon	MBNA	U.S. Bank
America Online	Microsoft	uBid
AOL	MSN	Usefulbill (fake company)
Bank One	NatWest	Verizon
Barclays	Paypal	VISA
Bendigo Bank	People's Bank	VISA
Citibank	Phishing	Washington Mutual
Citizens Bank	Regulations.gov	Washington Mutual Bank
Earthlink	Shadowcrew (billing	Wells Fargo
eBay	problem)	Westpac
e-gold	Sovereign Bank	Westpac Bank
FDIC	Spyware	www.ibillingservices.com
Fleet Bank	Suntrust	Yahoo!
KeyBank	TSB	

Figure 9.2.3

APWG documented phishing attacks.

This form of disruption is very time consuming and consumers must be careful not to fall into the clutches of these criminals. Other forms of computer assaults are more annoying than financially threatening.

9.3 The Annoying Types of Computer Assaults Affecting Personal Security and Privacy

- Spam
- Popups
- Denial of service attacks

The three major types of Internet intrusion are mainly annoying. In certain contexts, however, they can be financially devastating. An Internet catalog sales site, for example, would not be able to function with a denial of service attack, and therefore the employees might be sent home without pay. But, to most individuals these intrusions are just plain annoying.

SPAM

Spam uses legitimate email services over the Internet to barrage us with advertisements for anything from dating services, to financial products such as mortgages, to medications such as Viagra. According to the June 2009 State of Spam Report published by Symantec's Global Intelligence Network, approximately 90 percent of the email sent worldwide in May of 2009 was spam. With the numbers of emails estimated at between 32 billion and 100 billion messages per day, the number of spam messages has become an enormous financial drain on corporations and other organizations whose employees must spend their time filtering through these emails. In addition to employee time, additional costs include those related to the loss of bandwidth, reduced capacity of hard disk space, and a slower response rate for customer service. It should be noted that not all spam is sent to the corporate world. About half of all spam is sent to consumers.

According to the State of Spam Report, as of May of 2009, the most spam messages, nearly 28%, are used to entice the recipients to services such as creating free Web pages or other computer-related products. The next highest number of spam messages, or 23.5%, are related to health products and services. Pretty much every other product on the market makes up the product category with 17.7% of the spam messages sent. Although some believe that adult products and services are high on the list, these make up only 1% of all spam messages sent.

How do spammers get our email addresses? One way spammers obtain email addresses is by purchasing lists from organizations such as institutions of higher learning. These email addresses are widely available. Spam email is then sent to these purchased lists. Once the person who has received the email clicks on a link embedded in the email, the spammer then knows that the email address is viable and that the recipient actively reads his or her email. The email address is recorded and then sold to others.

Another way spammers find email addresses is through the use of bots, spiders, and agents as discussed in chapter 8. These programs can be designed to filter through Web sites recording email addresses. These programs are pretty smart! They can now find email addresses with the format of "username@address.topleveldoman", "username at address dot topleveldoman", and any combination thereof where username is your username and topleveldomain is the top-level domain as in .com, .org, or .edu. This means that if you have a personal Web site with your email address, and even if you think that you are crafty and can outsmart the email harvesting programs, eventually, these programs will find your email address as well.

Yet another way your email address can be collected by spammers is when you sign up for certain types of services over the web that require an email address. The email address is purportedly used to send back information to you, and may indeed send back the requested information. But, some of the more unscrupulous of these companies will sell your email address to spammers. Responding to spam also lets the spammer know that your email address is valid.

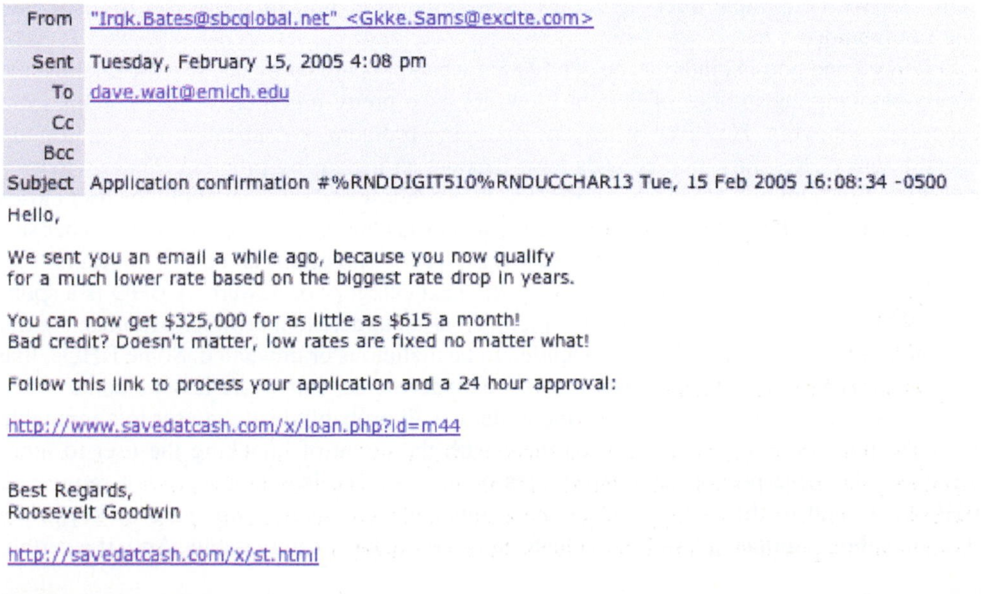

Spam is a noun describing "unsolicited commercial email messages." Historically it came from a Monty Phython's Flying Circus sketch in reference to the Hormel Foods' product Spam. It was also a Usenet term describing the flooding of a newsgroup with inappropriate or irrelevant messages.

From	"Irqk.Bates@sbcglobal.net" <Gkke.Sams@excite.com>
Sent	Tuesday, February 15, 2005 4:08 pm
To	dave.wait@emich.edu
Cc	
Bcc	
Subject	Application confirmation #%RNDDIGIT510%RNDUCCHAR13 Tue, 15 Feb 2005 16:08:34 -0500

Hello,

We sent you an email a while ago, because you now qualify
for a much lower rate based on the biggest rate drop in years.

You can now get $325,000 for as little as $615 a month!
Bad credit? Doesn't matter, low rates are fixed no matter what!

Follow this link to process your application and a 24 hour approval:

http://www.savedatcash.com/x/loan.php?id=m44

Best Regards,
Roosevelt Goodwin

http://savedatcash.com/x/st.html

Figure 9.3.1

Financial product spam

Once these email addresses are gathered then spammers go to work sending out spam. It should be pointed out that spammers don't do this for fun. It is a very profitable business because advertisers are willing to pay the spammer for the results: people buy the products. If no one purchased the advertised products, then spam would almost cease to exist.

The process of sending out the spam takes several forms. Sometimes the Trojan horse zombies mentioned in section 9.2 are programmed to receive email addresses and spam messages that are then sent out from the infected computer. Industry experts have estimated that zombies originated between 30% and 80% of the spam in mid 2004. Symantec Corporation's Vincent Weafer says that hackers controlling the zombies rent out the infected machines for 3 to 8 cents per PC per week. So indeed, if your computer were infected, it could be helping the spammers make money.

In another form spammers use their own servers to send out millions of spam emails. Before the CAN-SPAM (Controlling the Assault of Non-Solicited Pornography and Marketing) act of 2004, many of these spam hosts were in the United States; however, the penalties are quite severe so that almost all of the spam hosts have moved out of the U.S. As a result, spam has continued to rise in spite of this groundbreaking law. As of May 2009, 16% of all spam zombies reside in Brazil, followed by 8% in Turkey, 7% in Russia, 6% in India, 6% in the United States, 5% in Poland, then followed by numerous other countries with fewer spam zombies. As spam continues to be a profitable enterprise, little can be done to curb its spread throughout the world.

ADWARE

Adware is a form of software that is clandestinely downloaded to a computer. It then delivers advertisements in the form of **popups** (windows that pop up on the computer screen), pop-behinds (windows that pop up but are behind the current window), toolbars, banners and other forms.

Adware is a legal advertising and merchandising tool that uses popup ads, pop-behinds, cookies, and toolbar modifications to make the company's products visible to the surfing public. As opposed to spyware, adware requests that the user accept the program or enhancement before it is installed on the user's computer. These programs can be as annoying as spam, or as debilitating; such as when dozens of popups or pop-behinds get in the way of the user's productivity. Once installed, adware has the potential to become the more malicious spyware.

The serious nature of this problem is underlined by the fact that between 80% to 90% of all home computers in the U.S. have adware. What exacerbates the issue is that not all adware and spyware detection programs can eradicate abusive code. One problem is that there are different types of adware. And, each type of adware works differently. We will discuss four types of adware here: banners, popups and pop-behinds, Browser Help Objects (BHO), and tracking cookies.

Banners are the advertisements commonly found on Web pages. These banners are not always malicious. The advertisers pay fees to have their ads included on Web pages. The higher the visibility of the Web page, the higher the fee. Also, the more clicks on the ads, the higher the cost to the advertisers. Most of these ads are straightforward; they lead you to the advertiser's site. Others may, by clicking on the link, download embedded code to the user's computer with the intent tracking the user's Web habits or hijacking the user to a site that was not intended.

Popups and pop-behinds can be debilitating when popping up by the dozens. Luckily, the popup-blocking capabilities of current browsers have pretty much eradicated popups from becoming annoying. However, when one annoying problem is eradicated, another usually takes its place! Recently, pop-behinds have become an increasing problem. These windows automatically "pop-up" *behind* the current browser window and stay there until the user closes them. The pop-behind advertisers promote financial sites, movie rentals, books, and other services. These pop-behinds are often overlooked by security programs and popup blockers.

Browser Help Objects (BHO) make up the next category of adware. A BHO is a sponsored Web enhancement, which is often included as an update to a browser's toolbar. Again, like other adware, not all BHOs are intended to be malicious or unwanted. Some BHOs, like the Google search box, are welcome browser enhancements. Others are less welcome. Once again, clicking on one of these added menu items will probably lead the user to a reputable Web site. Others, however, are placed there with the intent of hijacking the user to more unsavory sites like pornographic Web sites or to other services that were not requested. BHOs can lead to the installation of malicious software such as spyware or keystroke recorders. For example, a BHO could possibly keep track of surfing habits. And, if a certain

Web site is visited, such as a financial institution, the BHO could install a program that records login keystroke information.

Cookies are coded text entries placed into a cookie file on your computer by the company or service provider that you visit. These cookies often retain information about you such as login information and user preferences. These cookies are intended to retain information about you so as to speed up services the company can provide to you. That is the intent of cookies. However, a growing number of tracking cookies, or malicious cookies, are retaining surfing habits and keystrokes. These malicious cookies are a growing source of adware. The Web habits of the user are compiled by third party providers, who in turn, sell this marketing information to other companies.

Widgets are also becoming a growing concern. Widgets, or gadgets, are small Web applications that sell themselves as being useful on-screen tools or entertaining distractions. These widgets have become very popular as more cell phones are being equipped with Web capabilities. A wide variety of widgets are available for download. Some examples include in-flight airline trackers, weather reports, tornado trackers, ski reports, dictionaries, tip calculators, bartender guides, language translators, and a whole host of games. However, some of these widgets may not be what they appear. These widgets have the potential of being adware hosts, which can return user preferences and marketing information.

There will always be new ways to attack unsuspecting computers as the approaches used in the attacks seem endless. This tendency makes it very important for computer users to become more savvy and investigate ways of keeping their private information private.

DENIAL OF SERVICE ATTACKS

The unavailability of a certain Web site may be an inconvenience to individual users. But, to a company doing business on the Web, it could prove to be very harmful. A **distributed denial of service attack** typically involves the use of thousand of computers sending requests simultaneously to a server with the intent of bringing the system down or causing irreparable harm to the company or organization.

Distributed denial of service is the act of sending tens of thousands of simultaneous bogus requests for Web pages to a particular Website. The server can't identify the bogus requests causing a delay, therefore legitimate requests can't be processed or are delayed a long time.

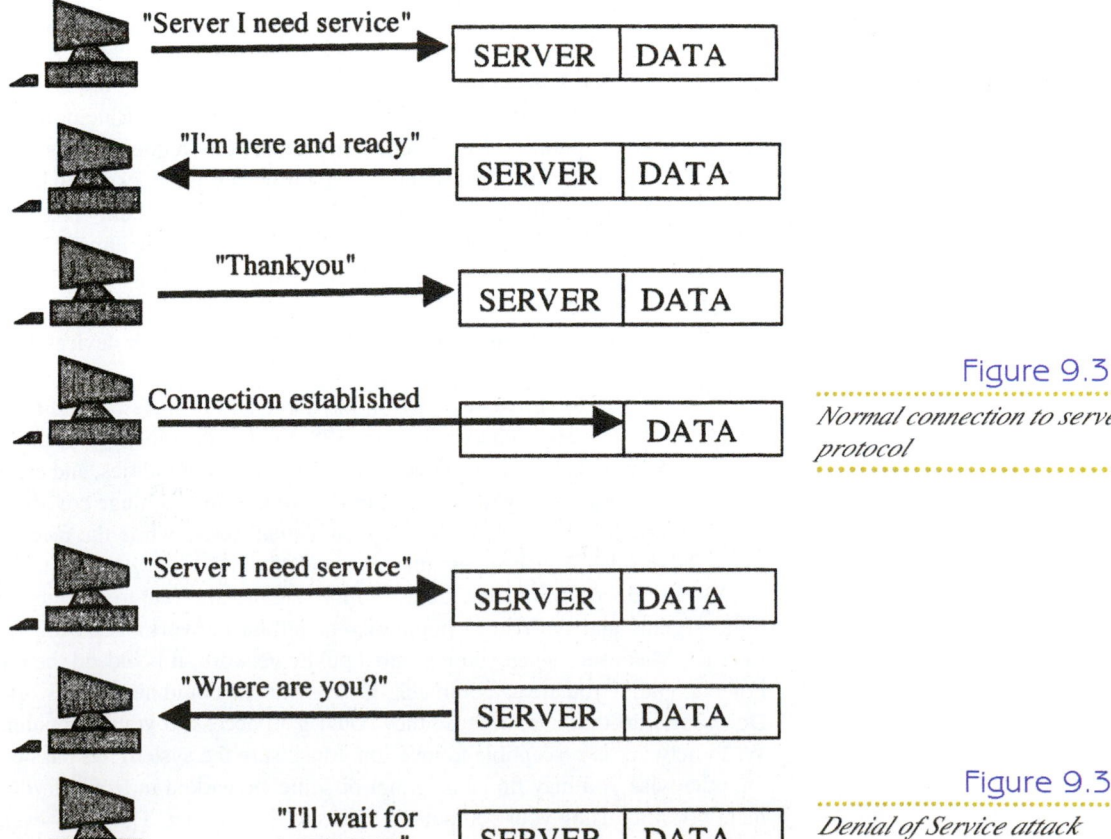

Figure 9.3.2

Normal connection to server protocol

Figure 9.3.3

Denial of Service attack (DoS).

Denial of service attacks (DoS) are not a new phenomenon. At the beginning of 2000, Yahoo! was the first major Web service to be compromised. Shortly after this, eBay, Amazon, Buy.com E*Trade, Datek Online, CNN.com, some financial institutions who would prefer to be nameless, and even the FBI's Web site were attacked. Services to these sites and more were brought to a standstill. It is presumed that the next major act of terrorism will be of this type of attack. Imagine attempting to bring down a government with one keystroke. How could this happen?

The normal response accorded a request from a user for service is outlined in Figure 9.3.2. The first action taken is the user requests some service of the company's computer server. The computer server responds to the request with an acknowledgement that it is ready to service the request. This process is often referred to as "authentication" or "hand-

Tech Talk

Wireless Standards: Bluetooth and Wi-Fi

There several short range radio frequency standards, commonly called wireless, for communication between devices. Two of them, Bluetooth and Wi-Fi, are the most common, and often used in conjunction with computers. Wi-Fi is used mainly for high-speed wireless access to the Internet or other local area networks up to about 300 feet. It is found in many public places, such as Starbuck's coffee shops and home wireless computer systems. Bluetooth, on the other hand, is low power and meant for fairly close range communication (30 feet), and is used primarily to replace cables on devices such as a keyboard, mouse, printer, or connecting on earpiece to a cellphone.

Both Wi-Fi and Bluetooth have security concerns. In particular, Bluetooth is subject to at least three types of incursion known as *bluejacking, bluesnarfing,* and *bluebugging.* These security breaches are possible because most of those using Bluetooth devices don't turn them off when moving about in public places. This means a hacker running Bluesniff can scan for local Bluetooth devices and possibly access them. For example, it is possible to use one Bluetooth cell phone to access someone else's Bluetooth cell phone and make calls through it. Knowing a Bluetooth device's modes and how they work is important. As an example, by just shutting off what is called discovery mode, often called promiscuous mode, the Bluetooth device will be invisible to other Bluetooth devices nearby. A well known security worker did a *bluesnarfing* experiment to see just how vulnerable the public is. He put his laptop in a briefcase with a special hidden antenna to pick up Bluetooth device signals, and set out into some public places. The laptop scanned the frequency range used by Bluetooth, probing cell phones carried by shoppers in their purses and pockets. In just a few minutes he picked up signals to almost 40 phones, and estimated it would only take only a few seconds to copy several of their address books. In this same vein, this famous security worker conducted "a similar experiment in the House of Parliament, where he had the opportunity (which he didn't take) to copy the address books and calendars of several prominent politicians. That excursion resulted in a mandate that all Bluetooth devices be turned off in the House of Parliament."

Wi-Fi is used for network access in the home and businesses, and has the potential for many consumer uses, such as replacing GPS (Global Positioning System) and cell phones. The transmitting and receiving devices have become commodities, and are even sold in Wal-Marts. They are very easy to install. A transmitting station's range covers an area the size of several football field and is no bigger than a small book, while the receivers that will plug into a PC or other device are as small as a matchbox.

Wi-Fi's security problems are even more significant, due to the increased range of the radio signals and the rise in popularity of public networks allowing free access to the Internet. Make sure when you log into a public network, it is indeed the one you think it is. For example, if you are at a Starbucks Cafe, someone could have a network called Starbuxs. Don't log into that one, because they could gain access to your computer. Even the home Wi-Fi network is susceptible to invasion. Make sure the system has password access turned on, otherwise you may find a neighbor or someone parked in front of your house or apartment invisibly using your computer's access to the Internet. They may even be one of those unscrupulous individuals out to destroy information on your hard drive!

shaking." Once the user's computer and the company's server agree to communicate, the user's computer is granted access to the data or Web page residing on the computer server.

The distributed denial of service attack attempts to confuse the company's server and keep its attention for a longer period of time thereby denying others service to the computer server. In this case, as shown in Figure 9.3.3, the computer is unable to authenticate the requesting computer's address and possibly wastes time trying to regain the connection. This process is simultaneously repeated thousands of times with the other computers as they try to confuse the server. Again, how could this happen?

These attacks quite commonly come from computers of unsuspecting users connected to the Internet. Trojan horses and worms, when executed, place time-coded instructions on thousands of computers. When the time is right, and the infected computers are connected to the Internet, the army of computers carry on the attack.

9.4 How to Protect Personal Security and Privacy from Hackers, Business, and Government

There are several fundamental safety rules for safeguarding a computer from the viruses, worms, Trojan horses, spyware, phishing, spam and adware. Some are common sense and don't require any expenditures, but a more complete defense can require the purchase of special software.

PROTECTION FROM VIRUSES, WORMS AND TROJAN HORSES

Research has shown that no one individual program can detect 100% of the viruses, worms and Trojan horses in circulation. This means for better protection at least two programs should be used. It also depends on the type of operating system and application software you are using. The Windows platform is the most vulnerable. This is because it by far the most commonly used operating system, and the unscrupulous hacker is trying create the "biggest bang for their buck." In most cases, this is because making headlines worldwide is a tremendous ego booster for them, and shows their hacker prowess. Even with only about 5% of the total market, Apple Computer's operating system is still under attack, but not to the extent that Window's systems are. Both platforms have freeware, shareware and commercial products to protect them against viruses, worms, and Trojan horses.

It should be noted that even with the best protection software, unless it is updated on a regular basis, then it quickly becomes useless. The bottom line is to install properly, which includes reading the documentation, and update often.

PROTECTION FROM SPYWARE AND ADWARE/POPUPS

Spyware is closely related to Trojan horses, and therefore some of what was said in the previous paragraphs is pertinent. Most spyware found today is considered somewhat legitimate, at least it is not against the law. It can be used collect personal and credit card information, and even take over operation of your computer.

The least harmful, yet annoying, are adware and popups. They cause the computer to slow down, and can make it almost unusable. There are many commercial and freeware programs such as Sunbelt Software's CounterSpy, Webroot Software's Spy Sweeper, Ad-Aware, and others, that can be used to root out installed adware. To be safe, more than one of these programs should be used to purge your computer. Spyware can be partially prevented with a series of precautions:

- Update operating system software using automatic updating
- Adjust your browser settings to control what can be transferred to your computer from Websites you visit, and to adjust the security settings
- Use a firewall
- Be careful in what and how you download

- Download from trusted sites
- Never click on "agree" or "OK" when closing a window unless you know what it means (you may be agreeing to install adware on your computer)
- Download freeware, shareware, or commercial spyware protection programs.

PROTECTION FROM UNAUTHORIZED ACCESS

Unauthorized access means that someone accesses your computer either over a network or directly without your permission. One of the two major types of unauthorized access is via some spyware or Trojan horse that has been downloaded to your computer. It could contain a program that, in a worst-case scenario, takes control of your computer to the extent that the hacker is virtually sitting at the keyboard. This takes a type of remote access program that was previously installed on your computer. Preventing this is done by not allowing any unauthorized downloads to occur. Again, you must only download from trusted sources and never click on "agree" or "OK" when closing a window unless you know what it means. Also make sure that firewalls are in place and configured for your needs.

The other unauthorized access is through an unprotected wireless network. If password security isn't turned on, then anyone within about 300 feet could be using your computer for Internet access, and maybe more unscrupulous behavior. Laptops are also vulnerable at public wireless networks, so make sure your laptop isn't set up for automatic connections to insecure networks and turn off all file and print sharing.

The Cutting Edge

RFID

Radio **F**requency **ID**entification (**RFID**) technology is one of the fastest growing computer technologies. It is being used in retail markets by companies such as Wal-Mart, and also to monitor industrial systems and the environment. RFID serves the same function as bar codes, but unlike the bar code, they don't have to be in the line of sight to communicate.

Technically, there are two types of RFID systems, active and passive. The most common and least expensive are the passive systems. The passive RFID system consists of a tag, referred to as a transponder, and a transceiver that collects the information regarding the tag. These tags can be paper thin.

Let's examine a hypothetical system to see how the system works. Suppose the application is a supermarket checkout. Each item in the store must have an RFID tag, which is put onto the package by the manufacturer. As you approach the checkout, a transceiver puts out a radio frequency signal that is picked up by the tag's antenna. This signal energizes the tag, which in turn will transmit information regarding the product it is attached to. The transceiver sends the information regarding all products in the bag or cart to a computer, which itemizes the items and creates a bill for the customer. The customer pays and leaves the store.

The transponder tag consists of an antenna and a miniature electronic circuit. In the passive case the electrical energy needed to make the circuit function is provided by a transceiver, which gives a burst of energy that the antenna picks up. This energizes the tag's circuit, which in turn transmits a signal containing data regarding the packages contents. In the active RFID system, a small battery is part of the transponder's circuitry.

The real advantages of this system are its relatively low cost, and the fact that radio frequencies can penetrate most materials. This eliminates the problem of line-of-sight reading. It can be used to tag pets, food, clothing, car keys, beer kegs, parts in manufacturing, shipping containers, and even humans. One novel idea used by Toyota and Lexus is the "smart key." This consists of a key fob with an active RFID circuit, which can communicate with the car within 3 feet. The driver can leave their keys in purse or pocket, and yet the doors will unlock and the car can be started without inserting a key.

The following table is a very short list of applications of RFID:

RFID   *(continued)*

APPLICATION	AREA OF USE
Human implant	Hospital & emergency identification
Car keys	Ignition & doors
Inventory control	Manufacturing & retail
Book ID	Library & retail checkout
Building keys	Access to buildings
Inventory control	Manufacturing & retail
Shipping & receiving	Manufacturing & retail
Regulatory compliance	All regulated areas
Returns & recall management	All product areas
Service & warranty authorizations	Retail sales companies
Toll booth	Prepaid passes
Access passes	Building & restricted area security

The active RFID tags can be designed to record information. In many ways this is similar to the CD technology where there are both read-only and read-write types of device. The read-only type of RFID tag usually contains things such as serial numbers or contents of the package. In certain applications this isn't enough. For example, a frozen foods manufacturer could put an RFID tag with sensors that monitor and record the temperature of the product as it passes through the delivery chain. Another example is the recording of the chain-of-custody that must be provided to the FDA, DOT or OSHA for hazardous materials, drugs, food and other regulated materials.

RFID is not without its problems. The main issues are privacy and theft. The tags can be manipulated relatively easily by hackers, disgruntled employees, or shoplifters. To illustrate the problem the German consultant Lukas Grunwald helped develop a program RFDump that would expose the frailties of the RFID system. With the right equipment, RFID tags can be read, altered, or even deleted using only a handheld, notebook or standard PC running Windows or Linux with an inexpensive plug-in tag reader.

Privacy issues are quite prominent in the case of the Japanese primary school that is putting RFID tags into the student's schoolbags and clothing. The city of Osaka decided that, in spite of privacy issues, it is better to be able to track all students and their movements. There is a lot of work to be done settling RFID privacy issues in applications such as this, and others even more invasive.

PROTECTION FROM PHISHING

One form of identity theft is enabled through phishing. This technique is only annoying, unless you fall for the scam. Typically, a well known bank's name and logo is used in an email spammed to you. It often refers to a security problem and you should immediately, or within 24 hours, sign on and verify your identity. A conveniently provided link is supposedly going to the bank. Although the link looks official, it is a setup to record all of the pertinent details for accessing your account. Don't ever give information over the Internet that is not through your own contact efforts. If you must, call the bank by telephone and ask about whatever problem was mentioned in the email.

PROTECTION FROM SPAM

Spam filters are often used by Internet Service Providers (ISPs), and can often be configured to your own needs. Spam is annoying, but can become more than that if you open, view attachments, or click on any links within the email. Spam filters can also be installed on your own computer, and it is possible to allow email from only specified email addresses. Unfortunately, if another computer has your email address and it is compromised, then you will get spam from that trusted address.

Chapter Summary

9.1 Introduction to Issues of Personal Security and Privacy

There are many topics in personal computer security, privacy and annoyances. Among them are using filters, firewalls, and other programs to protect personal computers.

9.2 Fundamental Concepts in Personal Security

Viruses, worms and Trojan horses have many things in common. The main difference is how they spread. Viruses need human help, either by opening an email or inserting a disk. Worms can spread without human intervention once they have been introduced to a network. Trojan horses don't automatically propagate and are usually attached to some legitimate program. Most often they are written to prove the prowess of a programmer. However, they are sometimes used by unscrupulous people to cause damage and create havoc on networks. Phishing or spoofing is an attempt to get sensitive information by tricking someone into revealing it. The newest member of the mix of malware is called spyware. This is software that can be accidentally authorized for installation. It will collect various information about the computer user and report it back to some central database. Spyware can also be used to commit crimes such as stealing credit card and bank account numbers with their passwords.

9.3 The Annoying Types of Computer Assaults Affecting Personal Security and Privacy

There is a whole class of computer assaults that are primarily annoying. The most common of these is email spam. Both legitimate and illegitimate companies send out millions of emails each day hoping to convince the recipient to buy whatever they're selling or marketing. Popups on the other hand are on the WWW and are also used to try and sell products. The software that creates the popups is clandestinely stored on your computer to receive and popup ads on the screen. Denial of service (DoS) attacks don't have any effect on your computer, but instead affect the Web site on the WWW that you may be trying to access. Flooding the site with millions of bogus requests for information essentially shuts it down.

9.4 How to Protect Personal Security and Privacy from Hackers, Business, and Government

Protecting oneself from all of the problems discussed in the first part of the chapter requires either software or hardware, and also changing personal computer habits. Rules of thumb include not opening email from someone you don't know to not being duped into giving personal information like bank account numbers and passwords over the Internet.

Key Terms

Key terms introduced in this chapter:

1. Adware, *262*
2. Agents & Bots, *252*
3. Back door, *257*
4. Banners, *262*
5. Bluebugging, *264*
6. Bluesnarf, *264*
7. Browser Help Objects, *262*
8. Chat rooms, *252*
9. Cookies, *263*
10. Cryptography, *252*
11. Data mining, *252*
12. Denial of service attacks, *263*
13. Email sniffing, *252*
14. Filtering, *252*
15. Firewalls, *252*
16. Instant Messenger, *252*
17. Lifelog, *252*
18. Parasitic computing, *257*
19. Phishing, *259*
20. Pop-behind, *262*
21. Popups, *252*
22. RFID, *266*
23. Search engines, *252*
24. Spam, *261*
25. Spoofing, *259*
26. Spyware, *257*
27. Trap door, *257*
28. Trojan horse, *255*
29. Virus, *252*
30. Webcam, *257*
31. Widgets, *257*
32. Wormhole, *257*
33. Worm, *254*

Matching

Match the numbers of the key terms introduced in the chapter to the following statements.
Each term may be used once, more than once, or not at all.

1. ___ Searching the Internet for data makes use of this tool.

2. ___ The act of pretending to be a bank or institution warning about possible problems, and then asking you to log in and verify your account information.

3. ___ A hidden entry point into software that allows someone to access or control the program.

4. ___ This is the term used to steal information from someones cell phone or computer that has blue tooth communications.

5. ___ A particular type of software that gathers information about a computer's activity is called by this name.

6. ___ This type of program was named this because it spreads like the human cold.

7. ___ Greek history contains references to the name of this type of malware.

8. ___ This type of program searches the Internet for information desired.

9. ___ This is an acronym for *radio frequence identification* that is used in industry.

10. ___ Unwanted and unsolicited email is called by this name.

True or False

Place either T or F on the line provided with each of the following statements. If a statement is false, you should be able to explain what changes would make it true.

1. ___ The technique called phishing is used to try and obtain sensitive information by using false identity.

2. ___ Agents are programs that only make airline ticket reservations.

3. ___ Cryptography is the field describing codes and secret messages.

4. ___ Filtering used in screening email can sometimes screen out desirable email.

5. ___ Internet search engines use spiders, bots, and agents to collect and index the content of the World Wide Web.

6. ___ Spoofing is another name for phishing.

7. ___ Denial of service attacks refer to when your computer is not working.

8. ___ Firewalls are used to prevent unauthorized access to your computer over a network.

9. ___ Chat rooms and instant messaging are somewhat related.

10. ___ Popups refer to a friend sending a message to you via instant messaging.

Multiple Choice

Answer the multiple-choice questions by selecting the best answer from the choices given.

1. This technology is used in tracking inventory.
   a. Agents
   b. Data mining
   c. RFID
   d. Webcam
   e. Firewalls

2. The process of trying to obtain sensitive information by using a false identity is called
   a. Filtering
   b. Phishing
   c. Bluebugging
   d. Email sniffing
   e. Data mining

3. The annoying ads that sometimes appear when browsing the Web are called
   a. Firewalls
   b. Lifelogs
   c. Spam
   d. Viruses
   e. Popups

4. Bluetooth technology is sometimes subject to
   a. Bluebugging
   b. Email sniffing
   c. Filtering
   d. Spam
   e. Spoofing

5. Communicating instantly with friends can be done using
   a. Parasitic computing
   b. Agents
   c. Instant messenger
   d. Spiders
   e. Trojan horses

6. The program that acts like an assistant in helping you is called a
   a. Bot or agent
   b. Firewall
   c. Trojan horse
   d. Worm
   e. Spider

7 Another term that is used instead of phishing is
   a. Bludbugging
   b. Email sniffing
   c. Parasitic computing
   d. Spoofing
   e. Filtering

8. Sensitive information passed over the Web can be protected by
   a. Filtering
   b. Cryptography
   c. Firewalls
   d. Agents
   e. RFID

9. One of the greatest problems affecting Internet efficiency is
   a. Spam
   b. Popups
   c. The chat room
   d. Instant messenger
   e. Spoofing

10. Search engines rely on this type of program to create useful databases.
   a. Popups
   b. RFID
   c. Spyware
   d. Filters
   e. Spiders

Exercises

1. Research the origin of the term Trojan horse.

2. Research the origin of the word spam.

3. Using a search engine like Google, find and make a list of examples of bots working on the World Wide Web

4. Use a search engine to find the viruses most reported about on the Web in the past few months. Make a list including: name and description.

5. How does the computer related virus get its name? What are the features of it that coincide with human viruses?

6. How does the computer related Trojan horse get its name? What are the features of it that coincide with the Trojan horse of Greek mythology?

7. Using a search engine find software that can help identify and eliminate programs that create popup ads. Download one of the freeware versions and use it on your personal computer. Describe what, if anything, was found by the program. Make sure the program you download is from a reputable company (check reviews).

Discussion Questions

1. What are the privacy issues related to RFID? Include a discussion regarding the tracking of both adults and children. How could RFID used in a library book compromise your privacy?

2. How can the public be educated regarding phishing?

3. Discuss and compare the issues with WWW filtering in the home, libraries, school computer labs, and businesses.

Group Project

How Vulnerable Are You?

We are all vulnerable to secret invasions of our security and personal privacy. Most of us, however, sit back in comfort, feeling only slightly threatened. We enjoy the benefits of our wonderful technological society without considering its dangers, until we become its victims.

Now is the time to take a good hard look at your own personal vulnerability to electronic attack, and determine how you can avoid its threats.

As a group discuss and create a your own "Electronic Vulnerability Profile." The Profile should have four columns, labeled like the ones in the following example. In the first column, enter any event or situation you feel presents an electronic threat to your privacy, security, rights or well being. In the second column, rate the severity of each threat on a scale of 1–10, with 10 being the most severe type of threat. In the third column, list the actions you might take to avoid the threat or render the situation harmless.

Here's an example of how your chart might look with its first entry:

Situation or Event	Threat or Danger	Threat Rating	Avoidance actions
1) Access and send personal email over a company Internet server	Provides danger of someone eavesdropping on my mail	4	a) Use company email only for company business b) Sign up for non-company ISP for home use c) Notify personal e-correspondents of new address. Encourage them to use it.
2)			

Hint #1

Having trouble listing your vulnerabilities? See if some of these describe you or your activities. If they do, add them to the chart.

1. Belong to a list-serve or electronic conference
2. Use or borrow disks belonging to friends
3. Lend disks, data, software to friends
4. Send or receive email with word-processed attachments
5. Use ATM machines
6. Use credit cards over the Internet or telephone
7. Send personal information over the Internet
8. Purchase goods and services online
9. Participate in Chat rooms
10. Download software, music or video clips

Hint #2

When you have finished listing your vulnerabilities (leave space, you'll most likely still find a few more), make up a defensive action plan with specific goals and deadlines for reducing your vulnerability. Adjust the threat ratings for each situation or event as you deal with its threats.

If you add up the ratings in the threat-rating column and divide that by the number of threats on the chart, you will get an overall average electronic threat score. Of course, your average electronic threat score will depend on how active you are using technology, and how dangerous your network activities are to your security and privacy. A score under 3, however, indicates a fairly good awareness of vulnerability, and a good threat management plan.

Bibliography

Cohen, Fred, Fred Cohen, "Computer viruses, theory and experiments," *Computers & Security,* vol. 6, 1987, pp. 22–35. http://vx.netlux.org/lib/afc01.html

Cohen, Fred, *On the Implications of Computer Viruses and Methods of Defense,* Invited Paper, IFIP-TC11, 'Computers and Security', V7#2, April 1988

chapter 10

Multimedia

TimeLine

1846 Joseph Farber produces synthesized speech with his Speech Organ.

1929 First color television signals are transmitted.

1962 Software is developed at Bell Labs to design, store, and edit synthesized music.

1962 Steve Russell, a graduate student at MIT, invents the first video game.

1963 Ivan Sutherland uses the first interactive computer graphics in his Ph.D. thesis, "Sketchpad: A Man-Machine Graphical Communications System," which used the light pen to create engineering drawings.

1972 A brain tumor is found by an experimental computerized axial tomography imager in Wimbledon, England.

1972 Nolan Bushnell founds Atari.

1973 The Alto, an experimental PC that uses a mouse, Ethernet, and a GUI, is developed at Xerox PARC.

1979 Sony and Philips develop digital videodisks.

1983 MIDI (Musical Instrument Digital Interface) concept is introduced.

1984 The MacPaint program gives computer graphics power to the personal computer audience.

1990 The Dragon speech recognition program recognizes 30,000 words.

1992 First MBone audio multicast is transmitted on the Internet.

1995 First completely computer-generated, full-length feature movie, *Toy Story,* is released.

2001 Audio toxic detection meter detects botulism and other food problems.

2003 Digital audio broadcasting is common.

2005 Digital cameras outsell 35 mm cameras.

Chapter Objectives

- Understand what multimedia is and how it is used.
- Recognize the importance of vision to the communication process.
- Understand how false-coloring is used in image enhancement.
- Know the difference between bitmapped and object-oriented graphics and how each is shown visually in both video and print forms.
- Understand how perspective and shading affect both two-dimensional and three-dimensional images.
- Recognize how blending can improve shaded surfaces.
- Know how animation is achieved with many images that differ only slightly.
- Know the difference between speech synthesis and speech recognition.
- Understand why recognition of disjointed speech is easier than recognition of continuous speech.
- Recognize the various audio formats used in computers.
- Know what MP3 is and how it impacts the WWW.
- Understand how MIDIs aid composers and performers in all aspects of the music industry.

Michael Newman/PhotoEdit

PUZZLER

You are responsible for the development of a commercial Web site. After doing some research on what other corporations are doing by browsing the Web, you notice something unusual. There is very little audio activity, which seems strange for a medium that supports it. Since you can't remember ever seeing a TV ad without sound, and the silent movies aren't produced in these modern times, the lack of audio on the Web seems rather strange. Two major questions come to mind:

1. Why isn't sound used very much on Web sites?
2. What options are there for having a Web site with audio capability?

10.1 What Is Multimedia?

The concept of multimedia is not new. In fact, silent films became multimedia with the inclusion of sound. The so-called multimedia revolution is not due to the inclusion of more media but the fact that it has become interactive. The key ingredients are hypertext and hypermedia, the links that make interactive use of media feasible. We covered hypertext and hypermedia in chapter 8. In this chapter, we'll turn our attention to **interactive multimedia.**

Interactive multimedia is the use of media such as text, graphics, animation, video, and audio in an interactive way that allows a participant to control it.

The five senses—sight, sound, touch, taste, and smell—are the mechanisms we use to communicate with others and our environment. Of these, sight is usually considered the most important. Second, and very close in importance, is sound. Most of the outside information entering our brains enters through our eyes and our ears. They are, indeed, input devices through which our world communicates with us. It therefore behooves us to examine visual and audio concepts in detail. This will allow us to understand their value to interactive multimedia.

In the next section we'll examine the visual domain—image manipulation, image creation, animation, and video. We'll follow with an investigation into the uses of sound media, including speech, music, and audio technology.

10.2 Visual Media: Manipulating Images

In chapter 2, "Metamorphosis of Information," we discussed the concept of digitizing images. We introduced the process of dividing an image into millions of pixels or picture elements and examined how gray-scale and color images are represented. In this section we will see how images can be either manipulated or created.

Modifying or processing images that already exist is less difficult than creating images when starting with a blank display screen or piece of paper. The process can be very creative and complex, but the proper tools make manipulating images relatively easy. There are three types of techniques you can use to manipulate images:

- Minor processing techniques
- Enhancement
- Restoration

PROCESSING EXISTING DIGITAL IMAGES

Many examples of digitized images are available, but none are more commonly seen than the satellite weather maps appearing on television news broadcasts and weather-related Web pages. Figure 10.2.1, showing Hurricane Daniel, is an example of a typical weather-map

Figure 10.2.1

The eye of Hurricane Daniel.

National Hurricane Center, National Oceanic and Atmospheric Administration

Graphics Formats from GIF to PNG

The most common type of image used by today's computers is bitmapped. These images consist of thousands of **pixels,** each of which has a number associated with it. How is this pixel information stored in a computer? There are a number of different forms, called file formats, in which these digitized images are stored. In fact, the program Graphic Converter, available in six human languages, converts among more than 100 different file formats. Each of these file formats has strengths and weaknesses. Let's look at just a few of them.

GIF. One of the most common formats is called GIF (Graphics Interchange Format). GIF was created by CompuServe and has two major strengths. First of all, it is in common usage, which means it's compatible with almost every computer. Another advantage of GIF is the capability to shrink the size of the graphics file; this is called compression. It makes use of a very fast compression algorithm that can shrink the files by up to a factor of 10. This is very important because graphics files tend to be very large, which leads to inefficiency when used in places such as the Internet. A major disadvantage is that it only has 8 bits per pixel, which means only one of 256 colors can be used for any individual pixel. Photographs, in particular, can be degraded from the original form. GIF is especially suited to graphic images such as cartoons, but photographic images can still be acceptable. Files with images in GIF have names that end in GIF, for example, MYDOG.GIF.

TIFF. Computer files that end in TIF or TIFF (Tagged Image File Format) are in a file format that was originally developed by the Aldus Corporation. The major use of TIFF is for large, high-quality or high-resolution images and photographs. It can use up to 96 bits for each pixel and also supports several compression schemes. There are some minor incompatibilities between programs using the TIFF system.

JPEG. Another fairly popular graphics format is JFIF (JPEG File Interchange Format). It is based on a compression scheme called JPEG (Joint Photographic Experts Group). The compression scheme makes use of several decades of research into human vision, which is used to throw out picture information whose absence won't be missed. This type of compression is called lossy compression because it is removing some of the information each time the image is compressed. JFIF file names usually end with the letters JPG.

PNG is the most recent of these common types of graphic image formats. PNG stands for Portable Network Graphics. Although not as commonly supported as the GIF format, the growing acceptance of PNG has been attributed to its flexibility and clarity. Both PNG and GIF formats are composed of bitmapped pixels (more about bitmapped later in this chapter). However, whereas GIF only allows for eight bits per pixel, PNG, depending on how the image has been set up by the software creating it, can be comprised of 8, 16, or 24 bits per pixel. Since the GIF format relies on a patented compression process and whereas PNG does not, more and more images are being stored in the PNG format.

image from the GOES-10 satellite. It should be noted that the image has an unnatural coloring. The artificial coloring shows the wind speeds, with red being the highest.

A close look at the weather maps used in most TV weather reports reveals outlines of the continental United States and coastline. When the satellite was digitizing the image from several miles above Earth, these outlines weren't there. How do they become part of the weather picture? As you probably guessed, they are the result of a computer program. By knowing the location of the satellite and the direction it is pointing, the computer program calculates where the continental boundaries lie. The outlines are then made by changing the tiny areas of the picture associated with these boundaries to a contrasting color.

Another series of satellites called the Landsat satellites is continuously circling Earth. They have sent back to Earth millions of pictures since the program first began. These pictures are not typical. They consist of up to seven different pictures of the same area taken at different frequencies, including infrared. It is like having a special camera with different filters, each of which lets only a certain frequency range through.

An example of one of these special pictures is shown in Figure 10.2.2, an image showing Cape Cod. This particular picture uses three of the seven frequencies available from the

Figure 10.2.2

Landsat 4 image of Cape Cod.

Courtesy and copyright of Verdian ERIM International, Inc., Ann Arbor, MI

Image enhancement is a type of digital image processing whose goal is to highlight or enhance particular aspects of an image or even change the structure of the image itself.

False-coloring or **pseudo-coloring** is an image enhancement technique that consists of changing the colors of an image, or assigns certain colors to the various aspects of an image. In the case of black-and-white images, colors are assigned to the various shades of gray.

Image restoration is the process of eliminating known but unwanted image flaws or degradations.

Thematic Mapper of Landsat 4. It gives a very realistic picture. If you look very closely, you can see the sandbanks and shoals just offshore in shallow water.

NASA and the U.S. Geological Survey (USGS) are teaming up as part of the Landsat Data Continuity Mission (LDCM) to send a new improved Landsat satellite into orbit. Their target date is set for July of 2011. The mission of the LDCM is to update the database of images taken by the Landsat satellites over the years and to use the images from these new satellites to compare past images with current images of and with images taken in the future. In keeping with advances in technology, additional equipment will be included on the new satellites. However, constraints include keeping some of the images taken by the new satellites to be consistent with the older Landsat images for comparison and analysis.

IMAGE ENHANCEMENT

Image enhancement is the formal name for changing an image from its original form. A common example of image enhancement is changing the normal visual colors of an image so as to emphasize detail. This is referred to as **false-coloring, or pseudocoloring.** False coloring was used in Figure 10.2.2. However, the colors were chosen to look natural.

This useful technique of false-coloring allows colors to be assigned in any desired way. Figure 10.2.3, for example, is a digital picture acquired in the late spring from the Nimbus-7 satellite. The false-coloring technique is used to color vegetation red and bare soil light blue. This coloring reveals that bare soil exists in the heavy farming area on the western edge of the thumb of Michigan, whereas the upper half of the lower peninsula of Michigan is mainly forest. From this image it is easy to understand how satellites can be used to investigate what is growing on the surface of Earth. Also note the light blue coloring in the lower-left portion of the image. This is the northern tip of the "bread basket" of the United States, where most of the nation's grain is grown but had not yet been planted when this image was produced.

IMAGE RESTORATION

Another image processing technique is **image restoration.** Imagine obtaining clear pictures where only a blur formerly existed, or being able to see something where previously no image existed.

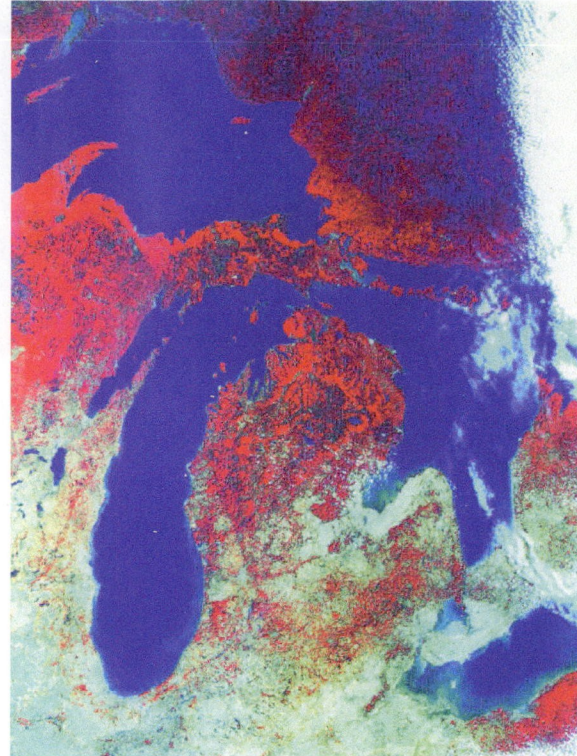

Courtesy and copyright of Verdian ERIM International, Inc., Ann Arbor, MI

Figure 10.2.3

Great Lakes area from the Nimbus-7 satellite. Red represents vegetation, and light blue is bare soil.

Image restoration is something that most of you have already seen, or at least you have seen its end result. Most of the satellite pictures sent to Earth in digital form must have some image-restoration work done on them. The need arises from many sources. For example, electronic "noise" may have resulted in false or incomplete picture information. The computer can be programmed to fill in missing details or change incorrect information as long as the source of the flaw or degradation is known.

An interesting example of image restoration of a different type is found in Figure 10.2.4. The upper photograph is a very fuzzy image of an unreadable license plate. The lower image is a restored version of the same photo. Notice how the letters and numbers are now readable. The computer program that accomplished this was written with the knowledge that the original license plate picture was unrecognizable because of incomplete information. The lack of picture information was due to being too far away.

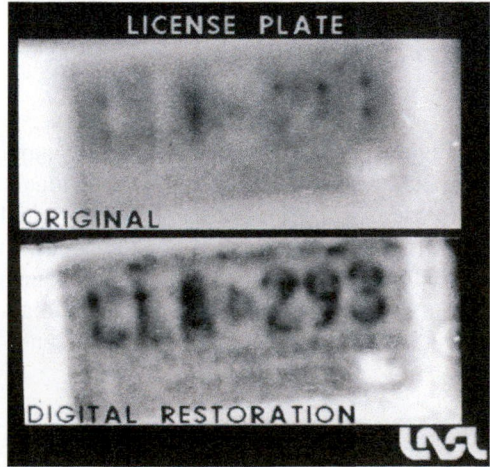

Figure 10.2.4

Restoration of license plate image.

Courtesy of M. Cannon and J. Trusse's Los Alamos National Laboratory

Imagery Courtesy of VisiColor, Inc., Denver, Colorado

Figure 10.2.5

Images of five interesting people.

Imagery Courtesy of VisiColor, Inc., Denver, Colorado

Figure 10.2.6

Composite image of the five people in Figure 10.2.5.

As a final example of image enhancement, Figures 10.2.5 and 10.2.6 illustrate major changes in the structure of an image. In Figure 10.2.5, there are images of five individuals. Look at them carefully. Now look at Figure 10.2.6, which is a composite of the five original images. The businessman has the hair of the "punk rocker," among many other changes. In fact, on close examination it seems that about the only things remaining of the businessman are his facial features. One wonders whether photographs can be trusted. Many tabloid magazines, for example, are known to have manipulated celebrity pictures for improved sensational effect.

IMAGES AND COPYRIGHT OWNERSHIP

Copying images from the Web opens up all sorts of copyright infringement questions. Who is the owner of the image once it is put into circulation on the Web? The answer is clear. The person who took the picture retains ownership of that image. Sure, a student may include the image as part of an assignment for a class with proper references. However, this does not mean that the student can include images on Web pages for personal enjoyment without obtaining proper copyright permissions.

The scope of copyright law is defined by U.S. Code Title 17 of the Copyright Act. Section 102 of the Copyright Act defines copyrightable subject matter as: "original works of authorship fixed in any tangible medium of expression, now known or later developed, from which they can be perceived, reproduced, or otherwise communicated, either directly or with the aid of a machine or device". According to the U.S. Copyright office, the types of works that may be copyrighted include:

1. literary works;
2. musical works, including any accompanying words;
3. dramatic works, including any accompanying music;
4. pantomimes and choreographic works;
5. pictorial, graphic, and sculptural works;
6. motion pictures and other audiovisual works;
7. sound recordings; and
8. architectural works;

According to Section 106 of the Copyright Act, the copyright holder retains the exclusive rights:

1. to reproduce the copyrighted works in copies or phonorecords;
2. to prepare derivative works based upon the copyrighted work;
3. to distribute copies or phonorecords of the copyrighted work to the public by sale or other transfer of ownership, or by rental, lease; or lending;
4. in the case of literary, musical, dramatic, and choreographic works, pantomimes, and motion pictures and other audiovisual works, to perform the copyrighted work publicly;
5. in the case of literary, musical, dramatic, and choreographic works, pantomimes, and pictorial, graphic, or sculptural works, including the individual images of a motion picture or other audiovisual work, to display the copyrighted work publicly; and
6. in the case of sound recordings, to perform the copyrighted work publicly by means of a digital audio transmission

Title 17 of the Copyright Act, then, provides a vehicle for those who create the works to retain a property interest and gives them the right to receive royalties for their works as well as decide who can and can't reproduce the works.

Photo sharing sites, such as Flickr, exist on the Web where anyone can upload images with the intent that the images can be used royalty free. This does not mean that the copyright owner does not give up his or her rights to copyright. But, it does mean that the person who put up the image agrees not to collect royalties for the images. Here lies the problem. Some of the images placed on Flickr were not placed there by the copyright holder. Instead, multiples of the same image are uploaded by people who do not retain the copyright. This is not the spirit of the Flickr photo sharing Web site. Also, finding images as a result of image searches on say Google or Yahoo! will certainly result in a mix of royalty free and copyrighted works. What this means is that there may certainly be financial consequences for using images found online for commercial or personal Web sites as well as in printed media. You should be very careful when using images from the Web and be sure to determine if the images are indeed royalty free or if copyright permissions are necessary.

This ownership of images and other copyrighted works spills into the educational realm as well. Whoever creates the work, no matter if it is a student or teacher, retains the right of copyright, unless, of course, a contract stipulates otherwise.

The "limitations on exclusive rights: fair use", is covered by section 107 of Title 17. The fair use concept allows reproductions of copyrighted works for the purposes of "criticism, comment, news reporting, teaching (including multiple copies for classroom use), scholarship, or research." The four factors that will determine fair use include:

1. the purpose and character of the use, including whether such use is of a commercial nature or is for nonprofit educational purposes;

2. the nature of the copyrighted work;

3. the amount and substantiality of the portion used in relation to the copyrighted work as a whole; and

4. the effect of the use upon the potential market for or value of the copyrighted work.

Even these limitations have "limitations!" For example, a teacher (or a student if it is part of an assignment) may make copies of an article for one class if it is a spur of the moment decision and if the article helps improve instruction of the topic covered in class. However, the teacher cannot make copies for several classes or make copies of the same article for more than the one term. Also, limits on the number of words from a book or poem are also clearly stated. In these cases, permission from the copyright holder would be necessary.

10.3 Visual Media: Creating Images

So far, we've reviewed how real-life images are digitized and then modified, smoothed, or false-colored. Here, we'll examine the artistic rules needed to create original images by computer.

Artists through the centuries have developed a set of fundamental rules for making images. Different sets of rules led to different artistic movements and individual styles. But there are universal rules that almost all of these schools of artistic thought have recognized. They consist of simple things such as hiding parts of objects that wouldn't normally be visible or violating this principle intentionally. In three-dimensional images, it is necessary to know the sources of light that illuminate the objects. In Rembrandt's portraits, for example, he used a particular style of illumination called Rembrandt lighting. Look at any Rembrandt portrait and notice that a light source seems to be located above and to the side of the subject, which leaves a triangle of light on the cheek.

CREATING LINE IMAGES

Because of the complexity of creating images, we will start with the simplest type of line drawings. Two major issues must be addressed when creating images that are made up of only straight and curved lines. The first is to create the image, and the second is to display it.

Creating images can be done by using drawing programs, such as Adobe Illustrator, that exist for almost every type of computer. These programs have many drawing-related features that help the user create images. There is usually a set of tools for drawing circles, ellipses, rectangles, squares, and curves through several points. Other tools usually available allow the artist to draw freehand, fill in with colors or patterns, outline objects, and perform other techniques. Figure 10.3.1 shows a caricature in the process of being drawn. Some of the tools used for making this drawing can easily be identified in the menu box along the left side, especially the straight lines and circles.

What are some of the uses for line drawings?

- Map making
- Architectural drawings
- Graphs (for example, a company's profit by year)
- Machine design plans
- Home decorator's layouts
- Model airplane plans
- Aircraft construction blueprints
- City population-density maps

VECTOR VERSUS RASTER GRAPHICS

Not all drawings are created equally. There are two fundamentally different types of line drawings: **bitmapped,** or *raster,* **graphics,** and **object-oriented,** or *vector,* **graphics.** Before we define these two different and often misunderstood concepts, let's examine bitmapped and object-oriented images of the same object. Figure 10.3.2 shows a simple line drawing of a daisy done in both forms using a typical drawing program. Each drawing was originally one quarter inch in diameter, and then enlarged to the size shown. Notice that the bitmapped daisy has uneven, somewhat jagged edges, whereas the object-oriented flower appears smoother. Both looked the same on the computer screen when they were first drawn but are, in actuality, very different.

Bitmapped, or raster, graphical images in the simplest form are those constructed by individual pixels that are black or white. The pixels can each be shades of gray or colored for photographic-looking images.

Object-oriented, or vector, graphical images are those that are stored in the computer as lines, curves, or geometric shapes. Formulas are used to indicate what to draw. The term **object graphics** is sometimes used.

Figure 10.3.1

Screen from the drawing program Adobe Illustrator showing many of the drawing tools available.

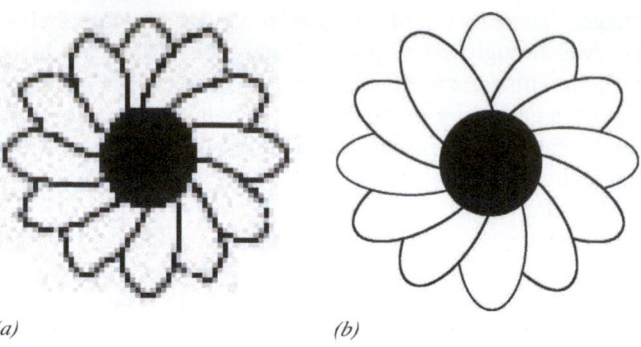

Figure 10.3.2

Images of a daisy in (a) bitmapped and (b) object graphics forms.

(a)   (b)

The bitmapped image was drawn by coloring individual pixels black or white. No information about the relationship of one pixel to another, or about one line to another, was stored in the computer. The image was saved only as a grid of pixels, some of which were black and some of which were white. When the image was printed, the exact pattern of pixels in the monitor image was reproduced on paper. Any changes to the image, such as enlarging it or modifying its shape, would require changing the size, color, or position of each dot in the image.

The object-oriented graphics image was handled differently. It was stored in a formula and then redrawn with the printing device's pixel size, which is much smaller. This makes the curves appear smooth. The main advantage over bitmapped graphics is that the objects can be moved or modified without changing each pixel independently; only the formula has to be modified.

To further emphasize the difference, suppose the same drawing program is used to make the two original images triple the size of the original drawing. The result in Figure 10.3.3 shows an even greater contrast between the two. Because the bitmapped information of the picture consists of only black and white pixels, the computer has no choice when enlarging the image. It must make each black pixel into nine black pixels, and each white pixel becomes nine white pixels. Because each old pixel is represented by three vertically and three horizontally, the image is three times bigger. However, the object graphics image just draws all lines at the original width but three times longer.

Figure 10.3.3

Enlargement of two images in Figure 10.3.2: (a) bitmapped and (b) object-graphic forms.

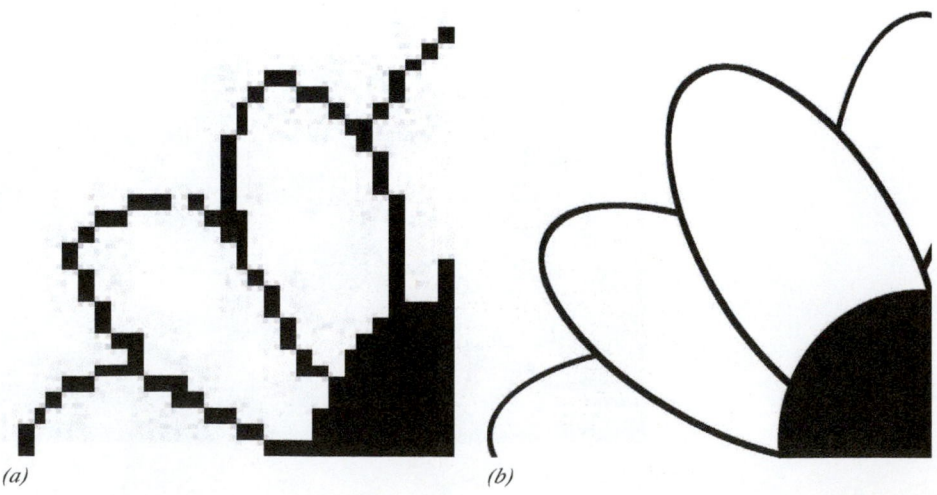

(a)   (b)

SOLID FORMS TO 3D

Although flat, two-dimensional line drawings are quite useful, three-dimensional pictures drawn in two dimensions involve more complex concepts that are quite familiar to art students. These concepts include curved surfaces, color, texture, and shading. The first two are probably already familiar to you, but texture and shading may not be. The texture of a surface can be best explained by example. The surface that looks like wood has a much different appearance than one that looks like fur. It is not hard to see the difference. However, shading is a little more difficult. Artists have worked with shading techniques to produce an endless variety of effects. Proper shading, for example, can make a scene look as if it is in direct sunlight or like a cloudy day. Let's start with simple, three-dimensional line drawings displayed on a flat surface such as a piece of paper.

Scenery, objects, and the human figure have all been the subject of computer line drawings. One interesting example involves the representation of airline pilots and an investigation into how their span of reach is affected by cockpit layout. Figure 10.3.4 shows several frames in a series of a pilot reaching for various control switches. By studying this type of image, the engineers who design cockpits of airplanes can see potential problems in the layout of instruments and controls.

There is one rather obvious peculiarity of this line drawing of a pilot in Figure 10.3.4. You can see through him! Is it possible to create better drawings of the pilot, which hide the lines that aren't supposed to be seen? The problem is referred to as the **hidden-line problem,** which is one of the classic problems in computer graphics.

The solution to hidden lines is well defined for most cases. How can they really be hidden if the only things hiding them are other lines? Of course, with some thought, we realize that the lines are really marking the edges of surfaces, and it is these surfaces that prevent us

The **hidden-line** or **hidden-surface problem** deals with how to hide the outlines or surfaces of a solid object that shouldn't be seen from the direction of the observation.

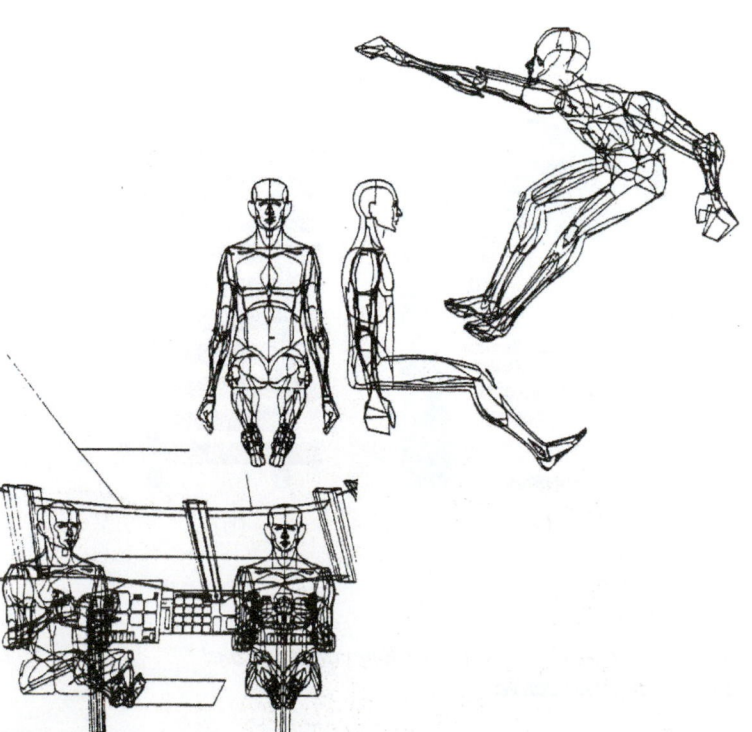

Figure 10.3.4

Studies of an airline pilot in action.

The Boeing Company

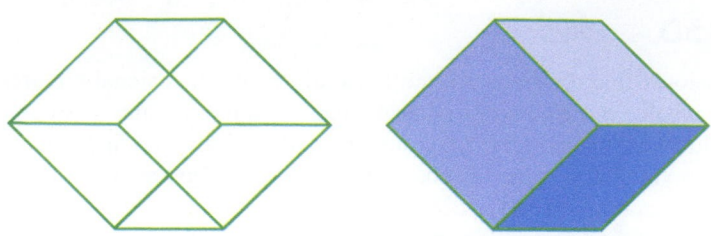

Figure 10.3.5

A box with and without hidden lines showing.

from seeing through the object. Figure 10.3.5 illustrates a box with and without the lines that should be out of sight if the box were opaque.

It's really no problem to remove these lines as long as our viewing direction isn't changed. However, this would be very limiting. In fact, one of the great powers of line drawings in computer graphics is the ability to view an object from different directions. Algorithms have been developed to allow the computer to draw objects as viewed from different directions as demanded by the user. These same algorithms hide the lines that should not be visible from the particular viewing direction.

Perspective is another important quality, which must be included to make drawings look realistic—that is, to make the image appear on paper the way it would actually look to the eye. Figure 10.3.6 illustrates a view overlooking some railroad tracks: (a) with perspective, and (b) without perspective.

Using the concepts of hidden lines and perspective, good-looking images can be drawn. Figure 10.3.7 illustrates an architect's line drawing of a home in two different views. Both

Perspective is the quality that allows three-dimensional images to be drawn on two-dimensional surfaces and yet retain their three-dimensional appearance.

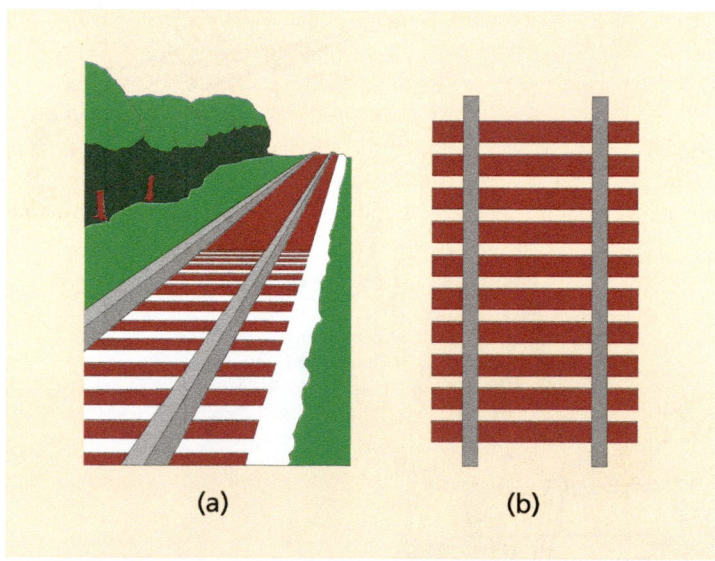

(a)   (b)

Figure 10.3.6

Image of railroad tracks: (a) with perspective, and (b) without perspective.

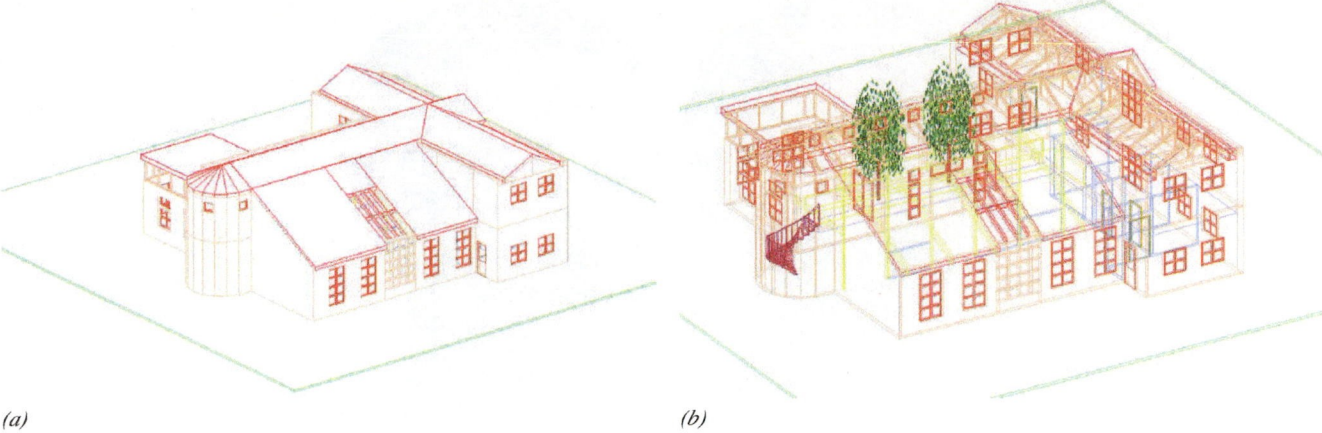

(a)   *(b)*

Figure 10.3.7

Architect's line drawing of a home: (a) without hidden lines showing, and (b) with hidden lines showing.

perspective and hidden lines are very important to this drawing. The computer that made this drawing used information about the dimensions of the home; then when the operator specified the position of the observer, the computer drew the image, taking into account both hidden lines and perspective.

Shading is used to make the image more realistic. Figure 10.3.8 shows an example in which the shading is very easy—each complete surface will have the same shading. By examining the figure, it can be seen that the sides facing away from the light source are darker than those facing the light. In this case, the light source is the sun. All scenes that mimic nature must have sources of light illuminating them. Most often, these light sources are the sun, reflections from a surface, or artificial lights.

A problem occurs when the object is constructed of curved surfaces because there are no flat, discrete surfaces to shade. One solution is to construct the curved surface out of many flat surfaces, as shown in the front view of the face in Figure 10.3.9.

Each of the facets (that is, flat sections) can then be individually shaded as necessary. Figure 10.3.10(a) shows the face with shading from a light above and to the left. This image is not very realistic, however. It can easily be improved by having the computer smear out or blend in the shading. Suppose, for example, that the region between two facets has shading

Shading is a technique used to give the appearance of illumination by some combination of light sources. It is used to make created images look like images humans are used to seeing or to take advantage of these effects.

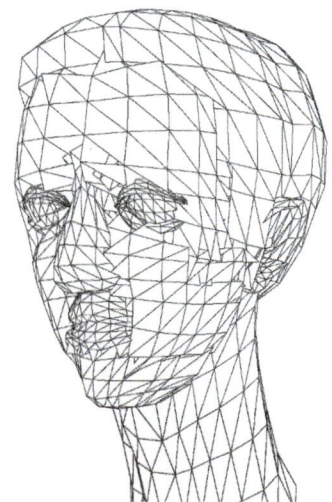

Figure 10.3.9

Construction of a human head from flat surfaces.

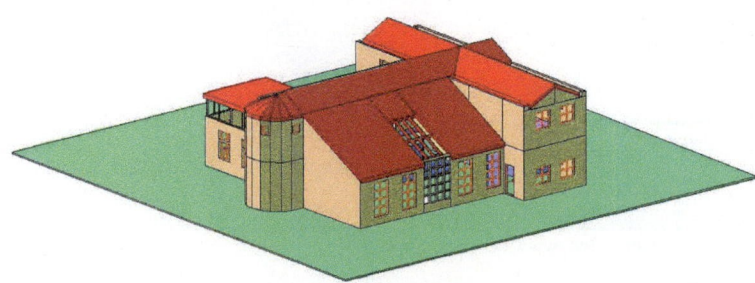

Figure 10.3.8

Shading used to give 3D effect to a building.

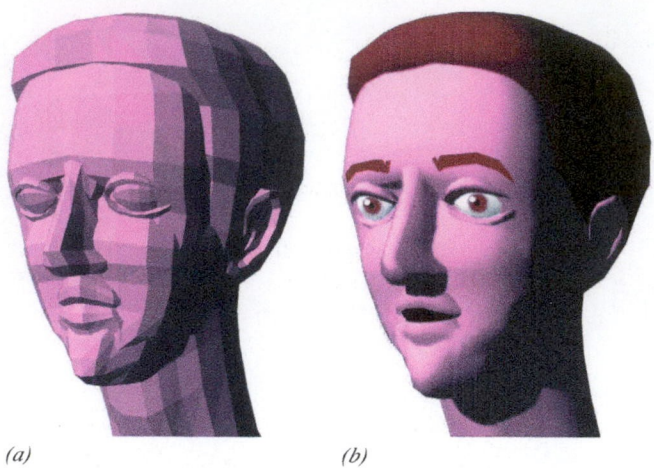

(a)   (b)

Figure 10.3.10

(a) Shading flat surfaces of the head; (b) blending facets to give a more natural look.

that is an average of the shadings. The shading can then smoothly vary to the original facet's value at the center of the facet. Figure 10.3.10(b) illustrates the result of the smoothing technique; the face looks more realistic.

Many graphics programs are available to the professional illustrator. With these powerful and complex programs, images of very high quality can be created. Incorporating perspective, shading, **texture,** and color—along with some illustrator talent—can result in images such as the sports car in Figure 10.3.11. This object-oriented graphics image with color is a high-quality example of a professional illustrator's work.

Texture is a property of a surface. It is observed and identified by humans through the reflection of the light off the surface. A shiny surface reflects light, for example, in a way that sometimes has a mirrorlike quality. Rough surfaces, on the other hand, reveal an unevenness.

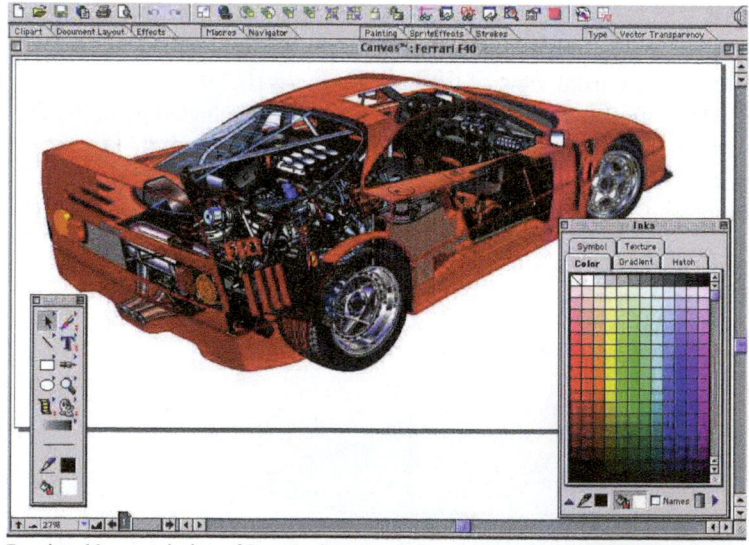

Reprinted by permission of Deneba Systems, Inc. www.deneba.com © 2000

Figure 10.3.11

Combining professional talent with a high-end graphics program gives spectacular results.

Tech Talk

Diplodocuses of the Jurassic in 3D

You may be familiar with the old-fashioned 3D viewers from the 1800s. Today, precise image manipulation using computers can produce a 3D effect without a viewer. Tatsuhiko Sugimoto's Creatures is a stereogram produced by Viz Communications. It is constructed using two side-by-side images that fool the brain into thinking the eyes are seeing a single 3D image.

To see a 3D image of a group of the genus diplodocus dinosaurs from the Jurassic period, place a fingertip on the bridge of your nose. While focusing intently on it, with crossed eyes, slowly pull your finger away.

Courtesy of VizCommunications, Inc.

It is important to discuss another aspect of graphics here. Most of the previous images exist in only one view, the one given in the figure. In looking at the architect's rendering of the building in Figures 10.3.7 and 10.3.8, however, it seems natural to allow the viewer to look at the building from another position. In fact, the architect's program used to create the building image actually has a three-dimensional description of the building in the computer. This internal description can be used to give pictures viewed from almost any angle chosen by the user of the architect's program. Figure 10.3.12 shows the building from a different perspective. The architect didn't redraw the building; the program redrew it so that it appears as shown from the new direction, which was selected interactively by the viewer.

Figure 10.3.12

View of the home from a different perspective.

10.4 Visual Media: Animation and Video

Moving images, whether they are created by hand, machine, or recorded as video, have a very important place in the communication process. In modern times animation started with picture-flipping using hand-cranked animation players and moved to cartoon cell animations on celluloid. The history is full of technological innovations, and the computer is proving to be the most important of them.

TRADITIONAL ANIMATION

Almost everyone is familiar with the Saturday morning cartoons on television. They portray animated figures that jump, run, swim, drive various contraptions, take pratfalls, get run over, smash and bash each other, and then return the next Saturday morning for more of the same. Who makes these films or videotapes, and how are they made? Thirty years ago, all cartoons had to have the figures drawn by artists. Then the animator would make them move by projecting the pictures, frame by frame. Now, full-length feature cartoons such as *Toy Story,* shown in Figure 10.4.1, are created completely by computer. To understand the process, it is first necessary to understand how motion pictures work.

If you have ever examined a strip of motion picture film, you probably observed that each of the pictures or frames is almost identical to those surrounding it. However, each frame does change very slightly. When you quickly view succeeding frames, the objects in the picture seem to move.

Graphics programs on computers can be used to draw these frames. The frames can then be stored individually in the computer. Special player programs can then view the animation on the computer screen or record them on videotape via special hardware and software on the computer.

Computer animation has moved into serious movie-making with movies like *Ice Age: Dawn of the Dinosaurs, Up, WALL-E, Grand Theft Auto, Shrek, The Lord of the Rings* Trilogy, *Toy Story, and Jurassic Park* to name a few. As an illustration of the process of animating the characters, we'll look at how Woody from *Toy Story* was created and animated. Woody began as one of dozens of hand drawn images created by Bud Luckey an illustrator who works at Pixar. Once the "right Woody" was selected, a clay model was created. This clay model served as a means of entering the three dimensional object into the computer where it would exist as a wire frame much like the one in Figure 10.3.9. The wire frame is moved by the computer, which calculates positions of each part viewed from a certain angle and distance. Then the computer covers the surface with a texture layer, which is added in a way that takes into account sources of light illuminating the figure. It is a fairly complex process that produces amazing results. A single frame from the movie is shown in Figure 10.4.1.

Figure 10.4.1

A frame from the cartoon movie Toy Story.

Neal Peters Collection

Figure 10.4.2

Scene from the movie Jurassic Park *showing a computer-created dinosaur.*

Another method of animating a character is by taking digital movies of a human, having the computer software analyze the points on the face and body, and then adding the animated character to the computer generated environment. To move the character, the computer software may be used exclusively, or a human model in a suit with sensor data points may be posed or asked to move in a certain way. These data points are then used by the computer to create more life-like motion for the animated character.

The computer used to create these animated films are not your average personal computer. These computers are fairly expensive and have very expensive proprietary software to create the incredible moving character. In some cases, these animated characters are combined with images of real humans and real scenery to look natural. One example of very realistic animated

Ivan Sutherland: Computer Graphics Guru

In 1965 Ivan E. Sutherland issued a challenge to researchers in the computer field. He said in his speech at an international conference: "Think of the screen as a window into a virtual world. The task of computer graphics research is to make the picture in the window look real, sound real, interact real, feel real." He was describing what is now referred to as virtual reality.

It was only two years earlier that he completed his thesis titled "Sketchpad: A Man-Machine Graphical Communications System" at MIT. This work pioneered concepts in interactive computer graphics that included zooming and the ability to make perfect corners, joints, and lines. It was the first GUI (graphical user interface).

Evans & Sutherland Computer Corporation

After graduation, he was inducted into the Army and went to work at NSA (National Security Agency) as an electrical engineer. Within a year, he was transferred to the Defense Department's Advanced Research Projects Agency (ARPA), where he headed the Information Processing Techniques office. At age 26, Lt. Sutherland's responsibility was to create sponsored research in computing with a $15 million a year budget.

After discharge from the Army, Ivan Sutherland became an associate professor at Harvard University. It was there in 1966 that he and graduate student Bob Sproull took on a Bell Helicopter project that turned into a virtual reality project. They used a head-mounted display, where the viewer could enter the room and look out windows on different walls of the room. To do this, the computer sensed the movement of the wearer's head and then created the appropriate view in the display.

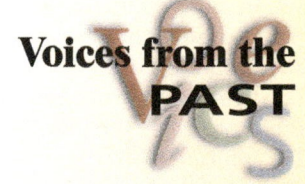

Voices from the PAST

character is Emily, by Image Metrics. Emily looks so real that it's hard to believe that she exists in the computer and is manipulated by software (To see a video of Emily, do a search on the Web with the keywords Emily and Animation.) It does not seem so incredible to think that some day soon, movies will be made without actors or scenic locations for filming.

SPECIAL EFFECTS AND MORPHING

Morphing is a special graphics technique used in animation. Starting with a beginning image, the technique will distort and change it frame by frame to the predetermined final image with a predetermined number of frames in between. The first commercially successful use of morphing was in Michael Jackson's 1991 video "Black or White." In this video millions of dollars were spent to morph many faces of different races, both male and female, from one to another. Morphing is currently being used in advertising with great effect.

The morphing technique is available to personal computers through software programs such as FantaMorph by Abrosoft, and Morpheus Photo Morpher™ by Morpheus Software, LLC. Some morphing software programs are free; others can be purchased for as little as a $30.00 to $100.00 depending on the number of features included as part of the package. The sample shown in Figure 10.4.3 is a morph from the face of Michelangelo's statue of *David* to a second image of his Madonna from *The Pièta*. It then continues with Leonardo da Vinci's *The Virgin of the Rocks,* and then to the final form of *Mona Lisa* also by Leonardo da Vinci. It was created by "Morph," one of the first morphing programs available for PC.

DIGITIZING AND MANIPULATING VIDEO

Early in the 1990s a digital video hardware system capable of capturing and manipulating video cost several thousand dollars. By the mid-1990s, low-quality, small-format video could be recorded and processed by the average personal computer with relatively inexpensive hardware. By the late 1990s, full-screen video was economically priced for the average personal computer user. Finally, by 2007, small handheld digital video recorders and cell phones with video capability became available at reasonable prices. This was the beginning of widespread use of video, not only in presentations but also over the Internet via the World Wide Web.

Video capture is the process of digitizing an analog TV signal. It is done using hardware that produces a digital form of the analog TV signal.

Basic Video Concepts   The majority of video today is digital. June 12, 2009 was the date set by Congress and regulated by the Federal Communications Commission to require that all full-powered television stations broadcast in digital format. The television stations, then, were able to send digital signals over the air. Those who previously received over-the-

Figure 10.4.3

A morph of images from David *to* Mona Lisa.

Gryphon Software Corporation

air analog signals through their television were forced to upgrade their televisions and antennas. This left many who were not prepared without television reception. Those people who had satellite and cable reception of television signals were not affected.

One major advantage of over-the-air digital television (DTV) is that the digital signal is not compressed. The programs are crisp and clear. The future of DTV has the potential to send multiple programs (multicasting) on one channel and will have the ability to be interactive. One major disadvantage of the digital over-the-air signal is that it has "all or nothing" reception. If anything blocks the signal, the viewer cannot watch the station. Also, a weak signal, or one that is just strong enough to view, may result in pixilated images where the image is broken up in pieces and where the television tries to fill in the gaps with larger pixels.

Analog video uses two broadcast standards developed over 50 years ago: the European (PAL), and the United States (NTSC) broadcast standards. They differ primarily in the number of horizontal lines that make up a single video frame or picture and in the number of frames per second that are displayed on the TV set. To digitize an analog video both hardware and software are needed to capture the analog video. So, if you plan on transferring any of your old VHS tapes to digital, you'll need to purchase the hardware and software that allows you to capture the analog video signal.

Video from digital cameras and DVDs are already in digital form. The digital video data are usually compressed by taking advantage of duplications of data that appear in the bitmap of the screen frame. Satellite and cable television still use compression techniques to send along digital signals to its customers. The schemes, or compression standards, are called codecs.

> A **codec** is a scheme for coding and decoding large amounts of data. First the data are coded, then they are economical and uncomplicated to store. To view the coded data, they must first be decoded.

Common CODECs

The Motion Picture Experts Group (MPEG) has had a great deal of influence on the codecs used for video, which also include audio. An early codec specified by the group is **MPEG-1.** It is one that was developed to handle slower media, such as video CDs, and deteriorates when high-speed action occurs, causing color smearing and digital artifacts, which are aberrations appearing in the playback. However, it has roughly the quality of VHS, and about 70 minutes of good-quality video with sound fit on a CD-ROM disc. With the advent of faster media hardware and computers, the Motion Picture Experts Group created MPEG-2 with enhanced features.

MPEG-2 is a full-screen codec standard that brings twice the quality of VHS and has four times the resolution of MPEG-1, which means a larger picture with equivalent quality can be displayed. MPEG-2 has been optimized for the higher demands of broadcast, satellite, and DVD video. Both MPEG-1 and MPEG-2 are based on the JPEG compression of the individual frames, which is discussed in the TechTalk box in this chapter. It takes a higher-end PC to play back MPEG-2 video files.

A third codec that deserves note here is **M-JPEG.** It requires more memory space than MPEG-2, but because each video frame is digitized separately using JPEG compression, it is easier to edit. This is because software implementations of M-JPEG, such as Adobe Premiere, allow a PC better access to the data. With the advent of DVD and the fact that all broadcast will eventually become digital, these codecs will become less important. Coding and decoding will be unnecessary because everything will already be digital.

DVD, the Digital Versatile Disc

DVD is an acronym that originally stood for "digital video disc" and then became "digital versatile disc." You can find details of how the DVD works in chapter 3, where we discuss its vast storage capacity of up to 17 gigabytes.

It is important to note that there are two forms of DVD. The first form—**DVD-Video** discs—was created with input from the Hollywood movie studios and is intended as the replacement for VHS videotapes. These DVD-Video discs are played on a special DVD player that also plays standard audio CDs.

The second form of DVD is called **DVD-ROM.** It was developed with a great deal of involvement from the computer industry and can be thought of as a very fast, large-capacity CD-ROM. The DVD-ROM player is usually built into the computer and can also play DVD-Video discs. However, note that DVD-Video players cannot play DVD-ROM discs.

> **DVD** or **digital versatile disc** is an optical disk storage technology that looks like the standard CD, but it is faster and has a much larger storage capacity.

HD DVD AND BLU-RAY   If you look at the spectrum of light projected by light passing through a prism, you'll notice that the colors split into Red, Orange, Yellow, Green, Blue, Indigo, and Violet (RPYGBIV). Each of these colors has their own electromagnetic frequency as shown in Figure 10.4.4. What HD DVD and Blu-ray have in common is that they both use the narrow, blue-violet end of the spectrum to read and write onto DVD discs. The result is that more data can be packed onto the disc because the width of the electromagnetic frequency of the light needed to read and write the data is narrower than that needed to read and write onto a regular DVD.

Because of the differences in the thickness of the protective plastic film used by Blu-ray and HD DVD, the methods used to record onto each disc is different. Blu-ray uses a thinner protective coating thereby being able to store the data in more layers. And, as a result, Blu-ray can store more data on a single disc. Blu-ray discs have the capacity to store 100 GB whereas HD DVDs can store only 45GB. Both Blu-ray and HD DVDs use the MPEG-2

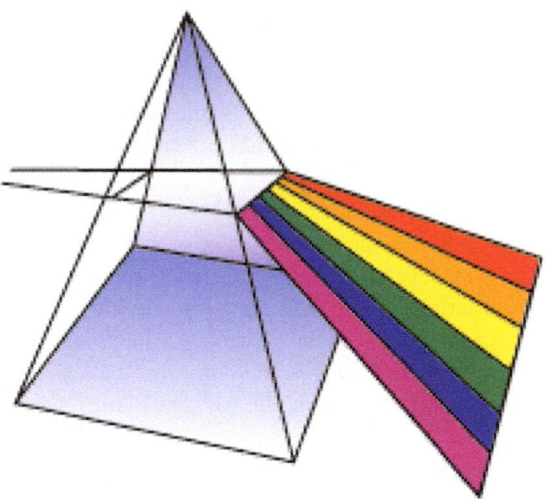

Figure 10.4.4

Figure 10.4.4 Light spectrum and electromagnetic frequencies.

compression format. Because Blu-ray discs are produced with a thinner protective coating than other DVDs, the cost to produce them is higher, at least, for the time being. At the time of the printing of this book, Blu-ray is winning the popularity race and is outselling media stored on HD DVD discs.

Digital Video Players   We still have to deal with the video files created with MPEG-1, MPEG-2, M-JPEG, or other codecs. One of the major needs is to have a cheap player that doesn't require the original digitizing hardware or additions to it. Several software products are available that simply play back video that was coded with one of these codecs systems.

One of the first software players on the scene was QuickTime from Apple Computer. It became a major milestone in digital video. It now runs under Macintosh, Windows, Windows-NT, and UNIX operating systems. It supports many of the codecs including MPEG-1, M-JPEG, Cinepak, Indeo, and MP3 audio.

Another popular software digital video player is Microsoft's Windows Media Player. It runs only under Microsoft's Windows operating systems and supports several formats including MPEG audio, WAV audio, MPEG-1, MPEG-2, and Apple QuickTime video.

STREAMING MEDIA

One of the most important concepts fostered by the Internet is **streaming media.** The concept is best explained through an analogy. When you view a TV program, the video information is being broadcast to you as it is being viewed. This is not the same as having a DVD disc, where you play back a previously recorded copy. Streaming media is the same idea. You are being sent a series of packets over the Internet that contains the program or real event. As they reach your computer, the packet information is displayed on your screen for video and would be heard over the computer audio system for audio.

You can pretty much find any kind of video online to stream to your computer or cell phone. The videos that you can find online include anything from political videos such as those showing the discourse in the streets of countries where other news media have been silenced, to live coverage of a tragic event such as the massacre of students at Virginia Tech, to "how-to" videos, to educational videos, to just plain videos meant to entertain. All that is required to create such a video is a small digital handheld video recorder or cell phone with video capabilities. The recorded video would then need to be uploaded onto a Web server where others can access the videos. The most common, and most viewed video streaming site is YouTube.

Streaming media is information in one of many different visual or audio forms that is sent from a server in packets to the requesting computer. Each packet contains parts of the medium that may be a recording or an actual live event. The information in the packets is then played back in the order sent, starting soon after a few packets arrive but before all of them have been sent.

10.5 Audio Media: Human Speech

The importance of audio media is not hard to find, whether it is the millions of CDs sold each day or the thousands of commercial radio stations in operation. We will consider two major categories of audio communication: human speech and music. The computer is intimately involved with both of them.

Research shows that speech is by far the fastest and most convenient way for humans to communicate ideas. Experiments comparing it with other methods of communication have shown that information is exchanged almost twice as quickly using speech as it is without speech. In fact, many researchers think that the development of human intelligence is very closely linked to the development of verbal communication and language. Therefore, indeed, vocal communication is worth our attention.

We'll focus on two activities: creating and recognizing human speech. We reserve a discussion of semantics or the meaning of the spoken words for chapter 13, "Artificial Intelligence and Modeling the Human State."

RECORDED SPEECH

One very simple method for creating speech is to record it and digitize it, as we explained in chapter 2. Early attempts at this process recorded individual words and then played them back. This method of speech production can be heard regularly in department stores and supermarkets. Some cash registers speak aloud each amount of money being entered, as well as the total amount owed, the amount tendered by the customer, and the change due.

Although digitized recording is the easiest way to produce human speech, the process requires a lot of planning. Let's use the talking cash register as an example. Before we can start, we need a complete list of the words and phrases our cash register must say aloud. This includes words needed to represent amounts of money: numbers such as *one, two, seven, ten, twenty, sixty,* and so forth, and words such as *dollar, dollars, and,* and *cents.* We also need some phrases, such as *your total is, your change is, thank you very much,* and so on. Every word and phrase needed for everything the cash register must say must be included.

After this list is complete, each word and phrase on the list must be spoken by a human and recorded. Each recorded word or phrase must then be individually digitized and stored separately in the computer's memory. The computer controlling the cash register must then be programmed to string together whichever digitized pieces of speech are needed to reproduce a complete utterance. Seven different digitized pieces must be strung together, for example, for a cash register to say, "Your total is ten dollars and twenty-seven cents."

The automated national telephone information service also uses speech composed of recorded words and phrases. In this case, longer phrases may be needed, such as, "this call may be dialed automatically for an additional charge," as well as the numbers from 0 to 9 and phrases such as "area code" and "the number is." When the information operator locates the number you requested in an electronic directory, the computer reads the number and then strings together the required digitized words and phrases, transmitting them to you via the phone line.

Some definite problems occur when using this approach to speech production. To recreate whole sentences of human speech using even a minimal vocabulary of recorded words would take a huge amount of computer memory, to say nothing of an extended period of time. In addition, many words would have to be recorded and digitized more than once. We say words differently at the end of a statement than we do at the end of a question. And words that occur in the middle of a sentence are often spoken with different pitch and volume levels from those that occur at the ends. Therefore, several digitized versions of each word might be needed to account for all possibilities. Because the number of words in any human language is enormous (English contains an especially huge vocabulary), the memory needed to store digitized versions of all words in all possible inflections is prohibitive.

Indeed, pure recording and playback is suitable for only a small number of voice applications. A different approach is obviously needed. Therefore, let us examine another, more useful methodology.

SPEECH SYNTHESIS: MAKING A COMPUTER SPEAK

Speech synthesis is the electronic production of sounds and sound patterns that closely resemble human speech.

The more general approach for producing human speech is commonly called **speech synthesis.** It is more general in the sense that without recording individual words, they can be synthesized or created out of building blocks made out of sound units.

The study of human speech has resulted in the categorizing of various sounds of any given human language into a finite number of sound units called **phonemes.** Different languages have different sets of phonemes. All words of any specific language are made up of different combinations of the phonemes of that language. As we noted in chapter 2, Table 2.5.1, American English has about 42 phonemes. Let's take another look at those phonemes in Table 10.5.1. Notice that English sometimes uses two letters to spell one sound, and sometimes one written letter might stand for two or more different sounds in different written words.

Phonemes are the fundamental sounds of any given human language. There may be two or more ways to spell any one phoneme. For example, the phonemes needed to pronounce the word *there* may also be spelled *their* and *they're.*

You may not agree with the number of vowel or consonant phonemes listed in Table 10.5.1. That's because we do not all say things in exactly the same way. Some speakers make a distinction between the vowels in *Mary, merry,* and *marry,* for example, but others don't. Some people think that *Wales* and *whales* are spelled differently because they begin with different phonemes; to others, the spelling difference is merely an annoying visual difference because they pronounce the two words exactly the same way. Such differences in splicing phonetic reality will become important when we try to teach computers to recognize and understand human speech.

Once the phonemes are chosen, as discussed in chapter 2, the computer program that is synthesizing the speech must modify them in three basic ways:

- Modify the pitch or **inflection** of each phoneme
- Select the appropriate **duration** for sounding the phoneme
- Splice the phoneme sound chunks together in the process called **elision**

The set of rules the computer software uses follows what we humans have learned to do automatically. The rules are simple but numerous and include things like raising the pitch at the end of an utterance that is a question.

Another issue that makes the process even more difficult is that most speech synthesis is done from written words. This brings in all of the rules for pronunciation and their exceptions into play.

After a string of phonemes is ready for output, the actual sounds produced are electronically generated. Although the voice production component does not resemble the human vocal system, the sounds it produces simulate those produced by the human vocal tract shown in Figure 10.5.1. Thus, it can produce both major types of human sounds: voiced and voiceless. **Voiced sounds** include all vowels and some consonants, such as *b, d,* and *g.* Examples of **voiceless sounds** are the sounds made by the consonants *p, t,* and *k.*

Voiced sounds in human speech are those produced by the vibration of the vocal cords in conjunction with specific positioning of the teeth, tongue, and the lips.

Voiceless sounds in speech are characterized by the lack of vibration of the vocal chords.

Table 10.5.1   *The phonemes of American English.*

Vowels	Consonants			
ee as in **bee**	p	**pea**	b	**bee**
i as in **mitten**	t	**tea**	d	**Dee**
e as in **make**	k	**key**	g	**gone**
eh as in **led**	f	**fee**	v	**vee**
ae as in **had**	s	**see**	z	**zip**
ah as in **father**	sh	**sheep**	zh	vi**si**on
aw as in **small**	tsh	**chest**	dzh	**jaw**
o as in **go**	r	**rate**	m	**me**
u as in **put**	y	**yet**	ëm	cha**sm**
oo as in **tool**	w	**Wales**	n	**not**
uh as in **the**	hw	**whales**	ën	Ed**en**
er as in ang**er**	h	**he**	ng	si**ng**
ai as in **while**	l	**lee**		
ou as in **how**	ël	crad**le**		
oi as in **toy**				
iu as in **fuse**				

RECOGNIZING SPOKEN WORDS

Speech recognition is inherently more difficult than speech synthesis. To better understand why, let's first look at some examples of problem areas. The following phrases are self-explanatory. Just say each pair out loud several times. Have someone else listen for any problems that may occur in recognizing which version was spoken. Remember that regional accents and speech impediments would complicate the situation even further.

I scream . . .

Ice cream . . .

or

The slip . . .

This lip . . .

How can a computer distinguish between similar sounding but different strings of phonemes? Before we discuss possible solutions to the apparent problems that these examples illustrate, let's examine the vehicle that carries the words.

A **voiceprint** is a visual plot of the frequency versus time of sound produced by a human speaker. It shows which frequencies of sound are present at each instant while a sound is being made.

The Voiceprint   The actual sound, which can be thought of as a stream of phonemes, can be visually recorded in what is called a **voiceprint.** Figure 10.5.2 is a voiceprint of a male speaker saying the word *said.* Examine it carefully and notice that it seems to be divided into two major components, in the left and center, followed by a less noticeable minor component on the right. The leftmost component is the *s* phoneme; the one in the center is the . . . *eh* sound. Finally, on the right, we see the pattern created by the . . . *d* phoneme. Say the word several times, slowly, to note the three phonemes that make up the sound structure.

If phonemes were the only components of vocal production, we could expect all voiceprints recording the same string of phonemes to look exactly alike. If this were true, voice recognition would be a simpler process. But, unfortunately, no two voiceprints are completely identical. That's because the exact sound of each human voice is determined by at least two qualities: **pitch** and **resonance.** These in turn depend on the unique way each individual voice is formed.

Pitch is determined by the number of cycles per second of a particular sound's vibration. The more vibrations per second, the higher the pitch.

Refer for a moment to Figure 10.5.1. Notice that three rather large cavities occur in the vocal tract, marked in this cross section as cavity A, cavity B, and cavity C. A vocal sound is created by vibration of the vocal chords, two flaps of membrane located below cavity C in a person's throat. The thickness of the vocal chords largely determines the pitch of the voice produced. Before emerging from the mouth, each vocal sound is amplified by cavities A, B, and C. The size and shape of these cavities (sometimes called resonating chambers) determine the resonance, or quality, of the person's voice.

Resonance is the reverberation or amplification of the voice in the cavities of the vocal tract. The larger the cavities, the deeper or richer the resulting resonance.

Because each individual has uniquely shaped vocal chords and resonating chambers, each has a uniquely individual voice. The implications for computer voice recognition are clear: If each and every voice is different, and if different individuals pronounce phonemes differently, how can a computer recognize similar words spoken by different people?

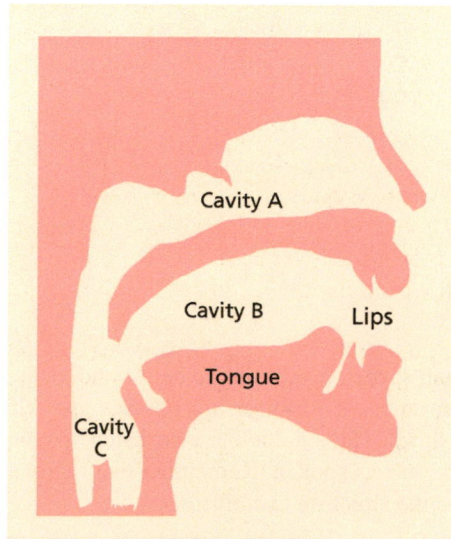

Cavity A

Cavity B   Lips

Tongue

Cavity C

Figure 10.5.1

A cross section of the human vocal system.

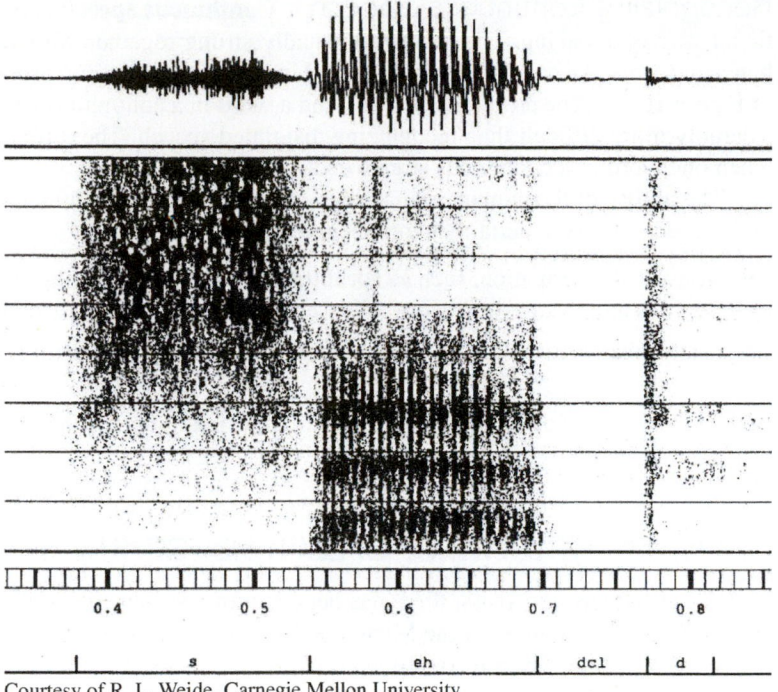

Courtesy of R. L. Weide, Carnegie Mellon University

Figure 10.5.2

Voiceprint of a male speaker saying the word said.

Recognizing Disjointed Speech

When words are spoken individually or separately, each segment of sound represents a single word. Recognizing individual words in a limited vocabulary is not too difficult a problem.

The simplest systems for recognizing isolated words are restricted to those individuals who have had a recording session with the computer. The individual must pronounce each word of the limited vocabulary several times. The speech recognition system in effect averages all pronunciations of each word to get a template of that word. After this recording session, the speech recognition system has "learned" its vocabulary and is capable of recognizing any of its limited number of words as long as they are spoken separately by the original speaker. The obvious disadvantages of this type of system are as follows:

- Each person must go through a recording session to train the computer.
- The process of speaking in disjointed speech is very unnatural.
- Any change in an individual's voice—caused, for example, by a head cold, sinus infection, or dental anaesthetic—may change the voice too much for the computer to recognize it.

Disjointed speech is when words are spoken one at a time with silence between words.

More sophisticated computer systems for recognizing **disjointed speech** can distinguish vocabulary words spoken by various individuals, as long as they all pronounced those words with reasonable similarity. Differing regional and foreign accents would not be easily recognized. A system of this type might divide the population of the United States into four groups—northern male, northern female, southern male, and southern female. Even with this division, words such as *nine* and *none* are still sometimes confused by speech recognition systems.

Note that this doesn't even begin to address the problem of homonyms—words that sound exactly alike—such as *I* and *eye* or *aisle, I'll,* and *isle.* Humans use the context of the conversation to figure out which word is appropriate. However, the main problem is that we almost never speak in disjointed speech. The words come in a continuous flow and usually with no silence between words.

Continuous speech is when words are spoken in a continuous stream of sound, usually with no pauses between the individual words.

Recognizing Continuous Speech

Continuous speech is our normal, conversational way of speaking. The words are usually strung together with varying or no pauses between words. An example of this is found in the words *Sue said it* shown in the voiceprint of Figure 10.5.3. The problem of identifying a word in a continuous stream of sound is considerably more difficult than recognizing disjointed speech. The difficulty is distinguishing when one word of a continuous stream ends and the next begins.

The ability of the human brain to recognize the words of continuous speech is not well understood. However, certain factors seem to be at work:

- Nonverbal information, such as vocal intonations, and nonacoustic information, such as gestures and facial expressions, are used to fine-tune speech recognition.

- Contextual information helps us clarify confusing similarities and misunderstood words.

- A combination of semantic and syntactic information helps the brain recognize continuous speech.

THE CURRENT STATE OF SPEECH RECOGNITION

Clearly, in the past ten years, there has been a dramatic increase in the speech recognition capabilities of computers. In the Microsoft XP operating system environment for example, Microsoft Word has voice recognition capabilities. It is recommended that the headset have noise reducing headphones and a good quality microphone. The software works much better if the recording is performed in a quiet room so that the microphone does not pick up distracting noises. After a training session (the more training the better), the user can enter an entire document and save the document by using voice commands alone. Sure, the Microsoft Word voice recognition application makes mistakes. But, if these mistakes are corrected immediately, the program will learn the corrected spellings and uses of the misinterpreted words and will be less likely to make the same mistakes again.

The Microsoft Vista operating system has brought major advancements over the XP version of voice recognition. With Microsoft Vista, voice recognition has become an operating system enhancement. Now, the user can use voice recognition for operating system commands as well as using it within applications. In Vista, voice commands can be used for instructing the operating system to open and close windows, open application programs, and save and retrieve files. When in a Web browser, voice commands can be used to command the computer to scroll up and down, click on specific links, and enter an address in the address box.

Figure 10.5.3

Voiceprint of male speaker saying, "Sue said it."

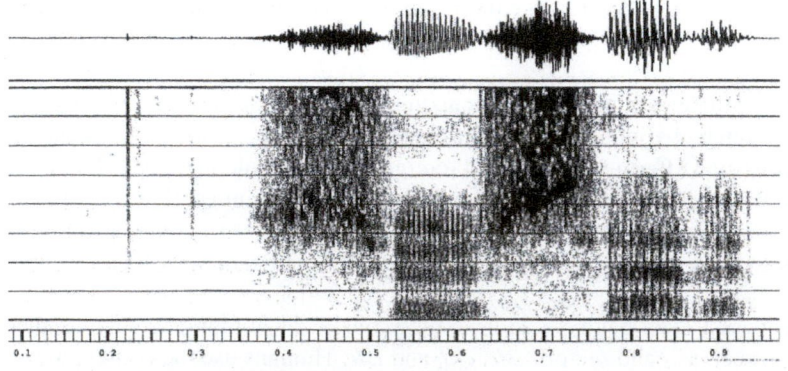

Courtesy of R. L. Weide, Carnegie Mellon University

Typical Speech Recognition Session: This Vista example is for a computer that is equipped with a headset with a microphone. The verbal commands listed here will open WordPad by leading the computer through the Start menu, then through the All Programs option, then opening the Accessories folder, then selecting WordPad to bring up a blank document.

"Start Listening"	The computer starts "listening"
"Start"	Pulls up the Start Menu
"All Programs"	Pulls up the "All Programs" menu
"Scroll Down"	Scrolls down the list if necessary
"Accessories"	Opens the Accessories folder
"WordPad"	Opens a blank document in WordPad
	A blank document opens and is ready for dictation.

A shorter alternative to the last scenario: Here, the command to Open WordPad is given directly to the operating system without the need to go through menu items.

"Open WordPad"	That's it! The computer knows to open the WordPad application.
	A blank document opens and is ready for dictation.

At this point, with a blank document open in WordPad, you can begin dictating whatever text you wish to include in the document. Commands like, "Scratch that" for deleting the last phrase spoken and "Delete that" for deleting the last word or punctuation, can be intermixed with dictation. The computer is now capable of recognizing the difference between commands and the dictation of text.

Other voice recognition application programs can also be used for translating spoken words into text. For example, Dragon Naturally Speaking does an excellent job of speech to text translation. In addition to using Dragon Naturally Speaking as a stand-alone application, some digital voice recorders include the program to take voice recordings made by the digital voice recorder and translate them into text. As an example of such a use, some professors at colleges and universities are recording their lectures using digital voice recorders. The professor can then use the Dragon Naturally speaking program that came with the recorder to translate the spoken portion of the recorded lecture into text and upload both the audio file and text file to a Web site.

No matter which version of operating system or speech recognition software program is used, the person speaking into the microphone must annunciate words and punctuation clearly or mistakes will be made. Training sessions are still an integral part of the process in teaching the computer to recognize our particular speech patterns. Even taking these issues into account, computers have come a long way in recognizing the words we speak. While our personal computers have *not yet* attained the level of becoming **conversational computers** where they recognize what we say and are able to communicate with us based on the *understanding* of what we *mean*, they are coming a lot closer to that goal. Some of the issues related to making computers understand what we mean will be covered in the chapter on Artificial Intelligence.

10.6 Audio Media: Music

It is impossible to ignore the effect that digital computer technology has had on the world of music. It started with the music synthesizer/keyboard that put thousands of orchestra musicians out of work in the 1980s. The impact of the compact disc as a recording/playback device continued the digital computer revolution in the music world. And now with the Internet, digital delivery of recorded music directly to your computer is shaking up the music industry. These three examples illustrate the profound effect computers are having on music.

THE COMPUTER AND RECORDED MUSIC

In chapter 2, "Metamorphosis of Information," we discussed the process of putting sound into the computer. More formally, this was referred to as representing sound in a computer, and one of the major concepts discussed was that of digitizing sound. Once a sound is digitized, it is transformed into numbers and can easily be stored on a CD or some other binary storage device, or even kept on your computer's hard drive. Let's take a look at the basic CD and DVD technologies.

The **compact disc (CD)** is a binary storage medium made of a plastic disc shape and containing up to 640 million bytes of data. The disc is "played" by a special-purpose computer called a CD player that will re-create the original sound on an amplifier.

Compact Disc Technology   There are two common places to save the millions of binary numbers that are needed to record even a short piece of music. One storage place is the **compact disc (CD).** Why has this revolutionary form of music recording swept the consumer music field? It's because CDs don't wear out like records and magnetic tape. After the numbers are recorded, they don't change. The only thing that can affect the quality is scratching the surface of the disc so that the numbers can't be read. In addition, compact discs can be produced from a master disc very inexpensively by the thousands or millions.

A microscopic look at the surface of a compact disc would reveal tiny craters or indentations in the surface. An indentation represents a 1, and the lack of an indentation means 0. To retrieve the binary numbers from the disc, a laser beam is reflected off the surface. When the beam bounces off the rough area around a crater, not much light comes back and this means the compact disc player receives a 1. With no crater present, the flat surface of the disc allows the beam to bounce back full strength, indicating a 0. Figure 10.6.1 illustrates the process. The CD player collects 44,100 binary numbers per second from the disc on each of the stereo channels and then transmits the appropriate voltages to the amplifier.

Technically speaking, the CD player is a special-purpose computer: It manipulates binary numbers under a program's control. Granted, it is a very special-purpose computer. You can't use it for word processing. On the other hand, its special purpose is enjoyed by millions of music lovers everywhere.

This CD technology has gone even further with the availability of low-cost CD-ROM recording machines, which are special-purpose computers that will transfer the binary numbers to a disc by burning the holes for the 1s. This means you can create your own CDs.

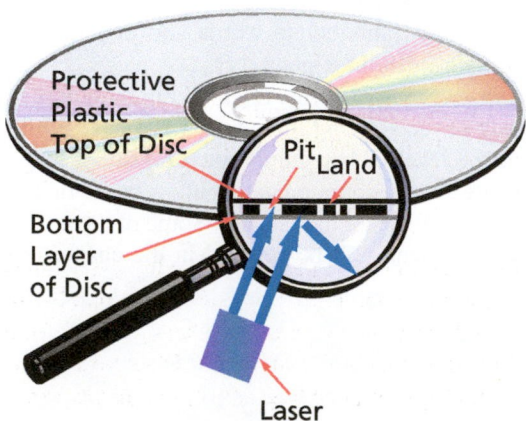

Figure 10.6.1

A schematic representation of a compact disc. The laser beam bounces off a crater and a flat land spot, indicating both a 1 or a 0.

Digital Versatile Disc (DVD)

The digital Versatile Disc (DVD) discussed in sections 3.6 and 10.4 has a lot more capacity than the CD format. From a commercial standpoint, audio recordings on DVD aren't as practical because they have too much capacity. In fact, a typical DVD using double layers on both sides could hold the equivalent of about 26 CDs. DVDs are technically similar to CDs, but with multiple layers. They are used mainly for digital video.

MP3 Compressed Music

The **file compression** technique called **MP3** is causing a revolution in the music recording/distribution industry. MP3 or MPEG Layer-3 is a standard defined by the Moving Picture Expert Group (MPEG). It compresses files using two techniques, one that discards information and, therefore, is called *lossy,* and one that shrinks the file using *lossless* techniques. In the lossy case, the standard takes advantage of human audio perception by essentially eliminating frequencies of sound we can't hear or that seem to be redundant. The masking of weaker sounds by strong sounds, for example, allows the elimination of the weaker sounds and the listener won't miss them. There are also several other effects that are too technical for this discussion. By throwing away information we are losing it; therefore, it is called lossy compression. The second technique consists of three schemes that are also too technical to discuss here. However, it should be mentioned that one of the schemes, Huffman coding, is a classic algorithm in computer science that is used for compression of all types of files.

Although MP3 was intended primarily for sending video over the Internet, the audio portion of the standard works quite well and has caused turmoil in the recording/distribution industry. This revolution is not because of the standard itself, but it is due to the files being compressed by a factor of about 11. This makes the recordings much easier to send over the Internet. Adding to this are programs that will find MP3 files for a particular piece of music you desire and facilitate downloading it.

> **File compression** is the process of making binary files smaller. This can be done without losing any information, which is *lossless compression.* Compression can also be done in a way that slight losses in information are acceptable, which is called *lossy compression.*

> The **MP3 (MPEG layer 3)** is an audio file compression technique that follows the standard adopted by Motion Picture Expert Group.

RECORDED AUDIO FORMS AND FORMATS

No one particular organizing force has mandated a standard for recorded audio. This means that there are many individual standards developed for special purposes or for specific computers.

Size and Quality of Sound Files

Sound files can be huge—often running to several megabytes in length. They can take several minutes to load on even a fast computer system. Although some types of sound files take less space than others, in general the smaller the file, the shorter the sound clip (in seconds) and the poorer the audio quality. Therefore, if you want to use a long piece of music on your Web page, you must sacrifice quality to keep the file down to a reasonable size. Here's an example: 16.5 seconds of music, recorded at acceptable quality, takes approximately 365 KB of space. High-quality sound takes up several times as much space. Low-quality takes less space but is often unsatisfactory, especially for music. Of course, using compression schemes will also make the files smaller, but then they must be decoded before being played.

Sound File Formats

Many Web viewers are confused by the several types of file formats that have been devised for storing digitized sound. To help understand this problem, it is useful to remember that most standards were developed for use with a specific computer platform. In Table 10.6.1 are a few popular sound file formats and the environments they originally ran on.

Hardware and Software Needs

Older computers and many Windows machines contain only low-quality speakers producing minimal sound. To play back Web sound with reasonable quality, these machines need a sound card and separate speakers. Some of the newer Pentium computers, designated "multimedia" machines, and most Macintosh computers come complete with a decent built-in sound system, needing only external speakers.

Table 10.6.1   *Common audio file formats.*

WAV	Originated with Windows 3.1
AU	Developed by SunAudio for UNIX systems
AIFF	Originated on the Macintosh
MPEG	Can be played on Windows, Macintosh, and UNIX systems
MP3	MPEG level 3, audio portion of video MPEG 3

To receive a sound file on the Web, it must be one that your browser can play on its own; otherwise special software must be added. Fortunately, the newer versions of popular browsers can play many of the standard file types using built-in utilities such as RealAudio's RealPlayer.

Despite these drawbacks, many Web pages can benefit from the addition of sound. A site describing different species of birds, for example, might include samples of bird songs. A musician or band would want a home site viewer to hear samples of their music. And an individual, like you, might want to greet visitors to your site in your own voice. Here are a few tips for effective use of sound on a Web site:

- If a sound clip is bigger than 500 KB, it's too big to use.
- Stick with good quality. CD and radio quality are acceptable; telephone quality and lower are not worth the time or effort.
- Stay with simplicity. Don't opt for stereo when mono does the job.
- Use standard sound file types whenever possible.
- Allow users to choose whether to listen to a sound.
- Use sound only when it is related to your page content: Gratuitous sound is considered by most viewers to be an intrusion.

PUZZLER HINT

Each of the compression schemes must have software to decompress and play the sound file. A browser would need to have the capability to play all of them, which isn't likely because this is too much software.

MIDI: A REVOLUTION IN MUSIC

One of the biggest changes in our musical recording and performance field is due to the musical communication standard that was created in 1982. Called **MIDI (Musical Instrument Digital Interface),** this standard makes possible communication of audio information between keyboards and drum pads, and from them to a computer-controlled mixer. The results are astounding and are a pinnacle in interactive multimedia.

The actual connection made between the computer and instruments is referred to as the **MIDI bus** because it behaves like an electronic expressway, 16 lanes wide. The bus carries electronic binary signals to instruments that are capable of decoding the signals and doing what is commanded. The 16 lanes refer to 16 channels, each of which can be dedicated to a particular instrument or to a group of instruments. The digital data for each channel travel over the MIDI cable so quickly that 65 separate 16-note chords could be played per second using all the attached MIDI instruments combined.

Each instrument connected to the MIDI bus usually has a very small, special-purpose internal computer with a built-in memory component. All MIDI instruments have three five-

The **MIDI bus** is the main communications channel for MIDI information that can consist of signals sent to as many as 16 different instruments or groups of instruments.

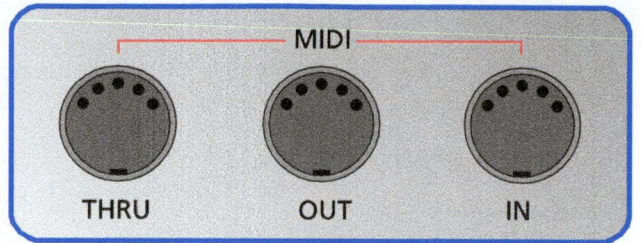

Figure 10.6.2

The three connectors necessary for a MIDI interface.

pronged connectors used to connect to the other MIDI instruments or computer via the MIDI bus. Figure 10.6.2 shows these three:

- **IN port.** Used to receive MIDI signals.
- **OUT port.** Used to send out MIDI signals.
- **THRU port.** Used to send MIDI signals obtained from the IN port on to other MIDI instruments.

Using MIDI Instruments

There are several ways to use a **MIDI instrument.** The simplest is to just use the instrument by itself. A MIDI synthesizer, for example, shown in Figure 10.6.3, needs only the connection to an amplifier with speakers and it can be played. Most synthesizers have a built-in amplifier and even speakers.

Using a MIDI instrument by itself doesn't fully utilize MIDI features. A slightly more complicated MIDI configuration would be to use one MIDI instrument as a master to a second MIDI instrument, called a **MIDI slave** instrument. In this configuration, the master not only can play its own notes, but it can also control the slave's notes. Therefore, only one musician is needed to play both instruments simultaneously, as shown in Figure 10.6.4. Note the MIDI drum is also a slave.

The **MIDI instrument** is a device that has the standard I/O port shown in Figure 10.6.2 and is controllable by the input signal coming over the MIDI bus.

Using a Sequencer

An even more effective configuration includes a MIDI **sequencer.** A sequencer can either be a computer with the proper sequencing software, or it can be a dedicated standalone sequencing device.

A sequencer can be thought of as a tapeless tape recorder. It records all the details of a musical sound (which keys are pressed, how long they are held down, how fast they are struck) and can play back exactly what was played by a human. However, most of its power comes from the fact that the recording can now be edited to change notes (that is, transpose), make tempo changes, and to modify just about everything including the type of sound (for example, change piano sound to that of a flute). A simple MIDI configuration including a synthesizer as master, a drum pad as slave, and a computer as sequencer is shown in Figure 10.6.5.

The MIDI **sequencer** is a device, usually a computer, that records and plays back MIDI signals.

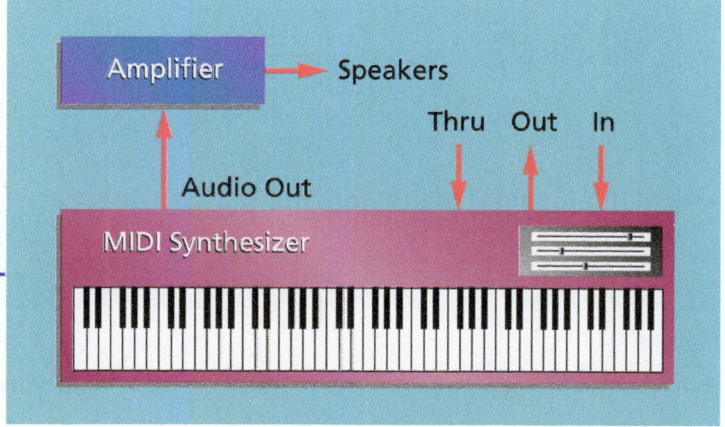

Figure 10.6.3

A MIDI synthesizer connected to an amplifier.

Figure 10.6.4

One way to exploit the benefits of MIDI is to set up a MIDI master/slave configuration.

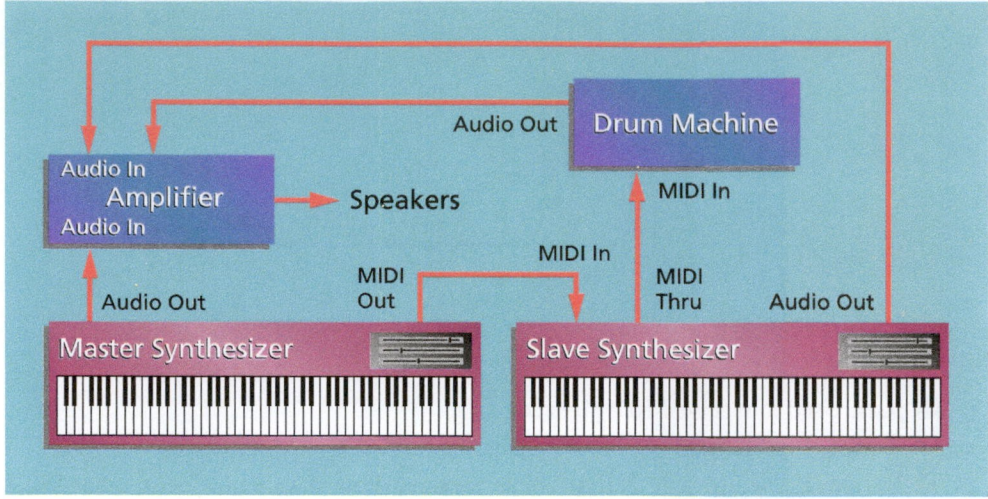

A **patch** is a MIDI-compatible binary description of a certain customized sound that the performer has prepared in advance. Most synthesizers have libraries of preset sounds stored in the memory of the synthesizer available on demand at any time during a performance.

To make the system more flexible, a general-purpose microcomputer with special software is most often used as the sequencer. This allows some very interesting possibilities. Most MIDI software allows the use of patches. **Patches** enable the musician to customize the sound that comes out of the musical MIDI system by feeding in binary directions for producing that particular sound. If one section of a performance needs a special sound, for example, the artist can create exactly the right sound in advance and store binary directions for producing it in the memory of the computer or synthesizer. Then the sound can be incorporated into a performance, when needed, as often as desired.

There is yet another very powerful use of a computer-type sequencer. Suppose you would like to produce background music for some of your home videos. Using a sequencer, you could play a MIDI piano on one of the channels of the MIDI system. Then while this is playing back, you could record with a second MIDI instrument on another channel along with the piano. The program that records these two instruments could then play both channels back together in perfect synchronization and enable you to play yet a third instrument along with the first two. At this point, you would have a musical background custom performed by a three-piece combo—you, yourself, and your alter ego. This could be continued until the total piece is done, incorporating, if you wish, the sounds of an entire orchestra.

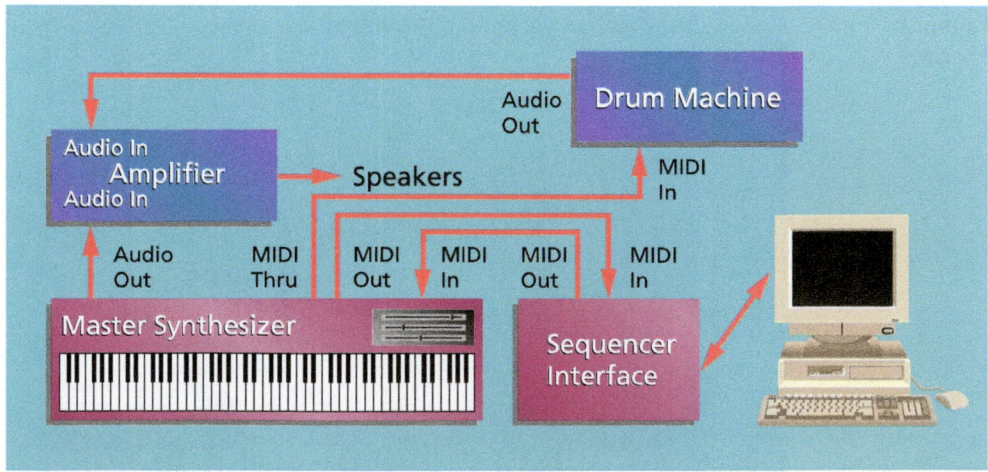

Figure 10.6.5

Another useful MIDI configuration is to attach the master and slave instruments to a computer, which then serves as a sequencer.

10.7 Software Applications: Internet Music and Audio

Downloading music and sound over the World Wide Web (WWW) is fun but possibly quite confusing. The issues involved are many and vary from ethics to marketing. The ethical issues deal mainly with September 2000 court rulings against using MP3s to copy music. In the marketing area there is a requirement that downloading be simple and automatic. These issues facing the neophyte are understood better by actually first experiencing the technology. We'll review three basic techniques for both downloading sound to your computer and listening to live audio over the WWW.

STREAMING AUDIO

The first means of downloading sound is similar to asking a radio disk jockey to play a song: You request a song, and the disk jockey plays it. You don't receive a copy of the song. Instead you receive a one-time playing of that song. Over the WWW, this technique is referred to as **streaming audio.** You make a request over the WWW by clicking on a button that sends a message to the Web site on whose home page the button is located, and then the Web site starts sending you the sound, which is immediately heard. You don't receive a copy of the sound. To experience this technique, your Web browser, such as Safari or Internet Explorer, must have the proper player software. If the browser doesn't already have the software capability to play the streaming file, then it is usually available in the form of a **plug-in.** In the WWW/audio world one of the most common plug-ins is by RealAudio and is called RealPlayer. In fact, many browsers have RealPlayer already installed. The basic concept of streaming audio is visualized in Figure 10.7.1.

SOUND FILES

Figure 10.7.2 illustrates a second technique to download sound over the WWW consists of sending a complete sound file, which can then be played. This technique is older than the streaming audio technique but has an advantage: It allows you to store the sound file on your computer. It doesn't need to maintain Internet communication to play, so once you have it on your computer you can play it at any time. The four most common types of sound files are:

- Wave format for Windows computers
- AIFF format for Macintosh

The **streaming audio** is an audio signal that is sent from a server in packets to the requesting computer. Each packet contains a part of the audio, which may be a recording or an actual audio event. The audio information in the packets is then played back in the order sent, starting soon after a few packets arrive but before all of them have been sent.

A **plug-in** is a piece of software that is added to your browser to give it a desired capability. Plug-ins are usually downloaded directly from the Web and automatically install themselves.

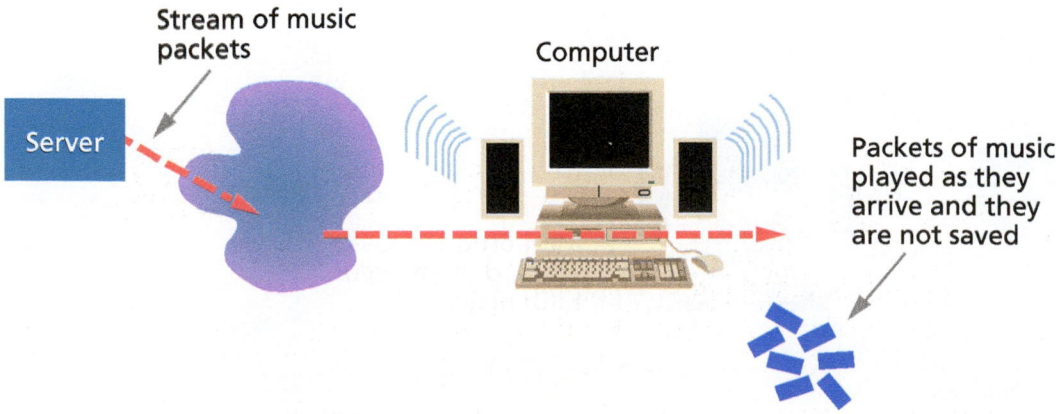

Figure 10.7.1

Streaming audio over the Internet.

Figure 10.7.2

Sending a file using FTP over the Internet.

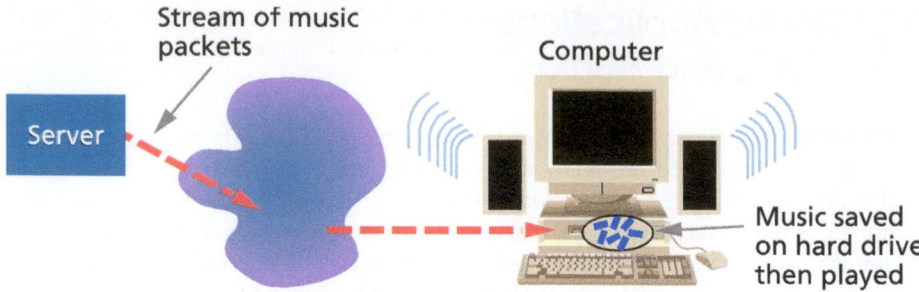

- AU format for Windows and Macintosh computers
- MP3 (MPEG level 3) for Windows and Macintosh computers

Wave, AIFF, and AU sound files are portable because they are recognizable by most audio applications. The MPEG format requires a player program. MP3 is the most recent format/compression scheme in use on the WWW today. It allows a 40-megabyte, 3-minute CD song to be compressed to about 3 megabytes and yet maintain close to CD quality.

MIDI FILES

The world of music performance has been changed forever by MIDI and music synthesizers. MIDI is a set of rules for sending sound information and the electronic specifications on hooking up MIDI instruments. It has led to another way of storing sound and music. However, unlike the forms of music mentioned previously, MIDI files don't contain the actual sounds. Instead they contain instructions on how to recreate up to 16 voices simultaneously. These voices may be the sound of a piano that has been previously stored and then played on command from the MIDI file. The major advantage of the MIDI file is that it is very small. The MIDI file can be played by a MIDI instrument or a MIDI player on a computer. If the MIDI player and associated sound-making hardware of the computer are of a high quality, then the MIDI file will also sound good. The MIDI files can be created by a performer on a MIDI instrument, in which case it is somewhat like a recording. The MIDI file can also be created by software that allows the creation of MIDI compositions. The important thing to remember is that a player program is needed to play the MIDI files on a computer. These are readily available on the Internet.

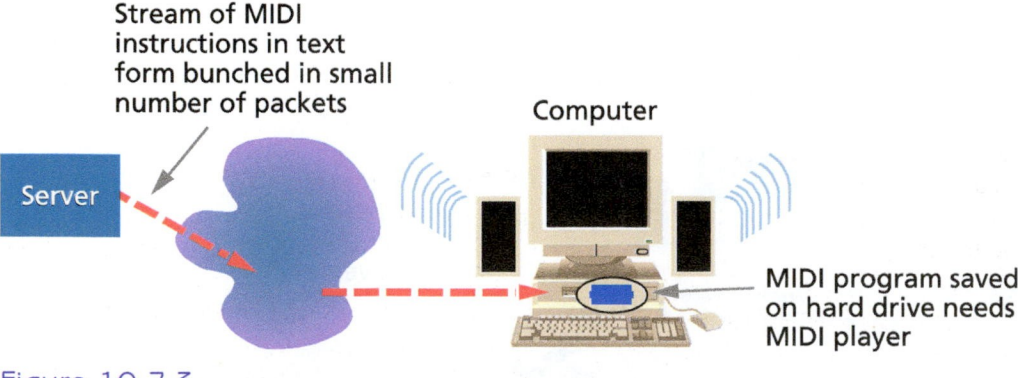

Figure 10.7.3

Sending MIDI audio over the Internet.

Figure 10.7.3 shows the process of playing a MIDI file that is part of a Web page. There are a lot of details about where the MIDI file gets temporarily stored and how it is played, but these are too technical for this discussion.

PUZZLER HINT

When considering audio for a Web site, there are several options. Unfortunately, they almost always require plug-ins, although standards will eventually solve this problem. The need for someone to obtain and install a plug-in makes the Web audio problematic.

Convergence

Convergence is the buzzword for the melding of telephones, fax machines, computers, audio, and television technologies into the foundation of the Internet. It is the goal of businesses, government, activists, engineers, and intellectuals interested in connecting every home and business to the Web of electronic services.

Computers can already double as fax machines. Televisions serve as information sources and services in hotels. And an alliance between two competing technologies for video on a disc in 1995 has produced DVD (digital video disc). With DVD a complete movie can be put onto a single disc. A hybrid entertainment center that combines the home computer, telephone, and television is converging just around the corner.

The new cutting-edge technology is actually eliminating the need for extra equipment such as fax machines. Currently, if you want to send a document to someone with an e-mail address, you don't need a fax; you attach the file and send it. There are also numerous fax software programs that allow one to send faxes straight from the computer desktop, or even from the beach with a portable computer via cellular phone.

A separate standalone fax machine is not the only piece of technology on its way to obsolescence. Others from the past, such as eight-track tapes or long-playing albums, are only a distant memory. Television sets are going digital, and it won't be long before the old analog home TV will also be a distant memory. In its place will be computer-controlled screen and entry device, which will take the place of the telephone, fax, TV, VCR, and other communication devices. The convergence of technologies will result in a new form of worldwide two-way communication.

Chapter Summary

10.1 What Is Multimedia?

Multimedia or multiple media is the term used to indicate the inclusion of two or more media such as static images, animation, video, audio, and other media of information. Interactive multimedia, where the participant can interact and control the media, is a revolutionary concept.

10.2 Visual Media: Manipulating Images

The static visual images common in our information age consist of digital files and can, therefore, be manipulated by the computer. These previously existing images could be satellite images, digitized photos, or any number of other visual forms. Digitizing might involve enhancing various aspects of the image by coloring them with colors that don't already exist: This is called false-coloring or pseudo-coloring. There is also a class of image processing done to restore images to some original form. Image enhancement is often used when the image has been distorted in some known way; the knowledge of how it was distorted may help restore it. Copyright ownership must be observed when obtaining and using previously created images.

10.3 Visual Media: Creating Images

Creating images is much different than working with existing images. The simplest would be two-dimensional line drawings. Then moving to three-dimensional line drawings on a flat surface, followed by covering the surfaces with textures, introduces many aspects studied by art students. To display these images on a computer, knowledge of how computers represent visual images is necessary. The object or vector graphic representation has many advantages over the bitmapped or raster graphics form, especially when manipulating 3D images and making changes.

10.4 Visual Media: Animation and Video

Many people have made animated cartoons by flipping a sequence of cards where the image changes from card to card. This is called traditional animation. The computer's power can be used to automate the process by creating some of the frames and filling in between frames. Add to that the computer's capability to color and duplicate and computer animation comes into its full glory with films such as *Toy Story*. Added to this common form are effects such as morphing that was used in older films such as the *Terminator* series. Finally, the computer can take original video, digitize it using a coding/decoding scheme called a codec, and play it back on a computer. All of this will change in the future with DVD and all-digital TV, which open the door for live streaming video.

10.5 Audio Media: Human Speech

Reproducing human speech is done in several ways. For a very limited number of words and phrases, playing back recordings of these words and phrases is acceptable. However, as the number of words becomes large, another scheme is necessary. By breaking human language into fundamental sounds called phonemes, reasonably good speech can be synthesized by stringing together the phonemes to make a word. Add to this the inflections and various tone changes and somewhat normal speech can be created. Recognizing speech is more difficult. Although it would be easier for a computer to recognize disjointed speech, it is not our natural way of communicating.

Computers are now much better at recognizing continuous speech but are not yet conversational computers.

10.6 Audio Media: Music

Music has existed for centuries and is very important to our culture. Using the computer to record, play back, and create music is often done. The result is digital music on a CD or on the computer's hard drive. There are other details of file formats such as the MP3 or MPEG layer 3 standard that are important. These various standards compress the audio using lossless or lossy techniques. The revolution that has changed the musical performance world is MIDI. MIDI instruments and recordings now have a major niche in the performance, recording, and playing of music.

10.7 Software Applications: Internet Music and Audio

There are essentially three ways to get music over the Internet. The first is called streaming audio and may require a plug-in on your browser. The quality is not up to CD standards, but it does give the feeling of being there. The second way is to download a complete digital file of the music. This entails the problems of formats, such as Wave, AIF, AU, and MP3. Once you have a copy, then you need a player on your computer that recognizes the format and will play it. The third possibility is MIDI files. These small files download very quickly, but the quality of sound will depend on your computer's musical synthesizing capability.

Key Terms

Key terms introduced in this chapter:

1. Bitmapped graphics, *281*
2. CD (compact disc), *300*
3. Codec, *291*
4. Continuous speech, *298*
5. Conversational computer, *299*
6. Disjointed speech, *297*
7. Duration, *295*
8. DVD, *291*
9. DVD-Video, *291*
10. DVD-ROM, *291*
11. Elision, *295*
12. False-coloring, *276*
13. File compression, *301*
14. GIF (Graphics Interchange Format), *275*
15. Hidden-line problem, *283*

16. Image enhancement, *276*
17. Image restoration, *276*
18. IN port, *303*
19. Inflection, *295*
20. Interactive multimedia, *274*
21. JPEG (Joint Photographic Experts Group), *275*
22. MIDI (Musical Instrument Digital Interface), *302*
23. MIDI bus, *302*
24. MIDI instrument, *303*
25. MIDI slave, *303*
26. MP3, *301*
27. MPEG-1, *291*
28. MPEG-2, *291*
29. M-JPEG, *291*

30. Object-oriented graphics, *281*
31. OUT port, *303*
32. Patches, *304*
33. Perspective, *284*
34. Phonemes, *294*
35. Pitch, *296*
36. Pixel, *275*
37. Plug-in, *305*
38. Pseudocoloring, *276*
39. Resonance, *296*
40. Sequencer, *303*
41. Shading, *285*
42. Speech recognition, *295*
43. Speech synthesis, *294*
44. Streaming audio, *305*

45. Streaming media, *293*

46. Texture, *286*

47. THRU port, *303*

48. TIFF (Tagged Image File Format), *275*

49. Video capture, *290*

50. Voiced sounds, *295*

51. Voiceless sounds, *295*

52. Voiceprint, *296*

Matching

Match the number of the key terms introduced in the chapter to the following statements.
Each term may be used once, more than once, or not at all.

1. ___ These are the small areas into which a picture is divided.

2. ___ This technique allows the live broadcast of audio.

3. ___ This technique refers to eliminating known flaws from a visual image.

4. ___ This technique refers to changing the normal visual colors of an image.

5. ___ This process entails processing a digital image to highlight particular aspects of an image.

6. ___ This type of line drawing is made up of individual pixels.

7. ___ This type of line drawing can be modified without changing each pixel individually.

8. ___ This concerns itself with how to hide lines that should not be seen from the direction of the observation.

9. ___ This technique is used to show that sides that are away from a light source are darker than those that are facing the light.

10. ___ This is the name given to the process of broadcasting visual and audio media over the Internet.

11. ___ This is the electronic production of sounds and sound patterns that closely resembles human speech.

12. ___ This allows computers to recognize and respond to human speech and sound patterns spoken aloud.

13. ___ These are the fundamental sounds of any given human language.

14. ___ This type of musical instrument can be controlled by a computer.

15. ___ This is the term given to the visible version of a stream of phonemes.

16. ___ The vibration of the vocal chords makes this type of sound.

17. ___ These sounds are characterized by the lack of vibration of the vocal chords.

18. ___ This quality of a human voice is determined by the thickness of the vocal chords.

19. ___ The size and shape of the cavities (chambers) determine this quality of a human voice in one's head.

20. ___ This storage medium allows the recording of music in the form of binary numbers.

True or False

Place either T or F on the line provided with each of the following statements. If a
statement is false, you should be able to explain what changes would make it true.

1. ___ Digitized pictures only have black and white pixels.

2. ___ Outlines depicted in maps (satellite images) are placed there by computer programs.

3. ___ Printed books store pixels differently than pictures displayed on TV screens.

4. ___ Color pictures require more memory to store than do black-and-white pictures.

5. ___ Satellites locate boundaries of countries by locating beacons on the ground.

6. ___ False-coloring means to change the colors of an image.

7. ___ Using the computer to alter a picture that was incomplete for some reason is an example of image restoration.

8. ___ In a bitmapped image, only the formula for the image needs to be changed.

9. ___ Graphic images stored as lines, curves, or geometric shapes are referred to as raster graphics.

10. ___ Perspective is a quality that makes a picture appear to be three-dimensional.

11. ___ Computer graphics can be used to reveal information that is not normally sensed by the human eye.

12. ___ Currently, computers can record only nonhuman audio sounds.

13. ___ The term given to the computer playback of recorded speech is called speech synthesis.

14. ___ The word *jar* is only made up of voiced sounds.

15. ___ The sound *sh* is voiceless.

16. ___ All human speech, no matter what language, can be represented on a voiceprint.

17. ___ The computer is more likely to recognize disjointed speech than continuous speech.

18. ___ MIDI instruments must be connected to a general-purpose computer before sound can be sent to amplifiers and speakers.

19. ___ Music played on a digital electronic musical instrument and stored within the computer cannot be altered from its original version.

20. ___ MP3 is the commonly used video compression scheme.

21. ___ Streaming audio is like listening to the radio in that you don't get a copy.

Multiple Choice

Answer the multiple-choice questions by selecting the best answer from the choices given.

1. This is the process that changes the color of an image.
   a. Image enhancement
   b. Image restoration
   c. False-coloring

2. This type of process is used to highlight or enhance particular aspects of an image.
   a. Image enhancement
   b. Image restoration
   c. False-coloring

3. This type of process eliminates flaws or degradations.
   a. Image enhancement
   b. Image restoration
   c. False-coloring

4. Another name for bitmapped graphics:
   a. Three-dimensional
   b. Object-oriented graphics
   c. Raster graphics
   d. Vector graphics

5. Another name for object-oriented graphics:
   a. Bitmapped graphics
   b. Three-dimensional
   c. Raster graphics
   d. Vector graphics

6. This type of line drawing would probably be used in more professional drawings, such as architectural drawings (may have more than one answer).
   a. Bitmapped graphics
   b. Object-oriented graphics
   c. Raster graphics
   d. Vector graphics

7. This piece of hardware's function is to copy an image and store it in the computer in its digital form.
   a. MP3 player
   b. Disk drive
   c. CD player
   d. Voice digitizer
   e. Scanner

8. This is a fundamental sound of any given spoken language.
   a. Phoneme
   b. Inflection
   c. Resonance
   d. Elision
   e. Pitch

9. This term is related to the frequency of sound.
   a. Phoneme
   b. Inflection
   c. Resonance
   d. Elision
   e. Pitch

10. From the group of sounds, choose the one that is voiced.
    a. *Sh*
    b. *Th*
    c. *F*
    d. *G*
    e. *S*

Exercises

1. Pick a rectangular object such as a desk and make a line drawing that shows all of the edges. Make a copy of it and then eliminate the lines that can't be seen in the actual object.

2. Which three Great Lakes can be seen in Figure 10.2.3?

3. Looking at Figure 10.2.5, list, if possible, at least two features taken from each of the five people shown in Figure 10.2.6.

4. Think of two or three legal or journalistic ramifications of the ability to produce composite images as shown in Figure 10.2.6.

5. Draw a simple straight-line image of a favorite object on a sheet of graph paper that is 50 squares high and 50 squares wide. When drawing the picture, make sure that the image can be traced without lifting the pencil. List the coordinates of each endpoint of the lines in the order determined by the tracing.

6. Draw your own animation using 3 ˘ 5 index cards. Make a flip book from these cards by stapling them together.

7. Explain why object-oriented curves look smoother than bitmapped curves.

8. What is the biggest advantage of object-oriented graphics over bitmapped graphics?

9. Identify several examples of words that sound the same but are entirely different in meaning (for example, *aisle* and *isle*).

10. Give several examples in which removing a suffix could lead to a totally different word (for example, *rating* should be *rate* and not *rat*).

11. Identify the phonemes in the words *shall, can't, mesmerize,* and *pumpkin.*

12. Write a list of all the talking computers you have encountered. Do you think they use digitized recordings of words and phrases, or do they build their own words from phonemes? Explain your opinion.

13. What issues are involved in having a cash register say, "Your total is $4,622.73."

14. List four difficulties of using phonemes for speech synthesis.

15. Explain the differences between disjointed and continuous speech.

16. Why is continuous speech difficult for computers to recognize?

17. What does a musical instrument need to connect to a MIDI system?

18. List three advantages of the digital instruments over their conventional counterparts.

19. List three advantages of the conventional instruments over their digital counterparts.

20. Pick a particular browser such as Netscape, Opera, or MS Explorer and check out its audio capabilities for streaming audio, acceptable audio file formats, and MIDI player. Write a paragraph or two describing what you found.

21. **PUZZLER** Make a list of the advantages and disadvantages of the three forms of audio on the Web: streaming audio, FTP files such as MP3, and MIDI.

Discussion Questions

1. You're a marketing person in the recording industry and would like to have a presence on the World Wide Web. As part of the marketing scheme, you would like to allow the potential buyer to hear your music products. Which of the three following techniques makes the most sense: streaming audio, file download, or MIDI? Discuss the pros and cons of all three.

2. The recording industry has been caught sleeping. In fact, the World Wide Web has become a place where pirated music is circulating with the use of the MP3 format/compression scheme. In most states it is allowable to make copies of your own CD in MP3 format. What's wrong with sharing these copies with friends? Putting yourself in the position of the artist and recording company, what is the effect of copying? Make comparisons between pirating music and pirating software.

3. How can you decide whether sound you hear from a cash register or other machine is synthesized speech using phonemes or a prerecorded digitized message?

Group Projects

1. A group of four students should select some event that interests them and create a brochure that announces the event. It should include text, photographs, and drawings. Each person should select one of the following assignments:

- Collect textual information
- Collect photographs (possibly take them)
- Do illustrative drawings for the design
- Be responsible for technical details (printing, digitizing, scanning)

All four should work out the design as a team. Suggestion: Use legal-size paper in horizontal orientation and then fold three times. This will give a trifolded brochure.

2. A group of four students form a design team to design an ideal audio world for the blind. The team should have at least one blind student. If that is not possible, however, each member of the team will consult with a blind person. The first step should be to design a survey form for the blind that includes questions such as the following:

- What is the most difficult problem you face?
- What ideas do you have for audio aids of any type?
- What are some annoying audio problems in your life?

The team should analyze the surveys and come up with a plan for a series of audio conventions and aids to assist the blind. These could include things such as sensors in public places that would activate a message or instructions. The sensor would be switched on by the blind person carrying a small transmitter in his or her shoe or cane. Keep in mind government allocation of the radio frequency spectrum for such devices.

Web Exercises

1. Try Out Streaming Audio: Use a browser with a RealPlayer or download a free RealPlayer from ReadAudio to visit Web sites that "broadcast" Real-Audio sound. Using a search engine with search words "realaudio" and "music" find some Web sites having RealAudio of interest to you.

Now, locate three Web sites that satisfy the following requirements:

- A Web site having sound clips (parts of a larger piece).
- A Web site that has a complete song performance.
- A Web site that has live audio such as a radio station, concert, and so on.

Record the URL and describe the Web site and the audio that you heard using a word-processing program.

2. Try Out Downloading Sound Files: Search the WWW for either Wave, AIFF, or AU sound files. Download at least two different types of sound. You can look under MP3, music, bird songs, and whale and dolphin sounds to find recordings. Now document the process using a word processor, presentation program, browser, or some application into which you can put both the sounds and text describing them.

You can get the downloaded sound into a file on your hard drive by selecting Save As under the file menu in the browser that just played the sound.

Go to http://mp3.com to download an appropriate MP3 player for your computer and then download some songs and sounds from the WWW. Combine at least one sample of MP3 in your presentation from the first part.

3. Try Out MIDI: Search the WWW for both a MIDI plug-in for your Web browser or a MIDI player that works independently of Web browsers. Download some MIDI files and try them out.

4. Go online and find a satellite image of New Orleans before Hurricane Katrina and a satellite image of New Orleans showing the flooding after Hurricane Katrina. A) Discuss how the two images differ. B) Discuss how satellite images can be used to warn us of other disasters such as this. (NOAA and NASA have these New Orleans satellite images available online for close inspection.)

Bibliography

Hacker, Scot. *MP3: The Definitive Guide.* Cambridge, MA: O'Reilly, 2000.

This book provides a complete guideline for developing and using MP3 files.

Keller, Eric, ed., *Fundamentals of Speech Synthesis and Speech Recognition: Basic Concepts, State of the Art and Future Challenges.* New York: John Wiley & Sons, 1994.

An expensive but very complete textbook for advanced undergraduate and graduate students.

Kientzle, Tim. *Internet File Formats.* Scotsdale, AZ: Coriolis Group Books, 1995.

A summary overview of file formats for sound, graphics, movies, and an overview of the subject of file compression.

Miano, John. *Condensed Image File Formats: JPEG, PNG, GIF, XBM, BMP.* Reading, MA: Addison-Wesley, 1999.

This is an easy-to-read study of the various file formats used in graphics and video storage.

Patterson, Jeff, and Melcher, R. *Audio on the Web.* Berkeley, CA: Peachpit Press, 1998.

This is a very readable and complete discussion of the audio file formats, streaming audio, and compression, and how they can be used on Web pages.

Penfold, R. A. *Advanced MIDI Users Guide.* New York: Cinzino, 1996.

An easy-to-read, complete discussion of MIDI and how it works. This book gives an intermediate-level technical view of MIDI.

Penfold, R. A. *Practical Midi Handbook.* New York: PC Pub, 1995.

An introduction to MIDI from a user's point of view. Very easy to read and understand.

Ratner, Peter. *3-D Human Modeling and Animation.* New York: John Wiley & Sons, 1998.

This book builds a bridge from traditional figure drawing, painting, and sculpture to the new field of creating and animating figures with electronic technology.

Watkinson, John. *MPEG-2.* Newton, MA: Focal Press, 1999.

This books explains the MPEG-2 format of storing video files and how it can best be used.

chapter 11

Databases: Controlling the Information Deluge

TimeLine

4000–1200 B.C.	Records of daily transactions are kept on tablets by the Sumerians, the first known civilization.
1801	Punched cards control the patterns of weaving in Joseph-Marie Jacquard's loom.
1896	The Tabulating Machine Company is established by Herman Hollerith.
1901	The keypunch machine first punches paper cards.
1931	A high school teacher, Reynold B. Johnson, first scores multiple-choice tests by sensing conductive pencil marks on answer sheets.
1967–1968	National Crime Information Center (NCIC) goes online with 95,000 pieces of information in five databases, handling 2 million transactions in its first year.
1971	All 50 states and Washington, DC, can access NCIC criminal data.
1980	The first database program for personal computers, dBase II, is developed by Wayne Ratliff.
1982	The computer is named "Man of the Year" by *Time* magazine.
1995	First Wiki site was created for the Portland Pattern Repository
1999	NCIC 2000 is launched, featuring terminals with scanners and digital cameras located in police cars for immediate access.
2003	Human Genome Project completes mapping of all 90,000 or so genes for massive database.
2012	Google completes digitizing 7 million books from the University of Michigan Library, and puts them on line.

Chapter Objectives

- Understand the implications of public access to the vast amount of data being generated daily.

- Understand the difference between data and information.

- Know the definition and uses of a computerized database.

- Identify several different methods for collecting data.

- Recognize several examples of remote electronic sensing.

- Appreciate the FBI fingerprint retrieval system as a highly organized database encompassing a large amount of data.

- Understand how statistics are used to analyze data in a database.

- Identify how sampling is used to choose data to be analyzed.

- Understand how samples can be skewed to give inaccurate results.

- Understand how false correlations can lead to erroneous conclusions.

- Identify the elements of a DBMS, from field to file.

- Identify several advantages of using a DBMS.

- Identify several disadvantages of using a DBMS.

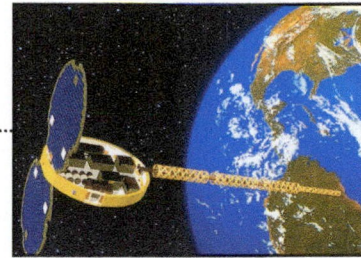

The Stock Market

Landmark Treasure Hunt

Later in this chapter you will find a satellite image of Washington, DC (Figure 11.2.4).

PUZZLER

Can you read the image well enough to identify some of our nation's most famous landmarks?

Study the image of Washington, DC, for a few moments. Resolution here is 30 meters per pixel, and a thin film of cloud makes the image a little hazy. Also, the image is falsely colored. Score 1 point for your answer to the following question:

Where is north?

Now give yourself three points for each of the following objects you can identify:

> The Lincoln Memorial
> The Reflecting Pool
> The Tidal Basin
> The Capitol
> The White House
> The Washington Monument
> Watergate Hotel
> The Jefferson Memorial
> The Smithsonian Institution
> The Pentagon
> Arlington National Cemetery

Compare points to see who in class was most successful.

11.1 Introduction: Information Overload

Have you ever wondered why the last third of the twentieth century was dubbed the beginning of the **Information Age**? Actually, there are two reasons:

1. We have been inundated with information: facts, figures, opinions, stories, pictures, records, and predictions—all carried forward with us into the twenty-first century.

2. The growing flood of information has been matched—even exceeded—by our growing dependence on it. Organized collections of information, called **databases,** have become essential in business, in government, and even in the mundane activities of our everyday lives.

The twenty-first century has continued both of these trends: the amount of available information and the uses we make of it increase exponentially. The accumulated knowledge of generations past, present, and future is overwhelming. How can we collect and store this knowledge, and how can we prepare it for effective use?

Until recently, most of our accumulation of information has been stored on paper. More than 15,000 different magazines, newspapers, and compact discs exist today. Figure 11.1.1 shows people scanning through some of them. All are sources of new information. In addition, experts estimate that Internet users create a terabyte of data *daily,* an amount equal to nearly 2.3 million 300-page books per day. We have amassed so much paper that we could circle the globe with it several times and still have some left over.

Fortunately, we no longer store the bulk of incoming information on paper. Computer technology provides many types of storage media that are more economical, longer-lasting, and easier to access. These include but are not limited to USB drives and hard disks, DVD discs, CD-ROM discs, and optical storage media. Before any storage medium is used, however, the data must be collected. We'll examine the role computers play performing three major tasks:

- Collecting data
- Retrieving data
- Analyzing data

To utilize information in any meaningful way, you must first gather it and organize it in a meaningful pattern. You must then be able to retrieve the information from storage efficiently and in a timely manner. Finally, you must be able to process the information and analyze it for content and impact.

Although the two words **data** and **information** are generally used interchangeably, the field of computing assigns to each a specific use. Computers process data; the resulting information is what people use. An accumulation of useful information can result in people making better decisions—personally, financially, or professionally. Before we can use infor-

---

For now, we'll define **database** as an organized collection of easily accessed information. A more complete definition appears on page 300.

A **datum** is a single idea or fact in raw form. **Data** is the plural form of datum. We use the plural form more frequently because facts and ideas seldom exist in isolation.

Information is data repackaged into a form we can understand and use. The repackaging may involve manipulating and organizing the data, analyzing their content, and producing usable results.

Figure 11.1.1

Books, magazines, CDs, and other media today fill our libraries with large amounts of information on any topic.

Mary Kate Denny/PhotoEdit

mation, however, we must first collect appropriate data and put them into a form the computer can read. The data then must be processed by the computer and stored in a manner that makes sense to people. Only then can we analyze the data and repackage them as information. It should be pointed out that one person's information may be data for someone else.

Sir Francis Bacon once said, "Knowledge is power." The computer puts an awesome amount of information and potential knowledge at our fingertips. Merely having access to masses of data, however, does not guarantee the power that Bacon envisioned. We need powerful tools to help manipulate data and make them usable. Today computer technology provides us with a broad range of analytic and reporting tools that help transform data into information that we can understand and use.

In order to include whatever data might someday be needed, a database must be very carefully designed. This is often done jointly by a database programmer and the users who will be working with the database. Together they must answer many questions before the database is established:

How can we efficiently collect large amounts of relevant data?

How can we reliably store these data for later use?

What media will we use to access the database?

How often will we need to access the data?

What format will we need the data in (text, numerical, visual)?

What security measures should we take to protect our data from unauthorized access and tampering?

What provisions should we provide for recovery from data disasters such as power failures, virus invasions, and potential data losses?

What types of reports will we need on a regular basis?

Can we design and build special-purpose reports on the fly?

Who is ultimately responsible for the content and accuracy of our database?

Over the years, human ingenuity has answered these and other database questions in many ways. Until the advent of the computer, we collected most data by hand, wrote or typed the data onto paper, and stored the records in file cabinets. As the data became more complex or numerous, we designed paper forms to make data collection easier and more accurate. Elaborate systems of filing evolved. One such system, for example, the **Dewey decimal system,** enabled the cataloging of books by subject matter. But even forms and filing systems could not keep up with the ever-growing flood of data needing collection and storage.

Now, let's examine the three major problems of information usage: collection, retrieval, and analysis.

11.2 The Technology for Data Collection

Collecting data is a task well known to all of us. Suppose, for example, that you wanted to find the best buy in a used automobile. You might collect your own data by finding newspaper ads about autos of interest and comparing their features and prices. Or, instead of collecting your own data, you may choose to purchase a copy of an already prepared paper database such as Consumer Guide's book, *The Complete Guide to Used Cars.* Whichever way you have collected your data, when you have enough, you can make a decision and select a car.

Either of these data collection methods would be satisfactory if all you needed were the price and reliability data for a single purchase. What would happen if you wanted automobile prices from all over the country for a project? Or, even more challenging, what if you wanted data from all over the world?

How would you, as a researcher, approach this data collection problem? You might collect the data manually by reading books or magazines. You might collect it from Web sites. You might even collect it from databases available at your school's library. Whichever way you collect data, at some point you'll have to organize it so that you can compare, analyze, and make decisions.

IN THE BEGINNING THERE WAS NOTHING

Early computers provided no means to collect data or to store it from one program execution to the next. You could, however, feed in accurate numerical data and produce accurate calculated results. Each piece of data needed for a particular calculation had to be input during the actual execution of the calculation program. Thus, the earliest forms of computer data were collected and stored on paper, outside the computer, and fed in only at the moment when they were needed by the computer's software.

MARK-SENSOR DATA COLLECTION SHEETS

One of the problems with the early types of data collection was that data had to be transcribed from question-and-answer forms to the cards before they could be used in the computer. What if the data could be collected in a form that the computer could read directly, without the necessity of transcription? That, of course, is the next important development: computer-readable **mark-sensor forms.**

To understand the impact of mark-sensor forms on the data collection and storage process, take a look at Figure 11.2.1 to see one of the world's most important and well-known data collection projects: the U.S. census.

A **mark-sensor form** is a sheet of paper used to collect responses to multiple-choice questions. The responder fills in small spaces indicating his or her answers to questions. A computer can then scan completed forms to read marks made on the form.

The usefulness of the computer in gathering data for the U.S. census is enormous. Needless to say, the mailings to more than 90 million households aren't addressed by hand! Database files of these addresses are stored in computer-readable form until the final list is ready. The mailed questionnaires are also in machine-readable form. This enables the person answering the questions to respond by filling in little printed boxes. Because the computer can sense or "read" which of the boxes have been filled in, the computer can process and store

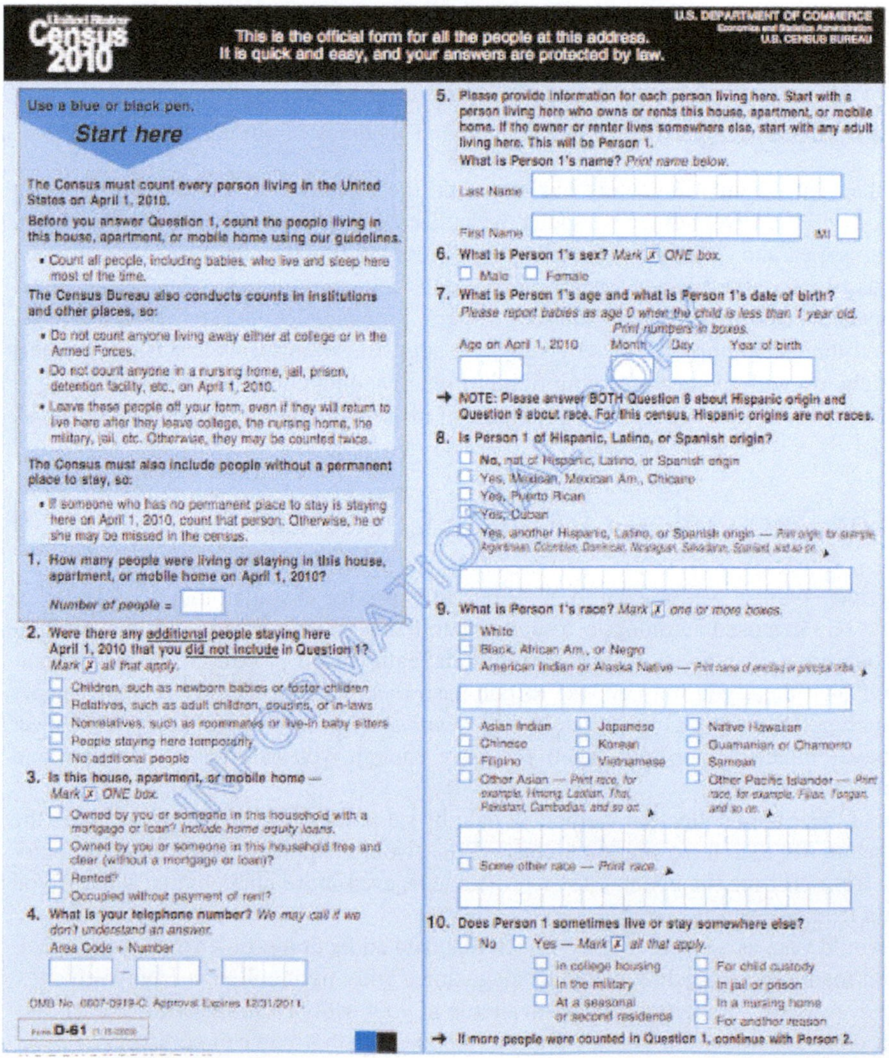
Census 2010

This is the official form for all the people at this address.
It is quick and easy, and your answers are protected by law.

U.S. DEPARTMENT OF COMMERCE
Economics and Statistics Administration
U.S. CENSUS BUREAU

Use a blue or black pen.

Start here

The Census must count every person living in the United States on April 1, 2010.

Before you answer Question 1, count the people living in this house, apartment, or mobile home using our guidelines.

- Count all people, including babies, who live and sleep here most of the time.

The Census Bureau also conducts counts in institutions and other places, so:

- Do not count anyone living away either at college or in the Armed Forces.
- Do not count anyone in a nursing home, jail, prison, detention facility, etc., on April 1, 2010.
- Leave these people off your form, even if they will return to live here after they leave college, the nursing home, the military, jail, etc. Otherwise, they may be counted twice.

The Census must also include people without a permanent place to stay, so:

- If someone who has no permanent place to stay is staying here on April 1, 2010, count that person. Otherwise, he or she may be missed in the census.

1. How many people were living or staying in this house, apartment, or mobile home on April 1, 2010?
   Number of people = ☐

2. Were there any additional people staying here April 1, 2010 that you did not include in Question 1? Mark ☒ all that apply.
   - ☐ Children, such as newborn babies or foster children
   - ☐ Relatives, such as adult children, cousins, or in-laws
   - ☐ Nonrelatives, such as roommates or live-in baby sitters
   - ☐ People staying here temporarily
   - ☐ No additional people

3. Is this house, apartment, or mobile home — Mark ☒ ONE box.
   - ☐ Owned by you or someone in this household with a mortgage or loan? Include home equity loans.
   - ☐ Owned by you or someone in this household free and clear (without a mortgage or loan)?
   - ☐ Rented?
   - ☐ Occupied without payment of rent?

4. What is your telephone number? We may call if we don't understand an answer.
   Area Code + Number
   ☐ - ☐ - ☐

OMB No. 0607-0919-C: Approval Expires 12/31/2011.

Form D-61

5. Please provide information for each person living here. Start with a person living here who owns or rents this house, apartment, or mobile home. If the owner or renter lives somewhere else, start with any adult living here. This will be Person 1.
   What is Person 1's name? Print name below.
   Last Name ☐
   First Name ☐ MI ☐

6. What is Person 1's sex? Mark ☒ ONE box.
   ☐ Male ☐ Female

7. What is Person 1's age and what is Person 1's date of birth? Please report babies as age 0 when the child is less than 1 year old.
   Print numbers in boxes.
   Age on April 1, 2010 ☐ Month ☐ Day ☐ Year of birth ☐

→ NOTE: Please answer BOTH Question 8 about Hispanic origin and Question 9 about race. For this census, Hispanic origins are not races.

8. Is Person 1 of Hispanic, Latino, or Spanish origin?
   - ☐ No, not of Hispanic, Latino, or Spanish origin
   - ☐ Yes, Mexican, Mexican Am., Chicano
   - ☐ Yes, Puerto Rican
   - ☐ Yes, Cuban
   - ☐ Yes, another Hispanic, Latino, or Spanish origin —

9. What is Person 1's race? Mark ☒ one or more boxes.
   - ☐ White
   - ☐ Black, African Am., or Negro
   - ☐ American Indian or Alaska Native —
   - ☐ Asian Indian ☐ Japanese ☐ Native Hawaiian
   - ☐ Chinese ☐ Korean ☐ Guamanian or Chamorro
   - ☐ Filipino ☐ Vietnamese ☐ Samoan
   - ☐ Other Asian — Print race, for example, Hmong, Laotian, Thai, Pakistani, Cambodian, and so on.
   - ☐ Other Pacific Islander — Print race, for example, Fijian, Tongan, and so on.
   - ☐ Some other race — Print race.

10. Does Person 1 sometimes live or stay somewhere else?
    ☐ No ☐ Yes — Mark ☒ all that apply.
    - ☐ In college housing ☐ For child custody
    - ☐ In the military ☐ In jail or prison
    - ☐ At a seasonal or second residence ☐ In a nursing home
    - ☐ For another reason

→ If more people were counted in Question 1, continue with Person 2.

Courtesy of the U.S. Census Bureau

Figure 11.2.1

Sample of the mark-sensor form used to collect data during the 2010 U.S. census.

almost all the responses. Transcription is needed only if the responder has used the wrong type of writing implement, filled in too many boxes, or damaged the form in some way.

REMOTE ELECTRONIC DATA SENSING

The U.S. census is certainly a very large data collection task, but in comparison to other types of projects, the amount of data collected is very small. For example, some satellites circling the globe collect millions of times more data in just one day than in an entire 10-year census! How can that be possible? How can so great a volume of data be collected in such a short period of

Collecting Data from Earth's Surface: A Satellite Update

Increased interest in geographic information and mapping has led to a frenzy of activity in designing and developing satellites equipped for remote data sensing. The results are sharper images than ever before at higher resolutions. Here is a short list of data imaging satellites:

- **Landsat 7**—Launched on April 15, 1999, Landsat 7 can now produce true-color or false-colored images with a resolution of only 15 meters per pixel. Using image acquisition software called ETM (Enhanced Thematic Mapper), Landsat 7 now produces incredibly clear images with sharply decreased signal noise.

- **Terra**—The first of NASA's new Earth Observing System (EOS) satellites was launched during April 2000. Terra circles Earth with a polar orbit, carrying a payload of five sensors to study Earth's atmosphere, oceans, life, and radiant energy.

- **IKONOS**—Space Imaging, of Denver, Colorado, launched IKONOS, the world's first commercial, high-resolution imaging satellite on September 24, 1999. IKONOS is in a sun-synchronous, circular low-Earth orbit. The black-and-white image of Montreal is evidence of the high-quality images IKONOS captures.

- **SRTM**—The Shuttle Radar Topography Mission was launched February 11, 2000. Its 11-day mission was to collect data resulting in the most accurate and complete topographical map of Earth's surface ever assembled. Each orbit collects data from a 240-kilometer-wide swath of Earth's surface. Images generated from these data have an absolute horizontal accuracy of 20 meters and a vertical accuracy of 16 meters.

- **NEMO**—Launched early in June 2000, NEMO was developed by STDC (Space Technology Development Corporation) in cooperation with the U.S. Navy. Much of the work done on the satellite was completed in Washington, DC, at the Naval Research Laboratory. Imagery data collected by NEMO will be used to study the coastal regions of the world's oceans.

- **EROS**—The first of Israel's Earth Observation Satellites (EROS) was launched late in the first quarter of 2000. It orbits Earth at an altitude of 408 km, completing one orbit in about 90 minutes. The resolution of the imagery acquired by EROS is a spectacular 1 meter.

Spacing Imaging LLC

This image of Montreal shows 1-meter resolution, giving clear, recognizable images of highways, an amusement park, and passenger vehicles.

Tech Talk

Remote electronic data sensing is a method of collecting information by electronic means without the direct intervention of a human. Communication between computer systems on earth and orbiting satellites is an example of this type of data collection.

time? The answer is that the satellite data are collected via **remote electronic sensing**, a method that doesn't directly involve human intervention. We will look now at two satellites that gather data several hundred miles above Earth and then send it to Earth via radio.

PUZZLER HINT

Sometimes finding landmarks is not as easy as it should be. For one thing, satellite images are not marked with the tourist signs we depend on when visiting a famous city. Another problem is we seldom see things from a bird's-eye view, very far up.

Help yourself by finding a good tourist map of Washington, DC, and its landmarks. A map that maintains relative scale of distances is best. Then check your compass points. Be sure your map is oriented in the same direction as the satellite image. Find any landmarks you missed earlier by comparing the map and the image. Give yourself only two points for landmarks you needed the map to find.

The satellite called Landsat 7 was launched on April 15, 1999. Landsat 7 can sense an object as small as 15 meters square from 500 miles above Earth's surface and sometimes can do even better. Figure 11.2.2 shows a color-enhanced image captured by Landsat 7 in May 1999. In it you can see a close-up photo of Washington, DC. The resolution on this photo is one meter. Although the day seems to have been a bit hazy, many familiar features of Washington are clearly recognizable. Images like this one are used primarily in geographic mapping, land use analysis, and population density studies.

The Hubble Space Telescope was deployed into orbit from the space shuttle in 1994. After several repairs and adjustments, it began transmitting high-quality data about outer space. The tremendous amount of astronomical data gathered by the Hubble Space Telescope is sent back to Earth at a rate of 85 million bytes per second (that is, 85 MB). The images it provides can be retransmitted to scientists all over the world.

Taking and sending satellite images from space is not the only example of data collection using remote electronic data sensing. Satellite systems are also being used to collect data in other ways as well. For example, transport companies are using global positioning systems (GPS) in their vehicles to track and record the speed of each vehicle in the fleet as

Figure 11.2.2

Satellite image of Washington, DC, captured by Landsat 7.

EROS Data Center, U.S. Geological Survey

well as where each vehicle is located at any given time. Also, cell phones have GPS chips in them. In case of emergency, a person only needs to dial 911. The emergency operator answering the call will be able to identify and locate the cell phone. In another example, radio-frequency identification (RFID) chips can be built into monitoring devices and have been used in conjunction with GPS to locate children, adults with dementia, or finding lost dogs.

BAR CODES

The bar code is another data collection innovation made possible by the magic of computers. A **bar code** is a series of short black vertical lines, some thick and some thin, that can be scanned or "read" by a computer input device called a **bar code reader.**

To understand the use of this method of data collection, let's look at the problem of inventory control in a large retail department store. Such a store may have many departments, including housewares, hardware, men's clothing, and toys. And each department may carry several thousands of different items in a variety of colors, sizes, and prices.

Before any of these thousands of items is placed on the shelf for sale, certain pieces of information such as brand name, price, size, color, and item number are all recorded in a computer database. Each item is then assigned a unique bar code. The bar code is printed on labels and affixed to the appropriate items. Whenever one of the labels is scanned with a bar code reader, as shown in Figure 11.2.3, the computer is able to match the item with its information.

When you select an item and bring it to the checkout line, the cashier uses a bar code reader to scan the data on the bar code label. Immediately, the price of the item appears in the cash register's window. The item's name and price are printed on the receipt tape, along with the quantity you have purchased and any applicable discount. In the computer's memory, the quantity of the item you bought is deducted from the number on hand. Thus, an accurate inventory count is maintained for stock replenishing purposes.

In addition to the major advantage of accurate inventory control, bar coding provides several smaller but important fringe benefits. Because the item's price is stored in the computer and accessed by bar code, the cashier does not have to type it in. Therefore, fewer errors can be attributed to inaccurate price entry. Also, because the price is in the computer rather than in the bar code, changes in pricing do not require changes in labeling. The new price of any item is entered into the computer. When its bar code is scanned, the new price is sent to the cash register window and the receipt tape.

A **bar code** is a unique combination of thick and thin printed bars that together identify a specific item in a merchant's inventory.

A **bar code reader** is an instrument used to scan a bar code and enter it into the computer. The computer then can access information such as description, price, size, color, and so on and use it to complete a transaction.

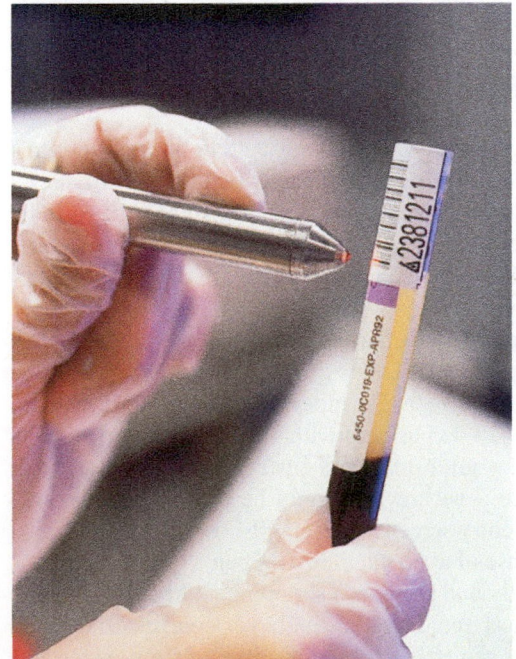

Figure 11.2.3

A handheld bar code reader is used to scan the code of a specific item.

David Polack/The Stock Market

DATA PROBE TOOLS

The collection of data electronically, without the error-prone intervention of humans, has extended into several fields in addition to sales, satellites, and census data. Meter reading is a good example.

The electric company places a meter on property to measure the actual amount of power used by each customer. A meter reader then comes around once a month to copy the numbers from the meters in his or her territory. The numbers collected by the meter reader determine how much money a particular customer will have to pay.

As population densities grew, especially in urban areas, and as wages for meter readers rose, utility companies found that they were unable to read every meter every month, and that the cost of each meter reading was too expensive. They also experienced a high number of reading/recording errors made by the human meter readers. So they looked for a cheaper, more accurate way to collect power-usage figures.

A **data probe** is an instrument that can be inserted into a utilities meter to read usage figures for that utility.

The solution they found was the data probe. A **data probe** is a keylike instrument that, when inserted into a power-usage meter, will electronically read and record the meter location and usage numbers into a computer. Because the human inserting the key does not have to see or write down the numbers, he or she spends less time at each meter, has fewer opportunities for error, and can visit many more meters in a day. This solved all three problems involving cost and accuracy of readings and allowed power companies to provide a higher level of service than was possible before.

VOICE RECOGNITION DATA ENTRY

This type of computerized data collection methodology is regularly used by regional salespersons and others who travel but must maintain accurate records and constant contact with databanks at a home office. **Voice recognition data entry** enables people to collect and record data merely by speaking into the microphone of a portable terminal. The receiving computer accepts the voice transmission and transcribes it into a form the computer can store.

Let's examine the case of a traveling salesperson using voice data entry. After spending a lengthy amount of time examining samples and catalogs, the client is ready to place an order. The salesperson sets up a portable terminal and enters into it the date, time, and customer name. As the client indicates each item and quantity, the salesperson speaks the item number and quantity into a small built-in microphone. When the order is complete, the salesperson types in a brief code. A printer attached to the laptop prints out an invoice, complete with price extensions, discounts if applicable, and total. The salesperson gives the invoice to the client and shuts down the laptop.

ONLINE INTERACTIVE DATA ENTRY

The last type of data entry methodology we'll discuss enables new data to be entered into a database directly from a Web browser screen. In this methodology, a company provides a user with an on-screen form, usually in a **secure environment.** The user fills in the form by typing data into a series of text boxes. When the form is completed, the user clicks on a Submit button. Data on the form are then added to the company's database. No further intervention by either the company or the user is needed.

A **secure environment,** in Internet terms, is a Web site that protects the security of the data being entered or displayed and the privacy of the user to whom the data belong.

The most common uses of interactive data entry occur in electronic commerce. Orders are taken, payment arrangements made, shipping instructions given, and confirmations sent, all using data entered and queried from an online screen. Consider a typical business transaction on 1-800-flowers, an online flower shop. To do business with 1-800-flowers, customers must first register, entering a username, password, e-mail and surface mail addresses, and credit card information. The registration form is secure—it cannot be read by others while data are in transit. Figure 11.2.4 shows a data entry screen at the 1-800-flowers.com Web site.

Registered customers can query a database of available items. When a desirable item is found, the buyer marks that item electronically and continues shopping. When all items are selected, an order form appears on the browser screen. After the buyer confirms the order, shipping information is requested. The buyer can either fill out a shipping form or retrieve information from a list of previously stored recipients.

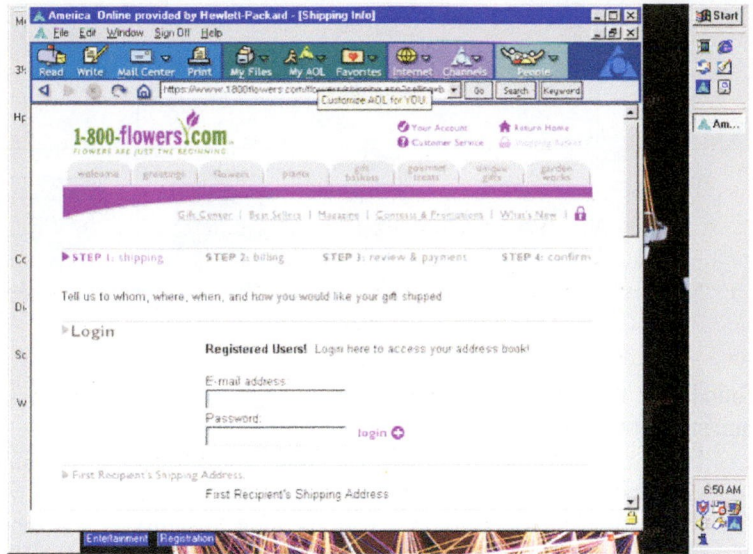

www.1800Flowers.com

Payment instructions are retrieved from the buyer's profile data and displayed on the screen. The buyer may either verify the payment methodology or modify it. Once payment methods are verified, the transaction is complete and is entered into a transaction file with a unique confirmation number. Later if the buyer has questions about the transaction, querying the database using the confirmation number retrieves the desired information.

11.3 Retrieving Data

Retrieving data after they have been stored is as complex a problem as collecting those data in the first place. Before computers came along, most data were stored on paper, of course, in file drawers and filing cabinets. Effective retrieval of those data depended on how well the files were organized. If the papers stored in the files were alphabetized or placed in some other logical order, retrieval could be simple and efficient. If the files were stored in random order, the retrieval could be agonizingly frustrating.

Similarly, computer data retrieval also depends on careful organization. In fact, organization of data is the single most important task of information retrieval. The FBI fingerprint database provides an interesting example of well-designed data organization and retrieval.

FBI FINGERPRINT PROCESSING: A STUDY IN DATA RETRIEVAL

Often our society demanded an absolute identification of certain individuals, whether for criminal or for security reasons. Because each person has unique fingerprints that do not change throughout life, the fingerprint has become indispensable as an identification aid to law enforcement and security agencies. Let's examine the collection, storage, and retrieval of fingerprint information. But first, a quick look at the history will help understand how the computer has revolutionized this process.

Historical Handling of Fingerprint Data
At its National Criminal Information Center (NCIC) near Washington, DC, the FBI maintained a paper database of over 270 million sets of fingerprints. This was before the 1970s.

Thousands of times daily, at locations across the country, a police officer booked a suspect, or a person applied for a position requiring security clearance. In either case, the person's fingerprints were taken. This was done by inking the subject's fingertips and then applying them, one finger at a time, to the collection card shown in Figure 11.3.1. Data concerning the person's name and other information are also entered onto the card. Completed cards were then sent to the FBI. One of the bureau's hundreds of expert fingerprint examiners would determine the print's **Henry classification** and then file it in the proper place.

The actual retrieval process involved taking the subject's full set of fingerprints and attempting to find a match with those already on file in the huge database. If a match was

The **Henry classification** system classifies fingerprints according to the patterns of ridges evident in the prints. The Henry system includes six major categories, each with several subsets. In all, the prints are organized into 1,024 different groups and filed accordingly.

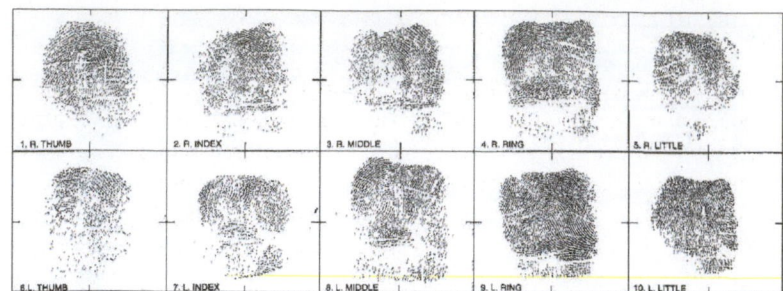

Figure 11.3.1

A typical fingerprint collection card.

found then the information on the cards was compared. The process was time consuming and subject to interpretations. This affected the search process.

In the early 1980s a computerized system, still based on the Henry classification, was implemented by many states and larger municipalities. This system was referred to as AFIS Matching (Automatic Fingerprint Identification System). It was thought that keeping the Henry system classifications was an advantage. Unfortunately, this still required many human interactions with the classification process, even though the computer was automatically scanning the fingerprints. Meanwhile, the Department of Justice and FBI continued to employ a manual fingerprint storage and retrieval system, even though by 1995 all states were using AFIS.

It was clear that the Henry-based AFIS system was an improvement over purely manual systems, but it just didn't fit well with computerization. This was mainly due to the Henry system's extensive and convoluted definitions of finger patterns that were extremely difficult to translate to the types of measurements that the computer was capable of doing. In addition, a technician was still required to examine the fingerprints before storing them on AFIS. More importantly, all ten fingerprints were needed to use the system. So when only one or two fingerprints were found the database couldn't be searched for matching prints.

These problems compelled the FBI to develop IAFIS (Integrated AFIS). By 1999 IAFIS was released and was a fully automated system. The new system had no connection to the Henry system of classification, and instead used pattern types that are based on ridge flow direction of the individual fingerprints. Each fingerprint pattern would yield a unique code. This means the complete database could be searched for a single matching fingerprint code. The IAFIS database is a huge flat file of fingerprint records, and searches of the database for matches are done primarily based on ridgeline counting.

In the past, using only full sets of fingerprints, it took days or weeks to search for a match in the manual database. Now with IAFIS matching time is less than two minutes, and the system has the capability of searching for a single finger's print, which is commonly referred to as a latent fingerprint. With the proper equipment this process can take place from a police patrol car's portable computer.

The FBI fingerprint retrieval system is just one of many examples of very complicated computerized information retrieval systems. All depend for speed and accuracy on effective organization of stored data. Other retrieval systems that might be of interest include the Library of Congress Catalog and the information retrieval system used by the Congress and by the executive branch of the U.S. government. Many articles regarding these two examples have been published.

VISUALIZATION OF INFORMATION FROM DATABASES

In section 11.2, many of the images revealed information that was not normally sensed by the human eye. In particular, the false-coloring of satellite images revealed information that couldn't be understood in any other way, especially if it were presented as a series of millions of numbers. This idea of taking any form of information and making it into a picture is called **visualization of information.** It is one of the fastest-growing areas in computer science. Whether it is blood flow in the heart, turbulence of a jet engine, or even stock market fluctuations, all can be visualized. Let's examine some interesting but simple examples.

Visualization of information uses many different techniques to transform any form of data into a visual image.

Biometrics: The New Wave of Identification

We live in a strange new world, where technology is increasingly reducing the amount of human interaction needed to produce goods, provide services, or communicate with our fellow beings. Where once we knew and recognized the people with whom we did business and shared ideas and social interaction, today they are strangers touched fleetingly over the Internet, never seen, never known, never even identified. Who are they? Are they honest? Reliable? Dangerous? Do they pose threats to our well-being? To our lives? To our children? Can they be trusted?

In such a world, individual identity verification takes on vital importance. Photographs, signatures, and other documents that traditionally serve as identification are no longer effective. We need identifiers that are unique and bound to the individual and that can be easily checked through repeatable, automated processes. Such identifiers exist and are called *biometrics*.

Although biometric technologies differ, their verification processes are similar. The person to be identified submits to a digital scan. The scan is then compared to a previously registered sample either stored in an electronic database or carried with the person as a token. An accurate match verifies the person's identity.

Here are some of the biometrics currently in use:

- Fingerprints—extensively used both as a crime fighting tool and as a means of identity verification of security officers.

- Hand geometry—reads the outline of the hand rather than fingerprints. Its best accuracy is achieved when the number of registered samples is small.

- Facial recognition—Encompasses several technologies: video or photo imaging, thermography (reading of the heat pattern emitted around the eyes and cheeks), and scanning the head's dimensions. Currently used at border crossings.

- Iris recognition—Video images are digitally processed and compared according to light and dark patterns in the iris itself. Inconspicuous and harmless, infrared iris scanners are being tested for use in automatic teller machines.

- Retinal scan—More intrusive than iris recognition, these require close-up infrared scanning through the pupil of the eye. The technique is used at some sensitive government installations.

- Active signature recognition—An electronic pad "reads" the speed, pressure, and direction of the writer's strokes, making flawless electronic hard-copy forgeries useless.

- Voice recognition—extends biometric identification and surveillance to the telephone. Early applications include home-detention monitoring and password-style security screening.

- DNA matching—Most trumpeted of all biometrics, DNA matching is now considered infallible. Current practice requires comparing live samples to a database of DNA profiles of approximately 600,000 known sex offenders.

Population Growth   One such interesting example involves the display of the population growth of the United States over a period of years. It is easy to read about how the West was settled and how the major population centers grew, but the computer drawings shown in Figure 11.3.2 give the information to the viewer more quickly and with greater understanding. The mountain-like spikes represent population density; the higher peaks represent greater population. In 1870, the effect of the Mississippi River on the population shift westward is striking. Except for the West Coast, which was accessible by water, all the population seems to end at this great river, which acted as a barrier. Looking ahead in time, the 1920 through 1960 illustrations show a lack of population where the Rocky Mountains prevail.

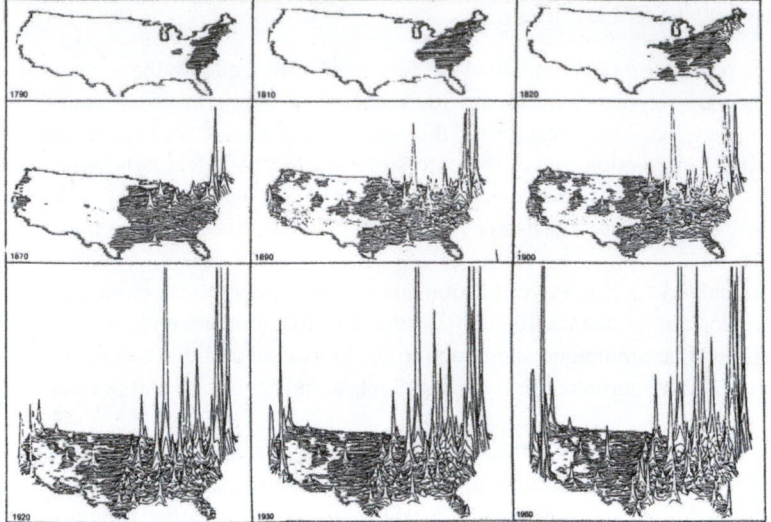

The Laboratory for Computer Graphics and Spatial Analysis at Harvard University

Another interesting feature is found in Figure 11.3.3, where the heavily populated northeastern United States is quite evident. Compare this region with Florida and California. Does this graphic image give you a different perspective? The northeastern U.S. population concentration is quite impressive.

The last image of the United States in Figure 11.3.4, shows a snapshot of an interactive map that accompanied an article by Nancy Gibbs that appeared in October 2006 on the Times.com Web site. A visual analysis of the map from 1979 shows some details. With further investigation online, actual census data from the beginning of 1980 confirms that the three most populated city areas were New York at 7,071,639, followed by Chicago at 3,005,072, and Los Angeles as third with 2,966,850. The map from October 2006 gives the actual numerical values without needing to do further research. By hovering the cursor over the map a balloon appears with the population details. From the 2006 map, we can determine that the three largest cities are New York with 18,747,300, followed by Los Angeles at 12,923,500, and Chicago coming in third at 9,443,400. The visual information derived from these maps is truly impressive!

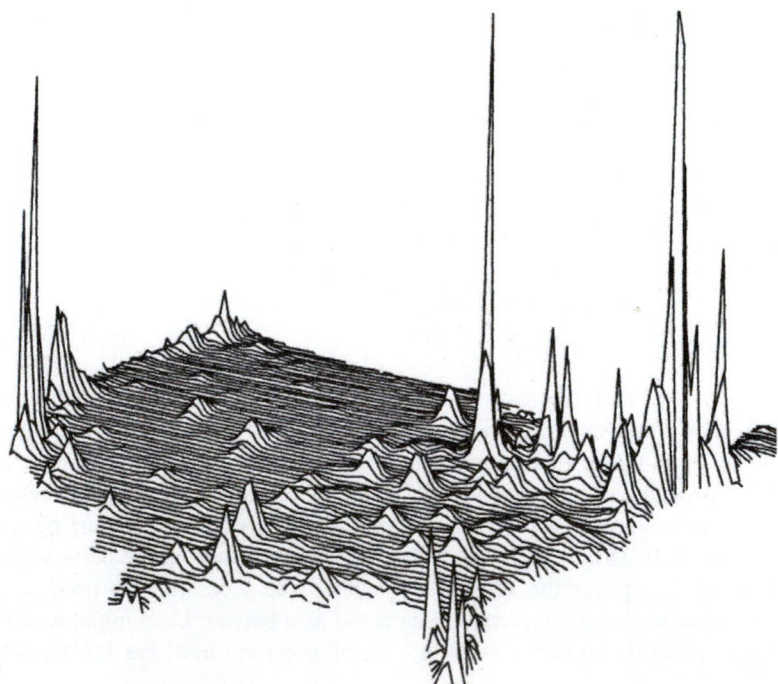

The Laboratory for Computer Graphics and Speech

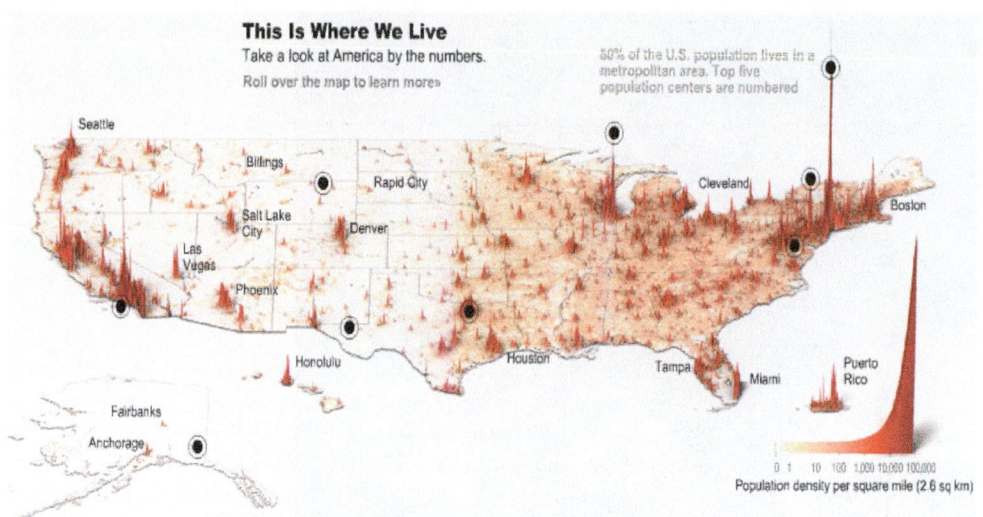

Time Graphic by Joe Lertola, Copyright 2006 Time Inc.

Figure 11.3.4

Population densities in the United States in 2006.

Knee Noises   Another interesting example of how three-dimensional line drawings can be used to display information that is otherwise almost impossible to see comes from the medical field. It involves the visual representation of knee noises for use in diagnosing and treating arthritis and other joint disorders. The diagnostic value of the noises made by the moving knee was first recognized in 1880. Unfortunately, the information obtained using a stethoscope was very difficult to interpret, especially if the doctor had to remember how the knee sounded from one week to the next. Add to this the problem of extraneous noise from such sources as skin friction, hand tremor, or snapping tendons. Indeed, the noises of interest were difficult to hear and discriminate. By using a sophisticated electronic system that canceled out the unwanted noises, researchers were able to isolate the information of interest.

There still remained the problem of recording the information in an easy-to-interpret form. This problem was solved using a computer program, which analyzes the digitized sound information and produces three-dimensional plots of the information. Figure 11.3.5(a) illustrates the mountain-like plots for a normal knee. Figure 11.3.5(b) shows a rheumatoid knee. As the patient bends the knee over a period of 3 seconds (one extension and one flexion), the illustrated data give the frequency of the noise, the position of the knee,

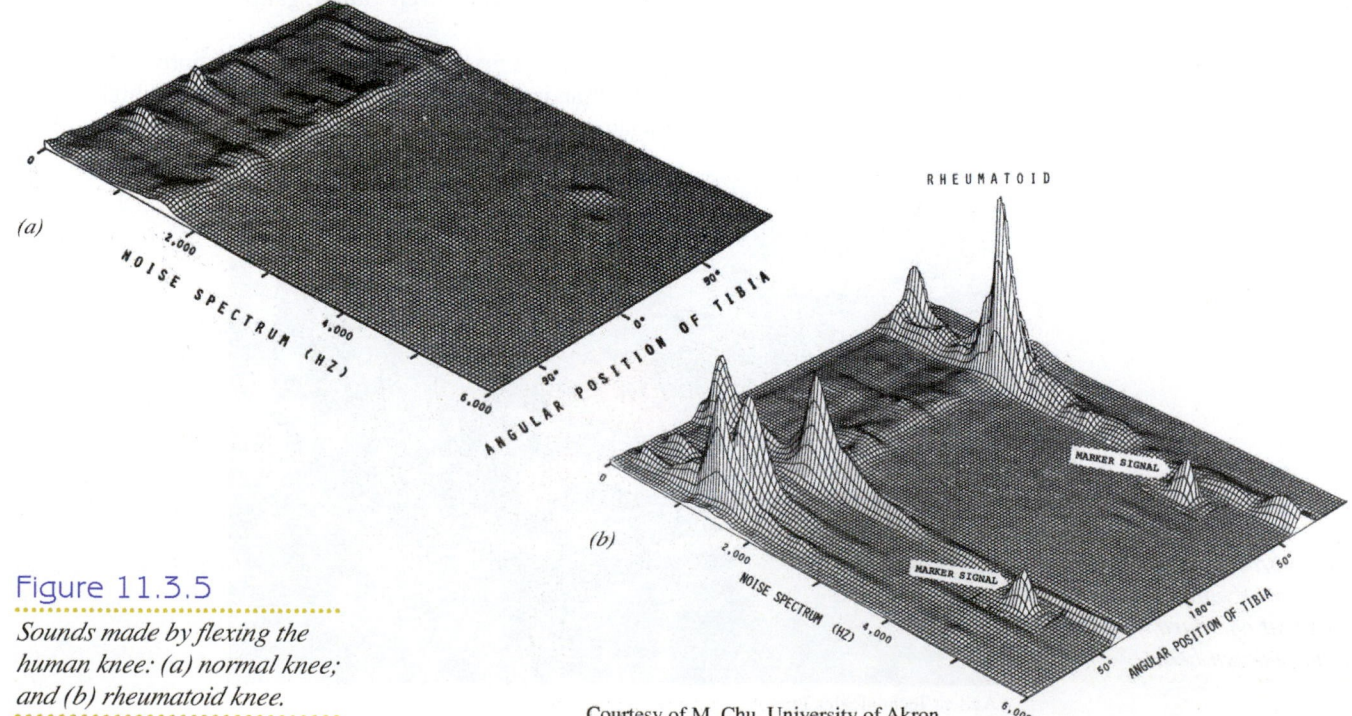

Figure 11.3.5

Sounds made by flexing the human knee: (a) normal knee; and (b) rheumatoid knee.

Courtesy of M. Chu, University of Akron

Figure 11.3.6

False-coloring clarifies the chain of storms experienced on August 5, 1995. Red indicates the greatest wind speed.

Courtesy of National Climatic Data Center

and the volume of noise, which corresponds to the height of these "mountain ranges." By looking at the diagrams, the extent and location of the damage to the affected knee can be determined. Then, by recording this information for a particular person over a period of time, the effectiveness or ineffectiveness of drugs and therapy can be evaluated.

A very common technique in the visualization of information is false-coloring, as discussed in chapter 10. A good example of getting extra information visually is found in the false-colored image shown in Figure 11.3.6. It is a weather image showing how false-coloring can be used to indicate wind speed. This very unusual weather condition, called the train of storms, shows several storm centers, four of which have either hurricane or tropical storm status. In this image, the deep red represents the greatest wind speed, with shading to yellow indicating lesser wind speed. Also note the green outline of the landmasses.

Ultrasound imaging is a medical diagnostic technique that provides visual images constructed from the sounds that reflect off various organs of the human body.

Heart Blood Flow

Ultrasound imaging uses computers and sound waves to open a "window" into the human body without making an incision. The technology provides visual images constructed from the sounds that reflect off organs in the body. Physicians can measure the size and view the action of the heart, fetus, liver, kidney, gallbladder, and eye without risk to the patient.

To make an ultrasound "picture," a gel is first rubbed on the skin to improve the sound transmission. Then a device with thousands of transducers that send out sounds higher than normal human hearing is held against the skin. The transducers, which also behave like

Figure 11.3.7

This ultrasound image shows the flow of blood through the different compartments of a living human heart.

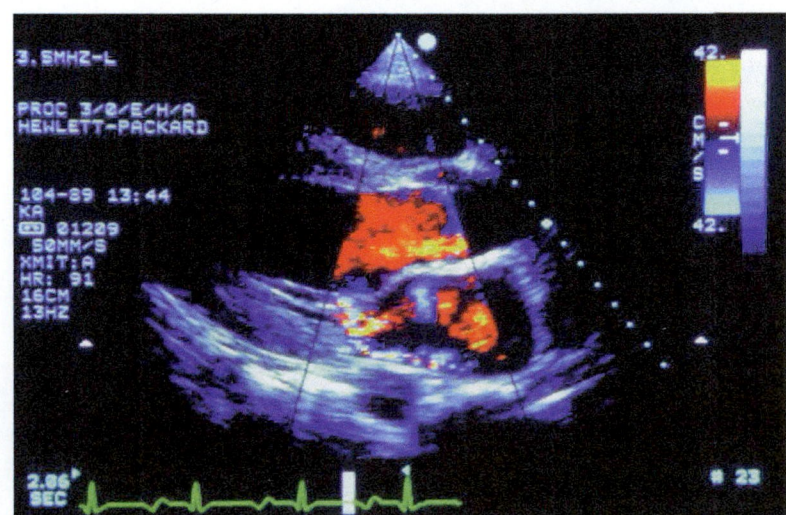

Agilent Technologies Inc.

small microphones, receive the reflections of the sound from the organs. Each one of the thousands of transducers represents a pixel of the image. The resulting black-and-white image can then be false-colored to make features more obvious. It works just like the sonar used in fish finders or submarines.

Motions of the blood in a heart can even be detected. For example, Figure 11.3.7 shows an ultrasound image made by a Hewlett-Packard machine. The blood flow images reveal a heart defect called mitral regurgitation. The blood flowing toward the transducer is colored red, and blood flowing away is blue. The defect can be seen as the red and blue mix.

11.4 The Role of Statistics: Transforming Data into Information

Notice that in the preceding two sections we discussed collecting and storing *data* but then used the term retrieving *information.* That's because whatever we retrieve from a database should be meaningful. The retrieval process involves the examination, summarization, and manipulation of data into information. The most commonly used method of transforming data into information is **statistical analysis.** Computer applications using statistics include such diverse subjects as the study of heart disease, lung cancer in smokers, average income of a U.S. family, and election outcome predictions. Figure 11.4.1 gives several examples of statistical data analysis.

Statistical ideas are important to database results and usage. Diverse computer applications cannot be fully appreciated without some basic statistical knowledge. Let's review some important statistical concepts.

PERCENTS

A number often quoted and sometimes misunderstood is the statistic called a **percent.** When someone says that 50 percent of the students in your class are seniors, this should indicate to you that half of the students in the class are seniors (and half are not). If there are 30 students enrolled in the class, 15 of them would be seniors, and the remaining 15 would be freshmen, sophomores, or juniors.

A **percent** (%) is a special type of fraction, representing a given number of parts out of the total of 100 parts that make up any whole. Examples: 25 out of 100 people would be 25 percent of the people; 20 percent of 10 dogs would be 2 dogs, or 20/100 of 10.

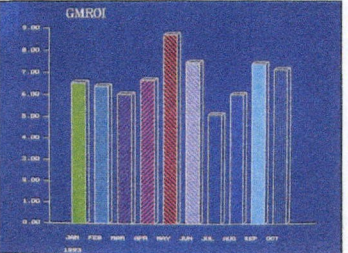

Information on receiving, on-hand and sales is expressed month by month, in either numerical or graphical form, clearly showing important market trends.

Five primary statistics are constantly monitored and always available: GMROI, Turn, Stock to Sales, Sell-through and Days of Supply.

Reprinted by permission

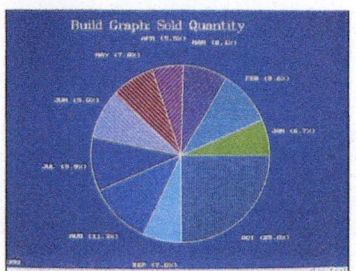

Information graphically displayed helps you quickly interpret the real situation.

Figure 11.4.1

Statistics are used to analyze collections of data and transform them into meaningful information.

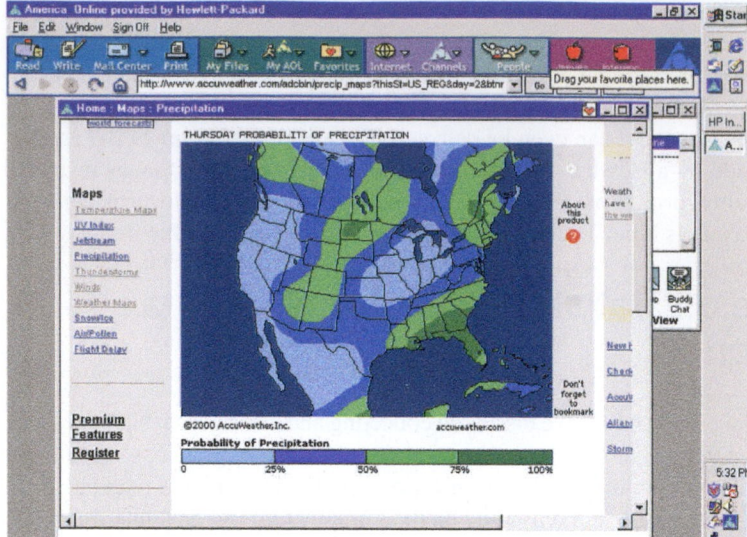

Weather Graphics Courtesy of AccuWeather, Inc.,
385 Science Park Road, State College, PA 16803, (814) 237-0309 © 2000

Figure 11.4.2

Weather predictions, often expressed as probabilities, are taken from computer-generated weather maps.

Probability is a numeric value given to a prediction of whether a specified event will occur. The value is usually expressed as a percent.

Sampling is the technique of predicting a total situation using a comparative few isolated cases collected by representative observations.

In a **normal distribution** 68 percent of all data values fall within a limited range near the center of the distribution, with the other 32 percent evenly spaced over the top and bottom ranges.

In a **skewed sample,** selection of the group participating in a survey supports some predetermined outcome. A skewed sample gives distorted results because the sample does not match the distribution of the population it represents.

In statistics, a **sample** is a small group of whatever data are being studied that is used to represent a much larger group.

PROBABILITY

It is difficult to give a definition of probability without seeming like a cat chasing its tail, but let's give it a try. **Probability** is our ability to predict whether certain events will occur. For example, many of us have heard the weather analysts predict a "50 percent chance of showers this evening." Figure 11.4.2 shows a computer-generated weather map used to predict the probability of precipitation. The prediction is based on the probability that certain patterns of observed weather will continue. Aside from the feeling that weather predictions always seem to be wrong, we should take the 50 percent probability prediction to mean that it is just as likely to rain as not to rain. In other words, if we looked back at all the days with a 50 percent chance of rain over the past year, we should see that about half of the time it actually did rain.

Suppose the meteorologist predicted a 50 percent chance of rain today and tomorrow, and further suppose that it doesn't rain today. Does that mean it will definitely rain tomorrow? Absolutely not! But, you say, in order to have 50 percent rain and 50 percent no rain in two days, it must rain one day and not the other. Why the discrepancy? Probabilities tell us that if we look at a large enough number of days where a prediction is 50 percent chance of rain, about one-half or 50 percent of these days will have rain.

IMPORTANCE OF PROBABILITY AND PERCENTS

As a society, we seem most comfortable making decisions based on numbers. We choose groceries by price and weight, clothing by size, and investments by profits. When we analyze data, we seek ways of expressing that analysis also in numbers. Even business and governmental decisions are based on numeric probabilities that certain events will happen. For example, lenders requesting personal information from a credit bureau are basing their loan approval on the probability (a numeric value!) that the individual will repay the borrowed amount. This probability is a numeric calculation the computer database system makes based on the personal data provided. An error in the data or mathematical calculations of the database program could unfairly cause a borrower to be denied a loan that he or she really has the resources to repay.

SELECTING DATA FOR STATISTICAL ANALYSIS

Often, it is impossible to gather all the data on a particular topic. The Nielsen Company, for example, releases a report that rates the popularity of various TV shows. It cannot possibly monitor every TV set turned on in the United States. Instead, it selects homes across the country that represent a cross section of the TV-viewing audience. Nielsen connects small computerized data collection boxes to television sets in its chosen representative homes. This **sample** is then used to rate the top television programs.

Although **sampling** is a very useful technique, a sample must be carefully selected to avoid predetermining statistical results. Suppose, for instance, that some Saturday morning Nielsen selected only homes with young children as the representative viewing audience. Needless to say, the cartoon shows would receive very high ratings indeed, giving a far different result than one would expect from a truly representative sample. The better chosen the sample, the better the analysis that will result. If the sample is randomly chosen, we can expect some semblance of a **normal distribution.** But if the sample is **skewed,** or distorted in some way, the data will reflect the distortion. For example, using only the data from monitoring Saturday morning television viewing would not give an accurate list of the top 10 TV shows.

CORRELATION

We are constantly being bombarded with news reports showing the correlation between certain habits and various diseases, such as cancer. A definite **correlation** or connection exists, for example, between lung cancer, age, and smoking habits.

> A **correlation** is a connection or relationship linking two or more pieces of information.

The analysis needed to investigate this correlation is too complicated to discuss here, and it definitely requires the aid of the computer. Let's analyze instead a much simpler correlation. The lengths of index fingers easily demonstrate correlation. Let's pose the following hypothesis:

Hypothesis: There is a correlation between index finger length and whether a person is male or female.

To test this hypothesis, we will measure the length of the index fingers of 100 men and 100 women. Table 11.4.1 shows the results of separate data for males and females. In general, we see that our hypothesis is proven: Females have shorter index fingers. This is not surprising; our intuition would have led us to the same conclusion because men in general are larger than women. Correlation analysis is really much more complicated than the finger-length example, but the idea contained in this example gives a taste of the real thing.

> **False correlation** or **false relevance** involves the assumption of a cause-and-effect relationship between two facts that seem to be related but are not.

Sometimes we assume a correlation between two true but unrelated facts. This is called a **false correlation** or **false relevance.**

A classic example is the direct correlation that may seem to exist between eating ice-cream cones and drowning while swimming. The correlation is false because there is no cause-and-effect relationship between eating ice cream and drowning.

Table 11.4.1 *Mean index finger lengths for males and females.*

Gender	Mean Index Finger Length
Male	72 centimeters
Female	68 centimeters

Fact 1: More drownings occur in the summer.

Fact 2: More people eat ice cream in the summer.

False relevance: People who eat ice cream are more likely to drown while swimming.

Here is another example.

Fact 1: All people breathe oxygen.

Fact 2: All people must die sometime.

False relevance: Oxygen must be toxic because 100 percent of people breathing oxygen today will die in the future.

The computer invasion has placed greater attention on statistical analysis of data than ever before. As a result, more people are aware of statistics and are gaining a greater understanding of statistical procedures. The computer's large capacity for data storage encourages a level of statistical accuracy and currency never before possible. Unfortunately, there are negative effects of computerized data analysis: human error and misuse. The most common problem is the misrepresentation of data. Remember: Garbage in = garbage out! A database is only as good as the data entered and the program used to extract the information. Computers only perform the functions. People enter, program, and explain the results.

11.5 Creating a Custom Database

Much of our everyday dependence on information today involves the use of already existing databases. Here are a few examples:

- If you work for a medium- to large-sized company, you probably receive a computer-prepared paycheck. The information on that check comes from the company's employee database, including your name, the gross amount you've earned, the amounts of various deductions, and the net amount printed on the check. If your check is automatically deposited to your bank account, the bank's name and address and your account number also are drawn from the same source.

- Do you use an ATM to get cash or deposit your check? You could not manage that unless your name and account information are in the bank's client database, and the pin-number you enter must match the one assigned to you in the bank's security code database.

- Corporate executives regularly use worldwide financial databases to determine future investment areas, where and when to target new market strategies, and where key customers are grouped.

- Federal funding for city and state programs, road construction, education, and many others is determined by the information reported in the U.S. census, one of the largest databases maintained by the federal government.

The Internet and the commercial market provide excellent tools to help you gather everyday usage. Not all information you might need, however, can be accessed through existing databases. What if specific information is needed that is not already in a database?

DATABASE STRUCTURE AND DESIGN

A **field** is a location in a database that contains one single specific piece of information.

Let's examine the arrangement of a typical database to understand how the various pieces of that structure are combined to create accessible information. The smallest piece of informa-

Credit & Payment History — FILE

Income & Employer

Identification & Address — FIELD — RECORD

First Name	Last Name	Street Address	City	State	Zip	SSN	Phone
John	Monroe	222 Alexander	Jefferson	MI	48161	777-00-7676	343-454-5678
Shannon	Jackson	123 Peach Lane	Carleton	MI	48117	313-65-9876	555-321-3452
Abdul	Botswain	22 Circle Drive	Clio	OH	48197	234-56-7890	555-456-1234
Kiernan	Smith	345789 Blanding	Jackson	FL	32075	456-78-9087	555-407-6543
Harmony	Valee	1943 Craig	Springs	CA	98076	654-76-1234	555-407-1234
Mitsu	Yamaha	765 Washington	Alma	GA	87654	777-007676	343-454-5678
Millie	Lintner	88 Sunshine Lane	Flower	HI	98765	313-65-9876	555-321-3452
Kurt	Lauckner	678 Physics Blvd.	Mathma,	MA	12543	234-56-7890	555-456-1234
Joan	Mrazik	123 Applebee	DeBary	FL	98077	456-78-9087	555-407-6543
Rachel	Witte	8907 Arts Drive	Savannah	GA	76543	654-76-1234	555-407-1234
Kristy	King	9876 Dingle	Ardvark	KS	65476	777-00-7676	343-454-5678
Nathan	James	786498 Hwy 66	Daalas	TX	87654	313-65-9876	555-321-3452
Angeal	Bays	East Lake Drive	Seavillle	MI	48765	234056-7890	555-456-1234
Jackson	Jones	222 Alexander	Jefferson	MI	48161	456-78-9087	555-407-6543
Sheryl	Lanb	123 Pech Lane	Carlton	MI	48117	654-76-1234	555-407-1234
Art	Piddle	22 Circle Drive	Clio	OH	48197	313-65-9876	555-321-3452

Figure 11.5.1

Structure of a typical database.

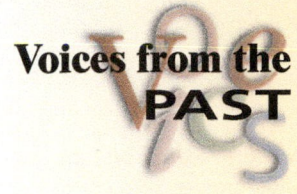

E. F. Codd and the Relational Database

In 1970 an English mathematician named Edgar F. Codd was working as a research scientist for IBM in the United States. He published a paper titled "A Relational Model of Data for Large Shared Data Banks." The paper defined the 12 rules that a relational DBMS should follow and formed the beginning of a new type of information management system called RDBMS (relational database management system). The RDBMS was flexible, gave greater capability to users, and was easy to modify. It was especially effective in managing large databases that needed flexible access. Dr. Codd received the 1981 Turing Award for this work on relational databases.

The first interactive operating system was another one of his accomplishments. Dr. Codd made use of the interrupt concept that was first implemented on the IBM Stretch computer. This enabled a person to interact with the computer from a keyboard instead of having to put stacks of cards with programs on them into readers that were then read in batches. Incidentally, the Stretch computer was the first supercomputer.

Dr. Codd also did some work in the area of self-replicating computers. Incidentally, John von Neumann preceded Codd in this area. In particular, he theorized a very complex self-reproducing machine called the universal computer constructor, or UCC. Dr. Codd made significant improvements to the UCC.

A **record** is a collection of related fields, all containing information about one individual or instance.

A **file** is a collection of related records, all of the same type, which store information about similar individuals or instances.

A **database** consists of a collection of records, each dealing with some aspect or part of a single overall subject. The files may be of similar or different types. They are connected only by topic and information usage.

A **DBMS (database management system)** is a software application that allows you to store, organize, and retrieve data from one or more databases.

A **relation** is a two-dimensional table made up of columns and rows of data. Each column stores the data in one field; each row stores the information in one record.

In a **relational database** data are stored in two or more two-dimensional tables that are linked together or related by common data fields.

tion accessible in a database is called a field, or **data element.** A **field** contains one particular piece of information. Some examples might be the first name field, the zip code field, and the social security number field.

A group of fields, all containing information about one instance or individual, is called a **record.** Therefore, a record might hold the name, address, phone number, social security number, and salary of one specific individual.

A group of records, all of the same type, is referred to as a **file.** For example, we might have a record for each student in a class. Those records, as a group, would constitute a class file.

It is important that the data in all the records in a given file be organized in the same way, as shown in Figure 11.5.1. That means two things:

Every record must have all the same fields as the other records in that file.

The fields must be arranged in the same way for each record.

Suppose, for example, that the layout for the student record in a class file is the following: Fname, Lname, Address, City, State, Zip, Phone. Every record in that file would contain the same list of information, arranged in the same order.

A group of files that are all related to each other, or are all related to the same subject, is called a **database.**

Gathering computerized data and organizing them into fields, records, and files will still not produce the usable results we are seeking. We still need some way of analyzing the data and transforming them into information. If we were to combine these structural elements with a query language and add programs for data modification, statistical analysis, and report formatting, we would have a complete package called a **DBMS (database management system).**

USING A RELATIONAL DATABASE SYSTEM

Although many different types of database management systems exist, those most commonly used today are based on the relational model. **Relational databases** use two-dimensional tables, called relations, to store the data. **Relations** are linked to each other by common fields. For example, suppose you wanted to store information about classes and the students enrolled in them. One relation, or table, could store the titles of the classes, their times and dates of meeting, and room numbers. Each class would also have a section number unique to that class. Another relation would have the names and student numbers for each student, and the section number of each class each student is taking. The section number field is the link that relates the two tables.

The success of the relational database model arises from two important features:

■ The structure of the relational model is simple and direct, allowing the user to store data in intuitively organized tables. This structure is flexible enough to fit a broad range of different database problems.

■ The relational database is especially well suited to the **client/server** environment in which most databases function. This environment usually uses two different computers connected by a network. The client machine sends a data request to the server, and the server computer responds by sending the requested information. The separation of the client and server allows the server to perform all database functions, freeing up the client to perform tasks of interface and application operations.

A **client/server** system usually involves two computers connected by a network. A database resides on one computer (the server), and the software needed to access data from the database resides on the other (the client). Separating the data from the access operations provides greater flexibility and data security.

Sometimes referred to just as a database system, a DBMS is a powerful software package for storing and accessing data. To understand how such a system works, let's use an example. Suppose you want to store on computer an index of the compact discs in your own personal music collection. Here's what you would do:

Step 1: Decide what information you might need about each CD. You might consider the title, artist's name, recording label, date of issue, titles of selections, and so on. You might also want to list the type of music and whether the performer is a vocalist, pianist, jazz band, or chamber orchestra. Each of these pieces of information would occupy one field in the record about one compact disc.

Step 2: After you have decided what information to include, you would then define the structure of your database. Commercially available database software packages provide a data definition screen, as shown in Figure 11.5.2, to assist with this task.

Step 3: Now you are ready to enter the information about each of your compact discs. Because it is important that you enter the information in the correct place and format, your DBMS program includes a data entry screen that guides you through this process. The data entry screen also provides a facility for correcting any errors you might make while typing in your data.

Step 4: You are now ready to reap the benefits of a computerized database. When you need information from your CD list, a query screen provided by your DBMS software will help you select exactly the information you wish to extract. If you planned your data storage carefully in step 1, you should be able to retrieve any combination of information you have entered.

Step 5: As you add CDs to your collection, or perhaps give a few away, you can update your database quickly and easily.

Figure 11.5.2

A data definition screen helps you to set up the fields needed to store your data.

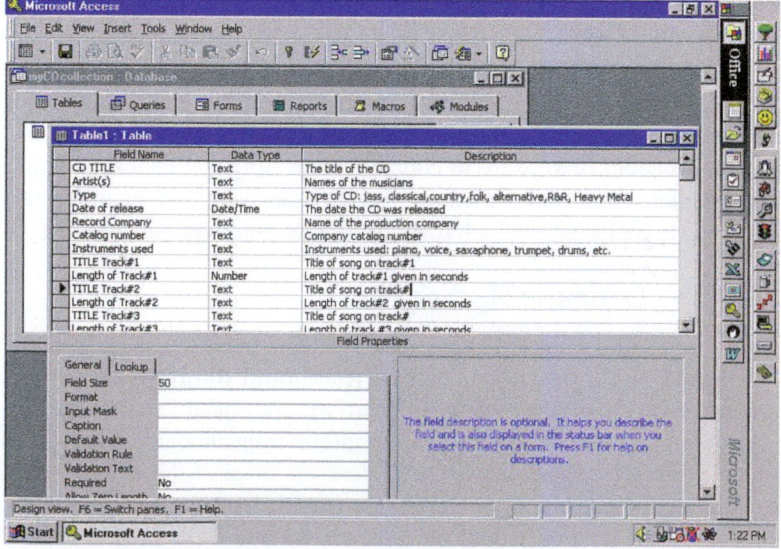

Screen shot reprinted by permission from Microsoft Corporation

Step 6: Finally, you can print out all or any part of your CD information in a format of your choice by using the report writing feature of your database program. You can decide which records to include, what information to display from each record, and how to organize these data. Some DBMS programs can also perform calculations as part of the printed report, providing a count of how many CDs are in each category of music, or total performance time of a number of selections (if you have included that information in your records).

DATA MARTS, DATA WAREHOUSES, AND DATA MINING

The enormous number of databases in existence and available today has generated a renewed interest in using information to enhance targeted marketing in the business world. Businesses now realize that creative use of information is a competitive weapon in the marketplace. The idea is to collect and consolidate data from many individual sources into centralized or distributed **data warehouses** or **data marts,** where users can access them all at once. Users can then apply the data they gather to, say, provide better customer service, do better marketing analysis in a more timely manner, or look at new combinations of data to help spot otherwise unrecognized problems or opportunities.

The process that makes such valuable use of data warehousing possible is called **data mining.** Data mining is searching for relationships and global patterns that exist in large databases but are hidden among the vast amounts of data found there. These relationships, when identified, reveal valuable knowledge about the database and the objects in the database, and about the real world as recorded by the database. The main problem in discovering meaningful relationships is that the number of possible relationships is very large. Checking every one of them for validity would be impossible by conventional search and query techniques. Thus, new search strategies, called **intelligent search** methods, are needed to mine the data. These strategies are taken from the area of artificial intelligence called machine learning. They include intelligent types of data representation, inductive learning, and rule-based knowledge systems. To better understand these concepts from artificial intelligence, look ahead to chapter 13, "Artificial Intelligence and Modeling the Human State."

> A **data warehouse** merges related data from many operational sources to provide an integrated information system spanning the data needs of an entire enterprise. A **data mart** is a limited type of data warehouse, usually oriented to a single subject or a single department's needs.

> **Data mining** is searching collections of databases to discover relationships and global patterns that exist among them, and applying these patterns to assist in management decisions.

> A computer operation is said to be **intelligent** if the computer appears to learn and develop its own structure for data organization, and its own methods for searching for and validating relationships.

PUZZLER HINT

You should by now be fairly familiar with the layout of the tourist areas of Washington, DC. Identify on the satellite image any other landmarks or attractions shown on your tourist map. Give yourself only one point for each one of these you can identify.

How did you do?

DATABASE ADVANTAGES

Some of the most important advantages of a database and its corresponding DBMS over other less organized systems of information are as follows:

- *Space saver.* Databases eliminate redundancy (that is, only one copy of each item of information need exist).

- *Increased accuracy.* One person can control or be responsible for certain data items, thereby lessening chances of human error.

- *Multiple use of data.* More than one department or group of people can use the same information.

- *Data integrity.* Special efforts can be made to make sure data items can't be changed accidentally due to computer failure, human error, or malice.

- *Time saver due to search abilities.* The option exists to look for data by title, keyword, subject, or field.

- *Easy use of data.* Users with different questions can find their answers in one database by changing the question.

ETHICAL HAZARDS OF DATABASE SYSTEMS

We have now had sufficient discussion of databases to understand one of the more important issues facing our society. Collecting information into large and easily accessible databases has raised the public's consciousness on several issues. Some practices make it easy to trick the general public through the misrepresentation of information. Other issues, such as invasion of privacy, pose a personal threat to our freedom and happiness. We will just skim the surface of these issues here.

Misrepresentation of Data

Everywhere we look today, we are assaulted by statistics. Television commercials assure us that a certain product is used by more doctors (more doctors than what? chimpanzees?). A cereal claims to contain 20 percent less sugar (less than what? maple syrup?). A company complains that its earnings have plummeted by 8.93 percent! (Is that from an all-time high?) Without a great deal more knowledge than the figures themselves, we cannot possibly know how accurate they are, or how much belief we should put in them.

Invasion of Privacy

It's easy to think of an example of an invasion of privacy. The computer is facilitating a very powerful means of invading privacy, the extremes of which could easily take the form of events in George Orwell's novel *1984*. Less exotic examples can be found almost every day in the newspapers and magazines.

Many large data banks can be found within the government. Some of these have been mentioned already, such as the U.S. Census Bureau and Internal Revenue Service (IRS) data banks. In general, these two data banks have a good reputation for honoring the privacy of the individual. However, several IRS employees were disciplined in the past for accessing the personal income tax files of some celebrities and selling the information to tabloids.

The desire to collect all of an individual citizen's data under a single universal identifier, or UID, has already been discussed in Congress. Your social security number is a prime candidate for a UID. If this were ever done, an authorized operator (with a single request) would be able to obtain an individual's records for tax, military, credit, medical, travel habits (via credit card information and passport usage), and just about any other recorded information imaginable. Indeed, the horrors of *1984* could still become a possibility.

11.6 Software Applications: Web-Database Connectivity

A few years ago, a business enterprise desiring to have a Web presence used static HTML-generated Web pages to present its image and products. Although that may have been adequate at the end of the twentieth century, the twenty-first-century business engaging in e-commerce needs the power and flexibility of **Web-database connectivity** and **data-driven Web sites.** This section will investigate the process of creating **dynamically generated Web sites** and some of their advantages and disadvantages. Figure 11.6.1 shows part of the dynamically generated eBay Web site.

WHAT IS WEB-DATABASE CONNECTIVITY?

Web-database connectivity is an interaction between one or more Web pages and the contents of a specific database. The Web pages are designed as templates, with image areas and text boxes to be filled in with data from the database. **Query-based programming** supplies the content from the database to complete the Web pages. In effect, this separates the design and layout of the Web page from the content to be displayed on that page.

Let's look at a theoretical example. Suppose you have an online business dealing in hand tools. Your available inventory contains 1,000 items. You want to display your merchandise in a Web catalog, with five items on a page. For each item, there should be an item number and name, a photo, a brief description, and a price.

Web-database connectivity enables the interaction between a Web page and the content of a specific database.

Data-driven Web sites and **dynamically generated Web sites** both refer to the ability to supply the content for a Web site dynamically, as the site is loaded onto a browser rather than statically when the site is designed.

Query-based programming uses a fourth-generation query language, such as SQL, to select Web content from a database and display it on a dynamically generated Web page.

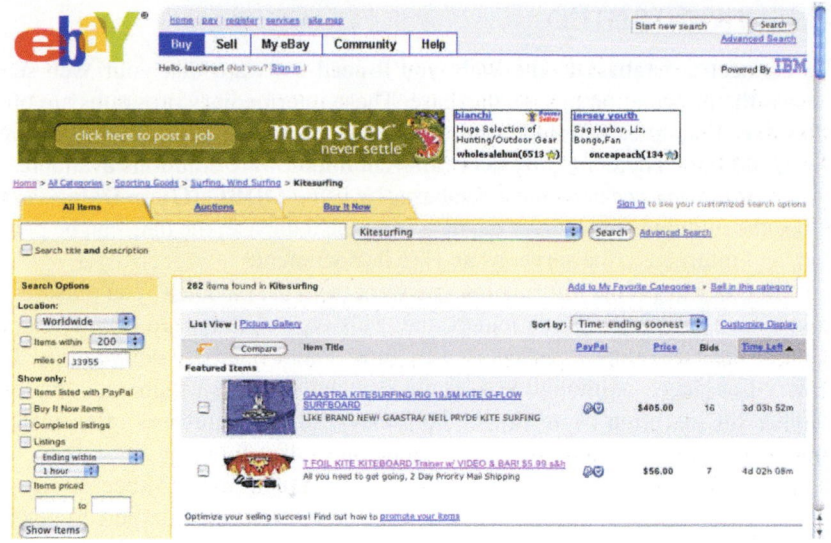

Figure 11.6.1

This eBay screen of search results is dynamically created by querying a database of available items to find those that match the key terms in the query.

You would need to create 200 different but similar static Web pages, each with its five items and images. This would be a tedious and time-consuming process, full of possibilities for errors and inconsistencies. To correct errors or update an item you would have to rework the particular Web page displaying the item. If your stock in an item ran out, you would have to rework its Web page again. You could spend a large portion of your busy life maintaining the Web pages of your online catalog.

To perform the same task using dynamic Web page generation and Web-database connectivity you would design the format and layout for one generic catalog page and use it as a template. Then, using some query-based programming, you would instruct the database to supply the content for each of the 200 pages of your online catalog. When a customer views your catalog in a standard Web browser, the pages of items are generated dynamically as needed. Page design would be consistent because all pages use the same template. Corrections and adjustments can be made in the database rather than on the Web pages, thus saving both time and money. The advantages for your online business are huge.

KEY ADVANTAGES OF WEB-DATABASE CONNECTIVITY

- Database information is universally available. Access to the information in a database requires only a Web browser and an Internet connection.

- Web site design and development are easier and faster, using fewer resources. Resulting Web sites are more consistent in appearance and less prone to errors.

- Web site maintenance is easier and more efficient. Design changes made on a template automatically update all pages generated from that template. Content corrections and changes can be made in the database rather than needing adjustment in the HTML.

- Adjustments and changes to Web pages can be made by any authorized person rather than needing the intervention of a Web developer.

- Because databases can store many types of data, Web pages could be designed to hold images, sounds, titles, descriptions, articles, books, numeric data, customer or employee data, and so on. Query-based programming can be used to calculate prices, totals, and discounts, can dynamically number pages or items, and even dynamically access links to other Web sites.

GETTING STARTED

Middleware is software that acts as an intermediary between a Web server and a database. It enables a Web server to collect specific data from a database and use them to generate dynamic Web pages.

ODBC (Open Database Connectivity) is a set of standards allowing information to be passed from a database to a dynamic Web page.

A **query wizard** is a tool or utility included within many major database management systems, which helps the user to frame requests for retrieving specific data from a database.

To connect a database to the Web, you'll need software that your Web server can use to access the information in your database. These intermediary programs are often called **middleware.** Examples of middleware include ColdFusion, Active Serve, Server Pages, PHP, Java, and Perl. There are dozens of different middleware solutions available.

Middleware accesses most databases by using **ODBC (Open Database Connectivity).** Once the middleware receives the data from the database, the data can be processed, formatted, and returned to the server as an HTML document.

In order to get the information you want from the database, you must request the data in a language the database can understand. This type of language is called a query language. One of the most popular, supported by most major database software, is SQL (Structured Query Language). Although SQL is not especially difficult to learn, complex queries could require the attention of an expert. Fortunately, major databases often include tools called **query wizards** to help frame queries in the most effective way.

Selection of an appropriate database program is the key to success using Web-database connectivity. Considerations you will want to address include performance requirements, such as speed of data access and the number of simultaneous database calls that can be made. Both are important concerns if you anticipate numerous consumers nationwide accessing your photo sales catalog. You must also consider the capacity of the database—number of records it can hold, cost, and platform availability. Not all databases support Macintosh and Linux computers, for example.

Let's take a very brief look at the capabilities of just one Web-database application program.

ORACLE HTML DB: AN INTEGRATED SOLUTION

Oracle HTML DB, a built in feature of Oracle's database log, is a complete, integrated solution for building, loading, and proactively monitoring Web-database applications and content-driven Web sites. Oracle is a popular high-end database program, used by Web industry giants such as Yahoo! and Auction Watch. HTML DB provides an efficient and effective way to "Web-enable" Oracle databases. Figure 11.6.2 shows an example of a dynamic Web page created with Oracle HTML DB. Here are a few tasks it can help you do:

> *Create and manage database objects*—This application allows Web developers to create, view, and edit database objects through an HTML-based interface. Some of the objects include tables, views, procedures, indexes, and packages.

Figure 11.6.2

Creating human resource Web page for company using a browser and HTML DB.

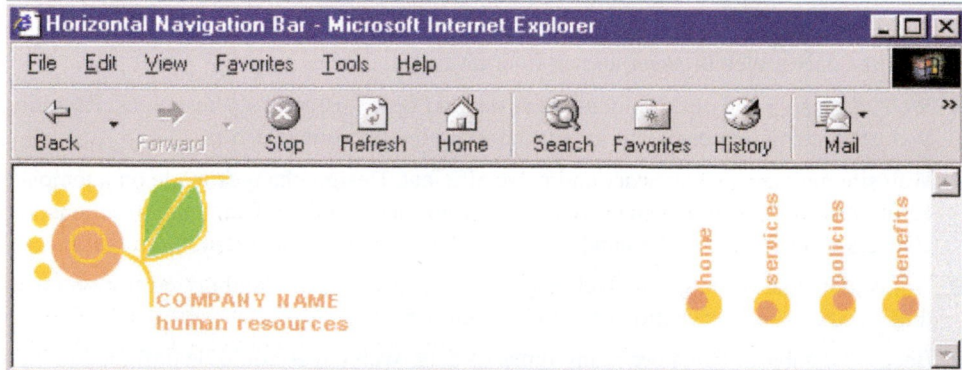

Oracle Corporation

Develop HTML components—Oracle HTML DB provides tools for creating HTML-based interfaces to database data. These interfaces include reports, forms, charts, calendars, menus, and frame drivers.

Build and maintain content-driven Web sites—Utilities and wizards simplify the task of Web page design and layout and help frame accurate queries for loading data into content-driven pages. The tools for managing HTML DB sites are contained within the sites themselves, enabling content creators to perform updates, corrections, and site-quality checks themselves, without relying on a Web master.

Track Web site and database connectivity performance—Performance-tracking facilities within HTML DB enable isolation and proactive resolution of performance problems. Prebuilt reports display individual components, Web pages and their users, as well as security and performance histories.

Manage database security—Oracle HTML DB provides tools to manage database users' accounts and privileges, as well as Web user registration and privileges and Web server settings throughout the WebDB interface.

In short, Oracle HTML DB is designed to ease the tasks of Web-database access and administration. Wizards guide database administrators and Web site developers through tasks step by step. By reducing the amount of technical knowledge required to produce content-driven Web pages, it makes information readily available to everyone who has permission to see it.

Chapter Summary

11.1 Introduction: Information Overload

As we enter the twenty-first century, the amount of information in the world continues to grow at unprecedented rates. The overwhelming quantity of data available makes their effective use extremely difficult. Only by harnessing computer technology can we collect, organize, and analyze data to enhance our understanding of the world around us.

11.2 The Technology for Data Collection

Organized collection of large quantities of data has always been a problem. As we have become more technologically sophisticated, we have devised effective ways to use computers for data collection. Early methods stored data on punched tapes and cards. More recent methodologies include data probes, satellite imaging, and dynamic Web-database interaction.

11.3 Retrieving Data

Effective retrieval of information is directly related to how well the stored data have been organized. The FBI's NCIC fingerprint database provides a case-study illustration examining collection and storage of both paper and digital data, along with high-tech computer methods harnessed for retrieval.

11.4 The Role of Statistics: Transforming Data into Information

The most useful techniques for transforming data into meaningful information often involve statistical analysis. Two common mathematical statistics are percents and probability. Because it is sometimes not possible to collect or survey all data on a specific topic, researchers use sampling to achieve representative results. Selecting a nonrepresentative sample can produce inaccurate or skewed results.

11.5 Creating a Custom Database

Creating your own database is sometimes necessary if you wish to collect and store data not already accessible in an existing database. After you determine exactly what data will suit your purposes, you must organize them by defining the fields, records, and files needed to sort the data as they are collected. The relational database is the most commonly used model for providing this structure. Once the data are stored, you can retrieve them as information using a query language to shape your information request. Data warehousing provides new ways to use the resulting information but necessitates use of data mining techniques to handle nearly unlimited possibilities. Regular periodic maintenance is needed to keep data accurate and up-to-date.

11.6 Software Applications: Web-Database Connectivity

A hot new technology allows the dynamic generation of content-driven Web pages through Web-database connectivity. Using application programs called middleware, a Web developer can create a Web page template and fill it with content from a database. The content is selected by queries, which retrieve the data and complete the pages. Advantages include huge savings in time and money previously invested in creating and maintaining static Web sites.

Key Terms

Key terms introduced in this chapter:

1. Bar code, *321*
2. Bar code reader, *321*
3. Client/server, *334*
4. Correlation, *331*
5. Data, *316*
6. Data-driven Web sites, *336*
7. Database, *333*
8. Data element, *333*
9. Data mart, *335*
10. Data mining, *335*
11. Data probe, *322*
12. Data warehouse, *335*
13. Datum, *316*
14. DBMS (database management system), *333*
15. Dewey decimal system, *317*
16. Dynamically generated Web sites, *336*
17. False correlation, *331*
18. False relevance, *331*
19. Field, *332*
20. File, *333*
21. Henry classification, *323*
22. Information, *316*
23. Information Age, *316*
24. Intelligent search, *335*
25. Mark-sensor forms, *318*
26. Middleware, *338*
27. Normal distribution, *331*
28. ODBC (Open Database Connectivity), *338*
29. Percent, *329*
30. Probability, *330*
31. Query-based programming, *336*
32. Query wizard, *338*
33. Record, *333*
34. Relation, *333*
35. Relational database, *333*
36. Remote electronic sensing, *320*
37. Sample, 330
38. Sampling, *331*
39. Secure environment, *322*
40. Skewed sample, *331*
41. Statistical analysis, *329*
42. Ultrasound imaging, *328*
43. Visualization of information, *324*
44. Voice recognition data entry, *322*
45. Web-database connectivity, *336*

Matching

Match the number of the key terms introduced in the chapter to the following statements.
Each term may be used once, more than once, or not at all.

1. ___ The age in which we are living is called this.

2. ___ This is a given thing or fact in a raw form.

3. ___ Data repackaged in a meaningful form become this.

4. ___ This filing system enabled the cataloging of non-fiction books by subject matter.

5. ___ This is a collection of interrelated data files or libraries organized for ease of use.

6. ___ This type of software serves as an intermediary between a Web browser and a database.

7. ___ This type of data collection is used to collect satellite data.

8. ___ This type of data storage is used to collect census data.

9. ___ This type of data collection device is often used for inventory control.

10. ___ This type of data storage sometimes has a person mark responses on the form using a graphite pencil.

11. ___ This type of data storage uses a keylike instrument that, after it is inserted into a meter, records the amount of utility service used.

12. ___ This type of Web page development enables you to fill in a template Web page from a specific database.

13. ___ This is the most commonly used method of transforming data into information.

14. ___ This special type of fraction refers to the number of parts out of the total of 100 parts that are in question.

15. ___ This technique is used to predict a situation by using a few isolated but representative observations.

16. ___ This is the connection or relation linking two or more pieces of information.

17. ___ This is what results when a sample is selected in a way that will result in a predetermined outcome.

18. ___ This involves the creation of a cause-and-effect relationship between two facts that seem to be related but are not.

19. ___ This is a collection of programs that allows immediate access to a database.

True or False

Place either T or F on the line provided with each of the following statements. If a statement is false, you should be able to explain what changes would make it true.

1. ____ Each day the equivalent of more than 300 books of information is created on the Internet.

2. ____ The reason why this period of time is called the information age is because we are now able to store mass amounts of information on computers.

3. ____ Because the terms *data* and *information* are used interchangeably by some, they now have the same meaning.

4. ____ Data are only a part of information.

5. ____ Only the Census Bureau uses mark-sensor forms.

6. ____ Bar codes are used exclusively for inventory control.

7. ____ In voice recognition data entry, a person speaks into a microphone attached to a portable terminal. Because voice recognition is very difficult for a computer, it must then be connected to a mainframe computer for decoding.

8. ____ A bar code reader is needed to "read" bar codes.

9. ____ With the advent of the computer being used to process fingerprint information for the FBI, fewer fingerprint technicians were needed.

10. ____ Forecasting the weather is an example of the use of probability to predict an event.

11. ____ Although research uses only a sampling of the population, it can still obtain accurate results.

12. ____ Web-database connectivity requires a physical, direct connection between a Web browser and the database that supplies its content.

13. ____ The connection between height and shoe size is an example of correlation.

14. ____ False correlation refers to having two related facts, both false, and making a connection between them.

15. ____ Kids carry books to school. Books contain a lot of information that kids can learn. The books make kids smart. This is an example of false relevance.

16. ____ A record contains information pertaining to the one person or instance in question.

17. ____ A file may contain many records.

Multiple Choice

Answer the multiple-choice questions by selecting the best answer from the choices given.

1. The age in which we are living is called the
   a. Stone Age
   b. Information Age
   c. Technological Age
   d. Second Renaissance
   e. Industrial Age

2. Cancer research has shown a connection between smoking and lung cancer. The two most important concepts used in making this connection are
   a. Correlation and skewed data
   b. Correlation and sampling
   c. Correlation and false relevance
   d. False relevance and sampling
   e. False correlation and sampling

3. This term refers to given things or facts in raw form.
   a. Field
   b. Record
   c. File
   d. Data
   e. Information

4. The definition of this term includes taking data and repackaging them in a meaningful form.
   a. Field
   b. Record
   c. File
   d. Data
   e. Information

5. Each field includes a single piece of this.
   a. Field
   b. Record
   c. File
   d. Data
   e. Information

6. This is a collection of related data elements.
   a. Field
   b. Record
   c. File
   d. Data
   e. Information

7. This is a collection of records, all the same type.
   a. Field
   b. Record
   c. File
   d. Data
   e. Information

8. This is a location in a database that contains one specific piece of information about one specific individual or instance.
   a. Field
   b. Record
   c. File
   d. Data
   e. Information

9. This is a collection of programs that allows direct access to the database.
   a. Database management system
   b. Archival information system
   c. Nonstandard system access
   d. Internal resource system
   e. File backup interpreter

10. Which of the following is not one of the important advantages of a database?
   a. Space saver
   b. Increased accuracy
   c. Less need for security measures
   d. Multiple use of data
   e. Time saver due to search abilities

Exercises

1. From the Internet, obtain a list of at least 10 data and document collections you can search to find information on some topic within your major.

2. If your library has a computerized catalog or bibliographic search system, perform a query on any topic of your choice and print out the list of references on that topic. Be sure to include the exact wording of your query at the top of the page.

3. **PUZZLER** Locate and examine Landsat images from your library resources (for example, *National Geographic Magazine*). Locate the image of a major city or land area with which you are quite familiar and identify recognizable landmarks.

4. Using a sheet of white typing paper and an ink pad, make a complete set of your own fingerprints. Identify (a) which fingers have the whorl pattern, (b) which fingerprints are in one of the other categories, and (c) which fingerprints don't fit any of the categories.

5. Carefully read a daily newspaper or weekly news magazine for one week. Cut out or photocopy all articles that you think relate to the privacy issue. Determine whether a computer was involved in each of the articles. Note: A computer-related newspaper will probably contain more of these articles than most regular daily publications. Don't mutilate library copies!

6. **PUZZLER** Locate the satellite image of Montreal in this chapter. Try to identify the following objects in the picture.
Amusement park entrance
Number of different rides in the park
Names or descriptions of specific rides, such as Ferris wheel, roller coaster, and so on
Number of vehicles on overpass

Number of trucks (as opposed to cars) in the image
Can you see any people? Where?

7. Design a small-scale database. Be sure to decide what information you need to store in each record and what fields of information you need. Use a DBMS program to define your database and enter 10 records.

8. Give five examples of how sampling and correlation are used to give useful results to our society (for example, the correlation between smoking and cancer).

9. Give three examples of false correlation from advertising (for example, TV and magazines).

10. Is it possible to recognize a content-driven Web page from your browser? List several criteria you think might help you determine whether you are viewing a static or dynamic Web site. Then browse the Web to apply and test your criteria. Can you identify five e-commerce sites that use static pages and five that use dynamic pages?

11. Make a list of all of the databases currently in existence that contain your name and identity.

12. Explain how the Dewey decimal system organized the library.

13. List at least three advantages of using bar code technology for inventory.

14. Using any Web search engine, find Web sites describing some of the middleware programs named in this chapter. Make up a chart describing each one and highlight similarities and differences. Be sure to include columns for price and platforms required.

Discussion Questions

1. Will humankind ever get to the point that the incoming data are just too huge, too unmanageable? What will we do when (if) that happens?

2. Discuss privacy and security issues as they pertain to interactive online data collection.

3. Do you think that a UID (universal identifier) that each person had attached permanently to himself or herself would be a good idea? If it could be electronically read from a distance, would this make a difference? Why or why not? How does this relate to fingerprints and other biometrics?

Group Project

A group of four students should prepare a survey on a subject of mutual interest. It can deal with student issues or interests, or general information. The survey should be at least 20 questions and can have either yes/no, multiple-choice, or numerical answers. If mark-sensing equipment such as that used on exams is available, design the questionnaire around that type of gathering system. Have the members of your class (your sorority, and so on) fill out the survey and return it to your group. Use an electronic spreadsheet to chart and analyze the data you collect. Do you see any correlations? Can you express your findings in percentages? Do you think your choice of sample skewed your results? Prepare and give the results in a presentation using an electronic presentation system.

Web Exercises

1. Create a database of Web sites with great satellite images. First, browse and search the Web for the Web sites of companies and agencies that provide satellite imaging. Here are a few acronyms to get you started: NASA, ERIM, GSFC, ERSI, EROS, SRTM, EOS. Most of these agencies will have lists of links you can follow to other imaging sites. Check out as many as you can. Then set up a database containing information you consider important or interesting about each of these sites. You should be able to query your database to pull out information the satellites have in common.

2. One of the largest data collection agencies in the United States is the Internal Revenue Service (IRS) that collects income taxes. Search the Web to find out how the IRS collects and stores its vast database of taxpayer information.

Bibliography

Adriaans, Pieter and Dolf Zantinge. *Data Mining.* Reading, MA: Addison-Wesley, 1996.

An overview of some of the tools and concepts for building an intelligent database.

Codd, Edgar F. *The Relational Model for Database Management: Version 2.* Reading, MA: Addison-Wesley, 1990.

The bible on relational databases, the industry standard—fairly technical.

Date, Chris C. *An Introduction to Database Systems (The Systems Programming).* Reading, MA: Addison-Wesley, 1994.

Another standard text on database systems, especially relational and object-oriented databases. Written for computer science students.

Garfinkel, Simpson. *Database Nation: The Death of Privacy in the 21st Century.* New York: O'Reilly, January 2000.

A strong commentary on the use of databases and their effect on security and personal privacy.

Greenwald, Rick and James Milberry. *Oracle WebDB Bible.* New York: O'Reilly, October 1999.

A great handbook on using Oracle WebDB to create and manage online data access and dynamic Web site design.

Maxymuk, John, ed. *Finding Government Information on the Internet.* New York: Neal-Schuman Publishers, 1995.

This book gives guidelines for finding a vast amount of free and useful government information via the Internet.

Morville, Peter, Louis Roisenfeld, and Joseph Janes. *The Internet Searcher's Handbook.* New York: Neal-Schuman Publishers, 1996.

Many, many tips and tricks on effective Internet search techniques.

Ramalho, Jose. *Developers' Guide to Oracle Tools.* Wordware Publishing, April 2000.

This books guides you through the steps to setting up and maintaining a business database using Oracle.

Simon, Alan R. *90 Days to the Datamart.* New York: John Wiley and Sons, March 1999.

Guidelines for converting company or department data into a functional data mart.

Tufte, Edward R. *Visual Explanations: Images and Quantities, Evidence and Narrative.* Cheshire, CT: Graphics Press, 1997.

This is a scholarly work showing how visual images are derived from different kinds of data and information, and how they can be used.

Wolff, Robert S. and Larry Yaeger. *Visualization of Natural Phenomena.* Santa Clara: Telos, 1993.

This book describes the techniques for collecting data from natural occurrences and converting these data into visually understandable information.

chapter 12

Simulation: Modeling the Physical World

TimeLine

1912–1965 Tidal predictions are made with the Coast and Geodetic Survey Tide-Predicting Machine No. 2.

1935 Parker Brothers buys the rights to the Monopoly game.

1952 A Univac I computer predicts the results of the presidential election.

1960 A computerized model of Earth's atmosphere is programmed by Edward Lorenz of MIT.

1966 Mainframe computers are first used to predict tides.

1968 Rvachev and Baroyan predict the spread of an influenza epidemic with a computer in the USSR.

1978 NRAO develops the Astronomical Image Processing System, the world standard for observers constructing images from radio telescope data.

1979 Mandelbrot simulates fractals with a computer.

1982 Mellott and Centrella develop the first simulation of the evolution of a universe using the "cloud-in-cell" model.

1984 The term *cyberspace* is coined in William Gibson's novel *Neuromancer*.

1987 The capability maturity model is designed by Humphrey and Sweet to predict a software developer's ability to produce reliable software.

1996 SimCity 2000 program sells 500,000 copies.

2009 The Folding@home project simulates human protein folding using over 4 million CPUs with an effective speed of over 4.1 petaflops.

2016 Simulation becomes widely recognized as the third branch of science along with theoretical and experimental science.

Chapter Objectives

- Know why time compression is necessary to predict the future.

- Understand how the quality of the model used directly affects the quality of the simulation.

- Recognize the uses of simulation.

- Identify whether a model of a system is continuous or discrete.

- Identify whether a model of a system is predictable or probabilistic.

- Identify whether a model of a system contains feedback.

- Analyze the Monopoly game simulation as an example of strategy building with a computer.

- Analyze the SimCity simulation as an example of long-term versus short-term planning in a feedback environment.

- Understand the significance of simulating protein folding.

- Understand how and why validation of a model is done.

- Know how simulation languages make writing simulations easier.

- Identify the specialized hardware necessary for virtual reality.

- Recognize situations in which virtual reality would be appropriate.

Owen/Black Star

PUZZLER

You've just been hired by a major corporation to investigate why sales forecasts far exceed the actual sales of its mass-market product. The company's sale of widgets, in fact, was only 7 million units. The forecast was for over 10 million widgets. This is a major catastrophe. If the problem isn't resolved the company could be "blown out of the water" by the competition.

Problem 1: What is the first thing that must be examined?

Problem 2: With which types of experts should you consult to correct the problem?

12.1 Reasons for Simulation

If it were only true, the Star Trek holodeck could save billions of dollars! *Star Trek* is a television series that started in the late 1960s and still has many fans called "trekkies." The Star Trek holodeck was capable of many amazing feats. The holograms could be projected into space, giving the effect of three-dimensional objects. In today's world the CAVE virtual reality system is a step in that direction; it will be discussed in section 12.7. In *Star Trek* the holodeck could be augmented with replicator technology, allowing actual substances to materialize: an apple, for example, that could be eaten. The holodeck's force beam technology allowed the simulation of solid objects, much like the more primitive virtual surgery simulations also in section 12.7. A real holodeck would make simulation even more valuable than it already is.

> **Simulation** is a technique used to mimic or imitate some phenomenon in a way that represents the real situation in most of its details.

Simulation is one of the most important concepts in modern technology. **Simulation** literally means *to imitate* or *to give the appearance of* something else. Typically, a physical or mathematical **model** is designed to behave like the object or event of interest; then by manipulating and working with the model an engineer, scientist, or architect can predict, understand, experiment with, and test it, or even use the model for training purposes. A physical model of an aircraft is used in the wind tunnel, for example, to investigate the aerodynamics of the outside shape of its fuselage and wings. Of course, the wind tunnel experiment will not help in designing the cockpit layout for ease of use by the pilots. On the other hand, to investigate the maneuvering of spacecraft by astronauts during docking, a physical model is impractical. In this case a mathematical model that takes into account the gravitational pull of Earth and other factors is possible. To better understand the whys and hows of simulation, let's look at the major reasons for using it:

> A **model** is a physical, mental, or conceptual system for simulation of some phenomenon. It leads to results that are identical or at least similar in many details to the real thing.

- forecasting or predicting the future
- accessing the inaccessible or impossible
- experimentation and testing
- education and training

FORECASTING OR PREDICTING THE FUTURE

Imagine that you have purchased an alarm clock radio. You would like to become familiar with its operation before letting it take over the responsibility of waking you up for your morning classes. To do this you compress time. That is, you turn the clock through a 24-hour period by hand in just a few seconds; you can then see how the clock operates during this period.

Monte Carlo Simulation

This technique, invented by mathematicians von Neumann and Ulam, is used to simulate certain types of real-life systems too complex or expensive to solve in other ways. It is named after the famous casinos at Monte Carlo because it makes use of pure chance to get answers. The military uses Monte Carlo methods in computer programs that simulate battlefield situations.

Jagjit Singh in his book *Great Ideas of Operations Research* shows how a chemical factory with only two loading docks for trucks can improve efficiency. When first observed, the situation had daily waiting times for trucks of 96 hours, and unloading crews experienced idle times of 50 man-hours. By using Monte Carlo simulation the effect of building extra loading bays and/or hiring more personnel can be examined without the cost of actually making the changes. In this particular example, it was found that by building an extra loading dock the daily waiting time of trucks was reduced to 25 hours, although the loading crew's idle time increased to 76 man-hours daily. But, because personnel hours are cheaper than truck hours, the extra loading dock would be a good decision. In this situation, and many others like it, the Monte Carlo simulation can determine in advance the effects of changes while costing relatively very little.

To predict the future, a model must compress time. Without **time compression,** simulating something like the depletion of Earth's resources over a period of 100 years would take 100 years, and by then it might be too late to matter!

The idea of using a model to predict the future is not unfamiliar. **Prediction** of the outcome of presidential elections, the weather, gross national product, yearly automobile production, the prime interest rate, the population of the United States, an eclipse of the sun by the moon, the price of a stock on the stock market, the pollution of the Great Lakes, the flooding of river basins, the pollution of the atmosphere, and the deer population in a national forest are all examples of using time compression in simulation. It should be noted, by the way, that not all predictions are correct! Early during election day 2000, some analysts predicted that Gore would clearly take the state of Florida. Actually, Bush took the state. On the other hand, some events, such as eclipses of the sun by the moon, can be predicted within seconds of their actual occurrence.

The incorrect prediction of a presidential election brings up an extremely important point: Predictions are only as good as the models used in the simulation. An incorrect model that may not take all effects into account invariably gives erroneous results.

Time compression is necessary when forecasting or predicting the future. It is equivalent to speeding up the clock.

PUZZLER HINT

The model in the company was created by an external company. If it is suspect, what should you do?

It should be clear that it is often impossible to know everything to include in the models used for simulation. Who could have predicted the seemingly reasonless rise in gasoline prices during the summers of 2000 and 2008? This is contrary to the 2005 gas prices that were predicted reasonably close to what really happened.

ACCESSING THE INACCESSIBLE OR IMPOSSIBLE

Many simulations are necessary because it is impossible to gain knowledge in any other way. We often resort to **simulating the impossible** to understand a system or event. Observing the collapse of a star, resulting from gravitation, to form a neutron star or black hole is impossible, for example. To understand the collapse of a star, astrophysicists create a mathematical model. Then a computer can perform the billions of calculations to determine what happens.

One 3D-animated simulation, developed by Engineering Animation, Inc. (EAI), realistically depicts the detonation that destroyed the Alfred P. Murrah Federal Building in Oklahoma City, Oklahoma, on April 19, 1995. EAI worked with explosive expert Kenneth Waltz and one of the original architects of the Murrah Federal Building, James Loftis, to scientifically depict the detonation and its damage to the building's structure.

After looking at the scene before and after the incident using videos and photographs, Waltz and Loftis combined their experiences to track the bomb's path and show the impact and devastation to the building. Loftis drew on his firsthand knowledge of the structure and design of the building and helped EAI determine the dimensions of the building's structure as well as its surroundings. Waltz determined the force of the shock wave based on his estimate of the bomb's force and on his years as an explosives investigator.

Five frames from the final result of the animated simulation are shown in Figure 12.1.1. They depict the site of the federal building as it appeared just after the bomb detonates unleashing a powerful shock wave and a fireball. The building is engulfed in a cloud of fire,

Courtesy of Engineering Animation

Figure 12.1.1
Five frames from a simulation of the Oklahoma bombing.

smoke, and dust. As the shock wave penetrates the interior structure of the building, massive concrete floor slabs are pushed upward before they collapse.

Also, it is sometimes physically impossible to try all the possible combinations or ways of doing things. Intuition may help a chemist select just the right temperature, elements, and proportions to make a new compound. But intuition doesn't always lead to results.

EXPERIMENTATION AND TESTING

Can you imagine what the total cost of developing a large airplane would be if it were necessary to build several complete full-size models? As each model was tested, design flaws would be corrected in the next full-size model, but it would take a lot of trials. Obviously, this is not the way to design and develop airplanes. Instead, very complicated mathematical models are run on computers for **experimentation and testing.** These models indicate design flaws that can be corrected and the new model can be "flown" or tested in the computer. When all the flaws seem to be gone, then a full-sized model can finally be constructed. Of course, it will probably still have some problems, but generally they will be minor and can be corrected as more aircraft are built. This is considerably cheaper in terms of both money and human life.

Figure 12.1.2 shows an example of how computer simulation can be used to test a new type of bridge railing. Instead of crashing several dozen automobiles at various angles and speeds, which is both costly and dangerous, it is possible to give the computer program the information. The program will draw individual frames for an animated "cartoon."

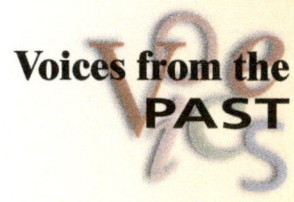

Voices from the PAST

Herbert A. Simon—Simulating Human Cognition

Born in 1916 in Milwaukee, Wisconsin, and receiving his Ph.D. in political science from the University of Chicago, Herbert A. Simon has had many illustrious honors. The most impressive is his Nobel Prize in Economics awarded in 1978. It was given to him "for his pioneering research into the decision-making process within economic organizations." More fundamentally, he indicated: "My central research interest is in building and testing theories of human cognition, using computer simulation models."

This interest in simulation had its beginnings when Dr. Simon felt that the social sciences needed the same mathematical rigor and foundation that the "hard" sciences found so successful. The desire to

Corbis

accomplish this caused him to comment: "I would prepare myself to become a mathematical social scientist." Research ranging from computer science to psychology, economics, and administration with philosophy as a major thread tied it all together. The unifying theme was his interest in human decision-making and problem-solving processes, and how these affected social institutions.

Dr. Simon has put a great emphasis on the area of simulating human thinking. By using the tools of computing and techniques of artificial intelligence he has made great contributions to this area. These efforts started back in 1954, when he joined with Allen Newell to attack the difficult processes in human problem solving by simulating them on the computer. This became a lifelong practice as he states: "Gradually, computer simulation of human cognition became my central research interest, an interest that has continued to be absorbing up to the present time."

An autobiography of Herbert Simon appears on the Nobel Foundation Web site. The quotations cited here were taken from that source.

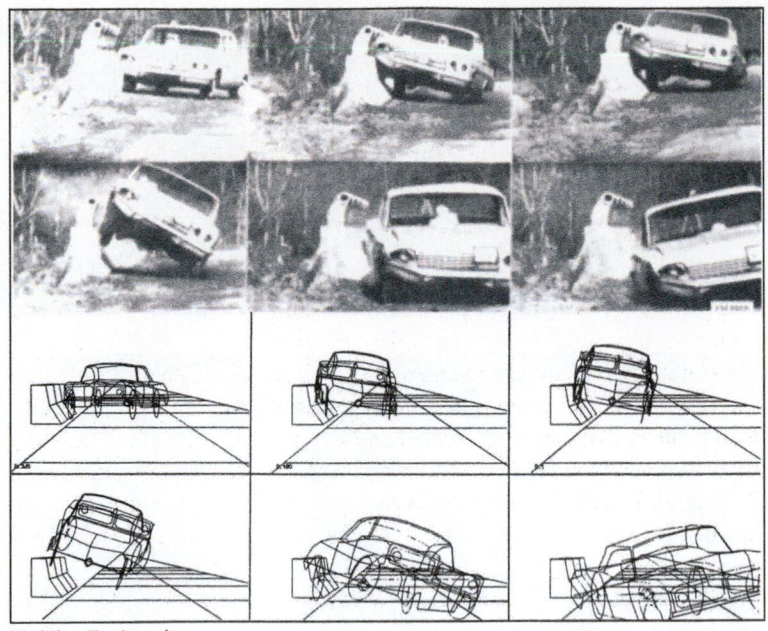

Veridian Engineering

Figure 12.1.2

Simulation of an auto crash.

Researchers can then study the films and make necessary changes. An important point to remember is that testing the simulated model of a complicated system is often more feasible than testing the real thing.

Sometimes, of course, computer simulation is not the best method for developing a new product design. It is much cheaper and quicker to design a flying disk for playing Frisbee by building several versions, for example. Then the best design is chosen on the basis of a test of the actual flying disk.

Another very important aspect of simulation is experimentation. It is sometimes disastrous to experiment on the actual system being tested. The U.S. economy, for instance, is very sensitive to changes in certain areas. Yet the federal government has the power to change taxes and prime interest rates, regulate rates for railroads and automobile gas mileage requirements, and control many other critical variables. How does the government decide to make a change in some sensitive areas? As you might guess, many decisions are made on the basis of how models of various parts of the U.S. economy behave. Unfortunately, the models don't always describe accurately how the economy really works. This is because there are so many unknown and unpredictable events that affect the economy; therefore, no model of the U.S. economy can be entirely complete. How could something such as the assassination of President Kennedy be predicted, for example? How could the effect of his death be incorporated into any model?

EDUCATION AND TRAINING

Among the most valuable uses of computer simulations are **education** and **training.** The following examples show how simulations allow greater flexibility and are often better than traditional methods for education and training.

It is often quite difficult to give the benefit of years of experience to people learning some complex skill. Diagnostics in medicine takes years of experience, for example, usually done on the job. But the simulation of patient-doctor relations can be extremely useful. One such interactive simulation involves the prospective doctor and a simulation that models an emergency. By typing into a computer, the doctor can request the vital signs such as pulse and temperature of the simulated patient. The time element is also incorporated; if the doctor takes too long, the "patient" dies! Records of how well the prospective doctor diagnosed and treated the various "patients" can be kept for progress reports.

Figure 12.1.3

Aircraft landing simulation.

Courtesy of Evans and Sutherland Computer Corporation

Interactive simulations are also used in military training. Aircraft landing simulation, in particular, is one that is particularly intriguing. Figure 12.1.3 shows four snapshots from a training session of a jet landing on an aircraft carrier. The person at the controls of the imaginary moving airplane causes the picture to change. This particular system can also include other moving aircraft to simulate even more complex events. The pilot sees the other aircraft and has to make decisions, which in turn affect the picture being shown. This constitutes a good example of a feedback loop, which we'll discuss in the next section. It allows pilots to have preliminary flight training at considerably less cost than practicing with real aircraft. Evans and Sutherland developed the software for the interactive landing simulator illustrated in Figure 12.1.3. Table 12.1.1 lists several popular interactive simulation activities.

Table 12.1.1   *Areas of simulation activity.*

Nuclear Power Plant	Fish Farm Management
Health Care Delivery	Traffic Light Timing
Steel Mill Scheduling	Financial Forecasting
Sales Forecasting	Railroad Operations
Armed Forces Logistics	Space Shuttle Reentry
Nuclear Waste Disposal	Taxi Dispatching
Bus Scheduling	Airline Maintenance
Job Shop Scheduling	Harbor Design
Ambulance Dispatching	Inventory Reordering
Police Response	Election Predictions
Urban Traffic System	Manufacturing
Ship Pilot Training	Library Layout Design
Airport Design	Bank Teller Scheduling
Electronic Circuit Design	Consumer Brand Selection
Mail Distribution	Facility Layout
Weather Prediction	Human Heart Functions
Sailboat Hull Design	Auto Suspension System

12.2 Building a Model

We've used the word *model* several times. What is a model? As mentioned earlier, the model of an object or system imitates the appearance or behavior of the system in question. There are many types of models, both physical and computer simulated. All of these share some general characteristics.

Models can be characterized as continuous or discrete systems. However, a combination of continuous and discrete systems is also common. Models of **continuous systems** are those for which the observable characteristics vary in a smooth or continuous manner, as contrasted with **discrete system** models that vary in steps or jumps.

In simulating the landing of a rocket on the moon, for example, the quantities such as velocity, engine thrust, and deceleration are all smoothly varying. In other words, these quantities don't jump from one value to another value but change smoothly from one to the other.

A simple example of a discrete system is the modeling of traffic at an intersection. There can be 1 or 23 cars passing through the traffic light, but not 1.5 or 7.6 cars. Fractions of cars don't make any sense. The number of cars "jumps" in units of 1 car.

Models of systems can also be categorized as being either **predictable** or **probabilistic.** The mathematical model of the solar system used to predict the eclipse of the sun by the moon is predictable. This is also true of the model of the orbit of a satellite.

Probabilistic systems, on the other hand, are those that are not predictable. The model for a roulette wheel is completely unpredictable, for example (unless, of course, it is dishonest). The model for traffic flow in the downtown area of a city is also probabilistic. It is almost impossible to predict when a shopper will decide to go home.

Another characterization of system models is the feedback versus nonfeedback feature. *Feedback* is a general term denoting the feeding back or recycling of actions or results of a model as input to itself. An automobile driver system is of the feedback type, for example. When a driver tries to avoid an object in the road, as in Figure 12.2.1, a turn away from the object is started. The eyes of the driver feed back information about how the turn is progressing. If the turn isn't sharp enough, the driver increases the turn. This system of recycling information is just one of the many human feedback examples. It is often referred to as a feedback loop. The figure of the driver illustrates a closed feedback loop. If the driver were suddenly blinded by the glare of the sun, the **feedback loop** would be opened, probably resulting in an accident.

As you might guess, these classifications are not always easy to determine. In fact, some of the more complicated models have combinations of all of the foregoing characteristics: discrete and continuous, predictable and probabilistic, feedback and nonfeedback. To better understand some of these characteristics, let's look at two examples in detail: the Monopoly game and a city management simulation called SimCity.

Models of **continuous systems** have quantities that vary smoothly or in a continuous manner.

Models of **discrete systems** have quantities that vary in steps or jumps.

Predictable systems have models that predict exactly what will happen.

Probabilistic systems have models that contain unpredictable features.

Models that feed results back to the input are referred to as systems with a **feedback loop**.

Figure 12.2.1

Driver feedback loop during an emergency turn.

12.3 Monopoly Game Simulation

A vast number of applications for simulation exists but none that will have a more familiar setting than simulation of that world-famous game, **Monopoly.** Invented by Charles Darrow in 1933, Monopoly is now marketed in 25 countries and has sold more than 80 million copies in the United States alone.

In this section, we'll investigate a simulation that will help develop some winning strategies for Monopoly. The ideas first appeared in an article "How to Win at Monopoly," by mathematician Dr. Irvin R. Hentzel.

Moves by each player are controlled by the random toss of dice or instructions given by randomly shuffled cards. The reliance on randomly chosen input ensures that the game is probabilistic, not predictable. It is also discrete rather than continuous. Is there any feedback in the system? It depends, of course, on how the system is defined. If the system includes the players, there is definitely feedback. As moves are made, the players observe the game's progress and then make decisions on what properties to buy. If, on the other hand, the system is defined not to include the players but only the die tosses and board play, it does not have a feedback loop.

The simulation we consider here will model only the board play; in other words, the model will do no decision making. Using a general-purpose computer, a program can be written that performs all the basic plays of the game: tossing dice, moving pieces on the board, allowing property purchases, checking ownership for possible rent payment, and drawing Chance or Community Chest cards. A group of players can then sit around a terminal and let the computer toss the dice and perform other functions, while they make decisions about whether to buy property. As most players would probably agree, the presence of the actual board and money is more satisfying than having the computer simulate them. But remember, this is an exercise to illustrate how computers can be used to simulate systems! Here is a detailed list of Monopoly activities the computer must simulate:

- toss dice
- move game pieces
- allow real estate purchases
- allow hotel purchases
- allow house purchases
- draw Chance card if necessary
- draw Community Chest card if necessary
- toss second time if doubles
- toss third time if doubles on second toss
- go to jail if third toss is doubles
- collect $200 upon passing GO
- check for rent payment
- keep records of each player's assets (cash and real estate)
- allow mortgaging
- get out of jail on doubles
- get out of jail after third toss
- go to jail if player lands in GO TO JAIL square
- pay luxury tax when landing on luxury tax square
- pay income tax when landing on income tax square

PROGRAMMING GETTING OUT OF JAIL

To understand the process of writing a program to play Monopoly, let's examine the problem of getting out of jail.

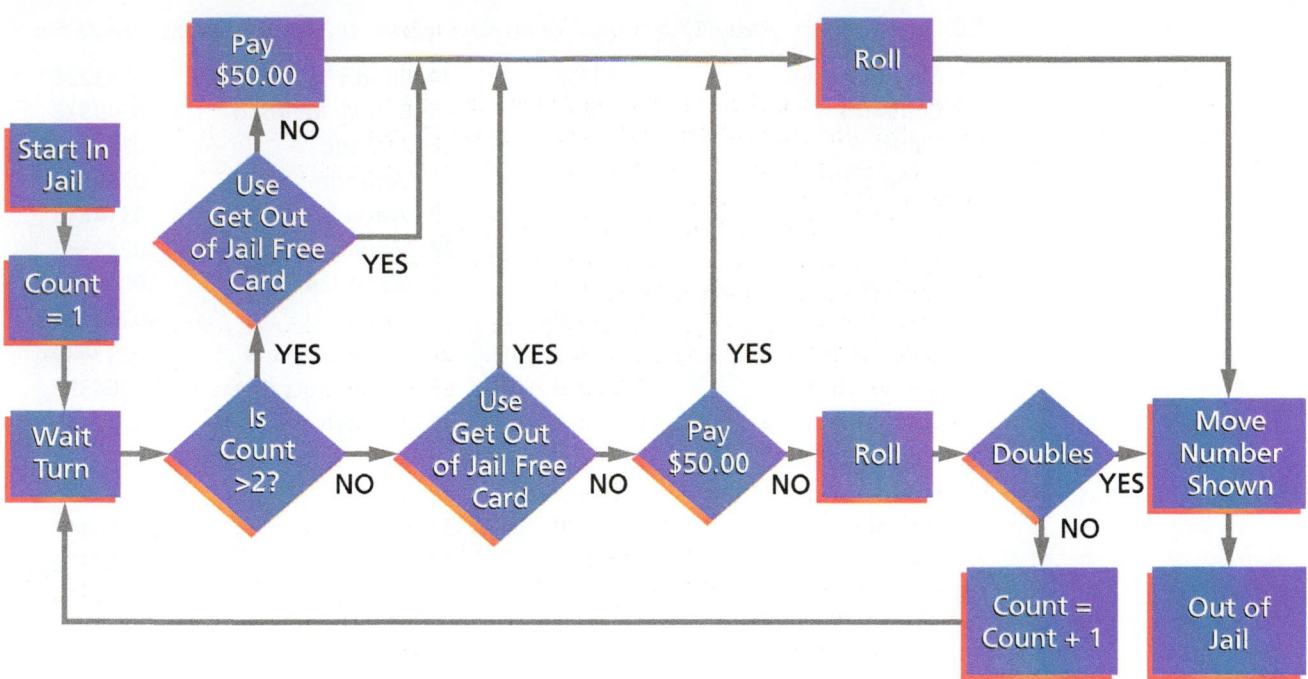

Figure 12.3.1

The flow of play showing getting out of jail.

The general flow of play is best illustrated by a flowchart as shown in Figure 12.3.1. It represents the process of getting out of jail.

To develop a strategy for Monopoly, certain types of information about the game are absolutely necessary. What information is necessary to help decide whether to build houses evenly on two or more of your monopolies, for example, or to build up only one of them? Of course, if you knew that your opponent is 30 percent more likely to land on one of them, then it is obvious that this monopoly should be developed first. Obtaining these probabilities is somewhat difficult from a purely theoretical point of view. But if we could simulate the play of many games and record how often each of the properties is landed on, then we would have the information necessary. Figure 12.3.1 is only part of the general scheme for a computer program that would play Monopoly. A complete flowchart of all the details is too much to consider here.

PROBABILITIES OF THE GAME

Professor of mathematics Irvin R. Hentzel made a study of the probabilities of landing on various squares in Monopoly. To calculate these probabilities a mathematical model was formulated, and resulted in Table 12.3.1. The calculations assumed that all Chance and Community Chest cards are in play and also that players elect to throw doubles to get out of jail.

Examining this table, we see that the property most often landed upon is square 24, Illinois Avenue, but there are several other properties with probabilities close to this value. In fact, the top five properties most often landed on are Reading Railroad, Tennessee, New York, Illinois, and B. & O. Railroad. At first glance, you might think that these are obvious candidates for ownership and development. However, what you should keep in mind is not merely how often an opponent may land on the square, but also how much it costs to develop the property and the return on that investment. A study of the expected return on investment is necessary.

Table 12.3.1   *Probability of landing on each square as computed by the simulation.*

1	Mediterranean	.0238252	24	Illinois	.0355236
2	Community Chest	.0210683	25	B. & O. Railroad	.0343378
3	Baltic	.0241763	26	Atlantic	.0301120
4	Income Tax	.0260343	27	Ventnor	.0298999
5	Reading Railroad	.0332449	28	Water Works	.0314613
6	Oriental	.0253014	29	Marvin Gardens	.0289385
7	Chance	.0096756	30	Go to Jail	.0000000
8	Vermont	.0259620	31	Pacific	.0299534
9	Connecticut	.0257326	32	North Carolina	.0293420
10	Just Visiting	.0253909	33	Community Chest	.0264392
11	St. Charles Place	.0303370	34	Pennsylvania	.0279291
12	Electric Company	.0310260	35	Short Line Railroad	.0271871
13	States	.0258042	36	Chance	.0096825
14	Virginia	.0287890	37	Park Place	.0244447
15	Pennsylvania Railroad	.0312800	38	Luxury Tax	.0243572
16	St. James Place	.0318117	39	Boardwalk	.0294734
17	Community Chest	.0272474	40	Go	.0345904
18	Tennessee	.0334833			
19	New York	.0333734		*Jail Probabilities*	
20	Free Parking	.0335340	J(1)	Sent to Jail	.0444049
21	Kentucky	.0310290	J(2)	In Jail 2 Turns	.0370041
22	Chance	.0124010	J(3)	In Jail 3 Turns	.0308368
23	Indiana	.0304690			

To calculate the return on investment, taking into account the probability of landing on that particular property, we need only multiply the probability of landing on a property by its rent; do this for each property in a monopoly and sum the results. Of course, the rent varies with how many houses or hotels are present. Figure 12.3.2 shows the yellow Monopoly deeds, for example, for which rents are $22, $22, and $24.

As houses or hotels are added, the rents go up. Calculating with all of the details for each house added to the group, a graph such as shown in Figure 12.3.3 would result.

Note that a maximum of three hotels can be erected on the yellow monopoly, one on each property. Therefore, even though additional capital is available, only $103.74 can be expected as return per turn from $2,250 capital invested.

Doing this calculation for all of the monopolies results in Figure 12.3.4. Examination of this figure will help you develop two strategies for winning Monopoly.

DEVELOPING A WINNING STRATEGY

On examining Figure 12.3.4, we see that for small amounts of investment capital, railroads are a good investment. Suppose, however, $2,000 of investment capital was available; then the expected return from railroads is only about $30, whereas investing the additional

Figure 12.3.2

Yellow Monopoly deeds.

Monopoly® & © 2000 Hasbro, Inc. Used with permission

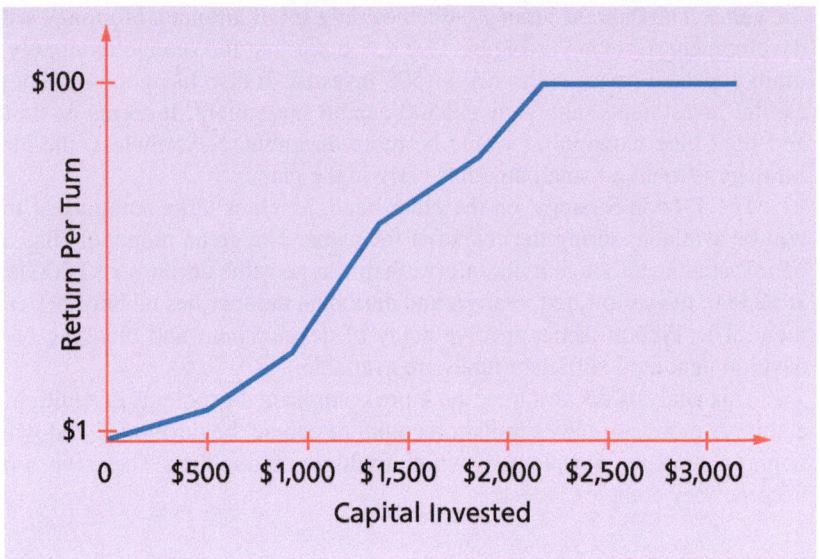

Figure 12.3.3

Yellow Monopoly's return per turn versus capital invested.

monies in the yellow monopoly would yield $103.74 and the green monopoly would yield an expected return of $87. It seems that a player's investment plan depends on how much money he or she has available or will have available for capital investment.

This leads to a pair of strategies devised by Professor Hentzel: the Peasant and Tycoon strategies. A player should first estimate how much money can be raised over the course of

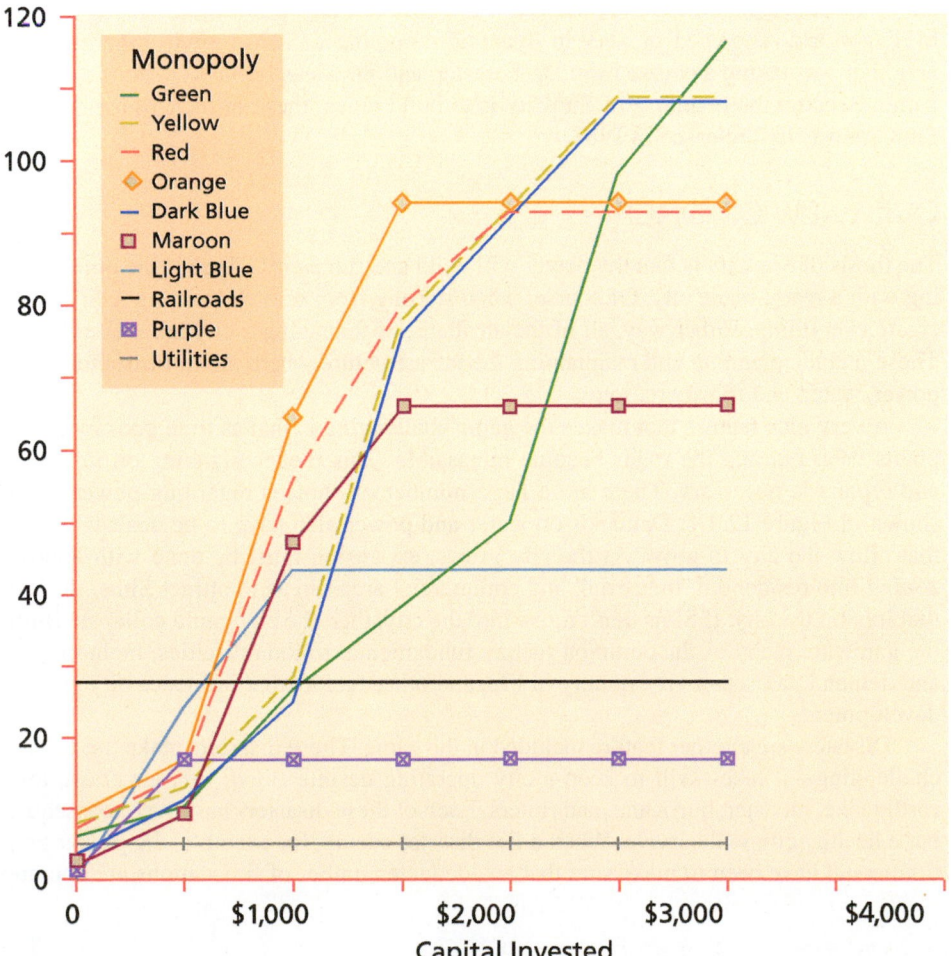

Figure 12.3.4

Return per turn as a function of capital investment on all the monopolies.

the game. The Peasant Strategy assumes only small amounts of money will be invested for development. Looking at Figure 12.3.4, we see that the orange monopoly reaches a maximum expected return with only $1,500 invested. It also has good expected return at lower capital investments, although at $500 capital investment, it seems as though the railroads and light blue monopolies would be more desirable. Nevertheless, the idea in the Peasant Strategy is to invest small amounts early in the game.

The Tycoon Strategy, on the other hand, assumes large amounts of investment capital will be available during the course of the game. The green monopoly has the highest return on investment, although it doesn't reach this large value until over $2,500 is invested. In fact, at $2,000, the yellow, red, orange, and dark blue monopolies all have better return on investment. The Tycoon tactics involve delay of development and blocking of your opponent's development until sufficient funds are available.

This analysis doesn't treat the more complicated problems of multiple monopoly ownership. A more complex simulation could, of course, be developed that would shed light on winning strategies for players owning multiple monopolies. These types of analyses could become very complex indeed.

12.4 SimCity: Simulation of City Planning

SimCity is the name of a game. If your definition of a game is an amusement or pastime, however, SimCity is more than a game. It is a simulation that architects and engineers could use to practice real city planning. The influences on the author Will Wright for creating SimCity are varied. First there was Stanislaw Lem's science fiction anthology *The Cyberiad,* which is about two constructor robots who try to outinvent each other and in the process create civilizations. Another influence was more indirect, and it involved Dr. Jay Forester of MIT, a world-renowned pioneer in dynamic modeling of urban environments. Wright's neighbor was taking a course from Dr. Forester, and the ideas fit nicely with the developing game. Because the objective of SimCity is to build cities, these influences are noteworthy. SimCity was first released in 1987.

OVERVIEW OF SIMCITY

The thesis of SimCity is that the player will build and run a city. There is the option of starting with a ready-made city. Of course, when starting from scratch building a city you must create everything. Either way, all of the attributes of managing a city are well represented. These include planning and maintaining the infrastructure where the infrastructure includes power, water, and transportation.

A very nice feature that makes the game challenging is that as time goes by the power plants wear out and the roads become impassable. This means planning on replacements and repairs is necessary. There are a large number of choices regarding power plants, as shown in Figure 12.4.1. Demands on water and power also have to be dealt with in ways that allow the city to grow. As the city grows, expansion must be done with appropriate zoning into residential, industrial, and commercial areas so as to attract Sims, the citizens that inhabit the city. If Sims don't move into the city, then the city could collapse. Built into the game are many of the common factors fundamental to today's cities, including supply and demand, tax sensitivity, quality of life, and other factors that influence city growth and development.

Disasters are another feature included in the game. These disasters make the game more challenging—it takes skill to keep a city operating despite flood, fire, air crash, tornado, earthquake, monster, hurricane, and rioters. Each of these disasters has severe consequences, but a healthy city will survive. When a fire disaster occurs, for example, the proper preparation would have been to make sure that an adequate number of fire stations are operational.

Reprinted by permission of Maxis

Figure 12.4.1

Oil, gas, coal, and wind electrical power generating plants.

Neophytes can turn off disasters, which makes SimCity easier to play. Figure 12.4.2 shows a fire disaster.

Consistent with all cities is the ability to tax and then spend the revenue on building schools, hospitals, recreation areas, seaports, roads, power plants, airports, police departments, and fire departments. If the taxes are raised too high, however, people will move away and the city will shrink. This will lead to the problems that are typical of today's real-life cities.

The model used to simulate the cities of SimCity is one that exhibits some of the interesting properties of all cities. As an experimental investigation of certain aspects of the model, let us construct a new city with two commercial zones. However, one of the zones will have very good access through a road completely surrounding it. The other will only have a single road going alongside. Figure 12.4.3 shows that after 10 years, the commercial

Figure 12.4.2

A fire disaster in action.

Reprinted by permission of Maxis

Figure 12.4.3

How roadways affect the growth of a city.

zone with the better access has a much larger residential community that has formed around it. Both commercial zones had the same amount of property zoned residential around them. This shows that the SimCity model seems to follow the normal course of development experienced in real life. This example also helps to reinforce a variation of an old adage "build a good city and they will come." It implies that if planning is done correctly by today's standards, then people will inhabit the city and both industry and commercial activity will flourish.

PLANNING DETAILS IN A FEEDBACK ENVIRONMENT

There are many details to master when planning a city. To view one aspect of this complexity, take a look at an existing city in SimCity 2000. The roadways and other transportation have already been done, but the water supply is minimal. A series of three screen shots from the city are shown in Figure 12.4.4.

In Figure 12.4.4(a), the city has grown to include residential, commercial, and industrial development. Figure 12.4.4(b) shows the original zoning plan: residential (green), commercial (blue), and industrial (tan). When zoning is done, the Sims—citizens that inhabit the city—will make use of the land according to the zoning restrictions. However, several factors affect development, including access, water, power, and even desirability. Land zoned residential next to a coal-burning power plant will not develop quickly, for example, because it is considered less desirable. The water factor can enter into development when the supply is limited, as is the case with new development. Only minimal water is automatically supplied when the Sims build, but the infrastructure for water is supplied. This underground water infrastructure is shown in Figure 12.4.4(c).

You can see the complexity of this simulation by examining the water systems. As was already indicated, the Sims built the underground water systems as the land was developed for residential, commercial, and industrial properties. Supplying water to existing water pipes can be done in several ways. Pumps may be added, as was done in Figure 12.4.4(c). Pumps installed some distance from freshwater supplies show up as wells, dependent on the water table, which is lower in the dry season. Pumps placed near freshwater rivers and lakes will produce three times more water, unless next to saltwater, where they produce the same as inland wells. A desalinization plant is needed to treat saltwater used for drinking. One way to deal with water shortages is to build water treatment plants to clean and recycle the water. Another strategy involves using water tanks to store water during the wet season for use in the dry season.

Water has other uses. It can help development by providing transportation and shipping. Recreation can also be developed on the waterfront. Recreational areas, stadiums,

(a) Reprinted by permission of Maxis

(b) Reprinted by permission of Maxis

(c) Reprinted by permission of Maxis

Figure 12.4.4

(a) A typical city.
(b) The zoning in effect for the city.
(c) Water system infra-structure for the city (blue—adequate, red—inadequate).

parks, and green space provide a quality of life that attracts people and will allow the city to flourish.

STRATEGIES AND THE MODEL

Strategies of many types can be used to play this game. However, some general long-range goals should be developed in advance. Suppose, for example, that the long-term objective is to grow the population as large as possible. In this case game designers indicate that you should "zone densely, keep control of crime, and watch the newspapers for public opinion and important inventions." Other possible objectives include maximizing city income or even creating an ideal city to live in. The latter objective is of a personal nature, but it's your choice.

The model itself is contained in the algorithms that control the interactions between the features that you create. These features should include:

- A residential zone where the Sims will live
- An industrial zone where the Sims will work
- A commercial zone where the Sims will shop and conduct business
- A power plant to supply power for all the foregoing activities
- Power lines to bring power to the various areas
- A transportation infrastructure so the Sims can get from place to place

With these basic features, the city will grow. However, the model has much more to it than these basics. The additional features that make SimCity even more complex are the algorithms that take into account the following:

- Zoning that has different density levels
- Multiple means of transportation including subways, trains, water, and air
- A water system including pumps, tanks, reclamation, and desalinization
- Landscaping for quality of life
- Police and fire stations
- Schools
- Recreational facilities

Feedback is an important attribute that adds complexity to a model. SimCity has feedback incorporated at many levels. As your city is growing, for example, some decisions are made on the basis of what you see happening. The feedback is actually quite complex and has many feedback loops, which make the game exciting and eventful. As each decision is implemented, its effects ripple through the city.

The traffic density model is another complex attribute of the model recognized by urban planners as the most impressive part of SimCity. Inside the SimCity program is an algorithm that implements the traffic density model. The traffic density model uses a technique referred to as recursion. Simple formulas aren't used to obtain the traffic density in a single calculation. Although too difficult to go into here in this discussion, recursion is used extensively by computer scientists. But the outcome of the traffic density model is something with which we can all identify. It relates to the fact that traffic always seems to expand to fill new roads and freeways. This is something everyone has experienced!

One of the most important criticisms of SimCity is that it is not very realistic. How many cities do you know that are run by a single person? In any normal city it is not likely that a single person can decide to raise taxes, build schools, build recreation complexes, or even zone property. Controlling activities of a city is usually done by several individuals in some type of a city council, possibly with other groups that act as checks and balances. With this single criticism out of the way, it can be said that SimCity is a very comprehensive model of city growth and management.

12.5 Simulation of the Process of Life: Protein Folding

WHAT IS PROTEIN FOLDING AND WHY IS IT IMPORTANT?

DNA is the basis for all types of biological activity, in other words, life. For humans, their DNA is a string of approximately 3 billion base pairs, and contains the complete plan on how to create the person it came from. This huge string segmented into about 20,000 to 25,000 segments called genes. These genes will instigate the biological process of forming proteins (strings of amino acids) that, in turn, may become
    —Structural parts of the humane body bone, and blood
    or
    —Act as active participants in bodily processes.

The genes also form enzymes that will promote the actions causing biochemical reactions. For these proteins to carry out their specific task, they must have the proper shape created by "folding" the protein. This process of protein folding is of great interest in understanding the human body and also medical research. By understanding the folding process it is hoped that diseases such as Alzheimer's disease, cystic fibrosis, Mad Cow disease, many cancers, and Huntington's disease can be better understood and may be cured with that knowledge. Researchers theorize that some forms of cancer are due to misfolding of the proteins. It is considered by many that understanding protein folding is the next major advance in understanding the process of life. The DNA represents the building blocks or plan, and proteins represent structure and processes of living things.

There are literally hundreds of projects around the world that are attempting to simulate protein folding. The intense research is driven by the desire to understand how living biology works. These research projects use many types of models and variations hoping to get some insight on how the real living system works by trying to simulate it. Since the process of how a protein folds upon itself is intimately related to the foundation of the problem, a large number of projects are focused on protein folding.

The idea is to mimic the folding of any one of thousands of proteins. Each protein has almost infinite ways of folding. In real life the actual folding process can take place in millionths of a second. The Folding@home simulation discussed later in this section models proteins that fold in 5 to 10 millionths of second.

All of these projects respect a fundamental goal of protein folding: fold the protein so it is in a stable state (e.g., the free energy is minimized). In other words, given this string of several hundred amino acids, the goal is to fold it so that it occupies a form with the lowest energy. By analogy, if two magnets are oriented so they attract, then they will have lowest energy when not held apart. They will then be touching. There are situations where folding will cause parts of the string to repulse each other (analogous to magnets oriented so they repel when forced together). This may or may not be allowed depending on the overall energy needed to assume the "fold."

THE FOLDIT@HOME PROJECT

Extreme amounts of computing power, such as supercomputers or grid computing, must be utilized to model protein folding. One such project, foldit@home , dates back to 2000 at Stanford University, and is under the supervision of Professor Vijay Pande. It relies on volunteers to donate use of their computers, either as a screen saver or dedicated to foldit.@home. Some notable features of the foldit@home project:

- Over 4 million CPUs participating

- CPUs run under a variety of operating systems: Windows, Mac OS X, Linux, ATI & Nvidia graphics processing units, and Playstation 3 game processors

- Playstation 3 game processors are 40 times faster than most personal computers, which means that they can process more information in a shorter time than most personal computers.

- Effective speed of the grid is 5 petaflops (petaflop—is a million billion floating point operations per second). This is much faster than the typical super computer.

The basic idea is that volunteers install a program, called a client, on their personal computers or game machines. Periodically, this client program will communicate with the foldit@home server and will send completed computations to the project server. During this process, the volunteers' computers will receive new computations to be completed. Most of the client programs run in the background of the volunteers' computers (see multitasking chapter 6), or can be dedicated to full time use. Each of these client programs is written especially for the volunteers' computer, whether it is a PS3, Windows or Macintosh. To make it more appealing, foldit@home can track their individual or team's contributions to the overall project. A more visual and "hands on" approach can be played in the form of a game.

THE FOLDIT GAME: USING HUMAN BRAIN POWER

Another project in Seattle makes use of human brainpower. David Baker and his team were using grid computing for several years to simulate protein folding through the project Rosetta@home. With 86,000 clients in 2006 he had the equivalent of a 77-teraflop super computer. Progress, however, was good but slow. In 2007 he had the idea of using the human powers of intuition and spatial reasoning. With the help of a computer graphics expert the team created a game that modeled a protein in 3-D using graphical colored shapes. The long string of amino acid molecules form a backbone with groups of atoms, called sidechains, hanging off each amino acid. Figure 12.5.1 shows a typical view of a small protein. The tubular ribbon like structure represent the string of amino acids. The blue and brownish pink appendages represent small groups of atoms called sidechains.

Figure 12.5.1

The view of a typical small-unfolded protein showing basic structure.

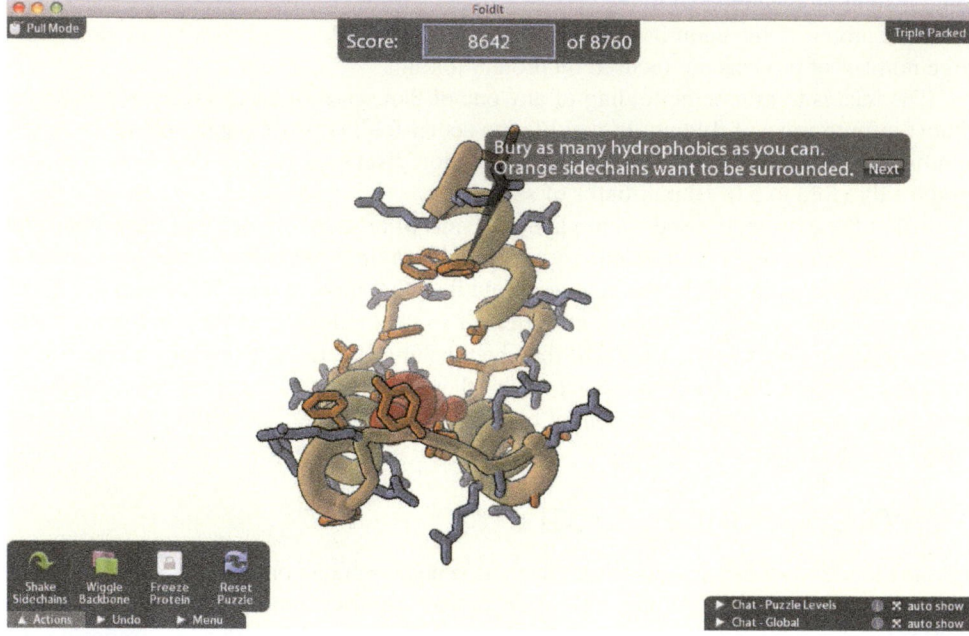

The model that simulates the folding process allows the user to bend, rotate, pull, and wiggle the amino acid anywhere along its' length. The rules in the model for the game "are based on physics—opposite charges attract, atomic bonds have limited angles to rotation, and the parts of the molecule that stick to water tend to point outward." In the process of manipulating the 3-D model the closer the user sticks to these rules the more points are awarded. A higher score reflects better folds. Figure 12.5.2 shows a compression of the protein of Figure 12.5.1, and but it was overdone and caused the score to go to zero.

Figure 12.5.2

Over manipulation of the protein of Figure 12.5.1 shows score going to 0.

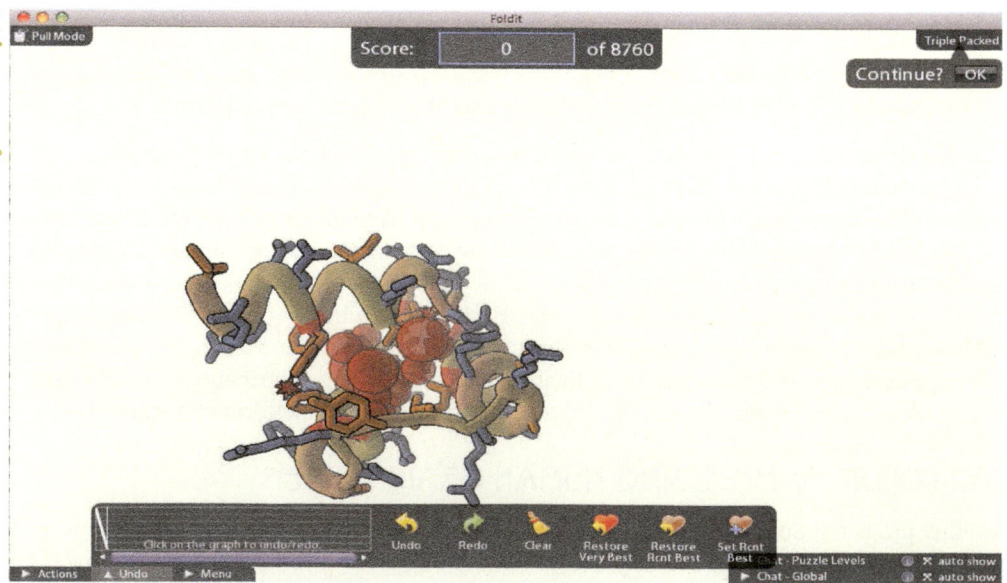

Note the red spheres in the figures, they represent voids, which should be reduced in order to make a better score. The "spiky" looking spherical shape is a conflict that must be resolved. Undoing this "over folding" Figure 12.5.3 shows another attempt that has a higher score.

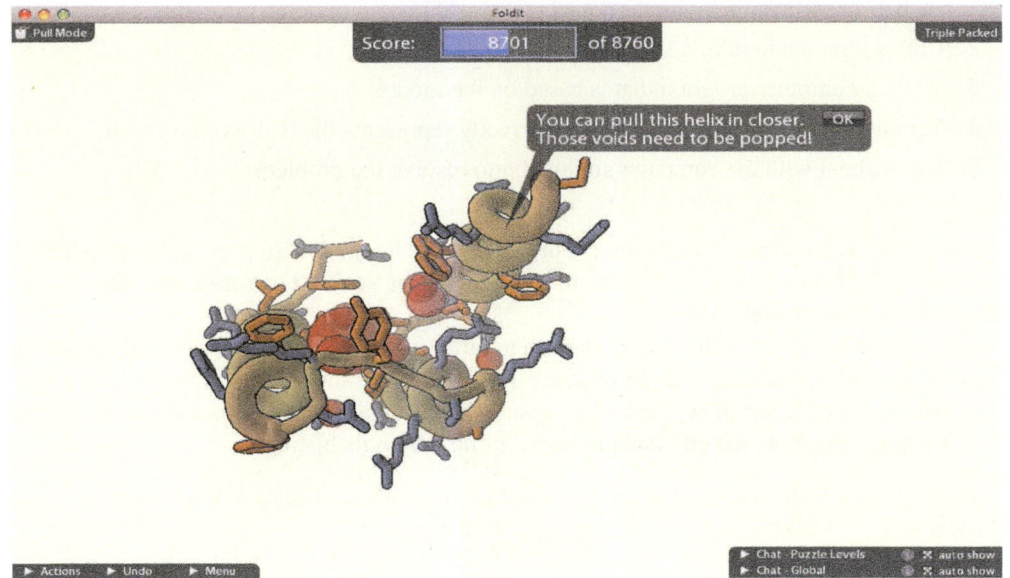

Figure 12.5.3

A better fold of the protein in Figure 12.5.1 shows a higher score.

The game was designed so that potential protein-folding prodigies would participate and move the field of protein folding ahead. Such is the case of the 13-year-old boy who beat out a 43 year old Parisian. When asked how he made his folding decisions, he replied that it looked right. Human intuition wins again!

To aid in making changes to a sample protein, tools are supplied by the game. A few of the tool options are listed here.

Lock

Rebuild

Rubber Bands

Shake Sidechains

Tweak

Wiggle

With more than 100,000 gamers playing Foldit, it is hoped that the understanding of protein folding will be advanced. The importance of protein folding is evidenced by its notoriety.

12.6 Design and Implementation of Computer Simulations

Before any simulation is designed or implemented, its purpose must be established. Usually it is necessary to simulate an event or physical object in order to solve some particular problem. Sometimes there are other reasons, such as the need to train with lifelike conditions. Whatever the objective, a simulation must have a reason for existing, whether it is for education, problem solving, entertainment, or even high-level governmental decision making. After the goals have been generally established, then the total system must be defined and analyzed so as to make apparent the interrelationships or interactions among its various parts. Then the goal should be completely restated in terms of the analysis just completed. Experts say that five basic tasks must be performed in setting up a computer simulation:

1. Determine if simulation is feasible. To do this examine the cost and other alternatives such as experimenting with the actual real-world system or doing mathematical analysis.

2. Create a model to mimic the real situation.

3. Write a computer program that is based on the model.

4. Validate and verify that the program correctly represents the real-world system.

5. Experiment with the computer simulation to resolve the problem.

A model is **verified** or **validated** when it is proven to be a reasonably accurate representation of the system being simulated.

As we've already seen, a simulation is only as good as its model. To prevent the possibility of erroneous results from a simulation, the model must be **verified** or **validated.** This should be done with any simulation.

Imagine spending millions of dollars on a traffic flow simulation, only to find out that it doesn't model the actual situation of interest. This was the unfortunate outcome for a real city that installed a complete traffic flow system based on a computer simulation. When the system was turned on, the city had the worst traffic jam in its history.

PUZZLER HINT

Keep in mind that any simulation must be validated before its actions can be trusted. Examine the validation history of your sales forecast program. Did the company that wrote the sales forecast program validate it? If so, what should you ask for?

Sometimes historical data can be used to validate models used for prediction. Start the simulation at an earlier time, for example, and see if it predicts the situation at present. If the simulation predicts what actually happened, then the model is probably a useful instrument.

SIMULATION LANGUAGES AND MODELING SYSTEMS

Simulations can be written in any number of computer languages, such as Visual BASIC, Smalltalk, C++, and Java. Even electronic spreadsheets can be used to develop very sophisticated simulations. For very complex simulations, however, these general-purpose languages are sometimes too difficult to work with because they offer too few tools to the programmer.

To make writing simulation programs easier, several simulation languages have been invented. What is a **simulation language**? An analogy with automobile repair might help explain what is meant by simplifying the writing of simulation programs. Imagine trying to fix an automobile engine with just two screwdrivers and an adjustable wrench rather than a complete set of mechanic's tools.

A new type of simulation-modeling system has surfaced over the past few years. It is very closely connected to the concept of object-oriented programming systems. These modeling systems usually have a graphics orientation. One example is a program called Extend, which is a general-purpose, library-based simulation program created by Imagine That, Inc. The programmer can build libraries of icons that represent the behavior of elements in the system being modeled. Figure 12.6.1 shows a cedar bog lake ecological system as modeled in Extend.

The cedar bog lake model involves "the annual cycles of solar energy, plants, herbivores, and carnivores, sediment, and the energy transfer to the environment in a lake ecosystem." The mathematical equations that give the relationships between the various constituents in the bog were based on research of an actual cedar bog lake located in Minnesota. Researcher R. B. Williams was able to model the lake in a set of six equations. Since they involve calculus, the details are beyond the limits of this brief summary.

Figure 12.6.1 graphically symbolizes the simulation of the cedar bog lake. The herbivore fish population eats the plants, which are a result of solar energy and organic nutrients that both carnivores and herbivores supply. The eagles (carnivores) prey on the fish (herbivores). The six equations are represented by the six icons (sun, plants, fish, eagle, plant production, and solar energy supply). The relationships between them are shown in the connections. Note that the labels used in the figure represent the actual quantities of plants, herbivores, carnivores, organic material and energy transfer.

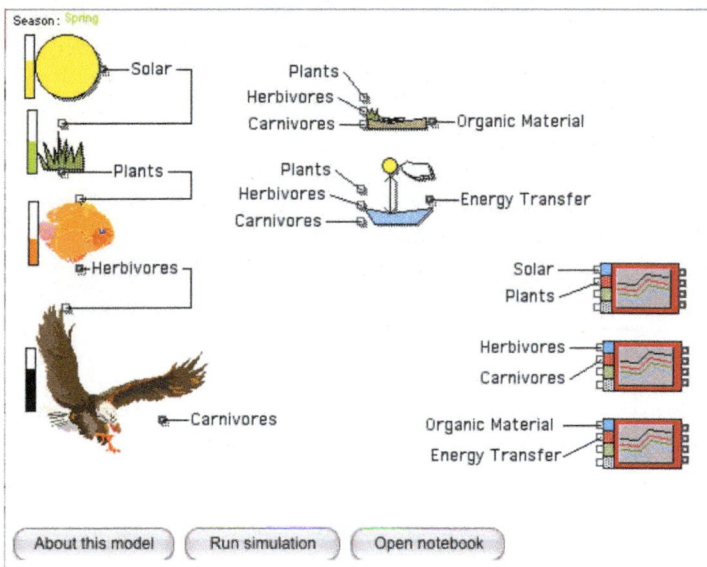

Figure 12.6.1

Graphical representation of a cedar bog lake with predator and prey interacting.

One of the equations represented by the symbol in the upper center of Figure 12.6.1 is expanded in Figure 12.6.2 and has the quantities of plants, herbivores and carnivores that go into making organic material. In words the equation consists of adding 2.5 times the volume of plants, 6.1 times the herbivores living, and 1.9 times the carnivores active. These quantities are then added up over time and result in a certain amount of organic matter, which provides food for the plants to grow. There is a lot of feedback going on, especially in the other equations.

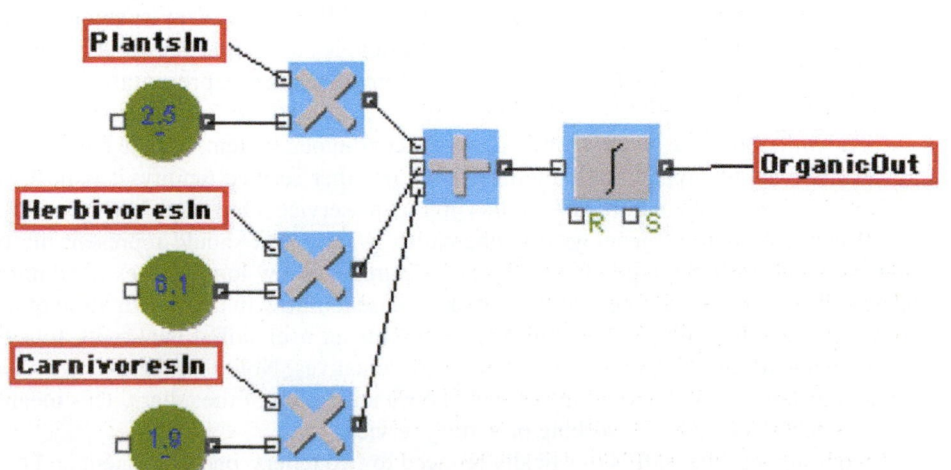

Figure 12.6.2

Graphical representations of the equations that calulates the amount of organic material produced.

Note the red boxes on the right of Figure 12.6.1. They represent the results of the simulation, and are accessed by clicking on the Open notebook button at the bottom of the figure. The resulting data is shown in Figure 12.6.3, which is a the result of a two year run of the simulation. Because of time compression, this was calculated in just a few seconds.

In the top graph of Figure 12.6.3, note the seasonal amount of sun energy transferred to the bog. In the two-year period there were two longest days of the year and two shortest days of the year, which are represented by the two peaks and two valleys in the yellow graph. In the middle graph the classic predator/prey population swings are visible. This can be observed by noting as the blue line goes up this means more food is available for the predator and their population will grow with the abundant supply of food.

Figure 12.6.3

Data from the cedar bog lake over a period of two years.

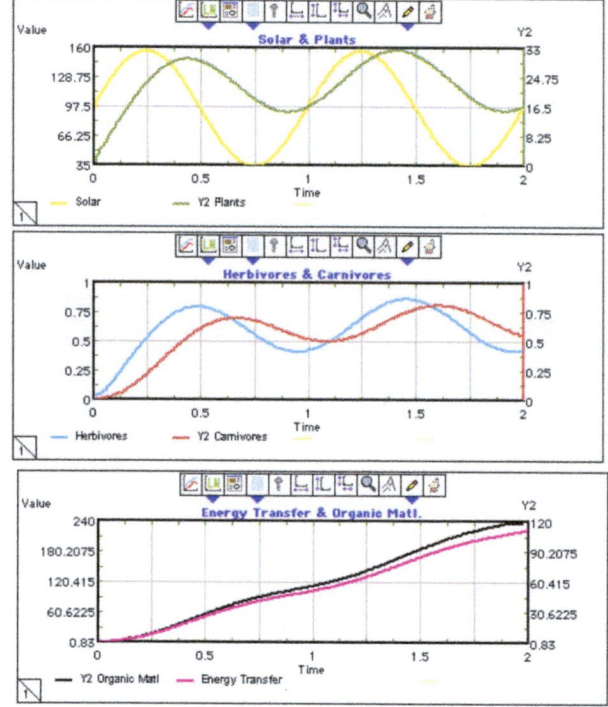

The Extend simulation program can be used for many other simulations. It is not restricted to ecological studies. Suppose you are responsible for designing a new bank. How many teller windows should be constructed? It depends on how many customers are to be served and also what services they need. In the example simulation shown in Figure 12.6.4, four tellers, two loan officers, and two customer service representatives will serve customers.

The cedar bog lake was the simulation of a continuous system, but the bank simulation is a discrete simulation. When building a bank or other service facility, it is necessary to determine the optimum number of stations giving the service. One way to do this is to obtain actual customer data or generate it mathematically. The data should represent the typical flow of people with the type of service they require, and how long it takes to complete the service. Assuming one car per patron, it makes sense to throw in an investigation of parking spaces needed. Figure 12.6.4 graphically represents an overstaffed bank with four tellers, two loan agents, and two customer service representatives. Note that the average wait time for a teller was 1.1437 minutes and there is a 66% utilization of the tellers. This means 34% of the time tellers were not working providing service.

Now suppose the staff is drastically reduced to two tellers, one loan agent and one customer service representative. Figure 12.6.5 shows the understaffed bank with five people waiting for a teller and an average waiting time of about five minutes. The tellers are almost

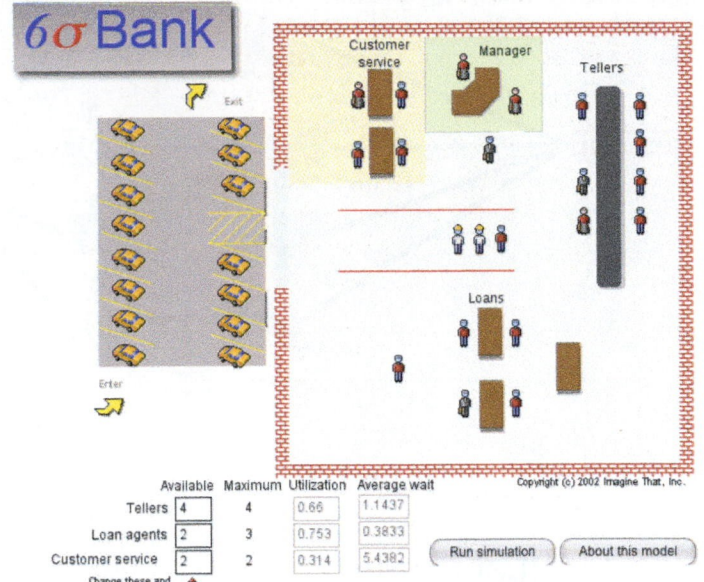

Figure 12.6.4

Graphical representation for a simulation of an overstaffed bank.

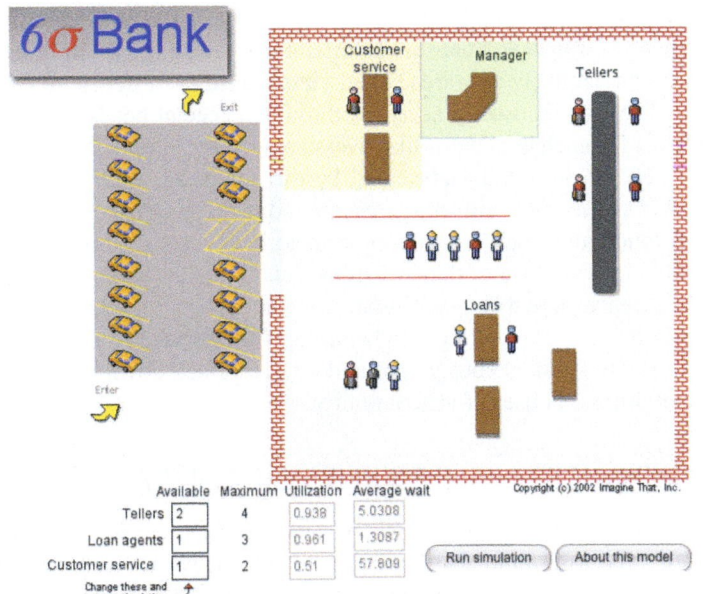

Figure 12.6.5

Graphical representation for a simulation of an understaffed bank.

always busy with a 93.8% utilization of their services. How many people left because they couldn't find parking? The simulation could also yield this type of information as needed.

The model itself is implemented in a flow type diagram, part of which is shown in Figure 12.6.6. One small part of this diagram is the *teller 2 box* that has the green circle. This means there is a delay time for the customer occupying the station. The delay time can be randomly selected or come from actual customer data. The diagram in the figure and all of the other diagrams determine the flow of the customers through the system. An animation feature can be used to see the process actually taking place.

After experimenting and examining the data, the bank designer can make decisions about how many tellers and other service people are needed. Even the number of parking lot spaces can be determined for optimum bank service.

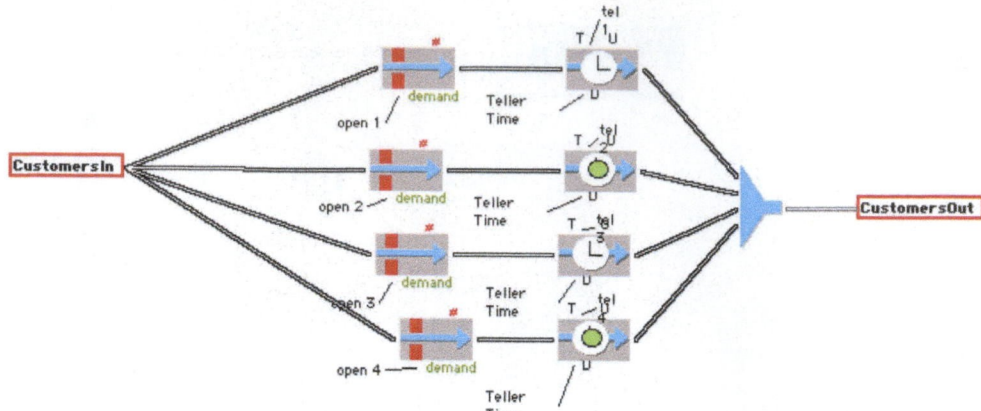

Figure 12.6.6

Graphical representation of the customer flow diagram of the teller stations.

12.7 Virtual Reality

The need for simulating the image of objects that we see in everyday life is growing each year. Both industry and the military need to train people in the use of complex systems. The demands for new and unusual entertainment are endless. These are only two of hundreds of uses of a relatively new area called **virtual reality** or **artificial reality.**

Virtual reality and **artificial reality** describe a situation in which an individual has a three-dimensional view into a world that doesn't exist except in the computer.

The view is usually accessed through a special headset, which consists of a miniature TV set for each eye, worn like oversized glasses. The visual images seen by the wearer of the headset are totally fabricated by the computer. With the proper sensors attached, the viewer can interact with and move around in an imaginary world. Other senses such as hearing, touch and smell are sometimes also included in a limited way. Virtual reality systems are being developed so that individuals can share the same imaginary environment with others. Science-fiction author William Gibson in his book *Neuromancer* generalizes this virtual or artificial world, calling it cyberspace. **Cyberspace** is a fictional place where millions of people can simultaneously visit and interact. Back down to earth, let's examine the current capabilities and uses of virtual reality.

FUNDAMENTALS OF VIRTUAL REALITY

A virtual reality system consists of very sophisticated software and some specialized hardware. The minimum hardware would be a viewing system. This must deliver a three-dimensional image to the individual. Figure 12.7.1 shows a person wearing a special headset, which consists of small TV-like screens, one for each eye.

A computer generates a left-eye picture and a right-eye picture. The illusion of three dimensions is relatively easy to create. All that are needed are a few well-chosen cues and the brain can fill in the details. Also needed is a way to interact with the virtual space. Most virtual reality headsets have sensors that can sense when the wearer turns his or her head; this will cause the scene being viewed to shift just as a real scene changes when we move our heads. Another common interaction device is a special glove worn by the viewer. The glove is shown in Figure 12.7.2. It has a series of sensors that are connected to the computer. Hand gestures with the glove may be translated to equivalent movements of a virtual hand in the virtual scene. Another possibility is that pointing your finger causes motion in the direction indicated.

Body suits, like the one in Figure 12.7.3, with a series of sensors can be used in some virtual reality systems to feed navigation information into the system. The Lycra suits have many sensors, which send body movement information to the computer. You could walk around in the virtual world. All of these devices are very expensive.

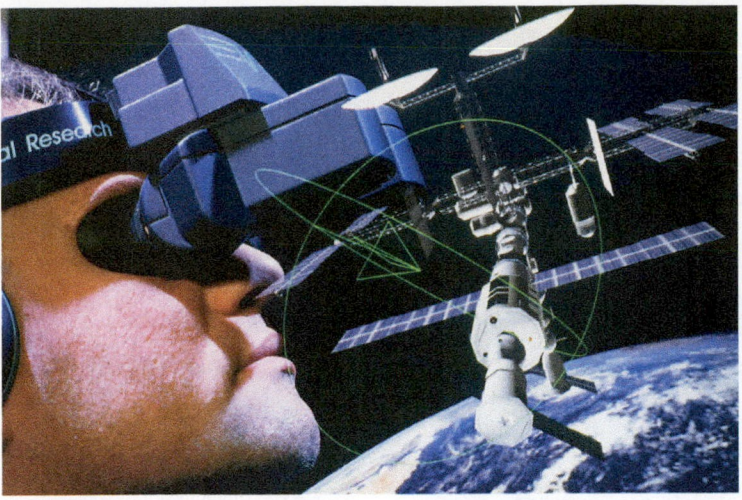

Corbis/Sygma

Figure 12.7.1

Virtual reality headset with a video display for each eye.

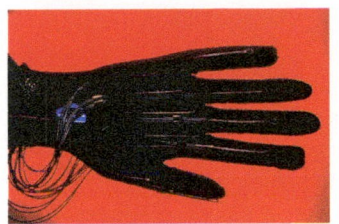

Bilderberg/The Stock Market

Figure 12.7.2

Glove with sensors used in virtual reality.

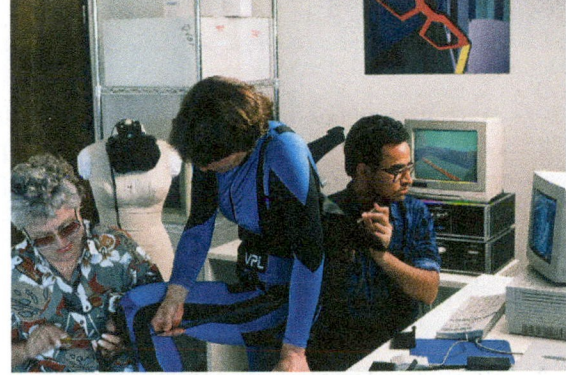

Peter Menzel/Stock Boston

Figure 12.7.3

Body suit used in virtual reality.

The classic virtual reality system uses the head-mounted display like the one shown in Figure 12.7.1. A second relatively inexpensive form is the video display with special glasses that separate the left-eye image from the right-eye image, but the viewer remains seated facing a display monitor. The third mode of implementing a virtual reality system is called CAVE.

CAVE AUTOMATIC VIRTUAL ENVIRONMENT

CAVE Automatic Virtual Environment (CAVE) was developed and introduced at the Electronic Visualization Laboratory at the University of Illinois–Chicago in 1992. An interesting note about its name is that CAVE is itself the first word of the acronym. Computer scientists refer to this as a recursive definition. Its name was influenced by "The Simile of the Cave" from Plato's *Republic*, where the ideas of perception, reality, and illusion are explored.

Physically CAVE installations consist of a 10' × 10' × 9' room, shown in Figure 12.7.4, where three of the walls and the floor are projection surfaces. Using specially designed shutter glasses, an image is formed on the booth's walls for the left eye, while the right eye is blocked from seeing. Then a fraction of a second later the booth's walls have images for the right eye, while the left eye is blocked. The shutters in the glasses are electronically controlled liquid crystal that can be blocked or made transparent alternately in synchronism with the projected images. Since the room is nearly a cube, then to make the images "look real," the pictures for left and right eyes need to be computed separately. This must take into account the distance of each object in the virtual scene from the viewer's eyes. The position of the individual eyeballs is known through special magnetic tracking so that the computer can compute the proper images. The computations needed to do this are detailed, and fairly expensive computers are needed.

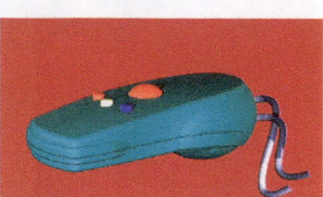

CAVE communications wand.

Figure 12.7.5

CAVE communications wand.

Figure 12.7.4

CAVE projection booth.

Electronic Visualization Laboratory

Communication for the viewer is accomplished through a wand shown in Figure 12.7.5. This wand allows the viewer to navigate the virtual space using a joystick, and to communicate with a set of three buttons that allow selecting options and setting modes.

CAVE is a fairly expensive virtual reality system; however, it has several advantages over the other two types of virtual reality:

- Higher resolution image
- Improved surround vision
- Reduction of geometric distortion
- Inclusion of real-world objects
- Virtual objects superimposed on real objects
- Multiple viewers can share and interact

This technology can have some very surprising and invaluable results. In the recent design for the expansion of a large international airport, CAVE simulation caused the discovery of a potentially dangerous and expensive design error. The control tower was visually blocked from seeing part of the runway. The modifications were made and the problem disappeared.

VIRTUAL SURGERY: A USE OF VIRTUAL REALITY

Imagine the following scenario: You are in Alaska and have an accident. Your condition requires expert surgery of a very specific nature. An expert surgeon is located in Los Angeles, but you can't be moved, and it is impossible for the surgeon to travel to Alaska. This situation is where the "virtual surgery station" can come to the rescue, and researchers are making it a reality.

Researchers have developed surgery-training workstations with a video monitor and special hand manipulators. Combined with features of a human body in its memory and special software, the surgeon can practice various types of surgery. After training on this surgery station, a switch can be flipped and now the surgery station becomes a remote surgery facility. This means the surgeon can sit at the surgery station with its manipulators connected via satellite communications to the operating room in Alaska. As the surgeon from Los Angeles moves the scalpel, robotic-like devices in Alaska do the job.

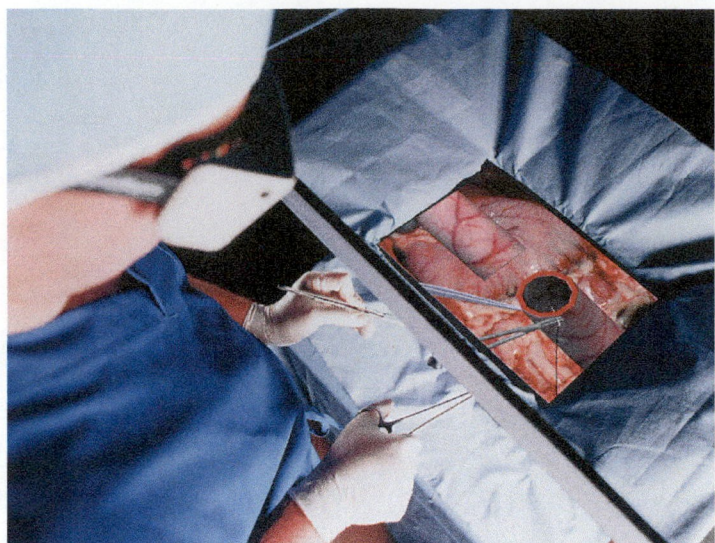

Boston Dynamics

Figure 12.7.6

Using simulated tweezers to manipulate simulated body parts.

Another interesting surgery project focuses on suturing tubelike organs, which include blood vessels, ureter, trachea, colon, and bile duct. This surgery simulation system allows the student surgeon to use simulated tweezers, needle-holder, needle, and thread. Figure 12.7.6 illustrates the use of tweezers to manipulate a simulated human-body, tubelike organ structure.

12.8 Software Applications: Electronic Spreadsheets as Simulation Tools

The electronic spreadsheet is an application that is available from many sources, including some freeware and shareware versions. But the basics of all of them are the same: They consist of rows and columns of cells that can contain numbers, text, and formulas. They differ considerably in features; the most notable include linking between spreadsheets, allowing huge spreadsheets, graphing, color, and built-in functions or formulas.

This section won't look at any particular product but will instead focus on uses involving the categories discrete/continuous, predictable/probabilistic, and feedback/no feedback.

CONTINUOUS SIMULATION MODEL

Systems that behave continuously can be modeled as discrete systems with the steps between values being very small. It is much like watching a movie film—the frames are static, but making the time between individual frames less than one-sixtieth of a second causes our eye and brain to think that the action is continuous.

We will not look at the actual spreadsheet for this first example, as it has several thousand cells. The Australian company Highland Oilfield Services created a very large spreadsheet enhanced with Visual Basic Macros. These macros are like mini-programs that the spreadsheet can use instead of calculating a single cell's formula. This particular spreadsheet, called Expres, simulates oil well production enhancement by using gas or water pressure in an adjacent well. More technically in language few can understand: "Expres is a standard three-phase, dispersed-flow, black-oil, finite-difference reservoir simulator." Figure 12.8.1 shows a static view of one frame of what can be shown as an animation. The pressure is increased at position row 21, column 21 of the grid with gas or water. The oil is being pumped out by the flanking well at row 5, column 5. This rather complex simulation uses Microsoft's Excel spreadsheet and makes good use of its graphics capability as can be seen in the figure.

Figure 12.8.1

One frame from an oil well simulation.

Supplied with the compliments of Highland Oilfield Serices Pty Ltd of Australia

PROBABILISTIC SIMULATION MODEL

In predictable simulations the general outcome is known and repeatable. By contrast, each time a probabilistic simulation is run, it will have different outcomes. It's much like a pair of dice—we know that two sides will be facing up after being thrown, but we can't predict exactly which ones they will be. Most spreadsheets have functions, which are special formulas that do more than what a single formula can do. For example, the random number generator in most spreadsheets is a function that calculates random values within a specified range. Figure 12.8.2 makes use of this function, which happens to be called RAND in Microsoft Excel, to simulate the toss of a pair of dice.

The formula used involves some arithmetic, but is worth looking at in detail. It is most illuminating to do this analysis step by step:

- When the Excel program sees the function called RAND() in a particular formula, it automatically calculates a fractional number between 0 and 1 and places it into the formula. Suppose the number calculated, for example, is 0.67781.

- The formula then multiplies the calculated number by the value specified between the parentheses (called the argument). The argument specifies the largest number to be generated. In this example, 0.67781 would be multiplied by 6, which would give 4.06686.

- The formula then calls another function, INT, to strip away the fractional part of the value, leaving the integer 4 in our example.

- Finally, the value 1 is added to the integer 4, giving 5 as the final result.

- Each time the RAND(6) function is used, a different number between 0 and 1 will be generated. Multiplying it by the argument (6 in our example), stripping off fractional values, and then adding 1 will guarantee that the result will be an integer between 1 and 6, thus perfectly simulating tossing a single die.

Figure 12.8.3 shows the same section of spreadsheet with the formulas that are in each of the cells. Note that the words "Toss," "Die#1," and "Die#2" appear because they are not formulas but text. This could be made much more sophisticated, but the results would be the same.

Tossing a Pair of Dice		
Formula: =INT(6 * RAND( ))+1		
	Die #1	Die#2
Toss 1	4	5
Toss 2	2	2
Toss 3	4	1
Toss 4	3	1
Toss 5	3	1
Toss 6	6	5
Toss 7	2	2
Toss 8	3	1
Toss 9	6	3
Toss 10	6	2

Figure 12.8.2

Die toss simulation using a random number function.

	Die #1	Die#2
Toss 1	=INT(6 * RAND())+1	=INT(6 * RAND())+1
Toss 2	=INT(6 * RAND())+1	=INT(6 * RAND())+1
Toss 3	=INT(6 * RAND())+1	=INT(6 * RAND())+1
Toss 4	=INT(6 * RAND())+1	=INT(6 * RAND())+1
Toss 5	=INT(6 * RAND())+1	=INT(6 * RAND())+1
Toss 6	=INT(6 * RAND())+1	=INT(6 * RAND())+1
Toss 7	=INT(6 * RAND())+1	=INT(6 * RAND())+1
Toss 8	=INT(6 * RAND())+1	=INT(6 * RAND())+1
Toss 9	=INT(6 * RAND())+1	=INT(6 * RAND())+1
Toss 10	=INT(6 * RAND())+1	=INT(6 * RAND())+1

Figure 12.8.3

Die toss simulation showing the formulas.

SIMULATION MODEL WITH FEEDBACK

Feedback adds a dimension that is used to deal with the issue of time. The equivalent of a clock must be somehow introduced because the process of running a simulation involves something happening that produces a later reaction. A fairly simple example that demonstrates this is the predator/prey problem discussed in section 12.6, where a special simulation program was used. A generic spreadsheet program can perform the same simulation but with a much less sophisticated look. Rather than revisiting that type of example, let's look at a different type of feedback, which is probably the most widely used type of feedback in spreadsheets. It is called the "what-if" simulation and involves the human user in the feedback loop.

Let's say you're going to take a backpacking trip, for example. Imagine you are going on a four-day camping trip and have only $45 to spend on food. To balance things out in your pack you need to have as close to 8 pounds of food as possible. From the list of breakfast, lunch, and dinner meals, you must choose three meals a day (a total of four breakfasts, four lunches, and four dinners) so that you get as close to the limits as possible. Notice that the more expensive foods weigh less! To select your meals, create a spreadsheet similar to

			BackPackTrip.xls			
			Backpacking Trip			
Amount	Meal	Meal Wt(lbs)	Meal Cost	Weight	Cost
2	Chicken Dinner	0.6	$5.50	1.2	$11.00
1	Lasagna Dinner	1	$4.75	1	$4.75
1	Stew Dinner	1.2	$2.50	1.2	$2.50
1	Bagel Breakfast	0.4	$2.85	0.4	$2.85
3	Pancake Breakfast	0.6	$2.32	1.8	$6.96
2	Sandwich Lunch	0.4	$4.56	0.8	$9.12
2	Soup Lunch	0.6	$3.21	1.2	$6.42
	Total Weight is	7.6		Total Cost is	$43.60

Figure 12.8.4

The what-if backpacking scenario.

Courtesy of Kurt Lauckner

the one in Figure 12.8.4. Then by changing the quantity of each of the meals, still maintaining four breakfasts, four lunches, and four dinners, you try to get selections in which the total cost is less than $45 and the weight is near 8 pounds. The first few times you may fail to meet the requirements. This is the what-if process. It is essentially saying "what if I make these choices, then do I meet the requirements?" The human running the spreadsheet is in the feedback loop.

To make this example more challenging and realistic, the calories for each of the meals should be included. By requiring a certain minimum caloric intake to maintain hiking strength, the problem becomes more difficult and could result in many trials to reach the monetary, caloric, and weight goals.

MOOs (MUDs Object Oriented)

In 1979 anthropologist Lucy Suchman studied Xerox accounting clerks and found that many of the practices used to get work done were not in any manual. Instead workers discussed problems, came up with innovative solutions, and passed the ideas to others "around the water cooler." At Xerox PARC one researcher, Pavel Curtis, looked closely at what are called Multi-User Domains (MUDs), which were an outgrowth of the Dungeons and Dragons role-playing games. He saw them as the "water coolers of the Internet." To further a seed of an idea he created MOOs, which are MUDs Object Oriented and were based on University of Waterloo student Steven White's work. Then in January 1991 LambdaMOO was launched at Xerox PARC. The idea of providing a "water cooler environment" for informal discussion, termed *storytelling,* was off and running. The idea is to provide an environment in which innovation and creative ideas can be shared and passed on. The director of Xerox PARC, John Seely Brown, believes that tomorrow's successful corporations will be "knowledge refineries," and as such, environments like the "water cooler of the Internet" must be nurtured and adapted to become part of the future. The importance of this research is evident in the hundreds of MUDs and MOOs around the world. The table that follows shows just a few of them.

PUZZLER HINT

During validation, you find out that the company that prepared the sales forecast used inaccurate and incomplete data. What should you do now? Create a plan of action. Who should be included in your expert consultants?

BioMOO	Weizmann Institute of Science, Israel	Professional community of biology researchers connected to the Globewide Network Academy.
CardiffMOO	Department of Computing Mathematics at University of Wales	Test bed for ideas related to research into the design of object-oriented programming environments.
ComMOOnity	The University of Illinois at Urbana-Champaign	Serves many purposes, including a test bed for research into collaboration technologies, a social gathering place, and a stable, fast environment for the expansion of MOO technologies.
Dhalgren MOO	Department of English, University of Washington	A small electronic community devoted to interdisciplinary discussion and research, the exploration of connections between art and technology.
El MOOndo	Pepperdine University Graduate School of Education and Psychology	It is aimed at K–12, with some rooms specially designated class meeting rooms for courses in graduate programs.
IPL MOO	School of Information, University of Michigan	Internet Public Library MOO— It is a public library for the Internet community and is intended as a model and laboratory for librarians and MOO folk to explore the possibilities of library services in MOO and virtual reality environments.
JHM MOO	Jay's House MOO	A place for research and development into information structures, tools for collaboration, and cohesive simulated environments.
trAce	Nottingham Trent University	Busy 24-hour online community for writers and readers across the world. We write, share our reading, critique each other's work, and discuss favorite books.
Lingua MOO	University of Texas at Dallas	Academic virtual community for teaching and research.
MediaMOO	MIT Media Lab	A professional community for media researchers.
LambdaMOO	Originally Xerox PARC	The first MOO ever! It started in 1991 and has over 6000 members. It is one massive virtual reality party, taking place in a mansion loosely modeled after the creator's home in California.
VROoM	Pepperdine University	The acronym stands for Virtual Rooms Offices and Meetinghouse and it is run by the Pepperdine Graduate School. It is mostly used for real-time conferences and meetings.

Chapter Summary

12.1 Reasons for Simulation

Simulation has a long history and has been extensively used in four areas: forecasting or predicting the future, simulation of the inaccessible or impossible, controlled experimentation, and testing, education, and training. To make use of simulation, a physical or virtual model must be created, and it often makes use of time compression. Most importantly a simulation is only as good as its model. It is often said that simulation is the third branch of science, along with experimental and theoretical science.

12.2 Building a Model

In the process of building a model there are three major contrasting categories: continuous versus discrete, probabilistic versus predictable, feedback versus no feedback.

12.3 Monopoly Game Simulation

One of the best-known board games in the world is Monopoly. Using simulation, a model consisting of a computer program can be used to devise strategies for playing the game. By examining the return per dollar of investment, the peasant verses tycoon strategy can be developed.

12.4 SimCity: Simulation of City Planning

SimCity is a simulation that is designed for the player to manage a city. People, called Sims, will move to the city and pay taxes, as long as services and other features such as schools, fire and police, recreation, shopping areas, and jobs are provided. All of the usual problems and decision options are present in the city: crime, power shortages, street deterioration, zoning, housing. The simulation has only one weakness: Real cities aren't run by a single individual but by political entities.

12.5 Simulating the Process of Life: Protein Folding

One of the potentially most fruitful computer simulations is protein folding. Proteins are the building blocks of life, and how they compact and fold upon themselves are the first steps in building blood cells, bone, and processes such as digestion.

Understanding proteins is considered to be the first step in conquering many human diseases. This research into protein folding uses the computer in massive grids and games.

12.6 Design and Implementation of Computer Simulations

When designing a computer simulation, five things should be done: determine if a simulation is feasible, build a model, write the computer program, verify correctness of the program, and use the program to resolve the problem. Specially designed programming languages and systems make creating simulations much easier than using general-purpose programming languages.

12.7 Virtual Reality

Virtual reality and artificial reality refer to the use of computers to simulate reality. The computer creates virtual worlds that don't exist and are viewed using special headsets or goggles. There are three approaches to this type of simulation: A computer creates scenes on two tiny video displays that are inside a headset worn by the user. A second technique is to wear special goggles that will make images on a display monitor seem three-dimensional. The third approach is to create a room whose walls are video projections of scenes that are created alternately for the left eye and then the right eye. This latter technique is called CAVE and uses special goggles that allow only one eye to see at a time. These virtual reality simulations are being applied to surgery and can be very effective in training and actual practice.

12.8 Software Applications: Electronic Spreadsheets as Simulation Tools

The generic spreadsheet can be used to do simulations involving continuous and probabilistic models with feedback. Comprehensive special simulation packages are already written using the more sophisticated spreadsheets with graphics. The what-if scenario is one of the most often used simulation techniques. The electronic spreadsheet is most appropriate for these what-if processes.

Key Terms

Key terms introduced in this chapter:

Matching

Match the number of the key terms introduced in the chapter to the following statements. Each term may be used once, more than once, or not at all.

1. ___ The literal definition of this is "to imitate or to give the appearance of something else."

2. ___ This is the equivalent of speeding up the clock.

3. ___ An example of this type of simulation would be to observe the collapse of a star due to gravitation that results in the formation of a black hole.

4. ___ An example of this type of simulation would be to observe the U.S. economy after making sensitive changes in certain areas.

5. ___ An example of this type of simulation would be to observe how well a new type of bridge railing would withstand an impact of different size vehicles from different directions and at different speeds.

6. ___ An example of this type of simulation would be to have a doctor practice a treatment plan based on symptoms displayed in a program that simulates an emergency room in a hospital.

7. ___ An example of this type of simulation would be to have a pilot fly a simulated jetliner in adverse conditions based on actual data from previous flights.

8. ___ This model has quantities that vary smoothly or in a continuous manner.

9. ___ This concept is necessary when forecasting or predicting the future.

10. ___ This fakes or gives the appearance of the system in question.

11. ___ This model can predict exactly what will happen.

12. ___ This model contains unpredictable features.

13. ___ This model has quantities that vary in steps or jumps.

14. ___ This model generates results, which it feeds back as more input for the simulation.

15. ___ This means that the model is proven to be a reasonably accurate representation of the system being simulated.

16. ___ This is another term for *verified.*

17. ___ This general name is given to a type of language that is often used to create simulation programs.

18. ___ This approach to virtual reality uses a projection system to put images on the walls of an environment in which the viewer is located.

19. ___ This gives an experience into a three-dimensional world that doesn't exist except in the computer.

20. ___ This is another term for *virtual reality.*

True or False

Place either T or F on the line provided with each of the following statements. If a statement is false, you should be able to explain what changes would make it true.

1. ___ Simulations are often created so that predictions can be made.

2. ___ Predictions are only as good as the model that is used in the simulation.

3. ___ We need to compress time in most simulations so that we don't have to wait, sometimes years, to see the outcome of the simulation.

4. ___ Before creating the simulation, we need to know as much as possible about the situation being modeled.

5. ___ Simulating car crashes using a computer has proven to be more costly and less feasible than using the real thing.

6. ___ The earth's orbit around the sun is an example of a continuous system.

7. ___ The time the "sun will rise" in the morning is an example of a probabilistic system.

8. ___ The game of Monopoly is an example of a probabilistic system.

9. ___ Counting the number of cars as they pass through an intersection is an example of a discrete system.

10. ___ The game of Monopoly is an example of a model that is both discrete and predictable.

11. ___ The models used in simulation must always be mathematical.

12. ___ A simulation program can never be proven to be a reasonably accurate representation of the system being simulated because changes always seem to occur to the simulation itself!

13. ___ Simulations are created using the same kinds of languages as other programs. (There is no difference in the type of language used.)

14. ___ The SimCity program allows the user to design or alter zoning and utility projects for make-believe cities.

15. ___ Part of the design and implementation of a computer simulation program is to determine whether the problem really requires a simulation in the first place.

16. ___ Using the Extend program, icons can be used to represent elements of a system being modeled.

These icons can then be manipulated to show the effects of the changes to the model in question.

17. ___ The Extend simulation is restricted to a predator/prey environment.

18. ___ In order to have a virtual reality experience you would need to wear special equipment.

19. ___ Virtual reality is an individual experience in which the computer interacts with one person at a time.

20. ___ Virtual reality is conducted in a three-dimensional environment.

Multiple Choice

Answer the multiple-choice questions by selecting the best answer from the choices given.

1. This is the same as speeding up the clock.
   a. Time compression
   b. Prediction
   c. Simulation of the inaccessible or impossible
   d. Experimentation and testing
   e. Education and training

2. This type of simulation helps people learn some complex skill that would otherwise be dangerous if "learning by doing" was taking place.
   a. Time compression
   b. Prediction
   c. Simulation of the inaccessible or impossible
   d. Experimentation and testing
   e. Education and training

3. This type of simulation allows people to manipulate designs based on very complicated mathematical models.
   a. Time compression
   b. Prediction
   c. Simulation of the inaccessible or impossible
   d. Experimentation and testing
   e. Education and training

4. This type of simulation allows people to gain insight into models that would be unobtainable in any other way.
   a. Time compression
   b. Prediction
   c. Simulation of the inaccessible or impossible
   d. Experimentation and testing
   e. Education and training

5. This type of simulation is used to forecast the future.
   a. Time compression
   b. Prediction
   c. Simulation of the inaccessible or impossible

   d. Experimentation and testing
   e. Education and training

6. This model has quantities that vary smoothly.
   a. Continuous system
   b. Discrete system
   c. Feedback loop
   d. Predictable system
   e. Probabilistic system

7. This model has unpredictable features.
   a. Continuous system
   b. Discrete system
   c. Feedback loop
   d. Predictable system
   e. Probabilistic system

8. This model feeds back input to itself.
   a. Continuous system
   b. Discrete system
   c. Feedback loop
   d. Predictable system
   e. Probabilistic system

9. This model has quantities that vary in steps or jumps.
   a. Continuous system
   b. Discrete system
   c. Feedback loop
   d. Predictable system
   e. Probabilistic system

10. This model results in outcomes that can be foreseen.
    a. Continuous system
    b. Discrete system
    c. Feedback loop
    d. Predictable system
    e. Probabilistic system

Exercises

1. Which of the following simulations must use time compression to be useful?
   a. Aircraft landing simulation
   b. Simulation of Earth's weather
   c. Simulation of fish hatchery management over a decade
   d. Automobile engine simulation
   e. Simulation of star formation
   f. Simulation of a nuclear reactor meltdown

2. All of the following simulations are subject to predictions based on uncontrollable random events. For each example that follows name one possible event that could cause the simulation to go awry.
   a. Simulation of a presidential election
   b. Simulation of automobile traffic flow in a city
   c. Simulation of a dial-a-ride city bus system
   d. Simulation of the steel industry to predict demands
   e. Simulation of a university's financial operations

3. Give an example not mentioned in the book that illustrates each of the following:
   a. Simulation of the inaccessible or impossible
   b. Simulation for experimentation or testing
   c. Simulation of education and training
   d. A continuous system
   e. A discrete system
   f. A probabilistic system
   g. A predictable system

4. Simulate the process of tossing a die
   a. Using a computer.
   b. By putting six slips of paper numbered 1 through 6 into a hat and drawing out one of them.
   c. By using the number on a license plate, dividing by six, and then taking the remainder plus one as the "die toss."
   d. By dividing a sheet of paper into six equal square areas and numbering them 1 through 6. Toss a coin onto the paper. The number of the square that the majority of the coin covers is your "die toss."

5. Discuss the results of problem 4. Do they seem to be equivalent to an actual die toss?

6. Simulate the tossing of a coin
   a. Using a real coin.
   b. By writing a program to simulate the tossing of a coin. Hint: Use the random number generator.
   c. By putting two slips of paper with *head* written on one and *tail* written on the other into a box and drawing out one of them.
   d. By dividing a sheet of paper into as many squares as is convenient. Label half of them with an *H* and the other half with a *T*. Toss any object that is small enough to fit within the squares onto the paper. The toss will represent head or tail depending on which square the majority of the object covers.

7. Suppose a certain machine can give you a random number (x) between 0 and 1 (e.g., .42317, .71123, .00121, .98791, . . .). Assume that the random numbers are evenly distributed (i.e., just as many less than .5 as there are greater than .5).
   a. Show how a random 0 or 1 can be obtained from x.
   b. Show how a random number 1 through 6 can be obtained from x.

8. List three examples of systems that can be viewed as both continuous and discrete. For example, the traffic flow in a city can be viewed in two ways. The actual motion of a car accelerating and decelerating is continuous, whereas the number of cars going through an intersection is discrete.

9. For each of the following examples, describe one factor that would keep the system from being predictable. For example, we can't predict the time of a transatlantic balloon flight because the wind speed cannot be exactly predicted.
   a. Grocery store cash register checkout line.
   b. Movement of the earth around the sun.
   c. Changes in the stresses of skyscraper structure.
   d. Growth and decline of the fish population in a lake.
   e. Launching a rocket on the moon.
   f. Simulation of an aircraft in flight.
   g. Simulation of cancer cell growth.
   h. Simulation of a computer system.
   i. Simulation of a mouse in a maze.
   j. Simulation of an automobile engine.
   k. Simulation of the game of Monopoly.

10. Find two examples of situations in your everyday life that involve feedback.

11. Name several areas in which simulation has been applied but has had relatively little success (e.g., weather, some city traffic simulations).

12. Write a short paragraph describing an example of an event from current news media (newspaper, magazine, radio, TV) that illustrates the unpredictability of normally predictable situations.

13. Examine Figure 12.4.4(a), pick out the following structures, and describe their position in terms of the words *lower left, center, upper right,* or similar notations:
   a. Mayor's house.
   b. Police station.
   c. Parkland.
   d. River.

14. **PUZZLER** Simulations are often affected by seemingly independent events. For the puzzler problem, state why or why doesn't each of the following affect the sales of a consumer product:

a. A shift in population density in your sales area.

b. A massive electrical failure in your sales area.

c. An increase in the prime lending rate.

d. A change in the color of your product (e.g., blue M&Ms or green ketchup).

e. A change in packaging your product from boxes to plastic wrappers.

f. A national or statewide election in your area.

g. A major change in the statewide unemployment rate.

h. A violent tornado or hurricane near your distribution center.

i. A violent tornado or hurricane 500 miles away from your distribution center.

j. The assassination of a major national celebrity or political figure.

15. Determine a means for validating the model of a die toss.

16. Find a formula that could be used for randomly giving numbers between 1 and 36 inclusive.

Discussion Questions

1. How much importance should be put on simulation of the U.S. economy?

2. Can a model be both continuous and discrete? Give an example.

3. Is the competing cities approach shown in Figure 12.4.3 better than investigating each city's organization independently of the other? Remember that the two cities in Figure 12.4.3 compete against each other for citizens.

4. Describe a virtual reality system to simulate attending a standard lecture class. Could you learn this way?

Group Project

A group of four students should design a series of experiments investigating the model underlying the SimCity simulation. For example, Figure 12.4.3 illustrates the effect that roadway access has on two cities' development. Each person should pick two effects to investigate. The group should meet to decide on the best city model that all experiments will use. Note that the two cities in Figure 12.4.3 have the same areas zoned commercial and residential; they only differ by the roadway access. Industrial zoning was placed exactly between the two cities. Ideas for investigation might include the effects due to the following: recreation, taxation, mass transit, airports, and many more. Before doing the experiments, the group should meet and review each other's proposed plan. Experiments on the cities already developed in SimCity may also be used as a starting point.

Web Exercises

1. Use the WWW to find a freeware or shareware copy of an electronic spreadsheet for your computer. Try it out and compare it to any commercial spreadsheet, such as Microsoft's Excel.

2. Find Web sites for SimCity and download any enhancements you find for it. These might include previously designed cities or software that allows you to drive through the streets and see them from the driver's viewpoint.

3. Search the Web for different versions of Monopoly. These versions are often associated with other cities, or entertainment such as the movie *Star Wars*. Make a list with descriptions of each of them.

Bibliography

Bucki, Lisa. *Learning Business Simulations with Microsoft Office 2000.* Washington, DC: DDC Publishing, 1999.

This book provides a beginners' guide to designing and implementing a variety of useful business simulations using current Microsoft software.

Chiu, Ben, Bruce Williams, Bill Hoscheit, and Rod Machado. *Microsoft Flight Simulator 2000 Official Strategies and Secrets.* Alameda, CA: Sybex, 1999.

This book includes instructions for take-offs and landings, understanding navigational data, and handling emergencies in the air.

Darzinskis, Kaz. *Winning Monopoly.* New York: Harper & Row, 1985.

An older book that helps in the development of strategy of the game.

Eastman, Charles M. *Building Product Models: Computer Environments Supporting Design and Construction.* Boca Raton, FL: CRC Press, 1999.

This book presents the concepts, technology, and methods used to develop a digital representation for architecture, civil engineering, and building construction.

Gibson, William. *Neuromancer,* reissue edition. New York: Ace Books, 2000.

This novel marks the beginning of the cyberpunk generation. Gibson's book has won many awards and is considered to be the first to introduce the world to cyberspace.

Krueger, Myron. *Artificial Reality II.* New York: Addison-Wesley, 1991.

A dated but easy-to-read historical perspective of the field. From the back cover: " . . . a revised edition of the 1983 classic by pioneer researcher Myron Krueger . . . the author describes his personal odyssey through the development of artificial reality technology, from the original vision through current applications and beyond, to his vision of artificial reality as a paradigm for future computer-human."

Lem, Stanislaw. *The Cyberiad.* New York: Harcourt Brace Jovanovich, 1985.

This science fiction book was influential in the creation of SimCity.

Levy, Perrie. *Becoming Virtual: Reality in the Digital Age.* New York: Perseus Books, 1998.

From Amazon.com: "Pierre Levy takes a fresh look at the whole idea of what is virtual. He's responding to the widespread belief, and sometimes even panic, that a digital society with emphasis on virtual interactions is necessarily depersonalizing. He takes particular exception to the notion that 'virtual' and 'real' are opposites. Instead, Levy argues that virtuality is one of four modes of existence, the rest of which he describes as reality, possibility, and actuality. Each is defined in terms of its relationship with its environment."

Schrage, Michael and Tom Peters. *Serious Play: How the World's Best Companies Simulate to Innovate.* Cambridge, MA: Harvard Business School Press, 1999.

This volume explains how the world's leading companies use modeling, prototyping, and simulation to stimulate and implement innovation.

Spear, Peter et al. *The Official SimCity 2000 Planning Commission Handbook.* New York: Osborne McGraw-Hill, 1999.

A complete strategy and planning book for SimCity 2000.

chapter

13

Artificial Intelligence and Modeling the Human State

TimeLine

1859 The principle of natural selection and its influence on the evolution of species is explained in Charles Darwin's *The Origin of Species*.

1920 Karel Capek uses the word *robot* (derived from the Czech word for compulsory labor) in his play *Rossum's Universal Robots*.

1937 The concept of the Turing Machine is introduced in Alan Turing's paper "On Computable Numbers."

1950 The Turing Test of machine intelligence is presented by Alan Turing.

1956 The concept of artificial intelligence is developed by John McCarthy, Marvin Minsky, and others attending a conference at Dartmouth College.

1959 The programming language Lisp (list processing) for artificial intelligence applications is developed by John McCarthy.

1959 A checker-playing program by Arthur Samuel performs as well as some of the best players of the time.

1960 The Perceptron computer at Cornell University learns by trial and error through a neural network.

1961 The first industrial robot is patented by George C. Devol. Its first use is to automate the manufacture of picture tubes for televisions.

1994 The use of DNA as a computing medium is demonstrated by Leonard Adleman of the University of Southern California.

2030 Raymond Kurzweil forcasts computer with intelligence indistinguishable from that of humans.

Chapter Objectives

- ➡ Recognize early attempts at machine intelligence.

- ➡ Understand how a computer's intelligence is tested with the Turing Test.

- ➡ Understand how models of the human brain make use of knowledge acquisition, knowledge retrieval, and reasoning.

- ➡ Understand how heuristics limit the search possibilities when trying to solve a problem.

- ➡ Recognize that exhibiting common sense is an attribute of very few computer programs.

- ➡ Appreciate how game-playing computer programs have aided our understanding of how humans make similar decisions.

- ➡ Know some of the problems related to natural language understanding by a computer.

- ➡ Discern how complex adaptive systems and artificial life try to model the natural situations of the world.

- ➡ Identify the basic premise of the genetic algorithm as solving all types of problems using a model of evolution.

J. O. Atlanta '96/GAMMA/Liaison Agency, Inc.

You just received your ticket purchase instructions for the 2014 Winter Olympics, but unfortunately they are in Russian, not English. You thought the whole world was speaking English—what an eye-opener! None of your friends speak Russian. How can you solve this problem?

PUZZLER

13.1 What Is Intelligence: Artificial or Not?

When the word *intelligence* is mentioned, almost everyone immediately thinks about human **intelligence.** For thousands of years the human species has pondered the complexity of the human brain and what it represents. Only recently has the scientific community begun to unravel its secrets. In this chapter, we'll show the attempts at creating intelligent systems using the computer and share some insights into the working of the human brain. A look at history is probably a good place to start our exploration.

Around 400 B.C. the Greek philosopher Plato's teachings included a theory that a perfect heaven rained down ethereal spirits that entered the body and were concentrated by the brain. Plato's student Aristotle didn't do much to improve on this theory; in fact, he concluded that the heart must contain the soul, and the brain's function was merely to cool the blood.

Other ideas of intelligence surfaced in the 1700s and 1800s when an object having human form would seem to mimic the intelligence of the human. In particular, **Maillardet's Automaton** (Henri Maillardet, 1805) was a drawing machine disguised as a young boy. Incidentally, for many years Maillardet's Automaton was dressed as a lady in green but has since been restored to its original male form. The small boy shown in Figure 13.1.1 kneels on a very large box that contains the bulk of the complex drawing machine's levers, ratchets, cams, and other mechanical parts. It could draw several complex images, one of which is shown in Figure 13.1.2. Because of its human form and the fact that he could draw such complex images, a certain feeling of intelligence was ascribed to the machine. Maillardet's Automaton now resides in the Franklin Institute, a museum in Philadelphia.

There are many other unusual, incorrect, or misleading examples of the attempt to understand intelligence, but it is more fruitful to return to the scientific investigation, which was more on the track of reality.

The Franklin Institute

Figure 13.1.1

Maillardet's Automaton as restored to the form of a little boy.

Figure 13.1.2

*Sailing vessel drawn by
Maillardet's Automaton.*

The Franklin Institute

The nervous system was discovered, but not understood, by the physician Galen while treating fallen gladiators. He discovered that gladiators with damaged spinal cords lost feeling in certain limbs but could often regain use of them. Then the scientist Galvani, using Benjamin Franklin's findings about static electricity, showed the famous jumping frogs' legs that indicated the electrical nature of the nervous system. The shocks from static electricity stimulated the nerves, causing the frog's muscle tissue to think the brain had sent the signal to contract.

Subsequently, the human central nervous system was found to be a very intricate continuous network of billions of **neurons.** The long axons that run throughout the body send communications by both electrical and chemical means. These interconnected neurons, called **neural nets,** stretch from the innermost portions of the brain all the way out to the sensory organs, such as the eyes and ears. The power of humans to perceive (for example, touch, hear, see, taste, smell) is not just in the brain but is spread throughout the body in the simultaneously operating neural nets associated with the various sensory organs. In effect, the mind is not all in the brain! Later in this chapter we will discuss the construction of intelligent systems modeled after the brain's neural networks. In the meantime, it would help our current understanding of intelligence to discuss criteria for intelligence. The latter is necessary because ultimately a discussion of computer or machine intelligence, commonly referred to as **artificial intelligence** or AI, must be addressed. The major question boils down to this: Can machines think? Before pursuing this weighty question, a discussion of intelligence is necessary.

What does it mean to be intelligent? The brilliant British mathematician Alan Turing (1912–1954) proposed a test, now referred to as **Turing's Imitation Game.** In its final form the imitation game is essentially an intelligence test of the computer. In phase one it consisted of having a man and a woman separated from a human interrogator, as shown in Figure 13.1.3.

The interrogator communicates with both individuals via a terminal-type device with a keyboard and a display to show the responses. The interrogator types questions addressed to either party without knowing which one receives the question. By observing the responses,

Interrogator

Truthful Woman

Lying Man

Figure 13.1.3

Phase one of Turing's test in operation.

the interrogator's goal is to try to identify which is the man and which is the woman. The rules of the test required the man to try to fool the interrogator into thinking he is the woman. Meanwhile, the woman tries to convince the interrogator that she is indeed the woman.

In phase two of the imitation game, the man was replaced by a computer, as shown in Figure 13.1.4. If the computer could fool the interrogator as often as the man did, then it could be said that the computer had displayed intelligence.

Interrogator

Truthful Woman

Computer

Figure 13.1.4

The Imitation Game phase two.

13.2 Modeling Human Intelligence

To appreciate the complexity of how humans store information and manipulate it, we'll now examine some attempts to model this capacity. It should be emphasized that these are human attempts to model something that is not completely understood.

MODELING THE HUMAN KNOWLEDGE SYSTEM

Intuitively it is clear that there are some necessary requirements for thinking. In fact, it seems plausible that thinking needs some basis on which to think. In other words, thinking involves using some knowledge (for example, facts and processes) about the circumstance in which the thinking is done. There must be something to think about! When you think about going out for a dinner at some exclusive restaurant, for example, many things must be known. Here are just a few of them:

> What clothes to wear
>
> What clothes are
>
> Dinner means eating
>
> Other people involved
>
> Who is going to pay
>
> You need enough money
>
> Take a shower
>
> Brush your teeth
>
> How to get to the restaurant
>
> When you leave (what time)

Literally thousands of small facts and situations must be known in order to think about going to dinner. How do humans keep all of this knowledge in their brains, and how do they access it? This is a most difficult question. It is not known how the human brain maintains its base

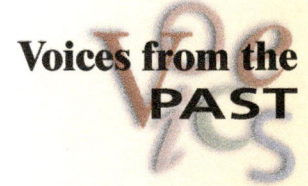

Voices from the PAST

Marvin Minsky—A Leader in AI

Since the early 1950s MIT Professor Marvin Minsky has been working to understand various aspects of human intelligence. He cofounded the MIT Artificial Intelligence Laboratory in 1959 with John McCarthy. In the early years the problems of how humans play games such as chess were thought to be the difficult problems. But as Professor Minsky has indicated by his statements and direction in research, the problem of understanding how humans use and manipulate common sense is far more difficult.

Marvin Minsky
The Image Works

In 1987 he published *Society of Mind,* which is his view of human intellectual structure and function. It represents a summary of the work he did in this area during the 1970s and the 1980s. The early work was done with Seymour Papert and combined insights from developmental child psychology with those of the research on artificial intelligence. This "society of mind" proposes that human intelligence comes from the interaction of many diverse, resourceful agents acting in their own interests.

Along the way to his "society of mind," Professor Minsky pioneered work on intelligence-based mechanical robotics and telepresence. He did original work in tactile sensing and visual scanning and built the first LOGO "turtle." In 1951 he also built the first randomly wired neural network learning machine called SNARC. In his 1974 paper, "A Framework for Representing Knowledge," Professor Minsky proposed the "frames and scripts" representation of knowledge.

of knowledge or how it actually works. Certainly the body of knowledge applicable to any given situation is large, and the thought network connecting that knowledge is complex.

One way to study complex systems is to build a working model of the system and observe it in action. Several major approaches are used to model the human knowledge system. They all make use of knowledge as just discussed. It cannot be said that any of them approaches the way the human brain works because it is not known exactly how the brain works. We will examine two of the approaches that are considered reasonably accurate representations of some of the thinking patterns of the human brain. None pretends to be a complete model of all brain activities.

Semantic networks consist of objects, concepts, or situations that people associate by some type of relationship. Examine the following sentence, for example:

A daisy is a flower.

The relationship between the concept daisy and the concept flower is expressed in English by the words *is a*. The words *is a* are so significant in a semantic network that they are usually written *isa*. We might label this type of relationship as membership. A daisy is a member of the group of objects included under the title flower. A semantic network is made up of a series of these interconnected relationships.

A small part of a typical semantic network relating a man named John to his belongings is shown in Figure 13.2.1. Notice how the network describes the relationship between John and his environment.

A second type of knowledge representation is expressed by rules. These systems use rules to store the knowledge, and that's why they are commonly called **rule-based systems.** Because the rules are usually gleaned from experts in the field being represented, they are often referred to as **expert systems.** A rule in an expert system that deals with everyday events, for example, might be the following:

IF (it is raining AND you must go outside)

THEN (put on your raincoat)

Because **production systems** attempt to emulate the experts in a particular endeavor, they have proven to be the most useful and widely used knowledge model in the commercial world. We'll discuss these later in the chapter.

These two knowledge representation schemes have significant deficiencies. However, they do help us understand how difficult it is to accurately represent human knowledge.

Modeling human intelligence involves a lot more than knowledge representation. For any of these models to work, they must be able to make use of this human knowledge in three different ways:

Semantic networks are designed after the psychological model of the human associative memory.

Rule-based systems or **expert systems** are knowledge bases consisting of hundreds or thousands of rules of the form: **IF** (condition) **THEN** (action). **Production system** is a term often used to describe a rule-based system.

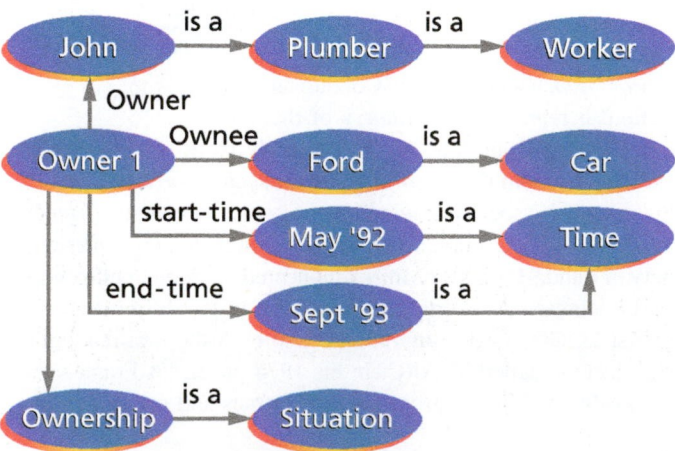

Figure 13.2.1

Simple example of a semantic network.

1. **Acquisition**—There must be some way of putting information or knowledge into the system because it is impossible to do anything without a base of information.

2. **Retrieval**—The intelligent system must be able to find the knowledge when it is wanted or needed. It does this by searching through the knowledge base.

3. **Reasoning**—The system must have the capability to use that knowledge through a mysterious process called thinking or reasoning.

Let's examine these three important intelligence functions in more detail.

KNOWLEDGE ACQUISITION

A fact, such as bees can sting, is an example of the simplest type of knowledge that can be acquired. Other types of knowledge, such as ideas, concepts, and relationships, are much more difficult for humans (or machines) to acquire. The idea that provoking bees causes them to sting, for example, could be inferred from the idea that teasing a dog results in being bitten. Before such an inference can be made, however, the dog-teasing idea must be integrated into the existing knowledge base, and the reasoning process called inference must be learned.

To better understand the process of **knowledge acquisition,** let's explore how a human "learns" a seemingly simple concept—the definition of a class of objects called "chair."

Actually, by the time you were in second or third grade, you already had a clear idea of what a chair was. If someone showed you a group of furniture items, you could pick out the chairs in the group unerringly. Suppose you had to describe a chair to some extraterrestrial being who had never seen one. What would you say? Here's a possible definition of chair:

> **Chair**—an object with four legs, a back, and a flat surface that you can sit on.

That sounds great—very functional and descriptive. It's certainly a good enough definition for the object we are talking about. Right? Let's send our extraterrestrial out to prove he's learned the concept of chair by pointing out some chairs he sees. Figure 13.2.2 illustrates three objects that our extraterrestrial student identifies as chairs. A brief look will show you that his understanding of chair is imperfect. The middle object is not a chair but a sofa. We had better rewrite our definition so that sofas and other objects similar to chairs, but not exactly like them, are left out. Here's our second try:

> **Chair**—a thing with four legs, a back, and a flat surface that one person can sit on at a time.

There! That's better. The sofa is now eliminated from our definition, as are settees, love seats, and benches.

Don't get too satisfied with the corrected definition. It is still not adequate. True, we have narrowed the definition to eliminate several objects that do not belong in the category called chairs. But is it broad enough to allow our extraterrestrial student to recognize all

Figure 13.2.2

Three examples of four-legged objects that we can sit on.

Figure 13.2.3

Several chairs that do not match our current definition.

examples of chair? A quick look at Figure 13.2.3 will show you that we are not yet done with our definition. These are chairs that our learner has failed to recognize because they do not fit our definition very well. One has no back, one has a pedestal instead of legs, one has rockers, one has a platform instead of legs, and the last defies description but is still a chair.

Here's a definition from *The American Heritage Dictionary of the English Language* that comes close to accommodating most of the pictures in Figure 13.2.3.

> **Chair**—a piece of furniture consisting of a seat, legs and back, and often arms, designed for one person.

Even this definition, however, does not adequately describe all examples of the concept chair. It is, in fact, impossible to devise a definition that describes all possible chairs while excluding objects that do not belong in this classification. The extraterrestrial learner might still have difficulties identifying a wheelchair, for example, or a chair lift.

At this point, we have defined chair to the best of our ability, and we have pointed out many examples for our extraterrestrial student to see. We must now count on his (its?) native intelligence to be able to generalize the concept to include other examples, by comparing each new chair to the examples stored in his memory. This ability to generalize, and to apply old definitions to new objects, is an important form of intelligent learning, or knowledge acquisition.

KNOWLEDGE RETRIEVAL BY SEARCHING

After knowledge has been acquired and stored in one's memory, the next task of intelligence is to be able to retrieve that knowledge and use it to solve problems. One way in which **knowledge retrieval** is done is to search the built-up knowledge base for the appropriate tidbits of information, and then relate them to the problem to be solved. The next discussion centers on ways in which a knowledge base can be searched to find information needed in solving a problem.

Brute-Force Search—Looking at Every Possibility

A **brute-force search** is one that looks at every possible solution before choosing among them.

Many advances in artificial intelligence have consisted of searching for ways of solving a problem and choosing among possible solutions for what seems to be the best solution. The **brute-force search** consists of looking at all possible solutions and then choosing an appropriate one. In playing the game of **Hexapawn,** for example, computers can base decisions on what move to make by looking at (that is, searching) all possible moves, and then selecting the best, whatever best means. The game Hexapawn is played on a 3×3 board with three white pawns and three black pawns. They start on opposite sides of the board and move just like chess pawns, which means they can move forward into an unoccupied square or they can move diagonally to an adjacent square occupied by the opposite color; the opposing pawn is then removed from the board. Whichever color reaches the opposite side first wins the game.

To explore the Hexapawn example further, examine Figure 13.2.4 in which all possible moves have been outlined in what is referred to as a game tree. This is part of the knowledge base for playing Hexapawn. Note that some moves are equivalent to others. The first move, for example, moving the white pawn forward, is the "mirror image" or essentially the same move on either edge. This is due to the symmetry of the nine-square grid used in the game. The game tree shows only the different moves (that is, all equivalent moves are not shown).

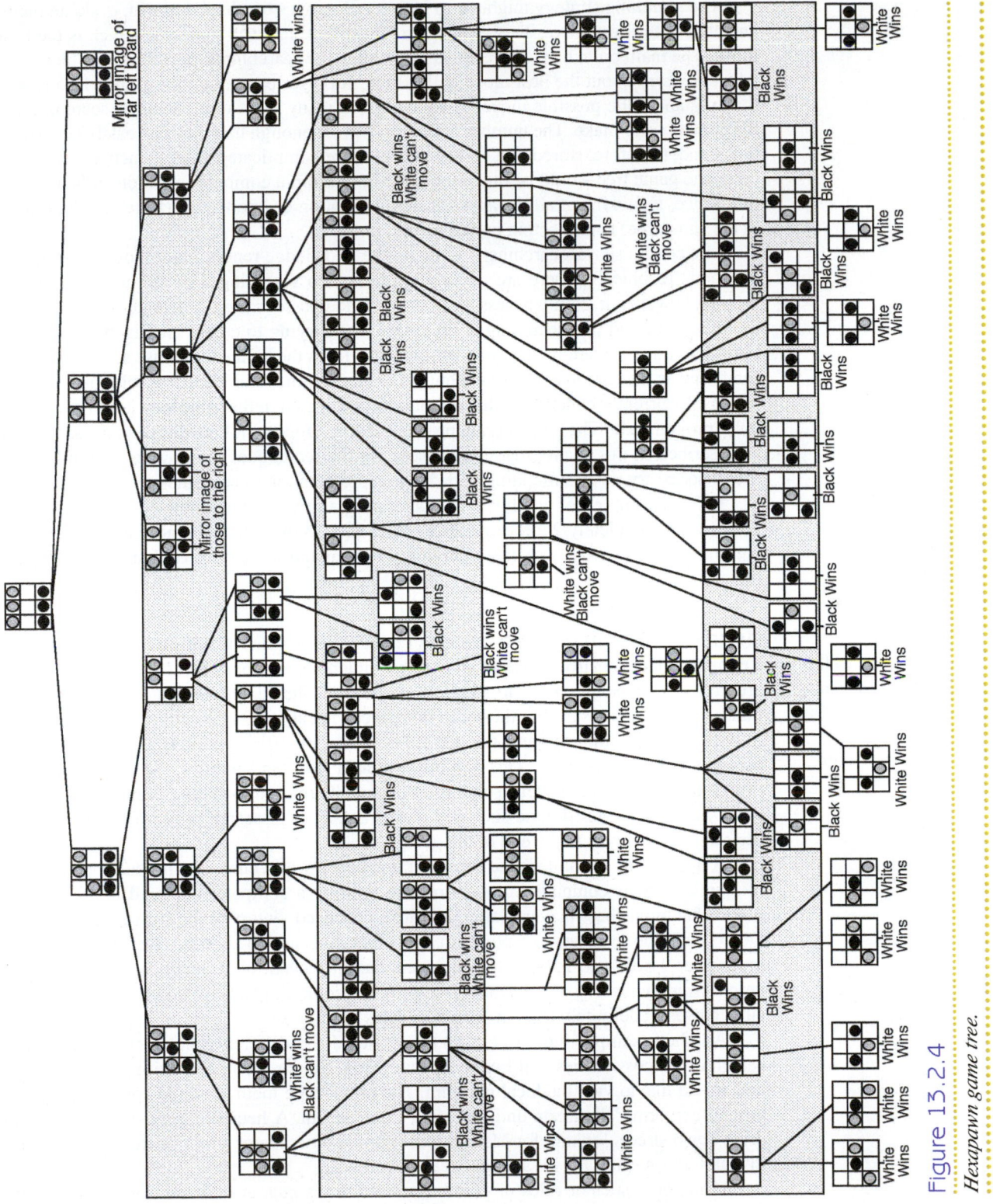

Figure 13.2.4

Hexapawn game tree.

391

The searching strategy might be to look for all moves that lead to a win, evaluate them, and choose the best move. This means there must be some way to decide which is the best move. The main point here, however, is to examine the searching aspect of the problem. So, let's not worry about the best move at this time. A player examining the game visually and thinking about the possible moves is equivalent in many ways to a computer searching for the next move to make. The number of moves is small enough that they can easily be written down and, therefore, stored in a computer. For more complicated games, such as chess, the complete game tree would be much too large to put into a computer all at once. Searching, in essence, is looking at all the appropriate information or knowledge (for example, moves in the game tree) and selecting one of them.

In a certain sense, searching is done on the knowledge representation of the system in question. Technically, there are many ways to do the searching. For the purposes of this chapter, however, it is only necessary to understand that searching is being done.

Keep in mind that searching is necessary when trying to create intelligent computers. How does this compare with human intelligence? Does the human brain use searching in the same way as the computer? How the human brain examines and identifies solutions to problems isn't currently understood. It certainly doesn't search in the same way as existing computer programs do. The human brain probably doesn't represent knowledge in the same way as described in this section. However, these are the techniques researchers currently have found necessary when simulating knowledge representation in computers.

Only the simplest of intelligent computer programs work with knowledge bases that can be searched completely. More complex systems such as those that diagnose individuals who are prone to heart attacks or chess-playing programs must use rules of thumb to find solutions to problems.

Heuristics are **rules of thumb** that are used to limit the number of items that must be searched in solving a problem. These rules of thumb aren't guaranteed to lead to a solution.

Heuristic Searching

The concept of **heuristics** or **rules of thumb** is important when a complete or exhaustive search of all possible situations is impossible. In other words, there are far too many solutions to do a brute-force search. The hexapawn game has only several hundred possible moves, and these can be reduced because of symmetry. Suppose we tried to write out the complete game tree for chess. There are 10^{120}, which is 1 followed by 120 zeros, possible chess plays. This is a huge number and can't possibly be written down or even searched through. Instead some rules of thumb are used to greatly reduce the possible plays that are examined. One such rule, for example, is to search only a few plays ahead instead of all the way to the end of the game.

A noteworthy example is the computer that beat a world chess champion. The first time the human versus computer competition was won by a computer occurred in 1997 when world champion chess player, Garry Kasparov, conceded victory to the IBM program called Deep Blue. The score was 3.5 points to 2.5 points. Kasparov had beaten Deep Blue the previous year 4 points to 2, but IBM engineers had improved the program. It should also be emphasized, in making a chess move, the program couldn't possibly search through all possible moves. It definitely used heuristics or rules of thumb.

Another example should help you understand the difference between a brute-force search of all possibilities and **heuristic searching.** Suppose you are visiting a small town and would like to visit the local museum. The brute-force method would consist of driving around exploring all streets until you find the museum. A heuristic approach might be to drive down streets looking for Main Street or some other major street because the museum in small towns is usually on a main street downtown.

Using heuristics or rules of thumb doesn't always guarantee a solution to a problem. Just imagine the museum in a small town that is located out of town at the nature center. This absence of a guaranteed solution should be contrasted with the algorithmic solutions to the problems in chapters 4 and 5. These algorithmic solutions are usually expressed in computer languages and give precise details on how to get a solution. It's guaranteed! Therefore, heuristic methods are quite a change from the usual way of solving problems using computers.

REASONING

With the ability to gather knowledge and represent it in our brain, the next step is to retrieve and reason with the knowledge. Reasoning is what we humans do when we solve problems. In the field of artificial intelligence, two types of reasoning are commonly used: shallow reasoning and deep reasoning. Shallow reasoning is based on heuristics (intuition) or rule-based knowledge. Deep reasoning deals with models of the problem obtained from analyzing the structure and function of component parts of the problem. Humans commonly apply deep reasoning, but computers for the most part do the shallow-type reasoning.

Reasoning is a difficult and important area of study in artificial intelligence. Just a few of the commonly known patterns of human reasoning include the following: probabilistic reasoning, fuzzy reasoning, inductive reasoning, and deductive reasoning.

The field of AI has also been challenged to consider another problem. How can the knowledge base be built up so that there is sufficient knowledge with which to reason? It would be too time-consuming or manually impossible to put all the knowledge of even a five-year-old child into the computer. One approach is to develop programs that learn.

LEARNING SYSTEMS

It's clear that to build knowledge bases by whatever means can be very tedious. For computer programs to become truly intelligent, they must be capable of learning on their own. After all, learning is one of the most prized attributes of intelligence. A commonly accepted classification scheme for learning is summarized as follows:

1. **Rote learning**—This corresponds to the memorization of facts, such as memorizing multiplication tables.

2. **Learning by instruction**—This is similar to the student/teacher relationship found in any classroom.

3. **Learning by deduction**—In this classification, deductive inference is used to transform knowledge into other forms. Deduction consists of drawing conclusions from certain premises. For example: *All cats are animals; this is a cat; therefore, this is an animal.*

4. **Learning by induction**—Inductive learning consists of several subcategories: learning by example, learning by experimentation, learning by observation, and learning by discovery.

5. **Learning by analogy**—This combines both deductive and inductive learning. In the case of the bee sting discussed earlier, being bitten by the teased dog could have made the individual learn not to tease bees.

These types of learning are used in writing intelligent computer programs that are capable of learning. Sometimes this concept is referred to as machine learning.

A very simple example of a **learning system** is found in a modification of the hexapawn game. Suppose the game tree of Figure 13.2.4 were enlarged so that a small container can be placed on each of the dozens of board diagrams. Assume the computer takes black. You will be the white player. After each move, put a red button in the box corresponding to the move that is made. If the computer wins, replace each red button with a dried pea. However, if you win, remove the red buttons and don't replace them with the peas. During each subsequent game, when the computer chooses a move, it should select the path that has the most peas in the boxes. If there aren't any peas, or if all paths have the same number of peas, then randomly choose among them. Eventually, the computer will choose paths that lead to winning. It is learning!

COMMON SENSE

It is interesting to note that when the field of AI was in its infancy in the late 1940s and 1950s, the problems that seemed to be the most difficult were playing chess and other intellectual games.

Contrary to this belief was one held by an informal research group from the mid-1970s called the Frames Group located in Berkeley, California. They would devote the first half-hour of their meetings to watching the TV program *Mork and Mindy*. Mork was an alien from the planet Ork who was played by Robin Williams and possessed remarkable reasoning powers. Because of his background, he didn't have an earthling's common sense. In one program, for example, Mork threw an egg in the air and said: "Fly, little bird, fly!" It so happened that on Ork spaceships were egg shaped and Mork, reminded of them, thought the egg could fly. Of course, viewers watching the program thought this to be very funny. It was this constant misunderstanding or lack of what we call common sense that made the program so amusing.

The concept of **common sense** is multifaceted. There are commonsense facts that must be in the knowledge base, and also commonsense reasoning must be included to make inferences from the knowledge base. Grappling with this area of AI has been exceedingly difficult.

Some progress, however, has been made through the tenacious pursuit of a computer program named Cyc (enCYClopedia) that exhibits and can apply common sense. Douglas Lenat and others have worked several years to develop Cyc into a knowledge base for commonsense reasoning. The project was started in 1984 at MCC (Microelectronics and Computer Technology Corporation) in Austin, Texas. It then split off under the name Cycorp in 1995. At that time Cyc started marketing some knowledge-based products with a core of about 1 million axioms. Using this knowledge base, Cyc can make commonsense decisions and observations. It knows, for example, that liquid in glasses should be carried rightside-up, when people die they stop purchasing things, and that trees are usually located outdoors.

The Cyc continues to be developed to "provide a 'deep' layer of understanding." Under the name the Cyc Knowledge Server, several components that are intended to be used by other programs can be identified. Among them are

The Cyc Knowledge Base

The Cyc Inference Engine

The Natural Language Processing Subsystem

The natural language component does some rather amazing things. On Cycorp's website several examples that Cyc "understands" are represented by the following sentences.

Fred saw the plane flying over Zurich.

Fred saw the mountains flying over Zurich.

Obviously, mountains don't fly. Cyc "understands" this fact and rejects the "flying mountain" interpretation, while many other language understanding systems would have a great deal of difficulty. The next section deals with some of these types of problems.

13.3 Natural Language Communication

Natural language communication using computers has been a goal of computer scientists for many years. The problems are many, and topping the list is the semantics of communication. Early experiments seemed to make great progress on the surface, but this was only a façade, enabled by human gullibility. The most noteworthy is ELIZA.

ELIZA: AN EXPERIMENT IN COMMUNICATION

The ELIZA program is a very early experiment in communication that is considered to be a classic example of the dangers of using computers in communication. It was written by MIT Professor Joseph Weizenbaum in 1965. ELIZA simulated the conversational style of a Carl Rogers category of therapist. This method of therapy is still used in treating cases ranging from mildly misbehaving children to psychotic adults. Using this style, the therapist mirrors the patient's conversation in a positive manner. The ELIZA program turned out to fool a lot of people, some of whom refused to believe it was just a computer communicating with them. Figure 13.3.1 is a conversation with ELIZA reported in a paper by Weizenbaum in the January 1966 *Communications of the ACM*.

All men are alike.

IN WHAT WAY

They're always bugging us about something or other.

CAN YOU THINK OF A SPECIFIC EXAMPLE

Well, my boyfriend made me come here.

YOUR BOYFRIEND MADE YOU COME HERE

He says I'm depressed much of the time.

I AM SORRY TO HEAR YOU ARE DEPRESSED

It's true. I am unhappy.

DO YOU THINK COMING HERE WILL HELP YOU NOT TO BE UNHAPPY

I need some help, that much seems certain.

WHAT WOULD IT MEAN TO YOU IF YOU GOT SOME HELP

Perhaps I could learn to get along with my mother.

TELL ME MORE ABOUT YOUR FAMILY

My mother takes care of me.

WHO ELSE IN YOUR FAMILY TAKES CARE OF YOU

My father.

YOUR FATHER

You are like my father in some ways.

WHAT RESEMBLANCE DO YOU SEE

You are not very aggressive but I think you don't want me to notice that.

WHAT MAKES YOU THINK I AM NOT VERY AGGRESSIVE

You don't argue with me.

WHY DO YOU THINK I DON'T ARGUE WITH YOU

You are afraid of me.

DOES IT PLEASE YOU TO BELIEVE I AM AFRAID OF YOU

My father is afraid of everybody.

WHAT ELSE COMES TO YOUR MIND WHEN YOU THINK OF YOUR FATHER

Bullies.

DOES THAT HAVE ANYTHING TO DO WITH THE FACT THAT YOUR BOYFRIEND MADE YOU COME HERE

Figure 13.3.1

A conversation with ELIZA.

The last statement by ELIZA is very convincing. The techniques used to write the program, however, are really quite simple. For example, the exchange:

Well, my boyfriend made me come here.
YOUR BOYFRIEND MADE YOU COME HERE

is a simple translation of the word *my* to YOUR and the word *me* to YOU. That is one of the simpler tricks. When no standard sentence pattern can be matched, the program will randomly pick some previously recorded information. This is what happened in the last sentence in Figure 13.3.1.

DOES THAT HAVE ANYTHING TO DO WITH THE FACT
THAT YOUR BOYFRIEND MADE YOU COME HERE

When humans see this type of response, however, they immediately think the computer really understands. But nothing could be further from the truth. In fact, Weizenbaum was so upset with people believing in his program that in 1976 he wrote the book *Computer Power and Human Reason.* In it he states: "Science promised man power. But, as so often happens when people are seduced by promises of power . . . the price actually paid is servitude and impotence."

SEMANTIC TRANSLATION PROBLEMS

The previous example helps to remind us that the semantics or meaning of the words being spoken is the goal in communication. It is necessary to have the computer understand the meaning, not just the words themselves. For example,

"The bark was irritating!"

is a sentence whose individual words don't tell the real story. Understanding words such as *irritating* is not simple because the sentence implies that there is an individual who was irritated. The computer would somehow have to determine this along with the understanding of the word *bark*. Is it the bark of a tree or the bark of a dog?

In fact, in the 1950s it was optimistically assumed that it would be relatively easy to have computers translate from one language to another. The semantic problem has certainly dulled this optimism. A classic example known as the Bar-Hillel paradox illustrates another even more difficult semantic problem:

The pen is in the box.

The box is in the pen.

These sentences convinced the linguist Yehoshua Bar-Hillel after nine years of struggling with this type of semantic problem that computer translation of languages is impossible. The sentences have identical syntax, yet the meanings can be interpreted completely differently. Most individuals interpret the first sentence as saying the writing instrument is in the box, whereas the meaning of the second sentence is that the box is in the playpen.

In spite of these problems there was still an overabundance of optimism in the area of language translation. It was thought that after only a few years' work, computer programs would be able to translate from Russian, Chinese, or any other language to English or vice versa. However, difficulties started to show themselves in sometimes humorous ways. An early attempt was made to translate the following English expression:

The spirit is willing, but the flesh is weak.

The translation to Russian and back to English had the humorous result:

The vodka is strong, but the meat is rotten.

These early results were not encouraging. They relied heavily on dictionary lookups and used simple word-for-word replacements. As the previous example makes very clear, more has to be done to get good language translations. The program must analyze the sentences not only based on the grammar and rules of the language being translated from, but also the language the sentences are being translated to. The words and phrases of a sentence must be translated in the context of the sentences coming before and after it. To create a world-class language translator takes millions of dollars and the efforts of hundreds of people-years.

However, through hard work and better understanding, language translation programs have come a long way. Evidence of this can be seen in the very useful language translation on the World Wide Web. Although the translation accuracy and interpretation are very crude, some of the programs in the last section of this chapter are still worth investigating.

PUZZLER HINT

Your Olympic tickets have a deadline, so time is of the essence. Try getting on the Web and look for the free language translation programs.

13.4 Expert Systems

In any field of endeavor there are some individuals who are experts. Their knowledge of the particular field is such that they can solve problems and understand the area intimately. We often call experts in to solve our own problems, such as: Why does my car lose power at about 60 mph? Section 13.2 introduced expert systems in the context of putting knowledge into a computer; this section will show how this stored knowledge can be used to model human intelligence.

EXPERT SYSTEM OVERVIEW

Expert systems are commercially a very successful domain of artificial intelligence. These computer programs mimic the experts in whatever field the programs were written to be experts. There are systems designed to be experts in many fields, such as the following:

auto mechanic expert

cardiologist expert

organic compounds expert

mineral prospecting expert

diagnostic internal medicine expert

engineering structural analysis expert

audiologist expert

telephone network expert

delivery route-finder expert

professional auditor expert

pulmonary (lung) function expert

weather forecasting expert

battlefield tactical expert

space-station control/life support expert

civil law expert

oil-rig drilling expert

toxic materials expert

The list goes on and on. Several thousand expert systems of various abilities exist. Some are trivial microcomputer-based experiments, but many are important commercial successes.

Expert systems are also called rule-based systems because the expert's expertise is built into the program through a collection of rules. The desired result is that the program functions at the same level as the human expert.

As previously stated, the rules that make up an expert system are typically of the form:

If (some condition), **then** (some action).

for example,

If (gas near empty **AND** going on a long trip),

then (stop at gas station **AND** fill the gas tank **AND** check the oil).

One of the largest and most successful expert systems was **XCON.** It was an expert system used by the former Digital Equipment Corporation to help configure the VAX family of minicomputers. When customers bought a computer, the system was customized to their needs. Of the thousands of combinations available for the VAX family of computers, the salesperson must pick all of the proper cables, connectors, interface boards, and software that will work with the customer's choice. This was a very difficult job until the expert system XCON was created. Using XCON, the salesperson indicates what hardware/software capability and layout the customer wants. XCON then fills in all of the details by specifying cables and other parts that are needed to make it work.

Typical expert systems will have thousands of these rules. In fact, the XCON expert system has over 10,000 rules that help in the layout and assembly of well over 400 parts and components.

STRUCTURE OF AN EXPERT SYSTEM

The **knowledge base** is the collection of rules that make up the expert system.

The **inference engine** is a program that uses the rules by making several passes over them. On each pass, the inference engine looks for all rules whose condition is satisfied. It then takes the action part or "then" part and makes another pass over all the rules looking for matching conditions. This goes on until no rules' conditions are matched. The results are all those action parts left.

Aside from the obvious human communication link to an expert system, there are two major parts, the **knowledge base** (set of rules) and the **inference engine** (rule interpreter). The simple expert systems only have rules of the type shown. With possibly thousands of these types of if/then rules, a controlling program is needed to interpret the rules. This is the inference engine. The inference engine will go through the knowledge base and find all of the rules that have the "condition" (*if* part) satisfied. Then it will use the "action" part (*then* part) and look for all of the additional rules that have it as a condition. This goes on until it can't find any more rules that have the current conditions. The final action part of the if/then is the answer from the expert system. The following example shows a simplistic situation:

> **Rule 1:** IF (it's raining outside), THEN (get an umbrella).
>
> **Rule 2:** IF (getting an umbrella), THEN (go to umbrella rack).

Suppose our extremely simple two-rule expert system was given the condition "it's raining outside," the inference engine would see that the condition in Rule 1 is satisfied, but no others. It would then make a second round using "get an umbrella" as the condition. The inference engine would then see Rule 2 and respond with "go to umbrella rack." Using this last response as a new condition doesn't give any further results. So, the final response to "it's raining outside" would be "go to umbrella rack."

Many other factors make this simplistic example almost incorrect, but the essence is there. The complexities become involved when there is uncertainty in which rule to use. Probability can then be invoked to use the *best* rule.

The preceding example used what is referred to as forward chaining, which means going from a rule's condition to a rule's action and using the action as a new condition and so on. Another concept called backward chaining goes in the other direction, looking for conditions that have certain actions.

Medical doctors, in effect, use both forward and backward chaining. When going to the doctor with some medical problem, for example, the first thing you would do is to tell the doctor the symptoms (for example, stomach pain). The doctor will come up with a tentative diagnosis, let's say an ulcer; this would be forward chaining. The doctor then may ask if you have eaten a green apple (he knows green apples give stomachaches), which would be backward chaining. In a diagnosis this is done literally hundreds of times in every patient's visit. But the doctor doesn't look at all the rules, only the most likely. The doctor wouldn't ask if you had just been shot in the stomach, for example, because that would have been obvious.

EXPERT SYSTEMS IN THE ARTS

With all of the emphasis on science and business it is important to note that expert systems have also made major contributions to the arts possible. In this next example we will focus

Bots and Intelligent Agents

As our world gets more and more complex, it is difficult for the average citizen to always know the right thing to do. It can be dangerous, for example, to sell your own house. If you forget even a single important word in the contract, then the buyer may back out or force you to pay for something not precisely indicated. That's why there are real estate agents, insurance agents, and other types of experts in a certain area.

The Internet has already produced the precursor of the intelligent agent. Called bots, as in roBOTS, they do menial tasks such as roaming the World Wide Web looking for things. As the following names indicate, they come in many different forms: Web robots, spiders, wanderers, worms, cancelbots, modbots, softbots, userbots, taskbots, chatterbots, knowbots, mailbots, bolo bots, warbots, clonebots, crashbots, floodbots, annoybots, hackbots, Vladbots, Turing bots, gossipbots, gamebots, conceptbots, roverbots, skeletonbots, spybots, spambots, and many others. The bots don't have the intelligence that is expected of the intelligent agent. However, bots that provide services and act as intermediaries between computers and humans could be considered a bottommost class of intelligent agents.

The artificial intelligence community is now developing computerized agents using the model of the human intelligent agents. Almost two decades ago, Alan Kay in his Knowledge Navigator proposed an early classic example of such an agent. His agent was to be a personal assistant that had access to electronic communications. In a simulation of how this agent might behave, the agent took phone calls, made appointments, and would do tasks such as locating individuals by phone or finding research materials. The agent appeared as a talking human form on the monitor screen of the computer. The human would give verbal instructions to the agent in continuous speech, and the agent responded as if it were human. Other researchers have proposed agents that scan the Internet for things of interest to the owner of the agent. This agent would then report back its findings.

more on the creative act of making art. We will examine the question: Is creativity a necessary ingredient of art?

Harold Cohen is an artist who contributes some answers to this question and raises still other new questions. His great success as a painter in England in the late 1960s gives him insight into the problems of art, with or without technology. It was with great courage he gave up the traditional artist's career to begin a new career producing art using computers and expert systems. His work with Stanford Professor Edward Feigenbaum led to the birth of AARON in 1973, an expert system that creates art.

What is AARON? What purpose did this work serve? Cohen stated that his purpose for working with AARON is to demystify the various functions in art-making that are often labeled as creativity. Many have viewed creativity as inspirational or even romantic; either view is certainly mysterious and unexplainable.

Cohen's work sets out to explore his own mental structures and decision-making processes and incorporate them into the collection of well over 1,000 rules called AARON. The rules include information regarding human anatomy and gravity. AARON is then set free to draw what it may draw. The program has only its own resources and the knowledge given it by Harold Cohen. Is it creating? It seems to be!

After over 30 years of learning through Cohen's adding new rules to the program, AARON can now even color the drawings. Cohen worked for many years to build a color theory that mimics his own and incorporated it into AARON. Figure 13.4.1 shows an example of AARON's art. As an interesting note, a PC version of the AARON program is now available as shareware over the Internet (www.kurzweilcyberart.com). AARON is a hefty program weighing in at almost 10 megabytes, and in screen saver mode produces an original work of art every couple minutes on a gigahertz PC.

Courtesy of Becky Cohen

Figure 13.4.1

A drawing created and colored by AARON.

13.5 Neural Networks

In the many years since Plato and Aristotle, curiosity about how the brain works has been piqued even more. Researchers who study the brain have found some very interesting and complex structures.

THE NEURON

One of the most fundamental of these brain structures is the nerve cell or neuron, which is the basic building block of the brain. Although there are several specialized types of neurons, they all have the same basic structure as shown in Figure 13.5.1.

Figure 13.5.1

The basic structure of an animal neuron.

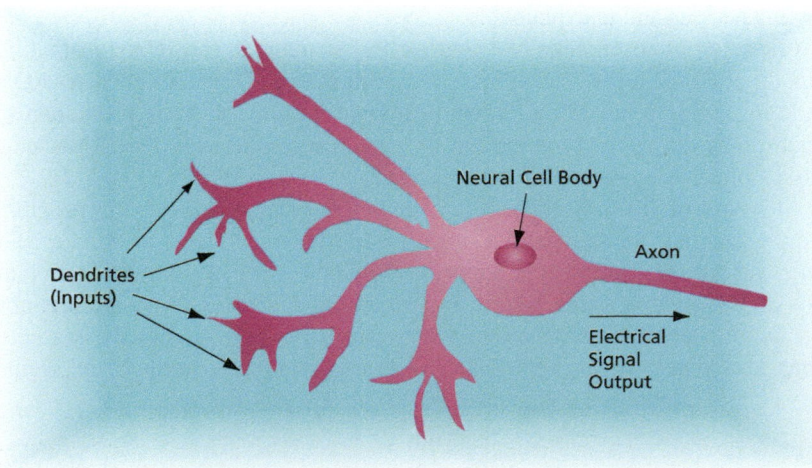

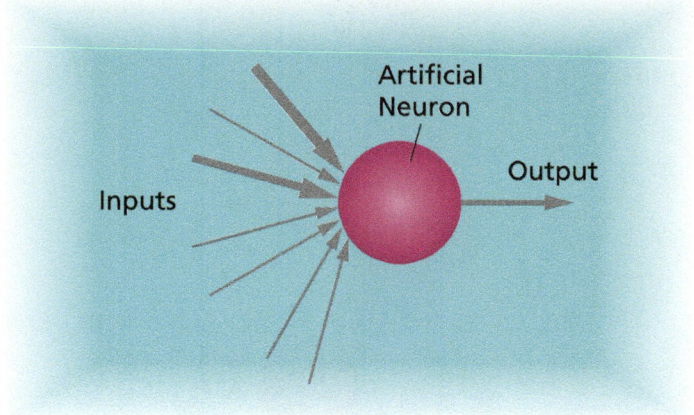

Figure 13.5.2

Artificial neuron with inputs of different strengths and one output.

The neuron has several inputs and one output. This means it can receive information from many other neurons but gives out only a single signal. In fact, neurons can receive input signals from 100,000 to 200,000 other neurons. These inputs are electrical pulses from other neurons, which can pulsate up to 1,000 times per second. The single output of a neuron (axon) is also electrical and can be connected to several thousand other neurons. Researchers' estimates of how many neurons are in the brain vary from 10 to 100 billion neurons. The brain can grow new connections and dissolve others that are insufficiently used.

The artificial models of a neuron are of two distinct types. One is electronic and the other is software running on a computer. The electronic version has electronic circuits that behave like a neuron, whereas the software version runs a program on a computer, which simulates the action of a neuron. Most research is done using the software approach. The following discussion pertains to either approach.

An **artificial neuron,** shown in Figure 13.5.2, looks very much like the real neuron. It has many inputs and one output. The artificial neuron is often called a **processing element.**

What are the inputs to the artificial neuron? The inputs are signals that are strengthened or weakened (that is, weighted), just as a real neuron's inputs are weighted. The width of the input line in Figure 13.5.2 indicates how much of the signal gets through to the neuron's center, where the signals are combined. Thick lines mean more of the signal gets through than for thin lines. If the sum of all of the inputs is strong enough, the neuron will fire, which means it puts out a signal to the output. In the case when a real neuron fires, it sends out a signal over its axon to other neurons.

Artificial neurons, commonly called **processing elements,** are modeled after real neurons of humans and other animals.

NEURAL NETWORKS

For many years researchers have been trying to build artificial brains. It should be emphasized that these artificial models of the brain are not copies of a human brain. About the only connection between the human brain and the researchers' models is the concept of the neuron. Researchers don't try to duplicate the human brain for many reasons. One is that it is too complicated. Also, the brain's details are still not completely understood. In fact, it should be noted that the vast capability of the human brain is still far beyond the computers we have today. It is estimated that the most powerful supercomputers have only enough speed and memory to give a little less brainpower than a leech.

In spite of the difficulty of the problem, scientists have used a small number of artificial neurons connected together to create a **neural network.** The results of a neural network with so few artificial neurons are remarkable.

The first neural networks of the 1950s were very simple, single layers of artificial neurons. Figure 13.5.3 shows a very simple, single layer of two neurons with three inputs. Note that all three inputs are connected to both neurons with different strength connections. Input 1, for example, has a stronger connection to Neuron 2 than it does to Neuron 1. This can be

A **neural network** is a collection of interconnected neurons. The output of one connects to several others with different strength connections.

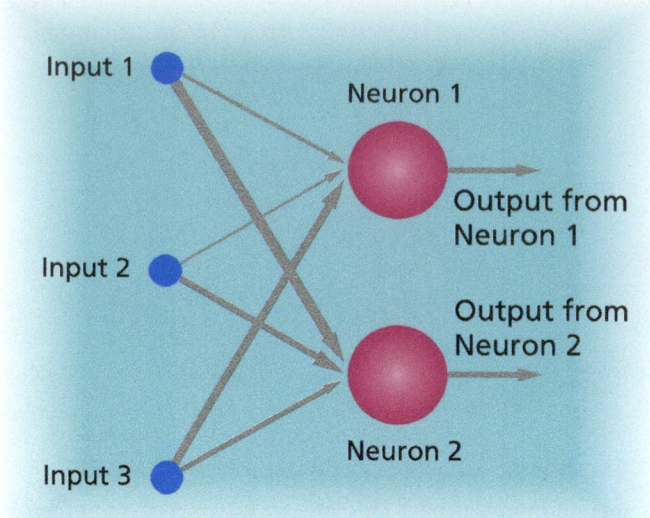

Figure 13.5.3

A single-layer neural network with only two neurons and three inputs.

seen by the width of the lines connecting Input 1 to the neurons. In other words, Input 1 has more effect on Neuron 2 than it does on Neuron 1.

The single-layer neural networks didn't have much success. In fact, advances in the field came almost to a standstill after the book *Perceptrons* by Minsky and Pappert that showed (in the late 1960s) the limitations of the approach used in neural networks. However, some researchers still pursued the neural network concepts. When the multilayer networks were created, progress was astounding. One of the more common types of neural network architectures is the three-layer neural network. Figure 13.5.4 shows a three-layer neural network. It has an input layer, an output layer, and a hidden layer. This is a very simple example; most neural networks have many more neurons.

Figure 13.5.4

A three-layer neural network with three input neurons, two hidden-layer neurons, and three output neurons.

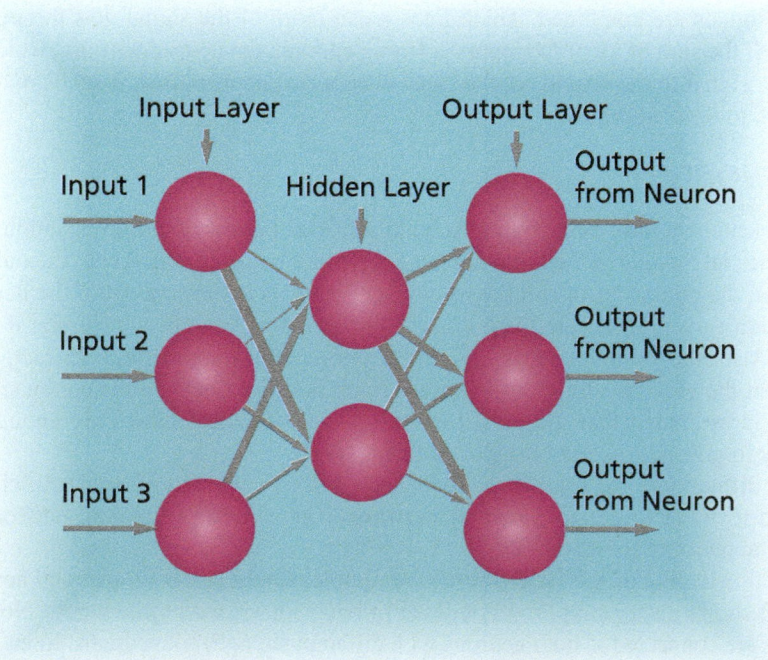

The connections made between the neurons in Figure 13.5.4 follow the rule that each neuron in one layer connects with all the neurons in the following layer with some weighting strength. Many other ways of connecting the neurons are possible, however. The neurons at the output layer could feed back to neurons in previous layers, for example, or input-layer neurons could be connected directly to output-layer neurons, or some of the connections could be left out altogether. Many of these various possibilities have been tried by the researchers with both successes and failures.

TRAINING A NEURAL NETWORK

A neural network does not have any knowledge in the beginning. Many techniques have been designed to impart knowledge to a neural network so that it can function. To better understand the process of training neural networks, let's look at both traditional programming and the expert systems that were discussed in the preceding section. Computer scientists Nelson and Illingworth in their book *Neural Nets* make an interesting observation.

When we write a program, the problem must be completely specified before we begin programming. The programmer analyzes the starting information or inputs (for example, a corporation's financial data) and the desired results (for example, how much can be spent on advertising). The process of programming is to specify precisely how every situation is to be handled. The program takes care of every event that can be foreseen by the programmer.

When developing an expert system, the programmer develops a set of rules that takes a certain input and gives a result. These rules form a chain of relationships between the input and output. But again, the programmer has to make sure all of the rules are in the system for it to function properly. In this case, the rules can be more general so that the specification isn't as precise as in writing a program.

By complete contrast, a neural network must be trained. There are no program steps or rules that a programmer must put into the network. In the beginning, no information is in the network. At the start of training, the weights or strengths of the connections between neurons are often randomly assigned. The neural network learns from experience by using many actual examples of inputs and expected outputs. This is much the same way humans do some types of learning.

The most common process for training a neural network is called **supervised training.** The process involves getting many examples of both input and output data from the area of interest, for example, credit information on an individual (that is, input) and whether he or she repaid loans or defaulted (that is, output). The credit information on many individuals and their records of payment are referred to as a training set.

An example of a very successful type of supervised learning is called back propagation. This method of learning is divided into two phases. In phase one the inputs are applied to the network, and the outputs are compared with the correct output. In phase two the resulting information about any error is fed backward through the network, adjusting the connection strengths to minimize the error.

There are many other types of learning rules and training schemes, but it is time to look at what all of this means. On to some real-world examples!

> **Supervised training** occurs when the neural network is given input data, and then the resulting output is compared to the correct output. The strengths of the connections between artificial neurons are then modified so as to minimize the difference or error in succeeding input/output pairs.

NEURAL NETWORKS IN ACTION

We'll examine just two of the hundreds of successful neural networks. The first is called the Mortgage Risk Evaluator. Data from several thousand mortgage applicants were used to train a neural network. This was done by applying each individual's credit data and loan result (that is, paid on time or default), one by one in pairs. This training took many hours. The patterns for a successful loan or default of the mortgage were contained in the data. By using the patterns inherent in the data, the neural network's weights were adjusted so that the output closely matched the actual output. Now, when a new applicant for a mortgage is entered as input to the neural network, the learned patterns will determine whether the person is a bad credit risk. The company that wrote the program, Nestor, even put in options to make the network conservative or optimistic. The success of the product was clear when a California financial institution began using the Mortgage Risk Evaluator neural network. *The New York*

Times reported that a test revealed the California company would have had a 27 percent increase in profits if it had been using the neural network the preceding year.

The second example is a combination expert system and neural network. It was designed to detect plastic explosives in luggage at airports. Plastic explosives give off a characteristic pattern of gamma-ray emissions when bathed with slow neutrons. A machine designed by Science Applications International Corporation can detect this gamma-ray pattern produced by the nitrogen in the explosive material. This machine was used from 1989 to 1994 to successfully check over 1 million bags at airports in New York City, Miami, London, and Washington, DC. Similar products are currently in use worldwide.

13.6 Evolutionary Systems

In 1950 the brilliant mathematician Alan Turing identified three attributes that are the basis for what is now termed *genetic programming.* They are familiar terms involved with Dawin's theory of evolution: *heredity, mutation,* and *natural selection.* We will examine the major efforts in using evolution to create or grow programs.

THE GENETIC ALGORITHM

The **genetic algorithm** or **simulated evolution** is a searching method that is based on the principles of genetics and evolution. It includes the equivalents of mutation, crossover, and chromosomes found in human genetics.

As the name implies, the **genetic algorithm** or **simulated evolution** mimics the processes in the genetics of living systems. It was created by John Holland of the University of Michigan in the mid-1960s, and it is meant to be a general solution to all types of problems. One interesting example is using a genetic algorithm to find some trading rules for the Standard and Poor's Composite Stock Index. The most important point to make in this discussion is this: Evolution creates the final result; there is no human programmer. A human puts together the system and specifies the desired result, but the details on how it is done are left to evolve.

An example illustrates the diversity of the genetic algorithm and its derivatives. John Koza, a leader in the field of genetic programming, developed a system that had tree-structured chromosomes in contrast to the string-shaped chromosomes of humans. Using some basic astronomical data, his system came up with Kepler's third law of planetary motion ("the cube of a planet's distance from the sun is proportional to the square of its period"). More interestingly, on the way to "rediscovering" Kepler's third law, Koza's system found a solution that Kepler had published 10 years earlier than his final one.

A difficulty with the genetic algorithm is that a coded representation of the problem must first be constructed in fixed-length character strings. This means the details of what the problem consists of must be known intimately. Then, with this knowledge, the detailed representation of the problem can be put into the computer for the genetic algorithm to work on.

The major problem with the genetic algorithm was the requirement of intimate knowledge of the system. A less demanding evolutionary approach is needed for problems in which only the goal and possibly some details of structure of the solution are known.

GENETIC PROGRAMMING

Genetic programming is a technique that follows Darwinian evolution. The evolution takes place directly on the programs in the population that are striving to reach the goal that is specified by the programmer.

Koza went on to develop **genetic programming.** It is similar to the genetic algorithm in only a general sense. They both use the concepts in Darwinian evolution. Genetic programming has somewhat less structure in the sense of organization restrictions to things such as fixed-length character strings representing the problem. In effect no limitation on some predetermined length is given. The representation is a program that can be of any length.

An example of genetic programming from Koza's work is creating a program to play the game Pac Man. The Pac Man game consists of the Pac Man that gains points by eating food, fruit, and monsters when they are in a vulnerable state. The four monsters can eat the Pac Man, whom they pursue, but with a limited attention span. The person controlling the Pac Man tries to get a high score. In Koza's example, the computer takes the place of the human and tries to obtain a high score.

This example was done using a group of 15 primitive tasks, three of which are as follows:

■ RGA—Retreat-from-Monster-A, which causes Pac Man to retreat from the nearest monster.

- AFOOD—Advance-to-FOOD, which causes Pac Man to advance to the nearest uneaten food dot via the shortest path.
- AFRUIT—Advance-to-FRUIT, which causes Pac Man to advance to the nearest moving fruit using the shortest path.

Each of these primitive tasks is implemented with several programming steps. The whole system is done in a programming language called Lisp. The nature of the Lisp language lends itself to genetic programming. Why this is true would entail a more detailed understanding of not only Lisp but also the details on how genetic programming works. The bottom line is that each primitive task consists of several programming instructions needed to implement it. Once the primitive tasks are programmed, it is no longer necessary to look at how they are programmed.

The simulation of the Pac Man game begins with the random generation of 500 programs. Each of these initial programs consists of a randomly generated list of the primitive instructions. Then all 500 of the programs are run, and a portion of the highest-scoring programs are kept. Some of them have an instruction or two randomly changed; others are randomly chosen and split into parts that are swapped with another program. The new set of 500 programs is run again, and the process starts all over again.

After 35 generations, one particular Pac Man program emerged and scored 9,240 points. For anyone who has played the game, this is a respectable score! It is truly remarkable that following the Darwinian theory of evolution, a programming technique could result in such a sophisticated program.

The Computer as an Inventor

Creating computer programs that can solve problems without help from humans is now a reality. However, critics of the computer have often said that the computer can only solve *toy problems*. They mean that any type of real-world problem is far too complex for the computer and evolutionary programming. Stanford University Professor John Koza took on this challenge by showing that a computer could create results that have been patented or infringe on a patent.

Most all would agree that creating something that can be patented takes intelligence, and the process of doing this often takes creativity. Neither of these attributes, intelligence or creativity, are thought to be possessed by computers. Koza chose the area of analog electrical circuits to do this experiment. He created an enhancement of his genetic programming that allowed the programs to have the fundamental circuit components: capacitors, resistors, and inductors.

The system starts with a high-level description of the circuit's properties but no general scheme for creating the circuit. In one case the objective was to design something called a low-pass filter for a stereo system. Everyone who owns a stereo system with a sub-woofer speaker has to have a low-pass filter; they are quite common. In this experiment and in several others 10 different patents issued by the U.S. Patent Office were either duplicated or infringed upon. The program even came up with an original circuit, one that duplicates the functionality of a patented circuit, and some would consider it to be a better design.

Koza proceeded to look at more complex circuits involving the transistor. The genetic programming system came up with the Darlington circuit patented by Sidney Darlington in 1953. This very powerful circuit is used quite commonly in the electronic circuit design field.

The question will always remain: Can computers create? The U.S. Patent Code states that novelty, usefulness, and difference from prior art are necessary to issue a patent. Considering these requirements and the fact that several of the circuits duplicated or infringed on existing patents, it seems as though the computer did create, and maybe it has some level of intelligence!

Another example from the financial investment world involves option pricing. A formal definition of what constitutes an option or option contract can be found in many places on the WWW. At the Web site of the Center for Financial Education a definition of the option contract is:

> **Option contract:** A unilateral contract giving the buyer the right, but not the obligation, to buy or sell a commodity, or a futures contract, at a specified price within a certain time period. It is unilateral because only one party (the buyer) has the right to demand performance on the contract. If the buyer exercises his right, the seller (writer or grantor) must fulfill his obligation at the strike price, regardless of the current market price of the asset.

Genetic programming has been applied to the pricing of options. Using the Standard & Poors 500 index options, the genetic programming system created pricing models. It did this by growing models that were programs used to make predictions. These models outperformed all but the Black-Scholes model, which is commonly used to calculate a theoretical call price for an option.

It is interesting to note that the Black-Scholes model is a well-defined mathematical model. It uses various factors such as stock price, strike price, volatility, time to expiration, and short-term (risk-free) interest rate as key values to determine a theoretical option price. This is contrasted with the genetic programming approach in which the data from the option index of Standard & Poors are used, and whatever the information the genetic programming approach uses is a mystery. The model itself is impossible to analyze: It just gives results.

13.7 Complex Adaptive Systems

Examples of complex adaptive systems are everywhere. The vast majority of them relate to living systems. Research on them has reached into many areas from predicting the weather to predicting fluctuations in the stock market.

DEFINING THE COMPLEX ADAPTIVE SYSTEM

A **complex adaptive system** is a collection of many parts individually operating under relatively simple rules and are highly interactive in a nonlinear way. The parts are self-organizing, operate in parallel, and exhibit emergent behavior. The system of parts evolves with natural selection operating.

Complex adaptive systems are challenging to define in a precise way. There are many examples of them, however, such as ant colonies, communities of bees, economies of nations, the world economy, political systems, cultural systems, the ecological system of an isolated island, and the ecological system of the world.

In spite of the difficulty in defining a complex adaptive system, there are some definite themes we can identify:

- They are nonlinear systems. The term *nonlinear* relates to mathematics. The solutions to nonlinear problems typically are almost impossible to find except through the use of the computer. Most physical systems in our world are nonlinear. Very small changes in a situation may result in completely different outcomes.

- They operate in parallel rather than serial; that is, several processes are executed simultaneously (for example, similar to a supercomputer rather than a von Neumann computer but even more complicated).

- They are evolutionary with natural selection involved. Darwin's theory of natural selection is an example.

- They have emergent behavior. This behavior is totally unpredictable but significant.

- The basis of the complex system contains some very simple rules. Each one of the thousands of parts of a complex system abides by these very simple rules.

- They are self-organizing. This means through various interactions, the individual parts will organize themselves much as ant colonies have developed.

Termite colonies in Australia are a beautiful example of a complex adaptive system that is reasonably easy to understand. The mounds built by the mound-building termites can be several feet high, as shown in Figure 13.7.1. Each termite has certain abilities that follow a rather

Figure 13.7.1
Termite mound found in Australia.

Nikolas DeRohan/Photovault

simple (compared to humans) set of behaviors. These behaviors can be modified over time by the chemistry of the mound.

The mounds are magnificent structures that seemingly just happen. There are no architectural plans or an engineering firm to guide its construction. Through the behavioral characteristics of the individual termites, however, the structure gets built. The termites just follow their simple set of rules. This is an emergent behavior of the colony of termites.

One very interesting emergent result is that the mounds have a form of air conditioning. The cooler air from below ground is circulated up through the mound. A complex air duct system emerges during construction.

It is tempting to think of the termite mound as being somewhat isolated from the surrounding landscape. To the contrary, they are integrated into a surprisingly interdependent community. They affect the types of plant that can grow above ground near the mound, and populations of mites and springtails flourish in the surrounding environment. On the other hand, the concentration of fungus spores and humus declines.

CHAOS

The word **chaos** is used to describe the situation in which things seem unorganized and unpredictable. For example, tiny changes in the starting point (for example, a small change in temperature) produce solutions to a problem that seem to have almost random or chaotic, unpredictable results. This sensitivity is sometimes referred to as the butterfly effect, which refers to the fact that a flap of a butterfly's wing could be the "seed" starting a hurricane.

In analyzing the chaotic behavior of certain systems, however, some structure is indeed found. The understanding of these behaviors is beyond this discussion. To get just a taste of the difficulties in learning about chaos, it is revealing to look at some of the names used in describing it. They include terms such as *attractors, strange attractors, bifurcation, deterministic chaos, state space, simulated annealing, fractals,* and many more.

In the process of simulating these systems on a computer, it is found that under certain conditions, things are totally predictable and there is no evidence of chaotic results. With changes in the conditions, chaotic results start to exhibit themselves. This is the point at

Chaos is a term used to describe a seemingly unorganized and unpredictable system, in which some unknown underlying principles are at work.

which interesting things begin to happen. In fact, it has often been said that *life exists at the edge of chaos*. This is the region of activity in which self-organizing begins and interesting behaviors occur. It is for this reason that scientists are very interested in understanding chaotic systems. They may help explain concepts of life on Earth.

ARTIFICIAL LIFE

What is life? Philosophers, religious experts, scientists, and many others have argued for hundreds of years over its definition. Rather than get into the problem of trying to precisely define life, it is probably more fruitful to take a broader view. Almost everyone would probably agree that stones or pebbles do not possess life. At the other extreme everyone probably agrees that humans are alive and possess that mysterious thing called life. In between there are life forms such as lichen, trees, sea slugs, worms, bees, ants, cockroaches, turtles, monkeys, dolphins, whales, and others. In addition, most humans would agree that these various forms possess life to differing degrees, more than stones but less than humans possess. The argument begins when we try to identify the point at which we say something is alive. It is probably most reasonable to accept what biologists see as the lowest forms of life, viruses and simple bacteria.

Artificial life or **a-life** is the name given to phenomena in computers that have attributes of life. Currently, a-life systems have simple rules followed by each of the thousands of constituent parts. With thousands or millions of interactions it is impossible to predict what behavior will emerge (that is, emergent behavior).

How does the computer enter into all of this? Later in this section, we'll discuss how the computer is used to study and support forms of life that are not carbon based, but silicon based. These forms of life are called **artificial life** or **a-life.** Because computers are constructed from components whose main ingredient is silicon, the common alternate term for artificial life is *silicon-based life*. Some argue that the first forms of artificial life are already here in the form of computer viruses. The several hundred computer viruses possess many of the attributes of the common cold viruses that we all know about.

To give further credibility to this new field of artificial life it is revealing to note the intellectual caliber of individuals concerned with this field. Some of the brightest minds of the past century have been involved. Heading the list is John von Neumann, the person most often identified with the invention of the stored-program digital computer. When von Neumann knew he was going to succumb to cancer (he died in 1957), he worked on two areas that were extremely important to him, one of which was the technology of life. He wanted to create a theory that encompassed both biology and computers.

His interest alone may not be sufficient reason to think of a-life as important. Other names connected with this field may indicate that something worthwhile indeed exists, names such as Alan Turing, Murray Gell-Mann, Heinz Pagels, E. O. Wilson, John Holland, Freeman Dyson, Norbert Wiener, John G. Kemeny, and E. F. Codd. The connection of these individuals is found through the many areas closely related to a-life, such as complex adaptive systems, nonlinear systems, chaos, and the genetic algorithm.

A quotation from theoretical biologist Stuart Kauffman is a good way to end this section. He says, "Artificial life is a way of exploring how complex systems can exhibit self-organization, adaptation, evolution, co-evolution, metabolism, all sorts of stuff. It is a mimic of biology, although biologists don't know it yet. Out of it will emerge some sort of strange companion theory to biology . . . a particular substation of how living things work. This emerging discipline may be getting at what the logical structure is for living things." (quoted by Steven Levy in his book *Artificial Life* New York: Pantheon, p. 124)

13.8 Software Applications: Natural Language Translation

The demand for language translation has become very big business. With the World Wide Web's global nature, Web pages appear in many languages, and e-commerce is the force that is causing the renewed interest in language translation. There are two distinct classes of translation software. One works while you are on the WWW and can be a direct translation of a complete Web page or parts of its foreign language text. The other is more of a stand-alone piece of software that is used to translate files of foreign language text.

WEB-BASED LANGUAGE TRANSLATION

One of the earliest Web translation free services is now part of Yahoo! and called Babel Fish. The basic idea of Web translation is that the user has some text to translate that must be pasted or typed into the translation box on Yahoo!'s Babel Fish Web page. The languages for the translation are selected from a menu and when the Translate button is clicked, the translation takes place. Figure 13.8.1 is a screen shot of the Babel Fish Web page and is accessed for free.

To check out the quality of the translation, the text from the classic example of section 13.3 was tested. Only this time the languages used are English and Italian. The original English text is:

The spirit is willing, but the flesh is weak.

The translation using Yahoo!'s Babel Fish came out in Italian as:

Lo spirito è disposto, ma la carne è debole.

Now taking this Italian text and cutting and pasting it back for a translation to English results in:

The spirit is arranged, but the meat is weak person.

This example points out the difficulty of using simple techniques for language translation. Another point should be made here: Babel Fish is primarily used in the cut and paste mode. It does, however, have a mode in which the URL of a Web page can be entered.

Some of the unusual names selected for Web sites have interesting stories behind them. Babel Fish is one of those (with its weird name it's not surprising that there is a story behind it). It comes from Douglas Adams's *The Hitchhiker's Guide to the Galaxy* where the Babel Fish is described in detail:

The Babel Fish is small, yellow and leech-like, and probably the oddest thing in the Universe. It feeds on brainwave energy received not from its own carrier but from those around it. The practical upshot of all this is that if you stick a Babel Fish in your ear you can instantly understand anything said to you in any form of language. The speech patterns you actually hear decode the brainwave matrix which has been fed into your mind by your Babel Fish. Meanwhile, the poor Babel Fish, by effectively removing all barriers to communication between different races and cultures, has caused more and bloodier wars than anything else in the history of creation. (pp. 59–61)

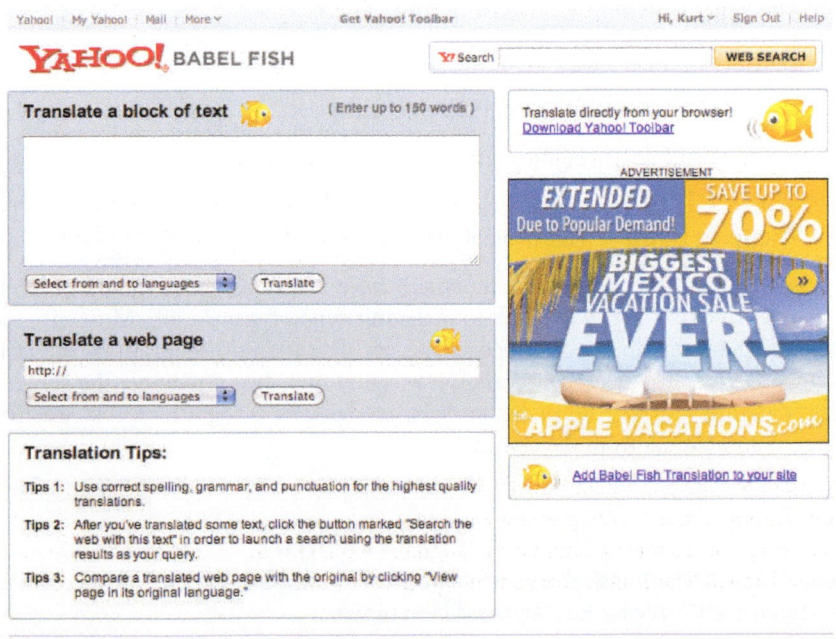

Figure 13.8.1

Yahoo!'s free Babel Fish Web site for translation of text.

Figure 13.8.2

FreeTranslation.com is a free Web site for translation of text and Web pages.

Another free WWW language translator is offered by Transparent Language under the name FreeTranslation.com. It not only allows you to enter a URL of a Web page, which it will translate with the language of choice, but it also does text entry for immediate translation to and from English. Shown in Figure 13.8.2, it is used to test our classic saying:

The spirit is willing, but the flesh is weak.

In this case FreeTranslation.com was used to translate the saying to German, yielding:

Der Geist ist bereit, aber das Fleisch ist schwach.

Taking the German translation and pasting it back into the translator for a German-to-English translation gives:

The spirit is ready, but the meat is weak.

As you can see, these translators still have a way to go. It should be pointed out that without context it is very difficult to make this type of translation. Most of us already know the saying, so that the translations seem poor. But the information that the translating program was given to make the translation was minimal. Just remember the sentence: The bark was irritating. Can you tell whether it is tree bark or a dog's bark that was irritating? Not without some hints from the context!

PUZZLER HINT

Babel Fish and FreeTranslation.com can help with Italian translation. Maybe you should try searching the WWW for Russian translation services.

Chapter Summary

13.1 What Is Intelligence: Artificial or Not?

Human intelligence has been the object of mystery and curiosity for thousands of years. Many unusual explanations and misunderstandings are in its history. As the quest for understanding goes on, we try to simulate this intelligence and understand what goes on when people think. How will we know when we have succeeded? Almost half a century ago, Alan Turing proposed a test for intelligence, which is now known as the Turing Test.

13.2 Modeling Human Intelligence

It is clear that for computers to think, they must have knowledge to think about. Putting this knowledge into the computer has been another time-honored quest. Two of the more successful attempts are semantic networks and expert systems. Once the framework for storing the knowledge is ready, then knowledge must be acquired to fill it. The next two stages are to retrieve and then reason with this knowledge. Many systems that learn have been created; however, a major problem they all have is dealing with common sense.

13.3 Natural Language Communication

One of the most important attributes of any intelligent system is to intelligently communicate. One infamous experiment was the program ELIZA, which fooled a number of people into thinking that it understood the flow of conversation. ELIZA was just the beginning. Many more discoveries of very difficult problems associated with understanding language were to surface. Language translation programs make good attempts at translation, but most efforts are not much more than word replacement using a dictionary.

13.4 Expert Systems

Expert systems became the first of several important commercial successes in artificial intelligence. Using a collection of rules in a knowledge base, a program called an inference engine will produce a result from some given conditions.

13.5 Neural Networks

The artificial neuron is roughly modeled after the human neuron. The artificial neurons are connected together in a network. These networks could be electronic neurons actually wired together, or more commonly, neurons simulated by software in a computer. Once a neural network is created, it must be trained. They are usually trained for very specific tasks, such as credit checks, bomb detection, or mortgage risk evaluation.

13.6 Evolutionary Systems

Evolutionary systems are based on Darwin's theory of evolution. Genetic algorithms and genetic programming are two very successful approaches. They have even created results that could be patented under U.S. patent law.

13.7 Complex Adaptive Systems

The research into systems in nature has focused attention on a class of interesting problems associated with complex adaptive systems. *Chaos* and *fractals* are terms often used in association with complex adaptive systems. What many consider to be the ultimate goal in this field is to create a form of artificial life or a-life.

13.8 Software Applications: Natural Language Translation

Interest in natural language translation has been given a boost by e-commerce. Language translation programs for use on the WWW are easy to use; however, the results are far from perfect. Translation programs are also available for general translation problems when not on the Internet. These PC programs are inexpensive and are used for translations between English, Spanish, French, German, Italian, and Portuguese.

Key Terms

Key terms introduced in this chapter:

1. Acquisition, *389*
2. A-life, *408*
3. Artificial intelligence, *384*
4. Artificial life, *408*
5. Artificial neurons, *401*
6. Brute-force search, *390*
7. Chaos, *407*
8. Common sense, *394*
9. Complex adaptive systems, *406*
10. Expert systems, *388*
11. Genetic algorithm, *404*
12. Genetic programming, *404*
13. Heuristic searching, *392*
14. Heuristics, *392*
15. Hexapawn, *390*
16. Inference engine, *398*
17. Intelligence, *385*
18. Knowledge acquisition, *389*

Matching

Match the number of the key terms introduced in the chapter to the following statements.
Each term may be used once, more than once, or not at all.

1. ____ This object had human form and mimicked human intelligence by having the ability to draw several complex objects using a combination of levers, ratchets, cams, and other mechanical parts.

2. ____ The human central nervous system was found to be a very intricate, continuous network of billions of these.

3. ____ These are interconnected neurons that stretch from the innermost portions of the brain all the way out to the sensory organs.

4. ____ This is another name for computer or machine intelligence.

5. ____ This model of thinking patterns of the human brain is designed after the psychological model of the human associative memory.

6. ____ This model of thinking patterns of the human brain is an emulation of an expert in a particular endeavor.

7. ____ This model of thinking patterns of the human brain consists of hundreds or thousands of rules of the form: IF condition, THEN action.

8. ____ This deals with the way of putting information or knowledge into the system.

9. ____ This deals with the ability of the system to be able to find the knowledge when it is wanted or needed.

10. ____ This deals with the ability of the system to use knowledge through a process of thinking or reasoning.

11. ____ This type of search looks everywhere for the solution to the problem at hand.

12. ____ This search limits the number of items that must be searched in solving a problem (selectively searching using rules of thumb).

13. ____ If this search technique is used, then it is not guaranteed that a solution to the problem will be found.

14. ____ This is what we do when we solve problems.

15. ____ This game is considered an intelligence test for computers.

16. ____ This simple game illustrates the problems facing game-playing programs including how computers choose to make the moves they do.

17. ____ This type of communication is the goal of AI programmers. The goal is not only to have the ability to recognize words but also to understand their meanings.

18. ____ XCON and AARON are examples of this area of artificial intelligence.

19. ____ This name is used to describe the situation in which things seem unpredictable and chaotic.

20. ____ This type of programming uses evolution.

True or False

Place either T or F on the line provided with each of the following statements. If a statement is false, you should be able to explain what changes would make it true.

1. ____ A feeling of intelligence was ascribed to Maillardet's Automaton because it was able to draw complex images.

2. ____ It was not until the twentieth century that scientific investigation into the nervous system took place.

3. ___ The mind is not all in the brain. (Human perception is spread throughout the body in simultaneously operating neural nets associated with the various sensory organs.)

4. ___ The purpose of Turing's Imitation Game was to test the intelligence of the interrogator.

5. ___ A supercomputer has more parts than a human brain.

6. ___ Computers need to be wired in a precise order whereas the human brain has a seemingly random order.

7. ___ Programming computers seems clumsy and inappropriate when compared to the largely self-organizing adaptability of the human brain.

8. ___ Semantic networks are reasonably accurate representations of some of the thinking patterns of the human brain.

9. ___ The rules that make up an expert system are usually gathered from experts in the field being represented.

10. ___ Every search routine performed by the computer will eventually find what the computer "thinks" is the answer to the problem.

11. ___ In a learning system, someone needs to manually input all of the information needed by the computer in order to solve a problem.

12. ___ Common sense is less difficult for the computer to learn than playing a good game of chess.

13. ___ When an inference engine runs, the result is inferred motion in a three-dimensional world.

14. ___ There has not and will never be a computerized champion chess player.

15. ___ It is difficult to program a computer to recognize the meaning of the words we speak.

16. ___ An expert system needs only a good set of rules to be an expert in any field.

17. ___ Researchers in AI have been striving to create a copy of the human brain to use as computer memory.

18. ___ Each neuron can receive only one input signal.

19. ___ In the same way that expert systems are trained, neural networks need a set of rules that takes a certain input and gives a certain result.

20. ___ Artificial life is the name given to phenomena in computers that have attributes of life.

Multiple Choice

Answer the multiple-choice questions by selecting the best answer from the choices given.

1. This type of learning combines both deductive and inductive learning.
   a. Rote learning
   b. Learning by instruction
   c. Learning by deduction
   d. Learning by induction
   e. Learning by analogy

2. Learning by example and learning by observation are two of the subcategories of this type of learning.
   a. Rote learning
   b. Learning by instruction
   c. Learning by deduction
   d. Learning by induction
   e. Learning by analogy

3. This type of learning corresponds to the memorization of facts.
   a. Rote learning
   b. Learning by instruction
   c. Learning by deduction
   d. Learning by induction
   e. Learning by analogy

4. This type of learning is similar to the student/teacher relationship found in any classroom.
   a. Rote learning
   b. Learning by instruction
   c. Learning by deduction
   d. Learning by induction
   e. Learning by analogy

5. This type of learning draws conclusions from a given set of facts.
   a. Rote learning
   b. Learning by instruction
   c. Learning by deduction
   d. Learning by induction
   e. Learning by analogy

6. These are commonly called processing elements.
   a. Artificial life
   b. Artificial neurons
   c. Chaos
   d. Complex adaptive systems
   e. Genetic algorithm

7. Some themes that identify this system include the fact that they are nonlinear, are evolutionary with natural selection involved, have emergent behavior, and are self-organizing.
   a. Artificial life
   b. Artificial neurons
   c. Chaos
   d. Complex adaptive systems
   e. Genetic algorithm

8. These systems seem to be almost random with unpredictable results.
   a. Artificial life
   b. Artificial neurons
   c. Chaos
   d. Complex adaptive systems
   e. Genetic algorithm

9. These systems have thousands or millions of interactions. It is impossible to predict what behavior will emerge.
   a. Artificial life
   b. Artificial neurons
   c. Chaos
   d. Complex adaptive systems
   e. Genetic algorithm

10. This searching method includes the equivalent of mutation, crossover, and chromosomes found in human genetics.
    a. Artificial life
    b. Artificial neurons
    c. Chaos
    d. Complex adaptive systems
    e. Genetic algorithm

Exercises

1. List several other facts that must be known and understood (whatever that means) before you could go out to dinner at an exclusive restaurant.

2. Write out 50 of the simple facts and actions that you think are necessary to start the day as you get up in the morning.

3. Explain why the mirror images in the game tree for the Hexapawn game aren't necessary to complete the game for all possible moves.

4. In teaching the computer to play Hexapawn, what would be the quality of the learning the computer is doing if you intentionally let it win with your poor strategy? Explain.

5. Draw the game tree for the game of Nim. Nim is a two-person game played with three piles of sticks or similar objects. There are one, two, and three sticks in each of the respective piles. The two players take turns selecting a pile and the number of sticks to take from it. At least one stick must be taken on each turn. Sticks can be taken from only one pile each turn. The player who takes the last stick is the loser.

6. There is a simple trick that will allow the first player in Nim to win every time. This player must always select a number of sticks so that the total number of sticks remaining is an odd number. Try this strategy out on an opponent who doesn't know how to play the game.

7. Make a list of at least six words that sound almost alike (e.g., *quick, lick, chick, click, pick, sick*).

8. Make a list of at least three words that sound identical but mean something entirely different (e.g., *I* and *eye*).

9. Think of two sentences which would give a computer problems in speech recognition because they sound the same. For example,

   "He walked to the store."

   "He walked to this door."

10. Do machines think? Why or why not?

11. Explain the difference between knowledge acquisition and knowledge retrieval.

12. Why is searching necessary in knowledge retrieval?

13. Which area of artificial intelligence enjoys the most commercial success?

14. **PUZZLER** Explain the difference between translating a Web page from one language to another, and translating a passage of text from one language to another.

Discussion Questions

1. In Turing's test called the Imitation Game, why is necessary to have two phases? Why not just have a computer and a human, and have the interrogator try to tell them apart?

2. The ELIZA program was written to act like a Rogarian psychoanalyst. Do you think it is ethical to use modernized versions of this program to providing low-cost counseling?

3. What is *your* theory on how the human brain searches for a particular piece of information? Can you explain the phenomena of trying to remember and failing, and then suddenly later the needed fact jumps into your consciousness?

4. Do any of the many examples of robots in the movies (Data from *Star Trek,* R2D2 and C3PO from *Star Wars,* etc.) exhibit what the book calls artificial life? Defend your answer.

Group Project

A group of four students should select a simple task such as making oatmeal for breakfast, answering a phone, or moving a box from floor to table. Each member will look at various aspects of the task such as description/definition of items encountered (e.g., oatmeal box), processes needed (e.g., pick up box), dissecting the task into related components, and coordinating the work of the other three members of the group. Use this knowledge to create a semantic network of relationships between things. It may even be necessary to create new types of relationships. Act out a typical scenario involving the task in front of the class. As the demonstration is carried out, a verbal commentary should be given by one or more members of the group.

Web Exercises

1. Using one of the WWW free translation services, such as Babel Fish in Yahoo! translate the expression: The spirit is willing, but the flesh is weak. First translate it to French and then back to English. Do this for two other languages. As the translations are done, cut and paste the results into a word-processing document.

2. Use both Yahoo!'s Babel Fish and FreeTranslation.com Web sites to translate the same paragraph of your choice to and from any language they have in common. Use a word processor and its cut and paste feature to compare the translations.

3. Find a passage written in some unusual language. Find a translation service on the WWW and translate your message. Document your efforts.

Bibliography

Adams, Douglas. *The Hitchhiker's Guide to the Galaxy.* Ballantine Books: New York, 1995.

This book is rich in comedic detail and thought-provoking situations and stands up to multiple reads.

Genetic Programming II: Automatic Discovery of Reusable Programs (Complex Adaptive Systems). Missoula, MT: Mountain Press, 1994.

This book is an extension of the 1992 genetic programming book. It deals with the problem of breaking down problems into smaller parts. It is an advanced book requiring knowledge of Lisp.

Johnson, R. Colin, and Chappell Brown. *Cognizers—Neural Networks and Machines That Think.* New York: Wiley, 1988.

An introductory text about the brain and artificial neural networks. It has historical events, mentions many of the major names in the field, and introduces the controversy of understanding consciousness.

Koza, John R. *Genetic Programming—On the Programming of Computers by Means of Natural Selection.* Cambridge, MA: The MIT Press, 1992.

The first of three volumes that give the results of many research projects using genetic programming. This is an advanced book for those with some programming background, especially in the Lisp language.

Koza, John R., Forrest Bennett, et al. *Genetic Programming III: Darwinian Invention and Problem Solving.* San Francisco: Morgan Kaufmann, 1999.

This book's main objective is to show that genetic programming can do what might be called creative work. It deals primarily with electrical circuits and illustrates how genetic programming can create patentable designs.

Kurzweil, Raymond. *The Age of Intelligent Machines.* Cambridge, MA: The MIT Press, 1990.

An all-encompassing history of artificial intelligence with many well-done illustrations. An introductory book that could be called a coffee table book with content.

Langton, Christopher, ed. *Artificial Life—An Overview.* Cambridge, MA: The MIT Press, 1995.

This is a collection of papers from the field of artificial life. Some of them are readable by novices in the field; however, the majority are fairly difficult reading.

Levy, Stephen. *A-Life.* New York: Pantheon Books, 1992.

A very readable history up to 1992, which gives detailed background about how various individuals contributed to the field.

Minsky, Marvin. *Society of Mind.* New York: Simon and Schuster, 1986.

This is Marvin Minsky's view of how the mind works. It is very readable and considered by some a landmark book in the field.

Simon, Herbert A. *The Sciences of the Artificial,* 3rd edition. Cambridge, MA: The MIT Press, 1996.

Simon uses examples from the fields of economics, management, computer science, psychology, and philosophy to analyze the relationships between thinking, human behavior, and computers. The book is accessible but certainly not light reading.

Glossary of Terms

Abacus: A calculating device that only holds information.

Access time: (1) The time it takes to get information from a device; (2) the time it takes to put information into a device.

Accumulator: This part of the arithmetic unit found in the CPU is a holding place for results of calculations.

Adware: A form of software that is clandestinely downloaded to a computer. It then delivers advertisements in the form of **popups** (a window that pops up on the computer screen), toolbars, banners and other forms.

Agents: Also known as intelligent agents, these software programs help humans deal with information overload.

AI (artificial intelligence): A branch of computer science involved in teaching a computer to learn from experience by storing information and applying it to new situations.

Algorithm: A detailed description of the exact methods used for solving a particular problem. It is essentially the solution to the problem and is usually implemented by a program. It should solve the stated problem in all situations.

Alpha testing: The first stage in testing of a software program, normally done within the company that created the program.

Analog computer: A computer that functions in continuously varying quantities and produces results that vary continuously.

Analog signal: A signal that varies directly with the input, such as a mercury thermometer.

Animation: The construction of images that appear to move, by rapidly presenting sequential pictures varying slightly from one to the next.

ANSI (American National Standards Institute): An organization that develops and maintains programming language standards for use by industry and computer manufacturers.

Applet: A short application program, usually written in Java, which adds enhancement or functionality to a Web page.

Application programs: Sets of computer instructions designed to perform a particular application or task, such as writing a document or maintaining a collection of related information.

Archie: An automated search service on the Internet.

Archival information: Large quantities of information stored on secondary memory devices for long periods of time.

Argument: *See* Operand.

Arithmetic unit: The part of the CPU where arithmetic is done.

ARPA (Advanced Research Projects Agency): A federal government research branch that influenced the formation of the Internet.

ARPAnet: The early network formed by ARPA to connect researchers. It was the backbone of early Internet development.

Artificial life: A-life or artificial life is the name given to phenomena in computers that have attributes of life. Currently, a-life systems have simple rules followed by each of the thousands of constituent parts. With thousands or millions of interactions, it is impossible to predict what behavior will emerge (that is, emergent behavior).

Artificial reality: *See* Virtual reality.

ASCII (American Standard Code for Information Interchange): A standard seven-bit code that represents letters, numbers, and special characters in the computer's memory.

Assembler: *See* Assembly language.

Assembly language: A low-level programming language whose instructions must be translated by an assembler before they can be executed.

Asynchronous transmission: Information is sent down the communications channel character by character.

Auto-dialer: Specialized software or hardware/software combination that systematically dials all possible telephone numbers within a given range.

Automated speech recognition (ASR): The recognition of spoken words by a computer.

Backbone: The main traffic route of a network, which is usually the fastest.

Back door, trap door or **wormhole:** A hole or special entry point deliberately left or created in a program by the programmer or hacker for future access.

Bandwidth: A measurement of the capacity of a network, usually given in bits per second.

Bar code: A series of machine-readable parallel lines of varying widths used to indicate product information such as price, brand, and size.

Bar code reader: A device that scans bar codes into a computer, so they can be matched with a database.

BASIC: An acronym for Beginners All-purpose Symbolic Instruction Code, a language developed to make it easier for beginners to program.

Baud rate: The number of times per second the state of a communication device or line can be changed.

Beta testing: The second stage in testing of a software program, usually done by sophisticated users outside the company.

Binary circuit: An electronic device that assumes only two states or conditions.

Binary number: A number made up of the symbols 1 or 0; a number in the binary numeration system.

BIOS: An acronym for Basic Input/Output System, this is the part of an operating system that deals with peripheral devices such as keyboards, displays, and disk drives.

BIT (*Binary digIT*): The smallest unit of information that a computer can recognize, can be either a 1 or a 0.

Bitmapped graphics: Graphics constructed of individual pixels that are black and white, shades of gray, or colored.

Blog or Web Log: An informal form of communication similar to a Web page that is continuously updated. It often allows two way communication and presents information in chronological order.

Bluetooth: A standard created to replace desktop cabling. It has a range of about 30 feet and is commonly used to allow connections between computers, keyboards, printers, cell phones and many other devices.

Booting: Turning on the computer and starting the operating system.

BPS (bits per second): The rate at which information (in the form of bits) is transmitted over a communications line.

Bridge: A device that connects two or more segments of a network.

Browser: *See* Web browser.

Brute-force search: A method of searching that looks at every possible solution before choosing among them.

Bug: An error or problem that arises with a computer or a program.

Bulletin board system (BBS): A special-purpose database residing on a single computer, accessible through a network. Its purpose is to provide information and allow users to put information into the BBS for others to access.

Bus network: A configuration consisting of a continuous wire to which all nodes on the network are attached.

Byte: A unit of data storage used to hold a set of bits (usually 8, 16, or 32, depending on the computer). A byte can hold the binary code for a letter, a digit, or a special character.

Cache memory: *See* RAM cache.

CAD/CAM: The acronym for computer-aided design and manufacture, a technology using highly specialized software to support product development and process control in industrial settings.

Card reader: An input device that reads information by sensing the holes on punched cards.

CAVE: An acronym for CAVE Automatic Virtual Environment. Wearing special goggles, the viewer sees realistic three-dimensional images projected onto the sides of a room (the cave).

CD (compact disc): A circular object containing digital information recorded and played back by laser.

CD-ROM (compact disc—read only memory): A compact disc whose data cannot be erased or modified.

CD-RW: The compact disk that cannot only be read but can also be written to using a special CD drive.

Central processing unit: *See* CPU.

Chaos: A term used to describe an unorganized and unpredictable system.

Character set: All symbols that are available in an encoding scheme used when storing characters inside a computer.

Chat room: A place on the Internet where users can communicate with others in real-time.

Chip: A miniaturized group of electronic circuits placed on a "chip" of silicon.

Client/server: Involves two computers connected by a network. A database resides on one computer (the server), and the software needed to access data from the database resides on the other (the client).

Client/server model: *See* Client server.

Clip-art: Computerized images available for inclusion in documents.

CMYK: The standard colors used in printing: cyan, magenta, yellow, and black.

Coaxial cable: A cable formed of two wires separated by insulation. One of the wires is formed into a tube; the second runs down the center of the tube.

Cognitive learning: Cognitive learning includes the acquisition of knowledge, such as facts, figures, and dates; and thinking skills, such as problem solving, analysis, and critical thinking.

Cold boot: Starting up the computer by turning the power on. The operating system in ROM looks for and loads the remaining parts of the operating system into RAM.

Command-line interface: An operating system interface in which commands are typed on a keyboard.

Communication cycle: Process in which one entity relays information to another. In turn, the second entity decodes that information and relays feedback to the first.

Communications channel: The path over which data travel from their source (creator) to the destination (receiver).

Compiler: A translation program that rewrites high-level instructions into machine code. The entire program is translated before execution.

Complex adaptive system: A system that has most of the following characteristics: nonlinear, works in parallel, evolutionary, based on simple rules, self-organizing, displays emergent behavior, and contains either biological or societal life.

Compressed format: *See* File compression.

Computer conference: An electronic meeting that can take place at the convenience of the participants.

Computer crime: Any illegal activity using computer software, data, or access as the object, subject, or instrument of the crime.

Concept-based search: This search uses a matrix of words commonly occurring together to select documents that fit a particular search query.

Connectionless: A network that uses packet switching to perform communication. It is in contrast to the direct-connect or connection-oriented networks.

Connection oriented: Direct-connect networks whose nodes have direct connections through either physical or wireless links.

Consumer profiling: The business practice of collecting consumer information from online-based activities and using that information to create targeted marketing efforts.

Content-driven pages: Refers to the ability to supply the content for a Web site dynamically, as the site is loaded onto a browser, rather than statically, when the site is designed.

Content filter: A program enabling a computer user to block objectionable Web content from being shown on his or her screen.

Context switching: Switching from one application to another.

Continuous speech: Words strung together with varying or no pauses between words.

Continuous system: A model that has quantities that vary smoothly or in a continuous manner.

Control unit: The part of the CPU that controls the flow of commands through it.

Conversational computer: A computer that recognizes and understands human speech and can respond meaningfully.

Correlation: A connection or relationship linking two or more pieces of information.

CPU (central processing unit): The collection of hardware parts responsible for controlling all activities of the computer system, for calculating all results, and for executing all instructions.

Crackers: Persons who break into other people's systems for either fun or profit, or with malicious intent.

Crash: An unplanned shutdown or failure of the computer to operate.

Credit doctor: A person who can cure your low credit rating by stealing a good credit history and selling it to you to replace your bad one.

Cryptography: The science of making messages unintelligible to all except those for whom they are intended.

CSnet: The Computer Science network was an early network that provided e-mail and Internet access to computer science departments at colleges and universities.

Cursor: An indicator on the screen that tells the user where he or she is typing.

Cut and paste: In word processing the process of taking out text (cutting) and moving it to another location (pasting).

Cyberspace: A virtual place where millions of people can simultaneously visit and interact.

Daisy chain: The way peripheral devices are connected together. One device is connected to the next, which is connected to the next, and so on.

DAN (desk area network): A network connecting devices within a single-user computer system.

DARMS (Digital Alternative Representation of Musical Scores): A graphical representation of music based on the position of symbols on a staff.

DAT (digital audio tape): Similar to a cassette tape in form. Information is stored digitally.

Data: A given thing, a fact. Often used to mean the facts that will be given to the computer to be processed. Technically, *data* is plural, and the singular is *datum*. However, *data* is often used as a singular noun.

Data bank: A comprehensive collection of libraries of data, usually holding archival information not often accessed.

Database: A collection of interrelated data files or libraries, organized for ease of access, update, and retrieval.

Data diddling: Swapping one piece of information for another of the same type.

Data element: One single fact or item in a database.

Data mart: A limited type of data warehouse, usually oriented to a single subject or a single department's needs.

Data mining: Searching collections of databases to discover relationships and global patterns that exist among them, and applying these patterns to assist in management decisions.

Data probe: The electronic collection of data by inserting an instrument into a device designed to output information in this fashion.

Data warehouse: Merges related data from many operational sources to provide an integrated information system spanning the data needs of an entire enterprise.

DBMS (database management system): A set of computer programs that controls the creation, maintenance, and utilization of databases.

Debug: To find and correct mistakes in a program.

Decimal system: Base ten number system generally used by our society in our daily lives.

Decode: The process of taking coded information and translating it to another usable form.

Defragmenting: The process of moving files on a fragmented disk so that all the available disk space is in one large block.

Desktop-publishing program: Specialized computer software for laying out text and graphics as well as manipulating fonts for printing.

Digital signal: A signal expressed in binary digits, for example, the data passed from the computer to a terminal or encoded on a compact disc.

Digitize: To convert data such as a photograph into binary numbers. A digitizer is a device used to convert a picture to numeric form.

Direct-connect network: Connection-oriented network whose nodes can be connected through either physical or wireless links.

Direct link network: A network such as the telephone switching system, in which a direct link is formed between two communicating parties.

Discrete system: A model having quantities that vary in steps or jumps.

Disinfectant: A program for detecting and eliminating computer viruses.

Disjointed speech: Words spoken individually or separately with definite pauses between them.

Disk cache: A type of memory that allows data normally accessed directly from a disk to move to the normal RAM memory where the CPU can obtain it more quickly.

Distance learning: An unsupervised independent mode of education where the instruction takes place via interactive video, e-mail, the Internet, and real-time electronic communication.

Distributed denial of service (DDoS): The act of sending tens of thousands of simultaneous bogus requests for Web pages to a particular Web site. The server can't identify the bogus requests, causing a delay.

Distributed processing: Using a network to allow an entity to decentralize its computing needs over several interconnected computers.

Documentation: The manual, description, and instructions that accompany software programs and hardware.

Document formatting: In word processing, actions that affect the appearance of a document, for example, setting margins and tabs and justifying text.

Domain name: The name assigned to a computer on the Internet.

Downloading: The process of receiving a copy of a program, document, or file from another computer

Drag and drop: The process of placing the mouse cursor on an object such as the icon of a folder or file and holding the mouse button down, then dragging the object to some location and dropping it (releasing the mouse button).

Driver: The name given to the program that allows communication between the operating system and a peripheral device.

DVD (digital versatile disc): A CD-sized disk that can contain up to 16 gigabytes of data, which is commonly used for video.

EBCDIC (Extended Binary Coded Decimal Interchange Code): A standard coding method for representing numbers, letters, and special characters, used primarily on mainframe computers.

Education factory: Unschooled students—raw materials—entered the education factory at age 5, were "processed" for 12 years, and were expected to emerge as finished products—adults for the workforce.

Electronic commerce (e-commerce): The online ability to buy, sell, and advertise goods and services.

Electronic computer: A device constructed from transistors that use electricity to function.

Electronic spreadsheet: A computerized ledger page arranged in columns and rows.

Electronic test generator: An application program that simplifies the tasks involved with creating, taking, and administering tests using computer technology and the World Wide Web.

Electronic wallet: Allows the user to prepay money into the wallet by sending a check or credit card payment to a service company. The wallet can then be used to pay for small purchases, up to the total amount available.

Elision: The sound of two words spliced so that when one of them ends and the next begins, the connection will sound natural.

E-mail (electronic mail): The process used to send messages from one user to another on a computer system or network.

Encryption: Translates the text of your message or other document into unreadable code, so it can be sent securely over a communication medium.

ENIAC: A digital computer built in 1944, programmed by using wires to connect relay switches.

Enterprise IP network: A TCP/IP network that operates inside a corporation.

Ethernet: A very fast local area network protocol.

Execute: To perform the instructions in a computer program.

Expert system: A system consisting of rules and an inference engine, which when given input can make decisions based on the rules. Also called a production system.

False coloring: Assigning different colors to specific shades of gray in a gray-scale image to make it more understandable to human eyes. Also called pseudocoloring.

False relevance: The assumption of a cause-and-effect relationship between two facts that seem to be related but are not.

Feedback system: A model that reacts to input.

Fetch/execute cycle: The operation in which an instruction is moved from internal storage to a special register for decoding, then executed.

Fetching instructions: The first state in processing an instruction, in which the instruction is copied from memory into the CPU and decoded.

Fiber-optic cable: A cable made of fine strands of glass fiber that carries digital signals using pulses of light instead of electricity.

Field: A location in a database that contains one specific piece of information.

file: A collection of records or data designated by name and considered as a unit. The records about employees of a company, for example, would be an employee file.

File compression: The process of making binary computer files smaller. Compressed files must be returned to their original state before they can be used.

File server: A computer dedicated to providing files to other computers on a network.

Find and replace: In word processing the process of finding a series of letters and other ASCII symbols and replacing them with another set of ASCII symbols, which are often words.

Firewall: A filtering program that scans all incoming documents and files and refuses to accept any found to be virus infected.

Flat file system: A system in which all files are in one big list with no subdivisions.

Flip-flop circuit: An electronic circuit that can be in one of two states or conditions, either flipped or flopped, which can stand for 0 or 1.

Flowchart: A series of visual symbols that represent the logical flow of a program.

Formatting a disk: Also called initializing a disk. Setting up a disk to be used by a particular operating system. *Note:* formatting a disk erases everything currently on that disk.

Forward chaining: The act of going from a rule's condition to a rule's action and using the action as a new condition, and so on.

Fourth-generation language: Computer programming languages, such as application generators, query languages, report writers, and data manipulation languages, which facilitate programming for a specific purpose.

Fragmented disk: Refers to a condition in which files are scattered on the hard drive in a way that there are many small chunks of available space instead of larger, more usable space.

Free downloads: Programs, images, sound, or video clips that can be downloaded from the Internet and used freely, without cost.

Freeware: Software that is totally free. It is legal to copy and distribute freeware without violating the author's copyright .

FTP (File Transfer Protocol): An Internet service used to transfer files from one computer to another.

Full-duplex transmission: A type of communication channel or line that allows transmissions in both directions simultaneously.

Fully connected topology: A term referring to a network in which every node has a connection to all other nodes.

Gateway: A computer that connects different networks, providing data flow from one to the other.

General-purpose electronic digital computer: A device constructed of binary electronic circuits that accepts many kinds of information, changes it in a way that is controllable by humans, and presents the results in a way readable by humans.

Genetic programming: A technique that follows Darwinian evolution. The evolution takes place directly on the programs in the population that are striving to reach the goal that is specified by the programmer.

Gigabyte: A unit of storage containing 1,073,741,824 bytes (about one billion bytes).

Gopher: A service that allows textual information access via the Internet.

Grammar checker: In word processing a program that finds grammatical errors and text and suggests replacements.

Gray-scale: A method of storing pictures in a computer, in which each pixel contains a value for a shade of gray.

GUI (graphical user interface): An operating system interface represented in pictorial form usually accessed with a mouse.

Hackers: Persons who use their considerable self-taught expertise to solve computer problems, extracting needed information and improving system performance.

Half-duplex transmission: A type of communication channel or line through which data can be transmitted, but in only one direction at a time.

Hardware: The electronics and associated mechanical parts of the computer. Each has a physical presence (you can see, feel, or touch it).

Hardwiring: A process of using a soldering iron to create electronic circuit boards with the connections needed to perform specific tasks.

Headers and footers: In word processing the name of text that appears at the top (header) or at the bottom (footer) of every page in a document, which often includes page numbering.

Henry system: Classifies fingerprints according to the patterns of ridges evident in the prints.

Hertz: A measure of the frequency of a sound or electrical signal, expressed in cycles per second.

Heuristic: A rule of thumb (a nonrigorous rule) that often gets a correct result but is not guaranteed to do so.

Hidden-line problem: A line in a graphic image that would not be visible if the surfaces closer to the viewer were opaque.

Hierarchical file structure: A filing system that organizes files in a treelike structure or hierarchy. Finding a file involves starting at the root or beginning of the structure and following a path through the hierarchy group by group until the file is found.

High-level programming language: A programming language that is independent of specific computer hardware.

Hollerith card: Keypunched cards used to hold information. *See also* Card reader.

Host: A computer that accepts remote logins.

HTML (HyperText Markup Language): A language used for Web page formatting and for setting up hypertext and hypermedia links.

HTTP (HyperText Transport Protocol): A set of rules residing on all computers using TCP/IP to communicate via the Web.

Hub: A device that connects several computers within a local area.

Human language: A language written by humans, intended to enable communication from one human to another.

Hypermedia: The concept of hypertext extended to include animation, video, visual, and other media.

Hypertext: A form of text that provides interactive access to related material located anywhere.

Icon: A small graphical picture representing objects or commands.

IDE: An acronym for integrated drive electronics, which are the controller electronics, usually on the motherboard of a computer, with a 40-pin socket that can be used for connections to peripheral devices.

Image enhancement: Processing a digital image to highlight or enhance particular informational aspects.

Image restoration: Processing an image to eliminate known flaws or degradations.

Imitation Game: Also known as Turing Test. This interrogation of the computer was designed to test for intelligence.

Industrial Revolution: A period of great technological advance resulting in industrial growth and productivity. It occurred during the late 1800s and early 1900s.

Inference engine: The part of an expert system that interprets the rules in the knowledge base.

Infinite loop: A set of computer instructions that repeats forever.

Information: Data repackaged in a meaningful form.

Information Age: The last half of the twentieth century. The term refers to the rapid growth in the amount of information accessible through the use of computer/communication technology, and to the increased dependence we have on that information.

Infrared: A light source used for wireless communications between objects such as keyboards and computers.

Inkjet printer: A type of printer that squirts the ink in tiny drops on the paper.

Input/output units: Devices connected to a computer, which take in information from the outside world, and, after it is processed, present results or messages via a printout or monitor screen.

Instant messaging (IM): A form of chat room where the chat participants can have their presence automatically announced to a pre-arranged group of buddies. Their "chat conversation" is shared among the buddies signed on the Internet, or one-to-one. This is done in real-time, which is analogous to "talking" in a group face-to-face.

Instant recalculation: A feature of electronic spreadsheet programs to refigure all calculations whenever a cell entry is changed.

Instruction decoding unit: This part of the CPU decodes instructions.

Instruction register: This part of the CPU is where an instruction is placed for analysis by the instruction decoding unit.

Instruction set: Those commands in a particular programming language that the computer can understand.

Intellectual property rights: The right of artists and writers to own and control the use of their "original works of authorship fixed in any tangible medium of expression."

Intelligent search: A computer search is said to be intelligent if the computer appears to learn and develop its own structure for data organization and its own methods for searching for and validating relationships.

Interactive multimedia: Two-way communication involving visual and audio information between humans and computers.

Interface: What the person working with the computer sees and experiences when using the computer.

Internet: An informally organized worldwide network connecting millions of computers using TCP/IP.

Internet address (IP address): A unique number that identifies each computer attached to the Internet.

Internetworking: A term used when direct-connect networks are connected together.

Interpreter: A program that translates a higher level language program into machine code, one line at a time, and executes each line immediately.

I/O units: *See* Input/output units.

IP (Internet Protocol): The protocol suite used by the Internet. IP along with TCP (Transport Control Protocol) consists of more than 100 protocols.

IRC (Internet Relay Chat): Internet chat rooms where people communicate in real time by typing messages, which are displayed to anyone currently logged into the chat room.

ISP (Internet Service Provider): A company or organization that offers connections to the Internet.

JavaScript: A scripting language designed for enhancing the functionality of Web pages.

JPEG (Joint Photographers Expert Group): A file compression scheme used to compress visual image files on the computer.

Justifying text: In word processing the process of stretching a line of text so that it touches both left and right margins.

K (Kilobyte): A unit of storage holding 1,024 bytes.

Keypunch machine: Used to punch holes in Hollerith cards. As each card was positioned and fed through the machine, holes were punched in it corresponding to the data typed in at the keyboard. Finished cards were carefully stacked in a holder.

Keyword search: This kind of search uses a technique called an inverted index, which indexes every word in every document it finds on the Web. To initiate this search, you type in some keywords relevant to your topic.

Knowledge: *See* Cognitive learning.

Knowledge acquisition: Using input (human's senses, computer's input units) to collect a base of information.

Knowledge base: A list of pertinent information on a given topic.

Knowledge retrieval: Efficiently finding information stored in the knowledge base.

LAN (local area network): A group of interconnected computers all within a short distance of each other (typically within one room or building).

Laser: A device capable of producing a tightly packed, narrow beam of high-intensity light.

License: The authorization to copy a program onto your hard disk for your own personal use.

Light pen: An input unit that allows the user to point to an object on a screen and activate the object so that it can be manipulated.

Link: A physical connection between nodes of a network.

Linux: An operating system based on the UNIX operating system and is open-source software, which means all of the details are available to anyone to make changes as they see fit.

Liquid crystal display (LCD): A visual display using a crystalline surface that is electronically controlled to display text and images, and is most often used on laptop computers.

Listserv or **newsgroup:** A cross between straight email and conferencing. It allows two way communication through mailing lists that are kept on the listserv server.

Loader: A module within the operating system that places into main memory the code of a program stored on a disk.

Loading a program: The process of copying a program or data found on an input device into the computer's memory.

Logic bomb: *See* Time bomb.

Logic error: A program error resulting from incorrect algorithm development.

Loop: A sequence of instructions repeated one or more times when the program is executed.

Low-level programming language: A programming language that is hardware dependent, written for a computer with a particular CPU.

Machine code: The "native language" of the computer, sometimes referred to as binary code.

Machine independent: Refers to a process or language that can be used on different types of computers.

Machine language: Binary code. The form that all instructions must be in before the computer can execute them.

Machine learning: The concept of using computer programs that are capable of learning.

MacOS: The operating system used by Apple Computer Company's Macintosh computers.

Macro language: A set of operations within a computer application that has been recorded for later execution in any document within that application.

Maillardet's Automaton: A mechanical drawing machine created in 1805, considered at the time to have some intelligence because it could draw complex images.

Mainframe computer: A large computer characterized by multi-processing and a high price tag.

MAN (metropolitan area network): A very fast network technology that can span areas as large as a major city.

Mark-sensor form: A sheet of paper with areas to be colored in by a user to indicate specific responses to questions.

Mechanical computer: A computer constructed of a combination of levers, springs, gears, cranks, pulleys, and so on.

Megabyte: A unit of storage containing 1,048,576 bytes (about one million bytes).

Memory: Any portion of a computing system where information to be used by the computer is kept for recall.

Menu-driven access: Allows you to view a selection—menu—of choices available from a particular screen.

Microcomputer: A small computer designed for a single user. A microcomputer typically fits on a desktop or even in a briefcase.

Microprocessor: The entire contents of a CPU designed to fit onto one single chip.

Middleware: Software that bridges the gap between database and content-generated Web pages.

MIDI (Musical Instrument Digital Interface): An industry standard for connecting musical instruments to each other and usually to a controlling computer.

Milnet (Military network): Originally part of ARPAnet and used for nonclassified military communication.

Minicomputer: A medium-sized computer characterized by higher performance than microcomputers, more powerful instruction sets, and a wide selection of available programming languages and operating systems.

M-JPEG: A scheme for coding and decoding large amounts of video data as compressed individual frames, which makes it easier to edit the video on a PC.

Mnemonic: An abbreviated name that reminds one of a full name, such as *sub* for *subtract*.

Model: A simulation that approximates or gives the appearance of the system in question.

Modem: An electronic device that takes binary data from a computer and converts them to analog form that can be sent over telephone lines. The receiving modem then converts the data back to binary form for the computer.

Motherboard: The collection of electronic circuits that make up the major portion of a computer, including RAM, ROM, CPU, and peripheral interface electronics.

Mouse: An input device used to send information to a computer. It usually involves a roller ball that manipulates an icon on the screen.

MP3: MPEG layer 3 is an audio file compression technique that follows the standard adopted by the Motion Picture Expert Group.

MPEG (Motion Picture Experts Group): A video compression scheme specifically for digitized video playback on computers

MPEG-1: A scheme for coding and decoding video data in slower media such as video CDs.

MPEG-2: A scheme for coding and decoding video data that have been optimized for the higher demands of broadcast, satellite, and DVD video.

MS-DOS: A command-line operating system developed by Microsoft Corporation.

Multimedia: The use of more than one medium or means to communicate information.

Multiprocessing: Computing done with more than one CPU. Also called parallel processing.

Multiprogramming: Running two or more programs at the same time on the same computer.

Multitasking: A form of multiprogramming in which one task is continued in the background while another is working.

Nassi-Schneidermann chart: A schematic representation of the organization of a computer program.

Natural language communication: The process of having the computer understand normal spoken language.

Natural languages: Computer languages that are very similar to human languages.

Network: Communication channels connecting a collection of computers, terminals, printers, switches, and other devices.

Network architecture: The logical connections and organization of the software that runs the network.

Network protocol: A collection of programs written to follow the rules for communication according to some prearranged scheme.

Neural network: An interconnected collection of neurons.

Neuron: An individual nerve cell, capable of receiving input from the environment or other cells and transmitting output to other neurons or to muscles and organs.

Node: A device with its own address on a network that can send or receive information over the network.

Nondestructive reading: Reading data from a storage location without changing or deleting the data.

Normal distribution: Data exhibiting a pattern as found in nature. The popular range of values tends to center around the average and forms a bell curve.

NSFnet (National Science Foundation network): Commonly recognized as the original backbone of the Internet.

Number crunching: The manipulation of large amounts of numeric data into useful calculated results.

Object code: The binary code produced when a machine language program is translated into machine code.

Object-oriented graphics: Pictures that are stored as lines, curves, or geometric shapes and can therefore be moved or modified easily.

Object-oriented programming language: A language that resembles human thinking in that it works on objects and their associated tasks.

ODBC (Open Database Connectivity): A set of standards allowing information to be passed from a database to a dynamic Web page.

Opcode (operation code): The part of an instruction that tells what operation is to be performed.

Open-source software: Software that reveals the complete, original source program so that knowledgeable users can customize it.

Operand: (1) A unit of data on which an operation is performed; (2) the part of an instruction that tells where to find the data or equipment to be operated on.

Operating system: A collection of programs that moves information around the computer and controls all of its activities.

Optical character recognition (OCR): Reading characters by machine directly from a printed document and translating them into machine-readable form.

Packet: A collection of bytes containing part of a message, a sequence number, where it came from, and where it is going.

Packet switching: The process of moving packets in a network from node to node until the destination is reached.

Palmtop computer: A small, fully functional computer that can be held in the palm of your hand.

Parallel: A transmission format in which all the elements of a word or message are sent simultaneously.

Parallel processing: *See* Multiprocessing.

Parity bit: A bit used to verify that the data bits of a message have been transmitted unaltered.

Passive multimedia: One-way communication using visual and audio forms to supply information to a human.

Password: Secret word or phrase used to prevent unauthorized people from accessing computer accounts, files, or equipment.

Patch: A customized sound that is prepared and stored in a MIDI-compatible form for recall later.

Path: Names any directories and subdirectories you have to go through to find a particular file.

Percent: A special type of fraction that represents the number of parts out of a total of one hundred parts.

Peripheral: Any piece of computer hardware that is not a part of the basic computer.

Person-months: A measure of project-working time. A person-month is equal to one person working full time (40 hours a week) for one month (four weeks).

Perspective: Alteration of the relative size and shapes of objects in an illustration to make it appear three-dimensional.

Phishing or spoofing: An old scam implemented on the Internet. It is usually in the form of an email that falsely represents a particular person or organization to get information such as bank account numbers and passwords.

Phoneme: A basic sound unit in spoken language.

PICS (Platform for Internet Content Selection): A set of technical rating standards for evaluating the content of digital materials.

Piggybacking: Invading a computer system by riding in behind a legitimate user with a password.

Pirated software: Software that a user does not have a legal right to have or use.

Pitch: A characteristic of sound determined by its number of vibrations per second.

Pixel: An abbreviation for *picture el*ement, the building blocks of a computer picture.

Plug-ins: Software that can be added to another program to give it additional capabilities, such as playing sounds.

Point-to-point network: A network whose connection is direct rather than indirect.

Popups: *See* adware

Port: A connecting path into and out of a computer; examples on a PC are the serial and parallel ports.

Predictable system: A system whose model can predict exactly what will happen.

Presentation software: An application program that assists in creating a multimedia presentation.

Primary memory: The main electronic memory where a program and related data reside when executed by the computer.

Probabilistic system: A system whose model contains unpredictable features or events.

Probability: A numerical value given to a prediction of whether an event will occur.

Problem: A task to be completed by a computer.

Procedural programming language: A computer language that expresses a problem's solution as a series of discrete instructions or steps.

Process control: The control of some process by a computer in real time.

Production system: *See* Expert system.

Program: A collection of commands or instructions for the computer to perform one by one.

Program counter: This part of the control unit found in the CPU contains the address of the next instruction to be executed.

Programming language: A language used by humans to communicate with computers.

Prompt: A character, word, or series of words that signal a user to give the computer a command or other input.

Protocol: Pertaining to networks, a protocol is a set of rules that must be followed by computers for them to communicate.

Protocol suite: A collection of programs that implement the protocols needed for network communication.

Pseudocode: A verbal shorthand method of detailing the steps of a program.

Pseudocoloring: *See* False coloring.

Psychomotor skills: Physical coordination and neuromuscular learning.

Query language: A fourth-generation computer language developed specifically to request information from databases.

QuickTime: A software technique used to convert standard video to a format that can be edited and played back on a PC.

RAM (random access memory): A part of the main memory of the computer. Its contents are not permanent.

RAM cache: Very fast memory that is used by the operating system to house the data and instructions that are currently being used. The CPU can then run faster than if it needed to access normal RAM, which is much slower.

RAM disk: A type of cache memory in which the operating system fools the application program into thinking it is accessing a disk, when in reality it is accessing the much faster RAM memory.

Random access: The capability of accessing memory without examining all the other information.

Raster graphic: Bitmapped graphic made up of pixels aligned in rows that make up a standard video display.

Rating: A description of some particular Internet content, using the terms and vocabulary of some ratings system.

Read only: Allows viewers to see, read, or print a Web page or Internet file but not to change it.

Real-time processing: Computing that involves humans interacting with the computer in a situation in which quick return of results is important.

Record: A collection of data items related to one person or instance that may be recalled as a unit. A record can be composed of different types of data.

Relation: A two-dimensional table made up of columns and rows of data. Each column stores the data in one field; each row stores the information in one record.

Relational database: In a relational database data are stored in two or more two-dimensional tables, which are linked together or related by common data fields.

Reliable program: A program that produces correct results with every possible value of appropriate data.

Remote electronic data sensing: Using a satellite to collect data from a great distance.

Resonance: The reverberation or amplification of a sound, such as the voice in the cavities of the vocal tract.

RGB: The standard display colors (red, green, blue) that make up each pixel; in the right proportions they give any color.

Ring network: A network consisting of nodes connected together to form a circle.

Robust program: A program that detects execution errors and notifies the user of possible problems without crashing.

ROM (read only memory): A part of the computer's main memory. It is permanent memory that cannot be changed unless you replace it.

Rote learning: The memorization of facts, such as memorizing multiplication tables.

Router: A network node, connected to two or more networks, that forwards packets from one network to another.

RSS (Real Simple Syndication): A protocol for web syndication, based on XML. It allows subscription to news feeds and blogs.

Rule-based systems: Expert systems that are knowledge bases consisting of hundreds or thousands of rules of the form: IF (condition), THEN (action).

Salami slicing: Involves spreading the haul over a large number of trivial transactions, like slices of salami in a sandwich.

Sampling: A technique used to predict a total situation by selecting a few instances to represent a larger group.

Scavenging: Searching through stray data and electronic garbage for clues that might unlock the secrets of a targeted computer system.

Scheduler: The part of the operating system responsible for determining the order in which resources, especially CPU and memory, will be assigned to process jobs.

Script: A script is a series of commands written to accomplish some task.

SCSI (Small Computer System Interface): The electronic interface to a computer that allows up to eight peripheral devices to be daisy-chained together.

Search engine: Web programs that provide the capability of searching the Internet for information..

Secondary memory: Memory units such as a floppy disk or hard disk that are used to store information to be loaded into RAM when needed.

Secure system: A secure system is one that protects the security of the data being entered or displayed, and the privacy of the user to whom the data belong.

Semantic network: In artificial intelligence, a representation of reality that consists of objects, concepts, or situations connected by some type of relationship.

Semantics: The exact content (meaning) of a language unit.

Sequencer: A computer or other electronic unit that acts as a recording device and allows the playback and modification of music after it is stored.

Sequential access: A method of obtaining information from memory by starting at the beginning of a list and proceeding item by item until the desired information is reached.

Serial: A transmission format in which data are sent one bit at a time in a stream.

Server: A dedicated computer that is part of a network. A server's hard drive contains files that are "served" to whichever computer requests them. The server normally also manages the network.

Shading: Assigning a gray-scale value to a face of a solid.

Shareware: Software that is legal to pass and copy but for which the user is expected to send money to the author if he or she keeps the software.

Simplex transmission: Transmission in which information can flow in only one direction, such as that between a keyboard and a computer.

Simulation: A computerized reproduction or image of a situation or set of conditions used to model a real-life situation.

Skewed sample: Data that are distorted and that misrepresent a total population.

Social interaction: The communication that occurs during relationships between people.

Software: The instructions that control the hardware and cause a desired task to be accomplished.

Software piracy: The unauthorized copying or use of software for which the user has not paid the appropriate licensing fee.

Solution: An answer to a computer problem.

Source code: A high-level language program before it has been translated into machine code by an interpreter, assembler, or compiler.

Spam: A noun describing "unsolicited commercial email messages." Historically it came from a Monty Phython's Flying Circus sketch in reference to the Hormel Foods' product Spam.

Special-purpose computer: A computer designed to be used in a very limited way.

Speech recognition: A computerized system designed to identify spoken words.

Speech synthesis: The electronic production of sound and speech patterns from a series of numbers previously stored in the computer's memory in digitized form.

Spell checker: In word processing, software that allows the user to select appropriate spellings and make needed corrections.

Spider: A program that follows links on the Web and records words on Web pages and follows any links found at a Web site.

Spoofing: *See* phishing

Spyware: A program that surreptitiously gathers data about your computer use or personal information. This information is sent back to a database controlled by an individual, company or the government.

Standalone filter: Mechanism for determining which sites should be blocked, along with software to do the filtering, all provided by a single vendor.

Star network: A network configuration consisting of nodes connected to a central node.

Statistical analysis: Manipulating data using numerical methods to make the data more meaningful as information.

Stored program computer: A computing device with memory that contains both a program and the information needed for computing by the program.

Streaming audio: *See* Streaming media.

Streaming media: Information in one of many different visual or audio forms that is sent from a server in packets to the requesting computer. Each packet contains parts of the medium that may be a recording or an actual live event. The information in the packets is then played back in the order sent, starting soon after a few packets arrive but before all of them have been sent.

Streaming video: *See* Streaming media.

Subdomains: Segments of a domain. They are separated by periods. The leftmost segment(s) identify the Web server for that computer. The rightmost segment is the top-level domain.

Subject search: *See* Topic search.

Supercomputer: A large computer characterized by incredible processing speed and multiple CPUs.

Supervised training: This occurs when a neural network is given input data and the resulting output is compared to the correct output. The strengths of connections are adjusted as necessary.

Surfing: A slang term used to describe the free-form navigation from place to place on the Internet by following hyperlinks on Web pages.

Switch: A node that connects networks of the same type.

Synchronous transmission: A method of communication in which information is sent down the communications channel in groups or blocks rather than one word at a time.

Syntax: The grammar rules of a natural or computer language.

Syntax error: A mistake violating the grammar rules of a computer language.

Systems programming: The development of system programs, which form the operating system of a computer.

Tags: Formatting instructions in HTML, the language that specifies the design and layout of Web pages. Each tag is delineated by angle brackets before and after to set the tag apart as complete.

TCP/IP (Transport Control Protocol/Internet Protocol): A suite of protocols consisting of more than 100 protocols for communication over the Internet

Teleconference: An electronic meeting held over a computer network that can take place at the convenience of the participants.

Telnet: A remote login service for Internet access. It allows a remote computer to connect to a computer that is part of the Internet and thereby gain Internet access.

Terabyte: A unit of storage containing about one trillion bytes.

Text analysis engine: Analyzes the content of a document's text and assigns a specific classification from its classification hierarchy. Searches are made by matching desired concepts to those of specific classifications.

Text entry: In word processing, typing a document, checking it for spelling errors, or modifying text by inserting or deleting.

Text file: A file consisting of 128 ASCII seven-bit codes for letters, numerals, punctuation, and special control characters.

Time bomb: A damaging software routine that can be triggered at some later time by the computer's clock or by a predetermined combination of events.

Time compression: Shortening the time a simulation takes compared to the time required by the actual activity.

Time sharing: A form of multiprogramming in which a number of users can interact directly and simultaneously with programs from terminals connected to one computer.

Topic search: This type of search begins with a list of classifications, which is further divided into a hierarchical system of several levels of subclasses.

Top-level domain: The rightmost segment of a WWW domain.

Traceroute: A software tool that allows tracing the path of packets on any network using TCP/IP protocol, including the Internet.

Training: Presenting input to a computer program, which, together with proper feedback about the program's output, enables the program to alter its assumptions or responses to later input.

Translation: The transporting of ideas, instructions and concepts from one language to another.

Tree network: A hierarchical network consisting of nodes connected at more than one level. Several nodes may be connected to a single node forming the next level.

Trojan horse: A program that pretends to be some legitimate program, game, email, image, or other file. They do not replicate themselves, but must have human assistance in getting downloaded to other computers.

Turing Test: *See* Imitation Game.

Twisted pair: A pair of connecting wires that are twisted together to help reduce electrical interference.

Ultrasound imaging: Medical diagnostic technique that provides visual images constructed from the sounds that reflect off various organs of the human body.

UNIX: A popular interactive operating system developed by researchers at AT&T Bell Laboratories.

URL (Uniform Resource Locator): The name given to the world-wide standard for expressing the unique address of a specific Web page.

USB (Universal Serial Bus): A serial electronic interface used for connecting peripheral devices to a computer.

U.S. Computer Software Copyright Act of 1980: Formally defines and protects the rights of software ownership.

Usenet: An older vehicle for sharing news about particular topics over the Internet, and provides a means of downloading movies, music, video and other file types. Topics that individuals may subscribe to are often referred to as **newsgroups.**

Vaccine: A program that searches your disk for viruses and notifies you of any that were found.

Validation: The process of checking out a software/hardware model to make sure it results in correct answers.

Vector graphics: Graphics stored by formula rather than in bitmapped form.

Verified model: A model that is proven to be a reasonably accurate representation of the system being simulated.

Veronica: A Gopher keyword search program that allows searching Gopher space for Gopher menus that have those words.

Version number: A series of numbers and sometimes letters with decimal points that designate the continuing revision process of programs. The larger the number the more recent the program.

Victimless crime: Any crime in which the victim cannot be easily identified, or when no real person seems to be hurt by the crime.

Video RAM (VRAM): Special RAM memory in which the video image is kept for refreshing the display screen.

Virtual classroom: A class that has no physical presence but meets only in cyberspace on the Web.

Virtual memory: An operating system feature that allows running programs that would otherwise be too large to run in the available RAM.

Virtual reality: A situation in which an individual has a three-dimensional view into a world that doesn't exist except in the computer.

Virus: A program intentionally designed to reproduce itself. It is attached to a host program or file and when program is executed or the file opened, the virus will find other hosts to attach itself to. Its effect ranges from harmless to very destructive. Human action is part of the process, whether it is inserting a disk, opening a file, or opening an infected email.

Visualization of information: Uses many different techniques to transform any form of data into a visual image.

Voiceprint: A visual representation of the sound frequencies made by a person speaking.

Voice recognition data entry: The collection and recording of data by speaking into a microphone of a terminal.

von Neumann computer: A stored program computer named after John von Neumann.

WAN (wide area network): A number of computer networks connected by communication channels of many different types and distances.

Warm boot: Reloading the operating system into RAM without disrupting power to the disk drives or power supply.

Web browser: A program that allows the user to browse or navigate the World Wide Web.

Web Log: *See* blog.

Web page: A document consisting of images, sound, or text whose display to a Web browser is controlled by HTML.

Web page builder: A type of application program that enables a user to design and edit Web page documents.

Web presence: A business is said to have a Web presence if it has its own Web site, usually including its trademark or logo, products or services available, philosophy, and policies.

Web server: A computer permanently connected to the Web, providing Web access to other computers networked to that server.

Web site: A group of related Web pages.

What-if forecasting: Examination of theories of the future on an electronic spreadsheet.

Wi-Fi: A standard created to allow wireless networking and access to the Internet. It has a range of about 300 feet and is often used in airports and coffee shops.

Word processor: A computer system designed to create, modify, and produce documents, using electronic text-editing and formatting software.

Workstation: A subcategory of computers, used by one person at a time, typically connected to other computers and storage devices through a network.

Worm: A form of computer virus that can replicate itself without human action or a host program. Once it is introduced to a computer or computer network, it spreads, consuming memory and communications bandwidth.

WWW (World Wide Web or Web): A communications protocol that allows multimedia access to the Internet.

WYSIWYG (What You See Is What You Get): A text manipulation program in which what is seen on the screen is what is printed on the paper.

XML: A Web page markup language that enables the programmer to define tags for data formatting.

INDEX

A

Abacus, 7–8
Access time, 64–65
Accumulator, 71, 135
Address, 49
Adobe Illustrator, 280
Adware, 262–263, 265
Agent and bot eradication programs, 252
Agents, 156
Akers, John F., 179
Algorithm, 108, 130
Alpha testing, 111
Altair 8800, 150
Analog computers, 13
Analog signals, 184–185
Animation, 288–290
Applets, 111
Application generators, 100
Application programs, 6. *See also* Software
  broader view of development, 112
  building, 107–112
  computer control, 200–205
  Internet and Web tools. *See* Internet and
    Web tools
  Internet music and audio, 305
  macros in, 102–103
  productivity tools. *See* Productivity tools
  scripting, 105–106
Archie, 216–217
Arecibo Observatory, Puerto Rico, 25
Arithmetic logic unit (ALU), 134, 135
Arithmetic unit, 71
ARPA (Advanced Research Projects Agency), 179, 191, 203,
  212, 225, 289
ARPAnet, 191, 212–213, 215
Artificial intelligence (AI), 166
Artificial Intelligence Lab, MIT, 126
Artificial reality, 368–369
ASCII (American Standard Code for Information
  Interchange), 35–36, 50, 75–78
Assembler, 101, 102
Assembly language, 98, 101, 138, 140–142
Asynchronous transmission, 187
Atanasoff, John Vincent, 79
Audio media, 293–304
  music, 300–304
  speech recognition, 295–299
  speech recording, 294
  speech synthesis, 294–295
Audio output devices, 73

B

Backbone, 213
Back door, 257
Bacon, Francis, 317
Bandwidth, 188
Baran, Paul, 191, 213
Bar code, 321
Bar code readers, 321
BASIC, 150
Baud rate, 185, 186
Bell Laboratories, 156, 166
Beta testing, 111
Binary code, 96–98
Binary devices, 12
Binary electronic circuits, 27–28
Binary numbers, 27–30, 31, 32, 33
Biological computers, 15
Biometrics, 325
BIOS (basic input/output system), 150–151
Bit (binary digit), 30, 76
Bitmapped (raster) graphics, 281–282
Bits per second (bps), 185, 186
Blog, 243
Bluetooth, 183, 264
Booting up a computer, 153–154
Bridges, 200
Broadcast standards, 291
Brooks, Rodney, 127
Brown, John Seely, 374
Bugs, 99, 110–112
Burn, 73
Burroughs Corporation, 164
Bush, Vannevar, 225
Bus networks, 188–189
Bytes, 64, 75–78

C

Cache memory, 162–164
Calculators, 7–9, 79
Cathode ray tube (CRT), 72
CAVE (CAVE Automatic Virtual Environment), 369–370
CD players, 62
CD-ROM, 60, 66, 69, 73
Cell phones, 10
Census Bureau, U.S., 5
Central processing unit (CPU), 15, 28, 69–71, 134–135, 162
Channels, 187–188
Chips, 70, 71
CISC (Complex Instruction Set Computer), 137